POLICY ANALYSIS
IN POLITICAL SCIENCE

POLICY ANALYSIS
IN POLITICAL SCIENCE

Edited by
IRA SHARKANSKY
University of Wisconsin

Markham Publishing Company / Chicago

MARKHAM POLITICAL SCIENCE SERIES
AARON WILDAVSKY, Editor

Acknowledgments

The idea and structure for this volume developed while I was teaching a course entitled "The Policy-Making Process" at the University of Wisconsin. My students were not reluctant to criticize the material that was offered to them, and thereby they helped me to select essays to be included in this book. Three colleagues were kind enough to comment on the initial selection of esssays and on the first draft of the introductory essay. They are Professors Kenneth Dolbeare and John Manley at the University of Wisconsin and Professor Robert Salisbury at Washington University. Each of them made this book at least a little better than it would have been. I accept responsibility for whatever shortcomings remain.

Madison, Wisconsin   I.S.
September, 1969

Contents

POLICY ANALYSIS
IN POLITICAL SCIENCE

CHAPTER 1

The Political Scientist and Policy Analysis

An Introduction by Ira Sharkansky

The design of this book is to introduce students to the "field" of policy analysis. Its purpose is to indicate the breadth of the concerns that lie within this field, and the variety of concepts, techniques of investigation, and findings that appear in its literature. This book should perform some of the functions of an introductory textbook, yet display the diversity of the field more successfully than an integrated text could. Indeed, the field of policy analysis currently reveals more diversity than integration. An anthology is the most appropriate volume for a beginning student.

This introduction illustrates the diversity in the field of policy analysis, yet also reveals its unity. There are several conceptions of policy. It would be futile and misleading to work toward a clear definition of *policy, policy process,* or *policy-making.* Political scientists who study these topics take different approaches and use specific definitions that are appropriate for their purposes. These definitions, however, do share certain meanings. We can express these terms simply, while admitting that some ambiguities exist. *Policies* are actions taken by governments. They include the provision of public services (*e.g.,* education, welfare, highways); the regulation of personal and corporate activities (*e.g.,* by the police, market inspectors, The Food and Drug Administration); the celebration of symbolic events (*e.g.,* Columbus Day, New Year's Day, the Fourth of July); and the control of the policy-making process or other political actions (*e.g.,* changing the filibuster rule in the Senate, requiring state officials to register Negro voters, combatting graft in the office of a district attorney). Although policies affect both international and domestic concerns, this book concerns itself solely with domestic policy. It eliminates analyses of foreign and military policies for the simple reason that they would carry us far beyond the boundaries of a manageable volume.

POLICY IN POLITICAL SCIENCE

Policy is not a new concern of political science. Our earliest writings considered the actions of public officials, the conditions that fostered certain

1

kinds of policy, and the implications of policy for other aspects of the political process. However, the current interest in policy departs from its predecessors, although it shares these basic concerns. Several new dimensions of policy analysis can be illustrated: a primary concern with explanation rather than prescription; sophisticated comparisons of the policies of different communities, states, or government agencies; the search for economic, social, and historical, as well as political and governmental, features to aid in understanding the policies that governments choose; and an effort to accumulate research to build theories about policy. These attributes of policy analysis are related to one another. The focus on explanation instead of prescription allows political scientists with different policy preferences to cooperate on common projects. The eclectic approach to the search for the "determinants" of policy is also beneficial because it is not bound by the overt concerns of political philosophy. The concern for additive theory-building stimulates scholars to make their own analyses relevant to the findings of their colleagues, and helps to integrate studies of different kinds of policy.

One of the most prominent features that distinguishes contemporary policy analysis from its predecessors is the concern with empirical analysis. The political scientists and other scholars represented in this volume display an overt concern with the evidence which supports their findings and with the uniformity of whatever findings they report. Policy recommendations—if they are made at all—are subordinate to description, analysis, and understanding. This is not to say that policy analysts are unconcerned with the world around them. Descriptive theory is valuable not only for its own sake, but also for its contribution to more successful prescription. The more we understand the policy-making process (that is, the more accurately we can describe it, account for differences in policies chosen, or differences in the effects of policies), the better we can inform those who would make suggestions for change. The work of description is not necessarily radical or conservative. It proceeds under the assumption that understanding will aid both the formulators and the potential adopters of reform in determining the likely consequences of their actions.

In their quest for understanding, many of the essays in this volume identify patterned relationships between components of the policy-making process. They compare different "levels" or "qualities" of a policy as they are produced by various states, communities, or government agencies to see what kinds of social, economic, or political factors are usually associated with each variety of the policy. The purpose is to determine what kinds of environmental characteristics may bring about a certain kind of policy or what may result from certain policies. Comprehension of these studies requires some knowledge of statistical tests: correlation, regression, and analysis of covariance. However, each piece contains clear description as well as sophisticated numerical analysis. By reading between the tables, even a beginning political scientist can gain some understanding of the findings and their importance in relation to other essays.

Policy analysis does not require the manipulation of "hard data" with sophisticated statistical techniques. Some areas of policy-making have so far proved not to be amenable to rigorous measurements. This is not to claim that measurement of some features of policy making is impossible; it is only that some topics of concern to the policy analyst have not yet been treated with rigorous quantitative tools; some insightful studies do exist which do not employ such tools. Some of these studies may provide preliminary descriptions that will help later scholars to quantify additional features of the policy process. The distinction that is sometimes made between "hard" and "soft" analyses seems untenable. Although some studies are more overtly quantitative than others, their conclusions are not necessarily more reliable or more important than the conclusions of studies which rely less on precise measurement. There are quarrels among the users of quantitative techniques which open some of their techniques to charges of unreliability or invalidity. The presence or absence of numbers in an essay is less important than other attributes: the breadth of relevant influences taken into consideration in analyzing a policy process, the use of the most substantial and trustworthy evidence that is relevant for the topic at hand, and the use of the concepts and tools of analysis that seem most likely to illuminate the forces that are important for the process at hand.

Policy analysts are wide ranging in their consideration of factors that might influence policies. They examine traits of administrative agencies and other official bodies, the level of economic development or the political culture which exists in an agency's jurisdiction, social and economic characteristics of voters or the agency's clients, and historical experiences. Another trait of policy analysts—their concern with relating their own investigations to the work of their colleagues—helps tie together this diverse collection of scholarship. In some of the pieces reprinted here there is an overt effort to bring together a wide variety of research and offer some theoretical linkages. In almost all of the pieces, the abundance of footnotes testifies to the writer's sensitivity to the work of others.

The works of political scientists who write about policy exhibit several distinct interests. Some develop theoretical frameworks that identify crucial lines of influence among the features of the policy process and bring together the work of many scholars. The essays in Part One are in this category: they either suggest a conception of policy, attempt to relate the work of several scholars to a common theme, or attack as unsuitable a conception of policy that has been offered elsewhere. The process of building a field of scholarship is not altogether harmonious. There are disagreements about the usefulness of another's work. No single essay in this book represents a "final thought" or "finished contribution." Each makes an offer to a continuing discussion among scholars that may gradually evolve into a set of ideas and findings that have wide acceptance. Part Two takes a slightly different approach to conceptual problems: it examines the difficulties involved in measuring policies—problems that occur prior to scientific analysis. We cannot agree about the results of research unless we first agree that the basic concepts are measured accurately. Many of the scholars who concern themselves with concepts and modes of analysis also try to identify the social and economic features, political behaviors, and governmental structures that affect policy. Parts Three to Five identify several features of the economy, individual actors, and government institutions that influence policy. These features do not seem to be of equal importance, and each feature does not operate with the same effect in all contexts. There are some surprises in the research findings, and some disagreements among investigators. Some writers assess specific policies and features of the policy-making machinery and determine which interests such policies benefit as well as whether or not they accomplish the goals they claim. This work is represented in Part Six, especially in essays about planning-programming-budgeting, legislative reapportionment, and the U.S. Selective Service System. Elsewhere in the book, essays about the "outputs" and "impacts" of policy and the results of government expenditure raise additional questions about the products of government policies. These studies find that conventional wisdom does not always describe the policy process accurately.

This collection should reveal some of the breadth that is possible in a study of "policy." Like studies in decision-making, group conflict, political system, and role, the treatment of "policy" is a focus that lends itself to many analytical purposes and unites the work of many political scientists. There are several fields of research not represented in this book which further illuminate the policy process. Electoral studies, for example, help us understand the selection of major policy-makers; studies of economic or political development provide information about the forces that alter the public resources of a jurisdiction and about the nature of its policy-making institutions and behaviors; studies of political socialization provide insights into the transmission of political norms from one generation to the next and suggest why some policy demands change and others remain stable. Policy also attracts the interests of scholars who are not political scientists. An article in Part Two of this book deals with questions of wide relevance within research methodology; its illustrations are not drawn from politics as much as from the psychological and sociological concerns of its authors. An essay in Part Six describes a policy-making tool of government agencies —planning-programming-budgeting—but is written by an economist who is interested in budget-making as a means of resource allocation.

An attribute of policy-oriented political science is its promise as a link between the work of academic political scientists and those persons (both officials and citizens) who formulate and implement government programs. Some of the work of political scientists designed to aid in understanding the policy process may be useful to those who toil as policy-makers. There have been several efforts to institute formal ties between academic political science and policy-making units of government. Some political scientists work as consultants with government agencies; others teach in programs designed to train policy-makers. Yet there is a continuing tension between the role of the academic political scientist and that of the practicing policy-maker. One strives for more complete (*i.e.,* general) understanding of the policy process, and the other wants specific recommendations for discrete problems. Nevertheless, the policy-oriented political scientist is joined to the policy-maker by a common focus. Some of the techniques of analysis and some research findings of the political scientist may aid the specific concerns of some policy-makers. Given the policy-makers' greater familiarity with their own needs for information, it may be their task—rather than that of the academicians—to know just which techniques and findings are useful in the policy process. As academicians, we may be able to offer no better general recommendation for the practitioner than that he acquire sophisticated training in policy-oriented political science, and reflect upon the academicians' work.

These essays may offer some ideas or information to government officials; they may also offer something for the students of political science who are interested in bringing about changes in public policies. Those students who charge that social scientists are not doing research relevant to current economic and social conditions have not read the kinds of research represented in these pages. The authors examine interactions among economic, social, and political phenomena—especially features which influence the policies of federal, state, and local governments. Each essay may not explain fully how policy is made or what the impact of a policy will be. At the very least, however, they illustrate the analytical procedures which can produce reliable, trustworthy information and this in itself is a potent tool in any policy-making process. Government officials and private citizens are in a better position to change policies if they can persuade the makers of policy that they have identified some tangible problems in current policies and that they can identify some alternative policies, the resources needed to implement each alternative, and the likely effect of each on the social or economic problems at hand.

The organizational framework of this collection does not stress policy-making at federal, state, or local levels of government. Instead, it focuses on generic features of policy-making processes that operate at each level. The goal of this research is to identify general principles that operate under many conditions, and then to specify important deviations from those principles that are found in different fields of policy, at different levels of government, or in individual states or localities. In a later section, some differences in the policy processes of federal, state, and local governments are noted. There are critical differences, for example, in their dependence on the economic resources available in the private sector and in their abilities to formulate policy independent of current economic conditions.

BASIC CONCEPTIONS IN POLICY ANALYSIS

A prominent feature of much recent policy analysis is its concern with "systemic" relationships among policy and other aspects of politics and economics. This writing relies heavily on systems theory. There are some different terms and concepts apparent in the essays of Part One. However, all systems theories start from the notion of interrelated parts. The principal assumption is that behavior does not exist in isolation. The observer of politics who is sensitive to systems theory continually asks himself: "What is related to what?" He searches for phenomena which interact with the current topic of interest, and his "system" shows how that topic receives and transmits stimuli in relationships with other factors. Thomas R. Dye focuses on "policy outcomes" and offers a model to explain them with reference to characteristics of political systems and socioeconomic development. Thus, policies are his dependent variables, and his independent variables are the political and socioeconomic characteristics likely to influence policies.[1] His research finds that socioeconomic factors are more important determinants of policy than are political factors. However, other writers have found that the relative influence of economic and political factors varies with the nature of the policy at issue, the level of government being examined, and the kinds of political elements that are considered.[2] Robert Salisbury and John Heinz offer a different approach to policy analysis. They look at different types of policies as independent variables, and search for the political processes that are affected by them. Their policy types are "distributive," "re-distributive," "regulatory," and "self-regulatory." Their principal argument is important: *different kinds of policy are likely to stimulate different kinds of interactions among other features of politics.* However, Salisbury and Heinz do not offer any concrete measurements of their policy types. Insofar as the "distributive," "re-distributive," "regulatory," and "self-regulatory" features are combined in individual policies, it may be impossible to determine what kinds of political features actually do exist along with each of these policy types. The third essay distinguishes "policy" from "output" and "impact," and treats policy as both a dependent variable responding to factors in the environment, and as an independent variable that affects the nature of outputs. A point that is mentioned less forcefully in other research is emphasized: policy is not a simple phenomenon, but may consist of different efforts in any one field of service (*e.g.,* education). Moreover, some of these efforts may fail to reinforce one another, or actually work at cross purposes. And policies may not have sufficient strength to work against the social and economic problems they are designed to attack; as a result, the outputs envisioned by policy-makers may never be produced.

THE MEASUREMENT OF POLICY

The essays in Part Two deal with some of the methodological issues encountered by policy analysts. The piece by Eugene Webb and his colleagues urges the use of multiple measures for any single concept. The title of their essay emphasizes an important aspect of policy analysis: *research is performed with surrogates of one's basic concepts, and not with the concepts themselves.* Policy is studied by examining measurements that seem to reflect government activities: expenditures, levels of welfare benefits, miles of highway in relation to population, and the ability of schools to attract their pupils through graduation. Likewise the social and economic attributes of a jurisdiction are measured by variables that seem to reflect these phenomena: personal income per capita, the level of adult education, and the percentage of people living in urban areas. Sometimes these variables are not accurate measures of the phenomena they are chosen to designate. Records may be faulty, so jurisdictions may actually have more or less of a given feature than is reported. Furthermore, the situation may be more complex than it is believed to be, and a single variable may be unable to reflect the subtleties that exist. Webb argues that researchers must triangulate on a concept with several measurements; thus, the faults inherent in any single measurement (which might bias research findings) can be revealed. Sharkansky's article identifies one problem that plagues much of policy analysis: the use of expenditures as measures of program performance. Several different measures of public service are employed and correlation analysis is used to test their associations with several measures of government expenditures and other public policies. The findings suggest that expenditures are poor measures of program performance. A number of other factors seem to affect the power of government spending and to limit the capacity of money to buy high quality performance.

DETERMINANTS OF PUBLIC POLICY

Parts Three to Five identify several factors that influence policy: the nature of a jurisdiction's economy, political culture and popular demands, and the traits of institutions and participants in the policy-making process. No effort is made to incorporate all of these determinants into a grand theory of policy-making. At this point, we can only list some forces that shape policy and assess the conditions under which each may be weak or powerful.

The Economy

Part 3 includes one essay which presents a strong argument for the influence of economic conditions on policy, and another that qualifies the economic–policy linkage. Dye's article on income inequality is only a piece in a lengthy bibliography that has argued for the influence of economic conditions on the policies of state and local governments. His most prominent work is *Politics, Economics and the Public: Policy Outcomes in the American States,* part of which is re-printed in Part One. In that book he writes that the level of economic development (measured by per capita personal income, urbanism, industrialization, and education) exercises a prevailing influence over the nature of state and local government policies. Dye's argument is persuasive, but tends to be exaggerated. A close examination of his statistics reveals their weakness. Of the 356 separate measures of association between an economic and a policy measure that he reports in his book, only 16 (4 per cent) are strong enough to indicate that an economic trait accounts for even half of the interstate differences in policy. This does not deny the role of the economy as a determinant of policy. Additional research has found that economic development is most powerful in its effect on local governments, and much less important in its impact on the policy decisions of state and national officials. Indeed, national officials have some opportunities to shape the character of economic development, and sometimes are the masters rather than the subordinates of economic conditions.[3] In the essay included in Part Three, Dye provides a more specific explanation of the economic–policy linkage than he does in his earlier book. He compares the influence of two different kinds of economic phenomenon: the *total level of resources* and the *distribution of resources* among various income groups. While the level of

Table 1

Relationships between Per Capita State and Local Government Expenditures and Per Capita Personal Income: Coefficients of Sample Correlation

1903	0.920
1932	0.839
1942	0.821
1957	0.658
1962	0.645
1964–65	0.558

total resources is more important for public policies, the distribution of resources is more important for political conditions. To the extent that policies depend on economic characteristics, they seem to get their support from the sheer level of resources available. The political traits of voter turnout and party competition, however, are more dependent on the distribution of resources among individuals; these aspects of citizen behavior may respond to the different life styles that citizens sense among themselves. Richard I. Hofferbert introduces a historical dimension into the analysis of the economic-policy relationship. He finds the influence of economic conditions declining over the 1940–1960 period. The data in Table 1 support this finding.[4] It shows a continuing decline in the relationship between economic development and public policy since 1902. Policy makers now seem far less dependent on economic conditions; there are many more opportunities for officials in low income states and localities to spend at high levels. Some of this increased flexibility may reflect changes in federal aid. Other research finds that federal programs aid the low income states disproportionately. By transferring revenues from "have" to "have not" areas, grants-in-aid make up for some of the resource differentials between rich and poor states. Also, state and local governments now have a more flexible tax structure. With state taxes on personal incomes and/or retail sales now used by over 40 of the states (no state used either tax at the beginning of the century), and an increasing number of local governments turning to these forms of taxation, policy-makers can tap an increasing proportion of the revenue within their own jurisdictions. Even the poorest states (*e.g.,* Mississippi, South Carolina, Arkansas, Vermont) have some pockets of wealth that can help support public services in their poorest counties.[5] Additional research shows that the economy is less important for policies where local governments have "reformed" governmental structures than where they are "unreformed." The characteristics of a reformed municipality (professional manager, non-partisan ballot, and an at-large election of council members) are neutral, by design, to the special demands of neighborhood communities or party organizations. In contrast, the policy-making elements of an unreformed city (elected mayor, partisan ballot, and ward-elected council members) are designed to reflect the economic demands of different population groups. As a result, the policies of unreformed governments are more likely to reflect the demands peculiar to their social and economic surroundings.[6]

Popular Demands and Political Culture

The part on popular demands and political culture includes a conjectural essay about state-to-state differences in culture and their impact on policies and an article that finds regional differences in public policy that are consistent with historical experiences and cultural norms. Daniel J. Elazar describes three types of political culture in the United States—Moralism, Individualism, and Traditionalism—and identifies the cultures that prevail in each of 228 areas. He explains the cultural differences by reference to patterns of initial settlement and migration along with contemporary features of industrialization and urbanism. He also offers some hypotheses about the influence of these cultures on public policy. Other research offers support for Elazar's hypotheses. States marked by "moralistic" cultures differ as predicted from "individualistic" and "traditionalistic" states in having higher levels of taxes, higher expenditures and service outputs in the fields of education, highways, and welfare, and larger, better-paid government bureaucracies. These characteristics are not simply the product of a state's level of economic development; they seem to reflect the weight of Elazar's "cultures," independent of this other influence.[7]

The paper by Sharkansky shows that one manifestation of political culture at work is the prevalence of policies that are consistent with the historical experiences and cultural norms of different regions. These findings persist despite different levels of economic development within each region. Although some states have progressed beyond their neighbors economically, they have generally maintained the kinds of policies that are characteristic of their region.[8] Some other research also finds long-standing constancy in the policies of state and local governments.[9] The routines of incremental budget-making appear basic to the persistence of these government activities. As shown in a later essay,[10] state governors and legislators tend to cut most severely the budgets of those agencies which request the largest increases. This keeps the budget of any agency—and the total budget of any state—from moving upward in a dramatic fashion. It is not impossible for individual governments to move out of their historic policy positions. Incremental budgeting, however, is a strong conservative force and inhibits dramatic innovations by government agencies.

Other research helps to clarify the influence of citizen demands and political culture on policy. A study of congressmen and their constituents that employs survey research finds that citizens' attitudes about civil rights are more important for the legislators' decisions than are citizens' attitudes about social welfare or foreign relations.[11] Another study finds that citizens may be especially well informed—even about complex issues—when they are debated by candidates for important offices; despite the obscure nature of tax proposals, people in different income brackets have identified and supported those features of the different proposals which offered them the greatest economic benefits.[12]

Individual Actors and Institutions in the Policy Process

The numerous pieces in Part Five testify to the importance attributed to people and institutions as the determinants of public policy. The literature of policy-making is heavy with case studies on the formulation of discrete policies, and with studies of individual institutions or persons in the policy process. Part Five contains some of the best examples of this literature, and combines it with some quantitative assessments about the importance of specific people or institutions to the nature of policies. The studies show that there is some opportunity to exercise discretion for the individual person. However, his opportunities are circumscribed by tradition, available resources, formal procedures, and the desires of powerful actors. Some areas provide more opportunity for the use of the individual will than others. Even the "best people" may not produce attractive policies under some conditions.

Part Five demonstrates some conflict regarding the influence of government officials in policy-making. Thomas J. Anton assesses several descriptive studies of budgeting in state governments, and concludes that the governor and the legislature play minor roles in expenditure decisions. For him, their actions are largely symbolic, having minimum impact on the level of spending. The manipulation of symbols and an obfuscation of tangible issues may exist in state (as well as in national and local) budgeting. However, another essay in Part Five reports some important deviations from Anton's findings. Ira Sharkansky and Augustus B. Turnbull, III, show marked differences in the budget roles of governors and legislatures in Georgia from those in Wisconsin, plus equally prominent differences in Wisconsin from one governor to the next, and between different kinds of administrative agencies. At least in Wisconsin, the interests and strengths of individual governors seem to affect their influence in state budgeting.

An essay by John Manley and an essay by Lewis A. Dexter discuss the burdensome nature of a legislator's job, his problems, and opportunities for making careful assessments of policy issues. Dexter focuses on the legislator's problems. The demands of policy analysis face stiff competition for his interests and his time. Moreover, each session of the legislature sees several prominent issues of policy put before the body. An individual legislator must not only reserve some time for policy analysis, but must also choose among several major issues that will attract his attention. Manley's article on the staff of the Joint Committee on Internal Revenue Taxation highlights one resource that legislators can use to maximize their investigation of policies. The staff of that committee—used both by the House Committee on Ways and Means and the Senate Committee on Finance—provides expert advice to the legislators; it enables them to assess the recommendations of the executive branch, and to formulate some of their own proposals for legislation. Legislative staffs have not attracted much attention from political scientists. Manley's article suggests, however, that to understand the role of the legislature in policy-making it is necessary to understand the ways in which the legislature collects its information. The committee and personal staffs are surely integral features in that process and deserve more attention than they have received.

Two items by John P. Crecine and Rufus P. Browning show that policies are made with both mechanical and individualistic procedures. Crecine reports his research on the budget decisions of three large cities (Cleveland, Detroit, and Pittsburgh), and finds decision rules that are so mechanistic that he can identify them and simulate their outcomes with a computer program. It is not simply that officials follow rigidly prescribed formal procedures: they also use some highly structured informal rules in making their decisions. Wage and salary requests tend to be rewarded more than equipment requests, for example, and new equipment tends to be favored more than requests for maintenance expenditures. Browning, in contrast, emphasizes some marked individual traits in the budget decisions of two agencies in the state of Wisconsin: an aggressive, growth-oriented welfare department and a lethargic labor department. He also identifies some of the factors which account for the differences between these two departments.

The essay by Anthony Downs differs from both Crecine's and Browning's in failing to couple its hypotheses with empirical data. Yet it suggests a number of factors that enter into an agency's change in policy. These factors include the officials' assessment of their performance under existing policies and their sense of marked change in their environment. Government officials do not always clearly perceive the performance of their current programs or the nature of their surroundings. They often employ mechanisms that deemphasize stress and that protect themselves from frequent changes in policy. The budget rules reported by Crecine are examples of these mechanisms. If officials can make their policy choices according to fixed rules, they need not make difficult choices among contending alternatives.

Lester Milbrath probes the influence of interest groups on the policy-making process. He does his research by asking participants in policy-making for their views of one another's influence. He finds no simple, clear pattern of ascribed influence; the identification of "powerful" actors varies with the nature of the issues and the officials who are questioned. Under most conditions, however, interest groups do not score high: they must compete among themselves, as well as with the predispositions and the considered policy judgments of the officials who make policy decisions. Most respondents rank the president, the executive branch, congress, and voters generally higher than lobbyists in the influence they exercise over policy-makers.

EVALUATION OF PUBLIC POLICY

Part Six deals with some problems of evaluating public policy. Two essays consider one of the most prominent devices that has been proposed in recent years to "rationalize" the policy-making process: planning-program-ming-budgeting. Another identifies some of the factors that can thwart one prominent reform (legislative reapportionment) even after it is imple-mented. Still another illustrates how political scientists can use their skills to propose reform, or to assess those reforms which are offered by others.

Murray L. Weidenbaum describes planning-programming-budgeting (PPB). He and other supporters argue that PPB can clarify the goals of government programs and indicate the relative costs and benefits of alternative ways of accomplishing the goals. Some commentators fear that it is limited in its usefulness to those kinds of programs with clear and non-controversial goals. As Ralph Huitt writes, the usefulness of PPB may be greatest in the military, where major goals (*i.e.,* deterrence of war, defense of country, and victory in war) are clear and widely accepted among the officials who make budget decisions. Elsewhere, the goals of programs are subject to intense controversy. In many cases different legislators and interest groups agree to support specific activities, but would conflict bitterly if they had to agree about the long range accomplishments of the programs. Even in the case of agencies with relatively unambiguous goals, the value of PPB is limited by the extent to which the costs and benefits of programs can be measured. The value of an American soldier's life, the life of an unlettered peasant in a foreign country, or the results of a research and development project must be considered in many phases of military planning, but they hardly lend themselves to simple or indisputable pricing. Some factors are worth more than their market price indicates.

Another objection to PPB is that it requires centralized decision-making by officials who assess information relevant to goals, resources, and prospective performance. Yet a prominent characteristic of American government is decentralized decision-making, with spokesmen of different government units or interest groups bargaining with one another. Huitt writes that a participant's definition of the feasibility of a policy is "a seat-of-the-pants judgment, based on (his) experience." The cost questions that Huitt's policy-maker asks himself are: "Will it 'go' on the Hill?" "Will the public buy it?" "Does it have political 'sex appeal'?"

Despite these constraints, PPB may be able to make a substantial contribution to policy-making. It will not oust political judgment and bargaining from the process, but it may focus disputes and provide the participants with a kind of information they have lacked in the past. This information includes output-oriented assessments of policy proposals—*i.e.,* assessments of things to be produced as well as of the money, personnel, technology, and other inputs that are to be invested in a program. Although PPB cannot adequately "price" inputs and outputs across the range of governmental programs, it may push budget makers' capacities in this direction. Decisions may never be completely "rational" or be based upon an "adequate" amount of information; but more information than decision-makers currently have and more sophisticated information about the costs and benefits of certain programs may narrow the range in which loose guesses and hopes have to take the place of understanding on the part of government officials.

The essay by Brett Hawkins and Cheryl Whelchel identifies some of the complex hurdles that a reform in the machinery of policy-making may have to surmount before it can "pay off" as expected. They show that legislative reapportionment does not represent a simple victory for urban representatives. The changes in legislative districting must manifest their influence through changes in the leadership structure of state legislatures. An increase in the number of urban legislators does not guarantee an increase in the proportion of powerful legislators who are from urban areas. In the case they present, the proportion of urban representatives in positions of leadership *actually declined after reapportionment.* This decline reflects the relative seniority of the rural legislators who survived reapportionment, and perhaps also an increase in dissension among urban legislators. As the numbers of urban legislators increased, so too did their diversity in terms of social status, race, and urban-suburban residence. Additional studies indicate that urban and rural legislators are not uniform in their policy preferences, even in those issues that bear upon urban problems.[13] Thus an increase in legislators from urban districts does not guarantee an increase in the legislators who will vote a pro-urban line when relevant issues come before them.

James Davis and Kenneth Dolbeare illustrate another kind of policy analysis that can be done by political scientists. They assess the policies of the U.S. Selective Service System by the standards of its official goals and—by a process of eliminating several alternatives—identify one proposal which should realize certain goals not achieved by the present program. On the basis of empirical data collected by the Selective Service System, the Defense Department, and their own survey of draft boards in Wisconsin, Davis and Dolbeare conclude that the System's goal of equity is not achieved (prior to 1967 changes in policy) on account of the high incidence of low income and black inductees. They further conclude that its goal of efficiency is not achieved because there is no systematic effort to define the civilian manpower needs of the country, or to meet these needs through the criteria that local boards use to grant deferments. The authors claim that political science research can examine a policy and define the conditions that might affect its success, the means that are available to policy-makers, and the likely effects and by-products of certain policies. They argue that the comparison of alternate proposals will support policy recommendations. They do not claim that the skills of a political scientist lead unerringly to one policy recommendation instead of others. They are persuasive in *rejecting* some policies by showing their inconsistency with current conditions, the means available, or desirable effects and by-products. They may be less successful in convincing a reader that their remaining alternative is a suitable draft policy.

WHAT'S NEXT? THE FUTURE OF POLICY ANALYSIS IN POLITICAL SCIENCE

When he has finished reading this collection, a reader might properly ask himself: "Where should political scientists go from here in the analysis of public policy?" This field is new as a subject of sophisticated social scientific analysis. The signs of its newness are the use of different terms to denote similar concepts; disagreements over assumptions and findings, some of which have not yet occurred to the scholars who disagree with one another; and the reliance on primitive measurements for complex concepts, with some of the measurements used for no apparent reason other than their availability. There is much work left to be done before we can understand the forces which affect the design and implementation of policy, or those which affect its success in coping with social or economic problems. Yet the work has begun, and this collection of essays testifies to its variety. Barring any breakthroughs in our ability to conceive or analyze policy-relevant phenomena, it is safe to predict that work in the immediate future will proceed along lines that are already evident.

By saying that research in the immediate future will continue present trends, we do not suggest that it will be devoid of innovation. There will be additional measurements collected for some of the same concepts that are currently being analyzed with rudimentary variables. These new variables will be designed to serve policy-relevant concepts, and will not simply be the left-overs of the census taker or the economic analyst. In this vein, there may be greater use of survey data. Instead of using "per capita personal income" to measure economic needs or demands, scholars might employ the results of interviews which ask citizens about their desires for public service.

As part of a trend toward greater precision in the selection of variables, scholars will probably study smaller policy-making units. In this way, they can observe the factors which have a direct bearing on individual policy-makers at work. Some steps in this direction are already being taken. Early studies of government spending were directed at the aggregate spending of state and local governments within each state. This was part of a tradition that political scientists inherited from economists interested in public finance. The total of state plus local spending is said to "control" for state-to-state variations in the proportion of spending responsibilities that are assigned to state or local governments. The price of this aggregation is the hiding of factors affecting the spending of state or local units. No officials actually make decisions about the combined spending of state and local governments. By "disaggregating" and examining the expenditures of state and local governments separately, political scientists gained an opportunity to examine the spending processes within the arenas in which decisions are made. Among the benefits from this research is the discovery that local government spending is highly dependent on the level of economic resources, while spending by state governments is relatively independent of economic constraints. Additional research has disaggregated even below the level of whole governments. By looking at the budget records of individual agencies, Crecine and Sharkansky and Turnbull have identified some decision rules that are used in local and state governments. These rules screen out innovative stimuli and minimize the growth which occurs in appropriations from one budget period to the next. These kinds of studies may be applied in additional state or local governments to test present results in different contexts. Such work can produce greater knowledge about the conditions that support or interrupt these rules of budget making and, by extension, the conditions that permit major innovations in government agencies.

Another trend that is likely to continue is the concern with the results (the outputs, outcomes, impacts, or effects) of specific policies, and with the results of changes in the machinery of policy-making. Among the pieces that represent this trend are the Hawkins and Whelchel study of post-reapportionment changes in the leadership structure of the Georgia legislature, and the Davis and Dolbeare study of selective service policy. There is nothing in the character of political science to keep its best practitioners from studying these kinds of problems. To keep the faith as social scientists, we need only base our conclusions on empirical evidence and clear standards. Hawkins and Whelchel made their judgments on the basis of data about Georgia legislators and the expectations of those who advocated reapportionment; Davis and Dolbeare made their judgments on the basis of government records, survey data, and the official goals of the Selective Service System. Further work can compare popular preferences (as determined by survey research) with the performance of certain programs, or compare changes in governmental programs over time with changes in the social or economic problems that the programs are designed to meet.[14] Each of these projects would be valuable in itself as a commentary about the utility of certain policies or certain reforms in the policy-making machinery. If studies of this kind are performed on a comparative basis, they would gain even more by defining both the general tendencies and the kinds of conditions that provoked deviations from these tendencies.

NOTES

[1] The "dependent variable" is typically the focus of one's analysis; it is the item which is assumed to *depend* on other items. These other items are termed the "independent variables"; for purposes of the analysis at hand, they are presumed not to depend on other factors. In reality, independent variables may be thought of as dependent upon some other factors, but these are excluded from analysis for the sake of clarity.

[2] See, for example, Ira Sharkansky and Richard I. Hofferbert, "Dimensions of State Politics, Economics and Public Policy," *American Political Science Review* (September, 1969) and Charles Cnudde and Donald McCrone, "Party Competition and Welfare Policies in the American States," *American Political Science Review* (September, 1969).

[3] Ira Sharkansky, *The Politics of Taxing and Spending* (Indianapolis: Bobbs-Merrill, 1969), Chapter V.

[4] Alan Campbell and Seymour Sachs, *Metropolitan America: Fiscal Patterns and Governmental Systems* (New York: Free Press, 1967), p. 57.

[5] Sharkansky, *op. cit.,* Chapter IV.

[6] Robert L. Lineberry and Edmund P. Fowler, "Reformism and Public Policies in American Cities," *American Political Science Review* (September, 1967).

[7] Ira Sharkansky, "The Utility of Elazar's Political Cultures: A Research Note," *Polity* (September, 1969).

[8] See also Ira Sharkansky, *Regionalism in American Politics* (Indianapolis: Bobbs-Merrill, 1969).

[9] Ira Sharkansky, *Spending in the American States* (Chicago: Rand McNally, 1968), Chapter III.

[10] Ira Sharkansky and Augustus B. Turnbull, III, "Budget-Making in Georgia and Wisconsin: A Test of a Model," *Midwest Journal of Political Science* (November, 1968).

[11] Warren E. Miller and Donald Stokes, "Constituency Influence in Congress," *American Political Science Review* (March, 1963).

[12] Sharkansky, *The Politics of Taxing and Spending, op. cit.,* Chapter II.

[13] David R. Derge, "Metropolitan and Outstate Alignments in Illinois and Missouri Legislative Delegations," *American Political Science Review* (December, 1958); and Herbert Jacob, "The Consequences of Reapportionment: A Note of Caution," *Social Forces* (1964).

[14] Kenneth Dolbeare, "Policy Analysis: Some Theoretical and Evaluative Pay-offs," Department of Political Science, University of Wisconsin, mimeo (1969).

PART ONE

Basic Conceptions in Policy Analysis

CHAPTER 2

A Model for the Analysis of Policy Outcomes

Thomas R. Dye

MODEL–BUILDING FOR POLICY RESEARCH

The study of public policy outcomes is one of the major responsibilities of political science. While the structure and functioning of political systems have always been a central concern of political science, the content of public policy is also an element of political life which political science must endeavor to explain. Policy outcomes express the value allocations of a society, and these allocations are the chief output of the society's political system. Policy outcomes, like election returns, roll-call votes, or court decisions, must be assembled, described and explained.

A central problem facing students of American state politics is not only *describing* the great variation in policy from state to state but, more importantly, *explaining* these policy differences. This work endeavors both to describe and to explain the policy choices of the fifty states in five of the most important areas of state policy-making: education, welfare, highways, taxation, and the regulation of public morality. Our central purpose is the explanation of these policy outcomes, and this involves examination of the relationships between policy outcomes and those social, economic, and political conditions which operate to shape them. No doubt many of the specific policy choices made by any state are a product of unique historical circumstances in that state. But this does not excuse students of state politics from searching for those conditions which appear most influential in determining public policy over time in all of the fifty states and for generalizations which help to explain why state governments do what they do.

What accounts for differences among the states in education, welfare, highways, taxation, and the regulation of public morals? What roles do urbanization, industrialization, wealth, and adult education play in determining state policies? What difference does it make in public policy whether a state is under Democratic or Republican party control? whether

Reprinted from Thomas R. Dye, *Politics, Economics and the Public: Policy Outcomes in the American States* (Chicago: Rand McNally, 1966), pp. 1–19, by permission of the publisher and the author.

a state is a one-party or a two-party state? or whether its voters turn out in large numbers on election day or stay at home? What are the policy consequences of malapportionment of state legislatures? These are some of the questions which must be dealt with in explaining public policy in the states.

The explanation of public policy can be aided by the construction of a model which portrays the relationships between policy outcomes and the forces which shape them.[1] A model is merely an abstraction or representation of political life: it should order and simplify our thinking about politics. Models appear in prose or in diagram or in mathematical notation, but often they are not made explicit. There seem to be many advantages, however, to developing an explanatory model of policy outcomes at the outset of any research into this area. Such a model can provide hypotheses about what policy outcomes should be under given circumstances. These hypotheses can then be tested against data derived from real political systems. If the hypotheses are proved correct, the model can be retained; if not, then the model can be modified or replaced by one that more closely corresponds to the real world of politics. For example, if a model indicates that welfare policy outcomes are partly a function of party competition, data on party competition and welfare policies can be examined to see if differences in the levels of competition produce differences in welfare policies. If it turns out that party competition and welfare policy are not related, then this relationship can be dropped from the original model and some other model can be constructed which does not hypothesize such a relationship.

The basic dilemma in model-building is how much to simplify reality. Certainly the utility of a model lies in its ability to simplify political life so that we can think about it more clearly and understand the relationships which we find in the real world. Yet too much simplification may lead to inaccuracies in our thinking about reality. If we include too few variables in our model or posit only superficial relationships, we may not be able to explain the policy outcomes which occur in the real world. On the other hand, if we include too many variables or posit overly complex relationships, our model becomes so complicated that it is not an aid to understanding. A model must simplify the relationships between policy outcomes and the forces which determine them, but it must at the same time be congruent with the real world of American state politics.

Another consideration in model-building is the ability of a model to aid in the design of policy research. A model should point out where to look for explanations of public policy and suggest the conditions under which we should expect to observe particular policy outcomes. A model should contain propositions about politics and public policy which can be directly tested in political research. It should be possible to devise operations using data from state political systems that will establish or discredit the validity of the model. In short, a model must be "researchable." Of course, no model will ever predict policy outcomes with unerring accuracy, but we should be able to develop predictions from models, so that, when results deviate from predictions, attention will be focused on the limitations of the model and the factors included in it.

Generally one thinks of any outcomes, including policy outcomes, as a result of *forces* brought to bear upon a *system* and causing it to make particular *responses*.[2] A model for the explanation of public policy outcomes, therefore, may describe relationships between socioeconomic inputs (forces), political system characteristics (systems), and policy outcomes (responses). These relationships can be diagrammed as in Figure 1.[3] This particular model assumes that the socioeconomic character of a society, that is, any condition defined as external to the boundaries of its political system, determines the nature of its political system. The political system is that group of interrelated structures and processes which functions to authoritatively allocate values within a society. Policy outcomes are viewed as the value commitments of the political system, and as such they are the chief output of that system.

Inputs are received into the political system in the form of both demands and support. Demands occur when individuals or groups, in response to perceived environmental conditions, act to promote goals, interests, or actions. Support is rendered when individuals or groups accept the outcomes of elections, obey the laws, and pay their taxes. The political

Figure 1
A Model for Analyzing Policy Outcomes
in American State Politics

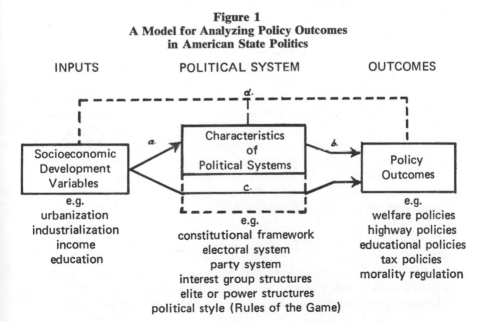

INPUTS   POLITICAL SYSTEM   OUTCOMES

system includes all of those institutions, structures, and activities which function to transform demands into authoritative decisions requiring the support of society. Any system absorbs a variety of often conflicting demands, and, in order to transform these demands into outputs (public policies), it must arrange settlements. The political system receives support insofar as it provides satisfying outputs and activates deeply rooted attachments to the system itself.

Linkages *a* and *b* suggest that socioeconomic variables are inputs which shape the political system and that the character of the political system in turn determines policy outcomes. These linkages represent the most common notions about the relationship between socioeconomic inputs, political system variables, and policy outcomes. They suggest that system variables have an important independent effect on policy outcomes by mediating between socioeconomic conditions and these outcomes. Linkage *c,* on the other hand, suggests that socioeconomic variables affect public policy directly, without being mediated by system variables. Of course, public policy is still formulated through the political system, but linkage *c* suggests that the character of that system does not independently influence policy outcomes. Hence the linkage between socioeconomic inputs and policy outcomes is unbroken. Feedback linkage *d* suggests that policy outcomes have some reciprocal impact on socioeconomic conditions and system characteristics.

Already the task of model-building has succeeded in directing our attention to an important problem in the explanation of policy outcomes. In exploring the relationships between socioeconomic variables, political system characteristics, and policy outcomes, we must ask whether or not differences in policy outcomes are *independently* related to system characteristics. Do system characteristics mediate between socioeconomic inputs and policy outcomes (as suggested by linkages *a* and *b*), or are policy outcomes determined without regard to system characteristics (as suggested by linkage *c*)? To state the problem in another fashion: Assuming that socioeconomic variables influence both system characteristics and policy outcomes, can system characteristics be shown to influence policy outcomes once socioeconomic variables are controlled? Of course, political systems are, by definition, the structures and processes which function to make public policy, but do the characteristics of these systems have any independent influence on policy outcomes?

POLICIES AND PREFERENCES

To explain policy outcomes in state politics we have selected an essentially *empirical* model, rather than a *normative* or a *prescriptive* model.[4] Policy outcomes, even though they express the value commitments of political systems, are treated in our model as facts. Our model does not enable us to proceed beyond *explanations* of state policies; that is, it does not provide *justifications* for state policies. Nor will it provide a basis for determining preferences among alternative state policies. It will not tell us what we *ought* to do in state government; at best it can only help us to understand *why* state governments do what they do. The failure to provide a guide for policy-making is a serious limitation of any empirical model. One must turn to normative models—models of "good government," "good welfare programs," "good educational systems," "good highway programs," "sound tax systems," and so forth—in order to find help in determining policy preferences.

This is not to claim that policy analysis can ever be completely value-free. Values play an important part in selecting the policies to be examined, in selecting the system characteristics to be studied, and in identifying the socioeconomic variables to be considered; indeed, values play a part in deciding to study state policy in the first place. The important distinction between an empirical and normative model is that the utility of the former is in helping to *explain* public policy, while the utility of the latter is in helping to *guide* public policy. By choosing to employ an empirical model, we are committing ourselves to the task of explanation rather than recommendation.

Our explanatory model is also distinct from the prescriptive model of Harold Lasswell and others of the "policy science" approach of a few years ago.[5] The policy science scholars were aware of the logical distinction between empirical and normative models. Yet they contended that the *relationships* between policies and preferences, that is, the relationships between instrumental policies and end values, were essentially empirical questions. As such, they were amenable to systematic inquiry not unlike the type of inquiry proposed in our model. They argued that, if certain end values are postulated, then the question of what policies would best implement these ends would be a question capable of scientific inquiry. They urged that prescriptive models be developed which would express the relationships between given end values and a particular course of public action. By clarifying relationships between means and ends, policy tools could be fashioned to help alter the course of "the world revolution of our time," whatever that phrase meant. While normative models would continue to concern themselves with definitions of "the good life," prescriptive models would describe the relationships between specific public policies and various definitions of the good life.[6]

In contrast to the models advanced by Lasswell and other proponents of a policy science, our explanatory model of public policy seeks merely to identify the major determinants of public policy choices. It does not consider what state policy ought to be, or even when it should be given a specified set of end values. It merely seeks to describe and account for differences in policy outcomes among the fifty states in relation to socio-economic input variables and political system characteristics. If an under-standing of the determinants of policy outcomes contributes in any way to rational decision-making, this is a by-product of the explanatory model and not its central purpose. In this regard our explanatory model differs from the prescriptive model of the policy scientists as well as other normative models.

ECONOMIC DEVELOPMENT AND POLICY OUTCOMES

Since a model is an abstraction from reality, it will never be completely congruent with conditions in the real world. It is inevitable that, in the process of simplifying reality, a model will fail to reflect all of the com-plexities of the real world. Simplification involves a reduction in the number of variables which are seen as relevant to the political process. From the almost unlimited number of real world conditions which influ-ence public policy outcomes, we can choose only a limited number for inclusion in our model, and, since it is impossible to consider all the environmental conditions which might influence policy outcomes, we shall never be in a position to explain completely the policy choices of all of the fifty states. In testing our model we shall be content to learn *to what extent* our model explains actual policy choices.

Students of politics from Aristotle to the present have recognized that a society's economic development helps to shape its political life. Eco-nomic development as defined here includes four closely related compo-nents of economic development: urbanization, industrialization, wealth, and education. Industrial societies require and support concentrations of people in urban centers in contrast to agricultural societies which are more extensive users of land. An industrial economy increases worker produc-tivity and produces a surplus of wealth. And a highly developed industrial economy requires educated rather than uneducated workers. In our model of public policy determination, economic development—urbanization, in-dustrialization, wealth, and education—is viewed as the crucial input variable which shapes the character of the political system and the kinds of policy outcomes it produces. There are good theoretical reasons as well as considerable empirical evidence to justify the selection of economic devel-opment, rather than any number of other environmental variables, as the principal input variable in our model.

Economic theory provides solid justification for postulating that eco-nomic development influences political system characteristics and policy outcomes.[7] Industrialization, whether in a planned or unplanned society, is said to result in increased specialization and demands for coordination. Coordination in a free enterprise economy is provided by the market mechanism and by corporate bureaucracies, but a great deal is also provided by government. Industrial development mandates the growth of public regulatory activity. The coordination demanded in our industrial society always involves certain inescapable difficulties: the expansion of some industries and contraction of others, overestimates and underestimates of economic conditions, and errors of judgment resulting in economic imbalances. In response to these dislocations, collective remedial action tends to increase, and added responsibilities are placed upon government. In addition, urbanization is understood to lead to a variety of social problems which are presumed to be amenable to collective action. This too implies added governmental responsibilities. Migration from rural to urban areas in response to the development of industry, the decline of agriculture, and the general search for economic opportunity by individuals and businesses also create governmental responsibilities. Economic development also involves expansion, at the state and local levels, of education, transportation, and welfare services, which are largely the responsibility of governments, as a result of dislocations and as an integral part of economic growth. Such expansion involves not only adjustment of state policies in these areas but also adjustment of the government tax and revenue systems which must finance all of these new responsibilities.

These linkages in economic theory appear to be well supported by empirical research. Recently, students of comparative government have attempted to isolate the *functional prerequisites* of political democracy and the socioeconomic conditions generating political stability and instability. Seymour Lipset in *Political Man* first used the term "economic development" to refer collectively to four related socioeconomic variables—industrialization, urbanization, wealth, and education.[8] Lipset studied the relationship between these economic development variables and the character of political systems in Western Europe and Latin America. Economic development variables and rates of change in these variables were shown to be related to stable democratic government as opposed to unstable democratic government or dictatorships. Robert Alford suggests that industrialization and urbanization encourage national political integration.[9] National political integration in turn affects other political system variables such as federalism, secularism in government, the emergence of national political parties, and class polarization in voting. Lyle Shannon correlated indices of economic development with self-government and non-self-government and showed that the latter type of political system is related to economic underdevelopment.[10]

Daniel Lerner utilized economic development variables to explain the stability of political systems in the Middle East and also introduced an additional dimension which affects stability, namely the disproportionate development of one or another of the indices of economic development. His views of the relationships between economic development and political system characteristics have already been cited by Lipset but they are worth quoting again at length:

> The secular evolution of a participant society appears to involve a regular sequence of three phases. Urbanization comes first, for cities alone have developed the complex of skills and resources which characterize the modern industrial economy. Within this urban matrix develop both of the attributes which distinguish the next two phases—literacy and media growth. There is a close reciprocal relationship between these, for the literate develop the media which in turn spread literacy. But, literacy performs the key function in the second phase. The capacity to read, at first acquired by relatively few people, equips them to perform the varied tasks required in the modernizing society. Not until the third phase, when the elaborate technology of industrial development is fairly well advanced, does society begin to produce newspapers, radio networks, and motion pictures on a massive scale. This, in turn, accelerates the spread of literacy. Out of this interaction develop those institutions of participation (e.g., voting) which we find in all advanced modern societies.[11]

These studies in comparative government have focused on the relationship between socioeconomic inputs and political system characteristics, but very few cross-cultural studies have explored the relationship between system variables and policy outputs. Phillips Cutright comments on this void in comparative research:

> Unfortunately, an inventory of the activities of national governments, or even a conceptual scheme to aid in their classification, is not at hand. Comparative studies of the outputs of national governments are limited by the lack of scales of these activities, and relatively little attention has been given to classification of the activities. Available indicators of government activities are not, however, being fully exploited.[12]

Cutright himself studied social security policy outcomes in 76 nations and the effect of economic development and national political organization on these outcomes. He found that, in spite of very great differences among nations in ideological orientation and type of political system, policy outcomes in the area of social security were strongly related to economic development. "Nations with high levels of economic development but with less than 'perfect' (i.e., democratic) political systems had government activities highly similar to those undertaken by democratic governments. . . . Similar levels of social security coverage are found in nations whose governments are thought to act in response to the popular will as occurs in nations whose governments are thought to act with less regard to public demands. It appears that the level of social security in a nation is a response to deeper strains affecting the organization of a society."[13] In terms of our model, Cutright is saying that social security policy outcomes among nations are more a product of economic development inputs than they are a product of political system characteristics.

It is clear that economic development merits inclusion in our model as a principal input variable. These studies in comparative national governments aid in the construction of our model of public policy outcomes, a model which hopefully can be transferred to the study of American state politics.

FIFTY STATES—A COMPARATIVE APPROACH

The development of an explanatory model of public policy, whether in international politics or American state politics, requires comparative analysis. Comparative analysis occupies a distinguished place in all political inquiry. Aristotle's studies were truly comparative, particularly if we remember that his definition of "constitution" included not only the political system of a society but also its socioeconomic character—the distribution of wealth, religion, education, and leisure. Studies which merely describe one political institution or event, without identifying or explaining similarities and differences among political data, cannot contribute substantially to the development of any explanatory theory of politics. Even the most insightful descriptions of specific political events cannot provide explanations which rise above the level of hunches. Roy Macridis explains that comparative study "entails the comparison of variables against a background of uniformity either actual or analytical for the purpose of discovering causal factors that account for variations."[14] Comparison, in other words, is an integral part of explanation. And all meaningful description is comparative; that is, facts can only be perceived when they are contrasted with some other element in the environment. Comparison is really basic to perception, conceptualization, explanation, thought, and expression.

Since comparisons are so critical to explanation, it follows that the value of the comparative approach is not limited to the study of national political systems. The comparative potential in American state politics is enormous, and it is a potential in which the more recent literature in American state politics has displayed significant interest.[15]

The American states provide an excellent opportunity for applying comparative analysis in non-experimental research. These fifty separate political systems share a common institutional framework and cultural milieu. All states operate under written constitutions which divide authority between executive, legislative, and judicial branches. The structure and operations of these branches are quite similar from state to state. All states function within the common framework of the American federal system. All states share a national language, national symbols, a¬d a national history. In short, important institutional and cultural factors may be treated as constants for analytical purposes.

This background of institutional and cultural uniformity in the American states makes it easier to isolate causal factors in our analysis of public policy outcomes. Comparative analysis of national political systems is made very difficult because of the many great institutional and cultural differences among national societies; it is difficult to isolate the reasons for variations in system characteristics or policy outcomes where vast differences exist in geography, climate, language, economy, history, religion, and so on. In contrast, when one focuses upon the American states many important independent variables are held constant, and the explanatory power of a single set of variables can be more clearly observed.

Of course the American states are not entirely alike, either with respect to socioeconomic development inputs, political system characteristics, or policy outcomes. And this too is an important asset in comparative research. In non-experimental research one cannot artificially manipulate variables in order to observe their effects; instead, one must find situations in the real world in which variations exist in the phenomena under study. The existence of variations from state to state in levels of economic development, political systems, and policy outcomes enables us to search for relationships between differences in policy outcomes and differences in levels of economic development or political system characteristics; and in order to test our model we must be able to observe the associated changes in these phenomena. It is the closeness of the relationships between variations in policy outcomes and variations in levels of economic development or political system characteristics which permits us to establish the utility of our model of policy outcomes. For example, if differences in policy outcomes are more closely associated with differences in economic development levels than differences in political systems, then we may infer that economic development is more of a determinant of policy outcomes than system characteristics. But if the closer association is between policy outcomes and system characteristics, then the opposite can be inferred.

Fortunately, if only for the sake of analysis, there are marked differences among the states in economic development levels.[16] In 1960 the median family income in Connecticut was two and one-half times what it was in Mississippi. Over 85 per cent of New Jersey residents lived in urban areas, while 65 per cent of North Dakota residents lived in rural areas. Only 1 per cent of the labor force in Massachusetts was engaged in agriculture, in contrast to 33 per cent in North Dakota. Kentucky adults averaged only an eighth-grade education, while adults in seven states averaged more than twelve years of schooling. This is sufficient variation to permit us to make observations about the impact of economic development levels on political systems and policy outcomes.

POLITICAL SYSTEMS AND POLICY OUTCOMES

Despite uniformity in constitutional framework, the political systems of the fifty states are remarkably varied. The comparative strength of the Republican and Democratic parties obviously differs. States can also be differentiated by the level of interparty competition and in the strength and functions of their party organizations. Furthermore, in some states conflict between rural and urban interests dominate state politics, while in other states conflict among regions, between legislature and governor, between liberal and conservative, or between labor and management may dominate the political scene. Some states are characterized by high levels of political participation, while in other states less than half of the eligible voters go to the polls. In some states the legislature makes the crucial decisions about public policy, while in other states the legislature simply rubberstamps the decisions of a strong governor, an influential party leader, or powerful interest groups in the state. In some states political alignments follow party lines, while in other states political battle lines reflect factional rivalries, competition among powerful interest groups, or conflict between liberals and conservatives or labor and industry. In short, state political systems can be quite different from one another.

Just as it was necessary to limit the number of environmental variables which could be included in our model, so also is it necessary to limit the number of system characteristics to be incorporated into it—another compromise with reality which we must make in the construction of a model.

Four sets of system variables have been chosen for inclusion in our model of policy outcomes, two reflecting characteristics of the party system and two reflecting characteristics of the electoral system. Party systems are represented in our model by several measures of the level of interparty competition in state politics and by measures of the division of Democratic and Republican party control of state government. Electoral systems are represented by several measures of the level of voter participation or turnout and by several measures of the degree of malapportionment in state legislative districts. All four of these system characteristics—the division of two-party control, the level of interparty competition, the level of voter participation, and the degree of malapportionment—have been hypothesized as influential in shaping policy outcomes in the American states.

What difference does it make in public policy outcomes whether a state is under Republican or Democratic party control? In the literature of American parties it has been argued that our two parties offer few policy alternatives.[17] American political parties are often regarded as "brokerage" organizations, devoid of ideology, and more inclined to adjust their policy positions to fit popular demands. Since parties in a two-party system must win a majority to hold office, each attempts to attract support from the moderate center of the electorate. In competing for this same market, parties are led to offer policy positions which are almost identical. This gives rise to the Tweedledee—Tweedledum image of American parties. In each state both parties tailor their policies to local conditions; politicians cater to the particular demands of their constituencies. The result is that the parties do not have any independent impact on policy outcomes. Parties merely reflect socioeconomic inputs, as do policy outcomes.

Herbert McClosky has challenged this view of the American party system. On the basis of survey material on the opinions of party leaders and rank-and-file members, he concludes that the parties are "distinct communities of cobelievers who diverge sharply on many important issues. . . . Republican and Democratic leaders stand furthest apart on the issues that grow out of their group identification and support—out of the managerial, proprietary and high status connections of the one, and the labor, minority, low status and intellectual connections of the other."[18] Of course this does not prove that these leaders act upon their divergent beliefs, but the implication in McClosky's work is that Democratic and Republican control of state government will independently affect policy. Support for this view is provided by Malcolm Jewell's compilation of data on party voting in state legislatures.[19] He found that on more than half of the non-unanimous roll-call votes in the legislatures of New York, Connecticut, Pennsylvania, Rhode Island, and Massachusetts, the majority of Democrats voted against the majority of Republicans. This is evidence of considerable party conflict in these states. William J. Keeffe reported that in both the Pennsylvania and Illinois legislatures the parties differed substantially on roll-call votes on major issues.[20] In both legislatures the Democratic party was more interested than the Republicans in labor, minorities, and social legislation, while the Republican party showed greater concern for fostering business and limiting the role of the government in regulating the economy.

On the other hand, there is evidence that in some states party voting is very infrequent and that the parties do not offer significantly different policy choices. The authors of *The Legislative System* obtained mixed results when they questioned legislators about what they thought the role of parties to be in legislative policy-making.[21] Over 90 per cent of New

Jersey legislators perceived considerable party influence. Ohio legislators were more divided: 51 per cent perceived considerable party influence, but 31 per cent saw little or no party influence. In California and Tennessee only 6 and 21 per cent, respectively, of the legislators perceived considerable party influence, and 40 and 57 per cent felt that parties exercised little or no influence.

Another possibility is that in some states it does make a difference which party is in office while in other states it does not. Analysis of party influence on roll-call votes in state legislative chambers suggests that interparty conflict on policy questions is more likely to occur in the urban industrial states in which the parties represent separate socioeconomic constituencies.[22] Party conflict over policy occurs in those states in which Democratic legislators represent central-city, low-income, ethnic, and racial constituencies and Republican legislators represent middle-class, suburban, small-town, and rural constituencies. In these states parties clash over taxation and appropriations, welfare, education, and the regulation of business and labor—in short, over the major social and economic controversies which divide national parties. Party conflict on policy questions is much less frequent in rural states where the parties must appeal to more homogeneous constituencies. These studies suggest that at least in urban industrial states, where the parties represent separate socioeconomic constituencies, it does make a difference which party controls state government.

The inclusion in our model of measures of Democratic and Republican party control allows us to explore these questions about the effects of partisanship on public policy. But in addition to the question of Democratic or Republican control of state government, there is also the separate question of the impact of interparty competition on policy outcomes. What difference does it make in public policy outcomes whether a state is characterized by highly competitive two-party politics or non-competitive one-party dominance?

A number of scholars have described and classified state political systems according to their levels of interparty competition: Ranney and Kendall, Key, Schlesinger, and Golembiewski, for example.[23] It seems clear that economic development affects the level of interparty competition. Golembiewski, in a study of relationships between a variety of "sociological factors" and state party systems, reported statistically significant associations between urbanism, income, and industrialization, and classifications of party competition among the states. Ranney and Kendall, Key, and Schlesinger have also indicated that one or more of the measures of economic development correlates closely with party competition in the American states. These studies tend to confirm the existence of the linkage between economic development and political system characteristics postulated by our model (linkage *a* in Figure 1).

On the other hand, the linkage between party competition and policy outcomes (linkage *b* in Figure 1) has *not* been systematically established. "Conclusions" about the effect of party competition on policy are mainly derived from a priori analysis or from anecdotal data. For example, it is often argued that competitiveness results in increased benefits for citizens because the parties are forced to bid for votes. Students of state party systems also feel that it is more difficult to hold factions responsible for policy choices than it is to hold competitive parties responsible. One-party factional systems may obscure politics for most voters and permit conservative interests to manipulate factional alignments. A large number of people who have little knowledge about the policies of various factions may be easily misled. Even if policy differences between parties are vague, there is at least the distinction between an *in-party* and an *out-party* which voters can identify at election time, and this is not really true in a one-party system. All of this implies that the policy choices of competitive states are different from those of non-competitive states.

Empirical evidence to support speculation about the effect of party competition on policy outcomes is meager. In *Southern Politics,* V. O. Key, Jr., finds that states with loose multi-factional systems with little continuity of competition tend to pursue conservative policies on behalf of upper socioeconomic interests.[24] States with cohesive and continuous factions pursue more liberal policies on behalf of less affluent interests. Duane Lockard observed among the six New England states that the two-party states (Massachusetts, Rhode Island, and Connecticut), in contrast to the one-party states (Maine, New Hampshire, and Vermont), received larger proportions of their revenue from business and death taxes, spent more on welfare services such as aid to the blind, the aged, and dependent children, and were better apportioned.[25] Neither of these studies, however, attempted systematically to hold constant for the impact of economic development while observing these policy outcomes. It was Dawson and Robinson who first attempted to sort out the influence of party competition on policy outcomes from the influence of economic development.[26] The focus of the Dawson and Robinson study was upon outcomes in welfare policy, particularly the average assistance payments to categories of welfare recipients. On the basis of rank orderings of the states, they found that increases in both party competition and levels of income, urbanization, and industrialization were usually accompanied by increases in welfare benefits. However, when wealth was held constant party competition no longer appeared to be closely related to increased welfare benefits. The authors concluded that "inter-party competition does not play as influential a role in determining the nature and scope of welfare policies as earlier studies suggested. The level of public social welfare programs in the American states seems to be more a function of socio-economic factors, especially per capita income."[27]

In short, there are good a priori reasons to believe that party competition does independently influence policy outcomes, but, on the other hand, there is some empirical evidence that suggests otherwise. There are some correlations between public policies and party competition, but they may be merely a product of the relationships between economic development and policy outcomes. The inclusion of party competition in our model of policy outcomes permits us to explore these questions.

The level of voter participation is also an interesting characteristic of political systems, and one which might reasonably be expected to influence public policy outcomes. Of course voting and non-voting have important meaning for the political system, since they represent levels of confidence in political institutions and degrees of support for the democratic rules of the game.[28] But we are more interested in the effect of high or low electoral participation on policy outcomes. Do states with consistently higher voter turnouts pursue policies noticeably different from those pursued by states with low turnouts, and can these policy differences be traced to the effect of voter participation?

There are good reasons to hypothesize that participation levels do influence policy choices.[29] Non-voting is most common among lower-income, lower-status, poorly educated groups. High voter participation is a characteristic of higher-status, higher-income, well educated groups. Non-voting is also characteristic of non-white populations; non-whites vote less often than whites even when income, status, and education attributes are the same. In addition, the Republican party draws its most reliable support from the higher socioeconomic groups who vote more frequently; low turnouts are said to hurt the Democratic party which draws its strength more heavily from lower socioeconomic groups. Certainly the outcomes of elections are vitally affected by turnout levels, and the presumption is that public policy is in turn influenced by the outcome of elections.

The final system variable to be included in our model of policy outcomes is malapportionment. Commentators on state politics have often implied that malapportionment seriously affects the policy choices of state legislatures. In the literature on state politics it is frequently argued that there are important policy differences between urban and rural constituencies and that malapportionment which overrepresents rural interests grants the rural constituencies a real advantage in policy-making. Charles Adrian has stated, "Malapportionment, in terms of population, has serious effects upon governmental policies,"[30] and V. O. Key has added, "it must be assigned a high rank"[31] among the factors which have led to the low status of state legislatures. Of course there is little doubt that malapportionment affects the character of state political systems or processes, but determining its effects on the content of public policy is a more difficult problem.

Proponents of reapportionment have been very enthusiastic about its consequences for policy outcomes. They have frequently attributed a lack of party competition, unfair distributions of state funds, conservative tax schemes, unprogressive educational policies, and penny-pinching welfare programs to rural overrepresentation; they expect to see these policies changed by reapportionment. Reapportionment, it is said, will help the states to come to grips with the important domestic problems facing the nation and so resume their rightful place in the American federal system.[32]

In contrast, a few scholars have urged more caution regarding predictions about the policy consequences of reapportionment. Duane Lockard referred specifically to the effect of malapportionment on policy outcomes in Massachusetts and Connecticut: "Do states with fair apportionment respond to urban appeals more readily? If anyone has made a systematic study of this, I am unaware of it, but limited evidence does not seem to indicate that the states with fair apportionment are any more considerate of urban problems than states with malapportionment."[33] Herbert Jacob was equally skeptical about the effect of reapportionment on public policy. In a study of the effects of malapportionment on party competition, highway funds distribution, and certain welfare expenditures, he found that conditions in malapportioned states were not noticeably different from conditions in well-apportioned states. He concluded, "it is improbable that it [reapportionment] will substantially invigorate state governments or dissolve the stalemates which sap public confidence in them."[34]

The impact of apportionment practices on policy outcomes in no way affects the moral or constitutional issues involved in state legislature reapportionment. The federal courts are committed to a policy of insuring to each citizen the equal protection of apportionment laws, regardless of whether or not, or how, reapportionment affects policy outcomes. But inclusion of apportionment measures in our model of policy outcomes enables us to predict the policy changes which may occur in the wake of court-ordered reapportionment. . . .

NOTES

[1] For a thorough discussion of the utility of models, see Herbert A. Simon and Allen Newell, "Models, Their Uses and Limitations," *The State of the Social Sciences,* ed. Leonard D. White (Chicago: University of Chicago Press, 1956); Paul Meadows, "Models, Systems, and Science," *American Sociological Review,* XXII (1957), 3–9; and James M. Beshers, "Models and Theory Construction," *American Sociological Review,* XXII (1957), 32–38.

[2] Hubert M. Blalock, Jr., *Causal Inferences from Nonexperimental Research* (Chapel Hill: University of North Carolina Press, 1964), pp. 7–9.

[3] This conceptualization is based upon David Easton's "An Approach to the Analysis of Political Systems," *World Politics,* IX (1957), 383–400; and his *A Framework for Political Analysis* (New York: Prentice-Hall, 1965), pp. 23–76. See also Richard E. Dawson and James A. Robinson, "Inter-Party Competition, Economic Variables, and Welfare Policies in the American States," *Journal of Politics,* XXV (1963), 265–89.

[4] The distinction between normative and empirical models is discussed in Vernon Van Dyke, *Political Science: A Philosophical Analysis* (Stanford: Stanford University Press, 1960), pp. 6–13, 104–7.

[5] Daniel Lerner and Harold D. Lasswell (eds.), *The Policy Sciences* (Stanford: Stanford University Press, 1960).

[6] See Harold D. Lasswell, "The Policy Orientation," in Lerner and Lasswell, *op. cit.,* pp. 3–15.

[7] See the discussion of economic development by James R. Elliot, "A Comment on Inter-Party Competition, Economic Variables, and Welfare Policies in the American States," *Journal of Politics,* XXVII (1965), 185–91. In establishing the theoretical linkages between economic development and political systems, Elliot cites the work of Bruce R. Morris, *Problems of American Economic Growth* (New York: Oxford, 1961); Walter Krause, *Economic Development* (San Francisco: Wadsworth, 1961); Charles P. Kindleberger, *Economic Development* (New York: McGraw-Hill, 1958); Benjamin Higgins, *Economic Development* (New York: Norton, 1959); Henry H. Villard, *Economic Development* (New York: Holt, Rinehart, and Winston, 1960); and W. W. Rostow, *The Process of Economic Growth,* 2nd ed. (New York: Norton, 1962).

[8] Seymour Martin Lipset, *Political Man* (New York: Doubleday, 1960); and "Some Social Requisites of Democracy: Economic Development and Political Legitimacy," *American Political Science Review,* LIII (1959), 69–105.

[9] Robert R. Alford, *Party and Society* (Chicago: Rand McNally, 1963).

[10] Lyle W. Shannon (ed.), *Underdeveloped Areas* (New York: Harper, 1957); and "Is Level of Development Related to Capacity for Self-Government?" *American Journal of Economics and Sociology,* XVII (1958), 367–82.

[11] Daniel Lerner, *The Passing of Traditional Society* (Glencoe, Ill.: Free Press, 1958), p. 60.

[12] Phillips Cutright, "Political Structure, Economic Development, and National Security Programs," *American Journal of Sociology,* LXX (1965), 537–48. Reprinted by permission of The University of Chicago Press. See also Phillips Cutright, "National Political Development: Measurement and Analysis," *American Sociological Review,* XXVIII (1963), 253–64; U.S. Department of Health, Education, and Welfare, Social Security Administration, *Social Security Programs Throughout the World 1961* (Washington: Government Printing Office, 1961).

[13] Cutright, "Political Structure, Economic Development, and National Security Programs," *op. cit.,* p. 548.

[14] Roy C. Macridis, *The Study of Comparative Government* (New York: Doubleday, 1955), p. 2.

[15] See, for example, Herbert Jacob and Kenneth Vines (eds.), *Politics in the American States: A Comparative Analysis* (New York: Little, Brown, 1965).

[16] U.S. Bureau of the Census, "United States Summary," *Census of Population 1960,* PC (1)-1C (Washington: Government Printing Office, 1960).

[17] For example, V. O. Key, Jr., *Politics, Parties, and Pressure Groups,* 4th ed. (New York: Crowell, 1958), Chapter 8; and Maurice Duverger, *Political Parties* (New York: Wiley, 1958).

[18] Herbert McClosky *et al.,* "Issue Conflict and Consensus among Leaders and Followers," *American Political Science Review,* LIV (1960), 426.

[19] Malcolm Jewell, *The State Legislature* (New York: Random House, 1962), p. 52.

[20] William J. Keefe, "Comparative Study of the Role of Political Parties in State Legislatures," *Western Political Quarterly,* IX (1956), 535–41.

[21] John C. Wahlke, Heinz Eulau, William Buchanan, and Leroy C. Ferguson, *The Legislative System* (New York: Wiley, 1962), p. 425.

[22] Duncan MacRae, "The Relation between Roll Call Votes and Constituencies in the Massachusetts House of Representatives," *American Political Science Review,* XLVI (1952), 1046–55; and Thomas R. Dye, "A Comparison of Constituency Influences in the Upper and Lower Houses of a State Legislature," *Western Political Quarterly,* XIV (1961), 473–80.

[23] Austin Ranney and Willmoore Kendall, "The American Party System," *American Political Science Review,* XLVIII (1954), 477–85; Joseph A. Schlesinger, "A Two-Dimensional Scheme for Classifying the States According to Degree of Inter-Party Competition," *American Political Science Review,* XLIX (1955), 1120–28; V. O. Key, Jr., *American State Politics: An Introduction* (New York: Knopf, 1956), p. 99; and Robert T. Golembiewski, "A Taxonomic Approach to State Political Party Strength," *Western Political Quarterly,* XI (1958), 494–513.

[24] V. O. Key, Jr., *Southern Politics in State and Nation* (New York: Knopf, 1951), pp. 298–314.

[25] Duane Lockard, *New England State Politics* (Princeton: Princeton University Press, 1959), pp. 320–40.

[26] Dawson and Robinson, "Inter-Party Competition, Economic Variables, and Welfare Policies in the American States," *op. cit.* See also the same authors' "The Politics of Welfare," in Jacob and Vines, *op. cit.,* pp. 371–410.

[27] Dawson and Robinson, "Inter-Party Competition, Economic Variables, and Welfare Policies in the American States," *op. cit.,* p. 289.

[28] Lester W. Milbrath, *Political Participation* (Chicago: Rand McNally, 1965).

[29] See Dawson and Robinson, "The Politics of Welfare," *op. cit.,* pp. 406–7.

[30] Charles Adrian, *State and Local Governments* (New York: McGraw-Hill, 1960), pp. 306–7. See also Daniel Grant and H. C. Nixon, *State and Local Government in America* (Boston: Allyn and Bacon, 1963), pp. 204–5; and Jewell, *op. cit.,* pp. 30–33.

[31] Key, *American State Politics, op. cit.,* pp. 76–77.

[32] See footnotes 30 and 31; in addition, see Commission on Intergovernmental Relations, *A Report to the President for Transmittal to Congress* (Washington: Government Printing Office, 1955), p. 39.

[33] Duane Lockard, *The Politics of State and Local Government* (New York: Macmillan, 1963), p. 319.

[34] Herbert Jacob, "The Consequences of Malapportionment: A Note of Caution," *Social Forces,* XLIII (1964), 261.

[35] Council of State Governments, *Book of the States 1962–63* (Chicago: Council of State Governments, 1963).

CHAPTER 3

A Theory of Policy Analysis
and Some Preliminary Applications

Robert Salisbury
John Heinz

This paper continues a line of inquiry which for the last several years has considered the question: How can we think about public policy decisions in ways that are (1) relevant to the development of empirical theory in the discipline, and (2) grounded in the data and techniques of systematic empirical investigation. This literature includes such work as that of Lowi and Froman regarding the theory development side, and the by now formidable array of Dawson and Robinson, Dye, Hofferbert, Sharkansky, and a number of others who have assessed the data.[1] Most if not all of these studies are set in a general frame which is at least quasi-Eastonian. Policy decisions are of central theoretical concern, viewed as the outputs of a political system which is responding to the inputs of resources, demands and supports. (This general orientation may be contrasted with the functional process orientation associated with Gabriel Almond and his colleagues wherein policy decisions receive comparatively scant attention in either the theoretical or empirical treatment.)

The thrust of a substantial number of the empirical studies of policy is that variations in the political system do not explain much of the variance in outputs. Rather than such classic political variables as party competition, apportionment patterns, or gubernatorial strength, the critical independent variables appear to be such items as income, urbanization, sectional or regional value orientations, and habit patterns regarding policy. Whatever relevance political system characteristics may have in other contexts, they do not greatly affect the *amount* of public expenditure in any of the numerous categories investigated once system resource variables are controlled.

It should be noted that (1) these findings deal mainly with expendi-

We are grateful to Robert H. Salisbury, John P. Heinz, and the American Political Science Association for permission to print this essay, which was presented at the 1968 American Political Science Association Convention, Washington, D.C., September 2–7, 1968.

tures and are concerned, at various levels of refinement of observation, to explain variations on a "more or less" dimension; (2) these findings are not asserted on theoretical grounds to have general validity—indeed there is contrary evidence for some earlier periods—but only to describe the situation, and the "normal" situation not the innovative one, as it has existed in recent American times; and (3) these findings accept and work within the policy categories "given" by the real political world and have therefore a low level of abstraction. Consequently, apart from the need for continuing refinement of this line of analysis, a number of major issues of policy analysis remains unsettled. One, which is perhaps the most completely unsettled, is the function of the political system in translating or processing demands into outputs. Hitherto the assumption underlying most discussion of this part of the process seems to have been that the political system accomplished its processing tasks by, in some sense, *representing* the demands and therefore securing outputs which would satisfy the demands. John Wahlke has argued persuasively that we have overstressed demand representation and underestimated the significance of supports.[2] Even this view, however, leaves the dynamics of the decisional system unclear since if decision-makers do not act by virtue of pressure on them, why, then, do they act? We shall not settle this issue here but only observe that it is opened, elevated to major theoretical importance, and left up in the air by the recent research on public policy.

A second issue which will be a major preoccupation of the rest of this paper is, in effect, what about all the policies which are not cast in the form of expenditures? How shall one analyze decisions which make or revise rules, establish or disestablish structures and programs, or administer justice in a court? A basic thesis of this paper is that there is a fundamental distinction to be made between decisions which allocate tangible benefits directly to persons or groups, as expenditures generally do, and decisions which establish rules or structures of authority to guide future allocations. Further, we shall argue, political system variables of the kind alleged to have little impact on the *amount* of expenditure may still have significant effect on the *kind* or the *distribution* of the amount.

I

There are by now several extant efforts at establishing a typology of public policy which would not simply accept the conventional categories of education, highways, welfare, etc. We shall not again review these, but we will indicate briefly the intellectual lineage of the typology proposed here. In a genuinely seminal essay Lowi argued that there are three fundamental types of policy: distributive, redistributive and regulatory; that these types are distinguishable mainly according to the degree of disaggregation of the treatment the policy in question provides to those groups it affects; and that there is some sort of developmental sequence that occurs in a technologically sophisticated system, roughly from distributive to regulatory policy.

Salisbury revised and extended Lowi's approach by suggesting that different policy types—distributive, redistributive, regulative or self-regulative—could be expected to emerge as outputs of various types of interaction between two key variables, the pattern of demand and the structure of the decisional system.[3] The two variables were placed on axes depicting the degree of fragmentation–integration in each. A highly fragmented demand pattern, *e.g.,* where each county seeks a subsidy for its roads, might interact with a fragmented decisional system, *e.g.,* most legislatures, and the result would be a distributive policy of the classic pork barrel variety. An integrated decisional system, a strong executive, for example, facing a relatively integrated demand of two conflicting groups, might be forced into choosing sides in what was interpreted as a zero-sum game.

Self-regulatory policy might be anticipated when an integrated group made demands of a fragmented decisional system with the policy decision being to delegate authority, say in the form of self-administered licensing authority, to the demand group. The fourth type, regulatory policy, was interpreted as resulting from the interaction of fragmented demand and integrated decisional system and was characterized by continuing governmental agency control over the demand groups. Characteristic of both regulatory and self-regulatory policies is ambiguity regarding winners and losers. The benefits are unclear because they are expressed in the abstract terms of rules and structures, and the tangible benefits themselves are deferred in a regulatory decision.

It was argued in that paper that political scientists have for generations been preoccupied with regulatory policy and particularly with constitutional policy, or policy decisions which establish or revise authority structures. It was argued further that in the American case the interactions of demand and decisional systems have tended historically to be concentrated in the distributive portion of the matrix, although modern times may have brought about somewhat greater aggregation of demand and integration of decisional systems, notably manifested in increased strength of the executive.

As we see it the major difficulty in the argument advanced previously lay in the conception of regulatory policy. More than the other three types identified, the meaning of regulation as distinguished from distribution was fuzzy to say the least. Perhaps this was a natural consequence of a conception which stressed ambiguity regarding beneficiaries as the criterion of classification, but we remained unsatisfied nevertheless. It will be recalled

that regulatory policy was asserted to result from the interaction of fragmented demand and integrated decisional system. Regulatory policies, such
as constitutional revisions, would thus be postulated to follow from diverse
group interests pressing claims upon a decisional body which was integrated enough to defer specific benefit decisions in favor of more general
rules. But the concept of integration in the decisional system is troublesome. Is a constitutional convention, or for that matter a Supreme Court,
more integrated a system than a legislature? Any measures of decision
system integration one might devise might have great trouble discovering
less unity on public works appropriations, undoubtedly a distributive
policy, than on constitutional changes. The terms integration and fragmentation are often used to identify significant features of decisional
systems but their empirical meaning is not clear.

On reflection, it appears to us that *any* decisional systems must
achieve some degree of integration in order to make *any* decision. The
minimum required is provided in the formal decisional rules; fifty percent
plus one, two-thirds, a constitutional majority, or what not. Informal
norms may add to or alter this minimum. But some measure of agreement
is essential. The agreement in a decisional system comes, however, at the
conclusion of the decisional process. And sometimes this process may be
arduous, sometimes easy. The question then is not the amount of integration achieved but rather how difficult or costly is it to achieve the requisite
coalition. From this perspective if we say that a legislature is likely to be
more fragmented than an executive agency, we mean that it is generally
more difficult or costly to organize the majority required for action in the
former than in the latter. And this alters our original argument considerably. We now regard the decisional system under scrutiny not as fixed
along an integration-fragmentation axis but as a variable whose functioning
is problematic. The more costly it is to organize decisional coalitions, the
more fragmented we may regard the decisional unit. But these costs will
vary depending on the type of policy under consideration. A legislative
majority can be organized more readily for some things than for others. So,
indeed, in any decisional systems. Can this observation be generalized and
linked to our earlier typology?

Let us do so in the following way. Let us conceptualize the linkages
between demand, and support as well, and a decisional system in terms of
cost-benefit ratios to decision-makers. That is, decision-makers will behave,
ceteris paribus, so as to optimize their cost-benefit ratios operating in
regard to a particular set of activities. The calculus involved will include
the value, positive and negative, to the decision-maker of acting so as to
confer benefits upon some relevant constituency; the costs of informing
himself about the substantive issue sufficiently to develop a position; and

the cost of investing time, energy, and resources in negotiating a favorable winning coalition. These costs will vary from issue to issue and individual to individual within a decisional system but we may generalize about their relative magnitudes and modes among institutions as well.

Now our initial formulation of this cost-benefit argument involves a fundamental distinction between two types of policy, allocative and structural. By allocative policies we mean decisions which confer direct benefits, material or symbolic, upon individuals and groups. Structural policies we take to mean policies which establish authority structures or rules to guide future allocations. The latter policies are more abstractly formulated and more ambiguous in their effect than the former. Allocative policies may vary along a distributive-redistributive axis; structural policies may vary as between regulatory and self-regulatory outcomes. We shall explore this further at a later point. For now let us assert our most *fundamental* hypothesis linking the cost-benefit calculus we described above to this distinction in policy outcomes:

> The more costly it is to organize the requisite coalition on an issue, the more likely it is that the policy outcome will be structural rather than allocative.

II

Let us consider a brief example. One state legislature receives the budgetary requests for the several state colleges and universities and makes the decisions about how much money each will receive. A neighboring state legislature makes a *de facto* delegation of authority to a state board of higher education to receive and adjust the budget requests for the state schools and ratifies the board's recommendations. In the former case the legislature makes an allocation decision, typically a highly distributive one in which each institution gets an incremental increase over its last appropriation. In the latter state, however, the legislature has, in effect, opted out of the allocation and instead chosen to make a structural, or regulatory, decision by establishing the state board. Why the different *types* of decision? Our explanation rests on the relative costs, as perceived by the decision-makers, of the one kind of decision as against the other. In the state where the Board makes the allocative decisions the key legislators no longer perceive much constituency–linked advantage to the old system. Where once the groups with the greatest active interest in higher education were concentrated in the districts containing the institutions, now the demand for expanded public higher education comes from everywhere and, indeed, there are state institutions of one kind or another almost everywhere. To logroll in this context would be exceedingly complex and individual legislators might find it very difficult to show their constituents where they had gained any advantage. For constituents as well as legislators it is vastly easier and more relevant to contemplate higher education in terms of a statewide system. Moreover, demand for higher education is not simply for places to accommodate Johnny. It is directed also toward developing the training and research facilities which are universally perceived as vital components of the state's economic growth. The demand is thus strong and steady but little tied to constituencies and hence to electoral benefits of interest to legislators. To make an allocative decision will be of small benefit to him. We may say that his constituency exchange values are low. At the same time, the growing magnitude and complexity of the state higher education system markedly increases information costs to the legislators. It becomes ever more difficult for them to learn enough about the problem to reach a policy preference of any substantive detail. And the diffusion of constituency interests helps to render the task of negotiating a winning coalition in the legislature uncertain and therefore potentially expensive. It has become more costly (and less beneficial) for legislators to allocate college and university monies, and so they opt out by creating a structural unit to do it for them.

Now why does the other state legislature continue to make its own allocations decisions? Reflecting perhaps a lower rate of economic growth and a less sophisticated urban and industrial base, the demand for higher education expansion is less vigorous. It continues to be fragmented regionally and expressed in ways that sustain viable legislator-constituent exchanges in the principally affected districts. Moreover, the slower pace of change makes it seem less difficult for key legislators to remain abreast of the issues. It is thus not so costly and more profitable to negotiate directly among themselves and the legislators do.

It is characteristic of many decisional systems to meet rising information and negotiation costs and/or declining exchange values by adopting *de facto* structural rules which call for the actual allocations to be worked out elsewhere. The deference paid legislative committees is a well-known example. Delegation to administrative agencies is another. The "agree bill" phenomenon described by Steiner and Gove,[4] wherein the principal demand groups work out their differences in advance, illustrates a type of self-regulative structural decision. Codification of the criminal code offers still another illustration.

An early President of this Association, Paul S. Reinsch, observed sixty years ago that American legislatures had never been particularly interested in code revision and tended to accept the recommendations of expert commissions.[5] He noted that this behavior could be observed as far back as the first thorough-going code revision in this country, which took place in New York in the 1820's under the sponsorship of Governor DeWitt Clinton. The same tendency has been observed somewhat more recently by Heinz in connection with the 1961 Illinois Criminal Code.

The Bar Association Committee responsible for the new Illinois Criminal Code was rather explicitly instructed by leaders of the state legislature that, wherever possible, controversies were to be resolved before the draft code was presented to the legislature. It was understood that compromises or agreements were to be reached with all important groups having serious objections to the draft, so that the legislature could give the matter minimum time and attention and avoid becoming embroiled. And that is what happened. The drafting committee consisted entirely of Chicago lawyers, with the exception of its secretary, Professor Charles Bowman of the University of Illinois School of Law. The result was quite a liberal and progressive code, by any standard, which rather closely followed in many respects the American Law Institute's Model Penal Code. In spite of its liberality, especially in the area of sentencing, the Code sailed through the legislature with a minimum of trouble—and, not coincidentally, a minimum of notice. On the one part of the draft code which gave rise to really serious conflict—the sex crime provisions—the drafting committee worked out a compromise which eliminated the problem before it got to the legislature. The drafters had substantially adopted the view of the Model Penal Code on both homosexuality and abortion—briefly, permitting private, consensual homosexual acts and therapeutic abortion. (These were, of course, very significant changes in the existing law.) The Catholic Church took strong exception to both of these proposals, but especially to the abortion provision. Before the controversy got very far, Professor Bowman sat down with the Church's lobbyist, one Mr. Claire Driscoll, and reached the rather simple agreement that the committee would instead recommend no change in the State's strict laws against abortion, in return for which the Church would cease its opposition to the homosexuality provisions. Both sides kept their agreement, and there was no trouble in the legislature.

Any legislature would have had great difficulty with these delicate issues had they attempted to work out the reallocations of legal status themselves. The structural decision to delegate and ratify was a great deal less costly to achieve and apparently did not cost much in exchange values.

The situation we have just described involved *de facto* delegations of authority by the legislature. In addition, of course, there are many examples of formally more complete and *de jure* delegation, as when a legislature (or a legislature plus the executive) decides to delegate a part of its Constitutional decision-making power to an independent regulatory commission. This kind of policy also appears to reflect the inability of the decisional system to meet the rising costs of making its own allocative policies. Often the demand may have become so intense and diffuse, as it was both for and against railroad regulation in the 1880's[6] that the legislature throws up its hands in despair. The same kind of thing happens when a patronage-dispensing system, having tired of creating "nine enemies and one ingrate" with every appointment, decides to set up a civil service commission. By taking such action, the decisional system either delays the time when it must choose whom to indulge and whom to deprive, or avoids the choice entirely.

Federal regulatory commissions make both structural or regulatory and allocative policy. Indeed, administrative law recognizes the distinction between the two types of decisions, terming the former "rule making" and the latter "adjudication." The reason why we class rule making as regulatory is obvious—in fact, the legal term is quite descriptive of our definition of the concept "regulatory." Most "adjudication" decisions, on the other hand, are allocative (distributive or redistributive) precisely because they allocate a television channel or an air route or whatever to one applicant rather than another. It is interesting that the Administrative Procedure Act in a sense recognizes and reinforces this pattern by requiring a more cumbersome decision process for rule making than for adjudication. The Act requires more steps in a rule making proceeding, and requires that more people become involved. In short, it invites a fragmentation of demand and makes the decisional process more costly to the interested parties. Thus, the characteristics which we would expect to find in a system producing regulatory policy have in this case been institutionalized by the Act as legal requirements of the system.

It will be apparent that the interpretation pursued here, though formulated independently, is closely akin to that recently presented by Adrian and Press.[7] Their more extended formulation of a cost typology stresses what we here have aggregated under two headings, negotiation costs and information costs. For our purposes, and without disputing the validity of their more detailed formulation, we shall treat most of their other costs as sub-types of our negotiation costs. Adrian and Press use the term information costs but appear to mean something else by it. Our use of information costs stresses information about the *policy* issue rather than, as with them, information about value orderings of other decision-makers. In effect, it is the cost of developing a value or preference ordering for oneself. Information of special relevance to our scheme is that dealing with the predicted impact of alternative allocations upon the objects of the policy: farmers, taxpayers, constituents, persons accused of crime, or whatever. Information costs include the cost to the decision-maker of finding out what, if anything, his constituents want—the cost of determining the exchange value. Adrian and Press do not include exchange values as part of their argument. We think that the value accruing to the legislator from his constituency of making or participating in making a policy choice is clearly a significant and variable part of his implicit calculations.

III

Let us move another step in the argument. From the basic hypothesis—if costs to decision-makers exceed some level, structural decisions will be preferred to allocation decisions—and from the above discussion what corollaries can be deduced? Let us briefly suggest several more to illustrate how the three cost-benefit components are worked into the general argument.

If demand is strong, relatively stable and district-specific—*e.g.,* for rivers and harbors improvements—information costs will be low, exchange values high (and costs therefore low), and allocative decisions will be preferred.

The more diffuse the demand, the greater the information costs (and under some conditions exchange values will also be low), and structural decisions, *e.g.,* delegation of authority, will be preferred.

If demand is strong and *ad hoc, i.e.,* confined to one issue and one segment of time rather than continuous and incremental, information costs will be high and structural decisions, *e.g.,* granting permissive authority to the *ad hoc* demand group, will be preferred.

The more integrated (cohesive, unified, hierarchical) the decisional system, the lower the negotiation costs, and the more likely allocative decisions will be preferred.

The greater the procedural distance the decision-maker is from the site of the evidentiary record, the greater his information costs, and the more likely a structural or rule decision will be preferred.

Now let us proceed still another step, and, in doing so, forge another link to our original analytic schema. Once the choice is made between an allocative policy and a structural policy what additional *types* of choices are open to decision-makers? Here we would preserve the distinctions offered earlier. Allocative policies may range along a distributive-redistributive continuum. That is, they may distribute the resources in question equally among all the putative objects of policy, or they may distribute in any of a nearly infinite number of unequal ways, or they may redistribute resources so that some policy objects (districts, groups, firms, individuals, nations) are more or less explicitly deprived and others advantaged.

We are prepared to adhere to the earlier hypotheses also regarding the conditions governing the extent of redistribution. That is, redistributive policy is likely to result from relatively highly integrated demand operating on a relatively integrated (*i.e.,* where costs of reaching a decision are relatively low in proportion to the exchange values involved) decisional system. Demand integration refers to the unity of the groups demanding a policy decision. It does not refer to mere parallelism of interests, as when many districts desire defense contracts, but requires more explicit and usually organized unity of action pressing for the decision. We would also reassert our earlier contention that in the United States demand is seldom sufficiently integrated and/or decision costs are seldom low enough to eventuate in much seriously redistributive policy—at least not without side-payments to assuage elements of the demand structure. At the same time, however, much policy has moderately redistributive elements, and a large portion of the policy *proposals* advanced by various contending parties may be highly redistributive.

If the costs of decision are high, and a structural or regulatory decision is chosen, there remains open the question of whether it may be one granting self-regulation to the group whose demands precipitated the decision. Here we would argue, as before, that when the policy objects are heterogeneous, or uncertain, or simply numerous and unorganized, regulatory policy results. Where, however, the object group generates the policy demand, is clearly identified, and highly integrated the likely policy result is to grant the authority to engage in self-regulation. Again the classic case occurs in the area of professional and quasi-professional group licensing. The disputed issues of self-regulation policy are those where a group demands such a delegation of authority to itself, claiming a high degree of integration, only to have the policy-makers perceive additional interests which would be affected and which, while perhaps silent at present, might be provoked into action by such a policy.

Let us represent in diagrammatic form the two fundamental arguments made, the one in Salisbury's earlier paper and the present one. Figure 1 shows both axes representing the degree of fragmentation-integra-

Figure 1

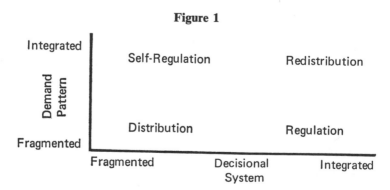

Figure 2

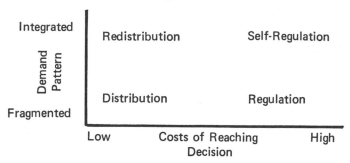

tion, one of the demand pattern and one of the decisional system. Figure 2 preserves the vertical axis from Figure 1 but presents the variable of decision costs along the horizontal axis. It will be noted that this alters the relationships among policy types along the lines and for the reasons indicated in the previous discussion. Let us turn to some further examples of policy decisions to see how the argument may be useful in organizing data.

IV

A theory of policy formation must, if it is to be comprehensive, account for policies made by all kinds of governmental agencies. Thus far we have concentrated attention on legislative decisions with a brief note on regulatory agencies. Let us now consider the courts with particular reference to criminal law policy.

All courts are relatively highly integrated decisional systems, as compared to legislatures, for example, and thus one might expect all courts to produce allocative policy decisions. But appellate courts, being more remote from the facts in question, ordinarily have higher information costs than do trial courts, and we argue that appellate courts are, consequently, more likely to produce regulatory or structural policy decisions than are trial courts. This is not to say that appellate courts *always* produce regulatory decisions. On the contrary, they produce a good many allocative decisions—as we shall shortly note—and this is consistent with the degree of integration of their decision-making structures. But the point is that appellate courts may produce policies of *either* of the two major categories, depending on the level of the information cost to them in a particular case. (Though the same is, of course, true of trial courts, it is less costly for them to produce allocative decisions because they are closer to the facts.)

Perhaps the classic case to illustrate an appellate court's information costs is the United States Supreme Court's decision in *NcNabb* v. *United States,* 318 U.S. 332 (1943). A very important step in the development of the law of confessions, that case held that a confession obtained after an unreasonable delay in arraignment could not be used at trial. In his decision for the Court, Justice Frankfurter made the flat statement that the McNabb brothers "were not brought before a United States Commissioner or a judge" during the two days they were held prior to their confessions. He was simply wrong. Though the record was silent on the point, the McNabbs *had,* in fact, been arraigned promptly. Thus, an important Supreme Court decision rested its rationale squarely upon a mistake of fact. (And given the legendary meticulousness and ego of Justice Frankfurter, one can imagine what his reaction must have been—especially since it came relatively early in his years on the Court.) No decision-making body can afford to have very many such incidents come to light, and especially not one where the expectation is so strong that the decisions will reflect a maximum of reason and informed deliberation.

Thus, the U.S. Supreme Court—like all appellate courts—will refuse to decide a case if it feels that the state of the formal record before it does not permit sufficient certainty about the crucial facts. For example, on the final decision day of its October 1967 term, (which was June 17, 1968) the Supreme Court announced its dismissal of the writ of certiorari it had previously granted in the case of *Wainwright* v. *New Orleans,* 88 S. Ct. 2243 (1968). That is, after granting certiorari, receiving briefs, and hearing argument, the Court decided that it was not going to decide the case. The reason was succinctly stated by Justice Harlan: "I find this record too opaque to permit any satisfactory adjudication. . . ." And Justice Fortas, with whom Justice Marshall joined, said:

Upon oral argument and further study after the writ was granted it became apparent that the facts necessary for evaluation of the dispositive constitutional issues in this case are not adequately presented by the record before us. It is also entirely clear that they cannot now be developed on remand with any verisimilitude. . . . Our jurisprudence teaches that we should decide issues on the basis of facts of record. (88 S. Ct. at 2244–45)

We would classify the action of the Supreme Court in the *Wainwright* case as a regulatory decision. The policy of "judicial restraint," along with doctrines of "ripeness," "mootness," "comity," "Waiver," and "exhaustion of remedies," are all structural rules the future benefits of which are uncertain.

On the other hand, many of the Supreme Court's most famous and controversial decisions, such as those which have changed the law of criminal procedure (*e.g., Mapp* v. *Ohio, Gideon* v. *Wainwright, Escobedo* v. *Illinois, and Miranda* v. *Arizona*), might well be classed as allocative decisions. In those cases, the allocation of many of the benefits and costs was relatively immediate. When what is at stake is whether defendants in all felony cases will receive advice of counsel, a decision requiring that it be provided to them constitutes, in a very real sense, a present allocation of a benefit to defendants (and perhaps the perceived deprivation of some law enforcement groups), even though subsequent action would be necessary before counsel was actually furnished to any particular defendant.

Not all of the great "landmark" cases produce allocative decisions. If the information costs to the court are too great, regulatory decisions will result. And, in fact, it seems likely to us that the information costs in important test cases are generally higher than in the cases that are of more limited significance. Almost by definition, a "test" or "landmark" case is one which is expected to lay down rules *for the future.* And because those cases are perceived to be important and of continuing significance, a premium is placed on knowledge of the probable impact of each of the various decisional options open to the court. In other words, information costs increase.

The matter of exchange values derived by a court is more difficult to ascertain. Without taking part in the discussion the literature offers regarding judicial "constituency" or interest representation, we can observe that judicial role orientations commonly lead to the conclusion that a particular allocation of benefits cannot or should not be avoided. If it were, values of importance to the judges would be lost.

Thus we would argue that in those major cases in which appellate courts render allocative decisions, they (1) feel that they have secured the necessary information (perhaps at high cost), and/or (2) feel that the benefits to be derived from an allocative decision outweigh the information costs. The "Brandeis brief" sometimes used in major cases (and *only* in major cases), and the numerous *amicus curiae* briefs offered and received in such cases, may be regarded as an attempt to meet high information costs. Moreover, the U.S. Supreme Court's opinions in cases like *Miranda* v. *Arizona* or *Brown* v. *Board of Education* are typically at pains to demonstrate that the Court is informed of all the facts of the social context relevant to its decision—in other words, that it has met the information costs. Conversely, where the information is inaccessible and the court does not feel that the benefits are sufficiently high, a court will not render an allocative decision, but will instead usually avoid deciding the issue—"judicial restraint," again, being a regulatory decision. For example, the U.S. Supreme Court's recent opinion in *Witherspoon* v. *Illinois,* 88 S. Ct. 1770, 1774–75 (1968), refused to decide the more sweeping of the two issues presented to it:

> The data adduced by the petitioner . . . are too tentative and fragmentary to establish that jurors not opposed to the death penalty tend to favor the prosecution in the determination of guilt. We simply cannot conclude, either

on the basis of the record now before us or as a matter of judicial notice, that the exclusion of jurors opposed to capital punishment results in an unrepresentative jury on the issue of guilt or substantially increases the risk of conviction. In light of the presently available information we are not prepared to announce a *per se* constitutional rule requiring the reversal of every conviction returned by a jury selected as this one was. [*Justice Stewart writing for the Court.*]

Trial courts, of course, also make regulatory or structural decisions— when they decline to take jurisdiction of an action, for example. As with appellate courts, we would argue that they do so when their costs, including information costs, are higher than the benefits they would anticipate from an allocative decision. Many judges have been dubious about the value to them and their self-images of entering certain controversial "political thickets." This may have been the situation when the United States District Court in Chicago late last June dismissed the civil suit brought by Dr. Jeremiah Stamler against the House Un-American Activities Committee. In that case, Dr. Stamler had been cited for contempt by HUAC, and he was asking for a declaratory judgment enjoining further proceedings by the Committee. The District Court rested its dismissal of the action on an extension of the Constitutional provision (Art. I, § 6) that Members of Congress cannot be held answerable in court for "any speech or debate in either House." The issue which had been raised, of course, was whether HUAC's proceedings constituted *legitimate* official action.

The more typical, run-of-the-mill trial court action, on the other hand, seems to us more likely to result in an allocative decision—either distributive or redistributive. Let us take as an example the lowly traffic court (assuming *arguendo* that the decisions which result can be called "policy"). The traffic court is a quite highly integrated decisional system. The decisions are made by a single magistrate who has a very large degree of discretion—usually, no transcript is made of the proceedings, so the magistrate does not even have to worry about the potentiality of an appellate court looking over his shoulder. The rules of procedure are notoriously loose. The defendant is usually not represented by counsel; somewhat more often an Assistant State's Attorney is present. Thus, in the typical case, the only persons present in court are the magistrate, a clerk, the defendant, other defendants in other cases, the complaining police officers, and perhaps a State's Attorney. The traffic court decisional system is thus highly integrated—and the demand pattern is too, at least when the defendant is not represented by counsel. When the defendant does not have counsel, little attention or weight is typically given to whatever he may have to say. Thus, all of the effective demand is from the State, for his conviction. And the result in the vast majority of cases is a redistributive decision, depriving the defendant of money and awarding it to the state. But if we introduce a defense counsel into the system, the result often changes dramatically. The demand pattern is more fragmented, and the decisions tend to be more distributive—*e.g.,* the defendant may still be found guilty but given a suspended sentence, or, instead of receiving a stiff fine or a license suspension, the defendant may be sentenced to go to traffic school.

The same is true of more serious criminal cases—misdemeanors and felonies. Very few criminal cases result in structural decisions which have any future effect. It is almost always a matter of deciding how to apply well-settled rules (regulatory policies) to the facts of a particular case. Something over seventy-five percent of all criminal defendants are convicted. And only a very small percentage of the total convictions are appealed. Thus, relatively few criminal cases ever reach the stage where the decisions are "reported" or have precedential value. Most criminal case decisions, then, lack future effect, and we would class them as allocative. These decisions may be either destributive or redistributive.

It does not often happen that a criminal trial court decides a case in a way that is redistributive in favor of the defendant—*i.e.,* a trial court does not often release a defendant who is regarded by the prosecution as "obviously guilty" of a serious crime. In our view, it is no accident that the decisions which raise the outcry that criminals are being turned loose typically come from appellate courts (and the outcry then may be raised even though the decision is not redistributive in favor of the defendant, but instead "regulates" the police, or is distributive when the State felt entitled to a redistributive result in its favor). Thus, when a trial court reaches a redistributive result in a criminal case, it is usually redistributive in favor of the prosecution. The defendant may certainly be deprived, and the prosecution may even be benefited in a very real sense—*e.g.,* the State's Attorney gets a good conviction record.

In explaining why trial court decisions in criminal cases may often be redistributive in favor of the State, but seldom in favor of the defendant, we would point again to the variable of the presence or absence of defense counsel. (The demands of the State may also vary in criminal cases, of course, and if the State reaches an agreement with the defendant, as in a negotiated plea situation, a distributive result may be expected.) *Gideon* v. *Wainwright,* 372 U.S. 335 (1963), may be viewed as a recognition of the fact that defendants tend to get lighter sentences when they are represented by counsel. And the research recently completed by Vaughan Stapleton and others on the effect of counsel in juvenile delinquency proceedings— comparing the treatment of juveniles represented by counsel with that of an unrepresented control group—confirms that observation even in a court which is in theory the "friend" of the defendants before it. Again, in our terms, the presence of defense counsel tends to fragment demand and to produce a more distributive policy result.

V

Let us finally attempt to illustrate our scheme applying it to a larger policy array—the major pieces of agricultural legislation proposed or passed, of the past twenty years. The initial task before us is to specify the major criteria by which to differentiate our several policy types. This we do in the following way, noting, of course, that many ambiguities and uncertainties remain:

Redistributive Policy

> Establishment of price support program
> Reduction or increase in mandatory price support levels
> Significant changes in groups covered when changes are controversial among the groups affected
> Limitations in level of support payment ceilings

Distributive Policy

> Addition of groups covered or benefitted by program without inter-group conflict
> Addition of program components of broadly applicable expected benefit, *e.g.,* soil bank and diversion payments, certain research programs, credit facilities expansion, etc.
> Extension of existing programs for short terms, one to three years, so as to maintain the status quo, usually in the face of impending redistribution of resources previously authorized but not yet implemented
> Limitation of time covered by authorization to not more than three years in order to leave open the option to renegotiate in Congress the existing benefit distribution

Regulative Policy

> Policies which vest discretionary authority in the Secretary of Agriculture to raise or lower price supports, to adjust acreage, or to sell surplus commodities without specific criteria to guide his decisions in these areas, so long as the discretion can in fact be used in either direction, up or down.

Policies which establish study groups to make recommendations on future policy.

Self-Regulative Policy

Policies which vest discretionary authority in farmers generally, or in commodity or geographical groups, to establish quotas, eligibilities, acreage allotments, benefit levels, or other benefit components.

*   *   *

The initial establishment of a farm price support program in 1933 was a substantially redistributive policy, taking resources from some groups in the population and allocating them to various classes of farmers. This result is in accord with our theoretical expectations since for a brief period farm group demand was highly integrated while the First Hundred Days presented an unusually integrated (low cost) decisional setting. Subsequent policy decisions have generally been distributive, however, as the diverse farm groups jockeyed for position. Controversy has centered on the level, range, and commodity coverage of supports; the extent and severity of growing and marketing controls, and on the range and impact of additional benefit programs to farmers. These conflicts have involved party, administration, and congressional leaders, farm organizations and commodity groups. During the 1950's the heart of the policy issue was high rigid v. flexible support policy, but many additional dimensions have entered the debate and we will try only to hint at some of these, showing how our theoretical argument leads us to view this tangled political struggle. From 1933 at least until 1961 the Administrations quite consistently proposed redistributive agricultural policies, varying in the extent of redistribution envisioned, in the particular groups to be benefitted by the proposed reallocation of resources, in the strategies and alliances employed and the willingness to accommodate divergent groups, and in success. Beginning in 1961, and off and on since then, administration proposals have tended to include substantial regulatory and, perhaps, self-regulatory elements in an effort to escape the impasse over conflicting redistributive proposals[8] and, at the same time, the growing money cost of farm programs and the threat of drastic redistribution implied by that cost.

Throughout most of this period we find that most of the key components of the Congressional system, especially in the House, and especially, of course, in the Agriculture Committee of the House, were strongly oriented toward distributive policy outcomes. For much of the period the Senate was more receptive to the introduction of flexible, *i.e.,* lower, support levels, but there, too, the price was often temporary deferment of lower supports or special treatment for one or more key commodities. Key legislators consistently defended the particular commodity interests of their constituents, and they were reasonably clear about the relationships between those interests and the policy issues under consideration. Their information costs were not high, therefore, and the benefits they perceived to accrue to them from effective constituency representation was substantial.

Had all or most farm groups generally shared the same policy interests there might have been relatively little difficulty in assembling the necessary votes to pass broadly distributive or even pro-farmer redistributive bills in Congress, regardless of what the USDA and the President desired. But, in fact, from the 1940's on these interests conflicted rather than united. The Farm Bureau and Farmers Union split; the Farm Bureau itself lost internal cohesion; commodity interests competed; regions with different commodity patterns developed conflicting interests. The proliferation of specialized policy interests accordingly made it increasingly difficult to organize a majority coalition for any program or package of programs in Congress. The growing fragmentation of demand, given the close and continuing linkage of commodity groups and representatives, thus increased the negotiation costs within the decisional system.

Yet this development, important though it is, should not be regarded as operating in isolation. Had it done so we would expect to observe a slow but steady growth of difficulty in assembling majorities to pass distributive policies, perhaps with the resultant policy vacuum filled by Administration efforts at securing regulatory authority to control farm policy administratively. To some extent the Eisenhower Administration consciously followed such a strategy, exacerbating commodity conflicts in order to secure greater discretion in dealing with surpluses. But the commodityization of farm policy demand has been greatly complicated by the concomitant partisanization of demand. Increasingly during the 1950's and still strongly in the 60's party unity has been striking in congressional voting on major farm legislation. Particularly has this been true of Republicans who on several occasions have demonstrated complete unanimity. Republican unity, usually in behalf of redistributive farm policy in the form of reduced controls and supports has been countered by substantial Democratic cohesion on the other side of the high rigid v. low flexible support issue that dominated farm policy debate for most of the Eisenhower years. But Democratic unity was, and is, less complete and much less committed to any particular redistributive policy line. Rather, the several key commodity groups, many led by influential Southerners, tended to negotiate distributive policy compromises, including on occasion benefits for urban Democrats to such as food stamps and promises on minimum wage bills. Democratic unity was problematic nearly every year depending on what agreement could be worked out and on how much leverage Republican opposition or a Republican administration might have. But in one way or another the Democratic majority was able to conclude agreements leading to policies that were mainly distributive. Democratic efforts at redistribution were vetoed by the President; Republican proposals were stymied in Congress; distributive compromises were passed. The only change in the 1960's was that Administration and Congressional majority were on the same side. The former sought to interject regulatory policy elements but generally settled for more distributive results. The greatest regulatory achievement was perhaps the four-year time period covered by the 1965 Food and Agriculture Act, longer than any previous authorization and thus giving more time for the Administration to seek administrative solutions to farm problems.

The persistence of distributive policies in agriculture has often been attributed to the strength of "the farm bloc," a mythical body of congressmen representing farm interest and organizations who allegedly get together on a bipartisan basis to secure subsidies and related goodies from an apathetic majority. In fact, farm policy disputes, since the Brannan Plan was proposed in 1949, have been highly partisan, major farm organizations have disagreed violently and consistently about most questions, and commodity interest have had a hard time to negotiate compromises among their divergent and often conflicting positions. Farm policy has remained so largely distributive because (1) non-farm Congressmen have generally opted out of the issue; exchange values derived from farm issues for them are low and information costs are high so they adopt a rule policy of party unity in support of whatever position their leadership, Administration or legislative, develops; (2) Democratic legislators from farm regions tend to dominate the relevant committees; they derive high exchange value from farm issues and have correlative low information costs; this balance is so strong that they are fully prepared to pay the very high costs of negotiating with one another to reach that agreement necessary for decision. Party unity or Administration support rules adopted by neutral congressmen greatly reduce the negotiating costs but the inter– and intra–commodity conflicts still make these high for Congress as a whole. Nevertheless, the exchange values are so great that the price is acceptable. That this continues to be true is partly the result of the fact that agricultural production is so fully bounded by geographical space. More than almost any other industry the specialized interests of, say, durum wheat or long-staple cotton producers have specific geographical referents and these are closely linked to the boundaries of legislative constituencies. Moreover, the demand for assistance to farmers through governmental programs has been strong and nearly continuous for decades, not always for the same programs but for policies adapted to the changing technology and economic structures of agriculture. The continuity of demands keeps information costs relatively low and the dynamic character of the industry maintains the exchange value to the congressmen of regular efforts at making new policy. And the geography of farming, specialized to locale, accentuates the exchange values as it reduces information costs. If agricultural production were to grow more sophisticated and flexible, as it has done to some extent, it might lose some of this geographical specialization and render the exchange values of legislators more uncertain. If a farm congressman found himself unable to determine what kind of program his constituents wanted, or if he was unable to discover any policy alternative he thought would do them any good, he might accept administrative regulation more readily.

Our model predicts that regulatory policy will result when demand is fragmented or diffuse and the costs of making allocative policy decisions are too high. Acceptance of party unity, Administration support or agriculture Committee leadership are all types of *de facto* decision rules that illustrate the point for some legislators within Congress, and the modest step toward granting the Secretary of Agriculture the authority to affect market prices by selling surpluses on the grain market is a recent example in substantive policy. But rule or structure decisions may also be self-regulatory if operative demand has sufficient unity and there are illustrations of this available too in recent farm politics. One was the Administration proposal in 1961 that commodity groups be organized to create their own programs which when certified by the Secretary of Agriculture would become operative unless vetoed by Congress within sixty days. The proposal foundered, partly because congressmen were still unwilling to delegate their authority and lose the exchange values and partly because commodity groups were neither so clear cut nor so unified as to be able readily to regulate themselves. Indeed, critics of the proposal alleged that because of the lack of definition among commodity groups it would be the USDA which would really make the policies, *i.e.,* it would be regulatory not self-regulatory. Another recent current of activity which aims at self-regulation is the NFO with its drive for collective bargaining between farmers and processors. NFO is explicitly opposed to government farm programs for purposes other than those necessary to permit the bargaining process to function, but they too depend on unity among farmers, *i.e.,* integrated demand, in order to make self-regulation of this type work to their advantage.

VI

Efforts at conceptualization often and properly may be faulted for their lack of specific indicators by which to test whether the formulation is merely an engaging metaphor or a genuine step toward empirical theory.

We acknowledge our vulnerability on this score. We have been concerned to explicate and illustrate our schema in the hope that it will seem both plausible and useful as a device to order a wide variety of policy data. In so doing we have incorporated a number of rather familiar propositions from the lore of political science—regarding delegation of authority, for example—and clothed them in language that places them into more contemporary modes of analysis. But this is not the same thing as utilizing unambiguous measures to test the hypotheses advanced. We must be content by pointing, if a bit lamely, to two elements of research strategy which our formulation indicates to be critical. One is that empirical research pursuant to our argument must concentrate much attention on the specification of decision costs. Here we are at one with an important current of the discipline, most recently exemplified by Adrian and Press. Secondly, our analysis points to an approach to the analysis of constituency —decision-maker interaction in terms that may be both feasible and fruitful; namely, in terms of exchange values derived from particular policy issues. Patterns of demand which are district–specific on the one hand, or diffuse on the other, continuous or *ad hoc,* and so on, represent potentially measurable ways of getting at this issue which has so often proved intractable to political scientists. We would simply conclude by voicing our agreement with the position that unless and until empirical specification is possible our schema remains in that overpopulated category of inelegant literature, the exploratory essay.

NOTES

[1] Most of this literature, though recent, is well known to students of public policy analysis. Theodore Lowi, "American Business, Public Policy, Case-Studies, and Political Science," *World Politics* (July, 1964), 677–715; Lewis A. Froman, Jr., "An Analysis of Public Policies in Cities," *Journal of Politics* (February, 1967); Richard E. Dawson and James Robinson, "Inter-Party Competition, Economic Variables, and Welfare Policies in the American States," *Journal of Politics,* 25 (May, 1963), 265–89; Richard I. Hofferbert, "Ecological Development and Policy Change in the American States," *Midwest Journal of Political Science* (November, 1966), 464–86; Hofferbert, "The Relation Between Public Policy and Some Structural and Environmental Variables," *APSR,* 60 (March, 1966), 73–82; Thomas R. Dye, *Politics, Economics, and the Public: Policy Outcomes in the American States* (Chicago: Rand McNally, 1966); Ira Sharkansky, "Economic Development, Regionalism and State Political Systems," *Midwest Journal of Political Science* (February, 1968), 41–62.

[2] John C. Wahlke, "Public Policy and Representative Government: The Role of the Represented" (paper presented to the Seventh World Congress of the International Political Science Association, Brussels, September, 1967).

[3] "The Analysis of Public Policy: A Search for Theories and Rules," *Political Science and Public Policy,* ed. Austin Ranney (Chicago: Markham, 1968).

⁴ Gilbert Y. Steiner and Samuel K. Gove, *Legislative Politics in Illinois* (Urbana: University of Illinois Press, 1960).

⁵ *American Legislatures and Legislative Methods* (New York: Century, 1907), pp. 316–17 and 322–23.

⁶ J. J. Hillman, *Competition and Railroad Price Discrimination—Legal Precedent and Economic Policy* (1968), describes the deliberate ambiguity of the Interstate Commerce Act as a device adopted to unload a conflict Congress could not resolve.

⁷ Charles Adrian and Charles Press, "Decision Costs in Coalition Formation," *APSR* (June, 1968), 556–64.

⁸ Robert Eyestone has recently examined farm policies of the past thirty-odd years and attempted to classify House Committee Reports according to criteria somewhat similar to ours. He, too, finds a significant increase in regulatory and self-regulative proposals over time though he interprets this finding in terms that are quite different from ours. "The Life Cycle of American Public Policies: Agriculture and Labor Policy Since 1929" (paper presented to the Midwest Political Science Association, May, 1968).

CHAPTER 4

Environment, Policy, Output and Impact: Problems of Theory and Method in the Analysis of Public Policy*

Ira Sharkansky

In recent years political scientists have shown great interest in the measurement and analysis of public policies. As might be expected in any burgeoning field, we have used different governmental contexts for our research, we have experimented with different concepts and terminology, and we have used certain measures for a variety of purposes. If policy is to continue as the focus of analysis, the field will profit from alternative approaches. However, each should spell out his assumptions, and attempt to justify them by demonstrating their theoretical or empirical pay-offs.

Richard Dawson and James Robinson provided the impetus for much of the current scholarship by their 1963 article on "welfare" policies.[1] Yet their service to the profession may have been balanced by a disservice in their failure to explicate boundaries around categories of policy. Their dependent variables combine measures of service levels or expenditures in education and employment security, plus measures of total government revenue, tax effort, federal aid, and percentage of revenue coming from death and gift taxes, as well as benefit levels in programs of public assistance. Their terminology suggests a legitimate borrowing from economics, where the concept of "welfare" is diffuse, and includes government activities contributing to public well-being. However, they and others have included all kinds of measures of government activity—and some private activity—together in one shapeless category. Sometimes this is labelled as welfare policy following the Dawson-Robinson term explicitly, and sometimes it is labelled simply as "public policy."[2] Some authors test policy measures from several fields against one set of independent variables. Because of this, they often fail to differentiate policy-making processes

We are grateful to the American Political Science Association for permission to print this essay, which was presented at the 1968 American Political Science Association Convention, Washington, D.C., September 2–7, 1968.

from one field to the next. Also, the practice of treating all policies in the same category masks relationships within the policy processes, and prevents scholars from seeing the impact of some types of government policy on other types of policy. A number of publications conclude that political conditions do not influence policy, but they overlook the obvious possibility that political decisions which shape certain policies (e.g., levels of government expenditure) may influence other types of policy (e.g., levels of public service).[3] If measures of spending and measures of service are treated equally as dependent variables, it is impossible to discern the interdependence of factors that actually influence each type of policy.

Several writers have conceived of policy categories that generate theoretical propositions.[4] Froman suggests we consider "areal" and "segmental" policies as standing in different relationships with elements of the political system.[5] Lowi suggests that we distinguish among policies that are "distributive," "redistributive," and "regulatory."[6] Salisbury adds "self-regulatory" to Lowi's list.[7] Eulau and Eyestone offer "adaptive" and "control" policies.[8] Although each of these suggestions has certain appeal, they may have prohibitive limitations. To my knowledge, Lowi and Salisbury have offered no empirical research using their categories and Eulau and Eyestone have not reported their results in a way that allows a reader to test the utility of their policy categories. Froman's effort appears unsatisfactory because his categories are not mutually exclusive and discrete. They require him to force the argument that municipal annexation and inter-municipal cooperation are "areal" in affecting the total population of a city, while urban renewal is "segmental" in affecting only a small portion of the population. In contrast, it appears likely that an annexation may affect only the neighborhood that is made part of the city, while an urban renewal project may affect a whole city through its impact on expenditures, taxes, and political controversy.

I have concentrated my efforts on analyzing levels of public service in the categories made popular by publications of the U.S. Bureau of the Census: education, highways, public welfare, health, natural resources, and public safety. The utility of these categories lies in their familiarity to authors and readers of political science. A great deal of data fits reasonably well into the appropriate categories, and policy-makers identify with their own field. Thus, we can merge interview data with government reports.

Even after the decision is made to concentrate research in the customary categories of service, it is necessary to subcategorize further in order to discern the operation of several mechanisms in the policy process. This paper looks within one field of service (elementary and primary education), and suggests some concepts and measurements that may clarify why some units of government provide more attractive services than others. Its principal concepts are "policy," "policy outputs," "policy impacts," and "environment." The units of analysis are school districts within the state of Georgia. Because we have data from only one state, this study must be viewed as exploratory. It is the first report from an extensive project that will examine service levels in the fields of education, highways, and welfare from a larger sample of states. Georgia is an attractive laboratory for this first effort. Because most school districts are contiguous with counties, we can use the economic, social and political data reported for each county in order to define the environment in which policy-making occurs.[9] Nevertheless, few social scientists have called Georgia "typical." Although these findings may prove to be representative of more extensive patterns, they must be viewed as tentative.

Thomas R. Dye's examination of "policy outcomes" in the field of primary and secondary education in his *Politics, Economics and the Public* employs some variables that are similar to ours, but he does not differentiate "policy" from "outcomes," and his units of analysis are combined efforts of state and local governments throughout the United States.[10] The fusion of policy and outcomes limits his ability to identify linkages between policy and outcomes, and the fusion of state and local government activities confuses the efforts of politically-distinct units. The state-plus-local aggregate is artificial, and not the arena in which policy-makers decide about the size of their budgets, the allocation of funds, or any other of numerous policy choices. The results of our within-state analysis differ markedly from the results of Dye's study of state-plus-local aggregates. The conditions that appear to distinguish among the policies of 50 state-plus-local governments do not similarly distinguish among the policies of Georgia school districts. Thus, aside from being an exploration of certain analytic categories, this paper also serves to compare the results of macro- and micro-analysis.

PUBLIC POLICY, POLICY OUTPUTS, POLICY IMPACTS AND ENVIRONMENT

In this paper we focus on four categories of phenomena relevant to policy in the field of elementary and secondary education. We differentiate between *public policy, policy outputs,* and *policy impacts* as three important dimensions of the policy process. In brief, public policy represents actions taken by government; policy outputs represent the service levels which are affected by these actions; and policy impacts represent the effect which the service has on a population.[11] A fourth element—the environment—represents the social, economic and political surroundings which both supply the impetus for educational policy and feel its impact. We shall clarify these concepts by identifying several components of public policy that seem likely to affect policy outputs and policy impacts. We also identify some features of the environment which may affect outputs and impact independent of public policy. Then we select independent and dependent variables that seem capable of depicting relationships between the environment, policy and outputs.

Policy

Among the manifestations of public policy that may shape the outputs of service are government expenditures, the interest which officials devote to a particular service beyond the formal requirements set down by law, the nature of the staff that is hired to produce the service, the size of each service agency, and the physical plant and facilities which are provided to the staff.

Expenditures are among the most evident of policy manifestations. Officials pay a great deal of attention to budget-making, and expenditures are widely viewed as a common denominator with respect to the items that actually produce services. Although spending by itself does not meet popular demands for service, spending does buy many of the things that produce services. Several observers have equated a government's level of service with its level of spending.[12] Sufficient funds may be a *sine qua non* for public services. However, several other determinants of outputs may be provided in generous or stingy proportions by different jurisdictions whose total budgets are nearly equal. By varying the allocation of funds between different factors, policy-makers may make a budget of a certain total more or less productive of service outputs. Because of this, some of the policies which have important effects on outputs may be statistically independent of aggregate spending levels.

In several fields of public service (including elementary and secondary education), the agencies which actually provide service to the public are bound by certain requirements that set minimum levels of policy. These may set a level of expenditure that the agency must raise from local sources, or define levels of training or experience that it must use in hiring technical or professional personnel. Presumably, agency officials can add to their own outputs by surpassing these minimum requirements. Additional expenditures of local funds, or strict hiring policies should enhance the performance of local school districts.

Several aspects of an agency's staff may have a bearing on the quality or quantity of service outputs. The nature of the training received by personnel, their sensitivity to clients' needs and their motivation for professional advancement may each affect an agency's ability to make the greatest use of its funds. Moreover, the simple factor of staff size, and its distribution among the principal and auxiliary tasks that are to be performed can also affect the potential for rendering service. Professional educators predict that the consolidation of small districts will add to the teaching skills available for each pupil, and increase the quality of school outputs. If expenditures are used to make salary levels competitive with those in other jurisdictions, they may facilitate the policy-maker's search for the "right combination" of training and motivation for each of the principal jobs within his organization. However, salary money alone does not guarantee success in obtaining a good staff. Indeed, the sensitivity of the leadership and its skill in using financial resources may be the key determinant that may (or may not) translate a good budget into a good staff.

The crucial dimensions of physical plant and equipment that may affect service-potential include compatibility with contemporary methods of providing service, flexibility with respect to the multiple needs and changing demands of clients, and durability in the face of heavy use. It is probably true that good education can be provided in an inadequate physical plant if the professional personnel are highly motivated and adaptable. But the nature of surroundings and the availability of modern equipment should contribute to the capacity of the staff to perform in a superior fashion. However, attractive plant and facilities cannot guarantee success. If quality facilities are available for only a limited range of the school's task, they may not have their maximum impact on overall performance. If the high school gymnasium sparkles while the library lacks up-to-date science texts, then the money spent on facilities may have a distorted influence on the school's output. The durability of facilities provides yet another dimension that may influence services. If the plant and equipment cannot stand up to the clients, then the cost of maintenance will deplete the investments that can be made on additional facilities or on an improvement in staff.

Outputs

It seems likely that favorable combinations of expenditures, staff and facilities will add to the outputs of a service-providing agency. However, there is no assurance that this will occur. Powerful elements in the environment may have a telling influence on outputs. Or different elements of policy may work at cross-purposes to each other. It is therefore necessary to measure outputs independently of policy and test the assumed relationships between them.

Depending on which type of service is at issue, outputs may be defined by the amount of benefits or services provided per client; the units of service in relation to the total population of the jurisdiction; the incidence of beneficiaires among people who are potential clients; the rate at which a program is performed; or by the frequency with which a population chooses to use a program. In the field of education, output may be measured by the attraction of pupils (clients) to school programs, or by the range of activities offered by a school district.

Impact

The impacts of policy outputs must likewise be defined for each type of public service. In general, they show the effect which a service has on a population. In the field of education, an impact may be measured by the intellectual skills acquired by students; by the earning power of former students; by the use of "cultured" forms of recreation; or by the intellectual skills imparted by former students to their own children. The study of educational impacts appears to be impractical in the present context. There is much inter-county mobility in Georgia, especially from rural areas to the cities. Our focus on individual school districts, and our lack of data for individual students or graduates will force us to overlook the impacts likely to be generated from the outputs of certain school districts.

Environmental influences

Several features of the economic, social and political environment of a jurisdiction can influence the kinds of policy decisions which officials make, and they can influence the translation of policy into outputs and impacts. Certain features of the environment may intervene between policies and their outputs, or between outputs and their impact on the community.

The elements of an environment that seem important for the outputs and impacts of public services include characteristics of the service's clients; market costs; the availability of manpower; economic conditions; and certain features of politics.

One of the most important influences on services may be the nature of the clientele. Their number, the severity of their needs, their motivation and their cultural and intellectual preparation can render the service expensive or efficient. Where primary and secondary school pupils come from culturally deprived families, their teachers will have further to go with a less receptive audience than is the case in school districts where the families are predominantly middle class, upwardly mobile, and apprecia- tive of the opportunities offered by education. Where the parents them- selves provide much of the preparation for reading and the understanding of abstract concepts, then school teachers can produce a superior graduate at much less cost than where they have to provide all the rudiments in the school building. In some cases, the nature of clients may cause the total expenditures made for a service to be substantially greater than the government expenditure. Where a PTA makes significant contributions for school libraries or recreational facilities, policy-makers may allocate an unusually high proportion of their budget to salaries or a more favorable teacher-pupil ratio.

The environmental features of market costs and manpower availability can influence the facilities or personnel that a policy-maker can expect to purchase with a given level of expenditure. Market costs for various skills and commodities can render them more or less expensive, and thereby alter the items that may be purchased with a given budget. The availability of manpower may influence the price of certain skills, or make it virtually impossible for policy-makers to obtain the types of skills needed for their outputs. Officials who locate institutions in unattractive surroundings add to their problems of manpower availability. Obtuse locations in rural areas or the slums may remove a school from professional talent, and make it necessary to pay higher than average salaries or settle for second-rate personnel.

Economic conditions within a jurisdiction may provide the wherewithal to support government budgets, and affect the character of clientele. A well-to-do community provides the resources for service expenditures without requiring oppressive levels of taxation. And where the community is wealthy, school children may benefit from supportive conditions at home and present less onerous demands to teachers and administrators. In this case, client-preparation may condition the outputs that are possible, and affect the impact that certain types of output can have within a community.

The political climate within a jurisdiction may be receptive or hostile to a particular service, and the officials elected to office may either facilitate or retard the efforts necessary to improve outputs. Politics may affect the allocation of expenditures among personnel or facilities, and within these categories to specific types of skills or equipment.

We can use the terminology of systems theory to clarify relationships between elements in the environment, public policy, policy outputs and policy impact. As these concepts are portrayed in Figure 1, they bear close resemblance to the concepts of *input, conversion, output,* and *feedback* that have been made part of our vocabulary by David Easton and others.[13] The inputs in our model are the factors in the environment that seem capable of influencing policy decisions. As in the case of systems theory, these environmental factors include demands for service, popular support for the government, and the economic and personnel resources that the community is willing to devote to public service. The decisions which result from interactions in the conversion process stand—in our model—as

Figure 1
Hypothesized Relationships Between Elements of the Policy Process

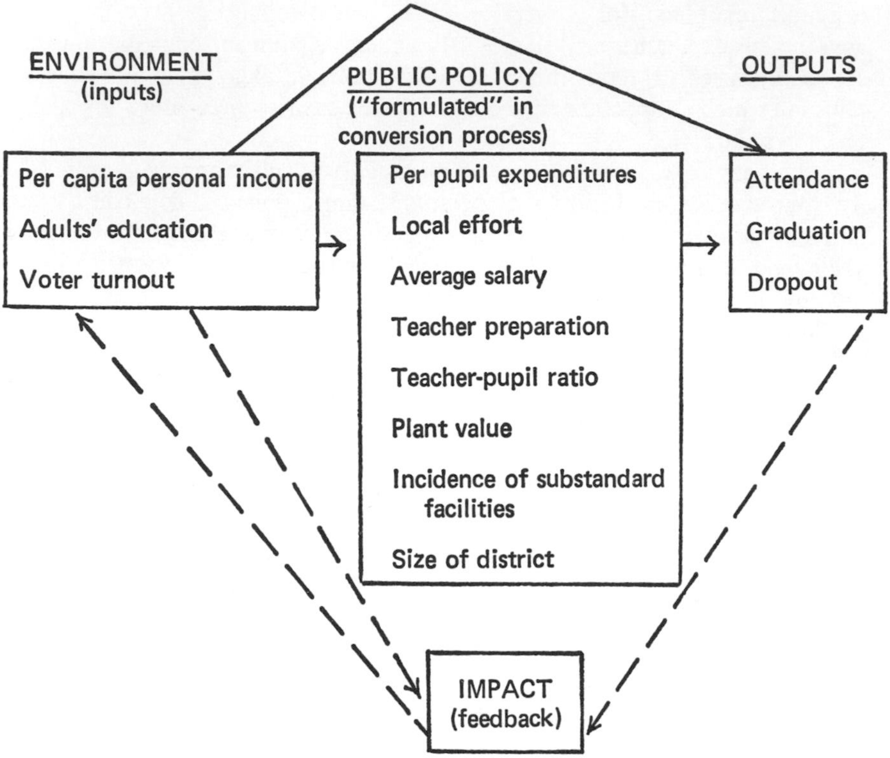

Note: Broken lines refer to relationships that are hypothesized, but not tested in this paper; terms in parentheses refer to equivalent concepts from systems theory.

policy. The linkages portrayed in Figure 1 show that policy and the environment can each influence the outputs of service. Both the nature of the outputs and elements in the environment can influence the impact which the service has on the population. Systems theorists frequently talk of the process by which policies feed back into the environment to condition the subsequent inputs from that environment to the decision-makers. Likewise, our notion of impact will affect the kinds of demands that come from the environment, and the nature of resources that the environment will be able to contribute subsequently to the policy-makers.

VARIABLES AND TECHNIQUES

The choice of variables to measure the phenomena depicted in Figure 1 was guided by an assessment of elements having likely importance within each category, and by the availability of data. The variables chosen for

Table 1
Measures of Environment, Policy, and Output*

Environment

 (*1*) Per capita personal income
 (*2*) Percentage of adults with at least a high school education
 (*3*) Percentage of adults voting in the 1964 Presidential election

Policy

 (*4*) Spending per pupil
 (*5*) Percentage of school expenditures coming from locally-raised revenues
 (*6*) Average teacher salary
 (*7*) Percentage of teachers with a certificate indicating 5 years of college education
 (*8*) Teacher-pupil ratio
 (*9*) Insured value per pupil of plant, facilities and equipment
 (*10*) Percentage of instruction rooms defined as substandard
 (*11*) Average daily attendance

Output

 (*12*) Percentage of enrolled students who attend daily
 (*13*) Incidence of high school graduates among population in high school
 (*14*) Incidence of reported drop-outs among population in high school

---

* Variables 1–3 come from the U.S. Bureau of the Census, *County-City Data Book, 1967;* variables 4–13 come from the Georgia State Department of Education, *Annual Report, 1965–66;* variable 14 also pertains to the 1965–66 period, but comes from a typewritten compilation of drop-outs prepared by the Georgia Department of Education.

each category are listed in Table 1. There are no variables listed for the *impact* of educational services in Georgia. As explained above, this category has defied search for appropriate measurements within the context of this study.

Variables for the *environment* measure the availability of economic resources within each school district, the likely interest of the population in educational services, and the involvement of the population in public affairs. Where a district scores high on personal income, adults' education and voter turnout, we expect that its school officials will be motivated to make high expenditures, show high local effort, pay high teacher salaries, maintain favorable teacher-pupil ratios, and be generous in their purchase of plant and equipment. Thus, there should be positive relationships between each measure of the environment and each measure of policy.

The policy variables cover several of the elements that seem likely to affect service outputs: spending, local effort, salaries, teacher preparation, the number of staff, the quality of facilities, and the size of the district.[14] The use of eight different policy measures will enable us to see if "policy" is a close-knit, unidimensional variable, or if its components divide themselves into numerous dimensions. The literature suggests that high scores on both the policy and the environmental variables should translate themselves into high scores on output. In order to assess the dimensions in policy and the relative importance of *policy* or *environment* on the measures of output, we shall use a combination of simple and multi-variate techniques.

The measurement of educational "output" involves some of the most controversial aspects of policy-analysis. Students come to class with a variety of intellectual needs and resources, and these characteristics influence the service that they do (and should) receive. Unfortunately, some of the traits that should be included in an analysis of educational output are not available. A sequence of test scores might reflect the nature of services provided by different school districts, but the Georgia school districts do not report comparable test scores for their students. The three variables that do measure output are limited in the behaviors that they assess. All measure the school's capacity to attract potential clients. The first measures average daily attendance, and the second and third measure the incidence of high school graduates and drop-outs.[15] Presumably, high scores on attendance and graduations, and low scores in drop-outs reflect the school's success in meeting students' needs—whether these needs be for the rudiments of literacy, preparation for further academic study, or placement in business or the trades.

A simple correlation matrix defines relationships among the policy variables taken two at a time. Interview data from a sample of school superintendents will reinforce our finds of multidimensionality of policy. A step-wise regression depicts the relative importance of each independent variable with respect to the measures of output and defines the success of several independent variables in accounting for variation in output. And coefficients of multiple-partial correlation show the relative importance of environment and policy in explaining variation in output.[16]

THE MULTI–DIMENSIONAL NATURE OF EDUCATIONAL POLICIES

There is strong support for the notion that educational policy is multi-dimensional. In the state of Georgia there is no single policy which can be described as "high regard for education." Different districts show wide variations in their relative scores for expenditures, local effort, salaries, teacher preparation, teacher-pupil ratios, physical facilities, and the size of school districts. Table 2 shows coefficients of simple correlation among these variables. Most of their interrelationships are positive, indicating that districts showing high scores on one trait tend to show high scores on the others. However, the coefficients are not strong enough to indicate a high degree of correspondence among the different scores. Many of the districts

Table 2
Coefficients of Simple Correlation Among the Measures of Policy

	(4)	*(5)*	*(6)*	*(7)*	*(8)*	*(9)*	*(10)*	*(11)*
(4) Spending	1.00	.39	.23	.06	.17	.34	−.08	.36
(5) Local effort		1.00	.51	.07	.02	.17	−.09	.71
(6) Salary			1.00	.10	−.09	.11	−.03	.54
(7) Teacher preparation				1.00	.17	.22	−.06	.15
(8) Teacher-pupil ratio					1.00	.28	−.05	.02
(9) Plant value						1.00	−.06	−.01
(10) Substandard facilities							1.00	−.02
(11) Size of district								1.00

Note: For the definition of each variable, see Table 1.

that score high on one dimension of policy score mediocre or low on other traits. The coefficients of Table 2 also point to the problems involved in assuming that expenditures represent an adequate measure of educational policy. Although there are positive coefficients between expenditures and the other measures of policy, not one of these relationships is strong enough to indicate that spending levels account for even 16 percent of the variation in another dimension of policy. Many districts showing similar levels of expenditure allocate their funds to different purposes. High scores on expenditure frequently coexist with low scores on other dimensions of policy.

The results of interviews with a sample of Georgia school superintendents reinforces the finding of loose connections among the several dimensions of educational policy. When 20 of the superintendents were asked to identify the components of "good" or "high quality" programs, they failed to show a uniform view of which policies would result in high quality services. Table 3 shows their responses arranged by the items they

Table 3
Responses of Georgia School Superintendents to the Question:
"What factors help produce good or high quality programs?"

	Number of Nominations	Average Rank
Qualified teachers	12	1.3
Adequate financing	14	2.2
Leadership	4	1.8
Supportive community environment	9	2.6
Curriculum improvement	6	2.7
Teacher-pupil ratio	3	1.7
Equipment, facilities	4	2.5
Inservice training	1	3.0
Auxiliary personnel	1	3.0
Other	1	6.0

Table 4
Coefficients of Simple Correlation
Between Measures of Environment and Measures of Policy

	Measures of Policy							
	(4) Spending	(5) Local Effort	(6) Salary	(7) Teacher Prepara- tion	(8) Teacher- Pupil Ratio	(9) Plant Value	(10) Sub- standard Facilities	(11) Size of District
Measures of Environment:								
(1) Income	.24	.70	.51	.13	−.03	.05	.13	.64
(2) Education	.35	.54	.40	.16	.03	.00	.20	.61
(3) Voting	.35	.32	.21	.11	.13	.28	−.07	.13

Note: For the definition of each variable, see Table 1.

named to produce high quality services.[17] Except for agreement among three-quarters of the respondents that "money" and "qualified teachers" are important, the superintendents spread their nominations among a large variety of responses. Few superintendents specified the allocation of "money" to specific purchases, or specified how they would select "qualified teachers." In education and perhaps other fields of public services, there is not agreement among practitioners about specific types of policy that will produce desirable outputs. As a result, school districts show different allocations of their resources among the dimensions of staff and facilities. Our coefficients of simple correlation show different allocations even among those districts that have similar social, economic and political characteristics, and make similar total expenditures.

ENVIRONMENTAL INFLUENCES ON POLICY

Districts that score high on the measures of the environment also tend to score high on policy measures. Table 4 indicates that populations that are well-to-do, well-educated and involved in politics tend to have large school districts, spend a lot for education, show high local effort, pay high teacher salaries, hire well-educated teachers, have a favorable teacher-pupil ratio, and valuable facilities. However, most of these relationships are weak, and several predicted relationships fail to exist. The strongest links between the environment and policy work to assure districts of large size, high levels of local effort, and high teacher salaries where populations are wealthy and well-educated.

INFLUENCES ON OUTPUT

Our measures of the environment and policy do not show their expected relationships with output. The coefficients of simple correlation reported in Table 5 show that only the teacher-pupil ratio and teacher preparation of all the independent variables perform consistently as predicted, and these relationships are not strong. The best relationship shows that teacher-pupil ratio accounts for less than 14 percent of the variation in one measure of output (attendance). In most cases the output measures vary from district to district without relation to policy or environment. Table 6 shows the results of step-wise regression analyses, and indicates that the full collection of independent variables accounts for only a portion of the variation in output. In no case is this explained variation—shown by the coefficient of multiple determination (R^2)—more than 36 percent of the total.

Several studies of state-wide data (using measures of state-plus-local government activity as the units of analysis) show a much closer corre-

Table 5
Coefficients of Simple Correlation Between Measures of Environment and Policy, and Measures of Output

	Output Measures		
	(12) Attendance	*(13)* Graduations	*(14)* Drop-outs
Environment:			
(1) Income	−.08	−.05	−.10
(2) Education	−.15	.02	−.29
(3) Voting	.03	.09	−.01
Policy:			
(4) Spending	−.26	.04	−.08
(5) Local effort	−.09	−.09	−.04
(6) Salary	.23	.01	−.03
(7) Teacher preparation	.27	.15	−.11
(8) Teacher-pupil ratio	.37	.33	−.20
(9) Plant value	.10	.09	.00
(10) Substandard facilities	−.16	−.05	−.16
(11) Size of district	−.07	.15	−.17

Table 6
Regression Coefficients, (Standard Errors), and Coefficients of Multiple Determination (R^2), Showing Independent Variables in the Order Loaded by a Step-Wise Program

	(12) Attendance
(8) Teach-pupil ratio	5.174 (.868)*
(4) Spending	−.152 (.048)*
(7) Teacher preparation	.139 (.039)*
(10) Substandard facilities	−.076 (.049)*
(9) Plant value	−.039 (.016)*
(6) Salary	.0001 (.000006)*
(2) Adult education	−.0007 (.0005)*
(3) Voting	.008 (.006)
(1) Personal income	3.809 (8.694)
(11) Size of district	.0000007 (.000003)
(5) Local effort	−.0009 (.044)
Constant R^2	.683 (.050)*
	.359

	(13) Graduation
(8) Teacher-pupil ratio	2.406 (.578)*
(5) Local effort	−.034 (.027)
(7) Teacher preparation	.033 (.026)
(9) Plant value	−.016 (.010)*
(3) Voting	.004 (.004)

Table 6 (continued)

		(13) Graduation
(6)	Salary	.000004 (.000004)
(4)	Spending	.017 (.031)
(11)	Size of district	−.0000001 (.0000002)
(10)	Substandard facilities	−.020 (.032)
(2)	Adult education	.0001 (.0002)
	**	
	Constant R²	.027 (.033)
		.157

		(14) Drop-outs
(2)	Adult education	−.003 (.0004)*
(1)	Personal income	15.233 (6.503)*
(8)	Teacher-pupil ratio	−1.539 (.650)*
(10)	Substandard facilities	−.050 (.036)
(11)	Size of district	−.0000003 (.0000003)
(4)	Spending	.022 (.036)
(5)	Local effort	.014 (.033)
(7)	Teacher preparation	−.013 (.029)
(9)	Plant value	.005 (.012)
(3)	Voting	.0001 (.005)
(6)	Salary	.000001 (.000005)
	Constant R²	.109 (.037)*
		.185

Note: For the definition of each variable, see Table 1. The independent variables here are numbered as in Table 1.
    * At least 1.5x standard error.
    ** Additional variables would drop F size below acceptable level.

spondence than we have found between environmental features and educational outputs. Our findings for Georgia may not be representative of micro-analyses using the school district as the basic unit. However, an examination of Dye's research on more widely-selected data shows a similar marked disparity between macro- and micro-analyses. In *Politics, Economics and the Public* (a study of state-plus-local aggregates), he finds a correlation of .59 between his measure of adults' education and per pupil spending, and a correlation of .43 between his measure of personal income and the teacher-pupil ratio. However, in his "Governmental Structure, Urban Environment and Educational Policy" (a study of local units), the comparable coefficients are only .04 and .01. Such environmental features as personal income and adults' education relate strongly with levels of output when 50 state-plus-local governmental aggregates are the units of analysis. But when examination turns to local units within the states, there may be little correspondence between levels of income and education, and levels of educational output.

Although neither the measures of environment nor the measures of policy provide a thorough explanation for differences in output among the school districts of Georgia, the measures of policy appear to be more influential than the measures of environment. This is evident in the coefficients of multiple-partial correlation reported in Table 7. They show the relationship of each class of variables with output, while controlling for the other class of variables. Policy measures show much stronger relationships with the outputs of attendance and high school graduation, and environmental variables show only slightly greater relationships with high school drop-outs. In reference to the diagram in Figure 1, it appears that the link between policy and output is more prominent than the direct link between environment and output. Policy seems to have an independent influence over output, and does not merely transmit influence from the environment.

The results of step-wise regression (in Table 6) provide a detailed indication of which variables show the strongest relationships with outputs. They reinforce the findings of multiple-partial correlation in showing that policy is more likely than environment to show independent relationships with the output. The teacher-pupil ratio, in particular, shows strong independent relationships with output. It was called first in the step-wise regressions for attendance and graduations, and it shows a high ratio of regression coefficient to standard error for each of the output measures. As expected, it has positive relationships with attendance and graduations, and a negative relationship with drop-outs. Perhaps a high ratio of teachers to pupils facilitates the identification of each student's peculiar needs, and the servicing of these needs by the staff.

Table 7
Coefficients of Multiple-Partial Correlation

	Output		
	(12) Attendance	*(13)* Graduations	*(14)* Drop-outs
Environment and output controlling for policy	.16	.10	.29
Policy and output controlling for environment	.59	.39	.25

Note: For the definition of each variable see Table 1. Environmental variables are #1–3; policy variables are #4–11.

SUMMARY AND CONCLUSIONS

This paper experiments with the concepts of *environmental* influences, *policy,* and *policy outputs.* With a combination of interview data and measurements of social, economic and political characteristics of Georgia counties, plus official reports about educational activities within each county's school district, we defined certain relationships among several measures of each concept. A fourth concept—*policy impacts*—was mentioned but not subject to empirical analysis.

The eight measures of policy prove helpful in illustrating the multidimensional character of educational policy. School districts that score high on one dimension of policy do not necessarily score high on the others. Neither the eight measures of policy nor the three measures of environmental conditions show strong relationships with any of the three output measures. These findings suggest severe limitations in our model—or in the variables used to measure each of the major concepts. Yet these findings also point to the weakness of alternate models, especially those which fail to differentiate between policies and the outputs of policies. Among Georgia school districts—and perhaps elsewhere—output levels are not identical with levels of expenditure, local effort in behalf of education, teacher salaries, teacher preparation, teacher-pupil ratios, school district size, or the value of physical plant and equipment. Policy-making is a complex phenomenon that reflects political and economic forces and perhaps many elements that do not lend themselves to readily-quantified, district-by-district measurement.

This study also suggests the value in looking beneath macro-analyses that investigate the artificial aggregates of state-plus-local government data. Macro-analysis may be valuable in pointing to policy-parameters that operate generally across the nation. However, the findings for Georgia school districts indicate that factors which explain the distribution of outputs at a macro level (the aggregate of state plus local governments across the nation) may not explain the distribution within a state.

NOTES

* The research for this paper was supported by grants from the Social Science Research Council: Committee on Legal and Government Processes; the University of Georgia Office of General Research; and the Graduate Research Committee of the University of Wisconsin. An earlier draft of this paper was presented at the Confer-

ence for the Measurement of Policies in the American States, University of Michigan, 1968.

[1] Richard E. Dawson and James A. Robinson, "Interparty Competition, Economic Variables, and Welfare Policies in the American States," *Journal of Politics,* 25 (May, 1963), 265–89.

[2] See Richard I. Hofferbert, "The Relation between Public Policy and Some Structural and Environmental Variables in the American States," *American Political Science Review,* 60 (March, 1966), 73–82; and Robert L. Lineberry and Edmund P. Fowler, "Reformism and Public Policies in American Cities," *American Political Science Review,* 61 (September, 1967), 701–16.

[3] See Dawson and Robinson, *op. cit.;* Hofferbert, *op. cit.;* Thomas R. Dye, *Politics, Economics and the Public: Policy Outcomes in the American States* (Chicago: Rand McNally, 1966); and Dye, "Governmental Structure, Urban Environment, and Educational Policy," *Midwest Journal of Political Science,* 11 (August, 1967), 353–80.

[4] Theodore Lowi, "American Business, Public Policy, Case-Studies, and Political Theory," *World Politics* (July, 1964), 677–715; Robert H. Salisbury, "The Analysis of Public Policy: A Search for Theories and Roles," mimeo., 1967; and Lewis A. Froman, Jr., "An Analysis of Public Policies in Cities," *Journal of Politics,* 29 (February, 1967), 94–108; Heinz Eulau and Robert Eyestone, "Policy Maps of City Councils and Policy Outcomes: A Developmental Analysis," *American Political Science Review,* 62 (March, 1968), 124–43.

[5] Froman, *op. cit.*

[6] Lowi, *op. cit.*

[7] Salisbury, *op. cit.*

[8] Eulau and Eyestone, *op. cit.*

[9] One hundred and twenty-seven of the Georgia counties have only one school district each; these county-districts comprise most of the 163 units in this study. Eight additional units are either the independent districts that cover cities over 25,000 population, or the counties outside of these cities. The remaining 28 units represent the summing of data for small city school districts and data for the non-city section of their counties.

[10] Dye, *Politics, Economics and the Public, op. cit.*

[11] If our focus was regulatory policy instead of levels of public service, then "output" would represent the character of actions that the regulatory agency took against firms or citizens; likewise, the policy-impact might represent the response of the firms or citizens to these outputs.

[12] Robert C. Wood, *1400 Governments* (Garden City: Anchor Books, 1961), p. 35; Jesse Burkhead, *Public School Finance* (Syracuse: Syracuse University Press, 1965), p. 50; Robert H. Salisbury, "State Politics and Education," *Politics in the American States,* eds. Herbert Jacob and Kenneth N. Vines (Boston: Little, Brown, 1965), p. 331.

[13] David Easton, *A Framework for Political Analysis* (Englewood Cliffs, N.J.: Prentice-Hall, 1965); see also the works cited above by Dawson and Robinson and Dye.

[14] The measure of district size (average daily attendance) allows a test of the expectation that school district consolidation will improve services by adding to the resources of each unit, and permitting a wider variety of educational offerings. School district consolidation has proceeded further in Georgia than in other states (see Note 9 above). However, consolidation has not yet reached the point where districts from different counties have been consolidated.

[15] We chose to measure the "drop-out" phenomenon from two angles. One measure relies on the data reported by school superintendents that reflect their knowledge of drop-outs. Insofar as some students may drop out during the summertime without coming to the notice of school authorities, however, an alternate

measure was used which shows the incidence of graduates among the high school population in a school district.

16 A step-wise regression program first selects the independent variable that shows the strongest coefficient of simple correlation with the dependent variable. In successive steps, it then selects additional variables that, when added to those already employed, add most to the proportion of the dependent variable that is explained. The program used was Roy R. Gillus and Steven Watt, *Multiple Linear Regression* (Madison: University of Wisconsin Social Systems Research Institute, March, 1966). Coefficients of multiple-partial correlation permit the identification of the proportion of the variance in a dependent variable that is explained by one group of independent variables (e.g., policy), while controlling for the influence of another group of independent variables (e.g., environment). For the simple computation formula, see Hubert Blalock, *Social Statistics* (New York: McGraw-Hill, 1959), p. 350.

17 The question asked: "What factors help to produce 'good' or 'high quality' programs?" The informants were then asked to rank the importance of those factors which had been named. We selected the sample of 20 superintendents from the 10 districts which showed the highest level of expenditures above the level estimated by a regression analysis of environmental characteristics against expenditures; and the 10 districts which showed the lowest level of expenditures below the level estimated by the same regression analysis. Thus, the sample reports the policy orientations of superintendents who are unusually high spenders, and those who are unusually low spenders. Eulau and Eyestone find a similar lack of agreement among city councilmen in the San Francisco area about the ingredients of policy, although councilmen agree about the basic goals their governments should pursue.

PART TWO

The Measurement of Policy

CHAPTER 5

Approximations to Knowledge

Eugene Webb
Donald Campbell
Richard Schwartz
Lee Sechrest

This survey directs attention to social science research data *not* obtained by interview or questionnaire. Some may think this exclusion does not leave much. It does. Many innovations in research method are to be found scattered throughout the social science literature. Their use, however, is unsystematic, their importance understated. Our review of this material is intended to broaden the social scientist's currently narrow range of utilized methodologies and to encourage creative and opportunistic exploitation of unique measurement possibilities.

Today, the dominant mass of social science research is based upon interviews and questionnaires. We lament this overdependence upon a single, fallible method. Interviews and questionnaires intrude as a foreign element into the social setting they would describe, they create as well as measure attitudes, they elicit atypical roles and responses, they are limited to those who are accessible and will cooperate, and the responses obtained are produced in part by dimensions of individual differences irrelevant to the topic at hand.

But the principal objection is that they are used alone. No research method is without bias. Interviews and questionnaires must be supplemented by methods testing the same social science variables but having *different* methodological weaknesses.

In sampling the range of alternative approaches, we examine their

Reprinted from Eugene J. Webb, Donald T. Campbell, Richard D. Schwartz, and Lee Sechrest, *Unobtrusive Measures: Nonreactive Research in the Social Sciences* (Chicago: Rand McNally, 1966), Chap. 1, pp. 1–34, by permission of the publisher and the authors.

Parenthetical notations refer to the author(s) and publication date of the work(s) cited. Full citations are given in the bibliography at the end of this article. If two works by one author were published in the same year, they are distinguished by the letters "a" and "b" after the year of publication.

weaknesses, too. The flaws are serious and give insight into why we do depend so much upon the interview. But the issue is not choosing among individual methods. Rather it is the necessity for a multiple operationism, a collection of methods combined to avoid sharing the same weaknesses. The goal is not to replace the interview but to supplement and cross-validate it with measures that do not require the cooperation of a respondent and that do not themselves contaminate the response.

Here are some samples of these kinds of methods:

The floor tiles around the hatching-chick exhibit at Chicago's Museum of Science and Industry must be replaced every six weeks. Tiles in other parts of the museum need not be replaced for years. The selective erosion of tiles, indexed by the replacement rate, is a measure of the relative popularity of exhibits.

The accretion rate is another measure. One investigator wanted to learn the level of whisky consumption in a town which was officially "dry." He did so by counting empty bottles in ashcans.

The degree of fear induced by a ghost-story-telling session can be measured by noting the shrinking diameter of a circle of seated children.

Chinese jade dealers have used the pupil dilation of their customers as a measure of the client's interest in particular stones, and Darwin in 1872 noted this same variable as an index of fear.

Library withdrawals were used to demonstrate the effect of the introduction of television into a community. Fiction titles dropped, nonfiction titles were unaffected.

The role of rate of interaction in managerial recruitment is shown by the overrepresentation of baseball managers who were infielders or catchers (high-interaction positions) during their playing days.

Sir Francis Galton employed surveying hardware to estimate the bodily dimensions of African women whose language he did not speak.

The child's interest in Christmas was demonstrated by distortions in the size of Santa Claus drawings.

Racial attitudes in two colleges were compared by noting the degree of clustering of Negroes and whites in lecture halls.

Before making a detailed examination of such methods, it is well to present a closer argument for the use of multiple methods and to present a methodological framework within which both the traditional and the more novel methods can be evaluated.

OPERATIONISM AND MULTIPLE OPERATIONS

The social sciences are just emerging from a period in which the precision of carefully specified operations was confused with operationism by definitional fiat—an effort now increasingly recognized as an unworkable model for science. We wish to retain and augment the precision without bowing to the fiat.

The mistaken belief in the operational definition of theoretical terms has permitted social scientists a complacent and self-defeating dependence upon single classes of measurement—usually the interview or questionnaire. Yet the operational implication of the inevitable theoretical complexity of every measure is exactly opposite: it calls for a multiple operationism, that is, for multiple measures which are hypothesized to share in the theoretically relevant components but have different patterns of irrelevant components (e.g., Garner, 1954; Garner, Hake, & Eriksen, 1956; Campbell & Fiske, 1959; Campbell, 1960; Humphreys, 1960).

Once a proposition has been confirmed by two or more independent measurement processes, the uncertainty of its interpretation is greatly reduced. The most persuasive evidence comes through a triangulation of measurement processes. If a proposition can survive the onslaught of a series of imperfect measures, with all their irrelevant error, confidence should be placed in it. Of course, this confidence is increased by minimizing error in each instrument and by a reasonable belief in the different and divergent effects of the sources of error.

A consideration of the laws of physics, as they are seen in that science's measuring instruments, demonstrates that no theoretical parameter is ever measured independently of other physical parameters and other physical laws. Thus, a typical galvanometer responds in its operational measurement of voltage not only according to the laws of electricity but also to the laws of gravitation, inertia, and friction. By reducing the mass of the galvanometer needle, by orienting the needle's motion at right angles to gravity, by setting the needle's axis in jeweled bearings, by counterweighting the needle point, and by other refinements, the instrument designer attempts to minimize the most important of the irrelevant physical forces for his measurement purposes. As a result, the galvanometer reading may reflect, *almost* purely, the single parameter of voltage (or amperage, etc.).

Yet from a theoretical point of view, the movement of the needle is always a complex product of many physical forces and laws. The adequacy with which the needle measures the conceptually defined variable is a matter for investigation; the operation itself is not the ultimate basis for defining the variable. Excellent illustrations of the specific imperfections of measuring instruments are provided by Wilson (1952).

Starting with this example from physics and the construction of meters, we can see that no meter ever perfectly measures a single theoretical parameter; all series of meter readings are imperfect estimates of the theoretical parameters they are intended to measure.

Truisms perhaps, yet they belie the mistaken concept of the "operational definition" of theoretical constructs which continues to be popular in the social sciences. The inappropriateness is accentuated in the social sciences because we have no measuring devices as carefully compensated to control all irrelevancies as is the galvanometer. There simply are no social science devices designed with so perfect a knowledge of all the major relevant sources of variation. In physics, the instruments we think of as "definitional" reflect magnificently successful theoretical achievements and themselves embody classical experiments in their very operation. In the social sciences, our measures lack such control. They tap multiple processes and sources of variance of which we are as yet unaware. At such a stage of development, the theoretical impurity and factorial complexity of every measure are not niceties for pedantic quibbling but are overwhelmingly and centrally relevant in all measurement applications which involve inference and generalization.

Efforts in the social sciences at multiple confirmation often yield disappointing and inconsistent results. Awkward to write up and difficult to publish, such results confirm the gravity of the problem and the risk of false confidence that comes with dependence upon single methods (Vidich & Shapiro, 1955; Campbell, 1957; Campbell & McCormack, 1957; Campbell & Fiske, 1959; Kendall, 1963; Cook & Selltiz, 1964). When multiple operations provide consistent results, the possibility of slippage between conceptual definition and operational specification is diminished greatly.

This is not to suggest that all components of a multimethod approach should be weighted equally. Prosser (1964) has observed: ". . . but there is still no man who would not accept dog tracks in the mud against the sworn testimony of a hundred eye-witnesses that no dog had passed by" (p. 216). Components ideally should be weighted according to the amount of extraneous variation each is known to have and, taken in combination, according to their independence from similar sources of bias.

INTERPRETABLE COMPARISONS AND PLAUSIBLE RIVAL HYPOTHESES

We deal here with methods of measurement appropriate to a wide range of social science studies. Some of these studies are comparisons of a single group or unit at two or more points in time; others compare several groups or units at one time; others purport to measure but a single unit at a single point in time; and, to close the circle, some compare several groups at two or more points in time. In this discussion, we assume that the goal of the social scientist is always to achieve interpretable comparisons, and that the goal of methodology is to rule out those plausible rival hypotheses which make comparisons ambiguous and tentative.

Often it seems that absolute measurement *is* involved, and that a social instance is being described in its splendid isolation, not for comparative purposes. But a closer look shows that absolute, isolated measurement is meaningless. In all useful measurement, an implicit comparison exists when an explicit one is not visible. "Absolute" measurement is a convenient fiction and usually is nothing more than a shorthand summary in settings where plausible rival hypotheses are either unimportant or so few, specific, and well known as to be taken into account habitually. Thus, when we report a length "absolutely" in meters or feet, we immediately imply comparisons with numerous familiar objects of known length, as well as with a standard preserved in some Paris or Washington sanctuary.

If measurement is regarded always as a comparison, there are three classes of approaches which have come to be used in achieving interpretable comparisons. First, and most satisfactory, in experimental design. Through deliberate randomization, the *ceteris* of the pious *ceteris paribus* prayer can be made *paribus*. This may require randomization of respondents, occasions, or stimulus objects. In any event, the randomization strips of plausibility many of the otherwise available explanations of the difference in question. It is a sad truth that randomized experimental design is possible for only a portion of the settings in which social scientists make measurements and seek interpretable comparisons. The number of opportunities for its use may not be staggering, but, where possible, experimental design should by all means be exploited. Many more opportunities exist than are used.

Second, a quite different and historically isolated tradition of comparison is that of index numbers. Here, sources of variance known to be irrelevant are controlled by transformations of raw data and weighted aggregates. This is analogous to the compensated and counterbalanced meters of physical science which also control irrelevant sources of variance. The goal of this old and currently neglected social science tradition is to provide measures for meaningful comparisons across wide spans of time and social space. Real wages, intelligence quotients, and net reproductive rates are examples, but an effort in this direction is made even when a percentage, a per capita, or an annual rate is computed. Index numbers cannot be used uncritically because the imperfect knowledge of the laws invoked in any such measurement situation precludes computing any effective all-purpose measures.

Furthermore, the use of complex compensated indices in the assurance that they measure what they are devised for has in many instances proved quite misleading. A notable example is found in the definitional confusion surrounding the labor force concept (Jaffe & Steward, 1951; W. E. Moore, 1953). Often a relationship established between an over-all index and external variables is found due to only one component of the index. Cronbach (1958) has described this problem well in his discussion of dyadic scores of interpersonal perception. In the older methodological literature, the problem is raised under the term *index correlations* (e.g., Stouffer, 1934; Guilford, 1954; Campbell, 1955).

Despite these limitations, the problem of index numbers, which once loomed large in sociology and economics, deserves to be reactivated and integrated into modern social science methodology. The tradition is relevant in two ways. Many sources of data, particularly secondary records, require a transformation of the raw data if they are to be interpretable in any but truly experimental situations. Such transformations should be performed with the wisdom accumulated within the older tradition, as well as with a regard for the precautionary literature just cited. Properly done, such transformations often improve interpretability even if they fall far short of some ideal (cf. Bernstein, 1935).

A second value of the literature on index numbers lies in an examination of the types of irrelevant variation which the index computation sought to exclude. The construction of index numbers is usually a response to criticisms of less sophisticated indices. They thus embody a summary of the often unrecorded criticisms of prior measures. In the criticisms and the corrections are clues to implicit or explicit plausible rival interpretations of differences, the viable threats to valid interpretation.

Take so simple a measure as an index on unemployment or of retail sales. The gross number of the unemployed or the gross total dollar level of sales is useless if one wants to make comparisons within a single year. Some of the objections to the gross figures are reflected in the seasonal corrections applied to time-series data. If we look at only the last quarter of the year, we can see that the effect of weather must be considered. Systematically, winter depresses the number of employed construction workers, for example, and increases the unemployment level. Less systematically, spells of bad weather keep people in their homes and reduce the amount of retail shopping. Both periodic and aperiodic elements of the weather should be considered if one wants a more stable and interpretable measure of unemployment or sales. So, too, our custom of giving gifts at Christmas spurs December sales, as does the coinciding custom of Christmas bonuses to employees. All of these are accounted for, crudely, by a correction applied to the gross levels for either December or the final quarter of the year.

Some of these sources of invalidity are too specific to a single setting to be generalized usefully; others are too obvious to be catalogued. But some contribute to a general enumeration of recurrent threats to valid interpretation in social science measures.

The technical problems of index-number construction are heroic. "The index number should give *consistent* results for different base periods and also with its counterpart price or quantity index. No reasonably simple formula satisfies both of these consistency requirements" (Ekelblad, (1962, p. 726). The consistency problem is usually met by substituting a geometric mean for an arithmetic one, but then other problems arise. With complex indices of many components, there is the issue of getting an index that will yield consistent scores across all the different levels and times of the components.

In his important work on economic cycles, Hansen (1921) wrote, "Here is a heterogeneous group of statistical series all of which are related in a causal way, somehow or another, to the cycle of prosperity and depression" (p. 21). The search for a metric to relate these different components consistently, to be able to reverse factors without chaos, makes index construction a difficult task. But the payoff is great, and the best approximation to solving both the base-reversal and factor-reversal issues is a weighted aggregate with time-averaged weights. For good introductory statements of these and other index-number issues, see Yule & Kendall (1950), Zeisel (1957), and Ekelblad (1962). More detailed treatments can be found in Mitchell (1921), Fisher (1923), Mills (1927), and Mudgett (1951).

The third general approach to comparison may be called that of "plausible rival hypotheses." It is the most general and least formal of the three and is applicable to the other two. Given a comparison which a social scientist wishes to interpret, this approach asks what other plausible interpretations are allowed by the research setting and the measurement processes. The more of these, and the more plausible each is, the less validly interpretable is the comparison. Platt (1964) and Hafner and Presswood (1965) have discussed this approach with a focus in the physical sciences.

A social scientist may reduce the number of plausible rival hypotheses in many ways. Experimental methods and adequate indices serve as useful devices for eliminating some rival interpretations. A checklist of commonly relevant threats to validity may point to other ways of limiting the number of viable alternative hypotheses. For some major threats, it is often possible to provide supplementary analyses or to assemble additional data which can rule out a source of possible invalidity.

Backstopping the individual scientist is the critical reaction of his fellow scientists. Where he misses a plausible rival hypothesis, he can expect his colleagues to propose alternative interpretations. This resource is available even in disciplines which are not avowedly scientific. J. H. Wigmore, a distinguished legal scholar, showed an awareness of the criteria of other plausible explanations of data:

> If the potential defect of Inductive Evidence is that the fact offered as the basis of the conclusion may be open to one or more other explanations or inferences, the failure to exclude a single other rational inference would be, from the standpoint of *Proof,* a fatal defect; and yet, if only that single other inference were open, there might still be an extremely high degree of probability for the Inference desired. . . . The provisional test, then, from the point of view valuing the Inference, would be something like this: *Does the evidentiary fact point to the desired conclusion . . . as the inference . . . most plausible or most natural out of the various ones that are conceivable?* [1937, p. 25].

The culture of science seeks, however, to systematize the production of rival plausible hypotheses and to extend them to every generalization proposed. While this may be implicit in a field such as law, scientific epistemology requires that the original and competing hypotheses be explicitly and generally stated.

Such a commitment could lead to rampant uncertainty unless some criterion of plausibility were adopted before the rival hypothesis was taken as a serious alternative. Accordingly, each rival hypothesis is a threat only if we can give it the status of a law at least as creditable as the law we seek to demonstrate. If it falls short of that credibility, it is not thereby "plausible" and can be ignored.

In some logical sense, even in a "true" experimental comparison, an infinite number of potential laws could predict this result. We do not let this logical state of affairs prevent us from interpreting the results. Instead, uncertainty comes only from those unexcluded hypotheses to which we, in the current state of our science, are willing to give the status of established laws: these are the plausible rival hypotheses. While the north-south orientation of planaria may have something to do with conditioning, no interview studies report on the directional orientation of interviewer and interviewee. And they should not.

For those plausible rival hypotheses to which we give the status of laws, the conditions under which they would explain our obtained result also imply specific outcomes for other sets of data. Tests in other settings, attempting to verify these laws, may enable us to rule them out. In a similar fashion, the theory we seek to test has many implications other than that involved in the specific comparison, and the exploration of these is likewise demanded. The more numerous and complex the manifestations of the law, the fewer singular plausible rival hypotheses are available, and the more parsimony favors the law under study.

Our longing is for data that prove and certify theory, but such is not to be our lot. Some comfort may come from the observation that this is not an existential predicament unique to social science. The replacement of Newtonian theory by relativity and quantum mechanics shows us that even the best of physical science experimentation probes theory rather than proves it. Modern philosophies of science as presented by Popper (1935; 1959; 1962), Quine (1953), Hanson (1958), Kuhn (1962), and Campbell (1965a), make this point clear.

INTERNAL AND EXTERNAL VALIDITY

Before discussing a list of some common sources of invalidity, a distinction must be drawn between internal and external validity. *Internal validity* asks whether a difference exists at all in any given comparison. It asks whether or not an apparent difference can be explained away as some measurement artifact. For true experiments, this question is usually not salient, but even there, the happy vagaries of random sample selection occasionally delude one and spuriously produce the appearance of a difference where in fact none exists. For the rival hypothesis of chance, we fortunately have an elaborated theoretical model which evaluates its plausibility. A *p*-value describes the darkness of the ever present shadow of doubt. But for index-number comparisons not embedded in a formal experiment, and for the plausible-rival-hypothesis strategy more generally, the threats to internal validity—the argument that even the appearance of a difference is spurious —is a serious problem and the one that has first priority.

External validity is the problem of interpreting the difference, the problem of generalization. To what other populations, occasions, stimulus objects, and measures may the obtained results be applied? The distinction between internal and external validity can be illustrated in two uses of randomization. When the experimentalist in psychology randomly assigns a sample of persons into two or more experimental groups, he is concerned entirely with internal validity—with making it implausible that the luck of the draw produced the resulting differences. When a sociologist carefully randomizes the selection of respondents so that his sample represents a larger population, representativeness or external validity is involved.

The psychologist may be extremely confident that a difference is traceable to an experimental treatment, but whether it would hold up with another set of subjects or in a different setting may be quite equivocal. He has achieved internal validity by his random assignment but not addressed the external validity issue by the chance allocation of subjects.

The sociologist, similarly, has not met all the validity concerns by simply drawing a random sample. Conceding that he has taken a necessary step toward achieving external validity and generalization of his differences, the internal validity problem remains.

Random assignment is only one method of reaching toward internal validity. Experimental-design control, exclusive of randomization, is another. Consider the case of a pretest-posttest field experiment on the effect of a persuasive communication. Randomly choosing those who participate, the social scientist properly wards off some major threats to external validity. But we also know of other validity threats. The first interview in a two-stage study may set into motion attitude change and clarification processes which would otherwise not have occurred (e.g., Crespi, 1948). If such processes did occur, the comparison of a first and second measure on the same person is internally invalid, for the shift is a measurement-produced artifact.

Even when a measured control group is used, and a persuasive communication produces a greater change in an experimental group, the persuasive effect may be internally valid but externally invalid. There is the substantial risk that the effect occurs only with pretested populations and might be absent in populations lacking the pretest (cf. Schanck & Goodman, 1939; Hovland, Lumsdaine, & Sheffield, 1949; Solomon, 1949). For more extensive discussions of internal and external validity, see Campbell (1957) and Campbell and Stanley (1963).

The distinction between internal and external validity is often murky. In this work, we have considered the two classes of threat jointly, although occasionally detailing the risks separately. The reason for this is that the factors which are a risk for internal validity are often the same as those threatening external validity. While for one scientist the representative sampling of cities is a method to achieve generalization to the United States population, for another it may be an effort to give an internally valid comparison across cities.

SOURCES OF INVALIDITY OF MEASURES

In this section, we review frequent threats to the valid interpretation of a difference—common plausible rival hypotheses. They are broadly divided into three groups: error that may be traced to those being studied, error that comes from the investigator, and error associated with sampling imperfections. This section is the only one in which we draw illustrations mainly from the most popular methods of current social science. For that reason, particular attention is paid to those weaknesses which create the need for multiple and alternate methods.

In addition, some other criteria such as the efficiency of the research instrument are mentioned. These are independent of validity, but important for the practical research decisions which must be made.

Reactive Measurement Effect: Error from the Respondent

The most understated risk to valid interpretation is the error produced by the respondent. Even when he is well intentioned and cooperative, the research subject's knowledge that he is participating in a scholarly search may confound the investigator's data. Four classes of this error are discussed here: awareness of being tested, role selection, measurement as a change agent, and response sets.

1. The Guinea Pig Effect—Awareness of Being Tested. Selltiz and her associates (1959) make the observation:

> The measurement process used in the experiment may itself affect the outcome. If people feel that they are "guinea pigs" being experimented with, or if they feel that they are being "tested" and must make a good impression, or if the method of data collection suggests responses or stimulates an interest the subject did not previously feel, the measuring process may distort the experimental results [p. 97].

These effects have been called "reactive effect of measurement" and "reactive arrangement" bias (Campbell, 1957; Campbell & Stanley, 1963). It is important to note early that the awareness of testing need not, by itself, contaminate responses. It is a question of probabilities, but the probability of bias is high in any study in which a respondent is aware of his subject status.

Although the methods to be reviewed here do not involve "respondents," comparable reactive effects on the population may often occur. Consider, for example, a potentially nonreactive instrument such as the movie camera. If it is conspicuously placed, its lack of ability to talk to the subjects doesn't help us much. The visible presence of the camera undoubtedly changes behavior, and does so differentially depending upon the labeling involved. The response is likely to vary if the camera has printed on its side "Los Angeles Police Department" or "NBC" or "Foundation Project on Crowd Behavior." Similarly, an Englishman's presence at a wedding in Africa exerts a much more reactive effect on the proceedings than it would on the Sussex Downs.

A specific illustration may be of value. In the summer of 1952, some graduate students in the social sciences at the University of Chicago were employed to observe the numbers of Negroes and whites in stores, restaurants, bars, theaters, and so on on a south side Chicago street intersecting the Negro-white boundary (East 63rd). This, presumably, should have been a nonreactive process, particularly at the predominantly white end of the street. No questions were asked, no persons stopped. Yet, in spite of this hopefully inconspicuous activity, two merchants were agitated and persistent enough to place calls to the university which somehow got through to the investigators; how many others tried and failed cannot be known. The two calls were from a store operator and the manager of a currency exchange, both of whom wanted assurance that this was some university nosiness and not a professional casing for subsequent robbery (Campbell & Mack, in preparation). An intrusion conspicuous enough to arouse such an energetic reaction may also have been conspicuous enough to change behavior; for observations other than simple enumerations the bias would have been great. But even with the simple act of nose-counting, there is the risk that the area would be differentially avoided. The research mistake was in providing observers with clipboards and log sheets, but their appearance might have been still more sinister had they operated Veeder counters with hands jammed in pockets.

We argue strongly for the use of archival records. Thinking, perhaps, of musty files of bound annual reports of some prior century, one might regard such a method as totally immune to reactive effects. However, were one to make use of precinct police blotters, going around to copy off data once each month, the quality and nature of the records would almost certainly change. In actual fact, archives are kept indifferently, as a low-priority task, by understaffed bureaucracies. Conscientiousness is often low because of the lack of utilization of the records. The presence of a user can revitalize the process—as well as create anxieties over potentially damaging data (Campbell, 1963a). When records are seen as sources of vulnerability, they may be altered systematically. Accounts thought likely to enter into tax audits are an obvious case (Schwartz, 1961), but administrative records (Blau, 1955) and criminal statistics (Kadish, 1964) are equally amenable to this source of distortion. The selective and wholesale rifling of records by ousted political administrations sets an example of potential reactive effects, self-consciousness, and dissembling on the part of archivists.

These reactive effects may threaten both internal and external validity, depending upon the conditions. If it seems plausible that the reactivity was equal in both measures of a comparison, then the threat is to external validity or generalizability, not to internal validity. If the reactive effect is plausibly differential, then it may generate a pseudo-difference. Thus, in a study (Campbell & McCormack, 1957) showing a reduction in authoritarian attitudes over the course of one year's military training, the initial testing was done in conjunction with an official testing program, while the subsequent testing was clearly under external university research auspices. As French (1955) pointed out in another connection, this difference provides a plausible reactive threat jeopardizing the conclusion that any reduction has taken place even for this one group, quite apart from the external validity problems of explanation and generalization. In many interview and questionnaire studies, increased or decreased rapport and increased awareness of the researcher's goals or decreased fear provide plausible alternative explanations of the apparent change recorded.

The common device of guaranteeing anonymity demonstrates concern for the reactive bias, but this concern may lead to validity threats. For example, some test constructors have collected normative data under conditions of anonymity, while the test is likely to be used with the respondent's name signed. Making a response public, or guaranteeing to hide one, will influence the nature of the response. This has been seen for persuasive communications, in the validity of reports of brands purchased, and for the level of antisocial responses. There is a clear link between awareness of being tested and the biases associated with a tendency to answer with socially desirable responses.

The considerations outlined above suggest that reactivity may be selectively troublesome within trials or tests of the experiment. Training trials may accommodate the subject to the task, but a practice effect may exist that either enhances or inhibits the reactive bias. Early responses may be contaminated, later ones not, or vice versa (Underwood, 1957).

Ultimately, the determination of reactive effect depends on validating studies—few examples of which are currently available. Behavior observed under nonreactive conditions must be compared with corresponding behavior in which various potentially reactive conditions are introduced. Where no difference in direction of relationship occurs, the reactivity factor can be discounted.

In the absence of systematic data of this kind, we have little basis for determining what is and what is not reactive. Existing techniques consist of asking subjects in a posttest interview whether they were affected by the test, were aware of the deception in the experiment, and so forth. While these may sometimes demonstrate a method to be reactive, they may fail to detect many instances in which reactivity is a serious contaminant. Subjects who consciously dissemble during an experiment may do so afterward for the same reasons. And those who are unaware of the effects on them at the time of the research may hardly be counted on for valid reports afterwards.

The types of measures surveyed in this monograph have a double importance in overcoming reactivity. In the absence of validation for verbal measures, nonreactive techniques of the kind surveyed here provide ways of avoiding the serious problems faced by more conventional techniques. Given the limiting properties of these "other measures," however, their greatest utility may inhere in their capacity to provide validation for the more conventional measures.

2. *Role Selection.* Another way in which the respondent's awareness of the research process produces differential reaction involves not so much inaccuracy, defense, or dishonesty, but rather a specialized selection from among the many "true" selves or "proper" behaviors available in any respondent.

By singling out an individual to be tested (assuming that being tested is not a normal condition), the experimenter forces upon the subject a role-defining decision—What kind of a person should I be as I answer these questions or do these tasks? In many of the "natural" situations to which the findings are generalized, the subject may not be forced to define his role relative to the behavior. For other situations, he may. Validity decreases as the role assumed in the research setting varies from the usual role present in comparable behavior beyond the research setting. Orne and his colleagues have provided compelling demonstrations of the magnitude of this variable's effect (Orne, 1959; Orne, 1962; Orne & Scheibe, 1964; Orne & Evans, 1965). Orne has noted:

The experimental situation is one which takes place within context of an explicit agreement of the subject to participate in a special form of social interaction known as "taking part in an experiment." Within the context of our culture the roles of subject and experimenter are well understood and carry with them well-defined mutual role expectations [1962, p. 777].

Looking at all the cues available to the respondent attempting to puzzle out an appropriate set of roles or behavior, Orne labeled the total of all such cues the "demand characteristics of the experimental situation." The recent study by Orne & Evans (1965) showed that the alleged antisocial effects induced by hypnosis can be accounted for by the demand characteristics of the research setting. Subjects who were not hypnotized engaged in "antisocial" activities as well as did those who were hypnotized. The behavior of those not hypnotized is traced to social cues that attend the experimental situation and are unrelated to the experimental variable.

The probability of this confounding role assumption varies from one research study to another, of course. The novelty of a test-taking role may be selectively biasing for subjects of different educational levels. Less familiar and comfortable with testing, those with little formal schooling are more likely to produce nonrepresentative behavior. The act of being tested is "more different." The same sort of distortion risk occurs when subject matter is unusual or novel. Subject matter with which the respondent is unfamiliar may produce uncertainty of which role to select. A role-playing choice is more likely with such new or unexpected material.

Lack of familiarity with tests or with testing materials can influence response in different ways. Responses may be depressed because of a lack of training with the materials. Or the response level may be distorted as the subject perceives himself in the rare role of expert.

Both unfamiliarity and "expertness" can influence the character as well as the level of response. It is common to find experimental procedures which augment the experting bias. The instruction which reads, "You have been selected as part of a scientifically selected sample . . . it is important that you answer the questions . . ." underlines in what a special situation and what a special person the respondent is. The empirical test of the experting hypothesis in field research is the extent of "don't know" replies. One should predict that a set of instructions stressing the importance of the respondent as a member of a "scientifically selected sample" will produce significantly fewer "don't knows" than an instruction set that does not stress the individual's importance.

Although the "special person" set of instructions may increase participation in the project, and thus reduce some concern on the sampling level, it concurrently increases the risk of reactive bias. In science as everywhere else, one seldom gets something for nothing. The critical question for the researcher must be whether or not the resultant sampling gain offsets the risk of deviation from "true" responses produced by the experting role.

Not only does interviewing result in role selection, but the problem or its analogues may exist for any measure. Thus, in a study utilizing conversation sampling with totally hidden microphones, each social setting elicits a different role selection. Conversation samples might thus differ between two cities, not because of any true differences, but rather because of subtle differences in role elicitation of the differing settings employed.

3. Measurement as Change Agent.   With all the respondent candor possible, and with complete role representativeness, there can still be an important class of reactive effects—those in which the initial measurement activity introduces real changes in what is being measured. The change may be real enough in these instances, but be invalidly attributed to any of the intervening events, and be invalidly generalized to other settings not involving a pretest. This process has been deliberately demonstrated by Schanck and Goodman (1939) in a classic study involving information-test taking as a disguised persuasive process. Research by Roper (cited by Crespi, 1948) shows that the well-established "preamble effect" (Cantril, 1944) is not merely a technical flaw in determining the response to the question at hand, but that it also creates attitudes which persist and which are measurable on subsequent unbiased questions. Crespi reports additional research of his own confirming that even for those who initially say "don't know," processes leading to opinion development are initiated.

The effect has been long established in the social sciences. In psychology, early research in transfer of training encountered the threat to internal validity called "practice effects": the exercise provided by the pretest accounted for the gain shown on the posttest. Such research led to the introduction of control groups in studies that had earlier neglected to include them. Similarly, research in intelligence testing showed that dependable gains in test-passing ability could be traced to experience with previous tests even where no knowledge of results had been provided. (See Cane & Heim, 1950, and Anastasi, 1958, pp. 190–191, for reviews of this literature.) Similar gains have been shown in personal "adjustment" scores (Windle, 1954).

While such effects are obviously limited to intrusive measurement methods such as this review seeks to avoid, the possibility of analogous artifacts must be considered. Suppose one were interested in measuring the weight of women in a secretarial pool, and their weights were to be the dependent variable in a study on the effects of a change from an all-female staff to one including men. One might for this purpose put free weight scales in the women's restroom, with an automatic recording device inside. However, the recurrent availability of knowledge of one's own weight in a semisocial situation would probably act as a greater change agent for weight than would any experimental treatment that might be under investigation. A floor-panel treadle would be better, recording weights without providing feedback to the participant, possibly disguised as an automatic door-opener.

4. Response Sets.   The critical literature on questionnaire methodology has demonstrated the presence of several irrelevant but lawful sources of variance. Most of these are probably applicable to interviews also, although this has been less elaborately demonstrated to date. Cronbach (1946) has summarized this literature, and evidence continues to show its importance (e.g., Jackson & Messick, 1957; Chapman & Bock, 1958).

Respondents will more frequently endorse a statement than disagree with its opposite (Sletto, 1937). This tendency differs widely and consistently among individuals, generating the reliable source of variance known as acquiescence response set. Rorer (1965) has recently entered a dissent from this point of view. He validly notes the evidence indicating that acquiescence or yea-saying is not a totally general personality trait elicitable by items of any content. He fails to note that, even so, the evidence clearly indicates the methodological problem that direction of wording lawfully enhances the correlation between two measures when shared, and depresses the correlation when running counter to the direction of the correlation of the content (Campbell, 1965b). Another idiosyncrasy, dependably demonstrated over varied multiple-choice content, is the preference for strong statements versus moderate or indecisive ones. Sequences of questions asked in very similar format produce stereotyped responses, such as a tendency to endorse the righthand or the lefthand response, or to alternate in some simple fashion. Furthermore, decreasing attention produces reliable biases from the order of item presentation.

Response biases can occur not only for questionnaires or public opinion polls, but also for archival records such as votes (Bain & Hecock, 1957). Still more esoteric observational or erosion measures face similar problems. Take the example of a traffic study.

Suppose one wanted to obtain a nonreactive measure of the relative attractiveness of paintings in an art museum. He might employ an erosion method such as the relative degree of carpet or floor-tile wear in front of each painting. Or, more elaborately, he might install invisible photoelectric timers and counters. Such an approach must also take into account irrelevant habits which affect traffic flow. There is, for example, a general right-turn bias upon entering a building or room. When this is combined with time deadlines and fatigue (Do people drag their feet more by the time they get to the paintings on the left side of the building?), there probably is a predictably biased response tendency. The design of museums tends to be systematic, and this, too, can bias the measures. The placement of an exit door will consistently bias the traffic flow and thus confound any erosion measure unless it is controlled. (For imaginative and provocative observational studies on museum behavior see Robinson, 1928; Melton, 1933a; Melton, 1933b; Melton, 1935; Melton, 1936; Melton, Feldman, & Mason, 1936.)

Each of these four types of reactive error can be reduced by employing research measures which do not require the cooperation of the respondent and which are "blind" to him. Although we urge more methodological research to make known the degree of error that may be traced to reactivity, our inclination now is to urge the use of compensating measures which do not contain the reactive risk.

Error from the Investigator

To some degree, error from the investigator was implicit in the reactive error effects. After all, the investigator is an important source of cues to the respondent, and he helps to structure the demand characteristics of the interview. However, in these previous points, interviewer character was unspecified. Here we deal with effects that vary systematically with interviewer characteristics, and with instrument errors totally independent of respondents.

5. Interviewer Effects. It is old news that characteristics of the interviewer can contribute a substantial amount of variance to a set of findings. Interviewees respond differentially to visible cues provided by the interviewer. Within any single study, this variance can produce a spurious difference. The work of Katz (1942) and Cantril (1944) early demonstrated the differential effect of the race of the interviewer, and that bias has been more recently shown by Athey and his associates (1960). Riesman and Ehrlich (1961) reported that the age of the interviewer produced a bias, with the number of "unacceptable" (to the experimenter) answers higher when questions were posed by younger interviewers. Religion of the interviewer is a possible contaminant (Robinson & Rohde,

1946; Hyman *et al.,* 1954), as is his social class (Riesman, 1956; Lenski & Leggett, 1960). Benney, Riesman, and Star (1956) showed that one should consider not only main effects, but also interactions. In their study of age and sex variables they report: "Male interviewers obtain fewer responses than female, and fewest of all from males, while female interviewers obtain their highest responses from men, except for young women talking to young men" (p. 143).

The evidence is overwhelming that a substantial number of biases are introduced by the interviewer (see Hyman *et al.,* 1954; Kahn & Cannell, 1957). Some of the major biases, such as race, are easily controllable; other biases, such as the interaction of age and sex, are less easily handled. If we heeded all the known biases, without considering our ignorance of major interactions, there could no longer be a simple survey. The understandable action by most researchers has been to ignore these biases and to assume them away. The biases are lawful and consistent, and all research employing face-to-face interviewing or questionnaire administration is subject to them. Rather than flee by assumptions, the experimenter may use alternative methodologies that let him flee by circumvention.

6. Change in the Research Instrument. The measuring (datagathering) instrument is frequently an interviewer, whose characteristics, we have just shown, may alter responses. In panel studies, or those using the same interviewer at two or more points in time, it is essential to ask: To what degree is the interviewer or experimenter the same researcher instrument at all points of the research?

Just as a spring scale becomes fatigued with use, reading "heavier" a second time, an interviewer may also measure differently at different times. His skill may increase. He may be better able to establish rapport. He may have learned necessary vocabulary. He may loaf or become bored. He may have increasingly strong expectations of what a respondent "means" and code differently with practice. Some errors relate to recording accuracy, while others are linked to the nature of the interviewer's interpretation of what transpired. Either way, there is always the risk that the interviewer will be a variable filter over time and experience.

Even when the interviewer becomes more competent, there is potential trouble. Although we usually think of difficulty only when the instrument weakens, a difference in competence between two waves of interviewing, *either increasing or decreasing,* can yield spurious effects. The source of error is not limited to interviewers, and every class of measurement is vulnerable to wavering calibration. Suicides in Prussia jumped 20 percent between 1882 and 1883. This clearly reflected a change in record-keeping, not a massive increase in depression. Until 1883 the records were kept by the police, but in that year the job was transferred to the civil service (Halbwachs, 1930; cited in Selltiz *et al.,* 1959). Archivists undoubtedly drift in recording standards, with occasional administrative reforms in conscientiousness altering the output of the "instrument" (Kitsuse & Cicourel, 1963).

Where human observers are used, they have fluctuating adaptation levels and response thresholds (Holmes, 1958; Campbell, 1961). Rosenthal, in an impressive series of commentary and research, has focused on errors traceable to the experimenter himself. Of particular interest is his work on the influence of early data returns upon analysis of subsequent data (Rosenthal *et al.,* 1963. See also Rosenthal, 1963; Rosenthal & Fode, 1963; Rosenthal & Lawson, 1963; Rosenthal, 1964; Kintz *et al.,* 1965).

Varieties of Sampling Error

Historically, social science has examined sampling errors as a problem in the selection of respondents. The person or group has been the critical unit, and our thinking has been focused on a universe of people. Often a sample of time or space can provide a practical substitute for a sample of persons. Novel methods should be examined for their potential in this regard. For example, a study of the viewing of bus advertisements used a time-stratified, random triggering of an automatic camera pointed out a window over the bus ad (Politz, 1959). One could similarly take a photographic sample of bus passengers modulated by door entries as counted by a photo cell. A photo could be taken one minute after the entry of every twentieth passenger. For some methods, such as the erosion methods, total population records are no more costly than partial ones. For some archives, temporal samples or agency samples are possible. For voting records, precincts may be sampled. But for any one method, the possibilities should be examined.

We look at sampling in this section from the point of view of restrictions on reaching people associated with various methods and the stability of populations over time and areas.

7. Population Restrictions. In the public-opinion-polling tradition, one conceptualizes a "universe" from which a representative sample is drawn. This model gives little or no formal attention to the fact that only certain universes are possible for any given method. A method-respondent interaction exists—one that gives each method a different set of defining boundaries for its universe. One reason so little attention is given to this fact is that, as methods go, public opinion polling is relatively unrestricted. Yet even here there is definite universe rigidity, with definite restrictions on the size and character of the population able to be sampled.

In the earliest days of polling, people were questioned in public places, probably excluding some 80 percent of the total population. Shifting to in-home interviewing with quota controls and no callbacks still excluded some 60 percent—perhaps 5 percent unaccessible in homes under any conditions, 25 percent not at home, 25 percent refusals, and 5 percent through interviewers' reluctance to approach homes of extreme wealth or poverty and a tendency to avoid fourth-floor walkups.

Under modern probability sampling with callbacks and household designation, perhaps only 15 percent of the population is excluded: 5 percent are totally inaccessible in private residences (e.g., those institutionalized, hospitalized, homeless, transient, in the military, mentally incompetent, and so forth), another 10 percent refuse to answer, are unavailable after three callbacks, or have moved to no known address. A 20 percent figure was found in the model Elmira study in its first wave (Williams, 1950), although other studies have reported much lower figures. Ross (1963) has written a general statement on the problem of inaccessibility, and Stephan and McCarthy (1958), in their literature survey, show from 3 to 14 percent of sample populations of residences inaccessible.

Also to be considered in population restriction is the degree to which the accessible universe deviates in important parameters from the excluded population. This bias is probably minimal in probability sampling with adequate callbacks, but great with catch-as-catch-can and quota samples. Much survey research has centered on household behavior, and the great mass of probability approaches employ a prelisted household as the terminal sampling unit. This frequently requires the enlistment of a household member as a reporter on the behavior of others. Since those who answer doorbells overrepresent the old, the young, and women, this can be a confounding error.

When we come to more demanding verbal techniques, the universe rigidity is much greater. What proportion of the population is available for self-administered questionnaires? Payment for filling out the questionnaire reduces the limitations a bit, but a money reward is selectively attractive—at least at the rates most researchers pay. A considerable proportion of the populace is functionally illiterate for personality and attitude tests developed on college populations.

Not only does task-demandingness create population restrictions, differential volunteering provides similar effects, interacting in a particularly biasing way when knowledge of the nature of the task is involved (Capra & Dittes, 1962). Baumrind (1964) writes of the motivation of volunteers and notes, "The dependent attitude of most subjects toward the experimenter is an artifact of the experimental situation as well as an expression of some subjects' personal need systems at the time they volunteer" (p. 421).

The curious, the exhibitionistic, and the succorant are likely to overpopulate any sample of volunteers. How secure a base can volunteers be with such groups overrepresented and the shy, suspicious, and inhibited underrepresented? The only defensible position is a probability sample of the units to which the findings will be generalized. Even conscripting sophomores may be better than relying on volunteers.

Returning to the rigidity of sampling, what proportion of the total population is available for the studio test audiences used in advertising and television program evaluation? Perhaps 2 percent. For mailed questionnaires, the population available for addressing might be 95 percent of the total in the United States, but low-cost, convenient mailing lists probably cover no more than 70 percent of the families through automobile registration and telephone directories. The exclusion is, again, highly selective. If, however, we consider the volunteering feature, where 10 percent returns are typical, the effective population is a biased 7 percent selection of the total. The nature of this selective-return bias, according to a recent study (Vincent, 1964), includes a skewing of the sample in favor of lower-middle-class individuals drawn from unusually stable, "happy" families.

There are more households with television in the United States than there are households with telephones (or baths). In any given city, one is likely to find more than 15 percent of the households excluded in a telephone subscription list—and most of these are at the bottom of the socioeconomic scale. Among subscribers, as many as 15 percent in some areas do not list their number, and an estimate of 5 percent over all is conservative. Cooper (1964) found an over-all level of 6 percent deliberately not listed and an additional 12 percent not in the directory because of recent installations. The unlisted problem can be defeated by a system of random-digit dialing, but this increases the cost at least tenfold and requires a prior study of the distribution of exchanges. Among a sample of known numbers, some 50 percent of dialings are met with busy signals and "not-at-homes." Thus, for a survey without callbacks, the accessible population of 80 percent (listed-phone households) reduces to 40 percent. If individuals are the unit of analysis, the effective sampling rate, without callbacks, may drop to 20 percent. Random-digit dialing will help; so, too, will at least three callbacks, but precision can be achieved only at a high price. The telephone is not so cheap a research instrument as it first looks.

Sampling problems of this sort are even more acute for the research methods considered here. Although a few have the full population access of public opinion surveys, most have much more restricted populations. Consider, for example, the sampling of natural conversations. What are the proportions of men and women whose conversations are accessible in public places and on public transport? What is the representativeness of social class or role?

8. Population Stability Over Time. Just as internal validity is more important than external validity, so, too, is the stability of a population restriction more important than the magnitude of the restriction. Examine conversation sampling on a bus or streetcar. The population represented differs on dry days and snowy days, in winter and spring, as well as by day of the week. These shifts would in many instances provide plausible rival explanations of shifts in topics of conversation. Sampling from a much narrower universe would be preferable if the population were more stable over time, as, say, conversation samples from an employees' restroom in an office building. Comparisons of interview survey results over time periods are more troubled by population instability than is generally realized, because of seasonal layoffs in many fields of employment, plus status-differentiated patterns of summer and winter vacations. An extended discussion of time sampling has been provided by Brookover and Back (1965).

9. Population Stability Over Areas. Similarly, research populations available to a given method may vary from region to region, providing a more serious problem than a population restriction common to both. Thus, for a comparison of attitudes between New York and Los Angeles, conversation sampling in buses and commuter trains would tap such different segments of the communities as to be scarcely worth doing. Again, a comparison of employees' washrooms in comparable office buildings would provide a more interpretable comparison. Through the advantage of background data to check on some dimensions of representativeness, public opinion surveys again have an advantage in this regard.

Any enumeration of sources of invalidity is bound to be incomplete. Some threats are too highly specific to a given setting and method to be generalized, as are some opportunities for ingenious measurement and control. This list contains a long series of general threats that apply to a broad body of research method and content. It does not say that additional problems cannot be found.

AN INTERLUDE: THE MEASUREMENT OF OUTCROPPINGS

The population restrictions discussed here are apt to seem so severe as to traumatize the researcher and to lead to the abandonment of the method. This is particularly so for one approaching social science with the goal of complete description. Such trauma is, of course, far from our intention. While discussion of these restrictions is a necessary background to their intelligent use and correction, there is need here for a parenthesis forestalling excessive pessimism.

First, it can be noted that a theory predicting a change in civic opinion, due to an event and occurring between two time periods, might be such that this opinion shift could be predicted for many partially overlapping populations. One might predict changes on public opinion polls within that universe, changes in sampled conversation on commuter trains for a much smaller segment, changes in letters mailed to editors and the still more limited letters published by editors, changes in purchase rates of books on relevant subjects by that minute universe, and so on. In such an instance, the occurrence of the predicted shift on any one of these meters is confirmatory and its absence discouraging. If the effect is found on only one measure, it probably reflects more on the method than on the theory (e.g., Burwen & Campbell, 1957; Campbell & Fiske, 1959). A more complicated theory might well predict differential shifts for different meters, and, again, the evidence of each is relevant to the validity of the theory. The joint comfirmation between pollings of high-income populations and commuter-train conversations is much more validating than either taken alone, just because of the difference between the methods in irrelevant components.

The "outcropping" model from geology may be used more generally. Any given theory has innumerable implications and makes innumerable predictions which are unaccessible to available measures at any given time. The testing of the theory can only be done at the available outcroppings, those points where theoretical predictions and available instrumentation meet. Any one such outcropping is equivocal, and all types available should be checked. The more remote or independent such checks, the more confirmatory their agreement.

Within this model, science opportunistically exploits the available points of observation. As long as nature abhorred a vacuum up to 33 feet of water, little research was feasible. When manufacturing skills made it possible to represent the same abhorrence by 76 centimeters of mercury in a glass tube, a whole new outcropping for the checking of theory was made available. The telescope in Galileo's hands, the microscope, the induction coil, the photographic emulsion of silver nitrate, and the cloud chamber all represent partial new outcroppings available for the verification of theory. Even where several of these are relevant to the same theory, their mode of relevance is quite different and short of a complete overlap. Analogously, social science methods with individually restricted and nonidentical universes can provide collectively valuable outcroppings for the testing of theory.

The goal of complete description in science is particularly misleading when it is assumed that raw data provide complete description. Theory is necessarily abstract, for any given event is so complex that its complete description may demand many more theories than are actually brought to bear on it—or than are even known at any given stage of development. But theories are more complete descriptions than obtained data, since they describe processes and entities in their unobserved as well as in their observed states. The scintillation counter notes but a small and nonrepresentative segment of a meson's course. The visual data of an ordinary object are literally superficial. Perceiving an object as solid or vaporous, persistent or transient, involves theory going far beyond the data given. The raw data, observations, field notes, tape recordings, and sound movies of a social event are but transient superficial outcroppings of events and objects much more continuously and completely (even if abstractly) described in the social scientist's theory. Tycho Brahe and Kepler's observations provided Kepler with only small fragments of the orbit of Mars, for a biased and narrow sampling of times of day, days, and years. From these he constructed a complete description through theory. The fragments provided outcroppings sufficiently stubborn to force Kepler to reject his preferred theory. The data were even sufficient to cause the rejection of Newton's later theory had Einstein's better-fitting theory then been available.

So if the restraints on validity sometimes seem demoralizing, they remain so only as long as one set of data, one type of method, is considered separately. Viewed in consort with other methods, matched against the available outcroppings for theory testing, there can be strength in converging weakness.

THE ACCESS TO CONTENT

Often a choice among methods is delimited by the relative ability of different classes of measurement to penetrate into content areas of research interest. In the simplest instance, his not so much a question of validity as it is a limitation on the utility of the measure. Each class of research method, be it the questionnaire or hidden observation, has rigidities on the content it can cover. These rigidities can be divided, as were population restrictions, into those linked to an interaction between method and materials, those associated with time, and those with physical area.

10. Restrictions on Content. If we adopt the research strategy of combining different classes of measurement, it becomes important to understand what content is and is not feasible or practical for each overlapping approach.

Observational methods can be used to yield an index of Negro-white amicability by computing the degree of "aggregation" or nonrandom clustering among mixed groups of Negroes and whites. This method could also be used to study male-female relations, or army-navy relations in wartime when uniforms are worn on liberty. But these indices of aggregation would be largely unavailable for Catholic-Protestant relations or for Jewish-Christian relations. Door-to-door solicitation of funds for causes relevant to attitudes is obviously plausible, but available for only a limited range of topics. For public opinion surveys, there are perhaps tabooed topics (although research on birth control and venereal disease has shown these to be fewer than might have been expected). More importantly, there are topics on which people are unable to report but which a social scientist can reliably observe.

Examples of this can be seen in the literature on verbal reinforcers in speech and in interviews. (For a review of this literature, see Krasner, 1958, as well as Hildum & Brown, 1956; Matarazzo, 1962.) A graphic display of opportunistic exploitation of an "outcropping" was displayed recently by Matarazzo and his associates (1964). They took tapes of the speech of astronauts and ground-communicators for two space flights and studied the duration of the ground-communicator's unit of speech to the astronauts. The data supported their expectations and confirmed findings from the laboratory. We are not sure if an orbital flight should be considered a "natural setting" or not, but certainly the astronaut and his colleagues were not overly sensitive to the duration of individual speech units. The observational method has consistently produced findings on the effect of verbal reinforcers unattainable by direct questioning.

It is obvious that secondary records and physical evidence are high in their content rigidity. The rescarcher cannot go out and generate a new set of historical rccords. He may discover a new set, but he is always restrained by what is available. We cite examples later which demonstrate that this weakness is not so great as is frequently thought, but it would be naive to suggest that it is not present.

11. Stability of Content Over Time. The restrictions on content just mentioned are often questions of convenience. The instability of content, however, is a serious concern for validity. Consider conversation sampling again: if one is attending to the amount of comment on race relations, for example, the occurrence of extremely bad wcather may so completely dominate all conversations as to cause a meaningless drop in racial comments. This is a typical problem for index-making. In such an instance, one would probably prefer some index such as the proportion of all race comments that were favorable. In specific studies of content variability over time, personnel-evaluation studies have employed time sampling with considerable success. Observation during a random sample of a worker's laboring minutes efficiently does much to describe both the job and the worker (R. L. Thorndike, 1949; Ghiselli & Brown, 1955; Whisler & Harper, 1962).

Public opinion surveys have obvious limitations in this regard which have led to the utilization of telephone interviews and built-in-dialing recorders for television and radio audience surveys (Lucas & Britt, 1950; Lucas & Britt, 1963). By what means other than a recorder could one get a reasonable estimate of the number of people who watch *The Late Show?*

   12. *Stability of Content Over Area.*   Where regional comparisons are being made, cross-sectional stability in the kinds of contents elicited by a given method is desirable.

   Take the measurement of interservice rivalry as a research question. As suggested earlier, one could study the degree of mingling among men in uniform, or study the number of barroom fights among men dressed in different uniforms. To have a valid regional comparison, one must assume the same incidence of men wearing uniforms in public places when at liberty. Such an assumption is probably not justified, partly because of past experience in a given area, partly because of proximity to urban centers. If a cluster of military bases are close to a large city, only a selective group wear uniforms off duty, and they are more likely to be the belligerent ones. Another comparison region may have the same level of behavior, but be less visible.

   The effect of peace is to reduce the influence of the total level of the observed response, since mufti is more common. But if all the comparisons are made in peacetime, it is not an issue. The problem occurs only if one elected to study the problem by a time-series design which cut across war and peace. To the foot-on-rail researcher, the number of outcroppings may vary because of war, but this is no necessary threat to internal validity.

   Sampling of locations, such as bus routes, waiting rooms, shop windows, and so forth, needs to be developed to expand access to both content and populations. Obviously, different methods present different opportunities and problems in this regard. Among the few studies which have seriously attempted this type of sampling, the problem of enumerating the universe of such locations has proved extremely difficult (James, 1951). Location sampling has, of course, been practiced more systematically with pre-established enumerated units such as blocks, census tracts, and incorporated areas.

OPERATING EASE AND VALIDITY CHECKS

There are differences among methods which have nothing to do with the interpretation of a single piece of research. These are familiar issues to working researchers, and are important ones for the selection of procedures. Choosing between two different methods which promise to yield equally valid data, the researcher is likely to reject the more time-consuming or costly method. Also, there is an inclination toward those methods which have sufficient flexibility to allow repetition if something unforeseen goes wrong, and which further hold potential for producing internal checks on validity or sampling errors.

13. *Dross Rate.* In any given interview, a part of the conversation is irrelevant to the topic at hand. This proportion is the dross rate. It is greater in open-ended, general, free-response interviewing than it is in structured interviews with fixed-answer categories; by the same token, the latter are potentially the more reactive. But in all such procedures, the great advantage is the interviewer's power to introduce and reintroduce certain topics. This ability allows a greater density of relevant data. At the other extreme is unobserved conversation sampling, which is low-grade ore. If one elected to measure attitudes toward Russia by sampling conversations on public transportation, a major share of experimental effort could be spent in listening to comparisons of hairdressers or discussions of the Yankees' one-time dominance of the American League. For a specific problem, conversation sampling provides low-grade ore. The price one must pay for this ore, in order to get a naturally occurring response, may be too high for the experimenter's resources.

14. *Access to Descriptive Cues.* In evaluating methods, one should consider their potential for generating associated validity checks, as well as the differences in the universes they tap. Looking at alternative measures, what other data can they produce that give descriptive cues on the specific nature of the method's population? Internal evidence from early opinion polls showed their population biases when answers about prior voting and education did not match known election results and census data.

On this criterion, survey research methods have great advantages, for they permit the researcher to build in controls with ease. Observational procedures can check restrictions only for such gross and visible variables as sex, approximate age, and conspicuous ethnicity. Trace methods such as the relative wear of floor tiles offer no such intrinsic possibility. However, it is possible in many instances to introduce interview methods in conjunction with other methods for the purpose of ascertaining population characteristics. Thus, commuter-train passengers, window shoppers, and waiting-room conversationalists can, on a sample of times of day, days of the week, and so on, be interviewed on background data, probably without creating any serious reactive effects for measures taken on other occasions.

15. *Ability to Replicate.* The questionnaire and the interview are particularly good methods because they permit the investigator to replicate his own or someone else's research. There is a tolerance for error when one is producing new data that does not exist when working with old. If a confounding event occurs or materials are spoiled, one can start another

survey repeating the procedure. Archives and physical evidence are more restricted, with only a fixed amount of data available. This may be a large amount—allowing split-sample replication—but it may also be a one-shot occurrence that permits only a single analysis. In the latter case, there is no second chance, and the materials may be completely consumed methodologically.

The one-sample problem is not an issue if data are used in a clearcut test of theory. If the physical evidence or secondary records are an outcropping where the theory can be probed, the inability to produce another equivalent body of information is secondary. The greater latitude of the questionnaire and interview, however, permit the same statement and provide in addition a margin for error.

So long as we maintain, as social scientists, an approach to comparisons that considers compensating error and converging corroboration from individually contaminated outcroppings, there is no cause for concern. It is only when we naively place faith in a single measure that the massive problems of social research vitiate the validity of our comparisons. We have argued strongly for a conceptualization of method that demands multiple measurement of the same phenomenon or comparison. Over-reliance on questionnaires and interviews is dangerous because it does not give us enough points in conceptual space to triangulate. We are urging the employment of novel, sometimes "oddball" methods to give those points in space.

BIBLIOGRAPHY

Anastasi, A. *Differential psychology*. (3rd ed.) New York: Macmillan, 1958.

Athey, K. R., Coleman, J. E., Reitman, A. P., & Tang, J. Two experiments showing the effect of the interviewer's racial background on responses to questionnaires concerning racial issues. *Journal of Applied Psychology*, 1960, *44*, 244–246.

Bain, H. M., & Hecock, D. S. *Ballot position and voter's choice: the arrangement of names on the ballot and its effect on the voter*. Detroit: Wayne State Univer. Press, 1957.

Baumrind, D. Some thoughts on ethics of research: after reading Milgram's "Behavioral Study of Obedience," *American Psychologist*, 1964, *19*, 421–423.

Benney, M., Riesman, D., & Star, S. Age and sex in the interview. *American Journal of Sociology*, 1956, *62*, 143–152.

Bernstein, E. M. *Money and the economic system*. Chapel Hill: Univer. of North Carolina Press, 1935.

Blau, P. M. *The dynamics of bureaucracy*. Chicago: Univer. of Chicago Press, 1955.

Brookover, L. A., & Back, K. W. Time sampling as a field technique. *Human Organization*, 1965, in press.

Burwen, R., & Campbell, D. T. The generality of attitudes toward authority and nonauthority figures. *Journal of Abnormal and Social Psychology*, 1957, *54*, 24–31.

Campbell, D. T. The informant in quantitative research. *American Journal of Sociology*, 1955, *60*, 339–342.

Campbell, D. T. Factors relevant to the validity of experiments in social settings. *Psychological Bulletin*, 1957, *54*, 297–312.

Campbell, D. T. Recommendations for APA test standards regarding construct trait or discriminant validity. *American Psychologist*, 1960, *15*, 546–553.

Campbell, D. T. The mutual methodological relevance of anthropology and psychology. In F. L. K. Hsu (Ed.), *Psychological anthropology approaches to culture and personality*. Homewood, Ill.: Dorsey Press, 1961. Pp. 333–352.

Campbell, D. T. Administrative experimentation, institutional records and nonreactive measures. In B. G. Chandler, E. F. Carlson, F. Bertolaet, C. Byerly, J. Lee, R. Sperber (Eds.), *Research Seminar on Teacher Education*, Report on Cooperative Research Project No. G-011 supported by the Cooperative Research Program of the Office of Education, U.S. Department of Health, Education, and Welfare, Northwestern Univer., August, 1963. Pp. 75–120. (Duplicated.) (a)

Campbell, D. T. From description to experimentation: interpreting trends as quasi-experiments. In C. W. Harris (Ed.), *Problems in measuring change*. Madison, Wis.: Univer. of Wisconsin Press, 1963. Pp. 212–242. (b)

Campbell, D. T. Pattern matching as an essential in distal knowing. In K. R. Hammond (Ed.), *The psychology of Egon Brunswik*. New York: Holt, Rinehart & Winston, 1965. (a)

Campbell, D. T. On the use of both pro and con items in attitude scales. Unpublished manuscript, 1965. (b)

Campbell, D. T., & Fiske, D. W. Convergent and discriminant validation by the multitrait-multimethod matrix. *Psychological Bulletin*, 1959, *56*, 81–105.

Campbell, D. T., & Mack, R. W. The steepness of interracial boundaries as a function of the locus of social interaction. In preparation.

Campbell, D. T., & McCormack. T. H. Military experience and attitudes toward authority. *American Journal of Sociology*, 1957, *62*, 482–490

Campbell, D. T., & Stanley, J. C. Experimental and quasi-experimental designs for research on teaching. In N. L. Gage (Ed.), *Handbook of research on teaching*. Chicago: Rand McNally, 1963. Pp. 171–246.

Cane, V. R., & Heim, A. W. The effects of repeated testing: III. further experiments and general conclusions. *Quarterly Journal of Experimental Psychology*, 1950, *2*, 182–195.

Cantril, H. *Gauging public opinion*. Princeton: Princeton Univer. Press, 1944.

Capra, P. C., & Dittes, J. E. Birth order as a selective factor among volunteer subjects, *Journal of Abnormal and Social Psychology*, 1962, *64*, 302.

Chapman, L. J., & Bock. R. D. Components of variance due to acquiescence and content in the F-scale measure of authoritarianism. *Psychological Bulletin*, 1958, *55*, 328–333.

Cook, S. W., & Selltiz, C. A multiple-indicator approach to attitude measurement. *Psychological Bulletin*, 1964, *62*, 36–55.

Cooper, S. L. Random sampling by telephone: a new and improved method. *Journal of Marketing Research*, 1964, *1*, 45–48.

Crespi, L. P. The interview effect on polling. *Public Opinion Quarterly*, 1948, *12*, 99–111.

Cronbach, L. J. Response sets and test validity. *Educational and Psychological Measurement*, 1946, *6*, 475–494.

Cronbach, L. J. Proposals leading to analytic treatment of social perception scores. In R. Tagiuri & L. Petrullo (Eds.), *Person perception and interpersonal behavior*, Stanford, Calif.: Stanford Univer. Press, 1958, Pp. 353–379.

Ekelblad, F. A. *The statistical method in business.* New York: Wiley, 1962.

Fisher, I. *The making of index numbers.* Boston: Houghton Mifflin, 1923.

French, E. G. Some characteristics of achievement motivation. *Journal of Experimental Psychology,* 1955, *50,* 232–236.

Garner, W. R. Context effects and the validity of loudness scales. *Journal of Experimental Psychology,* 1954, *48,* 218–224.

Garner, W. R., Hake, H. W., & Eriksen, C. W. Operationism and the concept of perception. *Psychological Review,* 1956, *63,* 149–159.

Ghiselli, E. E., & Brown, C. W. *Personnel and industrial psychology.* (2nd ed.) New York: McGraw-Hill, 1955.

Guilford, J. P. *Psychometric methods.* New York: McGraw-Hill, 1954.

Hafner, E. M., & Presswood, Susan. Strong inference and weak interactions. *Science,* 1965, *149,* 503–510.

Halbwachs, M. *Les causes de suicide.* Paris: Felix Alcan, 1930.

Hansen, A. H. Cycles of prosperity and depression in the United States, *Univer. of Wisconsin Studies in Social Sciences and History.* Madison, 1921.

Hanson, N. R. *Patterns of discovery.* Cambridge: Cambridge Univer. Press, 1958.

Hildum, D. C., & Brown, R. W. Verbal reinforcement and interviewer bias. *Journal of Abnormal and Social Psychology,* 1956, *53,* 108–111.

Holmes, L. D. *Ta'u: Stability and change in a Samoan village.* Reprint No. 7. Wellington, N.Z.: Polynesian Society, 1958.

Hovland, C. I., Lumsdaine, A. A., & Sheffield, F. D. *Experiments on mass communication.* Princeton: Princeton Univer. Press, 1949.

Humphreys, L. G. Note on the multitrait-multimethod matrix. *Psychological Bulletin,* 1960, *57,* 86–88.

Hyman, H. H., Cobb, W. J., Feldman, J. J., Hart, C. W., & Stember, C. H. *Interviewing in social research.* Chicago: Univer. of Chicago Press, 1954.

Jackson, D. N., & Messick, S. J. A note on "ethnocentrism" and acquiescent response sets. *Journal of Abnormal and Social Psychology,* 1957, *54,* 132–134.

Jaffe, A. J., & Stewart, C. D. *Manpower, resources and utilizations.* New York: Wiley, 1951.

James, J. A preliminary study of the size determinant in small group interaction. *American Sociological Review,* 1951, *16,* 474–477.

Kadish, S. On the tactics of police-prosecution oriented critics of the courts. *Cornell Law Quarterly,* 1964, *49,* 436–477.

Kahn, R. L., & Cannell, C. F. *The dynamics of interviewing: theory, technique and cases.* New York: Wiley, 1957.

Katz, D. Do interviewers bias poll results? *Public Opinion Quarterly,* 1942, *6,* 248–268.

Kendall, L. M. The hidden variance: what does it measure? *American Psychologist,* 1963, *18,* 452.

Kintz, B. L., Delprato, D. J., Mettee, D. R., Persons, C. E., & Schappe, R. H. The experimenter effect. *Psychological Bulletin,* 1965, *63,* 223–232.

Kitsuse, J. I., & Cicourel, A. V. A note on the uses of official statistics. *Social Problems,* 1963, *11,* 131–139.

Krasner, L. Studies of the conditioning of verbal behavior. *Psychological Bulletin,* 1958, *55,* 148–170.

Kuhn, T. *The structure of scientific revolutions.* Chicago: Univer. of Chicago Press, 1962.

Lenski, G. E., & Leggett, J. C. Caste, class, and deference in the research interview. *American Journal of Sociology,* 1960, *65,* 463–467.

Lucas, D. B., & Britt, S. H. *Advertising psychology and research.* New York: McGraw-Hill, 1950.

Lucas, D. B., & Britt, S. H. *Measuring advertising effectiveness.* New York: McGraw-Hill, 1963.

Matarazzo, J. D. Control of interview behavior. Paper read at American Psychological Association, St. Louis, September, 1962.

Matarazzo, J. D., Wiens, A. N., Saslow, G., Dunham, R. M., & Voas, R. B. Speech durations of astronaut and ground communicator. *Science,* 1964, *143,* 148–150.

Melton, A. W. Some behavior characteristics of museum visitors. *Psychological Bulletin,* 1933, *30,* 720–721. (a)

Melton, A. W. Studies of installation at the Pennsylvania Museum of Art. *Museum News,* 1933, *11,* 508. (b)

Melton, A. W. Problems of installation in museums of art. *Studies in museum education.* Washington, D.C.: American Association of Museums, 1935.

Melton, A. W. Distribution of attention in galleries in a museum of science and industry. *Museum News,* 1936, *13,* 3, 5–8.

Melton, A. W., Feldman, N. G., & Mason, C. W. Experimental studies of the education of children in a museum of science. *Publications of the American Association of Museums,* New Series, No. 15, 1936.

Mills, F. C. *The behavior of prices.* New York: National Bureau of Economic Research, 1927.

Mitchell, W. C. *Index numbers of wholesale prices in the U.S. and foreign countries: 1. the making and using of index numbers.* Bulletin No. 284. Washington, D.C.: U.S. Department of Labor, Bureau of Labor Statistics, 1921.

Moore, W. E. The exploitability of the "labor force" concept. *American Sociological Review,* 1953, *18,* 68–72.

Mudgett, B. D. *Index numbers.* New York: Wiley, 1951.

Orne, M. T. The nature of hypnosis: artifact and essence. *Journal of Abnormal and Social Psychology,* 1959, *58,* 277–299.

Orne, M. T. On the social psychology of the psychological experiment: with particular reference to demand characteristics and their implications. *American Psychologist,* 1962, *17,* 776–783.

Orne, M. T., & Evans, F. J. Social control in the psychological experiment: antisocial behavior and hypnosis. *Journal of Personality and Social Psychology,* 1965, *1,* 189–200.

Orne, M. T., & Scheibe, K. E. The contribution of nondeprivation factors in the production of sensory deprivation effects: the psychology of the "panic button." *Journal of Abnormal and Social Psychology,* 1964, *68,* 3–12.

Platt, J. R. Strong influence. *Science,* 1964, *146,* 347–353.

Politz Media Studies. *A study of outside transit poster exposure.* New York: Alfred Politz, 1959.

Popper, K. *Logic der Forschung.* Wien: Springer, 1935.

Popper, K. *The logic of scientific discovery.* New York: Basic Books, 1959.

Popper, K. *Conjectures and refutations.* New York: Basic Books, 1962.

Prosser, W. L. *Handbook of the law of torts.* (3rd ed.) St. Paul: West, 1964.

Quine, W. V. *From a logical point of view.* Cambridge: Harvard Univer. Press, 1953.

Riesman, D. Orbits of tolerance, interviews and elites. *Public Opinion Quarterly,* 1956, *20,* 49–73.

Riesman, D. & Ehrlich, J. Age and authority in the interview. *Public Opinion Quarterly,* 1961, *25,* 39–56.

Robinson, D., & Rohde, S. Two experiments with an anti-semitism poll. *Journal of Abnormal and Social Psychology,* 1946, *41,* 136–144.

Robinson, E. S. The behavior of the museum visitor. *Publications of the American Association of Museums,* New Series, No. 5, 1928.

Rorer, L. G. The great response-style myth. *Psychological Bulletin,* 1965, *63,* 129–156.

Rosenthal, R. On the social psychology of the psychological experiment: the experimenter's hypothesis as unintended determinant of experimental results. *American Scientist,* 1963, *51,* 268–283.

Rosenthal, R. Experimenter outcome-orientation and the results of the psychological experiment. *Psychological Bulletin,* 1964, *61,* 405–412.

Rosenthal, R., & Fode, K. L. Psychology of the scientist: V. three experiments in experimenter bias. *Psychological Reports,* 1963, *12,* 491–511.

Rosenthal, R., & Lawson, R. A longitudinal study of the effects of experimenter bias on the operant learning of laboratory rats. *Journal of Psychiatric Research,* 1963, *2,* 61–72.

Rosenthal, R., Persinger, G. W., Vikan-Kline, L., & Fode, K. L. The effect of early data returns on data subsequently obtained by outcome-biased experimenter. *Sociometry,* 1963, *26,* 487–498.

Ross, H. L. The inaccessible respondent: a note on privacy in city and country. *Public Opinion Quarterly,* 1963, *27,* 269–275.

Schanck, R. L., & Goodman, C. Reactions to propaganda on both sides of a controversial issue. *Public Opinion Quarterly,* 1939, *3,* 107–112.

Schwartz, R. D. Field experimentation in sociolegal research. *Journal of Legal Education,* 1961, *13,* 401–410.

Selltiz, C., Jahoda, M., Deutsch, M., & Cook, S. W. *Research methods in social relations.* New York: Holt, Rinehart & Winston, 1959.

Sletto, R. F. *A construction of personality scales by the criterion of internal consistency.* Hanover, N.H.: Sociological Press, 1937.

Solomon, R. L. An extension of control group design. *Psychological Bulletin,* 1949, *46,* 137–150.

Stephan, F. F., & McCarthy, P. J. *Sampling opinions.* New York: Wiley, 1958.

Stouffer, S. A. Problems in the application of correlation to sociology. *Journal of the American Statistical Association,* 1934, *29,* 52–58. (Reprinted in S. A. Stouffer, *Social research to test ideas.* Glencoe, Ill.: Free Press, 1962, Pp. 264–270.)

Thorndike, R. L. *Personnel selection.* New York: Wiley, 1949.

Underwood, B. J. *Psychological research.* New York: Appleton-Century-Crofts, 1957.

Vidich, A. J., & Shapiro, G. A. A comparison of participant observation and survey data. *American Sociological Review,* 1955, *20,* 28–33.

Vincent, C. E. Socioeconomic status and familial variables in mail questionnaire responses. *American Journal of Sociology,* 1964, *69,* 647–653.

Whisler, T. L., & Harper, S. F. *Performance appraisal: research and practice.* New York: Holt, Rinehart & Winston, 1962.

Wigmore, J. H. *The science of judicial proof as given by logic, psychology, and general experience and illustrated in judicial trials.* (3rd ed.) Boston: Little, Brown, 1937.

Williams, R. Probability sampling in the field: a case history. *Public Opinion Quarterly,* 1950, *14,* 316–330.

Wilson, E. B. *An introduction to scientific research.* New York: McGraw-Hill, 1952.

Windle, C. Test-retest effect on personality questionnaires. *Educational and Psychological Measurement,* 1954, *14,* 617–633.

Yule, G. U., & Kendall, M. G. *An introduction to the theory of statistics.* (14th ed.) New York: Hafner, 1950.

Zeisel, H. *Say it with figures.* (4th ed.) New York: Harper, 1957.

CHAPTER 6

Government Expenditures and Public Services in the American States

Ira Sharkansky

Much recent policy analysis is based on the assumption that the amount of money spent in a jurisdiction indicates the nature of services provided. This study seeks to test this assumption as it applies to the American states.

Among the studies that have attempted to explain the "outputs" of state and local governments by reference to political and economic characteristics, several have identified expenditures with services implicitly by mixing indicators of spending with indicators of services as the "outputs" to be explained.[1] Other studies have claimed explicitly that government expenditures reflect the "scope and character" or "calibre" or the "alpha and the omega" of public services.[2] A contrary argument is that "money is not everything." Such nonmonetary factors as the quality of personnel or the nature of the political environment may exert the greatest influences upon the quality or quantity of public services within a jurisdiction.

In assessing the relationship between spending and services, this study first defines static relationships between measures of spending and measures of public services. Secondly, it examines relationships over time in an attempt to discern if increases in government expenditures are likely to bring about increases in the quality or quantity of public services.

I. TECHNIQUES

One of the first problems encountered in the analysis of public services is the identification of services that are likely to respond to the expenditures of specific governmental units. In part, this is the problem of Morton Grodzins' marble cake. As he saw it, there are no major services that are solely the product of any one government level.[3] Rather, local, state and federal agencies share in the planning, financing, staffing and directing of

Reprinted from Ira Sharkansky, "Government Expenditures and Public Services in the American States," *American Political Science Review* (December, 1967), pp. 1066–77.

prominent domestic services. This is certainly true in the major categories of state and local services. For several fields, it is possible to go beyond Grodzins and note that they are the products of private efforts as well as the activities of local, state and federal governments. For example, officials in education, public welfare, health and hospitals, and natural resources seem likely to adjust their own services, in part, to the programs of private institutions within their jurisdiction.

Because of the public-private marble cake, it is virtually impossible to obtain measures of public services that are solely the outputs of particular governments. In order to cope with this difficulty, this study examines measures of services provided *within* each state. It relates these service indicators to measures of combined state and local government expenditures, and it evaluates these expenditure-service relationships in the light of measures pertaining to federal aid, private economic activity and other elements likely to influence services.

The study considers three measures of expenditures as having likely influence upon public services. Along with the other independent variables, they pertain to 1962:

 a) combined state and local general expenditures per capita[4]
 b) combined state and local general expenditures per $1,000 of personal income
 c) combined state and local general expenditures for each major function as a percentage of total general expenditures

Each of these measures is calculated for spending in the major fields of education, highways, public welfare, health and hospitals, natural resources (agriculture, fish and game, forestry and parks) and public safety. Variable *a* measures the money spent in relation to the population served by state services. Variable *b* measures spending in relation to economic resources. As such, it indicates the effort displayed by state and local governments in supporting the different fields of service. Variable *c* measures the relative success enjoyed by each field of service in competition with other services for government expenditures.[5] If the level of government spending actually reflects the quality or quantity of public services, then each of these spending measures should show positive relationships with service indicators.

Beside these measures of spending, 17 other independent variables were examined as having possible influence upon the nature of public services. After preliminary analysis, the following were selected for more thorough treatment:[6]

 d) Federal aid, i.e., Federal payments as a percentage of state and local spending for each service

e) the number of state and local employees per 10,000 population
f) the average salary of state and local employees
g) the percentage of state and local general revenue originating at sources other than local governments prior to intergovernmental transfers
h) per capita personal income
i) population

Variable *d* measures a source of outside money that might influence the nature of services within each state. Variables *e* and *f* measure the size and rewards of administrative units. Presumably, these features might influence services independently of expenditures. Variable *g* measures the centralization in state-local relationships.[7] The degree of centralization may influence the nature of services provided, or the efficiency with which expenditures affect services. Variables *h* and *i* are economic measures that relate strongly with other measures of economic activity;[8] they indicate the base of resources from which state and local governments and private groups draw in order to provide services.

Coefficients of simple correlation (Pearson's *r*) indicate the strength of simple relationships between each measure of spending and the measures of services. Yet coefficients of simple correlation do not indicate if the spending measures have independent relationships with public services. The problem of independence would occur, for example, if variables *a–c* showed positive relationships with public services only because variables *d–i* have stronger positive relationships with both the measures of spending and the measures of services. Partial correlation techniques, controlling for variables *d–i,* will provide a test for the independence of relationships between spending and services.[9]

Sixty-eight variables measure various aspects of public service quality or quantity within each state. Some variables measure the amount of benefits or services provided per client. Some measure the units of service in relation to the total population of the state. Some measure the incidence of beneficiaries among the people likely to use a service. Other variables measure the rate at which a program is performed. Others assess services by the frequency with which the state population chooses to use programs. Finally, some assess services indirectly by measuring the continued existence of phenomena that government activities are designed to control. The Appendix describes each measure of service. Because of space limitations, they are denoted in the tables by short titles only.

Since part of the analysis employs data from 1957, prior to Alaskan and Hawaiian statehood, only 48 states are included.

II. FINDINGS: STATIC RELATIONSHIPS BETWEEN EXPENDITURES AND SERVICES

The expenditure-service linkage does not appear to be strong. The coefficients of simple correlation reported in Table 1 show that 40 of the service measures (59 percent) have relationships with *any* of the expenditure measures strong enough to be statistically significant.[10] Yet there is a lower incidence of significant relationships between the service measures and all of the three expenditure measures. Of the 204 possible relationships between spending and services, only 78 (38 percent) are significant. Moreover, 37 of these relationships are negative! Only 41 (20 percent) of the simple relationships between spending and services are significant in the expected direction. Public officials may spend at high levels in the face of low service performance in the hope of elevating the level of services at some time in the future.

The relationship between spending and services appears even weaker when the influence of variable d–i are taken into consideration. Table 1 also reports coefficients of partial correlation between the measures of spending and service while controlling for measures pertaining to Federal aid, administration size and salary, state-local centralization and economic development. Only 23 (34 percent) of the service measures show significant partial correlations with any of the spending measures. Of the 204 possible relationships between the three spending measures and service indicators, 51 (25 percent) are significant, and 35 of them (17 percent) in the expected direction.

If government expenditures do not exert prevailing influence upon the quality or quantity of public services, what does explain the nature of services? For most of the service indicators considered here, the question must remain unanswered. For only 24 of the service indicators (35 percent) do the combination of a spending measure and variables d–i account for at least 50 percent of the interstate variation. These are the service indicators having a coefficient of multiple determination (R^2) of at least .50. The remaining 44 service indicators respond to elements not considered in the present study. Table 2 shows coefficients of partial correlation between the independent variables and each service indicator having an R^2 of at least .50. Measures of spending show significant, positive relationships with 15 of the 25 service indicators of Table 2. Only in the case of five service indicators, however, does a spending measure show a stronger positive coefficient of partial correlation than any of the other independent variables. Spending measures show their strongest positive relationships with payments for Old Age Assistance and Aid to the Blind, Agricultural

Table 1
Coefficients of Simple and Partial Correlation between
Measures of Spending and Services, 1962[a]

	Simple Correlation			Partial Correlation[b]		
	Spending Measure:			Spending Measure:		
	a	*b*	*c*	*a*	*b*	*c*
Education:						
teacher-pupil	41*	−01	−08	23	16	−02
BA teachers	00*	08	29*	−05	03	29
MA teachers	42*	06	35*	24	27	35*
vocational ed	−20	33*	12	−05	−05	04
school lunch	−35*	37*	08	11	12	10
rehab process	−39*	−07	−07	−34*	−38*	−11
rehab experience	−54*	−15	−05	−38*	−43*	−04
attendance	09	−01	06	−02	−14	−06
school term	17	−21	01	−04	−06	09
consolidation	−22	−18	−11	−25	−20	−07
median ed	76*	21	27	37*	33*	37*
5th grade ed	62*	−01	13	44*	24	19
high school ed	81*	28*	30*	48*	43*	43*
college ed	66*	17	34*	20	27	36*
school completion	25	−30*	15	−16	−22	−23
exam success	65*	08	16	40*	20	17
MA ed	18	14	00	02	04	−03
Dr ed	39*	−03	25	17	17	28
college enroll	07	09	−05	−05	−04	−08
own state enroll	05	09	−05	−05	−02	−07
Highways:						
total roads	41*	44*	47*	18	07	25
rural roads	−34*	−27	−18	07	−07	11
urban roads	43*	57*	57*	28	25	27
paved roads	−04	−21	−14	23	32*	26
4 & 6 lane roads	−25	−25	−27	−09	−13	−21
interstate miles	73*	59*	46*	37*	25	21
interstate completion	77*	60*	56*	51*	43*	40*
interstate progress	−34*	−45*	−39*	−04	−01	−02
road safety	−40	−55	−47*	01	04	−11
Public welfare:						
OAA recipients	−02	−07	−18	−13	−07	−11
MAA recipients	−08	−10	−14	−06	−07	−08
AFDC recipients	21	−07	02	24	27	29
AB recipients	00	−07	01	−05	−04	−03
APTD recipients	29*	17	17	26	23	26
OAA payment	36*	01	02	53*	50*	47*
AFDC payment	−21	−19	−13	41*	35*	38*

Table 1 (continued)

	Simple Correlation Spending Measure:			Partial Correlation Spending Measure:		
	a	b	c	a	b	c
AB payment	37*	−03	04	56*	52*	54*
APTD payment	18	−07	02	25	16	24
child welfare	08	14	06	13	14	09
Health & hospitals:						
hospital beds	24	−16	04	06	−04	−07
hospital bassinets	00	−07	−33*	06	−03	−10
mental hospitals	07	−11	−04	03	04	−02
mental treatment	20	−15	−04	−03	−11	−16
mental handicap hosp	−11	−14	−45*	−13	−19	−28
physicians	40*	−11	12	−08	−11	−19
dentists	33*	23	33*	20	21	26
child health	19	05	14	16	16	14
white infants	08	−14	17	−16	−11	−08
nonwhite infants	04	−15	−15	−13	−16	−22
Natural resources:						
extension agents	25	49*	35*	50*	52*	39*
ag researchers	62*	65*	54*	52*	49*	35*
soil conservation	−47*	−33*	−37*	−36*	−28	−30*
mapped conservation	−41*	−37*	−36*	−08*	−08	−10
ag conservation	−07	03	−06	13	17	04
parkland	43*	39*	27	20	15	03
park space	16	13	08	09	11	06
park visits	18	15	14	15	09	07
fish license	52*	60*	54*	42*	41*	34*
hunt license	49*	58*	48*	40*	40*	29
Public safety:						
murder	26	10	11	−33*	−30*	−37*
rape	−37*	−28*	−23	−02	00	−05
robbery	−43*	−34*	−40*	−01	−02	−06
assault	−11	−21	−27	−18	−18	−32*
burglary	−51*	−48*	−43*	−22	−25	−29
larceny	−65*	−59*	−43*	−42*	−39*	−38*
auto theft	−67*	−60*	−54*	−38*	−38*	−41*
paroles	20	22	16	22	21	10
parole success	−12	−12	−16	−02	00	−11

* Significant at the .05 level.
ᵃ For the definition of spending measures *a–c* see the text above; for the definition of service measures see the Appendix.
ᵇ With variables *d–i* controlled.

Researchers, Proportion of Interstate Mileage Completed, and College Graduates. Public safety spending shows strong relationships with crimes of Larceny and Auto Theft, but the direction of the relationships suggests that high crime rates lead to spending, rather than that spending acts upon the crime rate.

Measures of administration size, state-local centralization, per capita personal income and population show some consistent relationships with the service indicators of Table 2. The findings pertaining to administration and personal income suggest that relatively wealthy states with large administrative crops (relative to population) are likely to be high producers of public services. The findings about population suggest that elements generating public services are most likely to occur in states with small populations. The findings about state-local centralization indicate that a *decentralized* system seems to work in behalf of service outputs. Aside from the measures of expenditures, it is only the measures of administrative size and state-local centralization that show the strongest relationships with several measures of service. Per capita personal income shows the strongest coefficient of partial correlation only with school lunch, and population fails to show the strongest coefficient of partial correlation with any of the service indicators.

There are several possible explanations for the general lack of close ties between current measures of government expenditures and public services. The magnitude of funds previously spent in accumulating capital facilities or in assembling a staff of a certain calibre might influence the capacity of current spending to stimulate service outputs. A state may score relatively high in certain types of highway mileage despite relatively low current spending. The market costs of services or products may vary significantly from one area to another. In the case of several programs, private expenditures may affect the service levels and result in weak relationships between government spending and the indicators considered here. Economies of large scale operations may confound the simple relationship between spending and services. Certain characteristics of a program's clientele or its political environment may also influence the efficiency with which money produces services. In the field of education, for example, the family background of students may be a critical ingredient in the quality of services. Where the environment supports favoritism in the hiring of personnel or in the choice of sites for new facilities, then the ratio between financial inputs and outputs in desired services may be less than where "professional" criteria prevail. Measures of such characteristics may add considerably to the present capacity to explain interstate variations in public services.

Table 2
Coefficients of Partial Correlation between Independent Variables and Selected Service Indicators†

	Independent Variables								
	Spending measures			Fedl aid	Employees	Salary	Central.	Pers inc.	Population
	a	b	c	d	e	f	g	h	i
Education:									
teacher-pupil	23			−07	15	−21	−51*	25	−41*
teacher-pupil		16		−04	23	−16	−50*	26	−43*
teacher-pupil			−02	01	41*	−07	−48*	21	−47*
school lunch	11			−02	02	−23	17	−40*	11
school lunch		12		−02	03	−24	16	−20	12
school lunch			10	−01	15	−23	20	−39*	10
rehab experience	−38*			16	04	02	47*	12	−04
rehab experience		−43*		17	03	03	50*	−23	−06
median ed	37*			07	25	−01	−45*	15	−22
median ed		33*		10	35*	04	−45*	31*	−23
median ed			37*	08	63*	21	−41*	16	−29
5th grade ed	44*			08	−09	−16	−66*	32*	−44*
5th grade ed		24		14	10	−01	−62*	34*	−46*
5th grade ed			19	15	34*	13	−59*	27	−50*
high school ed	48*			11	29	−08	−49*	18	−27
high school ed		43*		14	40*	−02	−49*	39*	−28
high school ed			43*	13	71*	21	−42*	19	−35*
college ed	20			07	08	03	21	31*	05
college ed		27		07	08	01	18	38*	07
college ed			36*	03	35*	13	26	35*	05
exam success	40*			05	−05	−04	−58*	11	−37*

Table 2 (continued)

	Independent Variables								
	Spending measures			Fedl aid	Employees	Salary	Central.	Pers inc.	Population
	a	b	c	d	e	f	g	h	i
exam success		20		11	14	11	−54*	18	−40*
exam success			17	12	34*	24	−52*	08	−44*
Highways:									
interstate miles	37*			24	46*	05	09	−13	00
interstate miles		25		29	52*	05	05	−02	−03
interstate miles			21	31*	58*	09	08	−09	−02
interstate completion	51*			09	16	−07	09	21	−32
interstate completion		43*		14	24	−05	05	35*	−34*
interstate completion			40*	17	37*	05	12	25	−31*
road safety	01			−31*	−43*	07	−19	32*	−09
road safety		04		−32*	−45*	07	−19	32*	−09
road safety			−11	−26	−46*	03	−23	31*	−11
Public welfare:									
OAA recipients	−13			16	51*	−06	27	34*	−25
OAA recipients		−07		16	50*	−07	26	32*	−25
OAA recipients			−11	17	49*	−08	26	34*	−25
AFDC recipients	24			14	−23	40*	30*	38*	−03
AFDC recipients		27		14	−23	42*	28	41*	−04
AFDC recipients			29	12	−18	43*	31*	38*	−04
OAA payment	53*			−31*	19	26	−38*	−11	−17
OAA payment		50*		−31*	21	30*	−39*	−01	−16
OAA payment			47*	−34*	31*	33*	−35*	−13	−15

Table 2 (continued)

	Independent Variables								
	Spending measures			Fedl aid	Employees	Salary	Central.	Pers inc.	Population
	a	b	c	d	e	f	g	h	i
AFDC payment	41*			−36*	−06	46*	−43*	−10	−35*
AFDC payment		35*		−35*	−03	48*	−43*	−04	−34*
AFDC payment			38*	−38*	04	50*	−41*	−12	−35*
AB payment	56*			−17	15	23	−30*	21	−20
AB payment		52*		−16	18	27	−32*	29	−20
AB payment			54*	−22	29	31*	−28	18	−20
Health & hospitals:									
physicians			−19	−25	−21	09	11	33*	15
Natural resources:									
extension agents	50*			53*	24	−36*	−34*	−22	−09
extension agents		52*		57*	28	−32*	−37*	−05	−06
extensive agents			39*	50*	45*	−26	−27	−21	−09
ag researchers	52*			38*	44*	−08	−24	−03	−48*
ag researchers		49*		41*	49*	00	−27	09	−45*
ag researchers			35*	34*	62*	05	−17	−07	−45*
fish license	42*			42*	18	24	−48*	−43*	−32*
fish license		41*		44*	22	30*	−49*	−31*	−29
fish license			34*	40*	36*	33*	−43*	−42*	−30*
hunt license	40*			41*	21	09	−36*	−26	−27
hunt license		40*		44*	25	15	−38*	−14	−25
hunt license			29	39*	39*	19	−31*	−26	−26

Table 2 (continued)

	Independent Variables								
	Spending measures			Fedl aid	Employees	Salary	Central.	Pers inc.	Population
	a	b	c	d	e	f	g	h	i
Public safety:									
murder	−33*				05	42*	−50*	13	−41*
murder			−37*		−15	38*	−54*	14	−42*
larceny	−42*				−30*	−14	−38*	05	−03
larceny		−39*			−32*	−15	−37*	−21	−05
larceny			−38*		−45*	−27	−41*	00	−04
auto theft	−38*				−10	−08	−23	−06	05
auto theft		−38*			−11	−07	−22	−29	03
auto theft			−41		−30*	−19	−29	−08	05

* Significant at the .05 level.

† Selected are those combinations of a spending measure with variables *d–i* that account for at least 50 percent of the interstate variation in a service indicator; the partials shown represent the relationship between an independent variable and a service indicator while controlling for the influence of all other independent variables.

III. FINDINGS: RELATIONSHIPS BETWEEN
CHANGES IN SPENDING AND SERVICES

It is possible that changes in spending may exert great influence over changes in public services, despite the lack of strong relationships between current spending and the current level of services. Such phenomena as the level of private support for services, characteristics of a program's clientele or its political environment may remain stable over a period of several years so that increases in government spending can act upon the quality or quantity of public services.

In order to test the relationships between changes in expenditures and changes in public services, the analyses above were repeated using measures of 1957–62 percentage change in variables *a–i* and measures of 1957–62 percentage change for those service indicators where the data was (sic) available. The 1957–62 period was selected to take advantage of the data collected by the Census of Governments in those years. In general, both expenditures and service levels increased slowly during the period. Presumably, the five-year span includes some of the lag that may occur between changes in spending and changes in services. Table 3 reports coefficients of simple and partial correlation pertaining to changes in spending and services.

The analysis of change shows even fewer relationships between spending and services than the static analysis. Of the 45 service indicators for which measures of change are available, 14 (29 percent) show significant simple relationships with any measure of change in spending. Of the 135 possible relationships between changes in three measures of spending and services, 26 (19 percent) are significant. Twenty of the relationships (15 percent) are significant in the expected direction. When the influence of change in variables *d–i* is taken into account by partial correlation techniques, it is found that 11 (24 percent) of the service measures show significant relationships with any of the spending measures. Of the 135 possible relationships between measures of change in spending and services, 28 (21 percent) are significant. Twenty-one (16 percent) of the partial correlations are significant in the expected direction.

On the basis of the existing data, it is virtually impossible to assess the elements that do influence changes in public services. The coefficients of multiple determination derived from this analysis reveal that combinations of present independent variables explain 50 percent of the interstate variation for only three of the service indicators! It is possible that the five year time span built into the analysis is not long enough to allow changes in the independent variables to affect changes in public services. Or perhaps other elements subject to state by state measurement—beside those included in

Table 3
Coefficients of Simple and Partial Correlation between
Measures of Change in Spending and Services, 1957–62†

	Simple Correlation			Partial Correlation‡		
	Spending Measure:			Spending Measure:		
	a	*b*	*c*	*a*	*b*	*c*
Education:						
teacher-pupil	−01	−13	−03	−09	−15	03
vocational ed	−04	11	19	−11	−09	05
rehab process	−16	−19	−08	−21	−02	−02
rehab experience	−03	04	−24	−28	−27	−09
school completion	−14	−19	−21	−32*	−24	−20
exam success	−11	−23	−24	−21	−20	−27
MA ed	−07	−09	−11	−12	−11	−15
Dr ed	06	−11	−04	−09	−15	−07
college enroll	−12	−05	01	00	01	13
Highways:						
total roads	30*	26	23	06	05	05
rural roads	08	11	00	−02	02	01
urban roads	03	06	03	28	27	22
4 & 6 lane roads	13	07	20	05	05	14
interstate miles	−36*	−35*	−36*	−49*	−48*	−46*
interstate completion	−43*	−41*	−42*	−50*	−49*	−47*
road safety	−02	13	09	33*	33*	33*
Public welfare:						
OAA recipients	15	15	16	14	13	00
AFDC recipients	27	38*	39*	51*	53*	56*
AB recipients	12	19	31*	09	12	27
APTD recipients	−03	01	−02	12	13	−02
OAA payment	−01	23	16	01	29	17
AFDC payment	00	29*	38*	01	46*	53*
AB payment	−06	13	18	−03	18	18
APTD payment	30*	08	17	29	04	20
Health & hospitals:						
hospital bassinets	32*	31*	28*	38*	37*	33*
mental hospitals	00	01	03	08	08	08
physicians	92*	86*	89*	94*	90*	92*
dentists	92*	86*	89*	94*	90*	93*
white infants	25	27	28*	25	26	28
nonwhite infants	17	19	20	14	16	16
Natural resources:						
extension agents	−07	−05	28*	−05	−07	18
ag researchers	−03	04	−23	−05	−01	−18

Table 3 (continued)

	Simple Correlation			Partial Correlation‡		
	Spending Measure:			Spending Measure:		
	a	*b*	*c*	*a*	*b*	*c*
soil conservation	−16	−23	05	−14	−20	08
parkland	38*	38*	−23	37*	35*	−05
park space	25	14	−09	41*	32*	−26
park visits	16	19	−10	12	11	−24
fish license	−11	−04	−21	−06	01	−26
hunt license	15	21	−15	19	24	−18
Public safety:						
murder	11	12	05	16	17	15
robbery	10	09	06	14	14	11
assault	01	07	−01	07	07	07
burglary	02	00	03	05	05	07
larceny	06	00	02	−01	−02	−07
auto theft	01	−01	−03	−01	−01	−05
paroles	−08	−07	−04	−08	−07	−02

* Significant at the .05 level.

† For the definition of the spending measures *a–c* see the text above; for the definition of service measures see the Appendix.

‡ With changes in variables *d–i* controlled.

variables *a–i* are generally influential with respect to changes in services. Or perhaps marked changes in services typically result from the fortuitous combination of elements that do not lend themselves to state by state measurement. For example, changes in personnel within the executive or legislative branches of state government, or changes in local leadership may occur in ways that permit a sudden take-off of service levels.

IV. SUMMARY AND CONCLUSIONS

In contrast to the assumptions of several authors, it is evident that the levels of state and local government spending do not exert pervasive influence upon the nature of public services. There are many weak relationships and some negative relationships between current spending and services, and between changes in spending and changes in services. There are several possible reasons for the lack of expected relationships between spending and services. The level of private spending or previous capitalization may affect the present measures of services enough to obscure some of the influence from current government spending; market costs may vary from one state to another; economies of scale may affect the spending-service linkage; or the nature of clientele and political environment may influence the spending-service relationship.

The present findings should temper expectations about the results of current government spending. By themselves, however, they do not stand as an argument against increases in government spending. The findings are the product of gross analysis, employing the large categories of education, highways, public welfare, health and hospitals, natural resources and public safety. The results do not mean that focused increases in spending will fail to improve particular services or institutions. Furthermore, the findings do not strike at the variety of reasons for increasing public expenditures that do not assume an early increase in services. Such reasons include the desire to keep salaries of public employees equivalent to people in comparable nongovernmental positions; and the desire to improve staff or physical plant for the sake of obtaining service improvements over the long range or for the sake of avoiding a deterioration of services. The data here only warn that gross levels of spending do not reflect service levels, and that gross increases in spending are not likely to produce early gross improvements in services.

APPENDIX I

Each of the following indicators of public service seems capable of responding to the expenditures of state and local governments. They are defined so that high scores reflect high quality or quantity of public service. The short titles of each indicator are given in parenthesis. It is these short titles that are used in the Tables.

Education

number of teachers per 100 pupils (teacher-pupil) percentage of elementary teachers with at least the bachelors degree (B.A. teachers)
percentage of secondary teachers with at least the masters degree (M.A. teachers)
total enrollment in Federally-aided vocational education per 10,000 population (vocational ed)
percentage of school enrollment participating in the Federal school lunch program (school lunch)
number of persons in process of vocational rehabilitation per 10,000 population (rehab process)
number of persons experiencing vocational rehabilitation per 10,000 population (rehab experience)

average percentage of students attending daily in elementary and secondary schools (attendance)

length of school term (school term)

population per school district (consolidation)

median number of school years completed by persons 25 years and older (median ed)

percentage of persons 25 years and over with at least five years of school completed (5th grade ed)

percentage of persons 25 years and over with at least four years of high school (high school ed)

percentage of persons 25 years and over with at least four years of college (college ed)

percentage of eighth graders who graduate from high school four years later (school completions)

percentage of selective service registrants passing mental examination (exam success)

earned masters degrees per 10,000 population conferred by all institutions of higher education (M.A. ed)

earned doctors degrees per 10,000 population conferred by all institutions of higher education (Dr. ed)

enrollment in institutions of higher education per 10,000 population (college enroll)

enrollment of natives in their own state's institutions of higher education per 10,000 population (own state enroll)

Highways

mileage per capita of state-administered roads (total roads)

mileage per rural resident of state administered rural roads (rural roads)

mileage per urban resident of municipal roads (urban roads)

percentage of farms on improved (not dirt) roads (paved roads)

percentage of four or six lane miles among the Federally-aided mileage completed during 1963 (4&6 lane roads)

mileage per capita of interstate highways open to traffic by 1963 (interstate miles)

percentage of the designated interstate mileage completed by 1963 (interstate completion)

percentage of the designated interstate mileage completed or in progress by 1963 (interstate progress)

state residents per motor vehicle death (road safety)

Public Welfare

incidence of Old Age Assistance recipients among people over 65 and with
incomes of less than $2,000 (OAA recipients)
incidence of Medical Assistance for the Aged recipients among people over
65 and with incomes of less than $2,000 (MAA recipients)
incidence of Aid to Families of Dependent Children recipients among
people with incomes of less than $2,000 (AFDC recipients)
incidence of Aid to the Blind recipients among people with incomes of less
than $2,000 (AB recipients)
incidence of Aid to the Permanently and Totally Disabled recipients among
people with incomes of less than $2,000 (APTD recipients)
average payment per recipient of Old Age Assistance (OAA payment)
average payment per recipient of Aid to Families of Dependent Children
(AFDC payment)
average payment per recipient of Aid to the Blind (AB payment)
average payment per recipient to (sic) Aid to the Permanently and Totally
Disabled (APTD payment)
number of children per 10,000 child population receiving child welfare
benefits (child welfare)

Health and Hospitals

hospital beds per 10,000 population (hospital beds)
hospital bassinets per 10,000 population (hospital bassinets)
patients per 10,000 population in mental hospitals (mental hospitals)
net live releases from mental hospitals (mental treatment)
patients per 10,000 population in institutions for mental defectives and
epileptics (mental handicap hospital)
number of physicians per 100,000 population (physicians)
number of dentists per 100,000 population (dentists)
number of residents per child disability (child health)
percentage of white infants surviving their first year (white infants)
percentage of nonwhite infants surviving their first year (nonwhite infants)

Natural Resources

number of cooperative extension agents per 10,000 population (extension
agents)
number of agricultural experiment station researchers per 10,000 population (ag researchers)
percentage of farmland in soil conservation districts (soil conservation)

percentage of land in soil conservation districts that is mapped (mapped
    conservation)
percentage of cropland in Agricultural Conservation Program (ag conser-
    vation)
acreage per capita of state parks (parkland)
acreage per visitor of state parks (park space)
visits to state parks per 10,000 population (park visits)
number of fishing licenses sold per 10,000 population (fish license)
number of hunting licenses sold per 10,000 population (hunt license)

Public Safety

[note: each of the figures pertaining to crime are inverted from their usual
presentation to be consistent with the other service indicators. That is, high
scores on the following indicators reflect low crime rates and high public
service in the field of public safety.]
population per murder and nonnegligent manslaughter offenses (murder)
population per rape offense (rape)
population per robbery offense (robbery)
population per aggravated assault offense (assault)
population per burglary offense (burglary)
population per larceny offense (larceny)
population per auto theft offense (auto theft)
percentage of conditional releases from correctional institutions (paroles)
percentage of conditional releases *not returned* as violators (parole success)

The sources of these measures include Council of State Governments,
The Book of the States; U.S. Bureau of the Census, *Statistical Abstract of
the United States;* U.S. Office of Education, *Digest of Educational Statistics;* Federal Bureau of Investigation, *Uniform Crime Rates in the United
States;* U.S. Bureau of Prisons, *National Prisoner Statistics;* U.S. Bureau of
Public Roads, *Annual Report;* Social Security Administration, *Social Security Bulletin: Annual Statistical Supplement;* U.S. Department of Agriculture, *Agricultural Statistics;* National Education Association, *Rankings
of the States;* U.S. Bureau of the Census, *Census of Agriculture.*
    In gathering the data an effort was made to obtain measurements as
close as possible to 1962 for the static analysis, and as close to 1957 for
the analysis of change. In each case, it is assumed that the recorded data
provide reasonably accurate indications of fact. It is recognized, however,
that the quality of the data may occasionally disappoint the author's hopes.
For comments on the quality of specific measurements, the reader is referred to the sources noted above.

APPENDIX II

The results of factor analysis tend to confirm the findings in the text. Three principal factors result from the analysis of 68 service indicators. Their names derive from the indicators having the highest loadings with each, This is shown in Table A. Twelve of the remaining service indicators contribute weakly to these factors, and 29 others relate together in scattered factors that include from two to four indicators. The three principal factors include most of the indicators that show, by themselves, significant relationships with spending. As noted below, each of the principal factors show some significant relationships with spending. The variety of minor factors show only weak relationships with spending. Like the analysis of

Table A

Education—welfare	
exam success	.905
5th grade ed	.892
school completion	.871
AFDC payment	.790
OAA payment	.750
teacher-pupil	.745
high school ed	.693
mental handicap hosp	.690
median ed	.686
AB payment	.651
murder	—.865
Highway—natural resource	
total roads	.835
interstate miles	.790
ag researchers	.768
hunt license	.744
extension agents	.738
hosp bassinets	.736
soil conservation	.615
interstate progress	—.629
road safety	—.720
rural roads	—.787
Public safety	
rape	.894
auto theft	.890
larceny	.877
burglary	.857
robbery	.809
child health	.705

separate service indicators, factor analysis reveals services that appear to be linked with government spending. In not every case, however, are the linkages in the direction expected by those who see services dependent upon expenditures. Also, factor analysis reveals that many of the present service indicators show little relationship with government spending.

Because several ingredients in the major factors are not available for 1957, the factor analysis was not repeated in the consideration of changes in services.

For 1962, coefficients of simple correlation between the principal factors and the spending measures are shown in Table B.

Table B

	Education—welfare	Highways—natural resources	Public safety
Education spending			
a	.59*		
b	−.03		
c	.10		
Welfare spending			
a	.12		
b	−.25		
c	−.20		
Highway spending			
a		.67*	
b		.70*	
c		.64*	
Natural resource spending			
a		.44*	
b		.53*	
c		.43*	
Public safety spending			
a			−.57*
b			−.51*
c			−.39*
Total spending			
a	.61*	.34*	−.39*
b	−.09	.59*	.08

* Significant at the .05 level.

NOTES

* Grants from the Social Science Research Council and the University of Georgia Office of General Research provided funds to support this research.

[1] Richard Dawson and James Robinson, "Interparty Competition, Economic Variables, and Welfare Policies in the American States," *Journal of Politics,* 25 (May, 1963), 265–89; Thomas R. Dye, "Malapportionment and Public Policy in the States," *Journal of Politics,* 27 (August, 1965), 586–601; Richard I. Hofferbert, "The Relations between Public Policy and Some Structural and Environmental Variables in the American States," *American Political Science Review,* 60 (March, 1966), 73–82.

[2] See, respectively, Robert C. Wood, *1400 Governments* (Garden City, 1961), p. 35; Jesse Burkhead, *Public School Finance* (Syracuse, 1965), p. 50; and Phillip C. Burch, *Highway Revenue and Expenditure Policy in the United States* (New Brunswick, N.J., 1962), p. 34.

[3] Morton Grodzins, "American Political Parties and the American System," *Western Political Quarterly,* 13 (December, 1960), 974–98.

[4] "General expenditures" include all state spending for each major category except for insurance trust funds. The year 1962 was selected for all variables because of the data in the *Census of Governments, 1962.*

[5] See James A. Maxwell, *Financing State and Local Governments* (Washington, 1965), Chapter 2.

[6] Variables considered, but not retained were: percentage of per capita personal income paid in taxes to state and local governments; percentage of state and local general revenue originating at the state level prior to intergovernmental transfers; percentage of state and local general revenue allocated to the state level after tax collections and intergovernmental transfers; percentage of local general revenue received from the state; voter turnout in state elections; the David-Eisenberg measure of apportionment equity in state legislatures; a measure of party competition derived from Ranney's index of Democratic party strength; number of local governments per 10,000 population; percentage of population living in urban areas; percentage of labor force employed in manufacturing; and value added by manufacturing, per capita. Variables 2–4 of this list were dropped because they reflect the same phenomena as independent variable *g.* Variables 1, 5–8 were dropped because they fail to show strong relationships with either government expenditures or public services. Variables 9–11 were dropped because they reflect the same phenomena as independent variables *h* and *i.*

[7] Beside the state government, the principal non-local source of state-local revenue is the federal government. A high score on variable *g* indicates centralization because most federal contributions to local governments funnel through state agencies.

[8] See Harvey S. Perloff, *et al., Regions, Resources and Economic Growth* (Baltimore, 1960), Chapters 1–3.

[9] For an illustration of this technique, see Dye, *op. cit.* Also see Hubert Blalock, *Social Statistics* (New York, 1960), Chapter 19.

[10] Because the 48 states are not a random sample, the common tests for significance are not, strictly speaking, applicable. They will be used, however, to provide an arbitrary indication of relationships that appear "sizable."

PART THREE

Determinants of Public Policy: The Economy

CHAPTER 7

Income Inequality and American State Politics

Thomas R. Dye

The rapidly expanding research literature in comparative state politics typically measures its dependent and independent variables with references to means, averages, and per capitas for each state.[1] (For example, environmental inputs may be expressed as per capita personal income, percent of population living in urban places, median school year completed by the population over 25, etc.; political characteristics may be expressed as average voter turnout levels, percent of the total vote cast for the winning party, etc.; policy outputs are often expressed as per capita expenditures for education, average monthly payments for old age assistance, per capita tax revenues, etc.) With measures such as these, the comparative state politics research has systematically explored many of the linkages between environmental inputs, political system characteristics, and public policy outcomes.

Perhaps the most serious reservation regarding this research is its failure to examine distributive and redistributive aspects of state politics. Both dependent and independent variables are generally expressed as *levels* or *amounts* or *averages* for whole states; these can be neatly arranged for comparative analysis both longitudinally and cross-sectionally. But what about the *distribution* of wealth within a state? Or the *distribution* of public monies among high and low income groups, rural and urban populations, or other divisions within a state's population? The linkages between the distribution of resources within states, the distribution of influence within state political systems, and public policies reflecting distributional decisions, remain largely untested.

For example, scholars have explored the relationship between per capita personal income and levels of public expenditures and services in the 50 states.[2] Income consistently shows up as a very influential variable in determining expenditure levels of state and local governments, and also correlates nicely with party competition and voter turnout. But what is the

Reprinted from Thomas R. Dye, "Income Inequality and American State Politics," *American Political Science Review*, Vol. 63, No. 1 (March, 1969), pp. 157–62, by permission of the American Political Science Association and the author.

effect of *inequality in the distribution of income* on politics and public policy within states? Certainly there are good *a priori* reasons for hypothesizing that the degree of income inequality in a state affects both the character of its political system and the content of its policies. One would reasonably expect to find political differences between a state in which wealth is concentrated in the hands of a few, and a state in which wealth is more widely distributed, even if the median incomes of these states are similar.

Fortunately, economists have come up with a way of measuring income distributions within political systems. Income distributions may be observed by means of a Lorenz curve which shows the cumulative proportions of aggregate income (on the vertical or *y* axis) accruing to cumulative proportions of the population ranging in order from the lowest to highest income-earners (on the horizontal or *x* axis).[3] In a political system with perfect income inequality, income would cumulate in direct relation to cumulated proportions of the population. Perfect equality is represented on a Lorenz chart by a diagonal straight line rising from the lower left-hand corner to the upper right-hand corner. But in real political systems, the lowest income-earners earn a smaller proportion of the aggregate income than their proportion of all income-earners. Therefore, when cumulative proportions of the population ranging from lowest to highest income-earners are plotted against the proportion of aggregate income they actually receive, the result is a convex "Lorenz" curve. The greater the degree of convexity of this plotted curve, the greater the degree of inequality in the political system. The total area on a diagram which falls between the Lorenz curve, representing the actual income distribution, and the straight diagonal line, representing perfect income equality, expresses the

Figure 1
The Lorenz Curve of Income Inequality

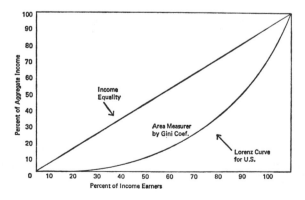

extent of income inequality within a political system. This area is measured by a Gini coefficient or Gini index, which ranges from a $+1.00$ (theoretical perfect inequality) to 0.00 (theoretical perfect equality).[4]

Gini indices for the 50 states and the United States are presented in Table 1.[5] Income inequality is greatest in Mississippi and least in Utah. The utility of this measure is obvious: It provides a single comparable measure for each state and permits us to systematically explore linkages between income inequalities and other measurable political system and public policy variables.

But before we turn to an examination of the relationships between income distributions and public policy, it is important to observe the relationships between income distributions and other environmental variables in the states. Table 2 shows that income inequality is closely associated

Table 1
Income Distributional Inequality
in the American States

State	GINI Coefficient	State	GINI Coefficient
1. Mississippi	.510	26. Minnesota	.431
2. Arkansas	.486	27. North Dakota	.430
3. Alabama	.478	28. New York	.429
4. Tennessee	.478	29. California	.427
5. Louisiana	.477	30. Colorado	.425
6. South Carolina	.474	31. Maryland	.424
7. Kentucky	.474	32. Illinois	.423
8. Georgia	.469	33. Rhode Island	.418
9. Oklahoma	.465	34. Montana	.415
10. North Carolina	.465	35. Indiana	.414
11. Texas	.464	36. Nevada	.414
12. Florida	.462	37. Massachusetts	.414
13. Virginia	.461	38. Washington	.413
14. Missouri	.459	39. Pennsylvania	.412
15. South Dakota	.456	40. Wisconsin	.412
16. Alaska	.456	41. Maine	.412
17. West Virginia	.451	42. Oregon	.411
18. Hawaii	.446	43. Michigan	.409
19. Arizona	.445	44. Ohio	.408
20. New Mexico	.440	45. New Hampshire	.407
21. Nebraska	.440	46. Connecticut	.404
22. Kansas	.439	47. New Jersey	.403
23. Iowa	.439	48. Idaho	.402
24. Delaware	.434	49. Wyoming	.399
25. Vermont	.434	50. Utah	.394

U.S. as a whole: GINI = .439

Table 2

Income Inequality and Economic Development in the States

Variable	Coefficient*	Variable	Coefficient*
Per Capita Personal Income	−.64	Median School Year Completed	−.69
Median Family Income	−.77	Nonwhite Population	.72
Urbanization	−.50	Industrialization Factor Score	−.35
Industrialization	−.36	Cultural Enrichment Factor Score	−.67

* Figures are simple correlation coefficients with GINI Index. All correlation coefficients reported in this study are product moment and not rank order coefficients.

with levels of income, urbanization, industrialization, and adult education in the states. The lower a state's median income, the greater the income inequality. Inequality is also associated with ruralism, agriculturalism, and lower adult education levels.[6]

Table 2 also shows the relationships between income distributions and two environmental factor scores derived by Richard I. Hofferbert.[7] These factor scores purport to show underlying dimensions of socio-economic variables in the states; Hofferbert employed factor-analysis to identify two independent environmental dimensions which he labeled "Industrialization" and "Cultural enrichment".[8] All of Hofferbert's base variables are per capitas, means, or averages for whole states; these factors do not include distributional variables. Apparently income inequality is negatively associated with both the "industrialization" factor and the "cultural enrichment" factor; an increase in industrialization or cultural enrichment is associated with a reduction in income inequality.

Table 3 shows the relationships between income inequality and several common political system variables in the states.[9] One may compare the coefficients obtained with the Gini index with the coefficients obtained with specific socio-economic variables and with factor-analyzed socio-economic dimensions.

Cross-sectionally speaking, an increase in income inequality is associated with a reduction in party competition for state office, a reduction in voter participation, an increase in Democratic voting for state offices, an increase in interest group strength, more fragmentation in state executive organization, and a reduction in the governor's formal powers. But what is even more noteworthy is the fact that the distribution of income is *more* closely related to these political system variables than absolute measures of

Table 3

Relationships between Income Inequality and Selected Political System Variables in the American States

Selected Political Variables	Coefficients Obtained with GINI Index	Compared to coefficients obtained with specific levels of:				factor scores for:	
		Income	Industrialization	Education	Urbanization	Industrialization	Cultural Enrichment
Party Competition							
Governor	−72*	66	18	61	29	−22	−63
Lower Houses	−61*	52	00	56	26	−19	−54
Upper Houses	−59*	51	03	49	30	−23	−52
Voter Participation							
Governor	−71*	52	05	49	17	18	53
Congress	−80*	66	09	63	26	19	60
Democratic Success							
Governor	66*	−56	02	−59	−22	−11	−60
Lower Houses	72*	−46	−10	−54	−05	−13	−52
Upper Houses	74*	−48	−03	−51	−15	−16	−51
Malapportionment							
Index of Rep.	06	21	−19	−18	−24	−03	−21
Urban Under-rep.	−47*	36	33	06	27	54	05
Apportionm. score	−32*	14	15	13	00	19	06
Interest Group Strength	42*	−42	08	−25	−06	−15	−21
Length of Constitution	30*	−20	03	−28	05	−04	−24
Elected St. Agency Heads	43*	−53	−42	−32	−28	−41	−26
Governor's Power Index	−42	60*	38	37	44	37	36

social and economic resources in the states or factors derived from such absolute measures. The coefficients obtained with the Gini index are higher than those obtained with measures of the level of social and economic resources or with environmental factor scores.[10] These admittedly rough calculations suggest that the *distribution* of social and economic resources within a state may be more important *politically* than the *level* of social and economic resources.

A different picture emerges, however, when we examine the relationships between income inequality and measures of the *level* of public spending and service in education, health, welfare, taxation and highways. While it is true that the Gini index correlates with a large number of policy outcome measures in these fields (see Table 4) the coefficients obtained with the Gini index are usually *not* as high as those obtained with specific socio-economic indicators or with factors reflecting environmental dimensions. (The only policy variables which are more closely related to Gini than to levels of socio-economic resources deal with centralization in state-local relations, e.g., state percent of total educational expenditures, state percent of total welfare expenditures, and the state percentage of total tax revenues. This means that income inequalities are associated with centralization of governmental spending and services at the state level.) This suggests that overall *levels* of public service in the states are more closely related to *levels* of social and economic resources than to the *distribution* of these resources.

The purpose of this note is to suggest that the distribution of resources within the states may have a significant impact on the character of political systems and the content of policy output. Levels of economic development are certainly influential determinants of politics and public policy, but it is also probable that the distribution of economic recourses also shapes politics and public policy in the states.

This brief exercise with a single measure of the distribution of resources suggests an interesting hypothesis for further study: The *distribution* of resources within American states is more important in shaping state *politics* than *levels* of socio-economic development; but *levels* of socio-economic development are more influential in determining *levels of public spending and service* in the states than the *distribution* of resources.

Table 4

**Relationships between Income Inequality and Selected
Policy Variables in the American States[11]**

Selected Policy Variables	Coefficients Obtained with Gini Index	Compared to coefficients obtained with specific levels of:				factor scores for:	
		Income	Industri-alization	Education	Urban-ization	Industri-alization	Cultural Enrichment
Education							
Per pupil Expenditure	−.61	.83*	.36	.59	.51	.45	.61
Educ. Exp. % of Income	.19	−.28	−.44*	.05	−.27	−.58	.12
State % Educ. Exp.	.45*	−.23	.18	−.35	.09	.09	−.39
Average Teach. Salaries	−.54	.88*	.64	.57	.69	.58	.53
Size School Districts	.36	−.18	.26	−.39*	.06	.04	−.43
Teacher-Pupil Ratio	.55	−.43	.19	−.50	−.12	−.05	−.56*
Drop-out Rate	−.62	.54	−.08	.60	.40	−.22	−.64*
Mental Failures	−.62	.46	.13	.70*	−.05	.20	−.66
Health & Welfare							
Unemployment Benefits	−.68	.80	.30	.67	.54	.39	.66
ADC Benefits	−.78*	.74	.26	.55	.61	.42	.56
General Asst. Benefits	−.68	.76*	.39	.43	.58	.55	.42
ADC Recipients	.41	−.30	.16	−.42	−.15	−.04	−.44*
Unemploy. Recipients	−.53	.58	.69*	.23	.39	.60	.23
Per Cap. Welfare Exp.	.04	−.01	.07	.07	.19	−.02	.12
Per Cap. Health Exp.	−.34	.56*	.39	.42	−.45	.27	.44
State % Welfare	.37	−.35	−.14	−.17	−.11	−.38*	−.12
State % Health	.09	−.08	−.07	−.14	−.30*	−.04	−.24
Taxation							
Total Revenue Per Cap.	−.50	.64	.03	.75*	.29	−.13	.75*
Per Cap. Tax Revenue	−.66	.76*	.23	.74	.59	.28	.77*

Table 4 (continued)

Selected Policy Variables	Coefficients Obtained with Gini Index	Compared to coefficients obtained with specific levels of:				factor scores for:	
		Income	Industri- alization	Education	Urban- ization	Industri- alization	Cultural Enrichment
Taxes % of Income	−.07	−.17	−.51*	−.16	−.15	−.45	.16
State % Taxes	.49*	−.33	−.08	−.24	−.28	−.39	−.32
Sales Tax Reliance	.13	−.15	−.01	−.18	−.03	−.08	−.12
Income Tax Reliance	−.05	.20	.02	.19	−.04	.08	.05
Highways							
Per Cap. Highway Exp.	.26	.01	−.51*	.36	−.37	−.54	−.36
State % Highway Exp.	.06	−.15	.04	−.03	−.29	−.30*	−.01
Highway Fund Diversions	.05	.06	.29	−.05	.42*	.31	.02
Rural-Urban Distribution	.29	−.38	−.45*	−.07	−.35	−.42	−.16
Highway User Revenue	.19	−.32*	−.20	−.26	−.04	−.12	−.17

* Highest simple coefficient among independent variables.

NOTES

* I am grateful for the comments and suggestions of John Q. Wilson, Department of Economics, Yale University; Elliot Morss, International Monetary Fund; and Edmund P. Fowler, Department of Political Science, York University.

1 See, for example, Richard E. Dawson and James A. Robinson, "Interparty Competition, Economic Variables, and Welfare Policies in the American States," *Journal of Politics*, 25 (May, 1963), 265–89; Richard I. Hofferbert, "The Relationship Between Public Policy and Some Structural and Environmental Variables in the American States," *American Political Science Review*, 60 (March, 1966), 73–82; Ira Sharkansky, "Economic and Political Correlates of State Government Expenditures," *Midwest Journal of Political Science*, 11 (May, 1967), 173–92; John Crittenden, "Dimensions of Modernization in the American States," *American Political Science Review*, 61 (December, 1967), 989–1001; Thomas R. Dye, *Politics, Economics, and the Public: Policy Outcomes in the American States*, (Chicago: Rand McNally, 1966).

2 See Note 1.

3 M. C. Lorenz, "Methods of Measuring the Concentration of Wealth," *Publications of the American Statistical Association*, 9 (1905), 209–19; see also Mary J. Bowman, "A Graphical Analysis of Personal Income Distributions in the United States," *American Economic Review*, 35 (September, 1945), 618–28.

4 Corrado Gini, "On the Measure of Concentration with Especial Reference to Income and Wealth" (paper delivered before the Cowles Commission, 1936); see also James Morgan, "The Anatomy of Income Distributions," *The Review of Economics and Statistics*, 44 (August, 1962), 270–80.

5 These Gini indices were computed by Thomas D. Hopkins from income distributional data for total families and unrelated individuals in 1959 from "General Social and Economic Characteristics," Table 65, U.S. Bureau of the Census, *U.S. Census of Population: 1960*, PC (1) 1C to 53C (Washington: Government Printing Office, 1960). See Thomas D. Hopkins, "Income Distributions in Grants-in-Aid Equity Analysis," *National Tax Journal*, 18 (June, 1965), 209–13. Slightly different Gini indices were computed from the same source by Al-Samarrie and Miller which correlate .89 (product moment) with the indices above and produce substantially the same results. See Ahmad Al-Samarrie and Herman P. Miller, "State Differentials in Income Concentration," *American Economic Review*, 57 (March, 1967), 59–72.

6 These findings parallel those of Al-Samarrie and Miller, who undertook a comprehensive explanation of income inequalities in the states. They regressed Gini coefficients on ten independent variables, including property income as a percent of total personal income, agricultural earnings as a percent of total labor earnings, median school years completed by persons 25 years and over, percent non-white population, and employment as a percent of population. Percent non-white turned out to be their single most explanatory variable; they did not employ a measure of family income. See Al-Samarrie and Miller, "State Differentials in Income Concentration," *op. cit.*

7 Richard I. Hofferbert, "Composition and Political Relevance of Major Socio-Economic Dimensions of the American States 1890–1960," *Midwest Journal of Political Science* (forthcoming).

8 The composition of Hofferbert's factors can be observed in the following factor loadings: "Industrialization"—value mfg. .91, pop. in mfg. .88, farm value .83, density .78, foreign .70, population .67, urban .66, telephones .65, number of employees .64, income .57, business failures .42, property .13, negro .07, illiteracy .04, pop. increase −.00, school years −.03, tenancy −.27, owner-occupied −.32, divorce −.33, acreage −.50, motor vehicles −.57; "cultural enrichment"—school years .91, property .79, income .73, motor vehicles .70, telephones .68, pop. increase .55, urban .52, acreage .49, divorce .43, business failures .29, owner-occupied .24, foreign-born .23,

population .05, farm value .02, value mfg. .01, density .01, pop. in mfg. −.13, number of employees −.35, tenancy −.47, illiteracy −.74, negro −.75. Hofferbert, *op. cit.*

[9] These political systems variables follow. Competition: one minus the percentage of votes cast in gubernatorial elections 1954 to 1964 for majority party, one minus the proportion of seats held by the majority party in the upper and lower chambers of the state legislature 1954 to 1964; voter participation: average voter turnout in gubernatorial elections 1954 to 1964, average voter turnout in congressional elections 1962 and 1964; Democratic success: The Democratic percentage of the two-party vote for governor 1954 to 1964, and the Democratic proportion of seats in the upper and lower chambers of state legislatures 1954 to 1964; malapportionment: the index of representatives suggested by Manning J. Dauer and Robert G. Kelsay, "Unrepresentative States," *National Municipal Review,* 44 (December, 1955), 571–75, updated to 1960; the index of urban under-representation suggested by Paul T. David and Ralph Eisenberg, *Devaluation of the Urban and Suburban Vote* (Bureau of Public Administration, University of Virginia, 1961); and the apportionment score suggested by Glendon Schubert and Charles Press, "Measuring Malapportionment," *American Political Science Review,* 58 (June, 1964) 302–27, with corrections published December, 1964, pp. 966–70; interest group strength: judgments of respondents reported by Belle Zeller, *American State Legislatures* (New York: Crowell, 1964) pp. 190–91; length of constitution, number of constitutional amendments, and number of elected state agency heads: see Lewis A. Froman, "Some Effects of Interest Group Strength in State Politics," *American Political Science Review,* 60 (December, 1966), 952–62; governor's formal power index: see Joseph M. Schlesinger, "The Politics of the Executive," *Politics in the American States,* eds. Herbert Jacob and Kenneth Vines (Boston: Little, Brown, 1965).

[10] Unfortunately, the degree of inter-relatedness between income inequality (Gini) and income levels (as well as other socio-economic variables) render partial correlations and beta values unreliable as a means of testing the independent effect of income inequality on political system variables or public policy. A simple comparison of the size of the correlation coefficients is probably the most efficient method of comparing income inequality with levels of socio-economic resources.

[11] The variables in Table 4 were selected from over 100 policy measures for which similar results were obtained. The specific measures in Table 4 follow. Education: per pupil expenditures in ADA 1961–62, educational expenditures as a percent of the total personal income 1961, state percentage of total state-local expenditures for education 1961, average teachers' salaries 1961–62, average size of school district 1961–62, teacher-pupil ratio, high school graduates in 1964 as a percent of 9th graders in 1959, percent of selective service examinees disqualified for failing mental test 1962; Health and Welfare: unemployment compensation average weekly payment 1961, ADC average monthly payment 1961, general assistance average monthly payment 1961, ADC recipients per 10,000 population 1961, per capita state-local welfare expenditures 1961, per capita state-local health expenditures 1961, state percentage of total state-local expenditures for welfare, state percentage of total state-local expenditures for health; taxation: total state-local revenue per capita 1961, taxes as a percent of personal income 1961, state percentage of total state-local tax revenue 1961, sales taxes as a percent of state tax revenue 1961, income taxes as a percent of state tax revenue 1961; Highways: per capita state-local expenditures for highways 1961, state percentage of highway revenues diverted to non-highway purposes 1961, percent of state highway grants going to counties rather than municipalities 1961, highway user revenues as a percent of total state revenue 1961.

CHAPTER 8

Ecological Development and Policy Change*

Richard I. Hofferbert

INTRODUCTION

Several recent reports of research in American state politics demonstrate a clear relationship between what may be called the "ecological development"[1] of the states and the nature of their public policies.[2] But while these studies offer concrete evidence for hypotheses heretofore substantiated largely by insight and guesswork, none of the correlations in this research is so strong or so comprehensive as to suggest a clear one-to-one relationship between any single ecological variable or composite of variables and the outputs of the state policy making machinery. Although the demonstration of such correlations is a fruitful first step toward explanation of the milieu within which policy makers work, there remains a large residual of unexplained variation between ecologically comparable states.

A thorough exploration of this residual is beyond the scope of the present article; however, it would seem that substantial guidance for future research and added insight into what we may already know could be gained from an examination of ecology-policy relationships over time. If one can demonstrate a change in the strength of these relationships over a reasonably extended period of time, it may be that this will, in turn, provide direction for further inquiry into the policy making process in the states.

The thesis which I am proposing here is that the states are becoming increasingly similar to one another along both the ecological and policy dimensions. This narrowing of the gap between the states serves to lessen the pressures in certain more or less basic policy areas for those states which have been trailing the field in the provision of "expected" governmental services. This lessening of pressure leads to an increase in latitude for choice and innovation by policy makers.

Reprinted from Richard I. Hofferbert, "Ecological Development and Policy Change," *Midwest Journal of Political Science,* Vol. X, No. 4 (November, 1966), by permission of Wayne State University Press and the author. Copyright © 1966 by Wayne State University Press.

THE PATTERN OF RELATIONSHIP

A few examples of the type of relationships that can be found between ecological and policy variables in the states are presented in Table 1.[3] Although most of the correlations shown in Table 1 are significant at the .05 level of confidence, there is substantial variation in the strength of the relationships. Therefore, one can hardly conclude that there is a completely deterministic connection between the type of ecological variables portrayed here and the manifest products of the policy-making machinery. Clearly, more generous policies do not simply pop out when ecological development reaches a certain level.

In a sense, these correlations leave a "black box" between ecology and policy. Human policy makers must act to achieve a given level of support for social services. And the choices they make vary between circumstances that are ecologically comparable.

A variety of hypotheses could be offered to explain both the strength of correlation between ecology and policy and also the variation in policy output between ecologically comparable states. The fact of ecological development means a more educated, more articulate electorate. It also may imply the sophistication of methods for communicating between citizenry and decision makers. And the most obvious product of ecological advancement is the growth of available resources which can be utilized by policy makers to provide a wide range of social services through governmental mechanisms. One such resource is the revenue base provided by economic affluence.

I am suggesting, however, that the resources made available by ecological development are not merely financial. There is too much variation in policy commitment by states of comparable economic ability for this thesis to be accepted as a total explanation of the variance in policy performance. Although limitations of this particular study do not allow for a more thorough investigation, some explanatory hypotheses might be worth considering.

Urbanization, high incomes, widespread education, etc., create a favorable climate for policy innovation. Technical skills and the demands of technically skilled people are vital tools for the office holder or group leader desiring to expand the role of the state as an instrument for collective purposes. Equally useful are the communications methods available to executive, administrative, and legislative leaders in ecologically advanced states. But there does seem to be a range for choice between innovation and inertia.

Such variables and processes as these are the likely occupants of the "black box" between ecology and policy. But further specification of work-

Table 1

Product-Moment Correlations between Selected Ecological and Policy Variables in The American States

Policy Variables	Ecological Variables					
	% Urban, 1963	Per Capita Income 1963	Non-Agri-cultural Employment, 1963	Literacy 1960	Owner Occupancy of Housing, 1960	Newspaper Circu-lation (Per 1,000) 1964
Per Capita Spending for Health and Hospitals by State and Local Governments, 1963	.411	.576	.530	−.052*	.476	.364
Per Capita Spending for Police Protection by State and Local Governments, 1963	.735	.813	.678	−.132*	.428	.499
Per Recipient Average Weekly Unemployment Compensation, 1963	.552	.736	.527	.423	−.110*	.402
Per Capita Debt of State and Local Governments, 1963	.527	.656	.477	.045*	.341	.373
Average Per Recipient Aid to Blind, 1963	.566	.634	.556	.358	−.136*	.569
Average Per Recipient Old Age Assistance, 1963	.380	.450	.344	.473	.128*	.369
Average Per Family Aid to Dependent Children, 1963	.466	.602	.447	.544	.020*	.466

* Relationship not significant at .05 level of confidence. All other correlations shown are significant at least at the .05 level. For a discussion of tests of significance with Pearsonian r, see Hubert M. Blalock, *Social Statistics* (New York: McGraw-Hill, 1960), pp. 302–09.

ing hypothetical constructs must await additional research. In the meantime, however, some assistance in ordering the variables for analysis may be gained from an examination of a few patterns of ecology-policy relationships through time. As the data are presented in Table 1, they are static and, in fact, provide no basis for speaking of "development" at all.

ECOLOGICAL DEVELOPMENT

In order to be able to label a particular set of affairs as somehow "developed," it seems reasonable to me that one must demonstrate: 1) the set of affairs so labeled has a prior state of existence in which it possessed different key characteristics or fewer or less of them than it now possesses; 2) other sets of affairs demonstrably akin to the former have a similar history or show clearly that they are somehow bent in the same direction.

In the case of the "ecological" development of the American states, it can readily be seen that some states have moved from a particular level to a "higher" level over time. It can further be seen that states "below" the advanced states are traveling the same route. Table 2 demonstrates this developmental pattern along a number of related ecological dimensions.

The direction of change within the individual regions is common. All are growing in population, becoming more urban, attaining higher personal incomes, and increasing the percentage of people owning their own homes. What is not readily revealed by this regional data is the relative rate of change among the states. Is the relative distance between the states along these ecological dimensions increasing, decreasing, or holding constant?

A convenient device for measuring the relative distance of subjects (in this case, states) from one another on a particular test is the Coefficient of Relative Variation.[4] Table 3 (on page 154) presents the Coefficients of Relative Variation among the individual states for several ecological variables over an extended period of time. The same data are graphically presented in Figure 1.

The most striking feature of Figure 1 is the marked tendency for the relative ecological variation between the states to decline over the years.[5] No doubt, there are several factors operating to bring about the increasing similarity of the ecological characteristics of the states. The exception seen with population growth may, in fact, be an element which helps explain the pattern among the other variables. There has been a process of selective emigration from poorer areas of the country into the industrial centers of the North and East. This would have a depressive effect upon the population growth in the poorer states while actually helping to raise the relative ecological standing of these areas compared to the areas of heavy immigration of unemployed persons, such as Negroes from the South.

153

Table 2

**Direction of Development of Selected Ecological Variables
in the American States, by Region: 1920–1960**

Region	% Urban					Population ('000)				
	1920	1930	1940	1950	1960	1920	1930	1940	1950	1960
New England	75.9	77.3	76.1	76.2	76.4	7,401	8,166	8,437	9,314	10,509
Middle Atlantic	75.4	77.7	76.8	80.5	81.4	22,261	26,261	27,539	30,164	34,168
E. No. Central	60.8	66.4	65.5	69.7	73.0	21,476	25,297	26,627	30,399	36,225
W. No. Central	37.7	41.8	44.3	52.0	58.8	12,544	13,297	13,517	14,061	15,394
South Atlantic	31.0	36.1	38.8	49.1	57.2	13,990	15,794	17,823	21,182	25,972
E. So. Central	22.4	28.1	29.4	39.1	48.4	8,893	9,887	10,778	11,477	12,050
W. So. Central	29.0	36.4	39.8	55.6	67.7	10,242	12,177	13,065	14,538	16,951
Mountain	36.5	39.4	42.7	54.9	67.1	3,336	3,702	4,150	5,075	6,855
Pacific	62.2	67.5	65.3	74.4	81.1	5,878	8,622	10,229	15,115	21,198

Region	Per Capita Personal Income					% Owner Occupancy of All Housing				
	1920	1930	1940	1950	1960	1920	1930	1940	1950	1960
New England	*	*	$757	$1,629	$2,465	39.2	46.2	42.0	50.9	59.1
Middle Atlantic			783	1,757	2,584	36.7	44.3	37.1	47.7	55.2
E. No. Central			667	1,660	2,375	51.4	53.4	49.0	60.0	67.7
W. No. Central			483	1,411	2,081	55.0	53.1	49.3	62.2	67.8
South Atlantic			459	1,204	1,849	40.8	41.8	40.5	52.1	61.0
E. So. Central			294	903	1,450	41.6	40.7	40.2	53.6	61.8
W. So. Central			383	1,194	1,786	40.7	39.0	41.3	55.8	63.7
Mountain			516	1,387	2,062	53.6	51.4	52.0	59.4	65.2
Pacific			784	1,786	2,612	46.7	48.9	47.2	57.2	60.2

* Comparable regional figures not available for 1920 and 1930.

Table 3
Relative Rate of Change in Selected Ecological Variables
in the American States: 1920–1963

		Coefficient of Relative Variation			
Year	% Population Growth	% Illiterate	% Urban	Per Capita Income	% Owner Occupancy
1920	69.7	84.8	48.4		16.2
				(1929) 29.6	
1930	71.2	98.6	39.6		14.2
1940	65.0		34.8	28.9	11.2
1950	103.9	61.2	22.4	19.4	9.3
1960	90.1	58.4	19.8	16.5	9.4
	(1963) 71.7			(1963) 16.0	

There are many other factors that are masked by the simple manner in which these data are presented. For example, the trend in owner occupancy of housing includes not only the movement of people in ecologically less developed areas toward acquisition of their own homes at an accelerated rate, but it also includes the growing tendency of people with moderate to high incomes in the urban areas to become apartment dwellers.

In any event, it is clear that the poorer states are getting richer at a

Figure 1

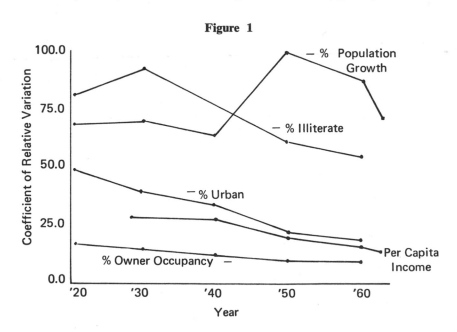

faster rate than the states which are already better off by absolute measures.

POLICY CHANGE

The data presented in Table 1 demonstrate a fairly strong relationship between certain facets of ecological development and the level of state support for a number of social services. We also saw that the states are becoming ecologically more similar over the years. What relationship is there between the increasing similarity of ecological patterns in the states and the nature of public policy?

It is not possible accurately to trace back public policy performance much before 1940, and in some cases records are inadequate even that far back. However, as may be seen from Table 4 and Figure 2, the same general contours are manifested with the directions of policy change as were evident with the ecological data. With the exception of general assistance payments, the relative variation among the states in the pattern of their public policies is declining. The states which provide the lowest levels of services and collect the fewest taxes per capita are increasing these activities at a faster rate than the states at higher absolute levels. Increasing similarity is evident in the policy realm to nearly the same extent that it is in comparative state ecology.

Again, the simplicity of the data may disguise the complexity of the processes at work. However, the comprehensiveness of the trend toward interstate similarity in policy commitment is strongly validated by these data. The indices employed include a summary revenue measure, policies heavily subsidized by federal aid (health and hospitals, ADC, highways), and functions performed almost exclusively with state and local funds (instructional salaries and general assistance). The evident trend, therefore, is not an isolated phenomenon characteristic of only particular types of state activity.

One factor that might explain part of the tendency of the states to become more similar in policy orientation is the redistributive effect of federal aid. However, most federal grant programs do not operate with an equalization formula, but rather are on a straight dollar matching basis. If redistribution of financial resources from rich states to poor states were the chief objective of federal aid, one would expect a strong inverse correlation between per capita federal assistance and the various indicators of ecological development, i.e., the poorer states would receive a relatively greater amount of federal aid than their more advanced counterparts. The actual correlations with a number of ecological indicators is shown in Table 5.

It is apparent from Table 5 that federal money does bring about some

Table 4

Relative Rate of Change in Selected Policy Variables in the American States: 1940–1963

Year	Coefficient of Relative Variation					
	General Assistance Average Monthly Per Case	Health & Hospitals State $ Per Capita	Aid to Dependent Children, Average Monthly $ Per Family	Per Capita State $ for Highways	Per Capita State Tax Collections	Average Salary, Instruc-tional Personnel
1940	(1944) 29.6		(1944) 39.1		(1942) 25.6	20.9
1945		(1948) 32.0		(1948) 32.1	(1947) 22.4	22.9
1950	32.4	(1952) 31.9	31.8	(1952) 32.4	(1951) 23.0 / 18.6	16.2
1955	32.5 / (1959) 42.9	(1956) 31.8 / 24.1	27.4 / (1959) 24.7	(1956) 25.7 / 26.3	(1959) 18.6	16.2 / (1958) 16.9
1960	(1963) 32.7	(1962) 25.2	(1963) 22.8	(1962) 27.5	(1963) 20.2	(1962) 13.7

Figure 2

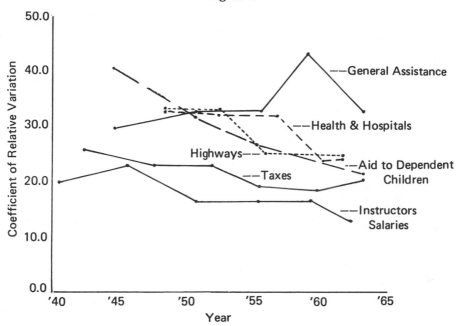

redistribution of resources and probably contributes to the increasing similarity of state policy patterns. But this element hardly offers a major or key explanation of the trend.

As with population growth among the ecological variables, one naturally wonders what accounts for the deviation of general assistance from the pattern of the other policy variables. (See Figures 1 and 2.) The states providing the lowest level of services (which are, by and large, also the ecologically most "underdeveloped") do not seem to be matching the rate

Table 5

Relationship between Selected Ecological Variables and Per Capita Federal Aid (by State) to States, Local Units, and Individuals: 1963

Ecological Variable	Correlation with Per Capita Federal Aid	Ecological Variable	Correlation with Per Capita Federal Aid
	r =		r =
% Urban, 1963	−.377	Literacy, 1960	−.082
Per Capita Income, 1963	.000	% Owner Occupancy of Housing,	
Non-Agricultural Employment, 1963	−.290	1960	−.197

of increased benefits through general assistance which is manifested where this function is supported more generously. Although the pattern seen with the other policies is evident in the last time period for the general assistance data, the overall pattern seems to be toward maintaining substantial variation among the states.

Several possible explanations may be suggested for this deviation of general assistance support from the pattern of other policies. For one thing, the general assistance program is the only facet of the system of direct welfare payments to needy persons which is wholly supported with state and local funds. Aid to the blind, the disabled, the aged, and dependent children are all heavily subsidized by federal funds. As noted above, federal participation may have some selective impact on the increasing similarity of state policy patterns.

The deviation of general assistance from the pattern, furthermore, may be related to the deviant variable in the ecological analysis, i.e., population growth. Many of the immigrants to the ecologically developed areas are unemployed persons who, in their former places of residence, were dissatisfied either with their personal ability to support themselves or with the level of public assistance provided them by poorer states. Although the time period of maximum variation in general assistance support (shown in Figure 2) lags a bit behind the crest of variation in population growth (Figure 1), there is probably some connection. The states receiving the greatest influx of unemployed Negroes from the South, for example, have responded, in most cases, with a greater commitment of their resources to various forms of public aid, including general assistance payments. The pressure for greater public support of low income persons in the states of most emigration has been correspondingly lessened. On the other hand, the data shown are for support per case. And it might seem that fewer cases would encourage the state with emigration of impoverished people (most of whom are moving from the South) to increase the per case support. One cannot, however, exclude from any speculation the fact that the majority of general assistance cases in the South are Negroes.

Again, however, despite an occasional exception, the trend is clearly toward greater similarity among the states in the general nature of their policies.

RELATIONSHIPS THROUGH TIME

The foregoing data present ample support for my major thesis, i.e., that the variation in ecological and policy characteristics between the states is declining. A further facet of this pattern of increasing similarity is that the strength of connection between ecology and policy declines as the overall variance along each dimension is reduced.

At the risk of making a rather hazardous jump from the raw correlations to the motives of the policy makers, it might be hypothesized that once adequate resources are available from ecological development and once certain minimum support levels have been achieved in a few substantive areas, the makers of policy are evidently freed from the restrictions of pressing need. Temporary expediencies, ideological predilections, or matters of momentary taste may find their reflection in public policies to a greater extent once the apparently expected national minimums of state commitment are achieved.

The declining strength of the ecology-policy connection is seen, for example, in the relationship between personal income and state tax collections. Figure 3 illustrates the co-variation between personal income in 1940 and per capita state tax collections in 1942 (the closest years for which I could find comparable data in the early 1940's). The nature of the

Figure 3

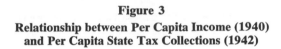

**Relationship between Per Capita Income (1940)
and Per Capita State Tax Collections (1942)**

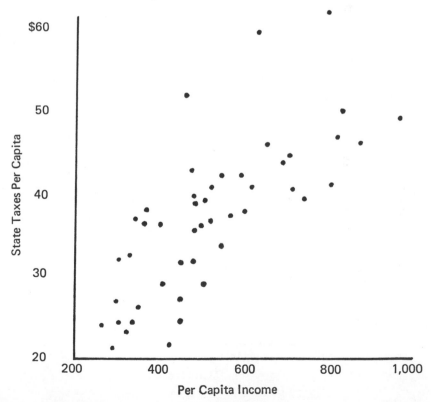

co-variation is clear from the scatter diagram and is further confirmed by a product-moment correlation of .754. As can be seen from Figure 4, however, the strength of the relationship becomes less as the absolute level of tax effort becomes higher and the relative variation between the states declines. The 1963 figures would indicate that once a certain level is achieved, the fact of relative economic well-being ceases to be a key determinant of the level of state taxation. In 1963, r = .375 between income and state taxes.

The same pattern, although to a lesser extent, may be seen with respect to a major spending activity of state and local governments. Figures 5 and 6 illustrate the relationship between per capita income and average salaries of instructional personnel in public school classrooms for 1940 and 1963 respectively. Although the scatter in 1940 is more heteroscedas-

Figure 4

**Relationship between Per Capita Personal Income (1963)
and Per Capita State Tax Collections (1963)**

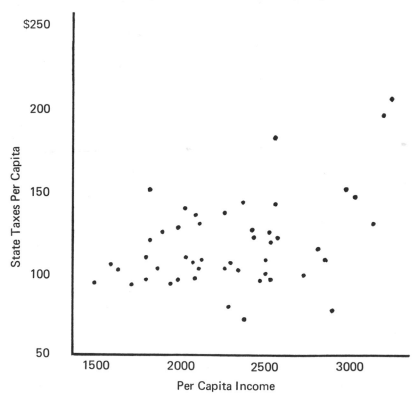

Figure 5
Relationship between Per Capita Personal Income
and Salaries of Instructional Personnel, 1940

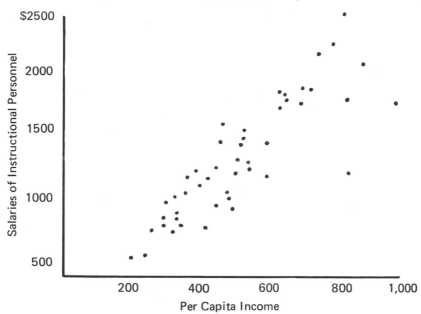

tic than 1963, the former correlation is higher (r = .850 for 1940 and .783 for 1963) due to the uniformly wide spread from the regression line in 1963.

Looking especially at the lower left part of the 1940 distribution (Figure 5), one can see that, at a certain low income level, the states simply do not go beyond a particular level of support for a given policy. But as resources expand, choice is correspondingly widened. And, as was demonstrated by the declining Coefficient of Relative Variation for instructional salaries (see Figure 2), as soon as ample resources become available to the less developed states, they seek to attain an "acceptable" level of support for major services (such as public education). However, as resource availability grows, additional commitments to the same activity become relatively less critical and more a matter of choice by policy makers.

Another way to see these same forces at work is to look at the share of available resources committed to particular state functions, as opposed to comparing per capita figures from state to state. The narrowing of the policy gap is to be expected, given the ecological pattern and the apparent

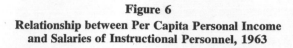

Figure 6
**Relationship between Per Capita Personal Income
and Salaries of Instructional Personnel, 1963**

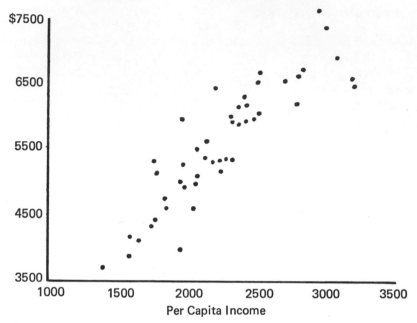

strength of ecology-policy correlations. All this says is that as the incremental resources of ecological development become available, policy makers commit a portion to program development and/or expansion.

But I would suggest, in addition to incremental resource allocation, there also may be operative a process whereby states seem to be emulating each other. An adequate test of this hypothesis would need to show such things as the frequency and nature of interstate communication and interaction between planners, administrators, and other policy makers in comparable functional areas. My observations of such personnel, while hardly comprehensive or necessarily representative, indicate that there are growing opportunities for professional contact across state lines. There are frequent national or regional meetings taking place or being arranged between state welfare administrators, commissioners of natural resources, highway personnel, budget directors, correctional officers, etc. It is difficult to believe that such events do not act as stimuli for the participants, particularly since the agendas of such gatherings are commonly arranged around specific problem areas and focus on methods of attempted solution in one or another state.

The actuality of invidious comparisons with the policy performance of other states (added to existing internal claims) may be serving as a goad to the less developed states. The response is to commit revenues to social services "beyond their means," in a sense. That is, the poorer states will tend to devote a higher proportion of their available resources to social services than is the pattern in economically more well-off states. That this tendency is present, but hardly overpowering, is evident in the various policy measures shown in Table 6, correlated with per capita personal income.

Although these correlations are not especially spectacular, they do all tend in the same direction. The fact that the less advantaged states seem to commit a larger portion of their available resources to social services indicates, of course, that there are more people in need of assistance in these states. But it also might make one wonder if there is not, in the minds of state policy makers throughout the country, such a thing as a "natural" level of support for the disadvantaged or for particular public activities. No matter how rich a state may be in revenue resources, public demands, technical skills, etc., the salaries of teachers in the public schools or the amount of monthly payments to the economically unfortunate are not likely to go very much beyond certain absolute levels followed in the rest of the nation.

The closeness of fit, therefore, between various indices of ecological development and the patterns of public policy in the states is likely to decline with the general diffusion of styles of life throughout the country.

This loosening of relationships may be further illustrated by looking at a few additional comparisons of correlations between ecology and policy over time. Table 7 presents the product-moment correlations of four policy

Table 6

State Commitment to Selected Public Policies as Per Cent of Personal Income, Correlated with Per Capita Personal Income

Policy Commitment as % of Personal Income	Correlated with Per Capita Income	Policy Commitment as % of Personal Income	Per Capita Correlated with Income
	r =		r =
State and Local Taxes, 1963	−.222	Welfare Expenditures of State and Local Governments, 1963	−.471
Spending of State and Local Governments for all Education, 1963	−.347	Health and Hospital Expenditures of State and Local Governments, 1963	−.105

Table 7

Correlational Trends: Income and Urbanism vs. Selected Policy Variables

Policy	Per Capita Personal Income		% Urban	
	1940	1963	1940	1963
	r =	r =	r =	r =
Average Salary of Instructional Personnel in Public Schools	.850	.783	.808	.843
Average Monthly Payment Per Family, Aid to Dependent Children	(1944)* .726	.602	(1944) .691	.466
State Tax Collections Per Capita	(1942) .754	.375	(1942) .588	.225
Average Monthly General Assistance Payment Per Case	(1944) .698	.703	(1944) .775	.664

* The figures in parentheses indicate the year for which the policy data could be obtained. All income and urbanism figures are for 1940 and 1963. All recent policy figures are for 1963.

variables with per capita personal income and percent urban measured in the 1940's and the early 1960's. In only two of the eight temporal comparisons does the strength of relationship increase. The correlation between instructional salaries and percent urban increased slightly between 1940 and 1963. The correlation between general assistance payments and personal income also showed a slight gain. The commitment of the various states to particular levels of general assistance payments already has been seen to deviate from the patterns of other policies. And I hesitate to speculate on the reasons for the increased strength of the relationship between urbanism and educational expenditures.

In all other cases, however, the predicted decline in the strength of ecology-policy relationships holds true.

CONCLUSION

Although there are fairly clear relationships between various ecological characteristics in the states and the level of commitment to a number of governmental services, the demonstration of such correlations does not, in and of itself, offer a comprehensive explanation of the factors which structure the formation of state policy. Such correlations provide a starting point for analysis rather than a logical culmination of inquiry. They do not specify the links between ecology and policy, i.e., the behaviors of the human actors who must ultimately make the policy decisions. Furthermore, the relationships which have been explored still leave a large area of unexplained variation in policy performance between ecologically comparable states.

The data presented here indicate that with overall ecological advancement there is decreasing strength of connection between ecology and the policy outputs of the states. And, although it is risky to jump from a portrayal of inanimate, aggregate statistics to assumptions about individual motives, it would seem that this decline in the strength of ecology-policy correlations is evidence of an increase in the potential for choice in the deliberations of state policy makers.

If this conclusion is an accurate assessment of current developments, it would seem to have strong implications for the study of state politics. Although there is still room for substantial work in refining and clarifying the gross relationships between ecology and policy, increasingly our attention should turn to studies of leadership behavior. As the latitude for individual decision making by governmental leaders is broadened, it becomes necessary to investigate the role orientation of these leaders. We also will need to look at the methods by which communication takes place between professional administrators across state lines and between these persons and elected officials within their own states. And, in order to place the entire process clearly within the context of the American states, it appears likely that we will need further insight into the conceptions of governmental purpose shared by interest group members and the electorate respecting technically complex public issues.

DATA SOURCES

Following are the sources for all the data contained in the various tables throughout this article:

Item	Table	Source
% Urban: 1920, '30, '40	2, 3, 7	U.S. Bureau of the Census, *Statistical Abstract of the United States: 1952* (Washington, D.C.: U.S. Government Printing Office, 1952), p. 30.
1950, '60	2, 3	*Statistical Abstract: 1965*, p. 16.
1963	1, 5, 7	National Education Association, *Rankings of the States, 1965*, Research Report 1965–R1 (Washington, D.C., 1965), p. 13.
Per Capita Income: 1929–'63	1, 2, 3 5, 6, 7	U.S. Dep't. of Commerce, Office of Business Economics, *Survey of Current Business*, 45 (April, 1965) p. 19.
Non-Agricultural Employment, 1963	1	*Statistical Abstract: 1965*, p. 224.

DATA SOURCES (continued)

Item	Table	Source
Literacy:		
1920, '30	3	*Statistical Abstract: 1937*, p. 43.
1950	3	U.S. Bureau of the Census, *Estimates of Illiteracy, By States: 1950*, Current Population Reports, Population Estimates, Series P-23, No. 6, p. 2.
1960	1, 3, 5	*Estimates of Illiteracy: 1960*, No. 8, p. 2.
Owner Occupancy of Housing:		
1920, '30	2, 3	*Statistical Abstract: 1937*, p. 48.
1940	2, 3	*Statistical Abstract: 1947*, p. 792.
1950	2, 3	*Statistical Abstract: 1957*, p. 774.
1960	1, 2, 3	*Statistical Abstract: 1962*, p. 759.
Newspaper Circulation:		
1964	1	*Statistical Abstract: 1965*, p. 525.
Per Capita Spending for Health and Hospitals by State and Local Governments: 1948–1963	1, 4, 6	Council of State Governments, *Book of the States* (Chicago), various biennial issues.
Per Capita Spending for Police Protection by State and Local Governments:		
1963	1	*Rankings of the States*, p. 52.
Per Recipient Average Weekly Unemployment Compensation:		
1963	1	*Book of the States, 1964–1965*, p. 561.
Per Capita Debt of State and Local Governments:		
1963	1	*Statistical Abstract: 1965*, p. 431.
Average Per Recipient Aid to the Blind:		
1963	1	*Book of the States, 1964–1965*, p. 418.
Average Per Recipient Old Age Assistance:		
1963	1	*Book of the States, 1964–1965*, p. 416.
Average Per Family Aid to Dependent Children:		*Book of the States* (various biennial issues).
1944–1963	1, 4, 7	
Population:		
1920–1960	2	*Statistical Abstract: 1965*, p. 12.
Population Growth:		
1920–1960	3	*Statistical Abstract: 1965*, p. 13.
1963	3	*Statistical Abstract: 1965*, p. 10.

DATA SOURCES (continued)

Item	Table	Source
General Assistance, Average Payments Monthly Per Case: 1944–1963	4, 7	*Book of the States* (various biennial issues).
Per Capita State Spending for Highways: 1948–1962	4	*Ibid.*
Per Capita State Tax Collections: 1942–1963	4, 6, 7	*Ibid.*
Average Salary of Instructional Personnel	4, 7	*Ibid.*
Per Capita Federal Aid to States, Local Units, and Individuals: 1963	5	*Rankings of the States,* p. 36.
State and Local Taxes as % of Personal Income: 1963	6	*Rankings of the States,* p. 37.
Spending of State and Local Governments for all Education: 1963	6	*Rankings of the States,* p. 47.
Welfare Spending of State and Local Governments as % of Personal Income: 1963	6	*Statistical Abstract: 1965,* p. 430.
Health and Hospital Spending of State and Local Governments as % of Personal Income: 1963		*Loc. cit.*

NOTES

* I wish to express my gratitude to Professor John Grumm of the Department of Political Science, University of Kansas, for generous advice and assistance in processing some of the data included in this study.

[1] At some risk, I prefer here to avoid a detailed exploration of the justifications for and implications of the "ecology" versus "policy" distinction. The variables I am here calling "ecological" have elsewhere been referred to variously as "input," "en-

vironmental," "socio-economic," etc. The idea of the relationship between men and their environment (including other men) seems to me to be best conveyed by "ecology." The trouble, of course, arises in determining when ecology stops and policy begins. This is the same problem faced by standard systems analysis when dealing with "feedback.' But conceptual sophistication is both a pre-condition and a product of empirical inquiry. The search for premature rigor often can serve as a barrier to further inquiry or as an emotionally gratifying substitute for it. The present state of our knowledge of comparative politics can ill afford either.

For some background on the intellectual evolution of "ecology" and guidance to the present usage, see Otis Dudley Duncan, "Social Organization and the Ecosystem," *Handbook of Modern Sociology,* ed. Robert E. L. Faris (Chicago: Rand McNally, 1964), pp. 37–82, and especially pp. 75–78.

[2] See, for example, Richard E. Dawson and James A. Robinson, "Inter-party Competition, Economic Variables, and Welfare Policies in the Ame.ican States," *Journal of Politics,* 25 (May, 1963), 265–89; Thomas R. Dye, "State Legislative Politics," *Politics in the American States* eds. Herbert Jacob and Kenneth Vines (Boston: Little, Brown, 1965), pp. 151–202; Richard I. Hofferbert, "The Relation Between Public Policy and Some Structural and Environmental Variables in the American States," *American Political Science Review,* 60 (March, 1966), 73–82.

[3] Sources for all the data contained in the tables are listed at the end of the article.

[4] For an elementary discussion of this particular device, see John H. Mueller and Karl F. Schuessler, *Statistical Reasoning in Sociology* (Boston: Houghton Mifflin, 1961), pp. 159–61. The computation formula for the Coefficient of Relative Variation is:

$$\text{CRV} = \frac{\text{AD}_{md}}{\text{Md}} \times 100,$$

where AD_{md} is the average deviation from the median and Md is the median.

The same procedure may be employed with the mean, dividing the standard deviation by the mean. AD_{md} employs arithmetic deviations, the sum of which (ignoring signs) is least when measured as deviations from the median. The standard deviation is computed with squared deviations, the sum of which is least when measured as deviations from the mean. If no further mathematical manipulations are contemplated, AD_{md} is preferable because of the simple method of computation. However, because signs are ignored in its computation, this statistic cannot be employed in further algebraic computations. Mueller and Schuessler note, "The Coefficient of Relative Variation is simple to compute, and particularly useful in comparative work, since it has the effect of norming for differences in absolute magnitudes and in substantive units of measure. It makes comparable sets of small and large values of the same kind, as well as values that are qualitatively different." *Ibid.,* p. 161.

[5] A more detailed analysis of this specific trend respecting personal income may be found in "Disposable Income by States in Current and Constant Prices," *Survey of Current Business,* 45 (April, 1965), 16–27.

PART FOUR

Determinants of Public Policy: Popular Demands and Political Culture

CHAPTER 9

The States and the Political Setting

Daniel J. Elazar

MARKETPLACE AND COMMONWEALTH
AND THE THREE POLITICAL CULTURES

The United States as a whole shares a general political culture.[1] This American political culture is rooted in two contrasting conceptions of American political order, both of which can be traced back to the earliest settlement of the country. In the first, the political order is conceived as a marketplace in which the primary public relationships are products of bargaining among individuals and groups acting out of self-interest. In the second, the political order is conceived to be a commonwealth—a state in which the whole people have an undivided interest—in which the citizens cooperate in an effort to create and maintain the best government in order to implement certain shared moral principles. These two conceptions have exercised an influence on government and politics throughout American history, sometimes in conflict and sometimes by complementing one another.

The national political culture is itself a synthesis of three major political subcultures which jointly inhabit the country, existing side by side or even overlapping one another. All three are of nationwide proportions, having spread, in the course of time, from coast to coast. At the same time each subculture is strongly tied to specific sections of the country, reflecting the currents of migration that have carried people of different origins and backgrounds across the continent in more or less orderly patterns.

Considering the central characteristics that govern each and their respective centers of emphasis, the three political cultures may be called individualistic (I), moralistic (M), and traditionalistic (T).[2] Each of the three reflects its own particular synthesis of the marketplace and the commonwealth.

Reprinted from Daniel J. Elazar, "The States and the Political Setting," in his *American Federalism: A View from the States* (New York: Crowell, 1966), pp. 85–104, by permission of the publisher and the author. Copyright © 1966 by Thomas Y. Crowell Company, New York.

THE INDIVIDUALISTIC POLITICAL CULTURE

The *individualistic political culture* emphasizes the conception of the democratic order as a marketplace. In its view, a government is instituted for strictly utilitarian reasons, to handle those functions demanded by the people it is created to serve. A government need not have any direct concern with questions of the "good society" except insofar as it may be used to advance some common conception of the good society formulated outside the political arena just as it serves other functions. Since the individualistic political culture emphasizes the centrality of private concerns, it places a premium on limiting community intervention—whether governmental or nongovernmental—into private activities to the minimum necessary to keep the marketplace in proper working order. In general, government action is to be restricted to those areas, primarily in the economic realm, which encourage private initiative and widespread access to the marketplace.[3]

The character of political participation in systems dominated by the individualistic political culture reflects this outlook. The individualistic political culture holds politics to be just another means by which individuals may improve themselves socially and economically. In this sense politics is a "business" like any other that competes for talent and offers rewards to those who take it up as a career. Those individuals who choose political careers may rise by providing the governmental services demanded of them and, in return, may expect to be adequately compensated for their efforts. Interpretations of officeholders' obligations under this arrangement vary among political systems and even among individuals within a single political system. Where the norms are high, such people are expected to provide high quality government services for the general public in the best possible manner in return for the status and economic rewards considered their due. Some who choose political careers clearly commit themselves to such norms; others believe that an officeholder's primary responsibility is to serve himself and those who have supported him directly, favoring them even at the expense of others. In some political systems, this view is accepted by the public as well as the politicians.

Political life within an individualistic political culture is based on a system of mutual obligations rooted in personal relationships. While in a simple society those relationships can be direct ones, societies with I political cultures in the United States are usually too complex to maintain face to face ties. So the system of mutual obligations is harnessed through political parties which serve as "business corporations" dedicated to providing the organization necessary to maintain it. Party regularity is indispensable in the I political culture because it is the means for coordinating individual enterprise in the political arena and is the one way of preventing individualism in politics from running wild. In such a system, an individual can succeed politically, not by dealing with issues in some exceptional way or by accepting some concept of good government and then striving to implement it, but by maintaining his place in the system of mutual obligations. He can do this by operating according to the norms of his particular party, to the exclusion of other political considerations. Such a political culture encourages the maintenance of a party system that is competitive, but not overly so, in the pursuit of office. Its politicians are interested in office as a means of controlling the distribution of the favors or rewards of government rather than as a means of exercising governmental power for programmatic ends.

Since the I political culture eschews ideological concerns in its "business-like" conception of politics, both politicians and citizens look upon political activity as a specialized one, essentially the province of professionals, of minimum and passing concern to laymen, and no place for amateurs to play an active role. Furthermore, there is a strong tendency among the public to believe that politics is a dirty—if necessary—business, better left to those who are willing to soil themselves by engaging in it. In practice, then, where the individualistic political culture is dominant, there is likely to be an easy attitude toward the limits of the professionals' perquisites. Since a fair amount of corruption is expected in the normal course of things, there is relatively little popular excitement when any is found unless it is of an extraordinary character. It is as if the public is willing to pay a surcharge for services rendered and only rebels when it feels the surcharge has become too heavy.

Public officials, committed to "giving the public what it wants," are normally not willing to initiate new programs or open up new areas of government activity on their own recognizance. They will do so when they perceive an overwhelming public demand for them to act, but only then. In a sense, their willingness to expand the functions of government is based on an extension of the *quid pro quo* "favor" system which serves as the central core of their political relationships, with new services the reward they give the public for placing them in office.

The I political culture is ambivalent about the place of bureaucracy in the political order. In one sense, the bureaucratic method of operation flies in the face of the favor system that is central to the I political process. At the same time, the virtues of organizational efficiency appear substantial to those seeking to master the market. In the end, bureaucratic organization is introduced within the framework of the favor system; large segments of the bureaucracy may be insulated from it through the merit system but the entire organization is pulled into the political environment at crucial points through political appointment at the upper echelons and, very frequently, the bending of the merit system to meet political demands.

THE MORALISTIC POLITICAL CULTURE

To the extent that American society is built on the principles of "commerce" in the broadest sense of the term and that the marketplace provides the model for public relationships in this country, all Americans share some of the attitudes that are of first importance in the I political culture. At the same time, substantial segments of the American people operate politically within the framework of two political cultures whose theoretical structures and operational consequences depart significantly from the I pattern at crucial points.

The *moralistic political culture* emphasizes the commonwealth conception as the basis for democratic government. Politics, to the M political culture, is considered one of the great activities of man in his search for the good society—a struggle for power, it is true, but also an effort to exercise power for the betterment of the commonwealth. Consequently, in the moralistic political culture, both the general public and the politicians conceive of politics as a public activity centered on some notion of the public good and properly devoted to the advancement of the public interest. Good government, then, is measured by the degree to which it promotes the public good and in terms of the honesty, selflessness, and commitment to the public welfare of those who govern.

In the moralistic political culture, individualism is tempered by a general commitment to utilizing communal—preferably nongovernmental, but governmental if necessary—power to intervene into the sphere of "private" activities when it is considered necessary to do so for the public good or the well-being of the community. Accordingly, issues have an important place in the M style of politics, functioning to set the tone for political concern. Government is considered a positive instrument with a responsibility to promote the general welfare, though definitions of what its positive role should be may vary considerably from era to era.[4]

Since the moralistic political culture rests on the fundamental conception that politics exists primarily as a means for coming to grips with the issues and public concerns of civil society, it also embraces the notion that politics is ideally a matter of concern for every citizen, not just those who are professionally committed to political careers. Indeed, it is the duty of every citizen to participate in the political affairs of his commonwealth.

Consequently, there is a general insistence that government service is public service, which places moral obligations upon those who participate in government that are more demanding than the moral obligations of the marketplace. There is an equally general rejection of the notion that the field of politics is a legitimate realm for private economic enrichment. Since the concept of serving the community is the core of the political relationship, politicians are expected to adhere to it even at the expense of individual loyalties and political friendships. Consequently, party regularity is not of prime importance. The political party is considered a useful political device but is not valued for its own sake. Regular party ties can be abandoned with relative impunity for third parties, special local parties, or nonpartisan systems if such changes are believed helpful in gaining larger political goals. Men can even shift from party to party without sanctions if the change is justified by political belief. In the M political culture, rejection of firm party ties is not to be viewed as a rejection of politics as such. On the contrary, because politics is considered potentially good and healthy within the context of that culture, it is possible to have highly political nonpartisan systems. Certainly nonpartisanship is not instituted to eliminate politics but to improve it by widening access to public office for those unwilling or unable to gain office through the regular party structure.[5]

In practice, where the moralistic political culture is dominant today, there is considerably more amateur participation in politics. There is also much less of what Americans consider corruption in government and less tolerance of those actions which are considered corrupt, so politics does not have the taint it so often bears in the I environment.

By virtue of its fundamental outlook, the M political culture creates a greater commitment to active government intervention into the economic and social life of the community. At the same time, the strong commitment to communitarianism characteristic of that political culture tends to channel the interest in government intervention into highly localistic paths so that a willingness to encourage local government intervention to set public standards does not necessarily reflect a concomitant willingness to allow outside governments equal opportunity to intervene. Not infrequently, public officials will themselves seek to initiate new government activities in an effort to come to grips with problems as yet unperceived by a majority of the citizenry.

The M political culture's major difficulty in adjusting bureaucracy to the political order is tied to the potential conflict between communitarian principles and the necessity for large-scale organization to increase bureaucratic efficiency, a problem that could affect the attitudes of M culture states toward federal activity of certain kinds. Otherwise, the notion of a politically neutral administrative system creates no problem within the M value system and even offers many advantages. Where merit systems are instituted, they tend to be rigidly maintained.

THE TRADITIONALISTIC POLITICAL CULTURE

The *traditionalistic political culture* is rooted in an ambivalent attitude toward the marketplace coupled with a paternalistic and elitist conception of the commonwealth. It reflects an older, precommercial attitude that accepts a substantially hierarchical society as part of the ordered nature of things, authorizing and expecting those at the top of the social structure to take a special and dominant role in government. Like its moralistic counterpart, the traditionalistic political culture accepts government as an actor with a positive role in the community, but it tries to limit that role to securing the continued maintenance of the existing social order. To do so, it functions to confine real political power to a relatively small and self-perpetuating group drawn from an established elite who often inherit their "right" to govern through family ties or social position. Accordingly, social and family ties are paramount in a traditionalistic political culture, even more than personal ties are important in the individualistic where, after all is said and done, a person's first responsibility is to himself. At the same time, those who do not have a definite role to play in politics are not expected to be even minimally active as citizens. In many cases, they are not even expected to vote. Like the I political culture, those active in politics are expected to benefit personally from their activity though not necessarily through direct pecuniary gain.

Political parties are of minimal importance in T political cultures, since they encourage a degree of openness that goes against the fundamental grain of an elite-oriented political order. Their major utility is to recruit people to fill the formal offices of government not desired by the established powerholders. Political competition in a traditionalistic political culture is usually conducted through factional alignments, an extension of the personal politics characteristic of the system; hence political systems within the culture tend to have loose one-party systems if they have political parties at all.

Practically speaking, traditionalistic political culture is found only in a society that retains some of the organic characteristics of the preindustrial social order. "Good government" in that political culture involves the maintenance and encouragement of traditional patterns and, if necessary, their adjustment to changing conditions with the least possible upset. Where the traditionalistic political culture is dominant in the United States today, political leaders play conservative and custodial rather than initiatory roles unless pressed strongly from the outside.

Whereas the I and M political cultures may or may not encourage the development of bureaucratic systems of organization on the grounds of "rationality" and "efficiency" in government, depending on their particular situations, traditionalistic political cultures tend to be instinctively anti-bureaucratic because bureaucracy by its very nature interferes with the fine web of informal interpersonal relationships that lie at the root of the political system and which have been developed by following traditional patterns over the years. Where bureaucracy is introduced, it is generally confined to ministerial functions under the aegis of the established power-holders.

THE "GEOLOGY" OF POLITICAL CULTURE

The three political subcultures arose out of very real socio-cultural differences found among the peoples who came to America over the years, differences that date back to the very beginnings of settlement in this country and even to the Old World. Because the various ethnic and religious groups that came to these shores tended to congregate in the same settlements and because, as they or their descendants moved westward, they continued to settle together, the political patterns they bore with them are today distributed geographically. Indeed, it is the geographic distribution of political cultures as modified by local conditions that has laid the foundations for American sectionalism. Sectional concentrations of distinctive cultural groups have helped create the social interests that tie contiguous states to each other even in the face of marked differences in the standard measure of similarity. The southern states have a common character that unites them despite the great material differences between, say, Virginia and Mississippi or Florida and Arkansas. Similarly, New England embraces both Maine and Massachusetts, Connecticut and Vermont in a distinctive way. These sectional concentrations can be traced for every part of the country, and their effects can be noted in the character of the economic interests shared by the states in each section.

The overall pattern of political cultures is not easily portrayed. Not only must the element of geography be considered, but also a kind of human or cultural "geology" that adds another dimension to the problem. In the course of time, different currents of migration have passed over the American landscape in response to the various frontiers of national development. Those currents, in themselves relatively clear-cut, have left residues of population in various places to become the equivalent of geological strata. As these populations settled in the same location, sometimes side by side, sometimes overlapping, and frequently on top of one another, they created hardened cultural mixtures that must be sorted out for analytical purposes, city by city and county by county from the Atlantic to the Pacific.[6]

Quite clearly, the various sequences of migration in each locale have determined the particular layering of the cultural geology of each state.

Even as the strata were being deposited over generations and centuries, externally generated events, such as depressions, wars, and internal cultural conflicts, caused upheavals that altered the relative positions of the various groups in the community. Beyond that, the passage of time and the impact of new events have eroded some cultural patterns, intensified others, and modified still others, to make each local situation even more complex. The simple mapping of such patterns has yet to be done for more than a handful of states and communities, and while the gross data which can be used to outline the grand patterns as a whole are available in various forms, they have been only partially correlated. However, utilizing the available data, it is possible to sketch with reasonable clarity the nation-wide geography of political culture (Figure 1).

POLITICAL CULTURE AND THE CONTINUING FRONTIER

The geography of political culture is directly related to the continuing American frontier. Since the first settlement on these shores, American society has been a frontier society, geared to the progressive extension of man's control over the natural environment and the utilization of the social and economic benefits gained from widening that control, i.e., pushing the frontier line back. The very dynamism of American society is a product of this commitment to the conquest of the ever-advancing frontier, a commitment which is virtually self-generating since, like a chain reaction, the conquest of one frontier has led to the opening of another.[7] It is this frontier situation that has created the major social and economic changes which have, in turn, forced periodic adjustments in the nation's political institutions, changes of particular importance to the role and functioning of federalism and to the character and particular concerns of intergovernmental relations.

Since the opening of settlement in 1607, the American frontier has passed through three stages: First came the *rural-land* frontier—the classic American frontier described by the historians—lasting roughly from the seventeenth through the nineteenth centuries. It was characterized by the westward movement of a basically rural population interested in settling and exploiting the land and by the development of a socio-economic system based on agricultural and extractive pursuits in both its urban and rural components. Early in the nineteenth century, the rural-land frontier gave birth to the *urban-industrial* frontier, which began in the Northeast and spread westward, in the course of which it transformed the nation into an industrial society settled in cities and dedicated to the spread of new technology as the primary source of the nation's economic and social

Figure 1

The Distribution of Political Cultures within the States

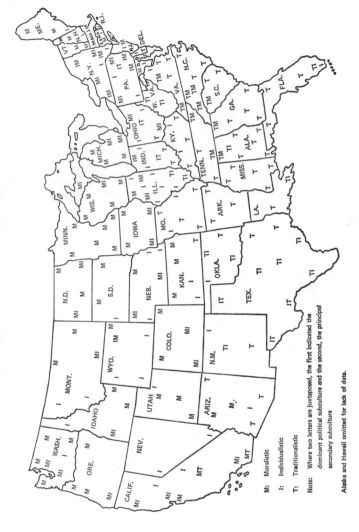

M: Moralistic

I: Individualistic

T: Traditionalistic

Note: Where two letters are juxtaposed, the first indicated the dominant political subculture and the second, the principal secondary subculture

Alaska and Hawaii omitted for lack of data.

forms. The dominant characteristic of this frontier was the transformation of cities from service centers or workshops for the rural areas into independent centers of opportunity, producers of new wealth, and social innovators possessing internally generated reasons for existence and growth. At first overlapping the land frontier, the urban-industrial frontier became dominant by the last third of the century. By the midtwentieth century, it had given birth, in turn, to the *metropolitan-technological* frontier which is characterized by the radical reordering of an industrial society through rapidly changing technologies and a settlement pattern that encourages the diffusion of an urbanized population within large metropolitan regions. These radically new technologies, ranging from atomic energy and automation to synthetics, and the accompanying suburbanization of the population influenced further changes in the nation's social and economic forms in accord with their new demands. Like the first two frontier stages, the metropolitan-technological frontier has also moved from east to west since the 1920's, becoming dominant nationally after World War II. Each successive frontier stage has opened new vistas and new avenues of opportunity for the American people. At the same time, each new frontier has brought changes in economic activities, new settlement patterns, different human requirements, political changes, and its own social problems that grow out of the collision of old patterns and new demands as much as they are generated by the new demands themselves.[8]

The basic patterns of political culture were set during the period of the rural-land frontier by three great currents of American migration that began on the east coast and moved westward after the colonial period. Each current moved, in the persons of the westward migrants, from east to west along more or less fixed paths, following lines of least resistance which generally led them due west from the immediately previous area of settlement.

Across the northern part of the United States thrusting westward and slightly southwestward is an area settled initially by the Puritans of New England and their Yankee descendants. The Puritans came to these shores intending to establish the best possible earthly version of the holy commonwealth. Their religious outlook was imbued with a high level of political concern, in the spirit of the ancient Israelites whose ideal commonwealth they wished to reproduce. From the first, they established a moralistic political culture.

After five generations of pioneering in New England, where they established several versions of their commonwealth in the several New England states, the Puritans had developed a set of deeply rooted cultural patterns. Then, moving westward into New York State, the Yankees began their great cross-country migration. Across New York, northern Pennsylvania, and the upper third of Ohio, the Yankee current moved into the states of the upper Great Lakes and Mississippi Valley. There they established a greater New England in Michigan, Wisconsin, Minnesota, and Iowa, and they attempted to do the same in settling northern Illinois. Beginning in the midnineteenth century, they were joined by Scandinavians and other northern Europeans who, stemming from a related tradition (particularly in its religious orientation), reenforced the basic patterns of Yankee political culture, sealing them into the political systems of those states. Pressing westward, Yankees settled Oregon, then Washington, and were the first "Anglos" to settle California. As Mormons, they settled Utah; then as abolitionists they settled Kansas. They became the leaders of the permanent settlements in Colorado and Montana and even moved into northern Arizona. In all these states, they were joined or followed by the same Scandinavian–northern European group and in each they established the M political culture to the extent of their influence. Within those states and the smaller ones colonized from them, the moralistic political culture flourishes today.

Groups of quite different ethnic and religious backgrounds, primarily from England and the interior Germanic states, settled the middle parts of the nation, beginning with the Middle Atlantic states of New York, New Jersey, Pennsylvania, Delaware, and Maryland. The majority of these highly diverse groups, which together established the basic patterns of American pluralism, were united by one common bond in particular—the search for individual opportunity in the New World. Unlike the Puritans who sought communal as well as individualistic goals in their migrations, the pursuit of private ends predominated among the settlers of the middle states. Though efforts were made to establish morally purposeful communities, particularly in Pennsylvania, the very purpose of those communities was to develop pluralistic societies dedicated to individual freedom to pursue private goals, to the point of making religion a private matter, an unheard-of step at the time. The political culture of the middle states reflected this distinctive emphasis on private pursuits from the first and, by the end of the colonial period, a whole system of politics designed to accommodate itself to such a culture had been developed with distinctive state by state variations, modified by moralistic traits only in Pennsylvania and by traditionalistic ones in Maryland and Delaware.

These groups also moved westward across Pennsylvania into the central parts of Ohio, Indiana, and Illinois, then on into Missouri. There, reenforced by immigrants from western Europe and the lower Germanic states who shared the same attitudes, they developed extensions of their pluralistic patterns. Since those states were also settled by representatives of the other two political cultures, giving no single culture clear predominance, pluralism became the only viable alternative. So the individualistic political culture became dominant at the state level in the course of time while the other two retained pockets of influence in the northern and southern sections of each state.

After crossing the Mississippi, this middle current jumped across the continent to northern California with the gold rush (an activity highly attractive to I types). Its groups subsequently helped to populate the territory in between. The areas of Nebraska and South Dakota bordering the Missouri River attracted settlers from Illinois and Missouri; the Union Pacific populated central Nebraska and Wyoming; and Nevada was settled from the California gold fields. Today there is a band of states (or sections of states) across the belt of the country in which the individualistic political culture is dominant.

The people who settled the southern tier of states were seeking individual opportunity in ways similar to those of their brethren to the immediate north. But, while the latter sought their opportunities in commercial pursuits, either in business or in a commercially oriented agriculture, those who settled the South sought opportunity in a plantation-centered agricultural system based on slavery and essentially anticommercial in orientation. This system, as an extension of the landed gentry agrarianism of the Old World, provided a natural environment for the development of an American-style traditionalistic political culture in which the new landed gentry progressively assumed ever greater roles in the political process at the expense of the small landholders, while a major segment of the population, the slaves, were totally excluded from any political role whatsoever. Elitism within this culture reached its apogee in Virginia and South Carolina; in North Carolina and Georgia a measure of equalitarianism was introduced by the arrival of significant numbers of migrants from the M and I cultures, respectively.

This peculiarly southern agrarian system and its traditionalistic political culture were carried westward by the Southern current. Virginia's people dominated in the settlement of Kentucky; North Carolina's influence was heavy in Tennessee; and settlers from all four states covered the southern parts of Ohio and Illinois as well as most of Indiana and Missouri. Georgians, with a mixture of other settlers, moved westward into Alabama and Mississippi. Louisiana presented a unique situation in that it contained a concentration of non-Anglo-Saxons rare in the South, but its French settlers shared the same political culture as the other southerners, regardless of their other cultural differences. Ultimately, the southern political culture was spread through Texas, where it was diluted on that state's western fringes by I type European immigrants, and Oklahoma; into southern Kansas, where it clashed directly with the Yankee political culture; then across New Mexico to settle better than half of Arizona and overlap the Yankee current in southern and central California.

The only major departures from the east-west pattern of cultural diffusion during the settlement of the land frontier came when the emigrants encountered the country's great mountain systems. The mountains served to diffuse cultural patterns because they were barriers to easy east-west movement. Thus, in the east, the Appalachian chain deflected the moralistic type Scotch-Irish southward from Pennsylvania where they were isolated in the southern mountains. There they developed traditionalistic patterns of culture over a moralistic base, and created special cultural pockets dominated by syntheses of the T and M cultures in the mountain areas of Virginia, the Carolinas, Georgia, and even Alabama.

In the west, the Rocky Mountains served to block the neat westward flow of the cultural currents and divert people from all three into their valleys from north to south in search of fortunes in mining and specialized agricultural pursuits. There the more individualistic types from all three subcultures diffused from Montana to Arizona, creating cultural pockets in all the mountain states of the west that in some cases—Wyoming, for example—altered the normal regional patterns of political culture.

The development of the urban-industrial frontier coincided with the arrival of other immigrant groups which concentrated in the burgeoning cities of the industrializing states. These groups, primarily from Ireland, Italy, eastern Europe, and the Balkans, also moved from east to west but settled in urban pockets adding new cultural strata to communities scattered throughout the country. Most of these settlers, though bound at first by traditional ties, soon adopted more individualistic attitudes and goals which brought them into the I political culture. Since most of them settled in cities, their cultural impact was less universal in scope but more concentrated in force. In some states (such as Massachussetts) they disrupted established cultural patterns to create new ones, in others (such as New York) they simply reenforced the existing I-dominant pluralism, and in still others (such as Illinois) they served to tip the balance between competing cultural groups.

NOTES

[1] For an analysis by political scientists of the national political culture in a comparative setting, see Gabriel A. Almond and Sidney Verba, *The Civic Culture* (Princeton: Princeton University Press, 1963).

[2] The names given the three political subcultures are meant to be descriptive, not evaluative. By the same token, the descriptions of the three that follow are intended to be models or ideal types not fully extant in the real world.

[3] It is important to examine this description and the ones following it very carefully after first abandoning many of the preconceptions associated with such idea-words as *individualistic, moralistic, marketplace,* etc. In this case, for example, nine-teenth-century individualistic conceptions of minimum intervention were oriented toward *laissez faire* with the role of government conceived to be that of a policeman with powers to act in certain limited fields. In the twentieth century, the notion of what constitutes minimum intervention has been drastically expanded to include such things as government regulation of utilities, unemployment compensation, and massive subventions to maintain a stable and growing economy—all this within the framework of the same political culture. The demands of manufacturers for high tariffs in 1865 and the demands of labor unions for workmen's compensation in 1965 may well be based on the same theoretical justification that they are aids to the maintenance of a working marketplace. Culture is not static. It must be viewed dynamically and defined so as to include cultural change in its very nature.

[4] As in the case of the I political culture, the change from nineteenth– to twentieth–century conceptions of what government's positive role should be has been great, i.e., support for Prohibition has given way to support for wage and hour regulation. At the same time, care must be taken to distinguish between a predisposition toward communal activism and desire for federal government activity. For example, many M types oppose federal aid for urban renewal without in any way opposing community responsibility for urban redevelopment. The distinction they make (implicitly at least) is between what they consider legitimate community responsibility and what they believe to be central government encroachment, or between "communalism" which they value and "collectivism" which they abhor. Thus, on some public issues we find certain M types taking highly conservative positions despite their positive attitudes toward public activity generally. M types may also prefer government intervention in the social realm—i.e., censorship or screening of books and movies—to similar government intervention in the economy.

[5] In this context, it should be noted that regular party systems are sometimes abandoned in local communities dominated by the I political culture to institute nonpartisan electoral systems in an effort to make local governments more "business-like" and to take local administration "out of politics." Such antipolitical efforts are generally products of business-dominated reform movements and reflect the view that politics is necessarily "dirty" and illegitimate. In this context, see Edward C. Banfield (ed.), *Urban Government* (New York: Free Press of Glencoe, 1961), Sections III and IV.

[6] A more detailed and elaborate discussion than can be given here of the origins and spread of the three subcultures will be found in the author's forthcoming book, *Cities of the Prairie*. Since the patterns of the political subcultures are tied closely to the patterns of the general subcultures in the United States, it is possible to gain some impression of the spread of the former from data prepared to illustrate the spread of the latter. One of the best sources for that data, though somewhat dated, is Charles O. Paullin's *Atlas of the Historical Geography of the United States* (Washington and New York: Carnegie Institution and American Geographical Society, 1932). The correlations between religious affiliation and political culture are clear and striking. Edwin S. Gausted's *Historical Atlas of Religion in America* (New York: Harper,

1962) includes maps showing the spread of religious denominations as of 1950, which are very useful in following the patterns of political culture as well.

[7] The frontier process emerging from the meeting of civilization and raw nature is a dynamic one; men approach the untamed area with a view to bringing it under their control because it appears to offer indefinite possibilities for expansion as well as a chance to begin from the beginning, to implement goals which appear difficult or impossible to implement in the civilized area about them. A frontier situation possesses the following elements: (1) the exploration of that which was previously unexplored and the development of that which was previously undeveloped; (2) a psychological orientation toward exploration, development, growth, opportunity, and change—often typified in the "boom" spirit; (3) an economy that is growing in scope and changing in character; (4) manifold opportunities for exploration and pioneering, coupled with a strong element of risk; (5) widespread freedom for people to engage in frontier-like activities and generally to have free access to the developing sector; (6) substantial movements of population in search of opportunity or improved living conditions; (7) an emergent or "unfinished" society that is continually responding to the advancing frontier by changing its social and settlement patterns; and (8) the creation of new opportunities on many levels of society as a consequence of pushing back the frontier. The basic statement of the frontier theory is still that of Frederick Jackson Turner and can best be found in his *The Frontier in American History* (New York: Holt, 1920). For an introduction to other aspects of frontier theory, see Nelson Klose, *A Concise Study Guide to the American Frontier* (Lincoln: University of Nebraska Press, 1964).

[8] The history and significance of the American land frontier has been set forth in great detail by Turner and his students. See, for example, Turner, *op. cit.,* and Ray Allen Billington, *Westward Expansion: A History of the American Frontier* (New York: Macmillan, 1949). Much less has been written about the urban-industrial frontier. Two good studies are John Kouwenhoven, *Made in America,* rev. ed. (Garden City: Anchor Books, 1962) on the role of the new technology of the midnineteenth century and Anselm Strauss, *The Image of the American City* (Glencoe, Ill.: Free Press, 1961) on the urbanization aspects of the urban-industrial frontier. Walt W. Rostow's *The Stages of Economic Growth* (New York: Cambridge University Press, 1960) provides a theory of economic growth that strongly supports the hypothesis presented here. The frontier aspects of the contemporary metropolitanization process have hardly been treated at all. The best discussion available is that of Samuel Lubell, *The Future of American Politics* (New York: Harper, 1952). See also, Daniel J. Elazar, *Some Social Problems in the Northeastern Illinois Metropolitan Region* (Urbana: University of Illinois, 1961). The author's forthcoming book, *Cities of the Prairie,* will contain an elaboration of the hypothesis presented here.

[9] One important study of the effects of these new migrations on American politics is Lubell, *op. cit.,* pp. 60–67, 75–78.

CHAPTER 10

Regionalism, Economic Status, and the Public Policies of American States[1]

Ira Sharkansky

In recent years, a number of scholars has examined the influence of current economic conditions on the expenditures and other policies of state and local governments. Among economists, Fabricant, Fisher and Sachs and Harris have found that the level of per capita personal income within the states has significant bearing upon the combined expenditures of state and local governments.[2] Among political scientists, Dye, Hofferbert and Dawson and Robinson have found that measures of economic development have more direct relationships with measures of expenditures and other public policies than do measures of certain political processes.[3]

The findings of these writers provide compelling evidence for the proposition that the activity of state and local governments depends partly upon current economic resources and economic needs within their jurisdictions. Yet economics alone does not provide a thorough explanation for interstate differences in public policies. The literature shows that economic conditions—as measured by various authors to include personal income, industrialization, urbanization and education—provide substantially less than one-half the statistical explanation for interstate variations in most measures of public policy. It is apparent that states frequently surpass or fail to reach the policy norms that generally are associated with their levels of economic activity.[4] Such deviations may result from historical experiences that stimulated citizens and/or officials to adopt unusually intense or indifferent attitudes toward certain policy issues. Some of these critical historical episodes may have been economic in their nature. Thus, policies of state and local governments may reflect previous accommodations to needs or resources that have been outmoded by changes in agriculture, commerce or industry.

It seems likely that a consideration of regionalism will add to the

Reprinted from the *Social Science Quarterly* (June, 1968), pp. 9–26, by permission of the publisher.

understanding of interstate differences in government expenditures and other public policies. Neighboring states in the various regions of America have experienced migrations, economic crises and ideological traumas at similar points in their histories, and these experiences may have helped set the patterns reflected in current government activities.[5] Moreover, state administrators and legislators often take account of regional norms in adjusting program levels within their own states. State research bureaus typically publish comparisons of their own states' activities with those of bordering states, and state administrators think in regional terms when they consider the experiences of other states as guides to their own policy decisions. Many public officials have a sense for interstate competition that inclines them to services no lower and taxes no higher than regional norms, and many perceive that neighboring states have problems that are most like their own and therefore most meaningful as sources of new policies.[6] Thus, the informal decision-making processes of government officials may produce a resemblance among the programs of regional partners that is greater than their current economic similarities.

Because regional partners tend to resemble one another economically at the present time, it is no simple task to separate the influences on states' policies that reflect their economic status from those that reflect non-economic attributes of their regionalism. However, many states deviate from the current economic norms of their regions. These intraregional economic deviations permit a statistical test for the importance of regional traits (other than current economic status) as correlates of public policies.[7]

This article seeks to define the relative importance of current economics and regionalism as influences on the public policies of state and local governments.[8] To do this, it employs simple, partial and multiple correlation techniques to define relationships between measures of economic characteristics and public policies. And by an analysis of covariance, using state scores on these economic characteristics and policies, together with three demarcations of American regions, it assesses the relative weight of non-economic regionalism on public policies.

Although the concept of regionalism promises some help in the explanation of public policies in the American states, it does not offer a great deal of specificity. The statistical techniques employed here show some relationship between the states' regional affiliations and their policies, while controlling for the states' current economic status. However, a common regional identification is a diffuse attribute that may include a variety of social or political characteristics, or common historical experiences. It is necessary to go beyond the analysis of covariance in order to identify the specific attributes of regional neighbors that seem to account for their current policies.

TECHNIQUES

Public Policies

The public policies considered here include levels of total government expenditures, intergovernmental payments and receipts, taxes, debt, and expenditure and service levels in the fields of education, highways and public welfare. The measures of expenditures include both state expenditures and the combination of state and local government expenditures per capita. Measures of intergovernmental payments and receipts include transactions between state and local governments, as well as relations between these governments and the federal government. The tax measures show government "effort" in terms of the available economic resources used, and the per capita revenues produced by taxes on real property, general sales, excises, individual incomes, motor vehicle licenses and current charges for services. The measures of educational service levels show the frequency with which state populations use various programs and the success of each state's candidates on a national examination. The highway measures show the incidence of certain types of highways in relation to traffic needs,[9] the safety record of state roads and the completion rate of each state's share of the Interstate Highway network. The measures of welfare programs show the average payments given to recipients of the major public assistance programs, and the incidence of recipients among the populations likely to need the services. In order to conserve space, the full title of each policy measure is shown only in Table 3, and short titles are given in subsequent tables. The measures of public policy, as well as the economic measures described below, come from widely available publications of the federal government and private organizations, and they pertain to the 1960–1962 period.[10]

Economic Status

The measures of economic status assess three different aspects of welfare, resources and living conditions that previous studies have found to be relevant for expenditures and other policies of state and local governments.[11] The specific measures are:
    a. per capita personal income,
    b. total personal income,
    c. percentage of population living in urban areas.
In this study, variable *a* is considered to measure individual welfare; variable *b,* the magnitude of economic resources; and variable *c,* a pattern

of settlement reflective of resources and life-styles. Each of these characteristics may affect both the needs for certain public services and the availability of resources to support services. Generally speaking, states scoring high
on one measure of economic activity also score high on the others.
However, as the co-efficients of simple correlation among variables *a, b*
and *c* (shown in Table 1) indicate, there is considerable "slippage" among

Table 1
Coefficients of Simple Correlation among Measures of Economic Status

	a	*b*	*c*
a. per capita personal income	1.00	.44*	.69*
b. total personal income		1.00	.58*
c. urbanization			1.00

* Significant at the .05 level

the characteristics. For this reason, the following analysis employs both
simple (product-moment) and partial correlation techniques to determine
the relative influence of each economic characteristic upon each measure of
public policy.[12]

Regions

It is no simple task to define the regions of America. In any single demarcation there are likely to be disputes about the assignments given to
"border states." To cope with the problem of regional definition this study
employs three demarcations of the states. The first two are used by Perloff,
et al., in their study of regional economic development.[13] Demarcation
#1 divides the 48 states into three regions, principally along the Ohio and
Mississippi Rivers. Because of economic affinities, however, Arkansas and
Louisiana are placed in the *Southeast* rather than in *Transmississippi*. East
of the Ohio River, Demarcation #1 follows the northern borders of West
Virginia and Virginia in dividing the *North* from the *Southeast*. Demarcation #2 subdivides two major regions of the first grouping: the *North*
becomes *New England, Mid-Atlantic* and *Great Lakes;* the *Southeast*
remains as is; and *Transmississippi* becomes the *Plains, Mountains, Southwest* and *Far West*. Demarcation #3 employs the principal divisions of the
U.S. Census Bureau: The *Northeast* includes New England plus the urban-
industrial states of New York, New Jersey and Pennsylvania; *North
Central* includes the Great Lakes and Plains states; the *South* includes the
eleven states of the Confederacy plus the border states of Delaware,

Maryland, West Virginia, Kentucky and Oklahoma; and *Transplains* includes the remaining states of the mountain, desert and Pacific coastal areas. The states included in each regional grouping are listed in Table 2.

Analysis of covariance permits the assessment of relative associations between measures of public policy, economic activity and regionalism. The

Table 2
Regional Groupings of American States

Demarcation #1	Demarcation #2	Demarcation #3
North	*New England*	*Northeast*
Maine	Maine	Maine
New Hampshire	New Hampshire	New Hampshire
Vermont	Vermont	Vermont
Massachusetts	Massachusetts	Massachusetts
Rhode Island	Rhode Island	Rhode Island
Connecticut	Connecticut	Connecticut
New York		New York
New Jersey	*Mid-Atlantic*	Pennsylvania
Pennsylvania	New York	New Jersey
Delaware	New Jersey	
Maryland	Pennsylvania	*South*
Ohio	Delaware	Delaware
Michigan	Maryland	Maryland
Indiana		Virginia
Illinois	*Southeast*	West Virginia
Wisconsin	Virginia	North Carolina
	West Virginia	South Carolina
Southeast	North Carolina	Georgia
Virginia	South Carolina	Florida
West Virginia	Georgia	Kentucky
North Carolina	Florida	Tennessee
South Carolina	Kentucky	Alabama
Georgia	Tennessee	Mississippi
Florida	Alabama	Arkansas
Kentucky	Mississippi	Louisiana
Tennessee	Arkansas	Oklahoma
Alabama	Louisiana	Texas
Mississippi		
Arkansas	*Great Lakes*	*North Central*
Louisiana	Ohio	Ohio
	Indiana	Indiana
Transmississippi	Michigan	Michigan
Minnesota	Illinois	Wisconsin
Iowa	Wisconsin	Illinois
Missouri		Minnesota
North Dakota	*Plains*	Iowa
South Dakota	Minnesota	Missouri

Table 2 (continued)

Demarcation #1	Demarcation #2	Demarcation #3
Nebraska	Iowa	North Dakota
Kansas	Missouri	South Dakota
Oklahoma	North Dakota	Nebraska
Texas	South Dakota	Kansas
Montana	Nebraska	
Wyoming	Kansas	*Transplains*
Idaho		Montana
Colorado	*Southwest*	Wyoming
New Mexico	Arizona	Colorado
Utah	New Mexico	New Mexico
Arizona	Oklahoma	Idaho
Nevada	Texas	Utah
Washington		Arizona
Oregon	*Mountains*	Washington
California	Montana	Oregon
	Idaho	Nevada
	Wyoming	California
	Colorado	
	Utah	
	Far West	
	Washington	
	Oregon	
	Nevada	
	California	

technique permits the identification of relationships between a dependent variable (a measure of policy) and a nominal variable (region) while controlling for interval variables (economic characteristics).[14] Each analysis of covariance reported below is performed three times: once with each of the three regional demarcations of the states. Where the findings show that region bears a significant relationship with policy that is independent of economic characteristics, the average scores of states in each region are shown. Finally, a limited effort is made to speculate about regional phenomena that contribute to distinctive levels of public activity.

FINDINGS

The measures of economic activity show the simple relationships with many measures of public policies that are expected on the basis of existing literature:[15] the greater the economic activity, the higher the level of government activities shown by state and local governments. The co-efficients of simple correlation, shown in Table 3, indicate that high (or low) levels of per capita personal income, total personal income and urbanization often associate with high (or low) levels of state and local government expenditures, tax revenues, indebtedness and levels of public service. Yet there are significant exceptions to this finding. Policies that

Table 3
Coefficients of Simple Correlation between Measures
of Economic Status and Public Policies

	Economic Characteristics		
	Personal income/ capita	Total personal income	Urbani- zation
Public Policies:			
(1) total state expenditures/capita	.14	−.26	.14
(2) state education expenditures/capita	.00	−.11	.03
(3) state highway expenditures/capita	−.03	−.41*	−.39*
(4) state public welfare expenditures/ capita	−.11	−.01	.09
(5) total state and local expenditures/ capita	.49*	.16	.34*
(6) state and local education expenditures/capita	.49*	.09	.32*
(7) state and local highway expenditures/capita	.03	−.35*	−.37*
(8) state and local public welfare expenditures/capita	−.02	.12	.16
(9) percent of state and local revenue allocated to state government	−.49*	−.64*	−.62*
(10) percent of state and local revenue from non-local sources	−.54*	−.49*	−.23
(11) federal aid as a percent of state revenue	−.46*	−.51*	−.54*
(12) federal aid as a percent of state and local revenue	−.59*	−.53*	−.60*
(13) state taxes as a percent of total personal income	−.54*	−.30*	−.35*
(14) state and local taxes as a percent of total personal income	−.23	−.06	−.12
(15) state and local property taxes/capita	.55*	.29*	.38*
(16) state and local general sales taxes/ capita	−.01	.18	.16
(17) state and local excise taxes/capita	.35*	−.06	.19
(18) state and local motor vehicle taxes/ capita	.22	−.18	−.11

Table 3 (continued)

		Economic Characteristics		
		Personal income/ capita	Total personal income	Urbani- zation
(19)	state and local individual income taxes/capita	.25	.13	.05
(20)	state and local revenue from current service charges/capita	.33*	—.04	.05
(21)	state and local government debt/ capita	.64*	.44*	.38*
(22)	percent of school enrollment participating in federal school lunch program	—.77*	—.41*	—.65*
(23)	enrollment in federal-aid vocational education program/10,000 population	—.56*	—.22	—.43*
(24)	persons in process of vocational rehabilitation/10,000 population	—.35*	—.25	—.34*
(25)	persons completing vocational rehabilitation/10,000 population	—.44*	—.26	—.40*
(26)	average percent of students attending daily in elementary and secondary schools	.04	.33*	.00
(27)	percent of 8th graders who graduate from high school four years later	.59*	.31*	.38*
(28)	percent of selective service registrants passing mental exam	.52*	.02	.33*
(29)	total mileage/capita of roads	—.25	—.47*	—.58*
(30)	mileage/rural resident of rural roads	.13	—.31*	—.16
(31)	mileage/urban resident of municipal roads	—.44*	—.53*	—.67*
(32)	percent of designated Interstate mileage open to traffic by 1962	.03	.02	—.19
(33)	percent of farms on paved roads	.46*	.31*	.38*
(34)	state residents per motor vehicle death	.46*	.42*	.59*
(35)	average payment/recipient Aid to Families of Dependent Children	.65*	.32*	.48*
(36)	average payment/recipient Old Age Assistance	.66*	.28*	.45*
(37)	average payment/recipient Aid to the Permanently and Totally Disabled	.29*	.37*	.33*
(38)	average payment/recipient Aid to the Blind	.55*	.29*	.56*

Table 3 (continued)

	Economic Characteristics		
	Personal income/ capita	Total personal income	Urbani- zation
(39) incidence of AFDC recipients among people with incomes of less than $2,000	.60*	.38*	.65*
(40) incidence of OAA recipients among people over 65 with incomes less than $2,000	.22	−.32*	.01
(41) incidence of APTD recipients among people with incomes less than $2,000	.11	.07	.32*
(42) incidence of AB recipients among people with incomes less than $2,000	.22	.34*	.21

* Significant at the .05 level

fail to show positive relationships with economic activity include state government expenditures, federal aid, tax effort, the centralization of state-local financial relations and several education and highway policies.[16]

Much of the economic-policy relationship that does exist depends on interstate differences in per capita personal income. This finding is evident in the co-efficients of partial correlation between per capita personal income and public policies shown in Table 4. They suggest that personal welfare is a more critical influence upon government decision-makers than the sheer aggregate of economic resources. This finding may reflect the political components in public decisions, whereby the individual needs and resources of taxpayers rather than the extent of urbanization or the total resources within a jurisdiction are the most salient considerations.[17]

By themselves, the three economic characteristics considered here leave unexplained much of the interstate variation in public policies. This is evident from the generally low co-efficients of multiple determination reported in Table 4. For only two of the 21 dependent variables do the aggregates of economic measures account for at least one-half of the interstate variation; these are the percentage of state and local revenue allocated to the state and the incidence of participation in the federal school lunch program. There remains a substantial component of public policies not explained by economics alone. Some of this unexplained variation is the effect of non-economic regional characteristics.[18]

There is considerable overlap between the concepts of regionalism and economic activity as they are used in this paper. Table 5 shows the average scores, by region, for each economic characteristic. Southern

Table 4
**Coefficients of Partial Correlation and Multiple Determination
between Measures of Economic Status and Public Policies**

	Coefficients of Partial Correlation			
	Personal income/ capita	Personal income	Urban- ization	R^2
Public Policies:				
(1) state expend/capita	.30*	−.29*	−.11	.15
(2) state educ expend/capita	−.02	−.15	.10	.02
(3) state highw expend/capita	.39*	−.29*	−.40*	.32*
(4) state pw expend/capita	−.24	−.06	.24	.07
(5) s + 1 expend/capita	.56*	−.11	−.09	.40*
(6) s + 1 educ expend/capita	.40*	−.17	.05	.26*
(7) s + 1 highw expend/capita	.45*	−.23	−.45*	.33*
(8) s + 1 pw expend/capita	−.19	.05	.20	.06
(9) s + 1 rev to state	−.08	−.45*	−.28	.51*
(10) s + 1 rev from non-local	−.30*	−.27	−.09	.38*
(11) fed/state revenue	.04	−.37*	−.17	.29*
(12) fed/s + 1 revenue	−.29*	−.28	.20	.46*
(13) state taxes	−.44*	−.11	.08	.30*
(14) s + 1 taxes	−.20	.02	.04	.06
(15) property tax	.43*	.07	−.03	.31*
(16) sales tax	−.18	.13	.16	.07
(17) excise tax	.33*	−.25	.04	.18*
(18) motor vehicle tax	.43*	−.19	−.28	.21*
(19) income tax	.29*	.10	−.20	.10
(20) current charges	.42*	−.13	−.19	.18*
(21) debt	.37*	.11	.26	.48*
(22) school lunch	−.58*	−.02	−.23	.62*
(23) vocational educ	−.41*	.07	−.10	.32*
(24) rehab process	−.17	−.06	−.10	.14
(25) rehab success	−.24	−.02	−.12	.21*
(26) attendance	.04	−.22	.40*	.16
(27) school completions	.44*	.05	.03	.35*
(28) exam success	.49*	−.25	−.01	.33*
(29) total roads	.27	−.23	−.49*	.41*
(30) rural roads	.36*	−.20	−.31*	.21*
(31) urban roads	.07	−.24	−.48*	.48*
(32) open I system	.22	.10	−.30*	.09
(33) paved roads	.34*	.14	−.06	.23*
(34) road safety	.08	.11	.35*	.36*
(35) AFDC payment	.50*	.03	.03	.43*
(36) OAA payment	.36*	.00	.11	.31*
(37) APTD payment	.08	.23	.08	.17
(38) AB payment	.46*	−.08	.20	.46*
(39) AFDC recipients	.28	.00	.37*	.46*
(40) OAA recipients	.36*	−.44*	−.01	.27*
(41) APTD recipients	−.15	−.14	.36*	.14
(42) AB recipients	.09	.27	−.04	.12

* Significant at the .05 level

Table 5

Average Scores, by Region, for Each Measure of Economic Status

	Economic Characteristics		
	Personal income/ capita	Personal income ($\times$ 1,000,000)	Urbanization
Regions:			
North	$2,538	$14,195	70.9%
New England	2,393	4,743	66.1
Northeast	2,504	13,818	71.3
Mid-Atlantic	2,793	21,184	76.7
Great Lakes	2,457	18,547	70.7
North Central	2,324	10,677	60.4
Plains	2,229	5,055	53.0
Southeast	1,699	5,833	50.0
South	1,880	6,565	54.7
Southwest	1,960	7,512	69.5
Transmississippi	2,260	6,889	62.0
Mountains	2,153	2,049	60.6
Transplains	2,335	7,033	66.4
Far West	2,749	15,525	71.8

regions take their customary place at the bottom of per capita personal income and urbanization, and the Mountain region scores lowest in total personal income. The Mid-Atlantic region scores highest on each economic scale. As noted above, however, there is economic heterogeneity within the regions. Thus, it may be non-economic aspects of regionalism that produce marked peculiarities in the public policies of state and local governments. An analysis of covariance provides a means for separating the influences on policies from the economic attributes of states and those regional attributes that are not economic in character. Table 6 shows the strength of regional differences while controlling for economics.

The co-efficients of Table 6 indicate that regionalism makes a substantial contribution to the explanation of public policies. In all but eight of the dependent variables, regionalism shows a significant independent relationship with policy while controlling for economics. Table 7 shows average scores, by region, on those measures where regionalism provides a significant independent explanation. By looking at the high and low scoring regions on these measures, it is possible to speculate about the historical backgrounds that have produced the current policies of certain regions.

One combination of traits that lends itself to historical explanation includes the components of government spending, state-local relations and property tax revenue. Several Northern and Eastern regions[19] show relatively low state spending and tax effort (variables 1–3 and 13), a heavy reliance on local governments (9 and 10) and high property tax revenues

Table 6
Analysis of Covariance: Intraclass Correlations between Region and Public Policies while Controlling for Economic Characteristics†

	Regional Demarcation		
	1	2	3
Public Policies:			
(1) state expend/capita	.06	.25*	.37*
(2) state educ expend/capita	.24*	.34*	.45*
(3) state highw expend/capita	.16*	.26*	.28*
(4) state pw expend/capita	.00	.00	—.08
(5) s + 1 expend/capita	.36*	.31*	.45*
(6) s + 1 educ expend/capita	.57*	.43*	.64*
(7) s + 1 highw expend/capita	.32*	.19*	.25*
(8) s + 1 pw expend/capita	.00	.00	—.08
(9) s + 1 rev to state	—.08	.22*	.24*
(10) s + 1 rev from non-local	.10	.35*	.45*
(11) fed/state revenue	.57*	.44*	.35*
(12) fed/s + 1 revenue	.11	.22*	.28*
(13) state taxes	.08	.22*	.24*
(14) s + 1 taxes	.08	.22*	.24*
(15) property tax	.34*	.28*	.39*
(16) sales tax	.05	.06	.08
(17) excise tax	.12	.20*	.23*
(18) motor vehicle tax	.44*	.22*	.15*
(19) income tax	—.09	.02	.00
(20) current charges	.49*	.35*	.31*
(21) debt	.11	.13	.23*
(22) school lunch	.30*	.21*	.09
(23) vocational educ	.40*	.21*	.29*
(24) rehab process	.10	—.03	.09
(25) rehab success	.46*	.28*	.45*
(26) attendance	.02	.07	—.03
(27) school completions	.55*	.64*	.59*
(28) exam success	.81*	.74*	.63*
(29) total roads	.13	.18*	.20*
(30) rural roads	.54*	.39*	.38*
(31) urban roads	.47*	.53*	.29*
(32) open I system	—.05	—.06	.01
(33) paved roads	.21*	.35*	.22*
(34) road safety	.56*	.46*	.54*
(35) AFDC payment	.36*	.20*	.33*
(36) OAA payment	.34*	.21*	.24*
(37) APTD payment	.38*	.21*	.23*
(38) AB payment	.13*	.24*	.08
(39) AFDC recipients	—.06	.02	.15*
(40) OAA recipients	.18*	.17*	.24*
(41) APTD recipients	—.01	.19*	.17*
(42) AB recipients	—.07	—.02	—.02

* Significant at the .05 level

† These data result from three separate analyses, each one made with a different regional demarcation of the states.

Table 7

Average Scores, by Region, on Selected Measures of Public Policy† ‡

Public Policies:	Demarcation #1			Demarcation #2								Demarcation #3			
	North	SoEast	Transmiss	New Eng	Mid-Atlan	SoEast	GrtLakes	Plains	SoWest	Mountns	FarWest	NoEast	South	NoCentral	Transplains
(1) state expend/capita	169	167	200	180	172	167	154	167	196	214	242	168	173	162	225
(2) state educ expend/capita	50	59	70	40	60	59	51	49	80	75	88	42	62	50	84
(3) state high expend/capita	49	44	61	59	40	44	46	56	49	78	60	50	45	52	67
(5) s + 1 expend/capita	326	256	354	328	329	256	321	326	311	372	424	329	268	324	385
(6) s + 1 educ expend/capita	120	93	140	111	123	93	128	127	131	149	161	113	100	127	154
(7) s + 1 higher expend/capita	61	52	76	74	50	52	58	78	58	89	72	65	53	70	77
(9) s + 1 rev to state	38	46	42	46	35	46	30	40	46	44	39	40	46	36	43
(10) s + 1 rev from non-local	54	68	59	55	55	68	51	52	67	61	60	52	67	52	62
(11) fed/state revenue	12	19	15	22	15	19	23	17	21	27	21	15	18	19	24
(12) fed/s + 1 revenue	13	19	18	16	10	19	11	16	19	22	16	14	18	14	20

Table 7 (continued)

	Demarcation #1				Demarcation #2							Demarcation #3			
	North	SoEast	Transmiss	New Eng	Mid-Atlan	SoEast	GrtLakes	Plains	SoWest	Mountns	FarWest	NoEast	South	NoCentral	Transplains
Public Policies:															
(13) state taxes	4.4	6.1	5.1	4.5	4.5	6.1	4.2	4.2	6.2	5.3	5.5	4.3	6.0	4.2	5.6
(14) s + 1 taxes	9.2	9.1	9.9	9.8	8.6	9.1	9.1	9.7	9.9	10.5	9.7	9.5	9.0	9.5	10.2
(15) property tax	116	54	107	125	101	54	120	121	74	115	107	124	58	121	105
(17) excise tax	43	40	40	47	45	40	35	35	41	36	51	46	41	35	42
(18) motor vehicle tax	9.5	6.2	12.9	9.6	8.9	6.2	10.2	12.8	11.4	13.5	13.6	9.3	7.5	11.7	12.8
(20) current charges	31	31	40	25	35	31	33	37	38	39	47	28	32	36	42
(21) debt	459	309	349	425	605	309	353	289	356	292	518	470	364	316	380
(22) school lunch	28	50	36	29	26	50	28	41	34	37	26	27	45	36	33
(23) vocational educ	130	315	231	120	109	315	161	214	241	229	253	107	297	192	223
(25) rehab success	55	111	48	55	70	111	40	48	48	59	33	56	102	45	45
(27) school completions	73	50	75	67	74	50	80	80	66	74	78	70	59	80	74
(28) exam success	83	59	90	84	79	59	86	91	81	94	89	83	64	89	90
(29) total roads	.033	.079	.075	.046	.032	.079	.020	.066	.066	.100	.068	.037	.073	.047	.084
(30) rural roads	.035	.039	.153	.032	.027	.039	.048	.138	.112	.203	.159	.032	.043	.100	.175
(31) urban roads	.0034	.0051	.0062	.0039	.0024	.0051	.0038	.0081	.0054	.0058	.0040	.0032	.0049	.0063	.0049
(33) paved roads	89	67	76	89	84	67	94	84	58	73	84	88	69	88	73
(34) road safety	5870	3710	3440	6840	6200	3710	4800	3760	3160	3090	3590	6650	3880	4190	3180
(35) AFDC payment	147	79	137	147	144	79	149	139	118	143	144	152	87	143	141

Table 7 (continued)

	Demarcation #1			Demarcation #2								Demarcation #3			
	North	SoEast	Transmiss	New Eng	Mid-Atlan	SoEast	GrtLakes	Plains	SoWest	Mountns	FarWest	NoEast	South	NoCentral	Transplains
(36) OAA payment	82	58	84	82	79	58	85	87	76	80	91	83	62	86	82
(37) APTD payment	91	57	79	93	83	57	98	81	81	71	65	92	62	88	70
(38) AB payment	91	61	91	100	82	61	89	89	88	82	107	96	66	89	92
(39) AFDC recipients*	1.9	1.1	1.6	1.7	2.5	1.1	1.6	0.9	1.7	1.7	2.5	2.1	1.2	1.2	2.1
(40) OAA recipients*	1.4	1.3	4.7	2.5	0.9	1.3	0.5	1.8	3.4	6.9	8.2	1.7	1.4	1.2	7.0
(41) APTD recipients*	7.6	7.2	9.4	8.6	7.9	7.2	6.0	4.4	7.2	13.8	14.8	8.5	7.0	5.0	13.1

* Index values showing relative interregional differences but not absolute values of regional scores.

† Policies selected are those where region shows a significant association with the policy, independent of economic characteristics.

‡ For the definition of each variable and its unit of measurement see Table 3.

(15). Southern states[20] score low on the combination of state and local spending (in keeping with their economic characteristics) but they score relatively high on the centralization of state-local relationships (9 and 10), state tax effort (13) and on some measures of state spending (1 and 2). The combination of state-local *decentralization* and heavy property tax reliance in Northern and Eastern regions reflects, in part, the heavy portion of responsibilities historically assumed by local governments in those regions. Religious groups that originally populated the Northern colonies brought with them a local government orientation, and settled their colonies in numbers large enough to support numerous viable local governments. State governments developed in the Northeast on top of a local government base that had operated for as much as 150 years before Independence. As Northerners moved west to the Great Lakes and Plains states they carried their local government traditions with them. Today, states as far west as Nebraska and the Dakotas have numerous local governing bodies that possess significant authority. The high use of the property tax in Northern states reflects their local government orientation and the development of the property tax since the 1930's as the possession of municipal, town and county governments.

While the decentralization of Northern states leads their state governments to spend less money than their economic situations would suggest, the centralization of state-local responsibilities in the state governments of the South promotes a relatively high level of spending and taxation at the state level and a low reliance on the real property tax. The continuing poverty in Southern states has contributed to their dependence on revenues collected and spent at the state level, but the state dependence of Southern policies has a colonial origin. The early period in the South differed significantly from that of Northern states; settlements in the South were relatively sparse, diffuse and centered economically on private plantations rather than in towns or cities. At the time of Independence there was much less of a local government base in the South than in the Northern colonies.

On the measures of educational policy, states in the Northeastern region score lower on the use of vocational education than is suggested by their economic characteristics alone, and states in the Mountain region score higher on the measures of exam success and school completion than is suggested by their economic characteristics. In the case of the Northeast's lack of vocational education, the explanation may lie in the heavy use of private education that is found in the area. States such as New Hampshire, Rhode Island, Massachusetts, New York, New Jersey and Pennsylvania are among the highest users of private education in the country; the parents who educate their children in parochial or other private schools generally remove them from contact with vocational programs. The high scores of Mountain states on the measures of school completion and exam success reflect the high performance of Utah (and to a lesser extent neighboring states) on these and other indicators of educational interest. Perhaps the educational orientations of Mormons have left their mark on the success of state and local education activities.

On the measure of payments for Aid to Families of Dependent Children, states in the Southeast score even lower than expected on the basis of economics alone. Southeastern states score low on all the welfare payments, but lowest of all (relative to other regions) on the measure of AFDC payment. This finding may reflect the racial effect that attaches to AFDC. More than in the case of other welfare offerings, Southern welfare officials must defend their AFDC programs against the attacks of conservative state legislators. As a former state welfare director in one Southern state told this author, "At one point we even had to tell the legislators that 40% of the AFDC beneficiaries were white."

Although there is a positive relationship between the measure of state and local government debt per capita and the economic measures (see Table 3), the Great Lakes states (among the nation's wealthiest) show relatively low scores on debt. This finding may reflect the fiscal conservatism that has prevailed in such states as Ohio, Illinois, Indiana and Wisconsin, leaving strong constitutional prohibitions or restrictions against the use of "full faith and credit" indebtedness.

SUMMARY AND CONCLUSIONS

This article has specified relationships among three measures of economic activity, regional location and forty-two measures for state and local government expenditures, taxes and indebtedness, intergovernmental financial relations, and levels of public service in the fields of education, highways and public welfare. Also, it has identified instances where regional phenomena make a significant contribution to the explanation of interstate differences in policy, that is independent of current economic characteristics of the regions.

The measures of economic activity, especially per capita personal income, show substantial relationships with most measures of public policy. However, economics alone leaves unexplained many of the policy characteristics of the states. Regional affiliations of the states show important relationships with most of the policy items considered here.

By itself, "regionalism" is not a satisfying explanation for public policies. Yet when they are viewed along with other information about the American states, the regional findings of this article provide important clues about the determinants of governmental activity. The saliency of the regional variable seems to reflect the importance of shared historical experiences and the regional orientation of state and local authorities. Insofar as public officials receive many of their policy cues from regional, rather than national reference groups,[21] it is necessary to weigh heavily the likelihood that historical experiences shared by neighboring states have had a lasting impact on public policies. The historic decentralization of government in the Northeastern states reveals itself in relatively low levels of state government expenditures and tax effort and a heavy reliance on property taxes. In contrast, a historic inclination to centralize public programs in the South shows itself in high state tax effort and a higher level of state government expenditures than is expected on the basis of economic conditions alone. Also in the South, the welfare program to aid families of dependent children seems to have run afoul of the region's racial biases, and that program is less well developed than other welfare activities.

This article makes no claim to identify the specific features associated with each region (independent of current economic levels) that provide the explanation of current policies. The speculations about the antecedents of several regional peculiarities provide only a few examples of the historical roots that might help to explain current policies. By searching for other policy roots in a regional framework, it may be possible to add substantially to the current understanding of state and local government activities.

While the focus of this study has been on static relationships between economics, regions and public policies in the American states, it has potential application for a broader range of experience. The findings in behalf of regionalism point to the staying power of government policies, and suggest limits to the impact that economic development may have on public policies.[22] To those who expect great changes to occur in government programs in response to increases in industrialization and personal well-being, this article should suggest some qualifications. Policies formed in the past may have considerable resistance to dramatic change, especially when they are accepted throughout a region and benefit from officials' inclinations to take their cues from regional neighbors.

NOTES

[1] Grants from the Social Science Research Council Committee on Governmental and Legal Processes and the University of Georgia Office of General Research provided the funds for this research.

204   *Determinants of Public Policy*

² Solomon Fabricant, *The Trend of Government Activity in the United States since 1900* (New York: National Bureau of Economic Research, 1952); Glenn W. Fisher, "Interstate Variation in State and Local Government Expenditures," *National Tax Journal,* 17 (1964), 57–74; Seymour Sachs and Robert Harris, "The Determinants of State and Local Expenditures and Intergovernmental Flow of Funds," *National Tax Journal,* 17 (1964), 75–85.

³ Thomas R. Dye, *Politics, Economics and the Public: Policy Outcomes in the American States* (Chicago: Rand McNally, 1966); Richard I. Hofferbert, "The Relation between Public Policy and Some Structural and Environmental Variables in the American States," *American Political Science Review,* 15 (1966), 73–82; Richard E. Dawson and James A. Robinson, "Interparty Competition, Economic Variables and Welfare Politics in the American States," *Journal of Politics,* 25 (1963), 265–89.

⁴ For example, it is generally in the wealthier states that state and local governments spend the highest amounts per capita. However, state and local governments in the relatively poor states of North and South Dakota spend above the national average, and governments in the relatively wealthy states of Indiana, Ohio and Illinois spend below the national average.

⁵ For a discussion of the political geology of America, see Daniel J. Elazar, *American Federalism: A View from the States* (New York: Thomas Y. Crowell, 1966), especially Chapter 4.

⁶ As part of a survey among budget officers of 67 major agencies in the Southern states of Florida, Georgia, Kentucky and Mississippi, an attempt was made to identify the states that served as the budgeteers' reference group. One question asked, "Have you or any of your colleagues contacted officials in other states in an attempt to learn how they deal with a particular situation that you have encountered in your work?" Where a budget officer answered in the affirmative, he was asked, "What states do you feel are the best sources of information?" The 67 respondents made 198 nominations of states that were their best sources of information. Most of their nominations (87%) were in the region that includes the 11 states of the Confederacy and the border states of Delaware, Maryland, Kentucky, West Virginia and Oklahoma; 35% of the nominations were states that bordered directly on the respondents' states! While it is conceivable that Southern officials are more parochial in their perceptions than those in other sections of the country, officials elsewhere (questioned informally about their reference-states) likewise referred primarily to states that are immediate or near neighbors.

⁷ The three states of northern New England are akin to several Southern or Western states in their levels of personal income and urbanization more than to Massachusetts, Rhode Island and Connecticut. Yet all the New England states have had common ethnic and religious backgrounds, as well as histories of early settlement and statehood, that may be critical for certain policy developments. In the South, Texas and Florida show several economic discontinuities with their neighbors; but the common background of Civil War, Reconstruction and racial tensions may have produced uniform regional responses to policy questions. In the Plains, Missouri and South Dakota show great differences in their present economic characteristics, but they both had frontier experiences that included grazing, wide-open towns and then settled agriculture. And in the Mountains the neighboring states of Colorado and New Mexico now exhibit markedly different levels of personal income and industrialization, but they had similar economic backgrounds of trapping, grazing and mining.

⁸ Some of the measures considered below combine the activities of state and local governments within each state. It is true that these actually mask decisions that are made in the arenas of state or local governments, but they are suitable in light of the combined participation of state and local authorities in the provision of major services. See Morton Grodzins, *The American System: A New View of Government in the United States,* ed. Daniel J. Elazar (Chicago: Rand McNally, 1966), Chapter 1.

[9] Philip H. Burch finds that population size is the best measure of traffic that is conveniently available, and it is used here. See his *Highway Revenue and Expenditure Policy in the United States* (New Brunswick, N.J.: Rutgers University Press, 1962), p. 23.

[10] Sources include: U.S. Bureau of the Census, *Statistical Abstract of the United States, 1964; Census of Governments, 1962: Compendium of Government Finances;* Council of State Governments, *The Book of the States, 1964–1965;* National Education Assocation, *Ranking of the States, 1963*. Because this study is part of a larger effort concerned with public policies throughout the twentieth century, the states of Alaska and Hawaii are excluded.

[11] See the sources cited above in Notes 2 and 3, plus Harvey S. Perloff, Edgar S. Dunn, Jr., Eric E. Lampard and Richard F. Muth, *Regions, Resources and Economic Growth* (Baltimore: Johns Hopkins University Press, 1962).

[12] The computer program employed is "Multiple Regression with Case Combinations: BMDO3R," *BMD Biomedical Computer Programs* (Los Angeles: University of California, 1965), pp. 258–75.

[13] Perloff, *et al., op. cit.* While the component states of Perloff's regions remain unchanged, his "West" is called "Transmississippi" here to eliminate confusion with other designations. For a similar reason, the region that the Census Bureau names "West" is called "Transplains" here.

[14] The analysis follows the procedures explained in Hubert M. Blalock, *Social Statistics* (New York: McGraw-Hill, 1959), Chapter 20. The computer program employed is "Analysis of Covariance with Multiple Covariates: BMDO4V," *op. cit.,* pp. 525–42.

[15] See Notes 2 and 3.

[16] The sizable negative relationships between economic activities and federal aid (variables 11 and 12) reflect the allocation formulae built into many of the grant programs; they redistribute economic resources from wealthy to poorer states. The negative relationships between economics and certain educational and highway service measures (variables 22–25, and 29–31) may reflect the program effects of these federal formulae. In education especially, it is the programs that receive much of their support from the federal government that show an inverse relationship with economic resources. The substance of these programs for inexpensive school lunches, vocational education and vocational rehabilitation seems particularly suited to populations that score low on measures of economic welfare and the magnitude of available resources. The negative relationships between economics and the highway programs may likewise reflect this federal effect, or they may reflect an allocation of funds by governments in developed states to construct relatively little total road mileage and in particular relatively little urban mileage.

The negative relationships between economics and the centralization of state-local finances at the state level (variables 9 and 10) may reflect the differential access of state and local governments to economic resources, and the economic dependence of the tax base that is legally available to local authorities. The temptation in a poor state to grant a high percentage of state-local financial obligations to state agencies results from the access of state authorities to the economic resources of the entire state. In poor states, numerous local governments (especially in rural counties) are hard pressed to support a satisfactory level of services on the economic base that lies within their jurisdiction. Perhaps because some localities must rely on state aid in such states, local governments generally are inclined to rely on the revenues of state-collected income and sales taxes in order to minimize the problems associated with high local property taxes. Moreover, the tax on real property is defined by state constitutions as the bulwark of most local government revenue systems, and this tax more than others (as demonstrated in Table 3) shows a substantial direct association with the level of economic activity. Public services in poor states, therefore, seem to rely on state financing because local officials face legal restrictions against their use of

206 *Determinants of Public Policy*

a non-property tax, and economic problems in raising substantial revenues from the property tax.

The lack of significant economic relationships with expenditures of state governments (variables 1–4) may reflect the fact that state governments are less dependent than local governments on economic conditions. As noted above, state authorities benefit from access to a more extensive and varied economy than local officials and from their legal opportunities to choose from a greater variety of revenue sources.

[17] An exception occurs in the case of highway expenditures and policies (variables 3, 7, 29–32). Here there are strong independent relationships with measures of urbanization. The dispersion of population that is characteristic of a rural state may present physical demands for extensive road networks (relative to population size) that are overwhelming in the perceptions of policy-makers.

[18] The analysis of covariance technique identifies instances of *significant* relationship between the dependent variables and the nominal characteristic (region) while controlling for economics. However, it does not identify the percentage of variance explained by the nominal characteristic. And used throughout this study, the concept of statistical significance is not, strictly speaking, correct. Because the 48 states represent a universe, rather than a sample chosen to reflect a larger universe, the tests of significance are useful only in pointing out relationships that may be considered "sizable."

[19] Including North, Northeast, Northcentral, Mid-Atlantic, Great Lakes and Plains.

[20] Including South, Southeast and Southwest.

[21] See Note 6 and the text preceding it.

[22] For a discussion of the influence from past spending decisions over current spending decisions, see the author's "Economic and Political Correlates of State Government Expenditures: General Tendencies and Deviant Cases," *Midwest Journal of Political Science,* 11 (May, 1967), 173–92; and "Some More Thoughts About the Determinants of Government Expenditures," *National Tax Journal,* 20 (June, 1967), 171–79.

PART FIVE

Determinants of Public Policy:
Individual Actors and Institutions
in the Policy Process

CHAPTER 11

Roles and Symbols in the Determination of State Expenditures

Thomas J. Anton

Despite growing appreciation of the significance of state government expenditures, relatively little is known about the manner in which state officials decide to spend public money. The few available reports, however, reach remarkably similar conclusions in different states, at different times. Agency or department officials, budget review officers, governors and legislatures take actions which appear to vary within rather narrow limits, regardless of the peculiarities of the state under consideration. These similarities of behavior on the part of financial officials in several states suggest the possibility of developing a model of expenditure decision-making that may have widespread relevance. My first purpose here, then, is to develop such a model, using the concept "role" to summarize actions which occur repeatedly and which appear to be structured by essentially similar goals. My second purpose is to assess the significance of the symbols around which these roles appear to be organized. Though necessarily tentative, such an assessment may help to clarify the characteristic responses of state actors to a common financial predicament.

ROLES

State Agency Officials

I take it that no one will be shocked by the proposition that the goals of those who administer operating agencies will vary along a continuum ranging from maintenance of currently-available resources to expansion of those resources as much and as quickly as possible. At the moment this

Reprinted from the *Midwest Journal of Political Science,* Vol. XI, No. 1 (February, 1967), pp. 27–43, "Roles and Symbols in the Determination of State Expenditures," by Thomas J. Anton, by permission of the Wayne State University Press and the author. Copyright © 1967 by the Wayne State University Press.

proposition rests mostly on faith, since adequately documented accounts of agency budget preparation in the states are exceedingly rare. On the other hand, my data provide supporting evidence with regard to agency officials in Illinois;[1] Allen Schick has reported findings of a similar nature in his survey of several eastern states;[2] and Rufus Browning has documented both extremes of the continuum in his study of two Wisconsin departments.[3] Browning quotes officials in the more expansive of his two departments as follows:

We don't hesitate to lay our problems on the line. I would not refrain from reflecting a need.

The budget is supposed to reflect the judgment of the administrator. There is no point in playing it cozy in trying to second-guess everybody along the line.

The budget should reflect only felt needs, nothing more, or less.

I usually put in something even if it has little chance of being approved. I think we should put all our needs before the department.[4]

I do not want to suggest that all agencies will be equally expansive; the data collected by both Browning and others demonstrate some considerable variety in agency aspirations. But I do have a good deal of confidence in the assertion that very few responsible agency administrators will be likely to request *less* money than is currently available to them. This is not simply because standards of service are rising, along with the increasing professionalization of state government. It is also, and in some sense more fundamentally, because budget requests are prepared by people whose organizational status is tied to, and reflected in, publicly available budget figures. To request a smaller budget than the current budget is to suggest that the job being done by the agency is not sufficiently important to warrant a greater claim on state resources and that the administrator in charge of that job is not sufficiently aggressive (or competent) to make the claim. Agency personnel, whose salaries are paid by public funds because they are presumably performing a needed public service, are threatened by the former implication, while the latter constitutes a direct threat to the agency administrator himself. As a budget officer once remarked to me, "We pay some of these men [hospital superintendents] better than twenty thousand each year and we expect them to be knowledgeable enough to know where and how things could be done better and to come in here with requests for improved and expanded programs. If they didn't, we'd probably think that we needed to get new people."[5]

The pressure for agency budget expansion is intensified by the public nature of budgetary decisions. However secretive the process of preparing requests may be within agencies, the final disposition of those requests will either be made in public or reflected in public documents such as budget books or appropriation bills. This forces the agency administrator to be attentive to several different public audiences. One audience is composed of the agency's employees, who will look to the agency budget for some indication of how well the chief administrator is protecting their—and his—status. Another audience is composed of the agency's clientele group, if there is one, who will judge the agency in terms of a budget in which they have a direct financial interest. The third, and probably most important audience, is composed of those officials who must review the budget request —particularly those officials who are elected to office.

Requesting an increase in funds is the surest method available to the administrator to satisfy each of these audiences. Such action affirms the significance and protects the status of agency employees, assures clientele groups that new and higher standards of service are being pursued aggressively, and eases the burdens felt by reviewing officials in dealing with programs about which they may have little knowledge. Should the proposed increase be eliminated, the agency administrator can hold reviewing officials to blame, without any harm to his own position, precisely because he has made an effort that is publicly documented. Should the increase be granted, the administrator can properly take credit for the expansion resulting from his initiative.

Budget Review Officers

Whether or not agency administrators are in fact expansive in the preparation of budget estimates, it is reasonably clear that the persons who review estimates believe them to be expansive. Once again we are indebted to Allen Schick's paper for the best evidence on this point. Schick's multistate examination of budget practices revealed what he called "the control orientation." Responding to the question "Which of these two functions do you consider *more* important for your budget office: (1) To serve as watchdog of the Treasury, or (2) To assist the agencies to perform their responsibilities more economically and effectively?" the officials interviewed by Schick indicated that the watchdog function was a more accurate description of actual budget practices. "According to this view," writes Schick, "there is so much built-in pressure for expansion that there must be a specialized agency with the task of saying 'No.' This responsibility falls upon the budget office which then must bear the onus of cutting departmental requests, curbing expenditures, and otherwise asserting central control."[6]

Recognizing the strength of built-in pressures to expand budgets, then, and believing that these pressures will be reflected in budget requests,

212   *Determinants of Public Policy*

reviewing officials naturally see themselves as "cutters." Having experienced the results of this orientation, agency administrators react in a time-honored fashion that Schick describes succinctly: "The agencies, anticipating a cut, over-estimate their needs and pad the budget, while the budget office, in the conviction that the budget is padded, makes deep cuts in the agency estimates."[7]

To explain the apparent negativism of budget review officials solely in terms of their mistrust of agency budget estimates, however, would be to overlook the personal and political stake they have in doing what they do. Review officers, too, must play to several audiences, including agency administrators, the governor, and the legislature. Their failure to make the cuts others expect them to make would challenge the grounds for the existence of specialized review agencies and thus threaten the jobs they hold. Moreover, so long as agency administrators cooperate by requesting increases over current appropriation levels, review officers can cut away at those increases, secure in the knowledge that they are doing no damage to ongoing operations. Budgetary reductions administered in this fashion may not reduce the cost of state government but they do protect the status of reviewing officials and they do help to generate public assurance that the diet of those who feed at the public trough is not overly rich.

These speculations about the meaning of budget review are buttressed by the general absence of an alternative philosophy of budgeting among the states and the general absence of the informational and institutional means of developing an alternative philosophy. Paul Appleby's justly-famous defense of budgetary negativism asserts the utility of special institutions to represent the values of "fiscal sense and fiscal coordination," but makes no attempt to specify the meaning of these values—apart from the assertion of strong opposition to "program and expenditure expansion."[8] Appleby calls this "a specialized way of looking at problems in decision-making," thus providing a rationalization for the convenient division of labor which I suspect exists in most American states: Agencies press for expansion using programmatic criteria while budget review officers attempt to negate expansion using financial criteria. But neither set of criteria produces the expected consequences. Significant programmatic and budgetary expansion takes place when money is available to fund it, while significant expenditure reductions take place when there is sufficient hostility to programs to force a cutback in expenditures. Meanwhile, since neither dramatic expansion nor dramatic reduction takes place very often, programmatic and financial justifications are used less as criteria for decisions than as symbolic shields, behind which agency administrators and budget officials both play a game of organizational status maintenance.

Governors

What does a governor have to do with the process by which his state's expenditures are determined? The best answer, it seems to me, is "very little." This conclusion is based, in part, on Shadoan's report that governors in some of the states she visited were singularly uninterested in what went into the state budget.[9] A far more important source of support, however, derives from documented accounts of the behavior of governors who were vitally interested in expenditures for which they were responsible: Freeman,[10] Harriman,[11] Rockefeller[12] and Kerner.[13] Fragmented and incomplete as these reports may be, they do offer some striking insights into the kinds of predicaments governors are likely to face and the regularities of their responses to such predicaments.

We all know, of course, that nearly all of the states have long since adopted the executive budget system, which authorizes governors to review agency spending proposals and holds governors responsible for preparation of what is supposed to be a comprehensive spending program. The pre-eminence granted by these formal arrangements, however, is seldom easy to achieve. The governor will probably come to his position without any direct experience in dealing with state finance. His own inexperience will thus provide a sharp contrast to the wisdom of the old hands who occupy administrative and legislative positions of influence, and who will probably regard the governor as an outsider—a "new boy," come to muddle in their affairs. Moreover, since the average length of service for most governors is less than five years,[14] the old hands can confidently think of the "new boy" as someone who is likely to be gone from the scene far in advance of their own departure. Neither the governor's lack of financial sophistication nor the ambiguity about his staying power is likely to encourage a warm reception from the old hands. The new boy must prove himself first, and he must do so in the face of a formidable array of obstacles.

The first—and probably most important—obstacle is the truly staggering complexity of the state's system of financial bookkeeping. Constitutional limitations, marvelously incoherent divisions of financial accountability, incomprehensible budget documents and, worst of all, an intricate maze of general funds, special funds, revolving funds, loan funds, trust funds, federal funds, local funds, all conspire to shroud the state's financial situation in mystery. Illinois, with only forty or so (the number changes from biennium to biennium) special funds to worry about in addition to the general purpose fund, is perhaps more fortunate than most states in this respect. But consider Connecticut, which finances expenditures from roughly 100 funds (only 5 of which are included in the budget), or

Wyoming, where no less than 168 special funds are used to support state spending.[15] The governor who hopes to fight for financial righteousness in these circumstances will surely be hard-put to locate the battlefield, let alone lead his forces to victory.

Given time, of course, any governor can come to some reasonably adequate understanding of these matters. But time is precisely what the governor does not have, at least in his first term. Presentation of the governor's budget typically is required at some point early in the legislative session following the governor's election to office and is typically the first major action taken by the governor. He will thus have no more than six to twelve weeks in which to learn what he must learn and incorporate that learning, if he can, into his first budget. Difficult enough in its own terms, this problem is made enormously more difficult by the realization that the old hands will be watching the new boy for signs of his political skill—as will the governor's political enemies and the general public. In view of the relative brevity of the governor's stay in office, impressions generated by his handling of his first budget are likely to remain influential during his entire tenure. Should these first impressions suggest less-than-adequate skill, the governor will have lost a good part of the battle almost before it began.[16]

Even assuming a willingness and competence to learn, however, the governor will probably conclude that there is very little he can do to control state spending. Other elected state officers, the legislature and the courts will be beyond his reach. Similarly, expenditures from special funds will be practically, if not always legally, impossible to control. Some idea of what this can mean for a governor may be gleaned from the fact that three-fifths of the states finance upwards of 50 percent of their total expenditures from such special funds.[17] What is left, then, is general fund expenditures, but since these are typically concentrated in two or three large programs or agencies—welfare and education, primarily—which cannot be abandoned, the proportion of the general fund open to significant influence by the governor may well turn out to be a minuscule part of total spending. And even this may be affected more directly by national economic trends than by anything the governor does or doesn't do; witness the experience of both Harriman and Rockefeller in New York.[18]

These situational constraints help to explain the curiously unreal quality of gubernatorial action. Governors typically campaign on platforms stressing, among other things, increased service (i.e., program expansion) and increased economy. Once in office, however, they typically find it impossible to accomplish either of these objectives. Freeman in Minnesota, Harriman and Rockefeller in New York, and Kerner in Illinois all promised to initiate new programs; all found, or claimed to find, their states in a condition of near bankruptcy; each had all he could do to find sufficient revenues to finance current operations, *after* putting aside plans for expanded activities.[19] A major factor in their inability to implement new programs, of course, was the built-in increase in the cost of existing programs. They all struggled to find more money for education because more students *were there,* waiting to be educated; they all struggled to find more money for state agencies because state personnel *were there,* waiting for salary-step increases; they struggled variously to find more money for activities such as welfare or capital construction because more clients *were there,* waiting to be serviced. Nothing the governors did or said affected these conditions. Instead, precisely the reverse was the case, for these conditions eliminated the possibility of either new programs or significant economies. The public statements of the governors nevertheless continued to use the rhetoric of "increased service and greater economy"—a curious and significant fact to which I will shortly return.[20]

By and large, then, governors do not "determine" expenditures, in the sense of looking at most state activities and deciding to reduce, continue or expand them. Rather, the exigencies of their situation force them to focus most of their attention on revenue, which typically must be increased just to keep pace with existing programs. This is an important—indeed crucial —problem, but it need not entail a very close examination of where state money goes. The need for more money can be established without difficulty in most states and, once established, the governor's attention is necessarily drawn to what he must regard as the more sensitive problem. Most states, after all, legally require a balanced budget. But even if legal obligation is absent, public concern for "fiscal integrity" will control the image pursued by the chief of state. Governors may be regarded as "money providers" or as "budget balancers"; only infrequently can they be viewed as "decision-makers" in the determination of state expenditures.

Legislatures

Like governors, state legislatures tend to focus what attention they give to state finance on the problem of revenue, and for similar reasons. Lacking the staff personnel required to cope with the intended and unintended complexities of state financial documents, legislatures typically know very little about what is contained in such documents. Constrained by constitution or by custom to dispose of major appropriations within a limited period of time, legislatures have little opportunity to do anything but approve the expenditures recommended by the governor. Occasionally a legislature will rise up, axe in hand, and begin chopping away indiscriminately at a governor's budget recommendations. However, such behavior is primarily aimed at the general public, which expects legislators to be "economy minded," and is easily circumvented by the executive. Thus, whether in Kentucky, where the last budget was introduced on Tuesday and passed by the following Friday,[21] or in New York, where the legislature normally requires only two days to approve the budget,[22] or in Illinois, where defeat for *any* appropriation bill is almost unheard of,[23] legislative participation in the determination of state expenditure is virtually non-existent.

On the other hand, legislatures are being drawn increasingly into the search for new revenue. For legislators, as for governors, the question of "who shall pay?" is more sensitive than the question "for what?" precisely because it fits more easily into the conventional platitudes which structure public expectations about state finance. Above all, legislatures must act in a "responsible" manner, by providing the governor with sufficient funds to operate the government—or else provide a publicly acceptable rationale for failing to do so. Since the general public knows very little about state programs, either choice (i.e., approving or not approving the revenue requested by the governor) can be rationalized as something which "provides necessary services," at "the most economical level," consistent with "efficient and sound management practices," taking care all the while to "maintain a favorable tax climate for industry" without sacrificing "equity" in the revenue structure. And since either choice can be so rationalized, the choice that is ultimately made will turn less on the activities to be supported at some higher level than on the question of who will be given credit or blame for providing that higher level of support. A legislature controlled by the opposition party can be expected to attempt to prevent the governor from receiving the credit for expanding activities or to blame him for increasing taxes—hence the common executive-legislative disputes over revenue. Legislative actions thus help to provide the money necessary for budgetary expansion, though the grounds for such actions seldom have anything to do with the activities to be financed by such expansion.

TOWARD A DRAMATURGICAL VIEW OF STATE EXPENDITURE POLITICS

These speculations persuade me that there are significant uniformities in the behavior of officials involved in determining expenditures for American state governments. A peek into the decision-making black box in most states, I submit, would probably reveal a system in which operating agency heads consistently request more funds, executive and/or legislative reviewers consistently reduce agency requests, governors consistently pursue balanced budgets at higher expenditure levels, and legislatures consistently approve higher appropriations while engaging in frequent disputes with the governor over revenues. From a process point of view, the operations of most of these systems could probably be summarized in terms which would closely resemble the "incrementalism" model developed by Professor Lindblom and others: marginal rather than fundamental changes, determined by piecemeal rather than comprehensive calculations.[24] From a structural point of view, the operations of these systems would probably not be inconsistent with the widespread belief that decision-making power has become concentrated in the hands of actors in the executive rather than the legislative branch of American governments.

Perhaps the most significant aspect of such systems is the contrast between what state officials actually do and the public statements or symbols used to rationalize their behavior. Agency administrators, I suggested, typically justify proposed budgetary increases on programmatic grounds, yet the frequency with which they propose increases for which they do not expect approval belies a rather difficult goal: protection against the adverse consequences of cutting a request that contains no increases that can be cut. In similar fashion, review officers—including the governor—justify the reductions they impose in terms of economy and efficiency, but their failure to prevent rapid and large-scale appropriation increases suggests that they, too, have a different operating goal: preservation of their peculiar status within an environment that knows no other justification for such a status. Governors and legislatures make use of both programmatic and management symbols, though their principal activities are aimed at increasing revenues in order to balance budgets which seldom show any evidence of either new programs or management efficiency. From budget request to final appropriation, every action is rationalized in terms which mask its true meaning.

In this sense the symbols themselves are deceptive, but it would be quite unfair to accuse state officials of a conscious intent to deceive. The realities of state politics are more complex than that. Reality number one is that states have lost effective control over their expenditures. Complex structures of special funds that are difficult to understand and more difficult to change, coupled with heavy investment in existing activities that must be continued, make up an expenditure base that leaves little room for innovation, particularly since this base contains built-in pressures for increases that strain state tax resources. Increases beyond those that are built in typically occur as a result of circumstances that, from the state point of view, are fortuitous: Congress passes a massive federal-state highway program that pulls the state to dramatically higher highway expenditures, a riot in the streets triples a state's expenditure for human relations programs, a massive campaign to "do something" about state mental health hospitals, led by private citizens, doubles state appropriations for such hospitals.[25] Initiative for such changes comes from actors in the external environment, who pull state actors along after the fact. Not infrequently, disagreement among state actors over the question of revenue enables the state to exercise a veto over the rate of expansion desired by external actors. But even here, the possibility of appeal to other sources of public funds—particularly federal aid—frequently permits these actors to soften the effects of a state veto. Thus state actors not only have given up a great deal of their power to initiate major changes in expenditure, but they also have lost much of their power to act as a brake on public spending.

Because the power to control the course of financial events has been lost, state actions designed to influence those events take on a peculiar quality of uncertainty.[26] A budget reviewer eliminates a request for funds submitted by an agency only to discover (perhaps) later that the activity for which the funds were requested has been carried on anyway, using some of the "free floating" money made available to the agency by the federal government. Who was responsible? Was it the agency head? Was it the federal government? Or was it the budget office, which failed to keep track of what was going on in the agency? A governor of the sovereign State of New York submits a budget full of new and expanded services, only to discover later that a moderate economic depression has eliminated the new revenue with which he had planned to finance the new services. Who was responsible for the failure to implement the governor's plans? Was it the governor, whose estimates of revenue turned out to be so wrong? Was it the Federal Reserve Board, or General Motors? Was it anybody? A governor of Illinois, anxious to conserve his state's dwindling financial resources, orders a "freeze" on the hiring of new employees, but discovers later that his order has reduced neither employees nor expenditures. Should the governor be held responsible for the failure of his directive? Should uncooperative agency heads bear the blame? Or perhaps it is the state's constitutional and legal system, which tolerates the existence of eighteen different personnel systems, many of which are beyond the scope of gubernatorial influence.[27]

These examples, of course, have been simplified to the point of caricature, but the caricature itself has a point, for in none of these cases is it at all clear that the actions of state officials had any significant impact on future events. Nor is it at all clear that future events would have been different in the absence of those actions. Expenditures for state employment might have been the same, whether or not the governor ordered a freeze; the activities of the State of New York might have been the same, whether or not new programs were proposed by the governor; agency activities might have been the same, whether or not a budget office reduction was imposed. From a public point of view, uncertainty about the effects of actions taken by state officials means that fixing responsibility for such actions is impossible: an appeal to some environmental force or internal complexity is always available to an official seeking to avoid responsibility, while his attempt to assume responsibility can always be challenged on the same grounds. And from the point of view of the actors themselves, uncertainty about the effects of their actions deprives them of an important source of feedback from the real world. How is a budget officer or governor to evaluate his judgments if they are not carried out? How can a governor evaluate his plans for new programs if they are not implemented? What, indeed, are the criteria of "success" or "failure" in a world in which budgets are balanced or unbalanced and programs initiated or stopped at least as much by uncontrollable external events as by the conscious actions of the officials who are presumably in charge?

The answer, it seems to me, lies precisely in the symbols used by state actors to rationalize and justify their public behavior: the budget as a symbol of Responsibility; the cut, as a symbol of Economy; and the increase, as a symbol of Service. What is at stake in the performance of the roles discussed above is not so much the distribution of resources, about which state actors have little to say, but the distribution of symbolic satisfaction among the involved actors and the audiences which observe their stylized behavior.[28]

To a mass public which has been taught to believe that there is "someone" in charge of the government and that there must be a "reason" for every governmental act, the budget document itself provides reassurance that these beliefs are valid. Prepared by a gubernatorial staff agency, presented with a ceremonial flourish that typically involves a joint legislative session to receive the governor's budget message from his own lips, and widely-publicized by the mass media as "the governor's" program, the budget is popularly identified with a single official, who is presumed to be the "someone" in charge. The guarantee that this program has been rationally conceived is provided by the great masses of figures contained in the document. Whether these figures result from careful calculation or, as is frequently the case, from more or less wild guesses is beside the point, for it is the specificity of the number rather than its source which warrants its rationality. However fuzzy the thinking behind any given figure may have been, its representation as a specific dollar-and-cents figure implies precise measurement of quantifiable factors, leading to this—and no other—sum.

For those who are closest to the centers of decision—and who are therefore in a position to know how unscientific the budget can be—it is not the document which offers symbolic satisfaction, but the process of putting it together. The constantly recurring cycle of financial activity provides an anticipated series of occasions for action, as well as a series of settings in which such action will take place. Visitations in the director's office, or the governor's office, legislative chambers, committee hearing rooms, and public forums of various kinds all provide settings in which the actors can display the behavior appropriate to their respective roles. The busyness of such activities together with the official secrecy which shrouds the decisions made in many of these settings reinforce the public impression that important matters are being dealt with by powerful men. It is similarly reinforcing for the actors themselves, whose long hours and frequently feverish work help to maintain their belief that the roles they play are in fact both powerful and important. In all these respects the budget, as document and process, creates symbolic satisfaction built upon the idea that affairs of state are being dealt with, that responsibility is being exercised, and that rationality prevails.

As the principal symbol of economy, the cut is especially favored by legislative actors, though it is in fact utilized more frequently by governors and budget officers. Governors and budget officers, however, have recourse to other powerful symbols of responsibility (i.e., the balanced budget, or "prudent management"), whereas legislative actors do not. The satisfactions derived from the cut are therefore largely monopolized by legislators. Grounded in the folklore of "rampant bureaucracy," building "empires" through "padded budgets" which "waste the hard-earned dollar of the taxpayer," and fed by the demand for "a dollar's worth of service for every dollar spent," the cut symbolizes a popular check on governmental excess. The cut may be specifically aimed at a program or a payroll, or it may be a meat-axe reduction designed to reduce all requests by some stated percentage. In either case it provides reassurances to legislators and to the mass public that their joint concern for economy has been implemented.

The overt and stylized distrust of public spending creates the need for another symbol to account for the obvious inability of state actors to prevent expansion of total state expenditures. The need is met by resorting to the imagery of "services" provided by the recurring increases. Since additional revenues are frequently required for the support of these expanding "services," opportunities for conflict are regularly provided. But since there is seldom disagreement over the propriety of performing the services (recall that most increases arise from built-in pressure for expansion), the issue involved in such disputes is not "what will be done?" but "who will receive credit?" for services that everyone accepts as necessary. A classic case involves the problem of state aid for local schools. When the governor and the legislature are on opposite sides of the political fence a good deal of maneuvering can be expected before the "credit" issue is resolved. Thus, a premature announcement by Republican legislative leaders in New York of a school aid plan more generous than the governor's forced Harriman's hand. According to Herzberg and Tillett, Harriman ". . . felt betrayed and explained with some heat that he did not want to be parsimonious toward the localities and certainly did not wish to appear less favorably disposed toward local education than the Legislature." Harriman's solution may be regarded as symbolic perfection: "The Governor immediately endorsed the Republican proposals publicly in a statement which seemed to suggest that he had expected such proposals, had agreed to them in advance, and had shared in their origin."[29]

Because revenues are so inherently unpredictable, their involvement in the symbolism of "increased services" frequently provides opportunities for the manufacture and distribution of an important subsidiary symbol: competence, or the lack of it. Revenue predictions can always be attacked as too high or too low, particularly where there exists a past record of inaccurate projections. The stylized forms in which such attacks and counterattacks are expressed typically involve legislative charges that: a) revenues have been miscalculated by the governor, b) needed programs can be carried on without additional expenditures, and c) gubernatorial incompetence or deceit explains the new revenue requests. Gubernatorial responses typically involve charges that a) legislators are "playing politics" with the poor, the school children, etc., b) new revenues are required to provide necessary services, and c) legislators are not fully informed (i.e., are incompetent).[30] An example taken from the most recent legislative season in Illinois provides a nice illustration of these symbolic themes.

Governor Kerner's budget for 1965–67 included the sum of $27 million for state participation in a federally-aided program of special education for the culturally disadvantaged. There was no disagreement about the desirability of the program but at the end of the session the Republican-dominated Senate deleted the $27 million state appropriation. Democratic reactions predictably lamented the failure to meet the needs of the people. Justification for the cut was summarized later in a press release issued by the Republican leader of the Senate. That release is worth quoting in some detail:

> Legislation establishing a special education program for underprivileged children was strongly supported by the Republican Senate during the past session and has become law.
> This program is wholly financed by federal funds but is administered by the State of Illinois. The Federal Education Opportunities Act passed recently provided $61.7 million for this program in Illinois this year. An additional $72.6 million is authorized for next year, bringing the total for the biennium to $134,300,000.

The Democratic administration in Illinois did not understand the financing of this program during the last session of the Legislature and apparently still does not. The Republicans in the Senate passed the bill establishing the program but deleted the state appropriation attached because of the massive allocation of federal funds. No state matching funds are required and in fact, if any state money were appropriated it would jeopardize future federal monies. The Federal law specifies that once state money is used, the same amount must be appropriated every year in the future for the program or the federal funds will be cut off.

Governor Kerner continues to lament that the program suffered when in truth, instead of the $27 million he would have allocated, the Republican Senate assured that Illinois will now receive over $134 million for the biennium without matching obligations.

Governor Kerner was uninformed about the relevant federal legislation and unaware of the financial operations of the program. The Republican task force will try to keep him better informed in the future.

Whatever the merits of the partisan position expressed in the press release, its significance here lies primarily in the symbols used to justify Republican behavior. Implicity, the Republican cut is justified because it reduces the state's financial burden. Explicitly, it is justified because it results in an even higher expenditure for this program than was proposed by the governor. Credit for this increased service is fully assumed by the Republicans, whose greater financial sophistication permitted them to overcome the incompetence attributed to the governor. What the program does, for what persons, is not an issue. Who can claim credit for the program is an issue—indeed, the only issue.

The willingness with which a traditionally conservative Republican leadership embraced federal participation in local education may seem surprising, but it provides a useful insight into the ambiguity with which state actors view the federal government. Virtually all state actors are verbally opposed to federal encroachment on state affairs, but on the other hand are quick to accept federal aid and the controls that are part of federal aid. In this case it is difficult to see what part the state can play in a program financed entirely from federal funds and utilized by local school boards who, we may surmise, are likely to be more responsive to federal requirements than to state officials who have no financial stake in the program. To the extent that the program narrows the scope of effective state responsibility it is a retreat from the principle of state control over state affairs. Yet the Republican senators who led the retreat mask it as a victory by alluding to their "sharpness" in getting something for nothing— "134 million . . . without matching obligations." Not unlike their small-town cousins, who pride themselves on their ability to "outwit" the "city-slickers," these state actors turn defeat into victory by "sharp deals" which "outwit" the slicksters in Washington.[31] Implicit symbolism of this sort, by preventing a full appreciation of state dependence on federal aid, helps to maintain the conviction that state actors have power. The reality behind the symbolism is quite different but, because it is not consciously recognized, it has little effect on state action.

To interpret state expenditure politics in symbolic terms is not to say that state actions are inconsequential. The consequences are real enough, but they are not the consequences we normally look for. Actors on the various stages of state politics are forced to act in situations which offer only a severely limited number of appropriate roles, none of which permit the exercise of full control over state finance. Lacking such control, but driven by the desire to maintain office and status, actors behave *as though* they are powerful by following a script written in terms of easily understood symbols. Rationally-derived Responsibility, Economy and Service are the principal symbols for which state actors compete and around which they organize their stylized behavior. If the tangible outcome of such behavior seldom corresponds to the symbols by which it is justified, nothing is lost, for it is not at all clear that tangible outcomes can be significantly influenced by anything done, or not done, by state actors. In this context use of these symbols provides a net gain, for they reassure actors and their audiences that powerful figures are engaged in important activities, in a significant governmental context. The extent to which these assurances have no basis in fact is both the source of state symbolism and the measure of the state financial predicament.

NOTES

[1] Thomas J. Anton, *The Politics of State Expenditure in Illinois* (Urbana and London: The University of Illinois Press, 1966), pp. 44–75.

[2] Allen Schick, "Control Patterns in State Budget Execution," *Public Administration Review,* XXIV (1964), 97–106.

[3] Rufus P. Browning, "Innovative and Non-Innovative Decision Processes in Government Budgeting" (prepared for delivery at the 1963 Annual Meeting of the American Political Science Association, New York, September, 1963).

[4] *Ibid.*

[5] Anton, *op. cit.,* p. 56.

[6] Schick, *op. cit.,* p. 99.

[7] *Ibid.,* p. 100.

[8] Paul Appleby, "The Role of the Budget Division," *Public Administration Review,* XVII (1957), 156.

[9] Arlene Theuer Shadoan, *Organization, Role, and Staffing of State Budget Offices* (Lexington: Bureau of Business Research, 1961), mimeo, p. 59.

[10] Thomas Flinn, *Governor Freeman and the Minnesota Budget* ("ICP Case Series," No. 60 [University, Alabama: University of Alabama Press, 1961]).

[11] Donald G. Herzberg and Paul Tillett, *A Budget for New York State, 1956–1957* ("ICP Case Series," No. 69 [University, Alabama: University of Alabama Press, 1962]).

[12] Clark D. Ahlberg and Daniel P. Moynihan, "Changing Governors—and Policies," *Public Administration Review*, XX (1960), 195–204.

[13] Anton, *op. cit.*, pp. 112–46.

[14] Joseph A. Schlesinger, "The Politics of the Executive," *Politics in the American States*, eds. Herbert Jacob and Kenneth N. Vines (Boston: Little, Brown, 1965), p. 209.

[15] Tax Foundation, Inc., *State Expenditure Controls: An Evaluation* (New York: Tax Foundation, Inc., 1965), p. 74.

[16] Ahlberg and Moynihan, *loc. cit.*, p. 195, offer a similar view.

[17] Tax Foundation, Inc., *op. cit.*, p. 74.

[18] Ahlberg and Moynihan, *loc. cit.*, p. 199, write: "The national economy, both on the downturn and the upsurge, fixed the limits of the real policy alternatives for these new governors as must be true in nearly all states."

[19] Flinn, *op. cit.*, provides a particularly effective account of the processes which forced Governor Freeman to abandon most of his new programs.

[20] Herzberg and Tillett, *op. cit.*, p. 30 write: "The public expression of these controversies often does not reflect candid consideration of governmental goals. To some extent, legislative and executive budget releases to the public have an academic character.

[21] Douglas Kane, "Our Streamrollered Assembly," *The Courier-Journal Magazine*, Sunday, February 20, 1966.

[22] Frederick C. Mosher, "The Executive Budget, Empire State Style," *Public Administration Review*, XII (1952), 73–84.

[23] Anton, *op. cit.*, pp. 147–77.

[24] Charles E. Lindblom, "Decision-Making in Taxation and Expenditures," *Public Finances: Needs, Sources, and Utilization* (Princeton: National Bureau of Economic Research, 1961), pp. 265–329; Aaron Wildavsky, *The Politics of the Budgetary Process* (Boston: Little, Brown, 1964).

[25] All these examples are taken from recent Illinois history.

[26] This discussion owes a great deal to Schlesinger's perceptive argument. *Op. cit.*, pp. 207–17.

[27] See Thomas Page, "The Employment Systems of the State of Illinois," *Illinois Government*, No. 7 (Urbana: Institute of Government and Public Affairs, 1960).

[28] The discussion which follows is stimulated by Murray Edelman's exciting work, *The Symbolic Uses of Politics* (Urbana: The University of Illinois Press, 1964).

[29] Herzberg and Tillett, *op. cit.*, p. 26.

[30] Murray Edelman offers an apt comment on the repeated use of cliches such as these, and others noted earlier: "Chronic repetition of cliches and stale phrases that serve simply to evoke a conditioned uncritical response is a time-honored habit among politicians and a mentally restful one for their audiences. The only information conveyed by a speaker who tells an audience of businessmen that taxes are too high and that public spending is waste is that he is trying to prevent both himself and his audience from thinking. . . ." Edelman, *op. cit.*, pp. 124–25.

[31] For an analysis of these themes in a small-town setting, see Arthur J. Vidich and Joseph Bensman, *Small Town in Mass Society* (Garden City: Anchor Books, 1960).

CHAPTER 12

Budget-Making in Georgia and Wisconsin:
A Test of a Model

Ira Sharkansky
Augustus B. Turnbull, III

This essay describes and tests a model of the state budgetary process with respect to the administrations of several governors and 43 separate agencies in Georgia and Wisconsin. By emphasizing the deviations from the model we assess the impacts arising from each state's political system, the style and strength of individual governors and occurrences peculiar to individual agencies.

Components of the model were suggested by existing research. From the budgeting literature we take the principle of *incrementalism*.[1] The budget-maker who follows incremental procedures simplifies his decision-making task by starting from the "base" of expenditures won by each agency during previous budget periods. Executive and legislative reviewers do not attempt a zero base analysis but focus attention only on the *increments* of new funds that agencies request. Incrementalism has two implications important for the model: first, reviewers generally cut only increments so if an agency were to request no increase over its current budget, its request would probably be approved as submitted; second, reviewers only respond to requests for increments; they are generally too harried to develop program innovations and impose increments on agencies that had not requested them.[2]

From the literature on executive-legislative relationships we take the principle of *legislative reliance on the governor's recommendations* which has its source in the relative skills and staff assistance available to the legislative and executive branches of state government. American state legislators are typically described as amateurs with minimum staff and little training or experience relevant for the review of administrative proposals.[3] Any staff expertise outside of the regular state agencies is likely to be found

Reprinted from the *Midwest Journal of Political Science,* Vol. 13, No. 4 (November, 1969), "Budget-Making in Georgia and Wisconsin," by Ira Sharkansky and Augustus B. Turnbull, III, by permission of the Wayne State University Press and the authors. Copyright © 1969 by Wayne State University Press.

in the governor's office, and most probably, in the unit responsible for reviewing agency budget requests. This condition is compatible with traditional doctrines of "proper" budget procedures. Budget reform literature frowns on agency attempts to submit independent requests to the legislature. It urges a "strong executive" with the staff assistance necessary to submit an integrated budget proposal to the legislature, and a legislature that responds primarily to the executive's recommendations.[4]

THE MODEL

The model includes three basic components: the agency as initiator of requests; the governor as making the first review of the agency request and providing recommendations to the legislature; and the legislature as the authority that defines each agency's appropriation. The model is dual in nature:[5] the first phase focuses on the percentage of an agency's request for new funds that is approved by the governor and appropriated by the legislature; because it is concerned with agency success in the current legislative session, it is labeled *short-term budget success*. The second phase focuses on the percentage of present expenditures that the governor recommends and the legislature appropriates for the coming budget period; because it is concerned with increases over time, it is labeled *success in budget expansion*.

The specific hypotheses derived from the model and tested by the analysis reported below are as follows:

Hypothesis 1: *In both phases of the model there are weak or nonexistent relationships between the sheer size of each agency's request and the recommendations of the governor or the appropriations of the legislature.* This hypothesis assumes a fixation of budget reviewers on the increments that are sought, rather than on the size of requests which include both new increments and the agency's base of current appropriation.

Hypothesis 2: *In short-term budget success there are negative relationships between the percentage increment that an agency requests, and the percentage of its request that the governor recommends and the legislature appropriates.* Presumably, those agencies which seek the largest increments will suffer the greatest cuts below their requests, while those requesting little or no increments above their base will suffer little or no cuts below their requests.

Hypothesis 3: *In success in budget expansion there are positive relationships between the percentage increment that the agency requests, and the percentage growth that the governor recommends and the legislature appropriates.* It is only by requesting growth that an agency will receive an increase in its budget, even though the increase received is cut below its initial request. Presumably, the agencies that request the greatest increments will receive the largest percentage growth over their current budget, while agencies requesting little or no increment will receive little or no growth in their budget.

Hypothesis 4: *In both phases of the model there are positive relationships between the measures of the governor's recommendations and legislative appropriations.* This hypothesis assumes the reliance of the legislature on the budget recommendations of the executive. Because of limitations in the legislators' own experience and in their staff assistance, and because of the principle that the executive should provide leadership in the budgetary process, we further hypothesize a more direct relationship between the governor's recommendation and legislature's appropriation than between the agency's request for an increment and the legislature's appropriation. Hence:

Hypothesis 5: *In both phases of the model the relationships between the governor's recommendations and the legislature's appropriations should be more direct than the relationships between the agency's request for an increment and the legislature's appropriation.*

Figure 1 is a graphic summary of hypotheses relating to each phase of the model.

TECHNIQUES OF ANALYSIS

Georgia and Wisconsin were selected for this test of the budget-making model for several reasons: the availability of comparable data over time; the states' considerably different political traditions, governmental structures and levels of party competition; and access to individuals who have been participants in state budgeting over the years.

For each state we have studied the longest span of time for which comparable data could be obtained. The time span for Georgia covers fiscal years 1964–69 including all fiscal periods since the adoption of "modern budgeting."[6] During this time Democrats controlled the Governor's office and the General Assembly although in recent years the Republicans have captured an increasing number of legislative seats, and have represented a threat to Democratic candidates for governor. Carl Sanders (1963–67) was a progressive Governor with a decade of prior legislative experience. Lester Maddox (1967–71) is a political fundamentalist who had never held elective office before being named Governor by the General Assembly.[7]

The time span for Wisconsin covers fiscal years 1958–67. Prior to 1958, needed data are unavailable and after 1967, a major reorganization

Figure 1
Model of the State Budgetary Process

Phase 1
Short-Term Budget Success

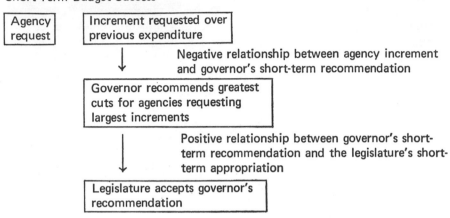

| Agency request | Increment requested over previous expenditure |

↓ Negative relationship between agency increment and governor's short-term recommendation

Governor recommends greatest cuts for agencies requesting largest increments

↓ Positive relationship between governor's short-term recommendation and the legislature's short-term appropriation

Legislature accepts governor's recommendation

Phase 2
Success in Budget Expansion

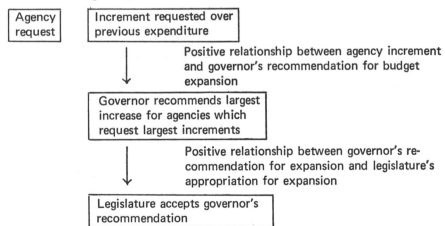

| Agency request | Increment requested over previous expenditure |

↓ Positive relationship between agency increment and governor's recommendation for budget expansion

Governor recommends largest increase for agencies which request largest increments

↓ Positive relationship between governor's recommendation for expansion and legislature's appropriation for expansion

Legislature accepts governor's recommendation

Note: the model hypothesizes no relationship between the agency request itself (sheer size) and the decisions of the executive or the legislature. There are also no direct relationships posited between the agencies' increments and the legislature's decision.

altered the responsibilities of state agencies thus making further comparisons impossible. The period includes the terms of four governors: Vernon Thompson (Republican); Gaylord Nelson (Democrat); John Reynolds (Democrat) and Warren Knowles (Republican). Thompson was the only governor whose party controlled both houses of the Legislature. Reynolds, and Nelson in his second term, co-existed with Republican legislatures. Knowles, and Nelson in his first term had party control in only one house. Each of Wisconsin's governors had previous experience in major elected offices.

In each state our analysis was limited to those agencies that requested at least $500,000 from the general fund for fiscal 1967 and that escaped major reorganization during the entire time span—26 agencies in Georgia and 17 in Wisconsin. This dollar limit removes small agencies from our sample thus eliminating many small dollar increments that loom large in percentage terms. Since earmarked money has been eliminated from our analysis, the focus is on the funds actually subject to budgetary decisions. With one exception (see Note 7) the analysis combines data for both years of each biennial budget period.

A variety of statistical techniques are used in testing the model's five hypotheses. Coefficients of simple correlation (Pearson's r) define relationships between the size of agency requests, the percentage increments requested, and the measures of the governor's recommendation and the legislature's appropriation. We use these coefficients to assess Hypotheses 1–4. We use the techniques of causal modelling to assess Hypothesis 5.[8] By examining separate sets of findings for each budget period, we not only make a general assessment of the model, but also assess continuity and change in budget procedures from one governor's administration to the next within each state. We also identify individual agencies whose experience deviates from the norm within each budget period. For this, we use a regression equation:

$$Y = a + b_1X_1 + b_2X_2 + b_3X_3$$

where Y equals the measure of budget success, X_1 equals the measure of the size of budget requested, X_2 equals the percentage increment requested, X_3 equals the measure of the governor's recommendation, and the a and b's are constants which when multiplied with the mean scores of the independent variables and added together approximate the mean score of budget success. By computing separate regression equations for each budget period and each measure of budget success, then using these equations in conjunction for appropriate independent variables for each administrative agency, we estimate budget success scores for each agency. Then by comparing real budget success scores with the estimated scores according to the formula

$$\frac{\text{actual score of budget success}}{\text{score estimated with regression equation}}$$

we identify the agencies whose budget success deviated markedly from that which was typical for the budget period. By seeking explanations for those cases where agency budget success is not consistent with the norm, we can identify certain types of phenomena that diminish the effectiveness of the model.

FINDINGS: GENERAL TENDENCIES

Generally speaking, the model works well. Hypothesis 1 finds uniform support. In every budget period considered there are only weak relationships between the sheer size of the agencies' request and the measures of the governor's recommendation and the Legislature's appropriation. The data of Table 1 support Hypotheses 2 and 3; it is the increment requested,

Table 1
Coefficients of Simple Correlation

State & Fiscal Yr.	Short Term				Expansion			
	A.I. & G.R.	A.I. & L.A.	G.R. & L.A.	R^2 of all items in L.A.	A.I. & G.R.	A.E. & L.A.	G.R. & L.A.	R^2 of all items in L.A.
Ga. 1969	−.75	−.85	.89	.87	.82	.82	.92	.86
Ga. 1968	−.89	−.82	.92	.85	.55	.17	.80	.75
Ga. 66–67	−.70	−.63	.92	.86	.62	.62	.96	.92
Ga. 64–65	−.89	−.83	.93	.87	.58	.54	.95	.90
Wis. 66–67	−.92	−.61	.60	.44	.26	.25	.57	.39
Wis. 64–65	−.52	−.06	.13	.05	.93	.52	.54	.29
Wis. 62–63	−.04	−.07	.53	.29	.93	.85	.88	.78
Wis. 60–61	−.58	−.57	.87	.76	.65	.56	.87	.78
Wis. 58–59	−.55	−.55	.12	.55	.84	.74	.84	.69

Notes: In order to conserve space, coefficients of simple correlation are not reported between budget size and the other variables; they are, as predicted, consistently low.

The R^2's reflect the influence of 3 independent variables: budget size, agency increment, and governor's recommendation. The definitions of each variable are shown below:

A.I. Agency Increment: agency request for the next budget period as a percentage of expenditure in the current expenditure.

G.R. Governor's Recommendation: (short-term) as a percentage of the agency's request; (expansion) as a percentage of agency's expenditure in the current budget period.

L.A. Legislature's Appropriation: (short-term) as a percentage of the agency's request; (expansion) as a percentage of agency's expenditure in the current budget.

Budget size: dollar amount of agency request.

rather than the sheer size of the request that concerns budget reviewers. Reviewers generally cut the requests of agencies that seek the largest increments, but they give increments only to the agencies which request them. It is also true, as predicted in Hypothesis 4, that legislatures usually respond favorably to the governor's recommendations. It is the agencies that he recommends for the greatest cuts or increases that typically receive these from the legislature. Moreover, the results of causal modelling most often indicate that the legislature is responding to the governor's recommendations instead of making its own assessment of agency requests. Although some legislatures seem to mix their acceptance of the executive's recommendations with a separate assessment of agency requests (see Model 3 in Table 2), there is no case in which a legislature shows primary reliance on its own assessment of an agency's requests (see Model 2 in Table 2).

DEVIANT CASES: IDENTIFICATION AND EXPLANATION

Although the model corresponds with reality most of the time, it is more successful in some contexts than in others. The hypotheses work better for Georgia than Wisconsin, and those pertaining to success in budget expansion work better than those pertaining to short-term budget success. Almost all of the sharp deviations from the model occur in the case of short-term gubernatorial recommendations and legislative appropriations indicating that budget reviewers may be creative in their short-term responses to requests, but seldom so creative, however, as to provide unrequested funds to an administrative unit. They are unlikely to impose expansion budgets on agencies which do not request them.

The difference between the model's success in Georgia and Wisconsin is evident not only in relationships between individual components of the model but also in measures that show the success of all the independent variables in accounting for agency-by-agency variations in appropriations. Coefficients of multiple determination (R^2) indicate that the independent variables consistently explain over 75 percent of the variation in the appropriations of Georgia agencies. The model attains this level of proficiency in only three of the 10 tests for Wisconsin.

Contrary to our expectations, we found that our model works well in the administrations of both Georgia governors. The budget recommendations of Lester Maddox, despite his reputation as a political amateur unable to work within the customary political process, were followed by the General Assembly to the same degree as those of his predecessor. The critical element in the Georgia findings appears to be the strength of the governor's office bolstered during the Sanders-Maddox transition by a

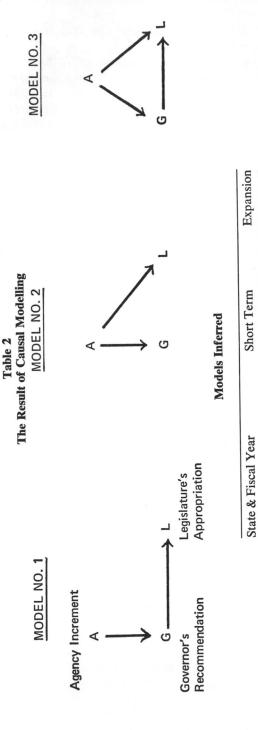

Table 2
The Result of Causal Modelling

MODEL NO. 1

MODEL NO. 2

MODEL NO. 3

Agency Increment

Governor's
Recommendation

Legislature's
Appropriation

Models Inferred

State & Fiscal Year	Short Term	Expansion
Georgia 1969	#3	#1
Georgia 1968	#1	#3
Georgia 1966–67	#1	#1
Georgia 1964–65	#1	#1
Wisconsin 1966–67	#3	#1
Wisconsin 1964–65	#3	#3
Wisconsin 1962–63	#1	#3
Wisconsin 1960–61	#1	#1
Wisconsin 1958–59	#3	#1

Inferences are made according to the techniques identified in Note 8. Detailed calculations are available on request from the authors.

professional budget bureau headed by a State Budget Officer who had excellent personal relationships with key legislators.

Like the typical southern governor,[9] the governor of Georgia has numerous formal and informal powers that influence the General Assembly generally to accept his recommendations.[10] For example, the General Assembly accepted the governor's recommendations for fiscal 1968 even when there was virtually no incumbent governor and considerable pressure for a show of "legislative independence" (see Note 7). Yet despite this "interregnum" we find the characteristically high positive relationship between these recommendations and the legislature's appropriations. It may be more accurate to speak of the legislature's weakness than the governor's strength as the crucial feature in Georgia budgeting.

In Wisconsin there is marked variation in the success of our model from one administration to the next. It appears these deviations reflect several items: the intensity of a governor's commitment to his policy preferences; differences in policy values between the governor and the legislature; the promise of new tax revenues; and the governor's tactics in presenting his recommendations to the legislature. The division of party control between the executive and legislature does not provide a consistent explanation for deviation from our model. Governors Thompson (1958–59) and Reynolds (1964–65) were alike in having the least acceptance of their short-term recommendations, but Thompson's party controlled both houses, while Reynolds' party controlled neither house. Moreover, Governor Nelson (1960–63) resembled Reynolds in having a legislature of the opposite party, but one Republican legislature accepted Nelson's recommendations, and another Republican legislature rejected Reynolds' recommendations.

Governor Reynolds was known for his social commitment and for the intensity of his conflicts with the legislature. The conflict ranged over a wide spectrum of issues that included tax policy and the confirmation of his appointments as well as budgeting. Our budget data show the governor's willingness to accept the requests of even the most expansionist agencies. He transmitted many of these virtually intact to the hostile legislature. Our data also show the governor's problems in getting his recommendations approved by the legislature. There is only a weak (.13) coefficient of simple correlation between his short-term recommendation and the appropriation of the legislature.

Nelson's second term (1962–63) presents an example of both a governor and a legislature departing from the usual practice of cutting agency budgets in inverse proportion to the requested increment. There are only weak relationships ($r = -.04; r = -.07$) between the increments that agencies requested and the short-term executive recommendations and legislative appropriations. According to participants, these actions occurred when a new tax seemed inevitable because of inadequate revenues. Under these circumstances both the governor and the legislature had several incentives to be unusually generous with some agencies. By accepting requests for large increments, the governor and legislature could gain the support of agencies and their clientele, and claim the mantle of policy–innovators. In addition, they could reinforce the justification for new taxes by permitting budget requests to mount even higher beyond the revenue-producing capacity of existing taxes.

The data discussed thus far support observations about the general effectiveness of our budget model, and the occasions that prompted deviations in the record of individual governors or legislatures. Next, deviations at a different level of analysis will be discussed. Our data come from the regression analysis described above and calculation of residuals for each administrative agency. They show the extent to which the record of *individual agencies* fails to resemble the norms established by the governor and legislature during each budget period. In order to conserve space, we shall omit the detailed tables from this report.[11]

These findings complement our earlier discussion in demonstrating many more deviations for agencies in Wisconsin than in Georgia where during the four budget periods only three agencies deviated from the norms by at least 15 percent on both measures of budget success. These few deviations seem to have resulted from atypically high requests which received less support than the model anticipated from either the governor or legislature.

During the five budget periods considered for Wisconsin, there were 20 cases of agencies deviating from the norm by at least 15 percent on both measures of appropriation. The major pattern that emerges shows that agencies identified with the unpleasant activities of taxation, law enforcement, and regulation tend to deviate more often, and negatively, than do agencies identified as providing attractive public services. Agencies in these categories[12] showed deviations on both measures of appropriation 30 percent of the time while other agencies deviated only 20 percent of the time. Moreover, the deviation of tax, regulatory and law enforcement agencies were negative 67 percent of the time, while the deviations of other agencies were negative only 30 percent of the time. Agencies with such negative images suffer from the complaints of those whose activities are curtailed by their efforts, and those who complain frequently are important in the economy and politics of a jurisdiction.[13]

Aside from this general tendency, participants in Wisconsin budget-making during the 1966–67 period suggested several explanations for deviant scores:

1) A negative deviation of the Tax Department's appropriation reflected executive and legislative reaction after two periods of generous budget growth. In fiscal 1962–63 and 1964–65 the department enjoyed large positive deviation. It increased staff and facilities in order to handle the new retail sales tax. By 1966–67, however, when the department requested a further increase, both the executive and legislative budget reviewers made large cuts.

2) A positive deviation in the Attorney General's appropriation for the 1966–67 budget period reflects an effort to centralize legal skills in the office of the Attorney General and two major cases: an investigation of local government corruption in Milwaukee County and an unsuccessful attempt to keep the Braves in Milwaukee.[14]

3) A positive deviation in the appropriation of the Department of Vocational and Adult Education reflects the intense interest of the governor (Knowles) in its program and the ability of a new governor to win legislative support for his pet program.

CONCLUSIONS:

This article tests a model of the state budgetary process over a period of several years in Georgia and Wisconsin. The principal deviations suggest the following conditions may upset normal budget procedures:[15]

1) A governor motivated to support agencies' initial requests even to the point of overlooking typical padding.

2) A realization by the executive and the legislature that tax increase is inevitable. At this point they may accept agency requests for sizable budget growth, both to earn agency and clientele support and to show that demands for new services make the tax increase essential.

3) The strong assertion of a governor in behalf of a favored program, and his ability (perhaps enhanced by the "honeymoon" effect of a recent election) to get the legislature's cooperation.

4) The willingness of a governor and legislature to permit major budget growth for an agency whose responsibilities are increased by major new program responsibilities; and conversely, the reaction against further growth on the part of an agency that has enjoyed recent and prolonged increases in its appropriations.[16]

5) Conflict between the governor and the legislature on some policies that spill over into budgeting lessens the legislature's willingness to accept the governor's budget recommendations.

6) A general predisposition against agencies with responsibility for taxation, law enforcement, or economic regulation.

NOTES

[1] See Charles E. Lindblom, "Decision-Making in Taxation and Expenditure," *Public Finances: Needs, Sources and Utilization* (Princeton: National Bureau of Economic Research, 1961), pp. 295–336; Thomas J. Anton, *The Politics of State Expenditure in Illinois* (Urbana: University of Illinois Press, 1966); John P. Crecine, *Government Problem Solving: A Computer Simulation of Municipal Budgeting* (Chicago: Rand McNally, forthcoming); Otto A. Davis, M. A. H. Dempster, and Aaron Wildavsky, "A Theory of the Budgetary Process," *American Political Science Review,* LX (September, 1966), 529–47.

[2] See Rufus P. Browning, "Innovative and Non-Innovative Decision Processes in Government Budgeting," *Public Budgeting and Finance,* ed. Robert T. Golembiewski (Itasca, Ill.: F. E. Peacock, 1968), pp. 128–45.

[3] For a description of the background, training and governmental experience of state legislators, see Malcolm E. Jewell and Samuel C. Patterson, *The Legislative Process in the United States* (New York: Random House, 1966), Chapter 5; and Thomas R. Dye, "State Legislative Politics," *Politics in the American States,* eds. Herbert Jacob and Kenneth N. Vines (Boston: Little, Brown, 1965), 151–206.

[4] A classic statement of this doctrine can be found in Frederick Cleveland and Arthur E. Buck, *The Budget and Responsible Government* (New York: Macmillan, 1920); subsequent statements can be found in Arthur E. Buck, "Financial Control and Accountability," *Administrative Management in the Government of the United States,* Report of the President's Committee on Administrative Management (1937); John W. Hanes, *et al.,* "Fiscal, Budgeting and Accounting Systems of the Federal Government: A Report with Recommendations Prepared for the Commission on Organization of the Executive Branch of the Government" (Washington: Government Printing Office, 1949); and Commission on Organization of the Executive Branch, *Budgeting and Accounting: A Report to the Congress* (Washington: Government Printing Office, 1955).

[5] We also experimented with another measure, the success of each agency in receiving its appropriations from the legislature in the previous budget period, for two reasons: to determine if certain agencies were characteristically successful in the budget process, while others were characteristically disappointed; and to determine whether the executive or the legislature base present decisions on decisions (on each agency) in the preceding budget review. Our preliminary findings suggest that—at least in the cases of Georgia and Wisconsin—there was no consistent relationship between budget success in one budget period, and success in succeeding periods. One difference between this research and that reported by Davis, Dempster and Wildavsky (see Note 1) is the availability of data for Georgia and Wisconsin on agency requests *and* the executive's recommendation. Because of this data our model includes two steps (the responses of the governor and legislature to the agency's initial request) that are not in their analysis.

[6] From 1931 to 1962, Georgia statutes permitted the governor to assign all revenue in excess of the latest legislative appropriation to the agencies as he saw fit. In the 1940's and 1950's, a period of infrequent appropriations and rising revenues permitted the governor great discretion in the use of state resources. A common allegation is that he "ran the state out of his hip pocket." In 1962, the budgetary process was modernized: biennial appropriations were made mandatory and the governor's powers over the surplus were sharply reduced. See Augustus B. Turnbull III, "Politics in the Budgetary Process: The Case of Georgia" (unpublished Ph.D. dissertation, University of Virginia, 1967); and by the same author, "Georgia Budgeting Comes of Age," *Georgia Government Review,* I (Fall, 1968), 1–4.

[7] Although most tests of the budget model combine data for both years of each biennium, we made separate tests for fiscal 1968 and 1969. These budgets were formally part of the same biennium, but the budget for fiscal 1968 was presented to

the legislature substantially as prepared by Carl Sanders in the absence of an officially certified victor in the 1966 election. Lester Maddox made a few changes in the fiscal 1968 budget, and then during the second year of his administration submitted a new fiscal 1969 budget to the legislature.

8 The general principle being followed here is that a linkage between any two variables in a triad may be inferred to be missing if their partial correlation (controlling for the third) approximates zero, or if their simple correlation approximates the product of the two other simple correlation coefficients. In the following diagram, for example, the linkage between variables A and L may be inferred to be absent if the simple correlation between A and L approximates the product of r_{AG} times r_{GL}. In this paper we follow the convention of inferring Model #1 if the differences between r_{AL} and r_{AG} times r_{GL} are less than the differences between r_{GL} and r_{AG} times r_{AL} for the alternate Model #2, and if the differences for only one of the two models is .10 or less. We infer Model #3 if the differences for neither #1 or #2 or for both #1 and #2 are less than .10.

MODEL NO. 1   MODEL NO. 2   MODEL NO. 3

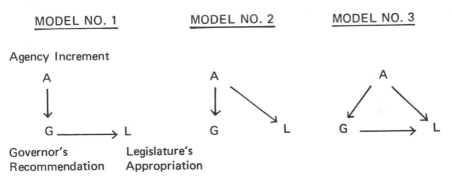

Agency Increment

Governor's   Legislature's
Recommendation   Appropriation

Model #1 indicates that the governor responds to agency acquisitiveness and the legislature responds primarily to the governor's recommendation. Model #2 indicates that the governor and legislature respond independently to agency acquisitiveness; and Model #3 indicates that the legislature responds partly to the recommendations of the governor and partly to agency acquisitiveness. For a more detailed explanation of techniques, see Hurbert M. Blalock, Jr., *Causal Inferences in Non-experimental Research* (Chapel Hill: University of North Carolina Press, 1964), p. 64 ff.

9 See Robert C. Highsaw, "The Southern Governor: Challenge to the Strong Governor Theme," *Public Administration Review,* 19 (1959), 7–11.

10 Aside from wide ranging powers of appointment, Georgia governors have had influence over which highways are to be built or resurfaced, over the awarding of contracts for state construction or insurance and determination of sites for the development of new state institutions, as well as in selecting existing institutions to be repaired or otherwise improved. Because the Georgia state government, like that of other southern states, supports many services that are provided by local units in other sections of the country, the governor's power can go deeply into fields concerned with local schools, county roads and the promotion of local industrial development.

11 These tables are available from the authors.

12 Attorney General, Audit Department, Department of Taxation, Industrial Commission, Public Service Commission.

13 See Murray Edelman, "Symbols and Political Quiescence," *American Political Science Review,* LIV (September, 1960).

14 Any equivalent costs in Georgia for getting the Braves were handled within regular budgetary limits!

[15] For a study which supports the general accuracy of the model, see Ira Sharkansky, "Agency Requests, Gubernatorial Support and Budget Success in State Legislatures," *American Political Science Review,* LXII (December, 1968). That article examines the budget experience of 19 states at one period in time. Unlike the present article, however, it does not examine deviations in the model with changes in the governor or with respect to the characteristics of individual agencies.

[16] See Ira Sharkansky, "Economic and Political Correlates of State Government Expenditures: General Tendencies and Deviant Cases," *Midwest Journal of Political Science,* XI (May, 1967), 173–92.

CHAPTER 13

Congressional Staff and Public Policy-Making: The Joint Committee on Internal Revenue Taxation

John Manley

Many students of Congress have observed that, due to the increased scope and complexity of governmental activity, congressmen need expert staff assistance if they are to legislate in an informed way and retain some independence of the executive branch and its expertise.[1] Confronted with multifarious demands on their time, the argument goes, legislators have a difficult time mastering the intricacies of substantive policy proposals; partly as a result, many policy-making functions theoretically reserved for the legislative branch have been transferred, in fact if not always in form, to the executive. Carried out to its logical conclusion this development would appear to culminate in the suggestion made by Samuel P. Huntington that Congress give up whatever lawmaking power it still has: "Explicit acceptance of the idea that legislation was not its primary function would, in large part, simply be recognition of the direction which change has already been taking. It would legitimize and expand the functions of constituent service and administrative oversight which, in practice, already constitute the principal work of most congressmen."[2]

Should Congress arm itself with a professional staff which may equip it to compete with the sources of information available to the executive and help it stem the tendency toward de facto executive lawmaking? Or should Congress recognize its inability to legislate and maximize the functions for which it is best suited: constituent service and administrative oversight? Or should Congress adopt, as a sort of via media, Representative Henry Reuss's (D.–Wis.) proposal for an American version of the Scandinavian ombudsman who would relieve congressmen of some of the details of constituent service and give them, it is hoped, more time for lawmaking activities?[3]

Like other questions of congressional reform the question of staff has

Reprinted from *The Journal of Politics,* Vol. 30, No. 4 (November, 1968), pp. 1046–67, by permission of the Southern Political Science Association and the author.

been raised before political scientists have produced descriptive and analytical accounts of the activities of the staff which Congress already employs. Shooting from the hip does not necessarily mean that one will miss the target but Ralph Huitt makes a persuasive argument that the low level of knowledge about how Congress works impedes the effectiveness of suggestions for change: "The difficulty is that too little is known about how Congress actually operates now and what the effects of various procedural and structural arrangements really are. *What we lack is a solid base of research which would make possible educated guesses as to who would be served by what kinds of changes and what the costs would be.*"[4] The most recent full-length study of the congressional staff provides, as one reviewer noted, "some useful background and some data, but the analysis remains to be done."[5]

The purpose of the present study is to analyze the role of one staff in the policy-making process. Because little is known about the staff of the Joint Committee on Internal Revenue Taxation, Part I sketches its origins and current status in terms of size and expenditures. Part II discusses the staff as a link between the two tax-writing committees of Congress, the House Committee on Ways and Means and Senate Finance, to the executive branch and to non-governmental groups. Attention is paid to the norms which are supposed to govern the staff's role vis-à-vis the committee members, the degree of conformity to these norms by the staff under two different leaders, and to the importance of how the Chief of Staff sees his job in relation to the competing blocs that are involved in making tax policy. Part III investigates the role of the staff in linking one of the committees, Ways and Means, to the executive branch and to non-governmental groups and individuals who are concerned with taxes. A final section discusses some variables which affect the staff's role and which may serve as starting-points for future research.

I

The Joint Committee on Internal Revenue Taxation (JCIRT), established forty-two years ago, is the oldest joint committee of Congress. As originally planned by the House in the Revenue Act of 1926 the "Joint Commission on Taxation," as it was called, was to be composed of five Senators, five House members, and five members appointed by the President to represent the general public. The job of the Commission was to investigate the operation, effects, and administration of the internal revenue laws with the purpose of simplifying the statute and improving its administration. Better phraseology and administration of tax law, not policy innovation, were the objectives of the Commission as envisaged by the

House.[6] The Commission, expected to last less than two years, received an authorization to spend $25,000 on clerical and traveling expenses; quarters were to be provided by the Secretary of the Treasury.[7]

The Senate drastically altered the House plan. Making liberal use of its authority to amend revenue bills passed by the House, the Senate called for a Joint Committee on Internal Revenue Taxation made up solely of congressmen: five Senators and five Representatives. The primary stimulus for this action was the sensational revelations of tax evasion aided by misconduct on the part of Internal Revenue Bureau employees, revelations which stemmed from the work of a select committee headed by Michigan Senator James Couzens. The new Joint Committee, *through its staff,* was designed to: (1) obtain information from taxpayers to assist in the framing of future revenue legislation; (2) gain a "closer insight" into the problem of the administration of the tax laws (a euphemism for preventing corruption in the Internal Revenue Bureau); and (3) gather data bearing upon revenue legislation.[8] The House receded on the Senate amendments and the Joint Committee, a combination watchdog and law-simplifying organization, was set up—with a staff.

Shortly after its inception the Joint Committee was given the job of reviewing large tax refunds planned by the Bureau of Internal Revenue. Today, the Joint Committee relies upon its staff (three of whom actually work in the Internal Revenue Service) to review the refunds. The Joint Committee, which has only an informal veto over refunds, acts mainly as an appellate court for IRS when the congressional staff and IRS cannot resolve a case. Under the current Chief of Staff, Dr. Laurence N. Woodworth, the Joint Committee has not yet reversed its staff; it did rule in favor of the Bureau under Woodworth's predecessor, Colin F. Stam, in rare instances.

In addition to checking on refunds the Joint Committee has met in recent years to discuss tax regulations and to be briefed on the computerization of tax returns, but it has not evolved into a policy-making body for revenue legislation. With no role in the general policy process the importance of the Joint Committee is that it serves as the institutional excuse for maintaining the joint staff, a body of experts which early in its history was praised for its work on the technical aspects of tax law.[9]

From modest beginnings, and with an uncertain future, the joint staff grew until for the period July 1, 1966 to July 1, 1967 it employed three dozen people at a cost of almost $440,000. Twenty of the 36 were professional staff, including three economists.[10] Most of these people spend their time helping the Ways and Means Committee and the Senate Finance Committee write tax laws; the staff needs of the Joint Committee as such are minimal.

II

It may be true that in some fields Congress needs more staff assistance but in the area of revenue legislation the Joint Committee staff provides the legislature with a professional, independent, highly reliable source of information. The few studies which mention the staff invariably cite its competence, expertise, and influence with congressmen. Two articles, one in *Business Week* and the other in the *Wall Street Journal,* stress the quality of the staff,[11] and in a well-known book Roy M. Blough observes that the members of the tax committees place "heavy reliance" on the Chief of staff and that the staff plays a "highly important" role in tax legislation.[12] A member of the Ways and Means Committee goes so far as to contend that, "Between the Joint Committee staff and the House Legislative Counsel, Congress has developed a more competent staff for drafting tax legislation than has the Treasury"[13]

Congressional experience with the Joint Committee staff is so favorable that this device has been taken as the model for changes in the legislative process. In the recent hearings before the Joint Committee on the Organization of Congress, for example, Senator John L. McClellan (D.–Ark.) used the JCIRT to support his proposal to establish a Joint Committee on the Budget. This arrangement, he felt, would give Congress the same type of technical assistance in the appropriations field as it enjoys in the revenue field, and as the Budget Bureau provides the executive branch.[14] The National Taxpayers Conference and the Tax Foundation stated that the JCIRT could be a precedent for a similar organization to deal with expenditures, and Senator Boggs used it as the prototype for a fully-staffed Joint Committee on National Strategy.[15] These proposals may never materialize but the fact that the JCIRT is taken as the model for further institutional innovations is evidence that in many quarters the view of the joint tax staff is a positive one.

What does the Joint Committee staff do for the tax committees which leads people to think that a similar device would be useful in different contexts? Are members of House Ways and Means and Senate Finance happy with the work of their staff; if not, why? What is the staff supposed to do for these committees and does it live up to congressional expectations?

The most obvious, and in some ways the most important, function of the Joint Committee staff is one of linkage: what continuity the tax legislative process has, apart from informal contacts between leading members of the committees, arises from the central role of the staff in both the House and Senate deliberations on tax bills. In the executive sessions of the Ways and Means Committee the staff is not merely on tap for the members but it is actively engaged in the examination of policy proposals made by the members, the Administration, interest groups, and lobbyists. After explicating for Ways and Means how individuals and groups will be affected by changes in the Internal Revenue Code the staff, and most prominently the Chief of Staff, crosses the rotunda and explains the bill to the Finance Committee, going through the same basic routine except that now there exists a detailed bill instead of the tax message with which Ways and Means normally begins. For many years, and until Russell Long (D.–La.) became chairman of Finance in 1965, about the only professional staff available to the Finance Committee was the joint staff.[16]

In performing its tasks for the Ways and Means Committee and the Senate Finance Committee the staff is expected to follow certain norms. Three such norms are: objectivity, bipartisanship, and neutrality. As a body of professional tax experts the Joint Committee staff is supposed to be objective in its handling of data, bipartisan in its handling of member requests, and neutral on public policy questions. "Our job," says the present Chief of Staff Laurence N. Woodworth, "is to see that members of Congress get the facts on both sides so they can make their own decisions."[17] "If I can come away from those meetings," he has said, "knowing that the committee has made its own decisions in the light of this knowledge, then I'm satisfied."[18] The staff's job, according to Ways and Means Chairman Wilbur Mills (D.–Ark.), is "to bring facts together for our use, to do the spadework for us."[19] A former Republican staff assistant noted the bipartisan nature of the staff: "When I tell Woodworth or those guys something I expect confidence and I get it." Recruited without regard to party affiliation ("I'm very proud of the fact that Mr. Stam [former Chief of Staff] never asked me my party politics and as far as I know never asked any other member of the staff.") the staff, as one aide put it, acts "as a coordinator for the Ways and Means Committee. We serve Curtis and Byrnes [Republicans], Boggs and Mills [Democrats], in addition to Senator Byrd." Woodworth has on occasion helped write the majority report on a bill and then turned around and helped the minority write its dissenting views.

Given the controversial nature of tax policy, given the well-known complexity of the Internal Revenue Code which puts a high premium on technical advice, given the difficulty of facing choices without forming opinions, and given the strategic role of the quartermaster corps in the conduct of any war it is not surprising that the staff, which obviously affects the decisions made by the policy-makers, has been criticized for failing to live up to the above norms. One norm in particular, that of neutrality on public policy, has, some policymakers feel, been broken by the staff, especially while Colin F. Stam was Chief of Staff.

"It has been estimated," Stephen Bailey and Howard Samuel note, "that Stam exercised more influence on the preparation of tax legislation than any other single person in the federal government."[20] Little known outside of Washington, Stam accumulated so much influence with the Ways and Means Committee and the Senate Finance Committee that only one (Harry Byrd) of 20 people interviewed by E. W. Kenworthy for his perceptive study of Stam was willing to have his views of the corpulent technician attributed to him.[21] Stam did not control tax policy, in Byrd's opinion, but he "has made very many vital decisions. He has made recommendations that have carried great weight with both committees."[22] For another piece of evidence in support of Stam's key role in the tax legislative process consider the tribute to Stam contained in the following remarks made by a Republican member of Ways and Means in 1953 in defense of the policies of the then chairman, Dan Reed (R.–N.Y.):

He [Reed] had the assistance of the best tax expert anywhere in the United States, and I refer to Mr. Colin Stam, who is the chief of staff of the Joint Committee on Taxation. . . . *These two gentlemen, Mr. Reed and Mr. Stam, have as much capacity to decide what is best in the tax field as anyone in this country.*
Mr. Reed and Mr. Stam agreed on a program, not that they were trying to force it upon anybody, but they advanced it as a suggestion.[23]

And, to cite but one more piece of evidence, a Republican Senator commented on Stam,

He'd been here so long that he wasn't like other staff men. He was the only staff man I knew who could tell a senator to go to hell without getting his face slapped. Not that he did it, understand, but there wasn't any of this subjugation or kowtowing which you sometimes see in the staff, no "sir" business. He was here when I first came in . . . and he cut quite a figure then.[24]

Inevitably associated with influence in Washington is controversy, and Stam had influence in the tax field despite his stated view of himself as a technician who merely supplied analyses and counsel to the decision-makers.[25] Not everyone would agree with the citation on his Rockefeller Public Service Award given "in recognition of distinguished service to the government of the United States and to the American people." Specifically, Stam's activity as Chief of Staff has been severely criticized by liberal Senators concerned with making changes or, as they see it, "reforms" in the internal revenue laws.

For these Senators not only was Stam of little help but his expertise was sullied because it buttressed, in the main, the views of their antagonists, men who were in effective control of both committees. Though Stam was certainly not the linch-pin in the conservative coalition which Senate liberals feel has controlled tax policy for many years, he was a conservative, he identified with the conservative leaders of Finance and Ways and Means, and his key position and acknowledged mastery of the Code were used to frustrate liberal attempts to "purify" the tax laws—so, at any rate, say the liberals.

"This fellow Stam was an autocrat, he played everything close to his vest, and I always felt that he was an ally of big business. Never trusted him." A Senate staff aide agreed with this view of Stam and complained about the assistance available to liberal senators: "First, they never offered help. They'd never come in and say, 'Here's an important bill, let's go over it.' Two, they were nominal in their assistance. And you couldn't trust it so we just went out and got our own." One disenchanted Senate liberal, who once asked Stam to leave the committee room, declared that he never had trouble getting help from Stam,

I just never got anything out of him at all. He wouldn't do any work for me. He was here 25 or 30 years and he never deviated from the line of Millikin, George, Harry Byrd. You could ask Stam if something was black and he'd say, "Well, there are several shades of blackness. . . ." On a tax bill he'd say, "This came up in the committee in 1862 and they thought . . . or in 1904 the committee did this," and when he was all done he hadn't said a goddamn thing except, "Therefore, we ought to take the bill as it's written."

He concluded, "I never did think Stam was reliable."[26]

It appears, then, that the impact of the staff's work leaned toward the conservative side under Stam's leadership—norms of neutrality and objectivity to the contrary notwithstanding. What the staff does to some extent affects what the committees decide, and even the conservative members of Finance admit that in Stam they had an important friend. "Colin Stam's personal philosophy," said a Senator in praise of the staff chief, "was that the tax law should be used for raising revenue and not for social reform. If that makes him a conservative then I suppose he's a conservative. I think this is Larry Woodworth's philosophy too, and it's certainly mine." Commenting on the demands for more minority staff, a Republican Senator confirmed the liberals' charges when he observed that on Finance the minority, plus the Byrd Democrats, had all of the staff they needed because Stam was a conservative. "Gore and Douglas and a few others were the ones who didn't have any staff," he chortled; "our coalition had the staff." In defense of Stam he ticked off a number of famous conservative Senators saying, "Stam's career was woven into theirs. He did nothing more than discharge the responsibilities given him by his employers." In further support of the breakdown of staff neutrality under Stam a member of the Joint Committee staff admitted that his former boss broke the rules:

"Quite frankly, on occasion, I think Mr. Stam, who used to identify himself pretty much with what the majority leadership of the committee felt, would really go too far in supporting their position. He'd become too committed."

Politics and policy preferences have, as reformer dissension shows, affected the role of the staff, its standing with its principals, and its relationship to the formulation of public policy. An institutional device such as the Joint Committee staff may not be an un-mixed blessing to all of the participants in the policy-making process; it may, depending upon such variables as the policy orientation of a Colin F. Stam, support one viewpoint over another. For one group of Senators the staff under Stam was merely doing its job for the majority; for the minority of tax reformers he was a bete noire. Their complaints about him testify to the high quality of the job he did for those with whom he identified; his expertise could—and apparently did—mean advantage for some and disadvantage for others.

Given the difficulty of remaining neutral in the policy-making process it would be tempting to look upon the above policy consequences of the staff attitudes as all but inevitable. Men in Washington form preferences, the political system is designed for the airing and resolution of preferences, and it may be unrealistic to ask any man to be a policy eunuch, especially one who must operate amid the competing demands which surround the tax legislative process. But the history of the joint tax staff since Stam's retirement and the ascendancy of Woodworth to the top position necessitates caution in accepting this conclusion. Perfect conformity to the norms of neutrality and objectivity is probably impossible but the degree of attainment and deviation varies with different individuals. And, experience shows, there is no reason to conclude that the staff *cannot* both serve and please diverse masters.

When Woodworth took over as Chief of Staff in 1964 he was aware of the liberal criticism of Stam and he took steps to restore the staff to its position as a useful aide to *all* members of the Senate Finance and Ways and Means committees. He assured Senate Liberals that he and his assistants stood ready to assist all members, regardless of policy considerations, and that, in effect, the staff would not play politics on revenue bills. Woodworth's campaign worked: the critics of Stam laud his successor. "I'd say the staff is 500 percent improved over what it used to be," said one liberal Senator. Hired by Stam in 1944, Woodworth is more skillful than his mentor in retaining the confidence of the factions that make tax policy. Whether or not he can always avoid all commitments to individual policy positions, or operate in such a way that although the staff research does in fact enhance one position at the expense of others he does not alienate any members, remains to be seen, but at present he is doing precisely that. "I honestly have no idea whether he's a Democrat or a Republican," says one long-time associate of Woodworth's. "He's about as straight down-the-middle as you can get."[27] If Woodworth can function in accordance with this inclination he may be able to play his role as he—and the congressmen—think it should be played.

It should be noted, in passing, that criticism of the joint staff has been found on only one side of the Capitol: the Senate. The Ways and Means Committee is populated with Democrats whose voting behavior is as liberal as the Finance Committee reformers, but there are crucial differences in style between the two groups. There are really no reform-minded liberals like Paul Douglas (D.–Ill.) (before his defeat) or Albert Gore (D.–Tenn.) on the House Committee, although some House members would no doubt vote for the same reforms—if pressed. The one Ways and Means member who in personal philosophy and public statements most closely resembles the Senate tax reformers is Chairman Mills, but in practice if not preachment he has been a disappointment: "Wilbur Mills has always been for reform right up to the opening day of Congress. . . . He pulled this three or four times until he found out he couldn't fool anyone anymore."[28] This statement, whether an accurate assessment of Mills or not, indicates that to date not much steam for tax reform has come from the House. Consequently, not much criticism of the staff for blocking reforms has come from the House either. The general attitude was probably well illustrated by a liberal Ways and Means Democrat who, in reply to a question about the criticism of Stam, dismissed it with the observation: "I think that's just a characteristic of some liberal Senators. They have to have something to complain about and if it's not the staff it's something else. I think complaining is their common denominator."

As a link between the two tax committees of Congress, in summary, the Joint Committee staff, as seen by the policy-makers, has had mixed results. Possessed of so much expertise that one House member was led to observe that "they are the legislators, we are the politicians," the staff has played its role appropriately under one head and inappropriately, in light of the norms which the members and staff espouse, under another. Having gone through the process on the House side the staff is equipped to inform the Senate Finance Committee on the technical—and political—problems involved in various sections of the bill. But it is a job which affects the kind of decisions made in the legislative process; as such, it is endowed with influence and, potentially, controversy. The existence of the former and avoidance of the latter is delicate business. Under Stam the expertise of the staff resulted in some disaffection; under Woodworth the expertise of the staff, in no way diminished, has been used in a more neutral—or less offensive—way. Time will determine whether or not this is a permanent revolution.

III

In addition to linking the Ways and Means and Senate Finance committees directly in the legislative process, the Joint Committee staff acts as an important point of contact between the committee and two key participants in the tax-making process: the Treasury Department and interest groups. In this section we will analyze the staff's relation with these actors, putting special emphasis on the initial stage of the process which revolves around the Ways and Means Committee.

Ways and Means—Treasury Department Relations

It is a maxim, by now, that although the Constitution separates authority among the three branches of government there is a good deal of overlap among the institutions and that, in fact, they share power and responsibility for legislation. To date, however, there are relatively few empirical studies of how the branches have bridged the formal separation and organized their interaction; there are even fewer studies of arrangements between individual congressional committees and related executive department agencies.[29] Congressional oversight of administration has received a fair amount of attention but much work remains to be done on the interaction between the branches in formulating policy, marking up bills, and striking a balance between the competing demands which are involved in the policy-making process.

One bridge between the branches is through the professional staff of Congress and its counterpart in the executive departments. For many years Joint Committee staff experts, under Stam and continuing under Woodworth, have worked with Treasury Department experts on technical tax problems in what are called staff "subcommittees."[30] A member of the Joint Committee staff summed up the purpose of these subcommittees:

We work very closely with Treasury people. Before a message is sent by the President we have these staff subcommittees composed of Joint Committee on Internal Revenue Taxation staff, Treasury people, and IRS [Internal Revenue Service] people. We discuss proposals drawn up by the Treasury's economists. These economists compose big ideas and general notions as to what Treasury ought to do on taxes—this is where it all starts. Then we get together in our subcommittee and discuss these ideas as to feasibility and technical possibility. Many times they aren't practical. We represent the Ways and Means Committee and let them know what the Committee may or may not accept. What we do in these meetings is kick ideas around, we brainstorm ideas.

The primary task of the subcommittee is to discuss, in a professional way, various tax proposals, the technical problems involved in drafting the language necessary to put them into effect, and the likelihood of congressional policy-makers responding positively or negatively to them.

Through the staff mechanism, then, the Ways and Means Committee members may learn what the Treasury Department is contemplating or not contemplating and Treasury receives technical assistance and valuable information about what the Committee is likely to accept or reject. Neither staff contingent has the authority to bind the policy-makers, of course, and the Joint Committee staff is careful about appearing to speak for its superiors. But policy questions are discussed, technical barriers to changing the Internal Revenue Code are resolved, and the subcommittees do serve as a way of combining the expertise of both staffs in the initial stage of the policy-making process. The prognostications of the congressional staff may or may not be heeded by Treasury. For example, in 1963 the joint staff warned the Department that Ways and Means would not approve the controversial proposal to limit itemized deductions to five percent of the taxpayer's adjusted gross income, but Treasury, committed to the five percent floor, proposed it anyway. The issue was not even put to a vote in Ways and Means. In other cases, however, the views of the congressional staff are taken into account when Treasury is deciding what to include in a tax message, and in this way the probable response of the Ways and Means Committee has a bearing on the initiation of tax legislation.

After the preliminaries are over and the Ways and Means Committee is in executive session, the Joint Committee staff, having spent hours in consultation with Treasury Department experts, is prepared to explain arcane tax proposals to the members. Since Ways and Means allows Treasury officials to attend and participate in its executive deliberations both staffs are involved in explaining the Treasury Department's proposals to the Committee. If the Secretary of the Treasury is especially well-versed in tax matters, as was Douglas Dillon on the proposal which became the Revenue Act of 1964, he will carry a large part of the burden of presenting the Department's case, and the Treasury staff will serve as a backstop to him. (One Committee member said Dillon spent so much time with the Committee in 1963 he began to wonder if the Secretary was using Ways and Means as a "hideout.") But the Joint Committee staff, playing the role of *Congress's* staff, ensures that the Committee hears all sides of the issues and, by so doing, the staff affects the decisions that are made. One staff man told how he helped a Committee member against Treasury:

Really, as far as I was concerned it was six of one and half a dozen of the other. Treasury was opposed to it but I pointed out that on the other hand these considerations could be taken into account and the Committee said since this is the case let's pass it. Later, after the Committee had done this, O'Brien [Thomas O'Brien, D.–Ill.] met me in the hall and he really went out of his way to thank me. He was very grateful and really all I had done was stated as near an objective opinion as possible.

As the above quote shows, when there is disagreement among the experts the Committee members are inclined to rely on their staff, not Treasury's. The general feeling is that the Joint Committee staff, which generates its own studies and data independent of the Treasury Department, has demonstrated that in a dispute with Treasury its studies are more reliable than the executive's. Two examples, one pertaining to the reduction of excise taxes, the other to raising the national debt limit, illustrate the Committee's faith in its staff and the ways in which the work of the staff affects policy outcomes.

In 1965, as part of a long-awaited excise tax reduction bill, the Administration proposed that the excise tax on automobiles be reduced in steps from ten percent to seven percent, and then to five percent by 1967 at which time the five percent levy would be permanent. Detroit's spokesman on the Ways and Means Committee, Martha Griffiths (D.–Mich.), proposed that the tax be removed altogether and at once, a proposal that would have cost the federal government over $1 billion in revenue. The Treasury Department, not wanting to increase the budget deficit by this much, opposed the Griffiths motion, and so did Chairman Mills. In the course of building his argument against the motion Mills argued that the Committee could not lift the automobile excise and stagger the tax on telephone service, so he asked Treasury how much reducing the telephone tax all at once would add to the deficit. Assistant Secretary Stanley Surrey replied that it would cost a half billion dollars. At this point Eugene Keogh (D.–N.Y.) asked how much a compromise proposal on the auto excise would cost and Mills then recognized Woodworth, the Chief of Staff. Woodworth informed the Committee that the joint staff figures showed that the federal budget deficit would be higher than that estimated by the Treasury, an observation which further argued against the Griffiths proposal. Representative Keogh asked a rhetorical question about whose estimates have usually been nearer the mark, Treasury's or the Joint Committee's staff, and Mills answered for Woodworth: the congressional staff. With the case made against the car makers' amendment Ways and Means voted. Griffiths, beaten on a voice vote, did not bother to press for a roll call. Mills, the Joint Committee staff, and Treasury, in concert, defeated the Griffiths amendment.

In the case of excise taxes the expertise of the Joint Committee staff buttressed the Treasury Department, but the congressional staff's work also helps the Committee take and support positions contrary to that of the Executive Branch. One such incident was the Committee's handling of the

1966 debt bill. On the basis of calculations about federal finances made by its staff, Ways and Means rejected the Administration's request for a $332 billion temporary limit on the national debt and recommended instead a $330 billion ceiling. The $2 billion cut was predicated on the joint staff's studies which showed that federal receipts would probably exceed the amount estimated by Treasury, the deficit would consequently be less than expected, and, therefore, a lower ceiling could be justified. The Committee's faith in its staff was not misplaced: a week after the House passed the bill Treasury Secretary Fowler acknowledged before the Senate Finance Committee that the Department, though squeezed, could live with the House figure.[31]

Thus Congress, through the staff of the Joint Committee on Internal Revenue Taxation, has a body of professionals which links its principal revenue-raising organs bicamerally, which serves as a communications link between the Ways and Means Committee and the Treasury Department, and which is so expert that the legislature has an in-house check on the expertise of the Executive Branch—so much so that the congressmen feel they can rely on their staff even in the face of conflicting information from the executive. Important as these functions are they do not exhaust the functions of the staff. One more aspect of the staff, its relations with interest groups, needs to be explored before one can appreciate the extent of the staff's services for the Ways and Means Committee.

Ways and Means—Interest Demands

Access to the Committee on Ways and Means is obtained in many ways. Members of the Committee act as the spokesmen for particular interests (e.g., the oil industry), the practice of holding public hearings on major bills is firmly rooted, and group spokesmen have on occasion been invited into the Committee's executive session to assist it in writing legislation (e.g., representatives of Blue Cross–Blue Shield were summoned to a closed meeting on medicare in 1965). Another line of access is through the Joint Committee staff. The staff is a common target for informed Washington lobbyists and the first stop for many constituent demands.

There is abundant evidence in the anecdotes which travel the Washington grapevine, the public record, and the perceptions of those involved in the policy-making process to support the observation that contacts between the staff and interested parties are frequent, legitimate, and important.

On the anecdotal level the story is told of Colin Stam that he carried so much weight with the formal policy-makers that a lobbyist who had difficulty getting to see him bought a dog and walked the canine around

Chevy Chase Circle in hopes of encountering the tax expert on his nightly dog-walking strolls. Apocryphal, perhaps, but the circulation of the story testifies to the importance of the staff to interest groups. "Nobody's been up to my neighborhood to see me yet," Woodworth has been quoted as saying,[32] but this may be because no one has yet had difficulty seeing him at the office.

Normally, access to the staff is not difficult. Stam, for example, used to hold quasi-hearings at which lobbyists would present their views on tax matters (a measure of his influence in the process), and Woodworth does the same. Many lobbyists have heard a member of Ways and Means or Senate Finance say, "See Stam" (and now, "See Larry"). Kenworthy quotes a tax attorney on how congressmen use the staff to winnow tax proposals and how the staff, contacted first, can reverse the procedure and assist a lobbyist:

The congressman says to the lawyer, "Go see Stam and then let me get a report from Stam." If Stam thinks there is no merit in the idea, the congressman will usually drop it. If Stam thinks there is merit, the congressman is likely to sponsor it.

An attorney will call on Stam to tell him what he would like to do and see whether it is in the cards. Stam may say, "Don't waste your time," or "You might be able to interest so-and-so in that." If Stam himself is interested he will explain the proposal to the congressman in friendly terms, without necessarily urging it, and so help put it across.[33]

"Stam's staff," as one Ways and Means member put it succinctly, "is very influential and that's why they are lobbied so much."

By receiving and analyzing tax proposals the staff increases the Committee's contacts with interested parties, which is an important part of the Ways and Means Committee's job, and at the same time it helps the members cope with the tremendous number of demands for changes in the Code. Many times, in fact, these demands are stimulated by the Committee itself as part of its legislative procedure. Prior to the passage of the 1954 Revenue Act, for example, the staff mailed a tax questionnaire to thousands of individuals and groups. Over 15,000 replies were received and over two dozen national associations did studies of various tax proposals before passage of the Act, the first major revision of the Code since 1939. So much of the work was done by the staff that one member, Jere Cooper (D.–Tenn.), argued that the Committee, with six weeks labor, still did not understand the bill reported to the House:

The staffs of the Joint Committee on Internal Revenue Taxation and the Treasury Department together have spent over two years preparing recommendations for the bill. Extensive hearings were held, and some 15,000 replies to questionnaires were reviewed preparatory to making recommendations to be included. In contrast to this, the committee deliberated on the bill for only six weeks. In my opinion, such a complete overhauling as this bill proposes to make involving the most complicated laws which Congress has ever written, would require at least one year to fully understand. . . .[34]

Another revealing example of the contacts between interest groups and the staff occurred in 1956 when the House considered a bill dealing with the renegotiation of government contracts. In this case the Committee did not make policy as much as it legitimatized the recommendations of the staff and business organizations. Thomas Jenkins (R.–Ohio) said of the bill:

> Mr. Speaker, this bill is the result of an exhaustive study by the staff of the Joint Committee on Internal Revenue Taxation. This study was conducted pursuant to statutory directive and lasted for many months. *Industry had a complete opportunity to present its problems to the staff.*[35]

Jenkins acknowledged that it may have been unfortunate that Ways and Means did not hold hearings but: "On the other hand, I believe that Mr. Stam and the joint committee staff did a magnificent job in developing these needed improvements in the act."[36] Small wonder that interest groups and individuals pay attention to the staff.

The testimony to the important role of the staff which is found in public record is, of course, the reflection of the staff's activities in countless private meetings with lobbyists and in the executive sessions of the Ways and Means Committee. When the members of Ways and Means descend from their dais and begin marking up a tax bill the staff becomes an integral part of the process. According to Thomas B. Curtis (R.–Mo.), when the doors are closed the staff represents the views of the people with whom it has been in contact:

The role of the Joint Committee staff is even more important during executive sessions when administration officials are the only outsiders present. Then the staff must represent the views of all other 'interests' whose positions are often discounted by the sometimes parochial outlook of Treasury and Internal Revenue Service officials and experts.[37]

The staff, in other words, brings to the discussion the results of its meetings and communications with people on the outside, thereby keeping the Committee informed on the views and arguments of those who will be affected by the Committee's decisions.

One example of this part of the staff's role will be cited. In 1965, when the Committee was considering President Johnson's proposed cut in excise taxes, the question arose as to whether or not the announcement of excise tax reductions would induce consumers to postpone buying certain items until the tax was removed, thus, in effect, creating a buyer's strike.

Woodworth reported to the meeting that the Joint Committee staff had contacted different industries to see if they thought a refund of any tax paid on such goods was needed to ward off a drop in sales. It first appeared, he stated, that the electrical appliance industry favored the refund idea, but consultation with the national organization of electrical manufacturers revealed that the only appliance to which the refund should definitely apply, due to the closeness of the summer selling season, was air conditioners. He also informed the meeting that many manufacturers were not too anxious to pass the tax cut on to consumers by way of lowered prices, and providing for a tax refund would increase the pressure on them to do so. This, together with the administrative burdens of handling the refund, argued against applying refunds to articles other than air conditioners. Ways and Means, guided by the information gathered by the staff from interested parties, decided to make the refund applicable to air conditioners.

Interest group representatives in Washington go where power is, or where they think power is, and the Joint Committee staff is not short-changed when it comes to contacts with lobbyists. A favorable response from the staff does not *assure* the same reaction from the tax committees, but with the complexity of tax legislation and the concomitant need of congressmen for expert guidance the likelihood of the decision-makers following the advice of the fact-finders is high. This does not mean that congressmen are captives of their staffs. By and large the staff probably reflects the views of the members more than it determines those views. But the above evidence shows that the staff can and does play an active role in the process. The input of the staff, one more variable for students of policy-making to consider, has received scant attention to date but it may warrant greater attention in the future.

CONCLUSION

From a case study of one staff it is impossible, of course, to answer the question of whether or not Congress needs more staff in order to compete effectively with the executive branch. All we can say is that in one significant area of public policy, revenue legislation, Congress is equipped to do much more than service constituents and oversee the bureaucracy. The House Ways and Means Committee is so well-equipped in this area that the Treasury Department usually presents its requests in the form of a tax message as opposed to a draft bill. The bill is the *product* of the Committee's work, not the start of it.

Having shown how the Joint Committee staff may affect the decisions of policy-makers, and discussed the linkage functions of the staff, we may speculate on some of the variables which are pertinent to the role of the staff. First in probable importance is, obviously, the nature of the subject matter handled by the committee. As the complexity of the decisions facing legislators increases so too does the likelihood that the staff will exert influence on the outcomes. Tax policy, infinitely complex, maximizes the importance of expertise. The importance of the staff is likely to vary on other committees with different tasks (e.g., the House Rules Committee, Government Operations).

Another factor that affects the influence of the staff is the scope of the decision. It is no accident that much of the criticism of Stam centered around his role in drafting and defending narrow tax provisions which helped particular industries, companies, or, in the case of Louis B. Mayer, one individual.[38] The more salient the issue is to a large number of participants the less likely the judgment of the staff will direct the decision. On purely economic grounds, for example, the Chief of Staff believed in the fall of 1967 that a tax increase was advisable but Chairman Mills led 19 other Ways and Means members in tabling the President's request until Congress and the President resolved the question of limiting federal expenditures. Staff studies, though not without some importance, bowed to the political barriers to passing a tax increase in the House.

Highly personal factors such as the relationship between the staff and leading members of the committees also deserve attention. There is in Congress a cadre of professional staff assistants who, like Stam, develop firm ties with influential congressmen, thus partaking of their sponsors' influence while they simultaneously contribute to it. Thomas J. Scott and Senator Carl Hayden, Oliver Meadows and Representative Olin Teague, Colin Stam and Representative Robert L. ("Muley") Doughton, John Barriere and Representative Albert Rains—these present and past relationships are important in the legislative process, too important to escape the attention of political scientists.

Other interesting questions about the role of the staff in the legislative process are not hard to imagine. On a committee such as House Post Office and Civil Service, for example, what are the consequences of having an unstable committee membership but a long-term professional staff director? How does the staff of a highly centralized committee (e.g., Ways and Means which does not work through subcommittees) differ from the Appropriations Committee which does almost all its work in subcommittees? Why is it that not one member of the current Democratic party leadership in the House has a staff confident other than House Parliamentarian Lewis Deschler? How do congressmen rely on the staff without becoming captives of the staff? Why are some highly capable men willing to refuse lucrative jobs outside of Congress in order to toil anonymously and at relatively low pay for congressmen? These questions, and others, will not be easy to answer but they appear to be sufficiently important to require some investigation.

It should be noted, in conclusion, that it is very difficult if not impossible to determine how much "power" the staff has in the policy-making process. On certain kinds of issues under certain conditions a staff man such as Colin Stam did indeed have power. But it was a curious kind of power. It depended upon the congruence between his judgment on policy and the judgment of the majority whom he served. In their frustration over the failure to change the internal revenue code one would expect the liberal critics of Stam to exaggerate his importance as a pillar of the status quo. Future research will demonstrate, I think, that Stam and other leading staff experts perform important functions in the legislative process but, in the final analysis, they take more cues from the formal policy-makers than they give.

NOTES

* This study is based on interviews with 23 members of the House Committee on Ways and Means, eight members of the Senate Finance Committee, five members of the congressional staff, and three high-ranking Treasury Department officials. Support was provided by the Congressional Fellowship program of the American Political Science Association (1963–1964), the APSA's Study of Congress under the direction of Ralph K. Huitt (research assistant to Richard F. Fenno, Jr., 1964–1965), and the Brookings Institution Research Fellowship Program (1965–66), all of whom are absolved of any responsibility for the content of the study. I would like to thank Professor Fenno for commenting on a draft of this paper.

[1] George B. Galloway, *The Legislative Process in Congress* (New York: Thomas Y. Crowell, 1953), pp. 605–12; Stephen K. Bailey, *Congress Makes a Law* (New York: Columbia University Press, 1950), pp. 61–64; Ernest S. Griffith, *Congress: Its Contemporary Role,* 3rd ed. (New York: New York University Press, 1961), pp. 86–89; Alfred de Grazia (ed.), *Congress: The First Branch of Government* (Washington, D.C.: American Enterprise Institute, 1966).

[2] Samuel P. Huntington, "Congressional Responses to the Twentieth Century," *The Congress and America's Future,* ed. David B. Truman (Englewood Cliffs, N.J.: Prentice-Hall, 1965), p. 30.

[3] See Reuss's statement before the Joint Committee on the Organization of Congress, 89th Cong., 1965–66, *Hearings,* pp. 80–100.

[4] Ralph K. Huitt, "Congressional Reorganization: The Next Chapter" (unpublished paper read at the annual meeting of the American Political Science Association, Chicago, September 8–12, 1964), p. 8. Emphasis added.

[5] Hugh Douglas Price, Review of Kenneth Kofmehl's *Professional Staffs of Congress,* in *American Sociological Review,* 28 (October, 1963), 859. Other studies of the staff which contain some helpful information are: Gladys Kammerer, *The Staffing*

of the Committees of Congress (Lexington, Ky.: University of Kentucky Press, 1949); James D. Cochrane, "Partisan Aspects of Congressional Committee Staffing," *Western Political Quarterly,* XVII (June, 1964), 338–48; Warren H. Butler, "Administering Congress: The Role of the Staff," *Public Administration Review,* XXVI (March, 1966), 3–13; Norman Meller, "Legislative Staff Services: Toxin, Specific, or Placebo for the Legislature's Ills," *Western Political Quarterly,* XX (June, 1967), 381–89.

6 U.S. Congress, House, Committee on Ways and Means, 69th Cong., 1st Sess., 1926, H. Rept. No. 1 to accompany H.R. 1, *The Revenue Bill of 1926,* p. 23.

7 *Congressional Record,* 69th Cong., 1st Sess., 1925, Vol. 67, Part 1, pp. 696–97.

8 *Ibid.,* Part 3, p. 2870.

9 See the remarks of Representative Collier, *Congressional Record,* 70th Cong., 2nd Sess., 1929, Vol. 70, Part 2, p. 1198.

10 *Congressional Record,* August 2, 1967 (daily edition), p. H9876.

11 "Where Tax Bills Run the Gauntlet," *Business Week,* June 11, 1966, p. 106; Arlen J. Large, "Help on the Hill," *Wall Street Journal,* June 25, 1965.

12 Roy M. Blough, *The Federal Taxing Process* (New York: Prentice-Hall, 1952), p. 64.

13 Thomas B. Curtis, "The House Committee on Ways and Means: Congress Seen Through a Key Committee," *Wisconsin Law Review* (Winter, 1966), 8.

14 *Hearings, op. cit.,* p. 477. McClellan's proposal has passed the Senate many times but to date leaders of the House Appropriations Committee have responded negatively.

15 *Ibid.,* pp. 1983, 1985, 800–01.

16 In justifying his successful request for more staff Long contended: "Under our Government the legislative branch is not supposed to be a lackey or the tool of the executive and is not to take the word of the executive on matters but should be able to acquire information itself." *Congressional Record,* April 20, 1966 (daily edition), p. 8239. He admitted that the Joint Committee staff does a good job but when they are working for Ways and Means the Finance Committee has only a secondary claim on their services. Long also argued that Finance has much nontax work to do and needs help which the joint staff cannot provide.

17 Quoted in "Where Tax Bills Run the Gauntlet," *op. cit.,* p. 106.

18 Quoted in Large, *op. cit.*

19 *Ibid.*

20 Stephen K. Bailey and Howard D. Samuel, *Congress at Work* (New York: Henry Holt, 1953), p. 342.

21 E. W. Kenworthy, "Colin F. Stam," *Adventures in Public Service,* eds. Delia and Ferdinand Kuhn (New York: Vanguard Press, 1963), p. 109.

22 *Ibid.,* p. 115.

23 *Congressional Record,* 83rd Cong., 1st Sess., 1953, Vol. 99, Part 6, p. 8493. Italics added.

24 After an apprenticeship with the Internal Revenue Bureau Stam joined the Joint Committee staff in 1927, became Chief of Staff in 1938, and ran it for a quarter of a century until his retirement in 1964. He suffered a stroke and died in January, 1966.

25 Kenworthy, *op. cit.,* p. 115.

26 Huitt reports similar complaints about Stam. See Ralph K. Huitt, "Congressional Organization and Operations in the Field of Money and Credit," *Fiscal and Debt Management Policies,* eds. William Fellner, *et al.* (Englewood Cliffs, N.J.: Prentice-Hall, 1963), pp. 452–53.

27 Quoted in "Where Tax Bills Run the Gauntlet," *op. cit.,* p. 111.

28 See Mills's plea for tax reform, "Are You a Pet or a Patsy," *Life,* November 23, 1959, 51 ff.

29 Notable exceptions include: J. Lieper Freeman, *The Political Process: Executive Bureau-Legislative Committee Relations,* rev. ed (New York: Random House, 1965); Richard F. Fenno, Jr., *The Power of the Purse* (Boston: Little, Brown, 1966), Chapters 6 and 7; James A. Robinson, *Congress and Foreign Policy-Making* (Homewood, Ill.: Dorsey Press, 1962), Chapters 5 and 6.

30 For brief descriptions of these subcommittees, see Blough, *op. cit.,* pp. 107–09, and Kofmehl, *op. cit.,* pp. 158–59.

31 Hobart Rowen, "Fowler Accepts House Dept Action," *Washington Post,* June 14, 1966. Before the Rules Committee, with Woodworth sitting behind him, Mills backed the Committee's action in these words: "I'm prone to believe that the staff itself may be more accurate than the Treasury."

32 Large, *op. cit.*

33 Kenworthy, *op. cit.,* p. 119.

34 *Congressional Record,* 83rd Cong., 2nd Sess., 1954, 100, Part 3, p. 3420.

35 *Congressional Record,* 84th Cong., 2nd Sess., 1956, 102, Part 9, p. 12726. Emphasis added.

36 *Ibid.,* p. 12726.

37 Curtis, *op. cit.,* p. 7.

38 For a study of special tax provisions see Stanley S. Surrey, "The Congress and the Tax Lobbyist—How Special Tax Provisions Get Enacted," *Harvard Law Review,* 70 (May, 1957), 1145–82. Surrey estimates that the Mayer amendment saved the tycoon about $2,000,000 in taxes. See also Philip M. Stern, *The Great Treasury Raid* (New York: Random House, 1963).

CHAPTER 14

The Job of the Congressman

Lewis A. Dexter

In the classical literature on democracy, notably in the writings of Burke, a lively debate concerned the question of whether the elected representative of the people should represent their interest as *he* sees it or as *they* see it. In either event, public opinion is regarded as pertinent, whether it be a constructive force guiding the representative's behavior or a corrupting force to which he makes concessions for the purpose of getting elected.

A neoclassical view of the democratic process, stemming from behavioristic political science, says in effect that it is naïve to think of legislators either as arriving independently at a decision in the general interest or as responding to the wishes of the general public. Organized special interests, according to this view, exercise the determining influence.[2] The general public, it asserts, lacks the capacity to make itself heard and, most especially, lacks the capacity to reward and punish legislators. The pressure groups which are articulate in presenting their views to Congress command attention because they, the pressure groups and not the general public, act to influence who will and will not be elected. In this view, organized pressure is the dynamo of politics.

One may well hold that all three models of the democratic process are correct in some instances and degrees. There are times when legislators out of their independent judgment arrive at decisions in the general interest. There are times when they respond to public opinion to the extent and in the sense they understand it, either because this corresponds to their ideal of democracy or because they wish to be re-elected. There are instances in which legislators succumb to the pressures of special-interest groups, as well as those in which they are under such pressures but resist them. A more sophisticated statement would hold that, in most legislative decisions,

Reprinted from Raymond A. Bauer, Ithiel de Sola Pool, and Lewis A. Dexter, *American Business and Public Policy: The Politics of Foreign Trade* (New York: Atherton Press, 1963), pp. 404–413. Reprinted by permission of Atherton Press, Inc. Copyright © 1963, Massachusetts Institute of Technology. Footnotes have been renumbered.

all three models apply to some extent. Often, the pressure of special-interest groups and of public opinion act as countervailing forces, offering the legislator independence in reaching a decision of his own choosing. Thus, what is involved is not a single process, but a set of interacting processes.

This would, in any event, seem a sufficiently complicated way of looking at things, and it is approximately the model of the democratic process which was in our minds when we designed our study and gathered our data. Yet, even this eclectic model proved insufficient when it came to understanding just what went on in Congress. It was an inadequate representation of the forces and processes at work there.

The flaw in that model of the legislative decision-process was that it postulates certain issues and certain alternative solutions to them as given. It assumes that these issues are somehow there in the legislative arena and that the legislator finding the issues before him must pay attention to them and reach decisions on them. It pictures the legislator as much like a student before a multiple-choice examination, in which he faces fixed alternatives and selects an answer among them. The model with which we started and, for that matter, most decision theory concerns that kind of situation of defined options. The question asked by such theory is what groups or interests or forces operate to determine a choice, the alternatives being pre-defined.

What we actually found, on the contrary, was that the most important part of the legislative decision-process was the decision about which decisions to consider. A congressman must decide what to make of his job. The decisions most constantly on his mind are not how to vote, but what to do with his time, how to allocate his resources, and where to put his energy. There are far more issues before Congress than he can possibly cope with. There are very few of them which he does not have the freedom to disregard or redefine. Instead of choosing among answers to fixed issues, he is apt to be seeking out those issues that will meet fixed answers. He can select those issues which do not raise for him the Burkean dilemma; that is, he can select those issues on which he feels no special tension between his own views and those of his constituents.

The issues or answers the congressman chooses to deal with are largely determined by the kind of job he as an individual wishes to do. The model of the legislative decision-process toward which we inevitably moved was one dealing with the congressman's choices about his career, his professional identity, his activities, rather than one dealing primarily with choices about his policies. It was also a model which took as the relevant criterion for choice the over-all needs of his position, rather than the views on specific policies held by special groups of the public. Any model is a simplification which accounts for only a part of the observations. What we are asserting is that looking at how a congressman defined his job helped us account for his behavior on reciprocal trade as much as did looking at the foreign-trade issue or at the involvements in it of his constituents and other groups.

We were thus forced to look at the Congressional process from a different perspective. What compelled us to do so was our own specific relationship to the problem under scrutiny. Frequently, social-science studies of public events proceed historically. The scholar begins with an event and seeks out antecedents that constitute a seemingly adequate explanation for the occurrence that is the focus of his interest. The actual nature of the consequent event serves him as a criterion of the relevance of prior events. He can ignore aspects which he might have thought relevant but for the wisdom of hindsight.

Our study was a historical one in the sense that we were interested in a single occurrence and its antecedent circumstances. But, since we were studying the event in the making, we could not use hindsight to know what would prove relevant to an event the ultimate shape of which we could not yet know. In the latter respect, our investigation was similar to an analyti-cal-predictive one. In a strictly analytic study dealing with the interrela-tionship of a limited number of variables, the scholar's theoretical interests serve as a criterion of relevance. He is free to ignore factors which fall outside his theoretical scheme so long as this scheme yields a satisfactory pay-off. In an analytical-predictive study, statistical predictions are made on the basis of a limited analytic model. If a sufficient proportion of events in a given category are (sic) predicted correctly, one is satisfied.

Our study was also different from these in that we were trying to anticipate ("predict" would be too pretentious a word) what was going to be significant in a single instance, and we could not remain content with the general validity of our model. Thus, we could not study the single event, the controversy over the Reciprocal Trade Act, by itself. We had to look at it in the context of the other things which were going on in Congress at the same time. As we shall illustrate at length, this is not a simple statement of the truism that "everything is related to everything else."

Our frame of attention had to include more of what was going on in Congress while the Reciprocal Trade Act was being considered than it would if we had had knowledge of subsequent events to guide us. This paper is a systematization of certain features of the Congressional process that came to our attention while we were thus trying to anticipate and understand the events as they were taking place. It is an essay on some aspects of the Congressional process and not a history of the passage of the Reciprocal Trade Act in 1954 and 1955.

CHOOSING A JOB

It is a cliché that the main job of a congressman is to be re-elected. There is much truth to it, but there are various ways of getting re-elected. Somehow, the congressman must do things which will secure for him the esteem and/or support of significant elements of his constituency. This he can achieve in many ways. He can seek for himself a reputation as a national leader, which may sometimes impress his constituents. He can work at press relations, creating and stimulating news stories and an image of activity. He can be a local civic leader, attending and speaking at community functions. He can make a reputation for himself in the field of legislation. In some states, he can be a party wheel horse and rely on the organization to back him. He can get people jobs and do social work and favors. He can become a promoter of certain local industries. He can conduct investigations and set himself up as a defender of public morals. He can take well-publicized trips to international hot spots. He can befriend moneyed interests to assure himself a well-financed campaign. He can befriend labor unions, veterans' organizations, or other groups with a numerous clientele and many votes. The one thing he cannot do is much of all these things. He must choose among them; he has to be a certain kind of congressman.

The reason he must choose is the scarcity of resources. Resources are various; they include time, money, energy, staff, information, and good will. All these have one common characteristic—there is never enough. They must all be budgeted and used with discretion. Opportunity is striking constantly or at least standing outside the door, but it is only occasionally that one has the wherewithal to capitalize on it. The skill of a congressman is to make the choices which, with the resources at hand, will get him the greatest results in doing the kind of Congressional job he has chosen to do.

Furthermore, his choices are not discrete. Choices on the use of scarce resources are never independent, for what is used for one purpose cannot be used for another. The choices are linked in other ways, too, for Congress is both a social system and part of a larger social system. The individuals with whom a legislator interacts in one transaction may be the same ones involved in another. The choice to spend time and effort in winning a particular friend can hardly be independent of another choice which would make of that person an enemy.

For these reasons, a rational congressman who has decided what kind of congressman he wants to be would then use his resources according to strategies consisting of whole packages of related acts. His stand on a particular issue would be far less dependent on what was specifically involved in that issue than on its role in a general policy or strategy on which he was working. Congressmen are no more rational political men than businessmen are rational economic men. Yet, to the extent that they are partially that and that a "maximizing"[3] model helps us understand their behavior, the model must be one relating continuing strategies, all aimed at achieving a certain kind of job success, not one dealing with strategies to maximize success on discrete issues. The skillful congressman—and, in this respect, most congressmen are skillful—makes his choices in terms of ways of living in a continuing political system. He constantly weighs his future relations with his colleagues.

A skillful congressman also takes account of the strategies of the other players in the Capitol arena and the rules of the game there. He is part of a multiperson game in which the goals of the different players vary and in which each defines them for himself; in which the pieces are the scarce resources which can be allocated; and in which the optimal strategies depend on the coalitions which can be formed, the procedural rules of the house in which the game is being played, and the power and the goals of the other players. Voting strategies depend on many things besides the pros and cons of issues. A senior senator, for example, can seek for himself the mantle of statesman with some chance of success, thanks to unlimited debate and his ability to balance special interests in one part of the state against those in another. A representative has far less chance of playing that particular kind of game. Again, a congressman can afford to vote the popular position in his constituency although he believes it wrong when he knows that there will be enough Congressional votes to defeat him anyway. He may have to vote his principles with courage when he thinks his vote is going to count. But, even then, he may, if skilled at parliamentary procedure, satisfy his constituents by dramatic votes and gestures at moments when they cannot succeed.

How a congressman defines his job, the importance of choice in the use of his time and resources, the continuing character of Congress as a social system, and the constraints of procedure and interaction form the substance of this essay. The congressman is typically thrust unprepared into a specialized milieu and confronted with a massive volume of highly technical legislation, with most of which he can deal only superficially. Counting on the assistance of a modest staff, he must work within the framework of a committee structure and is burdened with the additional task of servicing myriad personal requests from his constituents. These pressures combine to make time one of the congressman's most critical resources and the study of its allocation and husbanding a key to the legislative process.

ALLOCATING TIME

The scholar tends to approach his problem as though it had equal salience in the minds of men dealing with it on a practical basis. In reality, however, there are infinite demands on the congressman which he must meet with finite means. Both the scholar and the newsman often miss this point in their assumption that congressmen can pay attention to all issues of national policy. We began our study with two major interests: legislation and communication. We wanted to know what congressmen did about tariff legislation, and we wanted to know what and who influenced them in what they did. We tended to assume that the issues of public policy which were crucial to us were as crucial to the men with whom we were talking. Yet, few congressmen viewed tariff legislation as their primary concern, and the way in which many of them noticed what they read and heard about reciprocal trade was in large part a consequence of the fact that tariff legislation was simply one of several competing interests for them.

The low priority assigned tariff matters and the effect of that on what congressmen heard and did may be examined by considering their allocation of time. We could equally proceed by looking at the allocation of any other resource, particularly good will, for that is one of the most essential commodities in which a politician deals—there are limits to the frequency with which he can draw on his available fund of it. But let us look here at the consequences of the shortage of time in the congressman's life. A congressman is a member of what sociologists call a free profession, in that he makes his working schedule for himself. His job is undefined and free, not only in schedule, but also in content and in standards of achievement. As a result, he lives under a heavy burden of multiple choices, and, what is more, the choices he has to make are far more fateful than those most citizens make. The citizen may conceive of the congressman tackling his highly responsible choices with the same care and awe with which the citizen imagines himself tackling the few really responsible choices which he makes. But, by the very nature of their busy lives, congressmen cannot do this.

Let us consider the ways in which a congressman may occupy his time. He may concentrate on any of the following aspects of his job:

1. Legislative planning—the working out of legislation in committee.
2. Legislative criticism—an unpopular role in the House, but one common in the Senate.
3. Parliamentary procedure—specializing in rules and regulations for the conduct of Congressional business.

4. Legislative tactics—like Lyndon Johnson when he was majority leader, or James Byrnes in an even earlier period.
5. Investigation.
6. Public education—rallying support for causes through forums, speeches, articles.
7. Personal advertisement and campaigning—birthday and condolence letters to constituents, congratulations to graduating high school seniors, news letters, press releases, trips back home.
8. Seeing visitors and shaking hands.
9. Personal service—rectification of bureaucratic injustices; facilitating immigration of relatives of constituents; arranging military leaves, transfers, and hardship releases; helping confused constituents to route their inquiries to the right administrative offices; providing information on social security rights, etc.
10. Representation of local or state interests—Sen. Wiley (R., Wis.), ranking Republican on the Foreign Relations Committee, reported: "In 1939 on the occasion of the 75th anniversary of the Wisconsin cheese industry, it was my pleasure to preside over an appropriate celebration in Washington. It featured the world's largest cheese. . . . The cheese was eventually cut up and distributed . . . to Senators, Representatives, Congressional employees, newspapermen and others. . . . I am satisfied that advancing the interests of one of the foremost food industries of my state . . . is one of the jobs for which I was sent to Washington. . . ."[4]
11. Participating in national political organization or campaigning—for example, Sen. A. S. Mike Monroney (D., Okla.) has been chairman of the Speakers Division of the Democratic National Committee.
12. Development of local political organization and leadership—many senators are state political bosses, for example, the late Sen. Pat McCarran in Nevada.

A congressman might decide that his chief responsibility is, after all, legislation. Even so, there is far too much legislation for any particular legislator to attend to all of it. During the Eighty-third Congress, 1953–1955, which we were studying, the following legislative issues were among those considered:

1. Reciprocal Trade Extension acts of 1953 and 1954
2. Customs simplifications bills

3. Cargo Preference Act of 1954
4. Excise tax
5. Complete overhauling of federal tax system
6. Social security revision
7. Unemployment compensation measures
8. Appropriations measures
9. Amendment to the Constitution[5]
10. Civil service pay raises
11. The lease-purchase bill
12. Revision of health-welfare-grant formulas
13. Flexible price supports
14. Reduction of wheat acreage
15. Reduction of the Air Force
16. Establishment of an Air Academy
17. Building of twenty merchant ships
18. Upper Colorado development
19. Niagara Falls development
20. Highway aid
21. Commercial use of atomic-energy patents
22. Range improvements by private interests on public lands
23. Alaskan statehood
24. Hawaiian statehood
25. End of price controls
26. Revision of the Taft-Hartley Act
27. New health insurance law
28. Windfall profits
29. The Bricker amendment
30. Wiretap bills
31. Suffrage for eighteen-year-olds
32. Raising the federal debt ceiling
33. Tidelands oil
34. Sale of government rubber plants
35. Abolition of the Reconstruction Finance Corporation
36. The St. Lawrence Seaway
37. Special Refugee Immigration Law
38. Interest rate rise for Federal Housing Administration
39. Excess profits tax
40. Bill for twenty-six new judgeships
41. Witness immunity measures
42. Ten plans for government reorganization
43. Rise in postal rates.

In addition, during the Eighty-third Congress members of the Senate were confronted with a number of other time-consuming issues which were not properly legislative but were more important than many laws in terms of policy. Prominent among these were the censuring of Sen. Joseph McCarthy (R., Wis.), the proposal to unseat Sen. Dennis Chavez (D., N.M.), and the confirmation of appointments to major commissions, cabinet and diplomatic posts, and judgeships. Some appointments were highly controversial. The appointment and confirmation of ex-Representative Joseph Talbot (R., Conn.) to the Tariff Commission seems to have been regarded in many quarters as as great a protectionist victory as passage of the Fuel Oil Quota (Simpson) Bill would have been.

In the same session, the Senate and House conducted at least sixty-five investigations, some of which had specific legislative purposes. Finally, it should be considered that interested members of the House and Senate may and do devote long hours of work to legislative proposals that never reach the floor or achieve serious consideration in committee.

Only painstaking and continuous study can give a legislator command of the often complex details of any one of the many proposed pieces of legislation. Few congressmen can or do master more than a handful of them. A congressman with years of service may in time develop expertness in a particular field of legislation, but the best-informed of our lawmakers are fully acquainted with only a fraction of the bills that come before each session.

Furthermore, even if some particular legislation is the major focus of interest of a given congressman, usually, if he is to be re-elected, he cannot completely ignore other aspects of his job.[6] Said one administrative assistant:

> You know this business; it is like trying to deal with a great immovable beast or cleanse the Augean stables . . . you just cannot do much. . . . The Senator is now a member of fourteen important subcommittees, and he just cannot split up his time. . . . Now there is the [particular] subcommittee— . . . and all those questions are tremendous and vital questions. . . . Yet, you try to get these senators [members of the subcommittee] even to agree to meet at any one time and you cannot even do that . . . they are so independent and rushed and all doing things their own way.[7]

Not only is the congressman himself overcommitted, but he is surrounded by similarly busy men. A salient fact about the congressman's job is that what he does is invariably accomplished through other people, most of whom are as busy as himself. He becomes involved in a complex web of interdependence with colleagues and constituents as a result of the fact that each must work through the other to get what he wants, whether it be re-election, the passage of a piece of legislation, or service from a congressman. To anticipate a point which we shall develop later, it is highly naïve to think of a congressman as being under pressure from one direction or even as being under cross-pressure from two opposing directions. More typically, he is under simultaneous influence and demands from many directions, a large number of which are relevant to the issue with which the scholar or interest group is concerned only in that they compete with that issue for the congressman's time and energies.

However, our purpose is not to argue that congressmen are busy people but to show specifically that their busyness affected their reaction to the reciprocal-trade extension.

Busyness blocked effective communication of constituents' views to their congressmen. A congressman can seldom readily inform himself as to how his constituents feel about any issue. A sense of acting in the dark about public opinion plagued many of the legislators we interviewed. On the simplest level, communications with respect to foreign-trade policy had to compete with, and frequently were lost in, the welter of other communications. This is particularly true of conversations which congressmen and their assistants had with other people. In 1955, a senator's assistant commented:

> You know, so many people have come into the office in the last two weeks on all these things—rubber disposal, stock market, reciprocal-trade extensions, and taxes—I just haven't been able to keep in mind which was which; and I think it is pretty difficult for the Senator to keep track, too.

One representative who was very much concerned with the Reciprocal Trade Act complained about his impossible work load. He had recently been back to his district; he could remember vaguely that a number of people had talked to him about tariff and foreign-trade policy, but he could not recall who had wanted what.

Both these men belonged to the committees which handled reciprocal-trade extension. Yet, even for them, it was but one issue among many. They had no time to give more than a hurried glance to communications about it. As a result, they, too, had only the haziest notion of what public opinion in their constituency really was. The communications they received were poorly remembered and ill-understood. Most messages left only the impression that something had been said, not a clear recollection of what was said. We find that the net effect of communication was to heighten attention to an issue, rather than to convey specific content about it.

NOTES

[1] Based on Lewis Anthony Dexter, "Congressmen and the People They Listen To" (submitted in partial fulfillment of the requirements for the Ph.D. to Columbia University, 1959), here drastically condensed. The data arose mostly from interviews conducted by Dexter and the other authors. Dexter's major assignment in 1954–1955 was to observe and to interview on Capitol Hill. In all, about fifty members of Congress were interviewed, some several times. An equal number of closely affiliated persons, such as administrative assistants, were interviewed, some on a continuing basis. These interviews were supplemented by information from other sources. No attempt was made to tabulate the interviews, since they followed the journalistic principle of asking each man about those matters on which he had something interesting to say, rather than the survey principle of asking each man the same thing.

[2] Cf. Schattschneider, *op. cit.;* E. P. Herring, *Group Representation before Congress* (Baltimore: Johns Hopkins Press, 1929); D. Truman, *Governmental Process* (New York: Knopf, 1951).

[3] Actually, as already indicated, we believe Herbert Simon's concept of "satisficing" is more appropriate, though less familiar.

[4] Wiley, *Laughing with Congress* (New York: Crown, 1947), pp. 136–41. This book probably has the best treatment of the Congressional work load. It is one of the indispensable books about Congress for anybody trying to find out what Congress does. Especially valuable is Chapter VI, "The Office Inferno," particularly pp. 90–96.

[5] A resolution providing for the replacement of House members killed in a national emergency.

[6] For a variety of reasons, House members, if they are so minded, are freer to "take it easy" than members of the upper body. They represent a smaller constituency. Crucial decisions in the House are usually made by the leadership. Also, each member of the larger House is on fewer committees.

[7] A senatorial assistant rejected the idea of having an intern from the American Political Science Association in his office because "the intern has lots of ideas—mostly good—but every single one of them means more work." We should note that among the duties of a congressman is running his own office and staff. By 1959, House members received approximately $40,000 a year for the maintenance of staffs. They were permitted to employ as many as eight persons. In addition, members were allowed $1,200 per session for stationery, 2,700 minutes of telephone service, 12,000 words of telegraph service, $600 a year for official office expenses in the district, and $200 a year for air-mail and special-delivery stamps. Very few members employ as many as eight persons or spend quite the maximum. Few congressmen receive office space adequate for that number, and the use of a staff that large is likely to involve the personal financing of some office expenses.

The amount available to senators for staff purposes varies from state to state. The average expense appeared to be more than $50,000 a year. This usually permits the senator to employ two or three professional persons as legislative and administrative assistants and two or three clerks.

CHAPTER 15

A Simulation of Municipal Budgeting: The Impact of Problem Environment

John P. Crecine

---

1. ORGANIZATION OF PAPER

We can view the municipal resource allocation process, in toto, as a nearly decomposable system.[1] Simon and Ando, and Ando and Fisher have dealt with the case of a linear dynamic system and described conditions under which it is appropriate to aggregate variables and processes [10]. Essentially, by considering different time perspectives, certain systems can be shown to decompose into a series of analyzable, independent (in the short run) subsystems. It is contended that the simulation model of the municipal budgetary process discussed in this paper is such a subsystem embedded in a larger socioeconomic system.

We have shown elsewhere that the budgetary (sub-) system is internalized, having as its primary link to the larger environment the revenue constraint (tax rates × yields) [6, Chap. 10]. In addition, we have also demonstrated that the budgetary problem-solving system can be closely approximated by a set of linear functions [6, Chap. 8], thus approximating both the "nearly decomposable systems" and "linear" criteria of the Simon–Ando and Ando–Fisher works.

When there exists a nearly independent (sub-) system of (linear) equations[2] embedded in a larger system, the *ceteris paribus* assumption for that subsystem is reasonable for many purposes. In addition, one can analyze the *relative* behavior of variables in the subsystem by viewing the overall system as an aggregate index (i.e., level of revenues) [10, pp. 66–67]. This will be done.

In dealing with the "impact of the environment," we are justified in dividing the topic into two parts: (1) environment as contained in the

Reprinted by permission of the authors. Notations in brackets refer to the citations in the general bibliography at the end of this chapter, e.g., [9, pp. 66–67] refers to reference no. 9, pp. 66–67, in the bibliography.

"decomposable subsystem," and (2) the impact of the total system (external environment) on the long-run dynamics of the subsystem.[3]

We shall first discuss the overall system, locating in it the "decomposable subsystem" implicit in our simulation model of the budgetary process [6, Chap. 9]. The subsystem and relevant aspects of the *internal* environment will be discussed. Using the Simon–Ando [10] and Ando–Fisher theorems [1] on decomposable systems, we shall analyze the long-run dynamics of the budgetary simulation model.

2. TOTAL ENVIRONMENT: SYSTEM AND DECOMPOSABLE SUBSYSTEM

A review of the public expenditure literature reveals the general pattern of interaction found in Fig. 1. Generally, differences in per capita expenditures between cities are said to be explained by differences in tastes (white collar–blue collar employment distribution, median per capita income, population age distribution, value of housing), need (population density, and so on), ability to pay (industrial assessments, median income, assessed valuation, wealth, federal and state revenues), costs (population size—economies of scale, size of suburbs), political factors (party competition, owner–renter ratio, "power" structure), service standards[4] (national or regional norms), and precedent. In general, it is implicitly assumed that

Figure 1
Environmental Factors in Municipal Finance

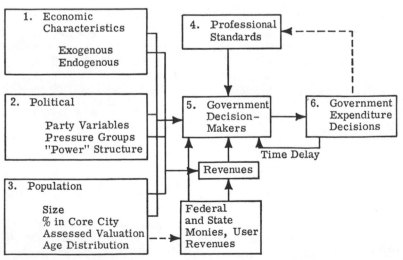

these environmental (external) factors drive the (governmental) decision system and determine expenditures. The exact nature of the "mechanism" that translates these external pressures and environmental determinants of public expenditure decisions is hardly ever specified.

In a very real sense it is clear that the immediate determinant of expenditures is "planned expenditures" or the budget.

An investigation of the decision process surrounding the municipal budget in three large cities (Cleveland, Detroit, and Pittsburgh) produced a simulation model describing a (sub-) system with the following characteristics:

a. The municipal budget is but one decision process in a sequence. The sequence might be described as follows—the revenue or level decisions, the budget or allocation decisions (municipal budget), and the actual expenditure or operating decisions. The elements in this hierarchy of decisions are separated by time and partly because of this are treated as largely independent problems. Each decision in the sequence forms a rigid constraint for the decision following it in the sequence. This administrative division of labor has the effect of making the municipal resource allocation problem a manageable one [see Fig. 2].

b. The structure of decision rules for formulating the municipal operating budget is basically the same, over time, in large cities with only the parameters varying between cities. (The model functions are of the same mathematical form, contain the same variables, and differ only in the constant terms or parameters.)

c. Three institutional rules or norms appear dominant in all municipalities tested:
   1. Balanced budget requirement in city charter (revenue constraint).
   2. Physical form of budget preparation sheets for departmental budget requests (forces historical comparisons).
   3. Uniform wage policy (one group of employees does not receive a wage increase unless all municipal employees are granted one—wages account for 65–80 percent of a city's total operating expenses); occasionally, the uniformed police and fire ranks are treated separately from the other city employees.

d. The decision rules used by members of the municipal governments appear to be internalized and to a large extent insulated from external pressures.

e. The decision system appears to be responsive only to special revenue opportunities, to long-run, cumulative "political" pressures, or to reasonably "catastrophic" events in the short-run.

f. Municipal operating budgets exhibit a great deal of organizational inertia.

g. The decision process can best be described as one in which the problem solver is faced with a great deal of uncertainty about future events and must satisfy a large number of fairly restrictive constraints, rather than as a process having a great deal of "political" content.

h. The general hypothesis that "the more 'complex'[5] the problem, the 'simpler' the decision rules used to solve it" is supported by the findings of this study.

i. "Last year's" budget represents a sort of equilibrium solution to the municipal resource allocation problem for city officials. "This year's budget" represents marginal adjustments to "last year's" solution to obtain "this year's" solution.

j. The lack of comparable performance data perceived by city officials (budgets and expenditures in one city "not the same" as "our situation") leaves the budget maker with little alternative but to use historical decisions as the primary reference point for current decisions [6, Chap. 6].

k. The decision-makers' cognitive maps of the process have as key variables the standard account categories and administrative units provided by the city's accounting system.

Assuming the model describes reality, it is clear that the budgetary process is relatively independent of sets of relationships and decisions occurring before and after the budgetary decision process. Such a causal hierarchy (see Fig. 2) is a decomposable—but not *completely* decomposable—system, as described by Ando and Fisher [1, p. 101; 2, p. 109].

Figure 2
Hierarchy of Decisions

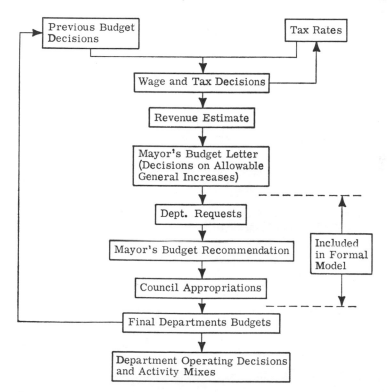

(T)his kind of assumption is equivalent to saying that our variables can be collected into sets *numbered* (from 1 to N, say) so that the variables in any given set are functions of their own past values *and* of the past-values of the variables in any lower-numbered set but not of the past values of the variables in any higher-numbered one. This sort of system is called *decomposable*. . . . Clearly, the dynamic behavior of any set of variables (in our case, those variables in the budgetary decision process) in a decomposable system can be studied, taking the behavior of variables in lower-numbered sets as given (i.e., the revenue constraint or tax policy) and without any regard for higher-numbered sets (the department's actual operations as opposed to appropriations). (Note, however, that the influence of lower-numbered sets *must* be explicitly recognized.) [2, p. 109].

This is precisely the kind of causal chain illustrated in Fig. 2. In our simulation model, the "revenue constraint" is a crucial variable, but "departmental operations" are not.

Within the budgetary process there are really three distinct subprocesses or subsystems: the formulation of department requests, the mayor's budget recommendation process, and the action of the council in making final appropriations.[6] These three subsystems of the budgetary subsystem also exhibit many of the characteristics of decomposable systems.[7]

We next move to an explicit discussion of the internal environment of the budgetary subsystem of municipal resource allocation.

3. INTERNAL ENVIRONMENT—OVERVIEW

The budgetary decision process can be thought of as an organized means for the decision-maker to deal with the *potential* complexity of the budgetary problem.[8] The most prominent feature of the "original" problem in terms of its contribution to complexity is an externally imposed constraint of a balanced budget—by requiring that, *at some level of generality,* all budget items be considered simultaneously.

A. Internal Environment—Role of Problem Complexity

We contend that the most prominent feature of the budgetary problem in terms of its *impact* on the internal environment is potential complexity. This argument is made in a heuristic spirit. We argue that the existence of potential complexity delimits the range of appropriate behavior. There are not many procedures that are both feasible in terms of individual cognitive and informational limitations and likely to produce a problem solution (balanced budget). Two classes of solution procedures come to mind:

1. Make separate judgments for each expenditure item (line item or

program). Add these to estimate total expenditures and change tax rates so that planned expenditures (budget) roughly equal planned revenues.

2. Gear the year to year adjustment in individual expenditure items to changes in anticipated revenues, holding tax rates constant (not yields).

Both procedures avoid rather than deal with complexity (interrelated decisions). We have found category 2 procedures in use.[9]

The "problem" referred to from this point on is the budgetary problem as seen by the actual decision-makers (department officials, mayor and mayor's staff, and council members). It is quite clear (from interviews) that the decision-makers *do not* see the problem as one of optimally balancing community resources or allocating funds among functions to achieve community goals. The problem is generally seen differently by different participants:

1. Department head—problem of submitting a budget request (to the mayor) that assures the department of funds to maintain the existing level of operations, is acceptable to the mayor's office, and provides for a "reasonable" increase if there is to be an increase in the total city budget.

2. Mayor—problem primarily of *balancing* the budget, maintaining existing service levels, providing for increases in city employee wages if at all possible, and avoiding tax increases. If the mayor has "extra" funds after dealing with the above problems, they will be used to grant portions of departments' supplemental requests.

3. Council—because of the complexity and detail in the mayor's budget and lack of council staff, the council's options are largely limited to approving (sometimes with very minor modifications) the mayor's budget.

Part of the way municipal decision-makers deal with the *potential* complexity of the municipal resource allocation problem is through their necessarily simplified perception of the problem as discussed above. Other simplifying heuristics observed were:

1. The operating budget is treated separately from the capital budget as a generally independent problem. The only behavioral connection between the operating and capital budgets is the "logical" elaboration of capital budgeting decisions in the operating budget.

2. The budget is formulated within a system of administrative units (department and bureaus) and account categories (salaries, supplies and expenses, equipment, and so on) that is extremely stable from year to year. This partial structuring of the problem "allows" most of the decision-makers to treat the appropriation question for one account category in one administrative unit as a (sub-) problem, separate from the overall resource allocation problem. Thus the overall problem is transformed into a series of smaller problems of determining appropriations for individual departments.

3. The revenue estimates are generally separate from expenditure estimates. That is, estimates of yields from a given tax are treated independently from expenditures. Although, on occasion, tax rates may be adjusted somewhat on the basis of preliminary calculations of *total* expenditure *estimates*, in order to balance the budget, tax *yield estimates* are seldom manipulated to achieve a balance.

4. The structure of the decision process itself represents a division of labor between department heads, the mayor's office, and the council— reflecting not only the administrative hierarchy but a set of simplifying heuristics for making a complex problem manageable.

5. Finally, an additional simplifying policy is found in all cities investigated. The presence of a uniform wage policy that maintains relative positions of employees within a city-wide civil service pay scale eliminates the potentially complex problem of deciding wage rates on an individual basis while attempting to maintain some kind of "similar pay for similar jobs" standards.

The *potential* complexity of the budgetary problem is created by the balanced budget requirement. The impact of this feature of the problem environment may be appreciated more fully by examining what the requirement of a *balanced* budget *could* mean. It would mean that the mayor not only would have to consider every budget item (of several hundred), but ". . . somehow the entire level of police expenditures (on equipment, for instance) would have to be justified in light of the implied preemption of health department services, public works, fire department expenditures, etc." [5, p. 789]. The mayor has neither the time, cognitive capabilities, knowledge, nor staff to make these judgements.

A simplified perception of the problem by the decision-makers "converts" the task to a manageable one. Complexity is further reduced by partitioning the problem into a series of manageable subproblems using the simplifying heuristics discussed above. This partition is of a particular kind—creating a system that is decomposable with subproblems arranged roughly in a "causal hierarchy," with solutions to one subproblem forming the givens for the next subproblem, and with little or no feedback between subproblems (see Fig. 3).

The hierarchic flow of decisions in the municipal budgetary process is illustrated in Fig. 4. The formal, simulation model consists of three submodels: DEPT, MAYORS, and COUNCIL (items A, B, and C, respectively, in Fig. 4).[10] The outputs of the departmental request submodels are inputs to the mayor's submodel and outputs of the mayor's submodel are inputs to the council appropriations submodel.

The outputs of each submodel correspond quite closely, in number

Figure 3
Fragmentation of Municipal Decisions

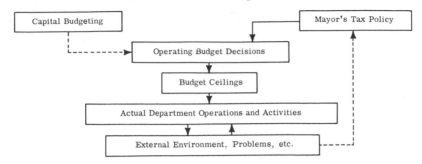

Figure 4
Overview of Decision Procedures

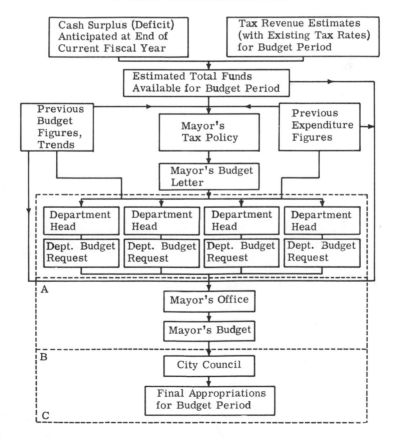

and level of detail, with the outputs (or decisions) found in the municipal budgetary process. In the model, each department included in the general fund or operating budget has requests for appropriations for each of two to five standard account categories—depending on the city involved. For example, the model produces, at each of the three stages of the decision process, dollar estimates for the City Planning Department as given in Table 1.

Table 1
Model Detail

Cleveland	Detroit	Pittsburgh
Personal services $\}$ X	Administrative salaries Nonadm. salaries $\}$ X	Administrative salaries $\}$ X Nonadm. salaries $\}$ Y
Materials Supplies Expenses $\}$ Y Equipment Repairs and improvements	Materials, supplies, and expenses $\}$ Y Equipment and repairs $\}$ Z	Materials, supplies, and expenses $\}$ W Equipment $\}$ U Maintenance $\}$ Z

Forty-four to 64 departments and administrative units are involved in the cities examined, with each unit having estimates for two to five accounts. Between 128 and 220 decisions are produced at each of the three stages of the model, for each year tested, in each of the three cities examined.

At this point one might legitimately ask two important questions:

1. Why are accounts categorized in the manner indicated?

2. Why is "dollars" the unit of resource allocation rather than men, number of street lights, and so on?

Both questions are "crucial" ones for a normative theory of budgeting. In a positive theory, however, the answers are rather straightforward— and essentially identical. People interviewed in all three cities think and talk in terms of "dollars"; they differentiate (at least in interviews) expenditures in terms of the same categories used in their city's accounting system. Apparently, dollar amounts provide the relevant reference points for dealing with the conceptual framework provided by the city's accounting system and provide the bases for the participants' cognitive maps of the process.

B. DEPT. Submodel

Role. The role of the department head is similar to that of the agency or bureau chief in the federal government as described in the Wildavsky study [12, pp. 8–21]. His objective is to obtain the largest possible amount of funds for his department and his purposes. Just as "Washington is filled . . . with dedicated men and women who feel that government funds should be spent for one purpose or another" [11, p. 414], so are municipal governments. In general, department heads, through experience and the process of socialization into their positions, and by "learning" that their request is likely to be cut by the mayor's office or council, tend to ask for more than they "expect" to get. This "padding" of the budget is one part of a system of mutual expectations and roles so prevalent in the internal environment. Department heads are expected to ask for more than they really "need"; the mayor's office is expected to cut these requests to balance the budget.

Context. The decisions we are speaking of set the limit on spending for the coming fiscal year. They are limits on manpower, supplies, material, and equipment. They are not program budgets in the sense that exact activity mixes are included in the municipal budget. In a sense, what we are talking about is an intermediate decision (see Fig. 3). This decision provides the constraints under which decisions about particular activities that a department will undertake must be made. The setting of *levels* of expenditures is just one aspect of the department head's continuing problems. Within a given expenditure ceiling, many different activity mixes can be utilized and activity-mix decisions can be disengaged from the level decisions. "Low ceilings, in short, can still permit several rooms" [11, p. 414].

DEPT. model characteritics. The role of the mayor's budget letter and the budget forms sent to the department head is a clear one and an important part of the decision environment. Together with the time schedule for submission of the completed budget forms, these items have the effect of structuring the department head's problem for him. Budget forms are typically sent to department heads about two months in advance of the presentation of the completed budget to the council. The department head usually has about one month before his completed request forms are due in the mayor's office.

The importance of the time deadline should not be underestimated. In that there is no moratorium on the department head's problems, budget compilation represents an additional workload. In the context of a myriad of nonbudgetary problems and duties, most department heads are more than willing to accept the problem structure provided by the budget forms.

Budget forms. Budget forms almost seem to be one of the physical constants of the universe [12, p. 59]. They are laid out as shown in Table 2.

Table 2
Budget Preparation Forms

	Expenditures Last Year	Appropriations This Year	Next Year's Request
Standard account 1	$54,321.00	$57,400.00	?
Itemization of 1	—	—	
Standard account 2	$43,219.00	$45,600.00	?
Itemization of 2			
.			
.			
.			
Standard account *N*	$ 100.00	$ 120.00	?
Itemization of *N*			

By structuring the department head's problem, the forms "bias" the outcome or decision in two ways:

1. They provide a great deal of incentive for the department head to formulate his requests within the confines of the existing set of accounts.

2. They provide for an automatic comparison between "next year's" request and "this year's" appropriation—which automatically determines that "this year's" appropriation provides one criterion or reference point for "next year's" request.

The Mayor's budget letter always contains instructions that reinforce the structuring of the problem provided by budget forms: to provide a ". . . written explanation for any change in individual code accounts," "(e)xperience for the years 1962 and 1963 is shown . . . to assist you in estimating your needs for 1965." "(U)nder the heading 'Explanation of Increases and Decreases' must be explained the factors . . . which make up the increase or decrease over or under," "the current budget allowance is shown above on this form."

The level of detail in line items has its influence on the department head's decision process also. (In one city studied, one of the line items listed a $3.00 current appropriation for "mothballs.") In general, each item broken out in the budget (each line item) "forces" one historical comparison and hence represents one more constraint the department request must satisfy. In the face of an increasing number of constraints (increasing as budget detail increases), it is not so surprising that the department head resorts to simpler decision rules to handle this potentially difficult problem. In addition, we would predict that the more detailed the budget (in terms of line items), the less change in requests (and appropriations) from year to year.

The need for effective budgetary control in the mayor's office, made more difficult by the presence of a small staff (small in relation to a similar organization in the private sector), is met by a large number of simple, historical comparisons and has, in many instances, resulted in a burdensome amount of detail—responded to by busy department heads with little change in budget behavior from year to year.

The "tone" of the letter accompanying the budget form has the effect of providing an arbitrary ceiling on the department's request (see Fig. 4). If the department total exceeds the "ceiling," the overage is generally submitted as a "supplemental" request. In addition, changes in salary *rates* through raises or promotions are submitted as a supplemental request (or not at all). Supplemental requests are accompanied with a detailed explanation and are treated separately by the mayor's office—and are always on the "agenda" when the department head meets with the mayor's office to discuss his requests.

So far we have discussed only the constraints a department head must satisfy and the procedures he must follow. There is, obviously, some room for maneuvering. Most of the department head's "calculations" involve figuring "what will go" with the mayor's office. This calculation involves using current appropriations as a base and adjusting this amount for recent appropriations, trends, discrepancies between appropriations and corresponding expenditures, and the like. The results of this "calculation" are then tested to see if they satisfy the constraints discussed above. Preliminary decisions are then adjusted until constraints are satisfied and the final request is entered on the standard budget forms and sent to the mayor's office for consideration.

Behavior not included in formal DEPT. model. The DEPT. model would indicate that (at least according to our theory) department budgetary behavior varies from department to department only by the relative weights assigned to previous appropriations, trends, and expenditures by the various department heads. Furthermore, it is contended (by the model) that these relative weights are stable over time. Missing from the formal model are notions of nonregular innovation (or change) by department administrators and notions of the department as a mechanism for responding to particular kinds of complaints from the citizenry—in short, the department is conceived of as explicitly responding to only the mayor's pressure.

Our model does not preclude innovative behavior or response to citizenry problems; it merely states that this takes place within a regularly changing budget ceiling.

Another "charge" the model is open to is that it fails to deal with "outside" influences at all. This is particularly true if by departmental responses to pressure one assumes that total (for the department) external pressure and influence is a thing that varies a good deal from year to year and that mechanisms for responding to that pressure would lead to irregular budget decisions reflecting this variation. If, however, one assumes that each department has, over the years, not only "made its peace" with the mayor's office, but with the extragovernmental environment, then the pressure-response mechanisms (i.e., constant responses to constant pressures) would also be reflected in the system of weights above. The model does not exclude a pressure-response kind of budgetary behavior, but has a good deal to say about the nature and context of the response (and pressure). The "pressure" from citizenry has two forms—increase municipal expenditures in a variety of areas and decrease taxes. Responses to the first kind of "pressure" or complaint may determine who's street is repaired first but not the total spent on street repairs for a year (within a very wide range of complaint levels). The result of the second kind of "pressure" is a strong tendency to hold the line on tax *rates*. The reasonableness of our characterization of "innovation" and "pressure" is reflected in the model residuals.

C. Mayor's Budget Recommendation Model

Role. The function of the Mayor's office relative to the budget is to fulfill the legal obligation of submitting a balanced budget to the city council for its consideration. The key word, of course, is "balanced." Most of the problem-solving activity and behavior in the mayor's office revolves around attempts to eliminate a deficit or reduce a surplus. Like most other organizations, subunit requests (stated needs) almost always exceed available resources. So vis-à-vis the departments, the mayor's office's role is that of an economizer, cutting department requests to the "bare minimum" in lean years and keeping the cost of government "under control" when revenues are more plentiful.

Characteristics of the MAYOR's model. The decision process in the mayor's office can usefully be thought of as a search for a solution to the balanced-budget problem. In a sense, the mayor has guaranteed the existence of a solution through use of budget guidelines set up in his letter of instruction to department heads. Approximately four months before the final budget is due for council passage, the mayor obtains preliminary revenue estimates from people in city government and from an outside source. Armed with a rough estimate of money available for expenditures in the next budget period, current appropriations, and a knowledge of "required" and predetermined budgetary changes for the coming year, the mayor is able to make a rough guess of the total allowable increase or decrease over current appropriations. From this figure, an estimate of the "allowable" percent increase (or decrease) is made and transmitted to department heads *via* the budget letter. (Only the output from this part of the process is explicitly included in our simulations model—"tone of mayor's letter.") In most instances, then, the "sum" of the budget requests reaching the mayor's office represents a "nearly" (within 10 percent) balanced budget.

The revenue estimate enters into the process at this point as an independent constraint to be satisfied. On very few occasions are revenue or tax *rates* changed to bring the budget into balance. In the municipalities investigated, there was no evidence of any altering of tax *yields* to balance the budget. Almost all tax rate increases are tied to general wage increases. Our formal model does not include the part of the decision process evoked when the revenue constraint becomes so restrictive (or loose) as to necessitate a change in tax rates (see Fig. 5). Tax rate decisions are made prior to sending the budget letter to department heads and are considered as given from that point on.

Just as the budget forms and account categories structure the problem for the department head, they also structure it for the mayor's office (items 1 and 3 below). ("Items" refers to numbered decision mechanisms in the General Mayor's Budget Recommendation Model flow chart.) The legal requirement of a balanced budget also helps structure the problem for the mayor's office and partially determines its role behavior. Together, the system of accounts and balanced budget requirement specifies the cognitive map of the decision situation for mayor's office participants.

Preliminary screening of requests.   As budget requests are received from departments by the mayor's office they are screened individually (item 4). The screening process reflects particular biases and relationships between the mayor's office and individual department heads (and departments). "Department heads are dealt with differently during the (budget) hearings. Some department heads can be depended on for an honest budget request. Others have a history of being less-than-realistic in their budgets."[11] Different perceptions of different departments are reflected in both model structure and model parameters (item 4). The interaction of perceptions and role (to cut requests) describes the preliminary screening process.

Figure 5
Mayor's Tax Decision Process

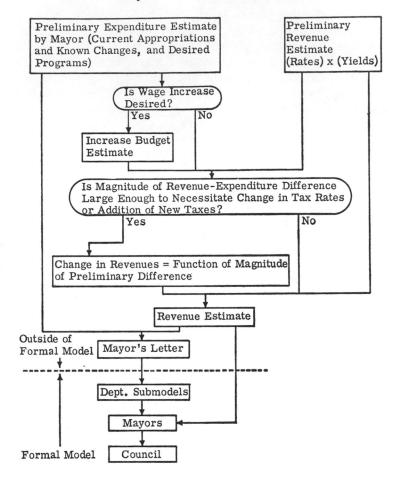

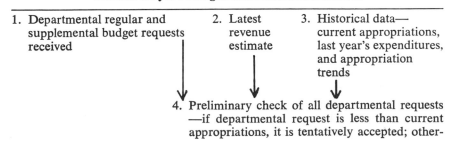

General Mayor's Budget Recommendation Model

1. Departmental regular and supplemental budget requests received

2. Latest revenue estimate

3. Historical data—current appropriations, last year's expenditures, and appropriation trends

4. Preliminary check of all departmental requests —if departmental request is less than current appropriations, it is tentatively accepted; other-

wise, a tentative "calculation" of the mayor's recommendation is made based on the department's regular and supplemental requests together with the change in appropriation from last year to the current year and the last available expenditure data

↓

5. Preliminary calculation of total budget—sum of preliminary calculations

↓

6. Check of preliminary total against revenue estimate to determine if a surplus or a deficit is anticipated. If "surplus," a set of "surplus reduction" routines is evoked. If "deficit," "deficit elimination" routines are evoked.

↓   ↓

Surplus reduction   Deficit elimination
procedures   procedures (go to 15)

↓

7. Calculate magnitude of anticipated surplus or residual

↓

8. Find total salaries and wages for the city (preliminary estimates)

↓

9. Is the anticipated surplus large enough to finance a minimum salary increase?

Yes ↓   No

10. If so, increase salary levels for all departments and reduce calculated surplus.

↓   ↓

11. Is there enough anticipated surplus left to distribute among departments?

Yes ↓   ↓ No

12. Consider the highest priority, nonsalary   Prepare final budget
account category (that has not yet been   recommendations (go
considered) starting with general expense   to 26)
accounts and ending with equipment
and maintenance accounts

↓

13. Increase the budget recommendation for the account category under consideration for all departments (until the surplus is exhausted) by granting a portion of each department's supplemental request. When (and if) money runs out, prepare final budget recommendations

↓   ↓

Money runs out
(go to 26)

14. Move to next highest priority account category and
go to 12. If all categories have been considered,
prepare final budget recommendations (go to 26)

Deficit Elimination Procedures

6.

6.

Surplus reduction
procedures 7–14

6.

6.

Deficit elimination
procedures

15. Consider accounts in reverse order of their
priority (consider equipment and maintenance first, salaries last)

16. Check, department by department, to see if the
preliminary budget estimate (mayor's) for the
account category under consideration is within
the limits (percentage of current appropriations)
implied in the mayor's budget letter to departments

Within limits

Outside limits

17. If within limits, no change
in preliminary budget estimate

18. Decrease preliminary
estimate of budget so
that it falls within
mayor's limits

19. Repeat 16–18 until deficit is eliminated or departments have all
been considered

Deficit
eliminated

All departments
considered

Prepare final
budget recommendation
(go to 26)

20. Consider next lowest
priority account (go to 16),
unless all account categories
have been examined

All account
categories
checked, for all
departments

Next lowest
priority account

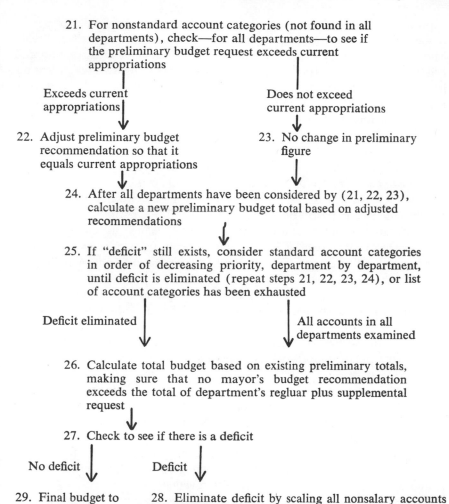

21. For nonstandard account categories (not found in all departments), check—for all departments—to see if the preliminary budget request exceeds current appropriations

Exceeds current appropriations

Does not exceed current appropriations

22. Adjust preliminary budget recommendation so that it equals current appropriations

23. No change in preliminary figure

24. After all departments have been considered by (21, 22, 23), calculate a new preliminary budget total based on adjusted recommendations

25. If "deficit" still exists, consider standard account categories in order of decreasing priority, department by department, until deficit is eliminated (repeat steps 21, 22, 23, 24), or list of account categories has been exhausted

Deficit eliminated

All accounts in all departments examined

26. Calculate total budget based on existing preliminary totals, making sure that no mayor's budget recommendation exceeds the total of department's regluar plus supplemental request

27. Check to see if there is a deficit

No deficit

Deficit

29. Final budget to council

28. Eliminate deficit by scaling all nonsalary accounts to make budget balance—proportional allocation of deficit (go to 26)

Basically, if the department request for a given account category is less than current appropriations, a preliminary, automatic acceptance of the request is made. If the request is larger than current appropriations, a request evaluation procedure is evoked that "calculates" or subjectively determines preliminary appropriation figures (item 4). A particular department can evoke one of four subjective evaluation procedures. The procedure evoked represents the cognitive map used by the mayor's office in dealing with that department.

The four basic procedures consist of two which arrive at a preliminary appropriation figure by making marginal adjustments in the departments' request figures—representing departments that submit "honest" or "realistic" budget estimates—and two which make adjustments in current appropriations to arrive at preliminary recommendation figures—representing less "realistic" or "honest" departments. The choice of procedures and parameter values was made on the basis of empirical tests using regression models. The four models used were:

1. Department head's request respected and adjusted by his supplemental request and current trends.

2. Department head's request ignored, and current appropriations adjusted to reflect recent trends and over or under spending in the past.

3. Department head's request used as a basis for calculation and changes in it are based on the magnitude of the requested change in appropriations, supplemental requests, and past change in appropriations.

4. Department request ignored and change from current appropriations based on previous changes and magnitude of underspending or overspending in the past.

The values of the estimated parameters represent the relative weights given to variables in the particular model by decision-makers in the mayor's office.

From the preliminary screening of requests outlined above (item 4), a preliminary budget total is compiled (item 5).

The next step in the process is to balance the preliminary budget. The "directives" issued by the mayor's office in the budget letter to department heads may be viewed as devices for guaranteeing that the budget will be "nearly" balanced. All alterations in regular departmental requests are aimed at balancing the budget. "Balancing techniques" are:

1. Raise tax rates or add a new tax to eliminate anticipated deficit.

2. Cut "lower priority" account categories (maintenance, equipment) to bring expenditures into line with revenues.

3. Grant a general salary increase and/or a portion of supplemental requests to reduce anticipated surplus.

4. Eliminate any "undesirable" tax or reduce tax rates to reduce anticipated surplus.

In general, strategies 1 and 4 are used when the anticipated discrepancy between revenues and expenditures is high, and techniques 2 and 3 are used if revenues and expenditures are reasonably close. The general tendency is to move toward a balance between revenues and expenditures by changing either revenue *or* expenditures, but not both. Only techniques 2 and 3 are a formal part of the model.

Surplus-elimination procedures. If a surplus is anticipated, several standard spending alternatives are considered in order of their priority:

1. General salary increase (items 8 to 10)
2. Grant portion of supplemental requests (items 11 to 14)
   a. general expense accounts (item 12)
   b. equipment accounts
   c. maintenance accounts

Although the formal model only includes the above alternatives, others are clearly evoked. It can be said with reasonable assurance, though, that the first alternative considered is a general salary increase whenever a surplus is anticipated.

The model is also "incomplete" in the sense that some departmental priority list obviously exists in granting of supplemental requests. Thus the sequence in which departments are considered (the order of departments in items 11 and 13) is important under a revenue constraint. The model's assumption that departments are considered in the order of their account numbers is a poor one, but not enough department request data existed to establish any other reasonable priority list. An analysis of the model residuals, however, failed to reveal any discernible pattern (or "list"). A priority list of account categories does exist though, and is shared by departments, the mayor's offices, and council. The salience of wage and salary accounts is readily discernible through interviews.

Deficit-elimination routines. If, instead of an anticipated surplus after the preliminary screening of requests, a potential deficit appears (the usual case), routines are evoked to eliminate the deficit. One routine not evoked in the formal model, but one of the alternatives sometimes evoked in practice, is the routine that says "raise taxes."

The alternatives are evoked in the following order:

1. Check preliminary recommendations (lower priority accounts first) to see if they are within limits on increases—bring all preliminary recommendations within limits.

2. Eliminate all recommended increases over current appropriations in nonsalary items, considering low-priority accounts first.

3. Uniform reduction of all nonsalary accounts to eliminate deficit, if all else has failed.

The order in which alternatives are considered represents a priority list for the alternatives (in order of their decreasing desirability) and a search routine evoked by the problem of an anticipated deficit (item 15).

The order of account sanctity for the mayor's office is identical to that of the department. This shared preference ordering is as follows: (1) administrative salaries; (2) nonadministrative salaries and wages; (3) operating expenses, supplies, materials, and so on; (4) equipment, and (5) maintenance, with maintenance and equipment the first accounts to be cut (and the last to be considered for an increase in the surplus-elimination routines) and salaries the last. This deficit-elimination procedure is executed only as long as a "deficit" exists. The first acceptable alternative (balanced budget) found is adopted and search activity is halted.

One item that is never reduced from current appropriations in the usual sense is salaries and wages. The salary and wage accounts are different from other accounts in that they represent commitments to individuals currently employed. There are no mass layoffs; rather, a freeze is placed on the filling of positions vacated by retirement, resignation, and death and scheduled step raises and salary increments are deferred.

Finally, either by reducing the surplus or eliminating a deficit, the mayor's office arrives at a balanced budget.

Behavior not included in formal MAYOR's model.   Perhaps the most prominent omission of problem-solving behavior is the lack of a priority list for departments. The model assumes that the priority list is ordered the same way as the account numbers. The overall importance of this faulty assumption is, of course, an empirical question. An analysis of model residuals suggests that it was not important or was reflected in estimated parameter values.

The entire budgetary process model we have constructed hypothesizes a stable decision structure between cities, and a stable decision structure over time within cities. Stability in decision structure between cities is "explainable" through problem similarity. Stability within cities reflects stable sets of relationships existing between positions and roles through processes of learning, reinforcement, and socialization. This assumption of stability and uniform socialization is predicted on an assumption that only a relatively few occupants of government positions change in a given period of time. The obvious exception to this situation occurs when an administration is defeated at the polls. This results in a complete reordering of position occupants and relationships. The gradual socialization, learning process will no longer hold. So, we expected and found the largest systematic model errors in those years corresponding to the start of a new administration.

Another kind of behavior not included in the model is the kind reflecting the mayor's response to external (to the government) pressure, influence, and constraints. Again, as in the DEPT. models, the MAYOR's model does not preclude a mayoralty response to requests for services from "powerful" interest groups or individuals. It only postulates that the response is *within* the budget constraint for the department involved. The model, as constructed, implies that either the "response to pressure" is systematic and regular over the years (implying a stable system of environmental "pressure" or "influence") and is reflected in the model parameters, or it does not enter the part of the budgetary process represented by our model at all. The only case where the "influence" of the external environment could be conceived of as imposing a decisional constraint is in the revenue estimate. Most systematic "pressure" from the business community concentrates on keeping tax rates constant, and not on particular expenditure items.

D. Characteristics of the COUNCIL Model

The role of the city council is a limited one. The primary reason is more one of cognitive and informational constraints than lack of interest. The city budget is a complex document when it reaches the council. The level of detail makes it virtually impossible to consider all or even a majority of items independently. The sheer volume of information to be processed limits the ability of a council, without its own budget staff, to consider the budget in a sophisticated or complex manner.

Perhaps a more important computational constraint is the balanced budget requirement. If there is no slack in the budget the mayor presents to council, any increase the council makes in any account category must be balanced with a corresponding decrease in another account or with tax increase. So, in the presence of a revenue constraint, the council cannot consider elements of the budget independently as is done in Congress. Davis et al. found that Congressional budgetary behavior could be described extremely well using a series of linear decision rules [8]. Behavior of this nature would not be possible if it were required that the sum of the changes in budgets made by Congress add to zero—i.e., the budget must add up to an amount predetermined by the President. Congressmen and Congressional committees also have staffs; councilmen do not.

Another reason for the limited effect of the council on the budget reflects the nature of the "pressures" they face. All interest groups, neighborhood organizations, department heads, and so on, feel that some department's budget should be increased. The pressures transmitted to council concerning the operating budget are of one kind—those advocating increases in the mayor's recommendations. The other side of the argument —curtailment of government activities—is seldom, if ever, presented to council. This countervailing influence enters the decision process not at the council level but generally through the mayor's office and, in particular, through the mayor's revenue estimate.

Given the above limitations, the council is "forced" to use the mayor's decisions as the reference points for their decisions. The constraints— "pressure," informational, and computational—coupled with a recommended budget with no slack to allocate (not enough difference between estimated revenues and recommended expenditures "to be bothered with") make it extremely difficult for the council to reject or change the mayor's budget significantly.

Overview. Generalizing, the entire model is one of a systematic, bureaucratic administrative decision process. The stability of the decision system is portrayed as evolving from the restrictive revenue environment, an assumed continuity in the actors manning the system, and an implied stable or nonexistent "community power network." The interaction of problem complexity and need for decision, combined with the lack of extragovernmental reference points or standards, produces a decision system which uses historical experience and precedent as its operating standards; a system which handles interest conflicts (high service rates, low taxes) by largely ignoring divergent viewpoints and using feasibility as the prime decision criterion; a system which handles complexity by fragmenting and simplifying the problem. By assuming (implicitly) that "this year's problem" is nearly identical to "last year's," "this year's solution" will be nearly identical to "last year's." It is a system that structures a complex problem, formulates alternatives and makes choices using simple decision rules.

4. EXTERNAL ENVIRONMENT—PROBLEMS IN ANALYZING EFFECTS

We wish to analyze the impact of various environments on a model of the municipal budgetary decision process. This creates many problems—how can we analyze the impact of the environment without also modeling that environment?

A. Decomposable Systems and Their External Environments

The works of Simon and Ando [10] and Ando and Fisher [1, 2] are relevant to our problem. To paraphrase Ando and Fisher:

> Political scientists are often concerned with the stability properties of a political system or institution considered in isolation: for example, the municipal budgetary process. However, there may be a somewhat uncomfortable feeling that this may not be a meaningful problem, since the models describing the political (sub-) system are themselves embedded in a far larger set of models describing the socioeconomic and physical universe. It follows that the movement of the political variables toward equilibrium may itself disturb variables (such as the local economy) which are assumed by the political model to be givens. Further, nonpolitical variables which political theory admits to be influenced by political ones may, in turn, influence the latter of the assumed

given nonpolitical variables and thereby hinder the political variables from reaching equilibrium. It follows that general equilibrium of the political variables (budgetary process), which is a partial equilibrium of the larger system, may be unattainable even if it is stable when considered in isolation.

The Simon–Ando and Ando–Fisher theorems suggest a general answer to this problem in the following way. Partition the set of all nonpolitical (socioeconomic) variables into: (1) those variables which theory assumes influences the budgetary process, but are not themselves influenced thereby; (2) those variables which are assumed to be influenced by, but which do not influence political or budgetary variables; and (3) those variables which are assumed to be unrelated to political or budgetary variables. We may disregard variables in the third category. Thus we visualize our budgetary theory as assuming that causal influences run from the first set to the budgetary or political variables to the second set with no feedbacks. The difficulty raised, however, is that there may in fact be weak feedbacks, since the assumptions of the theory are at best only good approximations. The Ando–Fisher theorem shows that *if these feedbacks are sufficiently weak relative to direct influences,* that is, if the theoretical assumptions are sufficiently good approximations, there exists a time span over which the behavior and stability of the political (budgetary) system can be analyzed in isolation without regard for the difficulties raised by the presence of such feedbacks. The length of the time span under which this analysis is valid is dependent on the relative weakness of the feedbacks to the direct influences.

Furthermore, the Ando–Fisher theorem asserts that when the time period under consideration is long enough to make it necessary for the influence of other parts of the socioeconomic and physical system on the political system (budgetary process) to be explicitly considered, there will come a time after which the political system (budgetary process) will always be in its own partial equilibrium (if, indeed, transitory outside influences ever disturb that equilibrium once it has been reached), that the variables in it (budget items) will be moving proportionately to one another, and that we can therefore represent the budgetary system as an index (total revenue or total budget) and can consider the influence of other parts of the social system on this index rather than on the political system (budgetary process) in its entire complexity [1, pp. 100–102].

What this means for our problem is that we can meaningfully study the movement of *budget shares* (not totals) in the long run by focusing on changes in total revenue *if* we can show that relatively weak feedbacks exist between parts of the budgetary process (budget items) and the remaining socioeconomic system. We have described the strong, direct influences in the internal environment of the budgetary process in the previous section. The measures of the goodness of fit of a model based primarily on an internal process are offered as strong evidence for this, elsewhere [5; 6, Chap. 8 and App.] and should not be at issue. Evidence of weak feedbacks from the external environment will be discussed briefly here.[12]

B. Weak Feedbacks between Budgetary System and External Environment

The model of budgetary decision making described above contends that the external environment has a rather minor role to play in the *allocation* of municipal operating funds, but exerts its major influence through the revenue total. If, in fact, our model is wrong and the assumed independence of individual budget items and external environment does not exist, the inappropriateness of the independence assumption should be reflected in the overall goodness of fit of our model and in the errors associated with individual budget items. In particular, if environmental corrections of the drifting, bureaucratic process are an important part of the "real" process, then at least some individual model errors ought to be associated with environmental corrections. Of the total set of model deviations for department totals [(predicted appropriations)—(actual appropriations)] for each year, in each city, a subset was chosen for close examination. The examined subset included:

  1. The five largest, absolute deviations in dollar amounts.

  2. The five largest, absolute deviations as a percentage of actual appropriations.

  The subsets of deviations (52 in Detroit, 89 in Cleveland, 51 in Pittsburgh) were then categorized by their perceived "causes." These "causes" were:

1. Change in external environment
   a. Intergovernmental transactions
   b. Catastrophic event, crises—reaction to focus of public attention
2. Changes in internal environment
   a. New administration
   b. Change in departments or functions
3. Lack of information (by model)
   a. Implications of capital budgeting decision
   b. Additional (ear-marked) revenue sources discovered
   c. Change in system of accounts
   d. Other (timing of elections)
4. Unexplained, miscellaneous, and other
   a. Missing data
   b. Improper accounting procedures
   c. Increased work load

"Causes" 1a, 3a, 3c, and 3d represent logical elaborations of other policies; 1b, 2a, 2b—when functions are not just transferred—3b, and 4c in most instances represent feedbacks from the external environment.

Causes were assigned to individual cases by examining budget hearing records, mayor's budget messages to the council, and newspaper accounts. The remarkable thing was, in nearly every instance where the simulation model identified a special case (i.e., produced a relatively large deviation), so did the mayor in his budget message! This, it would seem, argues more strongly for the *validity* of the process model than high goodness-of-fit measures [6, Chaps. 8 and 9 and App.].

It appears from an analysis of our residuals over time that environmental corrections:

1. are seldom (if ever) evoked directly to bring specific expenditure items "into line," *or*

2. are filtered through the revenue constraint [see Fig. 5], blurring the "cause" of increased (decreased) revenues and blunting possible direct impact on specific budget items.

In any event, environmental corrections appear to be more related to revenue changes than expenditure changes. Hence, their *impact* on expenditures appears to be a blurred one that is exercised through the administrative allocation and decision process rather than through any direct "expenditure-correction" mechanism.

Some *direct* environmental corrections were observed however. Negotiated contracts and changes in "ear-marked" revenue (state and user) provided some clear "corrections." The existence of Federal monies for municipal programs also appears to have "caused" a change in the "budgetary drift."

What seems to emerge from this study is an opportunity model of budgetary change. The broad "pattern of drift" is accelerated or depressed due to changes in general revenues. The "drift" in specific expenditure items changes in response to changes in "ear-marked" revenues or the terms of negotiated contracts. Rapid spurts of growth are observed in those areas where the city has the opportunity to expand activities because of the presence of revenues (Federal funds), rather than in areas having rapid changes or spurts in "needs." This also could be due to the fact that "needs" do not change in "spurts" either [5, pp. 813–814].

Based on the strong, internal relationships in the budgetary process and the existence of only very weak feedbacks between it and the external environment, it is reasonable (using the Simon–Ando and Ando–Fisher theorems) to analyze the relative, long-run relation of budget items by treating the external environment as an aggregate index (revenues).

C. Impact of External Environment

The properties of the model were tested using Detroit as the data base. The results of one set of tests are reported here (see [6, Chap. 10] for others).

The revenue constraint represents the impact of the external environment. The simulation model was allowed to run for a 10-year period under each of three revenue patterns:

1. Constant revenues.
2. Accelerating—10 percent increase per year.
3. Fluctuating—a "base" revenue increasing at 5 percent per year with a random fluctuation about this base to calculate revenue for a given year.[13]

The constant revenue assumption defines a very tight revenue constraint, whereas the accelerating-revenue condition specifies an extremely loose or non-existent constraint. The fluctuating assumption is more realistic and provides

Figure 6
**City of Detroit—Civil Defense Department: 10-Year Forecast
of Appropriations**

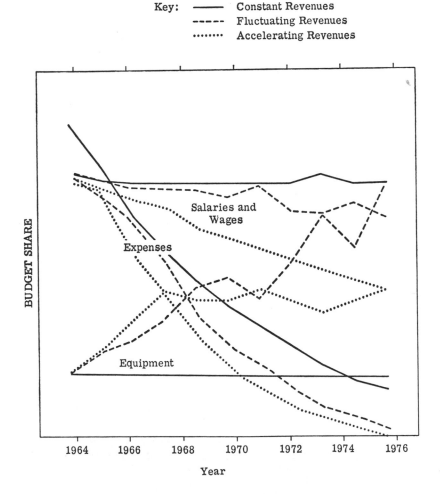

for moderate growth (on the average) with the spurts and occasional down-turn common in the last decade" [6, Chap. 10].

Time-series plots of the budget *share* for three departments in Detroit are shown in Figs. 6, 7, and 8. The dynamic behavior of all departments was plotted. The three presented here are typical.

Results of sensitivity analysis.[14]   Some general observations can be made. As the total budget size increases, the *share* (although *not* dollar amount) for wages and salaries nearly always decreases. The reasons for

Figure 7
City of Detroit, Recorders Court—Traffic Division:
10-Year Forecast of Appropriations

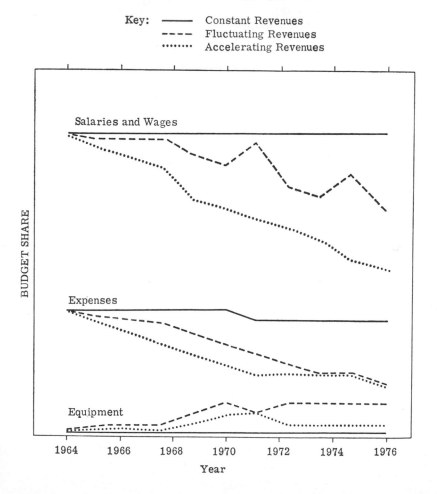

Key: ———   Constant Revenues
        ----   Fluctuating Revenues
        ········   Accelerating Revenues

this are not entirely clear. Perhaps this is an inevitable result of "automation" (one policeman in a patrol car can cover many times the area that he could on foot). It could reflect the fact that city revenues have really never grown more than 2 to 3 percent per year, if that. Employees are much harder to dispose of than equipment and other standard expense items. The reluctance of the model (and city administration) to take on employees at a rate of increase the same as (or higher than) the total budget might reflect a cautious approach to hiring. Employees involve long-run commitments of funds.

Another interesting phenomenon was noted. The constant and ac-

Figure 8
City of Detroit–Buildings and Safety Engineering Department:
10-Year Forecast of Appropriations

Key: ——— Constant Revenues
          - - - - Fluctuating Revenues
          •••••••• Accelerating Revenues

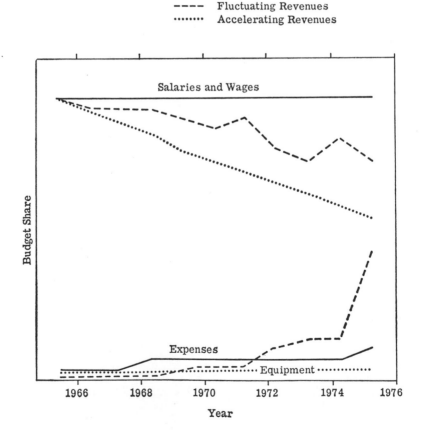

celerating revenue assumptions create a kind of funnel or envelope (see Figs. 6, 7, and 8) for appropriations, within which appropriations under fluctuating revenues usually remain. In most cases a change in revenue growth rate accelerates or depresses the trend in budget share for an account. Yet we note that some accounts break out of this envelope by obtaining a larger share of the total (in the model) under fluctuating revenues than under accelerating, whereas some receive an even smaller share than under a constant revenue situation. Are there any regularities in this deviant behavior? No department or group of departments seemed to be helped or hurt by fluctuating, erratic revenues to the extent that they systematically fall outside the constant-accelerating limits.

Table 3
Fluctuating-Revenue Accounts Outside
of Constant or Accelerating Limits

	Relation to "Limits"		
Account Type	Above	Within	Below
Salaries and wages	1	44	1
Materials, supplies, and expenses	8	33	4
Equipment	11	36	0

Table 3 suggests that the "expense" account fluctuates with fluctuating revenue more than "salaries," for instance. The 8 to 4 split suggests little in the way of consistent advantage for "expense" under fluctuating conditions, however. The equipment account is a different matter. One third of the departments (according to the model) were able to do better under somewhat erratic revenue conditions than under either stable or steadily expanding conditions. Of the 11 departments that somehow manage to use fluctuating revenues to their advantage by securing an increased share for their equipment account, *10 of the 11* time-series plots of fluctuating revenues "broke out of the envelope" in 1972–1973. What was so unusual about that year? Examining actual revenues used under the "fluctuating" assumption, we see that after a revenue decline (of nearly $7,000,000) for 1971–1972, the system received a sudden spurt in the form of an increase of more than 20 percent. Equipment accounts, for some reason, were able to siphon off more than "their share" of the increase. Interestingly enough, the eleventh case "broke out" of the constant-accelerating-revenue envelope in 1969–1970. This was a year with another sudden spurt in revenues (nearly a 20 percent increase). Once the equipment accounts reached this new plateau, the model implied they would stay there.

D. Conclusions—Role of Revenue Constraint

The experiments with the revenue constraint suggest some long-run, dynamic properties of our model:

1. Revenue increases (decreases) seem to accelerate or depress the *rate* of change in budget share for all accounts but do not usually change the direction of drift.
2. As the total budget increases, our model indicates that the *share* (*not* dollar amount) of wage and salary costs declines.
3. When the decision system is "kicked" through revenue changes:
   a. Salary and wages accounts are least responsive to the change.
   b. Expenses accounts are most responsive to the change and its direction.
   c. Some equipment accounts are responsive to accelerating revenues and are able to maintain their new levels after revenue acceleration tapers off.

Analysis of budget shares by accounts over time revealed, under changing revenue conditions, that a substantial reallocation of resources can occur. Although this change in budget share is an inertial one for most accounts, we have noted some interesting departures. The primacy of the revenue constraint in the reallocation of resources is our major conclusion.

5. SUMMARY

We have argued that:

1. Certain characteristics of the problem itself (potential complexity due to balanced-budget requirement) have limited the range of appropriate behavior.

2. Decisions are made by solving a hierarchy of subproblems where solutions to previous problems serve as constraints for problems following—the structure of the process decouples decisions, much as inventories create independent systems from an interdependent one.

3. Because the system is decomposable, and one of the systems is the budgetary process, we can analyze the budgetary (sub-) system independently.

4. ". . . if a nearly completely decomposable system is analyzed as though it were completely decomposable, the results obtained will remain approximately valid even in the long run as regards the *relative* behavior of the variables within any one set" [2, p. 108]. Therefore our analysis of the behavior of budget shares in the budgetary process under various revenue assumptions, "revenue" being the primary link between external and internal environment, is "approximately valid" in the long run.

A. Implications for Future Research

In assessing the impact of the internal or problem (short-run) and external (long-run) environments on the budgetary decision process we have confronted some interesting theoretical and methodological questions. It appears as if the Simon–Ando and Ando–Fisher theorems on decomposable systems might prove exceedingly useful in the development of an integrated, positive theory of governmental resource allocation that links influences of the larger socioeconomic environment with some realistic notions of how government officials reach decisions. A theory of municipal (or governmental) resource allocation which purports to describe the translation of economic characteristics, political variables, and population characteristics to government expenditure decisions (see Fig. 1) without explicitly dealing with the translation mechanism (government decision-makers) is inadequate.

NOTES

[1] This formulation is suggested by an apparent contradiction between my study of the municipal budgetary process ([5] and [6]) and other studies of public expenditures ([4] and [7], as two examples). My results suggest a highly internalized decision process where nearly all other studies seem to suggest a system in which the external environment largely determines outcomes. These results are reasonable if the budgetary process is a nearly decomposable subsystem of the overall resource allocation process in a municipality.

[2] Fisher and Ando [1, p. 93] conjecture that properties of nearly decomposable nonlinear systems have much the same properties as nearly decomposable linear systems. The linearity assumption should not be crucial to our analysis.

[3] It is hypothesized (and only discussed in this paper) that the very substantial differences between my model of the municipal budgetary process and more traditional models of public expenditures are really differences in degrees of aggregation and in time perspectives.

[4] Although few researchers explicitly discuss the existence or nature of a "service standard" or "expenditure norm," it is implicit in their works. The usual model of the municipal-expenditure-determining process is

$$\text{expenditure}_j = a_0 + \sum_{i=1}^{n} a_i X_i$$

where
j = expenditure category (function)
X_i = ith independent variable (external, exogenous)
a_0 = constant (empirically determined)
a_i = empirically determined regression coefficient for ith variable

The model is intended to explain intercity variations in municipal expenditures. It seems to me that the existence of a_0 implies some sort of a standard, and that it is not at all clear that it exists in anything like the form assumed in public expenditure studies (per capita figures, by U.S. Census functional categories). Use of the constant term carries with it a responsibility to explain what the constant means, where "it" comes from, and how this information gets transmitted from city to city.

[5] Where "complexity" is indicated by a large number of interdependent, real variables, by a high degree of uncertainty attached to "key" variables, and by non-linear relationships between real variables.

[6] The particular department-mayor-council form of government discussed here is not important. The *functions* are, however. Whether the mayor's function is performed by a city manager or a finance committee is not so important as the fact that the function is performed and in the indicated sequence.

[7] Although things such as department budget hearings after the department requests have been submitted, outright vetoes of the mayor's budget, or prior briefings of the council by the mayor would appear to contradict a decomposable-system formulation, it was found that vetoes hardly ever occur and briefings and hearings are pro forma events [6, Chaps. 5, 6, and 7].

[8] Here we use "complexity" in the same sense as Simon [9, pp. 478–9]. The *potential* pairs of interactions between variables in an n-variable system is n^2. Most social and natural systems, in fact, are very much less complex, involving considerably fewer nonnegligible interactions than n^2.

[9] Wildavsky [12] and Davis, Dempster, and Wildavsky [8] report similar findings in the federal budgetary process, as did Anton [3] for the State of Illinois.

[10] Note that the hierarchic system we have outlined (see [5; or 6, Chap. 4] for a complete description) contains all three forms of redundancy mentioned by Simon [9, pp. 478–9]: (1) Composed of only a few different types of subsystems (three) in various arrangements, (2) nearly decomposable, and (3) description can be recoded (programmed) to describe "laws" governing system dynamics.

[11] November 1964 interview with chief budget officer in one of the three sample cities. Name withheld on request.

[12] For a complete discussion, see [6, Chap. 9].

[13] $BASE_t = 1.05 \ (BASE_{t-1})$; $REVEST_t = BASE_t + Z$, where Z is a normally distributed random variable with mean zero and a standard deviation of $10,000,000.

[14] Paraphrase of [5, Chap. 10].

BIBLIOGRAPHY

1. Ando, A., and F. M. Fisher. "Near-Decomposability, Partition and Aggregation, and the Relevance of Stability Discussions," in A. Ando, F. M. Fisher, and H. A. Simon, *Essays on the Structure of Social Science Models*. Cambridge: M.I.T. Press, 1963.

2. ———. "Two Theorems on *Ceteris Paribus* in the Analysis of Dynamic Systems," in A. Ando, F. M. Fisher, and H. A. Simon, *Essays on the Structure of Social Science Models*. Cambridge: M.I.T. Press, 1963.

3. Anton, T. *The Politics of State Expenditure in Illinois*. Urbana: University of Illinois Press, 1966.

4. Brazer, H. E. "City Expenditures in the United States," *Occasional Paper 66*. New York: National Bureau of Economic Research, 1959.

5. Crecine, John P. "A Computer Simulation Model of Municipal Budgeting," *Management Science*, July 1967, pp. 786–815.

6. ———. *Government Problem Solving: A Computer Simulation of Municipal Budgeting*. Chicago: Rand McNally, 1968.

7. Davis, Otto A., and Haines, G. H. "A Political Approach in Public Expenditures: The Case of Municipalities," *National Tax Journal*, September, 1966, Vol. XIX, No. 3, pp. 259–275.

8. ——, M. A. H. Dempster, and A. Wildavsky. "On the Process of Budgeting: An Empirical Study of Congressional Appropriations," in G. Tullock (ed.), *Papers on Non-Market Decision Making*. Charlottesville, Va.: Thomas Jefferson Center, 1966.

9. Simon, H. A. "The Architecture of Complexity," *Proceedings of the American Philosophical Society*, 1962, Vol. 106, No. 6, pp. 467–482.

10. ——, and A. Ando. "Aggregation of Variables in Dynamic System," in A. Ando, F. M. Fisher, and H. A. Simon, *Essays on the Structure of Social Science Models*. Cambridge: M.I.T. Press, 1963.

11. Sorensen, Theodore. *Kennedy*. New York: Harper & Row, 1965.

12. Wildavsky, Aaron. *The Politics of the Budgetary Process*, Boston. Little, Brown, 1964.

CHAPTER 16

Innovative and Non-Innovative Decision Processes in Government Budgeting

Rufus P. Browning

We are in two kinds of trouble when we try to explain why a particular policy was chosen or why some particular sequence or class of policy choices was made. For one thing, we fail to deliver a truly exhaustive and precise explanation of why even the limited set of events we choose to study took place just the way they did. We are commonly unable to do more than speculate about a few elements of the dynamics of decision making. We gloss over the origins of important decisions. We report the time and place of a meeting but cannot explain why a particular choice was made and no other. We have many details but few data; inadequate guidelines for selecting data; and many difficulties in gathering data. Our suffering from ambiguity even in our descriptions of particular events is matched only by our distress at the uniqueness of the findings we are able to provide. The details spelled out in case studies of policy decisions seem to defy comparison.

These problems of uniqueness and of ambiguity are not unrelated—a good theory of complex decision processes would specify relevant variables and relationships among them so as to facilitate both the explanation of particular events and the comparison of disparate ones. In my own perusal of some particular budget decisions in a midwestern state government, I have relied heavily on the theory of organizational decision making set forth in Cyert and March's recent book, *A Behavioral Theory of the Firm*,[1] and in earlier work by Simon and others. I have relied on the theory to help me identify specific phenomena as the varying values of characteristics which are common to all government agencies rather than as events unique to a single case. While explaining a quite limited set of particular cases in some detail, I am using and suggesting ideas for approaching the explana-

This essay, which was presented at the Meetings of the American Political Science Association in New York City in September, 1963, is printed by permission of the American Political Science Association and the author.

tion of a broader set of events both in detail and at interesting levels of generality.

Most of my data stem from observation of decision sequences in two agencies and their twenty subunits, mostly decisions within the agencies, though I will also have something to say about the way in which the joint appropriations committee of the legislature makes up its mind. My assistants and I attended dozens of ordinarily confidential, private meetings on the budget, and we interviewed decision makers and other informants at great length at the time the decisions were being made. The agency functions we examined are financed almost entirely out of state tax revenues, not by federal grants, and they are mainly agency operations rather than aids to local communities. The agencies in which we spent most of our time are a Department of Welfare, where we concentrated on mental health and corrections programs; and a Department of Labor, with regulatory, investigative, promotional, and quasi-judicial functions in workmen's compensation, industrial safety, wages and hours, apprenticeship programs, and fair employment practices. As is obvious from this list of functions, the state is largely urban and industrial, though very strong agricultural interests are present, also.

Immersion in the budget process of these agencies flooded us with stupefying, paralyzing detail. Fortunately, the Simon-March-Cyert theory makes many assumptions which greatly ease the task of organizing and eliminating some of this detail:

(1) People tend to make repetitive decisions according to rather stable criteria, and we can separate these standard decision rules from the processes by which they change over time.

(2) Any choice can be exhaustively explained in terms of the alternatives considered, the perceived attributes of the alternative(s), and the standard rules applied to them.

(3) These decision rules are an operational expression of what we generally call an organization's goals or objectives, felt needs, fears, hopes, and the like; and to the extent that these phenomena have an impact on organizational choices—that is, to the extent that they are more than slogans—they may be defined in terms of decision rules.

(4) Decision rules specify satisfactory states of affairs corresponding to one or more of the perceived attributes of alternatives. A rule defines a branching operation such that following a comparison of the relevant attribute with the satisfactory standard, the alternative is rejected, accepted, or subjected to further evaluations.

(5) Perceptions of alternatives and their attributes are also regarded as relatively stable over time, or the patterns of communication by which

perceptions are acquired are stable, or both. Again, we can separate a limited set of items from the processes of communication, learning, memory, and organizational search by which the items change.

In what follows, then, we will discuss some sources of alternatives and objectives for agencies, and determinants of the processes by which agencies communicate with these sources and accept or reject the choices offered. Among the sources and determinants we will deal with are governors, legislators, clientele groups, similar agencies in other states or at the national level, professional reference groups, and the agencies themselves. We will touch also on agency strategies for gaining support.

1. GROSS DIFFERENCES IN THE BUDGET PERFORMANCE OF THE WELFARE AND LABOR DEPARTMENTS

The Department of Welfare, including other functions as well as the corrections and mental health programs discussed here, is one of the largest state agencies. It is known as innovative and progressive and aggressive; it has a reputation for knowing what it wants and getting it; it has expanded very rapidly since 1945. We may separate for illustrative purposes the mental health and corrections institutions from the central administrative apparatus of the Department of Welfare—central executive and staff operations, and line employees such as probation and parole officers working out of field offices which are not attached to institutions. In 1945, the Department of Labor and this Administration appropriation of the Department of Welfare were about equal (Table 1). (Labor has no institutions.) But in the time it took Labor to double in expenditures, to the biennium ended July, 1963, Welfare Administration multiplied its expenditures by 10 and the Institutions almost quintupled. (The disparity is actually even greater than these figures indicate since they do not include huge building programs for correctional and mental institutions.) Labor has gradually *lost* authorizations for personnel positions via the legislative expedient of eliminating positions which happened to be vacant at budget time, so that Labor's state-financed personnel have declined in number while Welfare's have more than trebled. Welfare has consistently asked for much more than Labor—since 1945, Welfare has twice requested biennial increases of 150% for administration—and consistently received much more, even though the percentage cut from Welfare Administration requests has been substantially larger than the cut from Labor requests.

It is not surprising that the Department of Labor has had a reputation of weak leadership in its field, a reputation for not wanting much and not

Table 1
Budget Performance of the Welfare and Labor
Departments Since 1945

	Department of Labor	Department of Welfare	
		Administra-tion	Instituti-tions
Expenditures in 1945–47 ($ mill.)	1.1	1.3	10.4
Expenditures in 1961–63 ($ mill.)	2.2	13.2	48.5
Change in employment financed by state taxes, 1945–63		182–167 (−7%)	1790–5608 (+213%)
Agency requests: average biennial % increase requested	16%	58%	27%
Growth: average % increase in biennial expenditures	11	40	24
Average % cut from requests	4	9	2

getting what it does want. Labor has been almost stable in the size and scope of its programs, while Welfare has revolutionized existing programs and added many new ones. Why this tremendous growth in one agency and its policies, so little growth in the other? Why was Welfare so innovative, spewing forth a flood of new policy proposals, and Labor so non-in-novative?

2. PUBLIC GOALS OF PUBLIC AGENCIES

Public goals are not the same thing as decision rules used to select specific policies. Public goals may remain stable for years while agency policies and decision rules for selecting policies undergo rapid change; or policies and rules may hold steady as the agency revises its public version of what it is doing and wants to do. Nevertheless, once we understand that we can not expect to find the origins of every agency decision in its public goals, it is useful to look at them because they tell us something both about how the agency rationalizes its activities to itself, and how it persuades others to support it. Rationalizations are often associated with specific aspirations, and the persuasiveness of public goals is one important aspect of an agency's ability to attain its aspirations.

The statements of purpose which preface the budget requests of the Welfare and Labor Departments are strikingly different in tone. The Department's request opens with a perfunctory reference to "administering laws in the fields of . . . ," and so on. Welfare's opening statement, in contrast, reads as follows: "The purposes of this department are to promote an integrated social welfare program which conserves human resources by providing just and humane services to . . . the mentally ill and retarded; by preventing dependency, mental illness, delinquency, crime and other social maladjustments; . . . and by providing for the rehabilitation of juvenile delinquents and adult criminal offenders." The Department of Welfare is explicitly not just administering the laws—it is promoting a program.

Although Welfare's request are included in the regular executive budget along with those of other agencies, the Department has a large enough staff that it is able to prepare its own version of its requests and the justifications for them. For the present biennium, this amounts to a book of more than 400 pages with many tables and single-spaced text, more than 80% of it devoted to mental health, corrections, and central executive requests. There is persuasive material throughout the document, but the opening letter of submission by the director of the department contains a particularly strong and broad statement of Welfare's public goals. Discussing those parts of the budget which provide "for the extension and intensification of services," he asserts that the object is "to do a better job of rehabilitation and treatment . . . by reaching more of the people requiring these services earlier and with a more intensive effort." Then comes a tie-in to potent social, moral, economic, and political objectives— "By so doing, we can reduce human suffering and waste and look forward to fiscal economy in the long run by shortening the span of dependency and the length of time in need of institutional care." Extension, intensification, do a better job, reach more of the people earlier, more intensive effort, reduce suffering, look forward to economy, shorten dependency and institutional care—every phase evokes the department's orientation toward the future, toward objectives it is moving to attain. This is the esprit of the department. And the objectives invoked are about as persuasive as they can be.

Among the specific requests for program improvements justified under these objectives are an additional half million dollars in state aids to communities to increase the number of community mental health clinics from 20 to 24 over two years; $400,000 for a new day care program for the mentally ill; $2 million to improve treatment programs at county mental hospitals; $300,000 for state mental health planning and promotion of community services; $1.4 million for clinical and ward staff in three state mental hospitals, partly to intensify treatment; $800,000 for treatment and ward care staff at colonies for the retarded, partly to intensify rehabilitation for release to community living; $500,000 for increased administrative and service workloads in support of these increased treatment programs; $130,000 for outpatient and day hospital programs; $150,000 for research on mental retardation; $230,000 to improve educational and recreational programs at correctional institutions; $200,000 for administrative and clerical support of correctional security and rehabilitation programs; and others.

In short, the Welfare Department has developed methods of generating (a) specific policy proposals, (b) persuasive justifications for them. These are problems which dominate the budget process for an agency that wants to go somewhere, cannot depend as a matter of course on powerful support from a favored group, and must cultivate broad support among diverse publics. (As they say in the department, prisons don't have alumni associations.) Whether or not an agency is successful in developing persuasive justifications, however, its anticipations of how the governor and particularly in this case the legislature will react to its proposals, and the effect of these anticipations on the agency's requests, are matters of interest. We need to specify, then, processes (1) for generating and choosing among policies which meet the agency's aspirations; (2) for eliminating or modifying requests which may get the agency into trouble, and (3) for insuring satisfactory levels of support for the remaining requests. The second of these processes refers to political penalties for making certain requests. For some agencies and agency heads, simple rejection of requests may be painful enough to prevent its making the request in the first place, but usually some other penalties are involved—public criticism, insult, and ridicule (public at least to one's colleagues and subordinates), loss of support for other requests, and loss of confidence from others with damage to future requests and to career chances.

Logically, this process—changing proposals preferred internally so as to avoid unwanted consequences of making them explicit requests—is a subset of the first. Agency aspirations include satisfactory standards for political consequences of making requests as well as standards for agency operations. It is useful to distinguish between avoidance aspirations and attainment aspirations, however, because quite different kinds of events affect them. Avoidance concerns may be strongly influenced by legislative action and offer therefore a means of legislative control, even when an agency gets its policy and budget proposals from outside the legislature. Obviously, the third process, agency procedures for insuring support, is also strongly affected by anticipations of legislative behavior, but there is quite a difference between anticipations which cut off certain requests altogether thus preventing them from becoming policy, and anticipations which cause agencies to work extra hard to elicit support.

3. SOURCES OF POLICY INNOVATIONS AND AGENCY COMMUNICATION WITH THEM

New policies do not fall out of thin air. Departments of government do not usually work out their problems in isolation. Legislators, clientele and other organized interests, corporate sellers of goods and services, researchers and consultants in academic life, and many others may be interested in the agency's policies, dissatisfied with existing policies, and more or less active in proposing new ones. If outside sources actively sell their policies, the innovative agency need only be a willing receptor. On the other hand, if outside sources generate alternatives but do not actively sell them, then the agency must make some positive effort to find them. The vigor of outside sources of new policies, the extent to which these sources sell their policies to the agency, and the extent to which the agency searches on its own for policy innovations are crucial variables affecting the direction and rate of agency innovation. It is of course possible, even likely, that various sources of policies will come up with similar solutions to similar problems. Nevertheless, that others support similar policies may be a strong reinforcement to an agency, both in deciding what it wants to do and in justifying what it decides upon.

In other words, innovation in a particular agency is likely to be more a social than an intellectual process, to depend more on communication and persuasion than on problem-solving. This is certainly true of the innovative Welfare Department, which is not so much an original thinker as a diligent searcher and vigorous organizer.

3.1 Intra-agency Promotion of Search for Innovations

The Welfare Department promotes active search for new policies at all levels. Divisions, institutions, departments within institutions are urged to ask for what they feel they need. They are persuaded to re-evaluate their objectives and progress toward them, and to develop coherent, justifiable programs. The department encourages new programs, accepts substantial portions of them, supports them vigorously before the legislature, and gets large parts of what it wants. It gets enough so that subunits are able to solve the problems of the moment—that is, to reach their most urgent objectives—and move on to new ones. The result of this happy sequence is that subunit as well as departmental goals rise rapidly and continuously. Subunits are generally enthusiastic about their progress and put much effort into searching for improved programs and more persuasive justifications.

Numerous comments from institutional administrators testify to the importance of departmental encouragement and support and of the legislative support which follows:

The department has always backed us up on everything we think we need. We have great confidence in their support. In fact, they are very grateful if we have ideas.

The state through the legislature and the department has subscribed to the program as expressed in its goals and has been willing to financially support the achievement of the goals. . . . We have had excellent financial support of all aspects of the program. . . . We were not restricted in any of our plans.

We try to impress on everybody that this is not just a chance to get more money, but to improve our program. And we try to get suggestions from all employees.

She appreciates a staff which has initiative. She always approves our requests.

I usually put in something even if it has little chance of being approved. I think we should put all our needs before the department.

The budget is supposed to reflect the judgment of the administrator. There is no point in playing it cozy in trying to second guess everybody along the line. The budget should reflect only felt needs, nothing more, no less.

We don't hesitate to lay our problems on the line. I would not refrain from reflecting a need.

In contrast, new budget requests from subunits of the Labor Department have usually been discouraged and almost always rejected in the past. A consequence of this was that some divisional administrators lost enthusiasm for making requests and attempting to justify them:

I have been conditioned by the attitude of the commissioners, I would play my cards thinking, "Would he kill this or not."

I've been around here long enough to think we can't get anything.

Our request measures up to what we think we can get.

I was in charge of preparing requests for additional personnel. It was discouraging because there was no support from the director. If you can't get support from your own director, you can't expect to get it any place else.

We've had three decades of conservatism.

The difference is obvious. Over the years requests by Labor subunits adjusted almost to coincide with the constraint imposed by stable expectations. In the Welfare Department, expectations, learned from past experience, of how the department and the legislature will treat budget requests, are not stable; they rise, and aspirations rise with them.

In turn, agency search for policy innovations is a direct function of aspiration levels. In the Welfare Department, where aspirations are high, where many problems are perceived and put up for solution, search is intensive. In the Labor Department, problems which call for solutions through budget requests are dimly perceived, poorly specified and left unsolved; aspirations (in the sense of criteria for selecting particular budget requests) are modest; and search is minimal. No goals means no problems means no search.

An extremely important group of sources of new policies—we will note shortly how important they are—are represented in the communications, in the literature and meetings, of a number of professions. Psychologists, psychiatrists, hospital administrators, nurses, social workers, criminologists, lawyers, engineers, economists, and others who specialize in one or another of Labor and Welfare's policy areas, produce policy recommendations and information about consequences of particular alternatives, in reports on what similar agencies elsewhere are doing and in reports of professional research. This material does not sell itself to agencies—they must search for it, dig it out for themselves. Even trivial gestures in this direction, such as reading three or four professional journals regularly, may take a surprising amount of initiative and effort (as we well know). More intensive search activity, for example sending large numbers of employees to professional conferences, is expensive as well; it uses resources which may be scarce and better applied to direct agency operations, and it uses them for a purpose which is particularly open to legislative attack.

Constraints on the resources as well as on the aspirations of the Labor Department limit sharply the search it undertakes among its professions, relative to Welfare's search for innovation among *its* professions. We can make some easy though potentially misleading and perhaps even somewhat inaccurate quantitative comparisons. The Labor Department now receives 11 professional journals, plus 5 proceedings of annual meetings. The Welfare Department, *in its central offices alone,* not including any of the institutions (where many more people are employed but the percentage of professionals is lower), has 128 subscriptions to a total of 105 journals. With respect to trips to out-of-state professional meetings at state expense, the Labor Department sent its employees on a total of 9 trips to 5 different meetings in fiscal 1961–62. The Welfare Department in calendar 1962 sent its personnel on 281 trips to 91 different out-of-state professional conferences; and these figures are from an incomplete listing of such trips. In addition, Welfare officials participated in at least 10 business meetings out of state not connected with a particular profession; and sent at least 20 people to 10 institutions or agencies in its field in other states, to find out about particular programs developed at these places. As one would expect, Welfare Department officials are much more conscious of professional standards than their Labor counterparts, and they are generally more aware of what similar agencies elsewhere are doing. Labor has much less well developed standards and, with some exceptions, knows little of what goes on in other states.

(These comparisons may be misleading because they reflect opportunities for fruitful search and the vigor of the relevant profession as well as the agency's propensity for search. One might assert that Labor does not search for innovations among its professions because they do not produce them. Lacking comprehensive knowledge of other states' labor departments and of the literature of Labor's policy areas, I can not disprove this hypothesis. A fair test would compare several agencies in the same policy field and therefore the same search opportunities rather than agencies in different fields. For instance, we would expect to find some variation among state mental health agencies in search activity, and a direct connection between these variations and agency budget requests.)

3.2 Passive Receptivity to Local Demands and Changing Technology

Explicit encouragment of innovation in the Welfare Department, and a budget process which consistently grants the department and its subunits substantial portions of what they want, incline them to be more receptive to demands for innovations as well as to search actively for them. Since it is easy to make requests, it is not difficult to respond favorably to other people's needs. Employees and clientele are encouraged to state their needs, and the institution is in a position to try to satisfy them.

Many requests get their impetus from the day-to-day behavior of inmates. An accident that might have been prevented if an attendant had been present, pleas from patients for help and therapy, aggressive behavior which could have been avoided if facilities for treatment or recreation had been available—events such as these trigger specific budget requests. Some requests come from relatives of inmates. Following a complaint from families of the mentally deficient in one institution that they were often unable to see a part-time chaplain, the institution put in a request for a full-time chaplain. Some requests come from employees for their convenience rather than for any clear policy purpose. Thus, employees made, and institutions forwarded to the department, requests for expansion of a little-used bus service operated by the institution for the employees, and for an automatic gate so that weekend staff would not have to go out in bad weather. Not all requests of this sort are accepted by the institution, particularly if they have already been rejected once by the department, but many of them are. It helps the institution head to get along with his staff if he can at least include their requests in the budget he submits to the department. He may not vigorously argue for them at the departmental budget conference, but by at least accepting and sometimes really supporting such requests, he obligates his subordinates to reciprocate. This dual function of the budget process is perceived quite explicitly at top levels of the department, too. It is recognized that the agency's operations are carried out by subordinates; that their cooperation is absolutely necessary if the department is going to move in new directions; and that one way to get this cooperation—that is, to get them to help you solve your problems—is to help them solve theirs.

Since every new request must be justified in writing in the Welfare Department, it might seem that local requests like those noted above would be troublesome for the institution. Actually, it always seems possible to tie them to a justification acceptable enough to indicate sincerity if not to prove need. Furthermore, many local demands genuinely satisfy departmental objectives; or to put it differently, some objectives are shared by the institutions and departmental executives. It is also true, however, that some of these are objectives that would not be attended to on the initiative of the department; if no request is made, the relevant objective is not acted upon or is taken care of in some different way. So even if we point out a large area of shared goals between the institutions and divisional and departmental executives, we must admit that many items get into the budget only because some subunit far down in the department or some outside source requested them, and institutional officials were willing to buck them up the line. The fact that the director of the Welfare Department agrees to include in his budget requests to the governor and the legislature a particular locally inspired request from an institution by no means indicates that the department would have taken care of the felt need which produced the request. Requests of local origin focus attention on objectives which would otherwise be neglected.

There are three basic departmental decisions on institutional budget requests. Some are rejected by the department. A second group, at the other extreme, are proposals which represent the department's highest priority goals. These are items the department will get into its budget by hook or by crook. If the institution directors concerned are willing and eager to put them into their requests, fine. If not, they may be persuaded or cajoled or instructed to include them. Or the central divisional offices may make a request themselves and assign the new personnel to the institutions. The third main set of decisions consists of acceptances of budget requests not inspired by the department. In the Welfare Department, because of its policy of encouraging innovation, because of its willingness to delegate responsibility to subunits, and because criteria for rejection and criteria for top priority requests leave such a large open area between them, this set of acceptances is relatively large. If the department's leadership was not itself so demanding, the zone of acceptance would be considerably larger. In an agency like the Labor Department, where constraints imposed by expectations of legislative behavior are much more limiting, the zone of acceptance is small. The size of this zone of acceptance and the ability of agency subunits to fill it up with local solutions to local problems may very substantially affect the allocation of budget increases.

In addition to employees and clientele, industrial firms comprise an important source of innovations to which the Welfare Department is likely to be more receptive than many other agencies, certainly more so than the Labor Department. Differences in the physical plant of the two departments are obvious. Ancient chairs, battle-scarred wooden desks and filing cabinets, and 10- to 15-year-old typewriters are much more common in Labor than in Welfare. Machine dictation has long been de rigueur in the Welfare Department, but most of the Labor Department's inspectors still write out their reports in longhand.

Potential budget items proposed to the Welfare Department by firms partly overlap with innovations communicated through professional channels. A pharmaceutical house selling tranquilizers to mental hospitals may be able to reinforce its advertising with articles in professional journals or statements by professional groups, and with favorable reports of experience elsewhere with its product. But many firms, selling products not so closely related to professional activities, rely on a sales force or on catalogues to communicate with the appropriate agency subunit. Since firms are mainly interested in selling things rather than services to the Department's institutions, most of the impact of innovation by firms falls on budget requests for repair, maintenance, and capital items. Thus, 13 wooden ladders of varying lengths are replaced by higher-cost magnesium ladders. (One hopes that the new ladders will be more durable than the old, and that they will make workers more productive and safer, as well as making their work easier.) A 12" garden tractor is replaced by a 24" one. A new cushion stuffer is justified on the grounds that the old one is outdated. Brush, broom, and dustpan are replaced by a shop vacuum cleaner. Muscle is replaced by a telescopic lift. Standard teaching equipment and methods are replaced by tape recorders, film and filmstrip projectors, television sets, and duplicating machines. A concrete cutting saw replaces some applications of air hammers, while a special machine for drilling through walls replaces them for that purpose. Automatic sprinkler systems are installed. A $400 paint mixer replaces hand mixing.

I would not imply that these are unprofitable changes—I have not tried to evaluate them. The point is rather that changes in technology, largely executed by business firms, change both standards and costs of living for government agencies, as they do for everyone else. Outlays for products subject to innovative effort by firms often run over 20% of an agency's budget. Major construction, which I have not examined but which has experienced rapid innovation and increase in cost, is sometimes a large proportion of an agency's operating budget. In short, technological changes and consequent requests by government employees for facilities which become standard in the skilled trades or in firms may account for a substantial portion of the total increment requested. Although acceptance of these changes may be justified on various grounds—increased productivity, for example, or on grounds that modern facilities are a necessary side payment to skilled employees—we may at least note that technological changes are likely to promote some agency subgoals more than others. The subgoals "Maintain a satisfactory physical plant" and "Make prisoners literate and skillful" both belong to the objective, "Rehabilitate criminals." Buying a concrete saw promotes the first of these subgoals; buying six weeks of skilled instruction at the same price does more for the second. Such a comparison is almost never made, to be sure. Repair, maintenance, and minor capital improvements are evaluated according to one set of criteria; expansion of the educational program, by other criteria. This flow of new products and the efforts of firms to sell them have the greatest impact on activities which involve new facilities rather than new personnel —a particularly significant point in view of the reluctance of some legislative bodies to grant increases in personnel, even while they permit facilities to improve. (The suggestion that some agency subgoals are promoted more than others because of the sales activities of business firms needs to be confirmed by further research, however—it may be that the only agencies which are able consistently to improve their physical plant are those which are generally wealthy.)

The cumulative effect of the local demands of clientele, and employees, and of changing technology and persistent sales effort by firms, is probably great. The readiness of agencies to accept alternatives proposed by these sources is a most important variable and one we often take for granted. It is true that these sources of innovation are fragmented. The changes they induce come in bits and pieces rather than in meat packages gift-wrapped in idealistic prose. But dozens of small alterations in an institution's staff, equipment, procedures, and buildings may have pervasive effects on recruitment, turnover, work performance, and clientele attitudes and behavior. Precisely how important these effects are remains to be established.

In this discussion of agency receptivity to local requests and to product innovations by firms, we have scarcely mentioned the Labor Department. The rate at which items from these sources enter Labor's budget requests is lower than for the Welfare Department. *Some* of this difference is due to differences in the rate at which local requests are made to the Labor Department and to differences in the volume of product innovations relevant to the department's functions. But the rate at which clientele and employees make demands on the Labor Department is itself a function, over the long run, of the department's receptivity to them; and in the one area in which Labor and Welfare are directly comparable (purchase of office equipment), Labor is much less willing than Welfare to request new products or new models of old products. As I noted above, the differences between the agencies in condition of physical plant are obvious. Furthermore, some kinds of office equipment are far from neutral tools. Dictating rather than handwriting reports may free substantial time for inspection. Automated record-keeping can alert an agency to problems that otherwise might escape its attention, and data made accessible can bolster requests weakened by the absence of supporting information.

Like the contrast between Welfare and Labor in rate of active search for innovations, the difference in receptivity seems to be a result of the adjustment of agency aspirations to its expectations of legislative treatment. An agency subunit which has trouble attaining its own main objectives is not likely to accept responsibility for meeting the local demands of others. And when potential requestors know in advance that requests are futile, they will not make them. [This does not mean that no demands impinge on the Labor Department, and it does not mean that the department never accedes to such demands—only that *local* demands by employees and clientele (in their unorganized state) are rarely made and rarely accepted.]

In addition to this damper on requests, there may be other differences in the relationships of the two departments to their immediate clientele which reduce the flow of requests. These differences are summarized in the difference between service and regulation—between doing something for people that they most urgently want, and doing something that recipients regard as against their interests. Welfare's clientele consists largely of the former, hence it is not surprising that the department receives from this source requests for expansion of services. But there is no reason for the firms which are inspected and regulated by the Labor Department to be interested in expanding its activities.

This difference should not be overdrawn, however, since an agency's relationship to its clientele is in part a creature of its own making. The Labor Department has beneficiaries of its operations—the employees of companies inspected for compliance with safety and with wages and hours regulations, and employees involved in workmen's compensation cases— but this clientele probably perceives the relation between its own objectives and the Labor Department's activities a good deal less clearly than Welfare clientele perceives the relevance of the operation of the state mental hospitals, for example. The Welfare Department's performance has shown its diverse clientele what it can do for them. As the department plays a larger, more active, more effective role in corrections and mental health programs, people's attention focusses increasingly on it. Labor's activities may have lacked both effectiveness and drama. Consequently, a public that might be interested in its programs, individuals who might stimulate the department to innovation by requesting solutions to local problems, is relatively apathetic and detached.

In sum, day-to-day experiences with clientele in the working lives of subunits, and innovations sold by firms, may bring specific problems and specific budget requests to the attention of lower-level employees and supervisors and administrators. The perception of events as problems to which solutions via the budget are appropriate, and the acceptance of specific demands, are subject to constraints which arise from the concern of agencies to avoid consequences of making certain kinds of requests before the chief executive and the legislature. These constraints result in lowered receptivity to local demands and local problems, cutting off and eventually attenuating these sources of innovation. Or the constraints sharply limit agency adoption of changing technology, with sometimes pervasive effects.

We have examined bits-and-pieces innovation. This kind of change lacks the title on the door—the connection to broad social objectives *follows* the decision. Pattern there may be to these innovations; of plan, there is little. For "policy" writ large, we must look to other sources.

3.3 Professions as Sources of Innovations in Policy

The main sources of new policies for the innovative, rapidly growing Welfare Department are neither local clientele demands nor shifting technology. They are the members of several professions, usually working in a non-industrial context—in universities, in private non-profit welfare institutions, and in government agencies in the corrections and mental health field in other states, in the federal government, and in other countries. The largest part of the Welfare Department's budget increase requests for program improvement goes for policies the department has taken over from these sources. These requests are also related most immediately to the public objectives of the department; they involve changes in the way the department handles its principal clientele, inmates of institutions and others under Welfare's supervision and care outside of the hospitals and prisons.

Above, I explained the public goals of the Welfare Department: reducing human misery and saving money in the long run. Then I listed some requested program improvements which were justified under these objectives—programs to enable the state mental health system to rely increasingly on county hospitals, local clinics, day care, and outpatient facilities, and to increase professional staffing for treatment and rehabilitation at all the institutions. We cannot hope to explain the choice of this set of means, or instrumental subgoals, by pointing to the public goals. There is nothing in the public goals to account for specific shifts in emphasis over a period of years, so we must go behind public goals to observe the sources of these requests, and then specify the rules with which the department picks and chooses among available alternatives.

We have already looked at how the Welfare Department dips continuously and eagerly into the stream of professional communications in search of policies. Perhaps it should not surprise us to find every one of the department's requests for new programs for the present biennium in the professional literature. I have yet to complete a systematic, comprehensive analysis of this literature, but even a casual inspection of a few journals and books in the mental health field, for example, reveals that they appear again and again in the form of recommendations or as reports on what is being done in some particular agency.

Furthermore, each of the mental health programs now being expanded or newly requested by the Welfare Department seems to have been around for a good long time. In 1937, a Citizens' Committee on Public Welfare in this state composed of both professionals and lay people issued a lengthy report with many recommendations. Some of these recommendations have long since been attained; others were rejected or ignored or became irrelevant. But among the recommendations, twenty-six years ago, were these: that programs for early diagnosis and treatment be established to prevent institutionalization; that a state-supported mental hygiene program operate in the counties, including psychiatric services; that the state adopt the American Psychiatric Association's minimum standards for the operation of mental hospitals; that individual treatment with expanded professional staff supplant mass custody in mental hospitals; that the county asylums be transformed into hospitals for diagnosis and treatment; that medical and field work staff be increased at the colonies for the retarded to intensify rehabilitation and to permit the return of more inmates to their homes; that the state expand diagnosis, treatment, and training at correctional institutions in academic, vocational, moral and civic, dental, psychiatric, medical, and recreational areas. Some of these proposals are identical to ones now being pushed in the Welfare Department budget; other are worked out in only somewhat less detail.

In the postwar period, the journal *Mental Hospitals,* a publication of the American Psychiatric Association, reports monthly on similar proposals in other states and other countries. The June, 1950, issue holds up Virginia's "Duke Report" as a model; it recommends expanded use of local mental health clinics. At about this time, too, one begins to find a significant new kind of article on mental hospitals, reporting on recommendations that have become working programs. One state reports that pressure on its mental hospitals is relieved by new clinics which see as many patients as are admitted to the hospitals. A city opens a 42-bed psychiatric unit in its hospital to develop treatment facilities at the local level. A state passes legislation to allow mentally ill patients to be kept in a local hospital for ninety days. Reports from mental hospitals all over the country testify to the effects of changes in professional staffing, in treatment programs, and in admission and discharge policies: one hospital reports on 80% increase in direct discharge rates over a 3-year period; another announces a 34% increase in patient turnover in 2 years, a 28% decrease in returns.

What this means, for one thing, is that for any single agency in the mental health field, there is very little new under the sun. Even the policy innovations of this Welfare Department, which considers itself one of the leading such agencies in the country, up at the top with California and New York, have usually been proposed repeatedly and tried out elsewhere. They are drawn from the recommendations and experience of a broad range of agencies in many places, not just from the few wealthy ones—money is essential to put new ideas into effect on a broad scale, but it is not so necessary, in large quantities, for the processes of thinking and organizing which produce an idea and try it out. I am told that the department even picks up many useful ideas from agencies and institutions which are not otherwise outstanding.

The people who devise new methods in this field are professionals. They undergo long formal training in their professions, they are committed to professional aspirations, they take pride in their standing as professionals. When they do something new, when they show results that other professionals might be interested in, they are eager to publish a description or to talk about it at a meeting. Other professionals, anxious to avoid being stick-in-the-muds, to avoid loss of professional status, and to do as good a job as possible, rush to inspect and adopt policies their colleagues are putting into effect.

This intensive professional activity constitutes a crucial difference between Welfare and Labor. Some professional associations specialize in areas of interest to the Labor Department, but they are much fewer in number, much less active in holding meetings and in publishing research and discussions of current problems and current solutions, and much less directly concerned with public policy than the groups with which Welfare regularly communicates. Professions in the mental health and corrections fields are more vigorous in producing and selling costly public policy innovations than those in the fields of industrial safety, workmen's compensation, apprentice training, and wage and hour regulation.

The key words here are "costly" and "public." With regard to cost, many policy changes proposed by professionals in Labor's policy areas do not involve governmental expenditures—for example, increases in the minimum wage do not necessarily require additional inspectors. Some additional educational and inspectional effort will be required for a time, but this can be and has been accomplished with existing staff. Policy innovations in corrections and mental health, on the other hand, tend to come in very expensive packages, involving massive and relatively high-salaried additions to professional staff and construction of new buildings. In short, professionals in the Labor field appear to have foregone objectives that require large budget requests—a constraint on aspirations which does not characterize the professions of social work, psychiatry, psychology, mental hospital administration, correctional administration and criminology.[2]

In addition to this difference in cost and therefore in budgetary impact of innovations proposed by professionals in the respective policy areas, there is a striking difference in orientation and content which is partly related to cost. Most of the professional journals to which the Labor Department subscribes address themselves to private industry rather than to public agencies. Officials of such organizations as the National Safety Council and the National Fire Protection Association are mainly heads of safety programs in manufacturing companies. Their journals are devoted to articles on safety devices, safety programs, and safety hazards and their cures in industry. This helps safety inspectors of the Labor Department keep up to date on new aspects of safety technology, but it doesn't help the department develop new programs for itself. What innovation there is in professions in Labor's policy area is directed toward the policies of firms rather than of governments. In contrast, the professions to which the Welfare Department belongs and listens operate almost entirely in areas where there is no distinction between public and private interests—for example, in the development of treatments for childhood schizophrenia—or in areas in which public agencies clearly dominate the field of operations, as in admission and discharge policies of large mental hospitals, the coordination of diverse facilities to meet the needs of a broad public, or almost the entire delinquency, crime, and corrections field.

In addition to setting objectives for future attainment, professions in the Welfare field, again in contrast to those in the Labor field, do a great deal to set standards for workload for professional employees. These standards have two major effects. In the first place, as workloads (in this case, mainly institutional populations) change, very sizable budget increases will be requested if the agency has a clear conception of how many employees of various kinds it wants for a given workload, keeps careful data on workload, and always adjusts requests to maintain workload standards. About 40% of the Welfare Department's requested increase for the current biennium is identified in the budget as workload change, as contrasted to only 12% for program change.[3] The financial impact of workload standards closely adhered to can be large.

Secondly, sticking closely to explicit workload standards is a prerequisite to the solution of current problems. Suppose you institute an intensified treatment program at a mental hospital. If the population in the hospital stays the same but time-consuming admissions work increases, you will lose ground in your attempt to intensify treatment—*unless* you perceive that part of your workload is changing, *and* insist that admissions rates are just as valid as the traditional, accepted population figures, *and* make the appropriate request to take care of the workload increase. Furthermore, failure to solve current problems will detract from your ability to handle future ones, and it will even prevent some future problems from being evoked at all, since it is commonplace that solutions to problems evoke new problems.

The professions which stand behind the Welfare Department are constantly pushing target workload standards. The department uses the standards to specify desirable staffing patterns and to justify its requests. It is acutely conscious of changes in the nature and quantity of its work. In the Labor Department, largely unaided by its professions, such changes go unnoticed, or if noticed, are poorly defined in terms of the public objectives of the agency. The Department is authorized by statute to set standards for frequency of safety inspection in factories, for example, but has not done so. Since there is no precise and persuasively justified workload standard, increases in workload do not trigger requests for more personnel.

In sum, by generating policy alternatives and setting standards, professions may have an immense impact on an agency's ability to maintain and raise its aspirations; therefore on its budget; therefore on public policies realized through the budget. For the Welfare Department, professions are far and away the most important sources of policy alternatives. And if professions in the Welfare field play as large a role as I think they do in developing innovations in public policy and putting them into effect, then problem-evoking and problem-solving in the professions are central to the policy making process.

3.4 "Political" Sources of Policy Innovations

Where do familiar public figures in our political landscape fit into this survey of sources of innovation—the elected chief executive, the legislative body, the organized interest groups? For the most part, they do not fit at all. They are not customarily sources of new policies for either the Department of Welfare or the Department of Labor. One minor program in the

Welfare Department was requested of it by the previous governor, but it is a small operation, not closely related to other major programs, and not even financed out of the department's budget. Furthermore, the program was suggested by the department itself in response to a request from the governor for ideas in an area of interest to him.

As for the legislature, both agencies report some contacts of the constituent case type, the legislator checking up on delay in a workmen's compensation case or on a constituent's problems in getting his mentally deficient child into a state institution. The legislature is not a source of policy innovations for these agencies.

Other than the professionals in and out of state employ, there are few organized special interest groups in the corrections and mental health fields in this state. They support the Welfare Department's programs, but they mainly support the department's proposals rather than generate ones of their own, at least in recent years. In the Department of Labor, a request for a new program did recently come from an organized group, but the case is so closely tied in with Labor's decision rules for acceptance of new policy proposals that we will discuss it under that heading.

4. DECISION RULES FOR PERCEIVED POLICY INNOVATIONS

Our lengthy emphasis on processes by which new policy alternatives are perceived reflects the impression (strongly reinforced by similar evidence about business firms) that these cognitive processes are fully as important to choice as processes by which goals are specified and applied. A specific choice often begins with an available alternative in mind rather than with a motivating objective. What people want does not determine what they know about how to get it.

The decision rules which may intervene between perception of an alternative and the decision to put it into the budget are diverse and numerous even within a single agency. What makes them researchable is that they are extensively factored. A department head plays a different game with the requests of his subordinates than they play in making them in the first place, and a different game than he plays with his own professional objectives or with requests from the governor. Requests for personnel evoke different criteria than requests for equipment; for clerical personnel, different than for treatment and rehabilitation positions; for large items, different than for small ones; from one institution, different than from another. This is only appropriate since decision criteria are expressions of objectives, and different kinds of requests from different sources affect different objectives. Rather than try to cover the field, we will discuss several cases which throw light on aspects of the topic.

4.1 A Construction Safety Inspection Program for the Labor Department

Problems are frequently perceived by comparing good performance in relation to an agency objective in an area in which the agency is active with poor performance in a closely related area in which the agency is not active. Labor Department statistics showed that the construction industry in this state had far and away the most accidents per million man hours, with proportionately high workmen's compensation assessments. Since one of the department's divisions already inspected industrial plants for safety in order to help prevent accidents to workers, it was an easy inference that the division should also inspect construction sites for safe practices in order to reduce fatalities and injuries among construction workers. Accordingly, the head of the division concerned discussed the matter with department officials over a period of several years. It took a change in the top levels of the department to bring about a decision to set up an advisory committee, with representatives of both the labor unions and the construction industry, to look into the matter. The committee looked over the evidence and recommended the establishment of a new construction safety section in the department. Both the contractors and the unions assured the department of their support, and the department subsequently requested the personnel for the proposed operation in the budget.

What are the crucial steps in this process? Someone in the department was interested in the proposal and brought it to the attention of higher officials. A change in the top levels of the department brought in an official with relatively high aspirations, a conception of the department as vigorous and innovative. His reaction was to test for the support of interested groups. When support was forthcoming, the request was made. One official noted, "We finally got some help on this from the associated general contractors, so we decided to go ahead with it." It is an axiom in the Labor Department that support from both industry and labor makes approval almost a sure thing. (The construction safety program was cut out by the legislature, however.) This test for support is a potentially strong constraint on Labor Department requests, and a basic difference between Labor and Welfare. The Welfare Department has learned by experience that it can get requests approved even without support from some magic set of groups, hence it does not subject its programs to the test of group support. Welfare's strategy relies mainly on direct persuasion rather than on accumulation of group support; the difference accords both with Welfare's continued favorable experience in obtaining what it requests and the relative absence of strong special interest groups in its environment. (But the absence of strong groups may be in part the result of Welfare's success on its own; satisfied groups have no reason to be active.) The difference in group-oriented strategies is associated also with contrasts in executive recruitment; Welfare recruits from professional ranks, Labor partly from partisan politics.

A further item of interest in this case: a representative for the contractors, when asked, suggested that 300 inspectors would be about right to cover the state. But as a Labor official pointed out, "Three hundred would be laughed right out of the hearing room." The official proceeded to make this request based not on some standard of need for inspection, but on rules of thumb that tended to make the request as unobtrusive as possible: (1) make it the same size as the (admittedly understaffed) industrial safety section; (2) make it small enough so that it will fit into some free (i.e., federally financed) office space available around the state, so that the cost of the new section will be lower than if space had to be rented. The ensuing request for 12 inspectors and 2 supervisors was cut in half within the department, not by a standard of need but by a calculation of legislative reaction—we would like to ask for all of them, "but you have to be realistic, after all." "We aren't being hard-nosed just for the fun of it. We are trying to pare down requests somewhat now so there won't be worse cuts later by the legislature." This implicit expectation—if you ask for a small amount, the legislature is likely to give you something, but if you ask for a large amount, the legislature might cut it all away—is totally absent from budget calculations in the Welfare Department. Welfare has decision rules which result in reduction of requests, but if they feel a large request can be justified, by their own standards, it is left in; if a small request cannot be justified, it is taken out. "I don't inhibit our material on some kind of second guessing. In deciding what to include there isn't anything I think of including for which there isn't a good case. . . . It's hard to draw the line. You can't make decisions on what you think will pass."

Testing for group support, making a request only after group support is forthcoming, requesting what you think you can get rather than what you feel able to justify—these decision rules may amount to constraints on innovation in public policy.

4.2 The Governor Initiates a Program

Although organized groups are not an overwhelmingly important part of the Welfare Department's environment, the governor is important, perhaps mainly because of his role in the budget process: "He has first crack at us. It is very difficult to get more than what the governor recommends." Consequently, requests from the governor are handled with deference. Such requests have not resulted in major Welfare policy innovations, especially compared to what Welfare generates on its own, but the way in which the governor's requests are handled illustrates a decision rule which is tied to the source of the request.

The governor was preparing a conservation program and wanted to tie it in with conservation of human resources, specifically with something in the juvenile delinquency field. "He asked us if we could give him some suggestions. Now, I consider that an order. As I see my job, I owe the governor a reply. We should know something about this, so I should volunteer the information. I find the time to do the work on this thing. I sent up two or three ideas, they took one of them. I consider this an initiation by the governor. He initiated it by asking that we give him some information on a problem." The result was a program in an area the department had only talked about without really planning to do anything at the time. The quick response with attractive, carefully worked out policy proposals, and the subsequent vigorous organization of the chosen program, had several effects. It focussed the department's attention on objectives which would not otherwise have been evoked in the form of a specific program. It resulted in a new policy. It insured that the policy would be administered by the department. And it presumably increased the governor's respect for and obligation to the department. A less enthusiastic response at any stage—different ways of handling requests from the governor, different modes of responding to a chance to raise aspirations—would have had quite different effects.

4.3 Problem, Solution, Problem Sequences in Mental Health Programs

As I noted earlier, most of the change in the Welfare budget, and almost all of its new programs, are obtained via professional communication channels from professional activity in similar agencies elsewhere. At the most general level, the major facets of the mental hygiene field are simple: intensify treatment, which is equivalent to asking for more professional staff; avoid institutionalization whenever possible, which is to say that patients who are no harm to anyone and are no longer being helped should be discharged; and promote local rather than highly centralized facilities for treatment of mental illness. But this summary list only summarizes; it does not indicate why a particular set of requests falling under one or more of these headings is chosen at a particular time, especially since all of the major new programs of the Welfare Department have been kicking around its professions for many years.

The point is that the standard, widely agreed upon problems and solutions to them in the mental hygiene field comprise a rather simple network. As one top executive put it, "It doesn't take long to figure out that if you can spend some money [on intensified treatment] and get the patients out of the institution, that in the long run, you will be saving money, and this is completely aside from the humanitarian aspects of the program. We just followed the road signs." Road signs tell you what direction to go to reach your objective. They do not determine who starts where. They do not determine how fast you go. They do not determine who gets there first. Where you are at the moment is determined by past events, and how fast you go depends on your skill as a driver, the power and durability of your machine, and your ability to obtain fuel, new parts, and other basic resources. Likewise, an agency's progress toward long run goals is determined by where it starts and by how it handles short run political and administrative problems—by what resources it can obtain from outside the agency, and by how skillfully it organizes the resources available to it.

To illustrate this process, we examine a network of objectives and problems and solutions occurring over time in the Welfare Department's mental health program. Figure 1 is a sequence of professional solutions to common problems in the field. The sequence proceeds roughly from top to bottom in time, with the exception of steps indicated by lines and arrows, which denote solutions which lead to new problems and policies which are solutions to several problems. Some problems and some solutions actually occurred at about the same time.

The sequence has several interesting features. In the first place, policy innovations are seen to be problem-oriented; that is, they are choices intended to reduce the discrepancy between some aspiration and the present state of affairs.

Secondly, solutions are evoked only by problems which are local to this mental health program as well as common in professional experience elsewhere. Problems do not require solutions unless they are felt locally and directly. Solutions to problems which can be foreseen but have not yet made themselves felt are usually postponed or reduced in scope: it is safer to avoid requesting and setting up a program that *may* not be needed after all; and it is easier to justify solutions to problems that are already upon us. Consequently, anticipatory solutions are infrequent, especially when massive resources are required, as when a new institution is built.

This factor is particularly important because new problems are often the result of successful solutions to old ones—the speed and effectiveness with which an agency moves to solve one problem will determine the time at which a new problem becomes urgent. For example, the tremendously increased volume of applications for admission to the state mental hospitals since 1945 depended in part on the great improvement in facilities and treatment programs in the hospitals in the postwar years. If admissions pressure had not been so great, the hospitals would have moved much more slowly to increase the discharge rate; and if intensified treatment

Figure 1
A Network of Problems and Solutions in the
Welfare Department's Mental Health Program, 1945–63

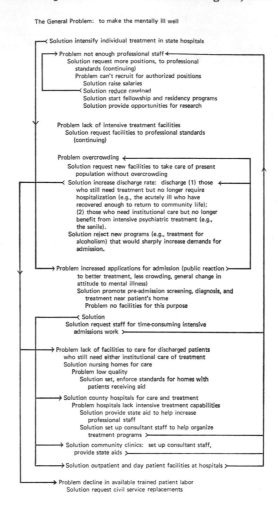

The General Problem: to make the mentally ill well

Solution intensify individual treatment in state hospitals

Problem not enough professional staff
    Solution request more positions, to professional
    standards (continuing)
    Problem can't recruit for authorized positions
        Solution raise salaries
    Solution reduce caseload
    Solution start fellowship and residency programs
    Solution provide opportunities for research

Problem lack of intensive treatment facilities
    Solution request facilities to professional standards
    (continuing)

Problem overcrowding
    Solution request new facilities to take care of present
    population without overcrowding
    Solution increase discharge rate: discharge (1) those
    who still need treatment but no longer require
    hospitalization (e.g., the acutely ill who have
    recovered enough to return to community life);
    (2) those who need institutional care but no longer
    benefit from intensive psychiatric treatment (e.g.,
    the senile).
    Solution reject new programs (e.g., treatment for
    alcoholism) that would sharply increase demands for
    admission.

Problem increased applications for admission (public reaction
    to better treatment, less crowding, general change in
    attitude to mental illness)
    Solution promote pre-admission screening, diagnosis, and
    treatment near patient's home
    Problem no facilities for this purpose

Solution
Solution request staff for time-consuming intensive
admissions work

Problem lack of facilities to care for discharged patients
    who still need either institutional care of treatment
    Solution nursing homes for care
        Problem low quality
        Solution set, enforce standards for homes with
        patients receiving aid
Solution county hospitals for care and treatment
    Problem hospitals lack intensive treatment capabilities
    Solution provide state aid to help increase
    professional staff
    Solution set up consultant staff to help organize
    treatment programs
Solution community clinics: set up consultant staff,
    provide state aids
Solution outpatient and day patient facilities at hospitals

Problem decline in available trained patient labor
Solution request civil service replacements

programs had not already been developed, it would have been difficult to
increase the discharge rate substantially. Finally, the increase in admissions
pressure has combined with the increased discharge rate to make the
development of local facilities for treatment of mental illness imperative
for pre-admission diagnosis and screening, non-institutional treatment
where possible, and post-release care to prevent return to the institution by
the discharged patient—imperative, that is, for executives willing to make

decisions and plunge into the administrative problems of trying to stimulate and regulate programs by independent local agencies. If any one of these problems had gone unperceived or unsolved, the department would probably be now less concerned with the development of local facilities than it is—it would still be working on prior problems. Many budget requests would not have been made, new policies would not have been adopted, facilities would not have been developed, and some of the mentally ill would have gone untreated.

The rate at which an agency proceeds through a sequence of problems, solutions, and new problems depends on many factors. At some points, the agency will have to request, justify, and obtain legislative authorizations and appropriations, but most of the factors have nothing to do with politics as we usually think of it.

Requests are determined in the Welfare Department by the conjunction of professional aspirations, local conditions, and professionally generated alternatives for choice. A prime determinant of both aspirations and alternatives is an agency's reference groups—the league in which the agency places itself. The Welfare Department, considering itself the equal of similar agencies in New York and California, gauges its performance by theirs, in terms of new results achieved, and new programs initiated. An agency which considers itself more in the same league with, say, its counterpart in Mississippi, obviously uses a different measure of its own attainment and will perceive a different set of problems as relevant to its circumstances.

Both before and after persuading a chief executive and a legislature to authorize and finance a solution to some problem, the agency faces the task of making various internal allocation decisions and of persuading often reluctant subordinates to support the new policies enthusiastically. These are important capabilities and not everyone has them or uses them willingly. Reorganization of lines of authority and communication and a variety of incentives and penalties may be involved. What may be a very substantial and time-consuming organizational effort will determine whether an objective is attained or foregone. The outcome, as in Figure 1, will evoke its own particular problems. What problems now exist depends on what problems were perceived and how they were solved in the past. Passage along such a problem-solution-problem sequence depends just as much on agency aspirations and organizational skill as on legislature approval. In fact, it has happened in the Welfare Department that a subunit's enthusiastic participation in a new policy was more difficult to get than legislative approval of the same policy, and strategies for dealing with subunits are at least as complex as strategies for dealing with the legislature.

5. AGENCY CONTROL OF PUBLIC POLICY

If the legislature tightly controlled the Welfare Department, none of the preceding would be very important. In fact, as we have noted, the department gets almost all of what it wants, if not this year, then next. The legislature and the governor largely acquiesce, apparently satisfied that the department's requests are worth paying increasingly large amounts for.

Why? An economist friend suggested to me that Welfare got more than Labor in the budget because it *should*. I agree that it should, but this begs the question of *why* we—and the governor and the legislature—think this way. It is, after all, not obvious on the face of it that preventing fatal and disabling accidents in industry is a less noble goal than helping the mentally ill out of their trouble. But we have been persuaded by a good many highly persuasive people, especially since the end of World War II, that we and our governments should and can do something about mental illness. In a flood of articles and books, scholarly and otherwise, in novels and in movies, we have observed the misery of the great asylums and witnessed the hope of individual treatment and recovery. Has anyone been persuading us of the need for government programs for industrial safety?

Governors and legislators share this experience with us, but they are exposed to additional persuasion as well. Almost all of the Welfare Department's budget tactics may be lumped together under the category of direct persuasion. The department works to persuade them of three things. It intones moral imperatives that most people would find very difficult to oppose. Then it lays out a budget which is in effect a plan, with much detailed persuasive material thrown in. This establishes a convincing link between the high-flying objectives and the dollar requests. The department's third persuasive thrust is to establish that the Welfare Department is expert and efficient, the ideal agency to entrust with the programs requested. This is accomplished mainly by showing very detailed knowledge of departmental policies and operations: "We do well in obtaining support because we always try to know about everything that is going on. If we don't, we can't make an interpretation of the program [to the appropriations committee, for instance]. . . . Our purpose is to be on top of everything."

And there we have the answer to the question—Why do governor and legislature acquiesce in Welfare's requests? They have been persuaded to. Professionals in the corrections and mental health fields have been persuading them for years, and home-grown professional public executives capped it off. The department has continuously raised the aspirations of the governors and legislatures it has served "under." The Welfare Department, backed by assorted professions and by the efforts of like agencies else-where, dominates policy initiation almost completely. It experiences some delay but only rare vetoes by the governor or legislature, so that little control is exercised over it via the anticipated reactions route. The Welfare Department largely controls state government policy in corrections and mental health, constrained by its professional ideology more than by legislative oversight or by executive leadership. Now, I am not saying that this is *bad*. I will sing no sad song of legislative impotence. My point is that we should know who's running the show, and we should know why they run it the way they do.

It is understandable why a really well-managed persuasive effort by an agency should be so successful. Legislators come to their jobs with relatively little knowledge of specific policies, and without well developed, thoroughly rationalized criteria for evaluating requests. A large portion of their communications, written and oral, about any particular program request is likely to emanate from the agency responsible for it. The agency supplies to the legislator a set of ready-made criteria for evaluating its own requests; if these justifications are well prepared, and if there is no strongly expressed counter-position, the legislator will find it easy to adopt them as his own. As one state legislator wrote a few years ago in *Mental Hospitals,* "Legislators seek supporting data to be sure that something is not being 'put over' on them. Yet in many instances they are unable to interpret the material when it is presented because of the occupational terminology and the statistical approach. Consequently they dare not assume the responsibility for making large increases or large reductions in the budget requests. This is true, session after session and the legislators vote—reluctantly in many cases—to approve all or most of the items submitted to them. . . . The result is that the growth and development of mental health programs rests for the most part on state executives."[4]

Many of the Welfare Department decision procedures that we have discussed—procedures for search, use of other agencies as reference group standards, rules for accepting proposals from various sources—are highly stable, changing only in response to some problem that they are not able to solve. The department's political tactics in the budget process are equally stable. Since the department enjoys great success, there is no reason to change them. These standard rules for persuasion specify the framework of public goals to which all requests will be tied and the persuasive activities that the department will perform. In general, almost all requests for new programs or for substantial numbers of a particular kind of personnel must be justifiable in terms of the objectives of rehabilitation and treatment. The pressure from the top level of the department for consistent justifications in these terms is so strong that requests from institutions presented for other reasons than these are sometimes left in the budget unchanged but with the justification entirely rewritten to emphasize rehabilitation and treatment.

Patterns of persuasive activities are equally stable. Department officials are always willing to speak to groups about the agency and its programs. The department director follows a routine in getting to know the legislators at each session. Introducing a new bill is accompanied by certain standard influencing activity. There is very little calculation in all of this, mainly the skillful execution of a well-adapted set of standard operations. As with other kinds of agency procedures and policies, there is some learning of budgetary procedures from professional sources and practices of other agencies. Techniques of program budgeting and workload measurement, which can be used to increase the persuasiveness of budget requests, are increasingly put into practice by the Welfare Department.

The Labor Department offers an interesting contrast. Moving in recent months to request new programs, the department has few standard procedures for budget tactics, and none that have been shown to be successful. There is a good deal more search, experimentation, and learning of new tactics here than in the Welfare Department. In the event of some success with these new procedures, they will quickly become standard, presumably.

6. CONCLUSION

In a political system in which an overwhelming proportion of policies are initiated in administrative agencies, and many of them are approved by elected officials, it pays to look at the origins of these policies and the processes by which they are generated. This is what we have been doing, at varying levels of detail and comprehensiveness, for two state agencies. We can say nothing about all administrative agencies on the basis of these cases, but we can note that this sort of analysis tells us a good deal about the dynamics of agency decision making that usually remains obscure to us.

We have shown that agency aspirations may be regarded as criteria for accepting or rejecting alternative policies. Choice depends on what alternatives are perceived, the characteristics of these alternatives, and the criteria applied to them. The criteria may refer to the source of the proposed alternative, to support for it from other sources, to its cost, to its justifiability, to the way in which it relates to problems the agency is trying to solve, and to a number of other characteristics. For the Welfare Department, criteria for evaluating policies frequently are part of a search for solutions to public problems. In the Labor Department, problems of justification and outside support for particular proposals are more likely to dominate choice.

Criteria (aspirations) may originate in diverse ways. In general, an agency learns through its own experience which criteria lead to success and the solution of problems, and aspirations adjust to success or failure in the long run. Aspirations are acquired also from the experience of other like agencies regarded as reference groups.[5]

Alternatives are similarly acquired through experience. A successful solution to a problem is a precedent for solutions to similar problems in the future, and this applies to solutions reached elsewhere as well as within the agency. The acquisition of both aspirations and new policies from outside the agency depends on communication channels that may or may not be used by an agency. Some sources of alternatives and policies, such as firms and local clientele, are likely to communicate with the agency; here the important variable is agency receptivity to specific requests. Communication with other sources may require active search by the agency, as in the case of professional groups and other like agencies elsewhere. Search tends to be problem-oriented and thus depends on the extent to which the agency's aspirations exceed present performance.

Justifications and persuasive tactics for policies generated and accepted likewise are developed according to standard criteria and are learned from the experience of the agency and its referents. The agency's ability to innovate freely by moving from one problem to another depends both on its success in persuading chief executives and legislators to grant its requests, and on its ability to organize available resources to solve each problem as it arises.

We need not attempt to prove anything by our use of examples to generate hypotheses, but I will mention one possible result of the application of this sort of analysis to a variety of policy making processes. It may be that the mental health and corrections fields are quite atypical in the extent to which professions dominate decisions, but this remains to be seen. If professions dominate policy initiation by agencies and agency initiatives dominate government policy, then I fail to see how we can support a theory of democratic politics, either descriptive or normative, which continues to place overwhelming emphasis on methods of conducting elections and the participants in them. Obviously, many other social decision processes, not authoritatively invoked in the Constitution, shape public policy and therefore determine the relation between policies enacted and the preferences of citizens. How important these processes are and how they work are questions for further research. The results might affect not only our view of ourselves but also our prescriptions for political development elsewhere.

Author's acknowledgments: To Ken Hoover, Richard Randall, and Bob Zimring for high quality research assistance; and to the Social Systems Research Institute and the Wisconsin Alumni Research Foundation for support.

NOTES

[1] R. M. Cyert and J. G. March, *A Behavioral Theory of the Firm* (Englewood Cliffs, N.J.: Prentice-Hall, 1963).

[2] One might argue that Labor's policies are inherently less budget-dependent than Welfare's, that innovations in Labor's policies naturally involve less additional expenditure than Welfare's. I do not think this is so, however. For one thing, Welfare initiates many policy changes other than those which appear in the budget; they are probably more innovative than Labor in this respect as well as in the budget. Secondly, anyone with a little imagination and a familiarity with public policies could easily think up a number of quite expensive policy innovations in the Labor field, or less expensive policies (in public tax funds) in the mental health field. Hence, I regard the avoidance of costly policies as a limitation on aspirations.

[3] This figure underestimates the actual cost in the present biennium of new programs, however, since an additional substantial amount goes to pay for operation over the entire present biennium of programs which were approved by previous legislatures but only operated in part of the previous biennium. The 12% figure for new programs also does not reflect the full future cost of new programs initiated in the present biennium.

[4] J. R. Hall, Jr., State Senator of Oklahoma, "How the Mental Hospital Budget Looks to the Legislator," *Mental Hospitals,* VIII, 6, p. 14.

[5] We have scarcely mentioned recruitment processes, but these are clearly basic, since they determine what aspirations, perceptions, and group referents agency employees and officials bring with them.

CHAPTER 17

The Basic Dynamics of Search and Change

Anthony Downs

INTRODUCTION

In all organizations, search (information seeking) is closely related to change in general. This is true because both organizations and individuals need additional information most when they are in relatively new and unfamiliar situations. Therefore, our exploration of search processes is inextricably bound up with our analysis of change. This chapter sets forth a basic model of search and change for both individuals and organizations.

THE DEPTH OF CHANGE

The behavior of both individuals and organizations changes constantly. However, during any given period when some elements are changing, others must remain stable, or there will be a loss of identity. For example, the specific behavior of an individual or bureau may be quite different on Tuesday from what it was on Monday, but the rules governing that behavior may be the same on both days. The first problem we encounter is distinguishing the depth of change involved.

Each individual's goal structure contains different layers of goals, varying from profound to shallow ones. Since the individual's behavior reflects his goals, we can identify the depth of his actions by relating them to specific layers in his goal structure. In this way, we can conceptually distinguish what depths of actions or goals are involved when an individual undergoes change.

Similarly, organizations have different structural depths. Our analysis recognizes four "organizational layers." The shallowest consists of the specific actions taken by the bureau, the second of the decisionmaking rules it uses, the third of the institutional structure it uses to make those rules, and the deepest of its general purposes.

In both individuals and organizations, change can occur at any depth without affecting layers of greater depth, though it will normally affect all shallower layers. Thus, a bureau can change its everyday actions without changing its rules; it can change its rules without shifting its rule-making structure; and it can alter its rule-making structure without adopting any different fundamental purposes. But if it adopts new purposes, all the other layers will be significantly affected. This means that change is largely a matter of degree, ranging from trivial shifts in everyday actions to profound alterations in purpose. Our analysis of bureaus will focus upon major changes in rules, structure, and purposes, rather than minor shifts in any of these elements or in everyday behavior. We will also show how "satisfactory" behavior is related to the maintenance of the existing internal structure of a person or an organization, and how the high cost of changing deeper layers creates personal and organizational inertia.

THE BASIC MODEL

In economic theory, there is a long-standing debate between theorists who believe that decisions are made (and hence change initiated) in a process of utility *maximizing* and those who believe they are made in a process of utility *satisficing* or *disjointed incrementalism*. Our own theory combines elements from all of these approaches.[1]

Our analysis of change is focused upon individual officials rather than upon the bureau as a whole, since individuals are the basic decision-units in our theory. Because they are utility maximizers, they are always willing to adopt a new course of action if it promises to make them better off, even if they are relatively happy at present. However, they cannot search for new courses of action without expending resources. Since the supply of these is limited, they tend to avoid further search whenever the likely rewards seem small *a priori* (that is, the expected marginal payoff seems smaller than the expected marginal cost). This is the case whenever their current behavior seems quite satisfactory in light of their recent experience.

Within this framework, our theory posits the following hypotheses:

1. All men are continuously engaged in scanning their immediate environment to some degree. They constantly receive a certain amount of information from newspaper articles, from radio and TV programs, from conversation with friends, and in the course of their jobs and domestic activities. This amounts to a stream of free information, since it comes to them without specific effort on their part to obtain it.[2] In addition, many officials regularly scan certain data sources (such as *The Wall Street Journal* or *Aviation Week*) without any prior idea of exactly what type of information they are seeking or will find. They do this not because they are

dissatisfied, but because past experience teaches them that new developments are constantly occurring that might affect their present level of satisfaction. This combination of unprogrammed free information streams and habitually programmed scanning provides a minimum degree of constant, "automatic" search. Every official in every bureau undertakes such search regardless of how well satisfied he is with his own current behavior or that of his bureau.

2. Each official develops a level of satisfactory performance for his own behavior or that of other parts of the bureau relevant to him. He may or may not in fact attain this level. However, he is not aware of any alternative behavior pattern that would both yield more utility and could be attained at a cost smaller than the resulting gain in utility. In other words, when he is actually at the satisfactory level, he is maximizing his utility in light of his existing knowledge.

Also, the satisfactory level of performance yields enough utility in relation to his recent experience so that when he attains it, he is not motivated to look for better alternatives. In short, he is not dissatisfied with his performance at this level. In this sense, the satisfactory level is a dynamic concept embodying not only his current, but also his past experiences.

3. Whenever the actual behavior of an official (or of a bureau section relevant to him) yields him less utility than the relevant level of satisfactory performance, he is motivated to undertake more intensive search for new forms of behavior that will provide him with more utility. He will designate the difference in utility he perceives between the actual and the satisfactory level of performance as the *performance gap*. The larger this gap, the greater his motivation to undertake more intensive search. He is already engaging in some search just by being alive; but in this case, dissatisfaction leads him both to intensify his normal search and to direct it specifically at alternatives likely to reduce the causes of his dissatisfaction.

His first step is to consider alternatives involving those variables he can most easily control. If one or more of these alternatives will move him back to the satisfactory level, he ceases his search and adopts the best of these alternatives.[3] If none of the alternatives contained in this initial set is able to return him to the satisfactory level, he enlarges his search and considers other alternatives involving variables beyond his own control.

He continues broadening his search for alternatives in discrete steps, pausing to evaluate each incremental set as he compiles it. This process continues until he either finds an alternative that restores him to the satisfactory level (or puts him onto some even higher level), or the cost of further search exceeds the cost of accepting a level of performance below his satisfactory level.

In searching for alternatives, he starts with those he initially believes will yield him the highest net utility and works downward, evaluating them in relatively homogeneous sets in terms of their likely net utility as he sees it. He considers his own goals in this process as well as those of the organization. Hence he regards any personal benefits to him as plus factors in his utility evaluation, and considers personal costs, large organizational changes, or computational difficulties as minus factors. Therefore, he is more likely to include the following types of alternatives in each set he analyzes than he is their opposites, other things being equal:

—Those that provide ancillary "side benefits" in terms of variables other than the ones whose drop from a satisfactory level caused him to initiate this intensive search.

—Those that are relatively simple and easy to comprehend.

—Those that involve marginal rather than major adjustments in the bureau's operations or structure.

—Those that do not depend upon estimations or consideration of highly uncertain variables, since such variables are difficult to use.

4. If intensive search fails to reveal any ways he can return to the originally satisfactory level, he will eventually lower his conception of the satisfactory level down to the highest net level of utility income he can attain.

5. Whenever his constant search process reveals the possibility that a new course of action might yield more utility than offered by his present satisfactory level of performance, he undertakes intensive search of this new course of action and any close substitutes for it that also promise to yield net gains in utility. Thus chance encounters with possibilities for improving his situation create potential performance gaps without any change in his current utility income. If his intensified search reveals that he can indeed make a net gain in utility by shifting to a new behavior pattern, he will make the shift that yields the largest net gain he is aware of.

6. Once he has adopted the new course of action and his net utility income therefrom has risen, he regards the new higher utility income level as his satisfactory performance level.

7. After he has either moved to a new higher level (which he now regards as the satisfactory level) or discovered he cannot improve upon his prior performance (which therefore remains his satisfactory level), he reduces his search efforts back to their normal "automatic" intensity. They remain at this intensity until he again falls below his satisfactory level, or encounters some specific reason to believe that particular alternatives might improve his position.

The above hypotheses form a theory of dynamic equilibrium involving (1) a tendency for the official to move toward a satisfactory position of equilibrium, (2) a constant stream of new inputs into the situation (both data and environmental obstacles to performance) displacing him from equilibrium and thereby initiating search, and (3) a process by which he continually redefines the locus of his equilibrium position to reflect his recent experience regarding what is really possible.

SEARCH ASYMMETRY AMONG INDIVIDUAL DECISIONMAKERS

The model of decisionmaking described above involves a certain asymmetry of search behavior. When the decisionmaker is in a state of equilibrium at his satisfactory level of performance, he conducts relatively low-intensity "automatic" search. As soon as his performance drops below this level, he initiates relatively high-intensity search even if he does not initially perceive any specific means of getting back up there. In contrast, he initiates high-intensity search when he is already at the satisfactory level only when he encounters specific reasons to believe that he might be able to go even higher.

This behavior appears to imply a "kink" in the decisionmaker's total utility curve at the level he currently regards as satisfactory. Below that level, relatively high rates of marginal utility seem to prevail, since he is willing to bear high marginal costs of intensive search in order to move back up along his utility curve. But once he reaches the satisfactory level, he cuts back his investment in search costs, which implies that marginal utility rates suddenly decline.

Two concepts explain this asymmetrical behavior in a manner consistent with traditional maximizing theory. These concepts are *uncertainty* and *structured behavior*. The utility function that any person perceives and acts upon is really his expected utility function; that is, his perfect certainty utility function discounted for uncertainty. Even if his total utility curve under perfect certainty were continuous and without kinks, his expected utility function would be kinked if there were a sharp discontinuity in his expectations or certainty at some point. The level of satisfaction is usually such a point. It is normally the highest level of utility that he has actually experienced in the recent past. Therefore, he knows what it is like to have that much utility, whereas he can only conjecture what it is like to receive more utility from the particular variables involved. This represents a sharp discontinuity in the concreteness of his knowledge at the highest level of utility he has recently experienced.

There may be another discontinuity at the same point based upon the structure of his behavior. When a person has experienced a certain utility income from some set of variables for a given amount of time, he begins to structure his behavior regarding those variables around that level of utility income. This idea is very similar to Duesenberry's concept of long-run consumption levels, or Friedman's permanent income hypothesis.

Once a person has structured his behavior—either as a producer or a consumer—around a certain utility income derived from a certain pattern of actions, it is initially to his advantage to regard any decline in utility income below this level as a temporary deviation rather than a permanent change. This allows him to avoid the costs of restructuring his larger behavior patterns in response to every change in his utility income.

However, the decline in utility income he has experienced often results from a permanent change in his situation. An example would be a drastic reduction of the appropriations to his bureau, causing across-the-board salary cuts. In such cases, he cannot avoid altering at least some part of his previous behavior structure. Either he must change jobs in order to restore his former income, or he must change his consumption pattern in order to retain his former job. But some changes are more costly than others. In particular, changes that involve the deepest layers in his goal structure are more costly than those involving more superficial layers. For some men, maintaining a certain consumption pattern for their families is more important than maintaining a particular job or career pattern; for others, the opposite is true. In either case, it is worthwhile for decision-makers who know they must change something in their behavior patterns to conduct intensive search to discover what particular change will be least costly.

Thus, whenever anyone experiences a significant decline in utility income, he will immediately intensify his normal search efforts. If he discovers that the decline is caused by a temporary change in his environment, he knows he will soon be restored to his former level of utility income without any change in his behavior. His search efforts will then drop to their previous intensity. If the change causing his lower income is a permanent one, he will continue his intensified search to discover his optimal response to that change. This response involves the least costs of restructuring his behavior. Once he has carried out this restructuring, his search efforts will return to their normal level of "automatic" intensity. He will then be at a new position of equilibrium on a level of utility income he has come to regard as satisfactory, though it may be different from the level he formerly regarded as satisfactory.

This process helps to explain the asymmetry of search behavior described above. If the decisionmaker's utility income from certain variables falls below the satisfactory level, the added costs of intensified search are doubly justified because, (1) they may enable him to go back to a higher level of utility income and (2) they may help him avoid or minimize the costs of restructuring his long-run behavior around a lower level of utility income. However, once his utility income stabilizes at a new equilibrium level, additional search may reveal ways he can raise his utility income, but it will not help him avoid restructuring his behavior.

It is rational for the decisionmaker to intensify his search behavior as soon as his utility falls below the satisfactory level, and yet not maintain equally intensive search behavior once his utility income is returned to that level (or has come to rest at a new equilibrium level which he then regards as satisfactory). The only exception is when he learns of some specific alternative that might cause him to move to a higher level. Then the expected returns from more intensive search rise so as to overcome the expected costs of having to restructure his customary behavior. This precisely describes the behavior patterns embodied in our theory.

The "sunk costs" of established behavior patterns also influence each decisionmaker's reaction to unexpected rises in his utility income. Rather than immediately changing his behavior patterns to suit the new higher level, he will usually wait to see whether the change is likely to last, and if it is large enough to offset the costs of shifting those patterns. In essence, the "sunk costs" embodied in his structure of behavior patterns constitute a "memory" which links his past behavior to his present actions. This link between past and present not only influences his search behavior, but also causes a lag in his adjusting what he regards as the satisfactory level of utility income to the levels he is actually experiencing.[4]

SEARCH ASYMMETRY IN ORGANIZATIONS

The above reasoning can also be applied to organizations. The actions, rules, structure, and purposes of an organization become built around certain customary levels of performance. Deviations from customary events cause repercussions of varying depth and cost, depending upon how large the deviations are and how permanent they are considered to be. It is easier to adjust actions than rules, easier to shift rules than change structures, and easier to alter structures than adopt new purposes.

Organizations, like individuals, are reluctant to accept any change in their environments—whether good or bad—as permanent if such acceptance would require them to make a significant alteration in their customary behavior patterns. It is usually more rational for them to continue these behavior patterns while conducting an intensive search to see whether the old *status quo ante* will return. Hence the costs of readjusting behavior patterns create a certain discontinuity of behavior at the level to which the organization or individual has become accustomed. This characteristic is commonly known as inertia.

If the organization cannot expect a restoration of the *status quo ante* without effort on its part, it will maintain intensified search while seeking to find the most effective response to this change. Other things being equal, it will select the response that involves the least profound change in its structure. Thus, it will prefer responses requiring it to change only its behavior to those requiring alterations in its rules, and it will prefer the latter to those that necessitate shifts in institutional structure. Only in the most drastic situations will it alter its fundamental purposes. Whatever adjustments it makes to the original change, it will eventually arrive at a new equilibrium point (assuming no further exogenous shocks occur). At that point, the organization will reduce its search efforts to their normal degree of intensity—though what constitutes "normal" may be slightly different from what it was originally.

The greater the depth of organizational restructuring required in order to change an official's satisfactory level, the slower he will be to make this change, and vice versa. To put it in economic terms, the greater the "sunk costs" that must be duplicated or replaced by any innovation, the greater the incentive to avoid innovations. For everyday actions search behavior patterns will closely approximate those posited in traditional maximizing theory, and hardly any discontinuity will be perceptible at the currently satisfactory level. But at the other extreme, striking asymmetry of search behavior may prevail when changes in the basic purposes of the organization are involved.

The satisfactory level itself need not be static. It can embody the decisionmaker's expectations of rising or falling utility income.[5] The important fact is that the satisfactory level serves as a link between the individual's (or organization's) past experiences, future expectations, and actual present behavior.

Search Problems in Bureaus

THE BASIC PROCESSES OF DECISION AND ACTION RELATED TO SEARCH

The preceding discussion presented the basic theory of how search and change are related. This section will examine the economics of search in greater detail. This section of the analysis may seem excessively detailed and rigorous, and perhaps even obvious. However, it is a necessary prerequisite to later, more significant sections, describing how search processes influence the substance of bureau behavior.

We assume that the decisionmaker starts in a position of equilibrium with no performance gaps. His steps in generating a new nonprogrammed action are as follows:

1. *Perception.* He obtains new information as a result of his automatic search.

2. *Assimilation.* The information he has received alters his image of the world.

3. *Performance Assessment.* When he compares this altered image of the world with his goals, he discovers a performance gap large enough to exceed his inertia threshold. In short, he believes he ought to do something.

4. *Formulation of Alternatives.* He designs a number of possible actions directed at reducing the performance gap.

5. *Analysis of Alternatives.* He then analyzes each possible action by testing it against his image of the world in order to discover its likely consequences.

6. *Evaluation of Alternatives.* He evaluates these consequences by measuring them against his goals.

7. *Strategy Formation.* If one or more of the actions appears likely to eliminate the performance gap, he incorporates it (or them) into a strategy of action under various conditions.

8. *Action Selection.* He then reexamines his image of the world to discover what conditions exist, and carries out the appropriate action in accordance with his strategy. (He may decide to do nothing, in which case he next acts as in step 13.b below.)

9. *Continuous Data Acquisition.* His information inputs during steps 3 through 8 are as follows:

   a. He receives a stream of information from his automatic search which constantly alters (or confirms) his image of the world.

   b. He may engage in special-project search aimed at discovering additional facts relevant to any of these. This constitutes the intensified search described in the previous chapter.

10. *Action Impact.* His action affects the world in some way, giving rise to new conditions therein.

11. *Action Feedback.* He receives information about these new conditions.

12. *Assimilation of Feedback.* This feedback information alters his image of the world once more.

13. *Performance Reassessment.* He compares this revised image of the world with his goals to determine whether any performance gap still exists.

a. If the gap has been eliminated, he is once more in a position of equilibrium and returns to his automatic level of search intensity.

b. If a performance gap still exists but is below his inertia threshold, he will probably continue some special-project search. However, he will not go through the action cycle again.

c. If a performance gap still exists and it exceeds his inertia threshold, he repeats the action cycle until either condition a or b above prevails.

THE SPECIFIC ECONOMICS OF ACQUIRING INFORMATION

The basic principle of rational action involved in search is that the individual should procure additional information so long as its marginal returns exceed its marginal costs. However, this proposition is an empty tautology unless we specify the returns and costs involved.

The Returns from Acquiring Information in General

The function of information is to help the decisionmaker improve his selection among possible actions. These actions are evaluated in terms of their likely impacts upon the performance gap, which can be stated in terms of changes in his utility. The net impact is the net gain or loss in utility caused by any action.

In many situations, uncertainty makes estimating the net impact of an action extremely difficult. However, the decisionmaker can use two concepts to grapple with such uncertainty. The expected value of an action's net impact constitutes a quantitative estimate of the action's likely effect upon his utility. Its variance measures his confidence in the accuracy of that estimate. Thus, the higher an action's expected net impact, the more promising the action appears. However, if the net impact also has a high variance, the decisionmaker may have low confidence in his estimate.

The individual decisionmaker is likely to use net-impact estimates both in analyzing the consequences of potential actions and in evaluating their impact upon his performance gap. Deciding how much information to procure in analyzing an action is intrinsically related to the potential impact of that action upon utility. Unless the action appears to offer some possibility of increasing utility, there is no point in finding out anything more about it. On the other hand, if it appears to offer such promise, one is justified in trying to obtain enough additional information about its effects to compare its net impact with those of alternative actions.

This means that in practice the person analyzing the consequences of any possible action is also continuously evaluating their net impact upon his utility. Only by doing so can he estimate the likely returns from further analysis, thereby deciding how much effort he should make to procure additional data. This leads to the important conclusion that it is impossible to separate the analysis and evaluation steps in the decision and action process without causing the allocation of either too few or too many resources to analysis.

The Returns from Acquiring Particular Pieces of Information

Up to now, we have shown how information derives general value from its roles in decisionmaking. Yet the choices actually facing the individual do not involve obtaining more information in general, but obtaining particular pieces of data. Clearly, he should acquire any piece with a marginal return exceeding its marginal cost. Its marginal return depends upon the effect it is likely to have upon his estimate of the net impact of an action. It could have any of the following effects:

—It might alter his opinion about what the action's consequences are likely to be without changing his degree of confidence in that (new) opinion. This means it would change only the action's expected net impact.

—It might alter his degree of confidence about the action's likely consequences, without changing that opinion. This means it would change only the variance of the action's net impact. Such a change in confidence alone could have very significant effects upon his behavior. For example, if the information raised his confidence enough, he might stop looking for more data about that action. Conversely, if the information lowered his confidence drastically, he might suspend any decision until he had further data.

—It might change both the expected value and the variance of the action's net impact.

—It might change neither.

The Costs of Acquiring Particular Pieces of Information

Whether the decisionmaker will translate his needs and desires for data into actual procurement depends in part upon the costs of doing so. These costs include the following:

—*Resource costs* of search, such as time, money, and effort.

—*Costs of delay,* such as the costs of carrying any operations that must be suspended while further information is sought and assimilated, and losses of the utility that would be gained from taking action immediately.

HOW ORGANIZATIONAL DECISIONMAKING DIFFERS FROM INDIVIDUAL DECISIONMAKING

Decisionmaking within large organizations differs from that conducted by a single individual for the obvious reason that it involves many persons instead of one. As a result:

—The various steps in the decision and action cycle are carried out by different persons.

—An organization must generate numerous conflict-controlling and consensus-creating mechanisms because its members have widely varying perception apparatuses, memories, images of the world, and goals.

—Organizational decisioningmaking involves the following significant costs of internal communication that have no analogs within an individual:
   a. Losses of utility due to errors of transmission.
   b. Losses of utility (for the ultimate users of the data) due to distortion.
   c. Resources (especially time) absorbed in internal communications.
   d. Losses of utility due to overloading communications channels in the short run.

On the other hand, organizations have such advantages over individuals as much greater capacity to carry out all steps in the decision and action cycle, extensive internal specialization, and simultaneous maintenance of a diversity of viewpoints.

We have made explicit these rather obvious differences between organizations and individuals because we will also use our basic conceptual scheme for individual decisionmaking in our analysis of organizational search.

BASIC PROBLEMS IN ORGANIZATIONAL SEARCH

The basic problems of organizational search include some that are not relevant to individuals. These problems are generated by tensions arising from four factors:

1. *The Unity of Search, Analysis, and Evaluation.* Search, analysis, and evaluation cannot be separated from each other without creating needs for almost continuous communications, irrational allocations of resources, or both.

2. *The Need for Consensus.* Bureaus operate on such a large scale that any significant decision almost invariably affects many bureau members and their activities. These intra-bureau repercussions are unlikely to be fully known to any one member (even the topmost official) unless he specifically seeks the advice of others. In essence, no one bureau member encompasses all the goals relevant to the bureau's whole operation. But evaluation requires measuring possible actions against one's goals (via the performance gap). Hence, evaluation is necessarily fragmentalized in every bureau.

3. *The Economies of Delegation.* Organizations can achieve huge economies of scale in search by assigning some of the steps involved to specialists. But this requires separating some of the steps in the search-analysis-evaluation cycle from others.

4. *Nontechnical Divergence of Goals.* Both delegation and the fragmentalizing of evaluation require giving certain powers of discretion regarding a given decision to many different officials. But officials always use some of whatever discretionary powers they have to benefit themselves and the bureau sections to which they are loyal rather than the bureau as a whole, thus introducing partly inconsistent goals into the theoretically unified search-analysis-evaluation cycle. This point is different from the need for consensus. The latter is required because a bureau is so large that no single member knows what all its relevant goals are. Hence consensus would be necessary even if all members had identical personal goals and ambitions. But nontechnical goal divergence arises from conflicts of interest that cannot be eliminated by knowledge alone.

In the remainder of this paper, we will explore specific aspects of the search processes in bureaus arising from tensions among these four factors.

HOW THE BIASES OF INDIVIDUAL OFFICIALS AFFECT THE SEARCH PROCESS

As each official goes through the decision and action process, he behaves somewhat differently from the way he would if his goals were identical to the formal purposes of the organization. Among his biases relevant to search are the following:

1. His perception apparatus will partially screen out data adverse to his interests, and magnify those favoring his interests.[6] The probability that important data will not be screened out by such biases can be increased by

assigning overlapping search responsibilities to persons with different and even conflicting interests and policy preferences, or assigning search tasks to persons who have no particular policy preferences and whose interests are not connected with the advancement of any bureau section.

2. In formulating alternative actions, each official will tend to give undue precedence to alternatives most favorable to his interests, and to those about which adequate consensus can most easily be established. The process of decisionmaking within a bureau involves significant costs. Some of these costs probably rise more than proportionately with the number of alternatives considered. Hence it is often more rational for a bureau to choose from a set of alternatives it has already assembled than to expand that set, even if such expansion might provide it with additional choices markedly superior to those now facing it.

This implies that the order in which alternative actions are assembled and evaluated may have an extremely important impact on what an organization eventually does. If the first set of alternatives considered contains at least one that closes the performance gap, the bureau may never discover other alternatives that would not only close that gap, but also provide a new higher level of performance.

As a result, any biases among officials that cause certain types of alternatives to be systematically considered early in the game will cause those types of alternatives to be adopted more often than they would be if officials were unbiased. Among such biases are the following:

—Since relatively simple proposals are much easier to discuss and obtain consensus about than complicated ones, officials will tend to consider such proposals first. This implies that over any given period, a bureau will tend to choose policies that are simpler than those it would choose if its members had perfect information about all possible proposals. Part of this simplification is a rational response to the costs of deliberation, but part results from officials' biases.

—Officials will tend to consider those alternatives that benefit their own interests before those adverse to their interests. Thus, a bureau will tend to select alternatives that are unduly favorable to the particular officials who are in charge of proposing alternatives. Incumbents are usually favored by actions that do not radically alter the *status quo*. Staff members are more oriented toward change so long as it does not injure their own interests or those of their line superiors. Hence bureaus in which incumbent office holders design proposals will tend to make unduly conservative choices. Those in which staff members design proposals will not exhibit this bias unless the proposals concern their behavior or that of their line superiors.

—The evaluation process in bureaus is fragmentalized; so officials proposing policies often need to obtain support from a number of others only marginally concerned. These officials usually bargain for a *quid pro quo* in return for their support. A common *quid pro quo* is including something in the alternatives that benefits them, even though it does not directly affect the performance gap concerned. Another is omitting from these alternatives anything damaging to their interests, even though it would benefit the bureau as a whole. The existence of such "territorial bargaining" has the following implications:

(1) A bureau will choose actions that unduly favor continuance of the existing allocation of resources and power among its subsections.

(2) Officials shaping alternatives will try to exclude marginal effects from their proposals so as to reduce the amount of consensus they need to achieve.[7] This will unduly narrow the impact of actions taken by the bureau. We refer to such behavior as the *shrinking violet syndrome*.

(3) The alternatives formulated will be irrationally affected by the particular organization of the bureau.

—If the initial set of alternatives assembled by an official has been rejected, he can either abandon the project, search for wholly new alternatives, or try to reformulate the rejected ones. If the latter include proposals strongly supported by powerful officials, he will tend to devote too much effort to reformulating those proposals.

—Officials will tend to propose alternatives involving as little uncertainly as possible in order to avoid complicated and conflict-engendering negotiations. Thus, over any given period, a bureau will tend to adopt actions that do not take sufficient account of future uncertainties.

The above analysis indicates that the need to establish consensus before making decisions has a tremendous influence upon the processes of search within a bureau. The more officials involved in a decision, and the greater the diversity of their views and interests, the more factors must be taken into account, the more alternatives must be explored, and the harder it is to get a consensus on any alternative.

This creates a dilemma for bureaus regarding search. On one hand, those who formulate alternatives often try to restrict the choices they consider to those that affect as few other officials as possible. This renders decisionmaking both faster and easier. But bureaus will systematically tend to consider narrower alternatives than they would if officials were unbiased.

On the other hand, if officials extend their range of search to encompass alternatives affecting a great many others, they will generate both extremely high costs of reaching a decision and a strong probability that the decision will support the *status quo* to an excessive degree. Thus it appears extraordinarily difficult to create incentives for the officials involved so that (a) they will extend their search for alternatives far enough to encompass all significant interdependencies, (b) they will make decisions relatively quickly and easily, and (c) those decisions will incorporate really significant changes in the *status quo* when warranted.

This situation results partly from a correct perception of the costs of change. If each part of a bureau merely had to consider changing its behavior every time an official anywhere else was making a decision that might affect it, the bureau would lose a great deal of its operating efficiency. Furthermore, it would become almost chaotic if it actually made changes in a high percentage of such cases. Hence resistance to suggestions of change is partly a rational behavior pattern for officials. But the biases of officials make this resistance excessive in terms of efficiently achieving the bureau's social functions.

There may be a partial escape from this dilemma for more significant decisions if the bureau's top officials can create some outside agency that will be free from direct operational responsibilities within the bureau, but quite familiar with its goals, rules, behavior, and routines. Such an agency can be used as an aid in searching for alternative courses of action, and for information useful in analyzing and evaluating alternatives. Ideally, its members should be familiar enough with the bureau to understand the interdependencies therein, but detached enough to propose changes involving major departures from the *status quo*. Such detachment normally results only when men have no direct operational responsibilities. The payoffs from such an arrangement can be very large.

THE IMPACT OF TIME PRESSURE UPON SEARCH

Search is greatly affected by the time pressure associated with a given decision. The cost of delay—that is, procuring additional information—rises sharply with pressure to act quickly. Under such pressure, a rational decisionmaker will decide on the basis of less knowledge than he would if time pressure were lower. Conversely, when there is little pressure to decide quickly, he can acquire a great deal of information before reaching any conclusions. Thus there is an inverse relationship between the extension of search and the time pressure on the decision. Whenever time pressure is high, the following will occur:

—A minimal number of alternatives will be considered. The more complex the decision, the smaller the number.

—Whenever only a few alternatives are considered, all the biases influencing the order in which possible alternatives are formulated become accentuated. Moreover, officials will tend to give primary consideration to "ready made" alternatives that have been thought out in advance. Since zealots will offer the pet policies they have been promoting for a long time, their ideas will have a much greater chance if being implemented than usual.

—The decisionmakers involved will try to restrict the number of persons participating in the decision and the diversity of views among them. Hence secrecy may be used simply to prevent knowledge of the decision from reaching persons who might want to be included in the deliberations if they knew the decision was being made. Furthermore, secrecy may enable more complex decisions to be made. If a great many people must be consulted in making a decision, it becomes difficult to communicate to each person the issues involved, the possible alternatives, and the responses and views of other consultants. But if secrecy restricts the number of persons consulted, those persons can consider much more complicated possibilities.

Clearly, the degree of time pressure has critical impacts upon decisionmaking. High time pressures usually spring from either crises or deadlines. The former are normally of exogenous origin, but deadlines are usually deliberate, hence they can be manipulated to exploit the effects of time pressure. For example, if a high-ranking official wants to restrict the number of people his subordinates consult on a given decision, he can place a very short deadline on it. Conversely, if he wants wide-ranging deliberations, he can give it a long time horizon.

"Gresham's Law of Planning" may nullify this strategy if subordinates are assigned both short deadline and long deadline tasks.[8] In order to complete their short deadline tasks, they may keep on postponing work on longer-run problems until once-distant deadlines loom in the near future. Therefore, extending search across a really wide and deep spectrum of possibilities normally requires assignment of long deadline tasks to officials or organizations separate from those responsible for short deadline tasks.

SEARCH EXTENSION AND ORGANIZATIONAL POLICIES

The foregoing analysis suggests a number of policies organizations can use to influence the degree of search extension in making a decision. These policies are set forth briefly in Table 1.

Table 1

Organizational Policies That Extend or Contract Search

Policies That Tend To Extend Degree of Search and Increase Diversity of Alternatives Considered	Policies That Tend To Contract Degree of Search and Narrow Diversity of Alternatives Considered
Allow a long time before conclusions must be reached	Enforce a very short deadline
Bring many people into decision making	Restrict decisionmaking to a small number
Insure that those involved have a wide variety of views and interests—even conflicting	Insure that those involved have similar views and interests
Reduce number of persons to whom final decision must be justified or intelligibly communicated	Increase number of persons to whom final decision must be justified or intelligibly communicated
Increase proportion of analytically skillful or highly trained persons participating, or to whom it must be justified or communicated	Decrease proportion of analytically skillful or highly trained persons participating, or to whom it must be justified or communicated
Isolate those making decision from pressures of responsibility for other decisions, especially short deadline ones	Assign the decision to those immersed in making other decisions, especially short deadline ones
Reduce proportion of extremely busy persons to whom decision must be intelligibly communicated	Increase proportion of extremely busy persons to whom decision must be intelligibly communicated

Our analysis also implies that the optimal degree of search extension depends both upon the nature of the problem and the time pressure for solving it. Other things being equal, the bigger the problem, the more likely that extension of search will be valuable, since potential savings from finding better alternatives are much greater.[9]

THE EFFECTS OF SEPARATING SEARCH, ANALYSIS, AND EVALUATION

When Separation Is Rational

Because of the inherent unity of search, analysis, and evaluation, there is strong pressure to keep the specialists carrying out these steps for any particular decision relatively close together in "organizational space." In many cases, each department has its own specialists in search and analysis assisting the people actually making decisions. Then the decisionmakers can advise the searchers about how much and what kinds of data they need. Moreover, there can be frequent communications between the producers and consumers of these data during the decisionmaking process. Even more important, the consumers of information must pay the costs of search. Hence such an arrangement minimizes misallocations of resources to search.

However, in certain situations, the economies of scale in search become enormous. The nearly complete separation of the producers and consumers of data is almost mandatory. Such economies occur when three conditions exist simultaneously.

First, the sources of relevant information are remote from the decisionmakers. By remote we mean relatively inaccessible in terms of space, technically specialized knowledge, cultural unfamiliarity, secrecy, or extreme fragmentalization in diverse locations. Second, the data required by persons working on one type of decision are also useful for persons working on other types. Third, the means of access to remote information can be used to procure data useful for different kinds of decisions.

The remoteness of data sources means that a large, indivisible capital investment of some type must be created in order to gain access to them. This investment can be a network of scattered foreign observers; the education of certain technical specialists; creation of linguistic, sociological, or political expertise; or a group of clandestine agents. The need for this large initial investment constitutes a forbidding "entry fee" which forces small-scale users to eschew such data altogether, or else to band together and establish joint search facilities.

Once the high initial cost of gaining access has been paid, a certain capacity is generated that exceeds the needs of any one user. In the case of spatial and cultural remoteness, access facilities can be used to gather a wide variety of specific data. An example is the network of State Department embassies abroad. Different users who have diverse data needs can be served by—and help pay for—these facilities. Other access facilities may produce a large quantity of a certain kind of information. This quantity may exceed the needs of any single consumer, but be useful to enough different customers to pay its total costs. An example is the global radio and press surveillance service of the Central Intelligence Agency.

When these conditions prevail, the development and operation of a jointly used search facility is the only economical way to provide for the many varied consumers involved. This facility can be operated by any one of the users alone, or it can be established as a separate agency. In our analysis, we will assume it is an autonomous search bureau.

The Impact of Separation upon Policy Formation

What types of problems does an agency face in deciding (a) what to search for with its existing facilities, (b) how many resources to expend searching for each item or type of item, and (c) what investments to make in creating additional access facilities?

Some of its major problems occur because it cannot judge the relative importance of acquiring any given piece of information. It is not the ultimate consumer of such information, nor can it charge the ultimate consumers money prices. No profit-making firm is the ultimate consumer of its products either, but such a firm can rationally allocate resources because it charges its consumers money for whatever it gives them. We will assume that the central search agency cannot use this mechanism. Instead, it asks the bureaus it serves to describe the relative urgency of their data needs.

Each bureau has no way of estimating how urgent its requests are in comparison with those of other bureaus, and the natural advocacy of each bureau's officials leads them to exaggerate the importance of their own needs. Hence the central agency is forced to make its own judgments about the relative importance of the needs of different bureaus. This it cannot do accurately unless its own personnel start becoming involved in the policy decisionmaking of its bureau clients. Since many officials within the search agency seek to increase their own power and that of their agency, such involvement is quite likely.

In this involvement, members of the central search agency may exhibit the following viewpoints regarding policy making in other bureaus.

1. In many matters they may act like statesmen. There is no *a priori* reason why the central search agency should have any particular substantive policy biases. Furthermore, the agency's members are encouraged to develop a broad viewpoint in order to choose among competing demands for information made by the various bureaus they serve.

True, insofar as this agency is attached to a particular political entity (such as the chief executive), it will be influenced by the political perspective of that entity. Even so, the search agency is partly prevented from becoming an advocate of any particular policy by its need to serve many different advocates of a wide variety of conflicting policies.

2. Members of the central search agency will inevitably seek to augment their own and the agency's power, income, and prestige. As a result:

—The agency will attempt to establish a monopoly over as many remote data sources as possible, partly by advocating "eliminating unnecessary duplication" of search facilities.

—It will exaggerate the need for secrecy in its operations to conceal discovery of how efficiently it operates.

—Its reporting will exaggerate those types of information likely to contribute to its significance. This significance derives from its usefulness to other bureaus, which will consider information most useful that both justifies existing policies and indicates enough change and instability to make larger appropriations desirable. The existence of external threats often performs the latter function. On the other hand, the governing party wishes to present a public image of competence and control of the situation. Hence the central search agency will tend to supply excessively alarming data to individual bureaus and excessively soothing data to the public in general.

—It will exaggerate the importance of expensive forms of search and analysis, and underplay that of inexpensive ones.

—It will overemphasize forms of search involving a great deal of analysis and evaluation by its own specialists.

3. Members of the central search agency may act as advocates for bureaus within the search agency. This will probably occur only if promotion of these liaison officials is controlled by the agencies in which they are working.

The Impact of Separation upon Resource Allocation

The bureau "customers" of the central search agency will have an ambivalent attitude toward it. They will ask it to furnish all information of any positive value, regardless of cost, since they do not have to pay for it. This conclusion has the following implications. First, no matter how large a data gathering and handling capacity the central search agency possesses, its facilities will always be overloaded. This results from the Law of Free Goods: *Requests for free services always rise to meet the capacity of the producing agency.*

Second, officials of the central search agency will develop nonpecuniary prices for their services. These are devices for imposing costs upon members of other bureaus who request information. They will be designed both to discourage requests and to provide rewards to central search agency members. Such "quasi-prices" will include demands for reciprocal favors, long delays, and frustrating barriers of red tape. This illustrates the Law of Non-Money Pricing: *Organizations that cannot charge money for their services must develop non-monetary costs to impose on their clients as a means of rationing their outputs.* Hence much of the irritating behavior of bureaucrats often represents necessary means of rationing their limited resources so they will be available to those truly anxious to use them.

Third, such rationing systems may result in irrational allocations from the viewpoint of society in general. Information seekers persistent enough to penetrate "quasi-price" barriers may not have needs that would be considered most urgent if all concerned had perfect information.

The other part of each information-using bureau's ambivalent attitude is its desire to "capture" some of the search agency's activities and incorporate them into its own program. This would bring its decisionmakers closer to their data sources as well as add to its total resources.

"SPREADING THE WORD" AND THE NOISE PROBLEM[10]

The Fragmentalized Perception of Large Organizations

Since an organization has no personality, only individual members can perceive or search. Therefore, organizational perception and search are inherently fragmentalized. Information is first perceived by one or several members, who must then pass it on to others.

Thanks to the ubiquity and speed of modern communications some information is perceived almost simultaneously by all members of even very large organizations. For example, over 90 percent of the entire population in the United States knew of President Kennedy's assassination within four hours of his death.[11] Similarly, if members of a bureau all read the same newspapers or watch the same TV programs, they may learn about a wide range of events almost simultaneously. Nevertheless, such high-exposure sources transmit only a small part of the information important to any bureau. A large proportion of the data it needs is initially perceived by only one or a few low-level members, who then transmit it upwards through channels.

Yet it is not clear just when the organization has perceived any particular item of information, for a statistical majority does not by any means comprise the substantive decisionmakers. We can say that the organization has been informed when the given information has become known to all those members who need to know it, so that the organization can carry out the appropriate response.

The Problem of Assessing the Significance of Data

There is a great difference between knowing a fact and grasping its true significance. The radar supervisor in Hawaii whose subordinate picked up returns from unidentified aircraft on the morning of December 7, 1941 knew that fact, but he did not grasp its significance. The number of facts gleaned every day by any large organization is immense. In theory, the screening process transmits only the most significant fact to the men at the top, and places them in their proper context along the way. But considerable distortion occurs in this process. Each part of the organization tends to exaggerate the importance of some events and to minimize that of others. This naturally produces a healthy skepticism among officials at the top of the hierarchy.

An inescapable result of this situation is a rational insensitivity to signals of alarm at high levels. This may have disastrous consequences when those signals are accurate. It is the responsibility of each low-level official to report on events he believes could be dangerous. However, the real danger of the supposed threat is not always clear, and his messages must therefore contain suppositions of his own making.

In organizations always surrounded by potentially threatening situations (such as the Department of Defense, the State Department, and the Central Intelligence Agency), officials at each level continually receive signals of alarm from their subordinates. But they are virtually compelled to adopt a wait and see attitude toward these outcries for three reasons. First, they do not have enough resources to respond to all alleged threats simultaneously. Second, experience has taught them that most potential threats fail to materialize. Third, by the time a potential threat does develop significantly, either the threat itself or the organizations's understanding of it has changed greatly. Hence it becomes clear that what initially appeared to be the proper response would really have been ineffective. Therefore, initial signals concerning potential threats usually focus the attention of intermediate-level officials on a given problem area, but do not move them to transmit the alarm upward.

Only if further events begin to confirm the dire predictions of "alarmists" do their superiors become alarmed too, and send distress signals upward. But higher-level officials also have a wait and see attitude for the same reasons, and it takes even further deterioration of the situation to convince them to transmit the alarm still higher. Therefore, a given situation may have to become very threatening indeed before its significance is grasped at the top levels of the organization.

This is one of the reasons why top-level officials tend to become involved in only the most difficult and ominous situations faced by the organization. Easy problems are solved by lower-level officials, and difficult situations may deteriorate badly by the time they come to the attention of the top level.

As Roberta Wohlstetter argued in her study of the Pearl Harbor attack, fragmentalization of perception inevitably produces an enormous amount of "noise" in the organization's communications networks.[12] The officials at the bottom must be instructed to report all potentially dangerous situations immediately so the organization can have as much advance warning as possible. Their preoccupation with their specialties and their desire to insure against the worst possible outcomes, plus other biases, all cause them to transmit signals with a degree of urgency that in most cases proves exaggerated after the fact. These overly urgent signals make it extremely difficult to tell in advance which alarms will prove warranted and which will not.

There are no easy solutions to this problem. With so many "Chicken Littles" running around claiming the sky is about to fall, the men at the top normally cannot do much until "Henney Penney" and "Foxy Loxy" have also started screaming for help, or there is a convergence of alarm signals from a number of unrelated sources within the organization. Even the use of high-speed, automatic data networks cannot eliminate it. The basic difficulty is not in procuring information, but in assessing its significance in terms of future events—from which no human being can eliminate all uncertainty.

NOTES

[1] The leading proponents of "satisficing" theory are Herbert Simon and James March. See H. A. Simon, "A Behavioral Model of Rational Choice," *Quarterly Journal of Economics,* 69 (1955), 129–38; and J. G. March and H. A. Simon, *Organizations* (New York: Wiley, 1958), pp. 47–52, 173–77. The term "disjointed

incrementalism" is from Charles E. Lindblom and David Braybrooke, *A Strategy of Decision* (New York: The Free Press of Glencoe, 1963). The latter work contains numerous references to earlier theorists who set forth the traditional "maximizing" approach.

[2] The concept of a stream of "free information" providing at least minimal data to everyone was advanced in A. Downs, *An Economic Theory of Democracy* (New York: Harper & Row, 1957), pp. 221–25.

[3] This sequence of search was suggested by March and Simon, *op. cit.*, p. 179.

[4] For further discussion of the economics of search, see George J. Stigler, "The Economics of Information," *Journal of Political Economy*, LXIX, 3 (June, 1961), 213–25; and Armen A. Alchian and William R. Allen, *University Economics* (Belmont, California: Wadsworth, 1964), pp. 548–55.

[5] March and Simon hypothesize that aspiration levels tend to rise gradually over time. This is consistent with our theory, although we are not incorporating it as one of our own postulates. See March and Simon, *op. cit.*, p. 183.

[6] Leon Festinger, *A Theory of Cognitive Dissonance* (Evanston, Illinois: Row, Peterson, 1957).

[7] This is related to the desire of decisionmakers forming a coalition to restrict membership in the coalition to the smallest number required to "win" in a given contest. Such restriction is a central theme in William H. Riker's book, *The Theory of Political Coalitions* (New Haven: Yale University Press, 1962). However, Riker confined his analysis to zero-sum-game situations; whereas the restrictions we are talking about also apply to non-zero-game situations.

[8] This "law" is set forth in March and Simon, *op. cit.*

[9] This principle is opposite to the situation described by C. Northcote Parkinson in his "Law of Triviality." It states that "The time spent on any item of the agenda will be in inverse proportion to the sum involved." However, the behavior depicted by Parkinson's law may actually embody rational short-run responses to the fact that items involving large sums are complicated and research into complexity is expensive, whereas small items are usually simple and often involve data already known to the persons concerned. See C. Northcote Parkinson, *Parkinson's Law and Other Studies in Administration*, pp. 24–32.

[10] Most of the ideas in this section have been developed by William Jones, to whom I am greatly indebted.

[11] Paul B. Sheatsley and Jacob J. Feldman, "The Assassination of President Kennedy: A Preliminary Report on Public Reaction and Behavior," *Public Opinion Quarterly*, 28, 2 (Summer 1964).

[12] Roberta Wohlstetter, *Pearl Harbor: Warning and Decision* (Palo Alto: Stanford University Press, 1962).

CHAPTER 18

The Impact of Lobbying on Governmental Decisions

Lester Milbrath

Perhaps the most difficult question about lobbying is that of the extent of its influence or impact on governmental decisions. No one has a definitive answer to that question. Yet an understanding of the influence of lobbying is essential to a full perspective on the topic. Still quite a number of observable facts contribute some enlightenment. In this chapter, all findings relevant to the impact of lobbying will be reviewed to provide as broad a perspective as possible.

Inquiring about the influence of lobbying is not the same as inquiring about the influence of pressure groups. Admittedly, the factors are highly related, but they are not identical. Some lobbying is carried out on behalf of individuals or corporations as well as groups. On the other hand, some of the influence of pressure groups is not exerted through lobbying (using a special envoy at the seat of government) or lobbyists. It will not be necessary to maintain a clear distinction between lobbying and pressure groups, but the reader should be aware that the primary purpose of this chapter is to evaluate the influence of lobbying, not that of pressure groups.

SOME CHARACTERISTICS OF INFLUENCE

Some characteristics of influence are relevant to the query of this essay. First, influence is not an absolute quantity of which an individual or an institution has a certain measurable amount. One can speak about influence in comparative terms (e.g., A has more influence than B) but even that can be done only with reference to a given issue or decision (B may have more influence than A on another decision). Influence, then, varies with the decisional setting, the roles of the actors, the diligence with which goals are pursued, and the tactics employed, as well as with the assets available to each contestant.

Reprinted from Lester Milbrath, *The Washington Lobbyists* (Chicago: Rand McNally, 1963), Chap. 17, pp. 328–58, by permission of the publisher and the author. Footnotes have been renumbered.

Second, influence does not automatically make itself felt; it must be exerted. Moreover, exertion entails some costs (time, money, attention, etc.) on the part of the influencer. The costs of exerting influence must be weighed relative to the value of the anticipated reward. Banfield[1] thinks of influence as analogous to money; it is a scarce resource which can be saved, invested, and spent. Some political actors have more influence assets than others, but assets must be carefully managed to avoid influence bankruptcy. It is "rational" for political actors to try to maximize their influence just as it is "rational" for economic actors to maximize their monetary assets or gains.

Third, political influence is necessarily focused on the decisional processes of authoritative decision-makers (government officials). Influence can be achieved only by affecting the perceptions of officials (short of replacing one official by another), and it must be conveyed via some kind of communication.

The perceptions of the policy process held by the official decision-makers and the values they try to achieve are of central importance. The problems involved in measuring the perceptions and values of officials, even assuming they would remain constant enough to be measured, are so great that one can make only very general statements: (1) The basic goal of officials is to maintain and enhance their position; achieving a "good record" is usually essential to that. (2) Assuming position can be maintained, officials tend to decide policy questions in accordance with their political philosophy. (3) Motivations of friendship, having a good time, making money, and so forth will generally be of lesser importance than the first two.

One could push to a more abstract analysis of influence by dealing with such questions as free will versus determinism, but that would take us far afield. In the other direction, one could press for a more specific level of analysis, but that would require dealing with many specific issues and actors and would not readily lead to a general understanding of the process.

Because influence takes place only in the decisional process of human beings, it is extremely difficult to measure. Most humans could not report accurately, even if they sincerely desired to, the proportionate weight they assign to various influences as they make a decision. Influence is generally measured by some less direct method. March[2] says three general ways to measure influence have been widely used: measuring attributed influence, measuring changes in opinions, and measuring interaction between actors. This study contains only measures of attributed influence and some measures of interaction between lobbyists and officials.

In this discussion of the influence of lobbying, three kinds of evidence relevant to the point will be presented. First is an analysis and pinpointing of where and how influence can be exerted; some supposed methods of influence fall by the wayside because they are too difficult or too costly to employ. For example, it is virtually impossible to steal or buy governmental decisions of any consequence in Washington. In seeking points at which influence may be exerted, it is relevant to examine the factors that officials consider as they make their decisions. Second is an analysis of lobbyists' evaluations of their personal success and the success of their organization and their selections of the most effective lobby organization in Washington; these are taken as partial evidence of attributed influence. Third, the influence of lobbying is compared to other forces also attempting to influence policy. Some lobbying cancels out other lobbying because groups oppose one another; some lobbying is simply overwhelmed by the power of non-lobbying forces.

FACTORS CONSIDERED BY OFFICIALS
WHEN MAKING DECISIONS

No executive branch officials were interviewed for this study. The pre-eminent motivation to maintain or enhance one's position is probably characteristic of both elected and appointed officials. However, for elected officials, it is oriented toward pleasing constituents; whereas for appointed officials, it probably is oriented toward following the directions of and attempting to please elected officials. This study has no data relevant to the latter generalization.

Congressional respondents were asked the following question:

Whenever a person must decide how he will vote on an issue or a bill, he must take several factors into account, such as: the wishes of his constituents, the views of interest groups, the recommendations of his colleagues and friends, and his personal feelings. Which of these kinds of factors are uppermost in your mind as you arrive at your decisions?

Members gave complicated and varied answers reflecting different backgrounds and different situations. Before discussing each factor more fully, some quotations from members will point up the complexity of the inter-relationships:

That is the sixty-four-dollar question to ask a member of Congress. I think it varies. If it is a question which affects the national security, why I invariably vote the way the best information for me indicates I should vote regardless of the constituents.

I take them all into account, but I almost always vote the way I personally decide. I don't make this decision naïvely, by the way. My own view is that it is good politics to take a personal position, and that is the way representative government should function. However, it is not as simple and clear-cut as that. Many times you may see an issue very clearly at the beginning of a session, and you know how you are going to stand on that issue, but by the time you get to the end of the session, it may become confused because there are so many compromises and changes. You wonder if the problem is being evaded and how you should really stand on it. . . . I would say by and large I have a view of my own before I am approached by an interest group. The lobbyist may bring me the first information on a "cat and dog bill"; those are bills without much consequence for the public. I don't remember a time when a position I had was changed by a contact. I do recall making at least one recognizable mistake each year I have been in Congress. The only one that ever upset me was one time when I voted on both sides of an issue; I voted for the bill and then voted to sustain the President's veto. I tried to explain it to the people in the next campaign and discovered it had no effect on my election; since then I haven't been too worried about making a mistake once in a while.

You haven't listed the most important one—that is, the merits of the legislation. There is an interaction in the mind of the legislator which considers all those factors. The attitude of every member is influenced by his over-all background and the nature of his constituency. Members are either born economizers or born spenders, and this is influenced by the nature of his constituency. Most members are more or less predisposed toward an issue before they get to it. We take a pretty common sense approach to the views of interest groups: Are they selfish or unselfish? How does opinion run in one's district? Is there undue advocacy or undue advantage? How the views are presented is a lesser factor but still a factor.

Your first claim is to your district or you won't be here next time. Second comes the desires of the President; I am his leader in the House, and I wouldn't desert the President or the aims of the administration unless there were a mighty weighty reason. I am a member of the team, and this is uppermost in my mind on most questions. I don't take the views of interest groups too seriously. Actually, I don't get too much pressure; I have a very good district in that respect. Maybe it is because I have been here thirty years; they know what to expect. Either they have confidence that I will do the right thing, or they figure it is hopeless—either way I don't get a lot of letters.

The number one factor is that you make sure it doesn't adversely affect the people you represent. If it doesn't hurt your people or you feel it might be good for them, you also try to weigh the public or the national interest and try to decide what the legislation will do over a long pull. If you decide it is a good bill and it is lasting, why this is a very persuasive factor in one's decision. What your colleagues think about an issue or a bill doesn't enter into your decision. All of these people have their own problems, and just because one guy is in favor of a bill doesn't mean you should be. He may have different problems with his constituency. What shall it profiteth a man if he vote to save the country and lose his own seat? . . . I do discuss certain problems with other members; these are men I have come to know and trust over the years.

It can be seen from the quotations that the wishes of a member's constituents are an omnipresent factor, and, in a broad sense, they are decisive. The desires of constituents might be conceived of as boundaries beyond which a member dare not step without suffering dire consequences. These boundaries might be very wide on certain questions and very narrow on others. If a constituency is vitally interested in a question—for example that of segregation (for a southern district)—the boundaries are very tight, and the representative can take only one action if he hopes to be re-elected. The folkways of the Congress recognize these restrictions, and a member who breaks with the leadership to please his constituency on such a tight matter will be forgiven. If a constituency is not so vitally interested, the boundaries are broader, and on some questions there are no boundaries at all. Lobbying has greater opportunities for influence when the constituency is not very interested and the decision-maker has greater decision latitude. If the constituents are interested and aware, their desires are undoubtedly the most important factor. A congressman put it this way:

Well, of course the views of the constituents are always uppermost in the politician's mind. We jokingly make a distinction between a politician and a statesman, but we are all politicians, too. As statesmen, we are delegated to represent not only the views of our constituents but also their best interests. If we could count on the people being properly informed, well then, their views would be all that is necessary, but unfortunately that cannot always be counted on. When you come up here they expect you to study and advise them, and I try to do so. I lead them a little bit, but in the end, their views tend to be uppermost.

A clerk for a congressional committee said:

If I had to select one as the most important day-in-and-day-out, I would say it is the appraisal of the member of what his constituents think. He may not know what his constituents think; he has no really good measure; but it is what he thinks they think that is important. Even if he believes his constituency is not too interested in a bill, he may try to parlay his vote on that bill into an advantage for him in his constituency on some other kind of issue. Ninety-nine per cent of the money spent on lobbying falls short because it ignores that fact. . . . To the extent lobbying can influence public opinion, it has some impact because voter reaction is the most important thing in Congress.

Most lobbyists also recognize the predominating influence of voter desires:

Most of what happens in the legislative area is at least 80 per cent determined on the day of election; in addition, much of the legislative activity throughout a session of Congress is actually a setting of the stage for the next election. It is impossible for a lobbyist "to make a silk purse out of a sow's ear." . . . You do not change a member of Congress by buying him or browbeating him or otherwise attempting to change him.

The smart lobbyist tries to demonstrate to a member that following a particular course of action will help him in his constituency. The member usually listens attentively to such information, but he also learns that he must view claims of constituency support with some skepticism. Reliable information about constituent desires is difficult to obtain. The leaders of large membership organizations generally claim that they speak for all their members, but this is a claim they can hardly substantiate.

You can't be a public official without having considerable knowledge in your own right, and you learn to discount what these groups say. I come from a farm district, and it makes a difference if the Farm Bureau is for or against a piece of legislation. But I have learned that the top people in these organizations often have views that are different from their members down below who are my constituents; therefore, I discount what they say a little.

Following constituent desires too closely can be harmful in certain cases. Constituents generally do not and cannot follow the development of information and arguments on an issue. The complexion of the issue may change, and the available alternatives may shift to such an extent that constituent desires provide little or no guidance. Many members also take the traditional Burkean perspective that constituents really elect a man's judgment and that it is proper to vote according to their own judgment even if it goes against the desires of the constituents. Members report that they feel compelled on occasion to vote against their constituents, especially if they believe it is for the good of the country:

It so happens that practically all of my votes are the way that the prevailing opinion is in my district. This is probably because my own philosophy of government is the same as that of the people in my district. However, there are times when we differ, and in such cases I vote the way my best judgment indicates. In the long run, this is in the interests of the people, and they do have an opportunity to express approval or disapproval at the next election. The Lend-Lease and defense acts early in World War II were opposed by 75 per cent of the people in my district; yet I voted for every one of them and in so doing I was performing my representative function.

There are two types of issues. When it doesn't involve a profound decision or doesn't strongly affect the government or there will be no great disparity in cost, I give the weight to what the people feel strongly about. There are other kinds of decisions that are weighty and will affect the security or solvency of the country. On those kind your own convictions are dominant. The people are very understanding even if you go against their wishes. If you frankly tell them that it wasn't wise for the country, they are not going to turn against you. You can try to educate them, but generally you can't make them change their mind. They may still be against you, but they will realize there are two sides to the question, and they will not turn against you.

If boundaries set by the constituents on an issue have left some decision latitude to the member, the next most important factor is likely to be his personal convictions about the issue. Most members have a long-established political philosophy which guides their decisions. Through their political philosophy they "know" what is good and bad for the country and the people. Furthermore, a man who has served in public office for some time has had to take a stand on most issues in the past. A prior stand tends to freeze his current position. A change from a past position can easily be interpreted as a tacit admission that the prior position was incorrect or possibly that undue influence was used.

On broader legislation which affects the lives and future of the people, I vote according to my philosophy of government. Some people in government stress the money values and some stress the human values. Without disregarding money values, my emphasis is on the human values.

When lobbyists work on broad national policy, their effect is very minor. Lobbyists are effective when they are urging what you are for and not effective when they are urging what you are not for. I have watched people come and go on the Hill here for fourteen years, and I have seldom seen a change in a fellow's basic philosophy even though he has been subject to all sorts of pressures.

Everyone has a political philosophy and is seldom talked out of it. If they have been re-elected, they feel it has paid off in getting them re-elected. Lobbying might have some effect on insignificant facets of legislation, but it doesn't have much effect on the philosophy of a senator. The longer a senator has been here, the more he is convinced the people back home like his philosophy and the less susceptible he is to lobbying. . . . You can pretty well judge in advance how a senator will vote on something because he has been voting that way for years. You really can't get them out of their rut, and the pressure groups tend to freeze them this way; they feel they must hold these people within the traces. If a senator kicks over the traces, the pressure groups generate indignation all over the country.

It is important to keep in mind that simple "yeas" or "nays" are not the only alternatives open to a member when an issue is up for decision. A wide range of actions is possible—from campaigning on the issue, to mere voting, to abstaining. Matthews[3] diagrammed nine alternative positions that a member might take on an issue. Most lobbying effort, then, is aimed not at conversion but at activating the favorable member or at least at ensuring that he remains committed and votes "correctly."

Every public official is interested in making a "good record." A "good record" is instrumental in maintaining and enhancing his position. It brings increased influence, which is important to all public officials. Further, when an official pursues policies that fulfill his political philosophy, he thinks that he is making a "good record"; this is important in satisfying his ego needs (his conception of himself). But no public official can make a "good record" by himself. He must have the cooperation of other officials. To obtain this cooperation, he must be prepared to bargain and must learn to play as a "member of the team." Former Speaker Rayburn is reputed to have said, "The way to get along is to go along."

The organization of a majority to get a bill passed requires some minimum amount of discipline and compromise. Once the "team" position on a given piece of legislation has emerged, the pressures for the members of the team to "go along" become rather intense. Failure to "go along" lowers one's standing within the team and lessens one's chances for advancement in the system; it may even result in negative sanctions such as withdrawal of campaign support or loss of preferred committee assignments, although Congress is generally reluctant to apply such severe sanctions. The major penalty for not playing as a member of the team is loss of reputation or standing, which provide influence or power. Certain members can be characterized as very powerful; their power generally derives from the respect they have gained from their fellow members as they have played by the rules on the team over the years. A non-team player never gains that respect and influence.

When a member's political party holds the Presidency, his team grows to include the presidential office and even the executive departments. His leader becomes the President, and much of the policy initiative flows from that quarter. Presidential and departmental recommendations become important influences on his voting decisions. These recommendations are backed by superior information and research as well as all of the influences associated with the team effort.

Officials cannot avoid making decisions though they generally must make them on the basis of somewhat imperfect information. To fill the gap, they usually welcome or actively seek out information. The need for facts provides lobbyists with their best opportunity to influence decisions. But even here, lobbyists must compete with many other sources of information and advice. Information and recommendations of colleagues are very important in this process. Officials are inclined to accept information and advice from a colleague if they respect his integrity and wisdom and believe that he has superior knowledge. The complexity of modern legislation and the norms of the institution encourage members to develop knowledge in depth in only a few legislative subjects.[4] In subjects about which they are not so well informed, members lean heavily on committee recommendations or on the advice of a member of the relevant committee.

Informal circles of friends with similar political philosophies spring up in Congress. Information on forthcoming developments is exchanged within them. Respect for one another's specialties within such a circle can be so great that the recommendation of the specialist in a certain policy area can determine the votes. of the entire friendship circle. One lobbyist said that at the time when he was a member of Congress he belonged to a circle of friends with similar political philosophies. Each member of the group served on a different committee, and they met weekly at lunch to report to one another on developments in their respective committees. Asked if he accepted the recommendations of his colleagues without further investigation, the respondent rocked back in his chair, thought for a full minute, and then said quite decisively, "Yes, by God, I did."

Staff assistants to decision-makers also exercise an important influence on the information and advice accepted by officials. Staffs not only process incoming information, they also take the initiative in digging out information. Staff persons are appointed by their superiors and are supposed to be alter egos for them, but since staff members are individuals, they may have some political convictions which intrude into the performance of their tasks. It is impossible to say with any precision how much decision-makers lean on their staffs; some are probably much more dependent than others. Dependence on staff recommendations probably increases if decisions involve technical or specialized questions and as decision-makers become more rushed.

Since officials have several alternative sources for information and advice, it is difficult to measure how effective lobbyist messages are. Officials do attend to lobbying information; they welcome it even if they do not feel very dependent on it. A rough indication of the value decision-makers place upon messages from lobbyist also can be derived from answers to the question of how often decision-makers come to lobbyists for information and advice.

Table 1 shows how often lobbyists have been solicited for their views and the kind of views sought. Twenty-four percent report that they have never been solicited; 44 percent say it has happened no more than ten times a year; 18 percent say it occurred eleven to twenty-five times a year; and 14 percent say it has been continual. Most lobbyists report that communications initiated by decision-makers are confined to requests for information to which the lobby organization has unique access or to views on issues on which the organization has strong and established opinions. A prime aim of most lobbyists is to develop confidential relationships with decision-makers which will provide regular opportunities to exert influence. These data suggest that no more than 10 percent of the lobbyists achieve this with even one official; only 9 percent are consulted frequently on a wide range of policy issues. There is no evidence in this table that lobbying messages are widely sought after by decision-makers.

The representatives of large organizations with considerable power at

Table 1
Decision-Makers' Solicitation of
Policy Views from Lobbyists

TYPE OF VIEWS SOLICITED	FREQUENCY OF SOLICITATION						
	Never	2 Times a year or Less	3–10 Times a Year	11–25 Times a year	On-going Activity	No re-sponse	Total
None	24						24
Inquiry confined to organizational views or information		13	25	15	8		61
Wide range of issues		2	2	3	3		10
Confidential conversations					3		3
No response		1	1			14	16
TOTAL	24	16	28	18	14	14	114

the polls, such as labor and farm groups, report being solicited for their views more often than other lobbyists. This again reflects the power of the constituents; the stand of an organization with power at the polls may be important information when an official is making a decision. Organizational executives and officers who are the spokesmen for their organizations are solicited more often for their views than lobbyists in other roles. Lawyers in private practice are seldom solicited. Lobbyists who have previously had confidential relationships with decision-makers tend to carry part of that confidence over to their new role; former office-holders, those with Hill experience, and those who are very active in groups, tend to be solicited more frequently. Political activity also seems to be rewarded by increased solicitation of one's views; political contributors, especially political fund-raisers, are solicited more than those who do not so participate.

These data do not precisely indicate the extent to which lobbyists are heard. However, where lobby groups have useful information, it is heeded; and when their stand has important political implications, it is heeded. But we must also say that many lobby messages fall on deaf ears. Decision-makers occasionally seek information and advice from lobbyists, but very few of these interchanges are on a confidential and wide-ranging basis. Very few lobbyists report, and none of the congressional respondents report, having such confidential relationships.

Looking back now on the factors that decision-makers consider as they make their decisions, we can more clearly evaluate the range of lobbying influence by inquiring into the probability that lobbying or lobbyists can affect these factors. Lobbyists and lobby groups have a very limited ability to control the selection of officials or to affect the likelihood that an official can keep or enhance his position. Lobbyists and lobby groups are reluctant to become involved in partisan politics. They also find it difficult and very expensive to try to manipulate public opinion; many of them have great difficulty manipulating even the opinion of their own membership. This is not the same as saying that groups have little influence on politics; they obviously do have considerable influence; however, the influence of groups is derived from the fact that members of groups are citizens and the political system is designed to respond to the influence of their votes.

In similar vein, lobbyists and the leaders of lobby groups cannot, by themselves, make an official look good or bad. They have little to say about whether an official makes a "good record" or not. They can, of course, offer support to or oppose an official, and that may have some little impact on his public image; but they do not have votes on bills that they can use to bargain with officials in the way officials bargain for one another's votes. They are not members of the team and do not have team norms and sanctions to use to control the behavior of officials. They have little or no success in changing the political philosophies of officials. Even their impact from supplying information and suggested policy alternatives to officials is diluted by the many alternative sources officials have for information and ideas.

The kinds of rewards and punishments that lobbyists are in the best position to offer have relatively low priority for the officials. It has been shown that entertainment and parties are not even considered a reward by most officials. Favors and bribes are not highly valued and are considered very dangerous by both officials and lobbyists. Lobbyists do have a kind of nuisance impact. They can make life somewhat unpleasant for officials who do not go along with them: It is embarrassing to vote against someone who is watching; it is difficult to vote against a group that has sent six thousand letters; it is hard not to listen to someone who is very persistent; it is hard to stand up to scorn by the public media. On small matters these nuisance factors may have considerable impact; they may even be decisive; but on matters of large public import such factors are rarely, if ever, of any great importance.

It has been suggested that the impact of lobbying on governmental decisions varies with the nature of the issue. On broad political issues commanding considerable public attention, the major determinant is the desire of the public. Lobbyists can do very little to affect the outcome, though they may influence the details of the bill or the specific language of small sections. If the legislation is specialized and affects only a small segment of the population, lobbyists are more likely to play a larger role. A member of the Ways and Means Committee of the House told a story about representatives of two large whiskey distilleries who came before the committee to argue about when the tax on whiskey should become due and payable. Each was seeking a competitive advantage over the other. There was no governmental or public interest to be served or disserved. The issue received no attention in the press. The committee listened quietly to the pleas from both sides and then made its decision (handed down its judgment). Lobbying may have been important on this bill, but was the bill really important?[5]

It is the demands of the people that start the country on a certain broad road policy-wise. Lobbyists may affect the language of the bills and legislation that come out in conformity with this broad policy, but they have little influence on the general outcome. They may not have any influence about the choice of the road to drive on, but they do have something to say about the way we drive on the road once we are on it.

I think lobbying plays a role in shaping the final content of a piece of legislation. We went out and slugged for an amendment to the highway act and got it tacked on. We couldn't affect the outcome of the bill very much, but in this technical way lobbying plays its role.

I think over the long haul that lobbying hasn't too much influence. I think they do have some impact on the details, and considerable impact on specialized legislation.

The lobbyists are really interested in the details, and this is where they have their effect. On over-all policy, however—the 1954 tax code for example —I don't think they are particularly effective. I suppose on broad policy if you get enough lobby organizations heading in the same direction, it has some effect. But once a coalition is built up on one side, it stimulates an opposing coalition on the other side, and Congress is caught in the middle.

Some observers argue that lobbyists have their greatest power when the issue is closely contested and switching a few votes here or there may turn the tide. It is rather superficial, however, to give lobbyists credit for the outcome if they have switched a few votes in a close contest. It ignores all the factors that originally made the contest close, the influences that created the firm stands of the persons lined up on both sides of the issue. In legislative votes, the factors that determine one vote are as important as those that determine any other vote. If two hundred House members, acting on their political beliefs, were to line up on each side of a bill and the tide were turned by a dozen votes that were influenced by lobbying, would it be correct to say that the votes of four hundred persons acting on political conviction were outweighed by the dozen acting on pleadings from lobbyists?

THE BALANCE OF POWER IN LOBBYING

An important factor attenuating the impact of lobbying on governmental decisions is the fact that nearly every vigorous push in one direction stimulates an opponent or coalition of opponents to push in the opposite direction. This natural self-balancing factor comes into play so often that it almost amounts to a law.[6] The great numbers of lobbyists in Washington may actually be a blessing instead of a threat to the governmental system. When groups push on both sides of an issue, officials can more freely exercise their judgment than when the groups push on only one side.

The theory that countervailing power will cancel out some of the one-sided strength and evil effects of lobbying is an old one in Washington and is criticized vigorously by some persons. One criticism is that certain interests, such as consumers, have no one to represent them and that, therefore, any pressure against the welfare of these weakly organized interests is not resisted adequately. Although there is some truth to that criticism, the point is often overstressed.[7] From time to time, consumer representatives are placed on boards and other decision-making bodies. More important, consumers, and any other poorly organized group, have a voice through constituent pressures and the vote. In addition, it is common for one of the organized interests to have an interest coinciding with unorganized interests.[8] For example, in the struggle over the tariff, the direct interest of the consumer is in free trade; the goods he purchases will be cheaper. Every time tariff decisions must be made, some organized interests lobby vigorously in favor of free trade.

A more telling criticism of the theory of countervailing power is that there is some danger that such an overwhelming coalition of groups may be organized on one side of an issue that the beneficial effect of competition may be outweighed by the irresistible force of combination.[9] This criticism can be overemphasized, too. If an overwhelming combination of powerful groups were on one side of an issue, the public would probably also favor that side of the issue. In such a case, the outcome would be completely in accord with our beliefs about how the political process should work. If the public were not behind the coalition of groups, the decision-makers would have sufficient public support to decide without being irresistibly influenced by the coalition.

When thinking about the theory of countervailing power, it is important not to think of decision-makers as inanimate objects which are manipulated by group pressures. Officials have beliefs and values of their own which are important guides to their decisions.[10] The group or coalition with the greatest numbers, or the most money, or the loudest noise will not necessarily prevail, especially if their prevailing is not in the public or national interest. As we saw above, the pressures of groups are but one of the factors considered by decision-makers—and by no means the most important one.

Another false notion in thinking about the impact of lobbying is the condemnation of all pressure as bad. It is a fact that life, especially organized community life, does not exist without pressure of one kind or another. Pressure is effective when it is backed by sanctions. The sanction with the greatest impact on the public official is the decision of the voters to support him or not. Every vote is a unit of pressure on a representative. Every communication from a constituent to his representative is a pressure. Our political system was designed to register those pressures, and we consider it proper when public officials respond to them.

All other forms of pressure derive meaning only as they are converted into voter pressure. If a lobby group can use money and other resources to convince the body politic that a certain policy should be followed, that conviction will be registered in pressure at the polls, and it will be proper for the system to respond to that pressure. We would not, in fact, want public officials who were insensitive to pressures at the polls. The only feasible and legitimate way to counteract political pressures is to form opposing groups and to try to convince the public that the original pressure group is wrong. If a group can sway the body politic, that is exactly what our system responds to and should reward.

ESTIMATIONS OF LOBBYING SUCCESS

Lobbyist respondents were asked to make several subjective evaluations of their success and of the contribution of lobbying to the policy-making process. In addition, they were to name the most successful lobby organization in town. Some consensus in this selection was expected. Lobbyists do not agree on the most successful lobby group in Washington; no organization received more than eight or ten choices. One reason for this is that judgments of success are very subjective. Different lobbyists use different standards. Some evaluate the percentage of bills passed that a group supported. This fails to come to grips with the question, however; one does not know whether the same bills would have passed if the lobby group had done nothing. Others use a broader criterion of long-range progress toward a distant goal. The subjective component of this kind of appraisal is readily apparent. Still others use a negative criterion of a group's ability to prevent potential damage to its interests.

Another reason for the lack of agreement on the most successful lobby group was that lobbyists naturally tend to choose a recent opponent as the strongest or most successful group.[11] Psychologically, one enjoys believing that one's opponents are strong. Like anyone else, lobbyists need to believe they are succeeding. The feedback from their activities, however, is very ambiguous and difficult to interpret. They naturally interpret their progress as favorably as possible; this helps to maintain their self-respect. Believing that one's opponent is very strong, a lobbyist who wins a point scores a striking success in his own mind. Even if he should be defeated, his deflation is minimized because one could not really expect much more when opposing such a strong adversary. About 15 percent of the lobbyists choose a major opponent as the strongest group in town. There are also psychological rewards for believing that one's own organization is the strongest in town; about 14 percent of the lobbyists believe that.

Despite the subjective difficulties in estimating group success, lobbyists tend to pick large membership organizations—like farm groups, veteran groups, and labor organizations (especially the railway labor unions) —as the most successful. About one-third of the lobbyists choose a large membership organization as the most successful.[12] This is consistent with the contention that power at the polls is the greatest power in lobbying. The American Medical Association and the oil and gas lobbies are the specialized groups most often listed as quite powerful.[13] The reputation of the AMA stands out quite sharply and stems largely from their successful public relations campaigns to label proposed national health insurance plans as "socialized medicine." Another source of the AMA's strength is their firm policy that the organization shall take public stands only on medical matters.

On the whole, lobbyists rate the success of their own organizations rather highly. None calls his own organization a failure, and only six report that they do poorly. About one-fourth think they have moderately good results, and about one-half say their results are good; only one-sixteenth think they are resoundingly successful. Respondents tend to estimate that the odds against great success are rather high. They made such statements as, "Considering the odds against us, I think we did rather well." Estimations of success vary with the kinds of goals the group sets for itself; usually these goals are broad and long-range—more than simply a successful outcome on particular bills. Naturally it is easier to obtain specific limited objectives than to realize broad long-range goals.

These varying goal standards for measuring organization success produced interesting results in the data. Most observers would agree that organizations with great power at the polls generally have lobbying power superior to those with little power at the polls. High-poll-power organizations, however, tend to set broad, long-range goals which are difficult to attain. Thus, representatives of organizations with high power at the polls are no more inclined to claim high success for their organization than representatives of organizations with less power at the polls. Rather significantly, few lobbyists claim outstanding success. If the total lobby setting results in a balancing of groups, we should find, as we do, that groups claim moderate success against strong odds. If a substantial percentage claims resounding success, it would signal that a balancing process might not be functioning.

It is a truism that it is easier to stop a bill at some one hurdle in a legislative passage than it is to get it over all the hurdles (eight or ten in a two-house legislature) and signed into law. From this observation it is often suggested that "defensive organizations" (those trying to maintain the status quo) will generally be more successful in lobbying than "offensive organizations" (those trying to change the status quo).[14] The organizations represented by respondents in this study were categorized according to whether the policy of the group was primarily designed to preserve the status quo in society or to change the status quo.[15] The results show no relationship between these categories and respondents' appraisal of the organization's success.[16] This suggests that the generalization that defensive organizations find more success than offensive ones must be examined more rigorously.[17] The lack of correlation between defensive-offensive postures and appraisal of organization success probably results from several factors. Group success depends on many factors in addition to defensive and offensive posture; it is also appraised by varying goal standards. In addition, the legislative process is not so neatly arranged that defensive organizations will nearly always attempt to defeat bills while offensive organizations will nearly always attempt to pass them. Both types of organizations attempt to pass some bills and to defeat others. This results mainly from the fact that numbers of bills are introduced on all sides of questions in each Congress.

One lobbyist for a deprived minority group attributes much of his organization's considerable success to the fact that there is basic and clearly recognizable justice in his pleas. He believes that decision-makers recognize this fundamental justice and that this prevails as they make their decisions. Yet, careful examination of the data does not show that organizations trying to correct a basic injustice have any more success at lobbying than other kinds of organizations. The success of this respondent's lobby group probably stemmed more from the fact that the rationale for the original injustice had disappeared and that no organization is pushing on the other side. In many other cases of injustice, the organization, or organizations, benefitting from the injustice is still active on the other side.

Lobbyists' estimations of their personal success are highly correlated with estimations of their organization's success. Most lobbyists report moderate or good results from their personal efforts; only two report poor results; and only three report resounding success. Most lobbyists take a rather long-range view of their efforts. One reports, "I have only been on this job for five years, and that's not long enough to find out how successful I will be." Lobbying success is very much dependent on tenure, since acceptability of messages from lobbyists by officials can be gained only if the lobbyist builds a reputation for reliability. Most lobbyists hold their job for some time and plan to make a career in lobbying. Feeling successful goes along with liking the work and planning to make a career of it. The lobbyist's feeling of personal success shows no relationship to the poll-power of his organization. This finding was not unexpected; lobbyists for weak organizations take that fact into account as they appraise their personal success, and lobbyists for strong organizations realize that organizational success is due to many other factors in addition to their personal efforts. It also seems to be generally true that every lobbyist aspires to more than he achieves; he must then decide what he might reasonably expect to achieve.

EVALUATIONS OF ALL POLICY INFLUENCES

In attempting to make an over-all evaluation of lobbying impact on governmental decisions, it is important to place lobbying within the setting of all the factors influencing public policy. The final question of the interview with respondents was:

> We all know that lobbying is just one factor in making public policy. The President, Congress, executive agencies, political parties, opinion leaders, and voters also participate in policy-making. How would you appraise the relative influence of these various forces as they operate in making policy?

More than half of the respondents pick the President or the executive branch as the most important factor in making policy; even lobbyists with experience on the Hill and congressional respondents tend to give first rank importance to the executive branch. About 20 percent of the lobbyists give the voters first rank importance. (These people tend to give unqualified approval to lobbying.) Many congressional respondents also rate voters first. Approximately 10 percent of lobbyists give first rank importance to Congress. Congress is most often named second (about 35 percent) and is followed closely by the executive branch (30 percent). Opinion leaders and political parties are named relatively few times.

Most important for our purposes, only one lobbyist gives first rank importance to lobbying, and only five rate it second. Congressional respondents also accord very slight importance to lobbying in making public policy; about half of them, in fact, place lobbying at the bottom of the list. It is rather striking that both the practitioners and the recipients of lobbying think that lobbying is of so little importance in making public policy. One lobbyist struggling with this question said:

> I don't know where in the world I would fit the lobbyists as a group. Some of them have been up here for years battling for lost causes. On the whole, and speaking of all lobbyists in general, I think they are a lot less effective than most people believe.

The tendency of the public to overestimate the impact of lobbying on public policy is curiously seductive. If one assumes that lobbying is bad and ought to have little or no influence on policy and then discovers that lobbying does have some influence, it is easy to leap to the conclusion that lobbying is powerful and exercises inappropriate influence. If, on the other hand, one assumes that lobbying is legitimate and then evaluates all the other influences on public policy, he concludes that lobbying has relatively little impact on policy when compared with the other factors. Persons who believe human nature is essentially evil seem to be able to find sinister influences everywhere; finding a few sinister influences in lobbying, they are overeager to condemn all lobbyists.

The strong influence of the President and the executive branch on public policy is attested to by some very knowledgeable leaders in Congress:

> You would almost have to put the President number one. He has such a tremendous command of the sources of information, this automatically gives him an advantage. Next I suppose you would put the sources of information such as the press, mass communications, political commentators, and other opinion leaders. The public opinion they create is reflected from the districts back into Congress. Congress has some leadership in policy but it is more difficult to pinpoint than the leadership of the President.

> Policy is made largely by the executive and the legislative party leaders; these two most important factors are somewhat influenced by the other factors. Lobbyists have very little to say on legislation so far as I can see. . . . I have known lots of party chairmen and the party, on the national scene is not very effective. I never saw a chairman who would swear he had any effect on policy whatsoever. Any attempts to influence policy would be instantly resented either by leaders in the executive branch or leaders of the legislative party in Congress.

> There is just no way of getting around it, the President is the dominant force in policy-making. The President is one man, and when he speaks he has

the attention of the world. He can mold public opinion, and he also tends to have the confidence of all the people. There is no one member of Congress who has that much respect. If it should become a popularity contest, the President will always win out. All policy is made from a view of what the public demands; political figures orient to it. I doubt if the lobbyist has much to say except when he gets down to specific language of particular sections of bills; he is not very effective on broad policy.

The lobbyist-son of a former President said:

The President is certainly the most influential—this is without any question. Second I would put the head of an executive department who is putting up a real fight and is backed by the President. The most important single element is the President's backing up of a fighting cabinet officer.

THE DANGERS OF LOBBYING

The weight of the evidence that this study brings to bear suggests that there is relatively little influence or power in lobbying per se. There are many forces in addition to lobbying which influence public policy; in most cases these other forces clearly outweigh the impact of lobbying. Voters set the broad trends of public policy which all the other influences on policy must follow. It is for this reason that so many forces battle to manipulate public opinion. Public opinion is a factor which sets the boundaries for the policy struggle. On certain questions the boundaries are closely restricted, and the policy decisions of officials must closely follow public demands. On other questions, the boundaries may be broader, leaving wider discretion to decision-makers and more possibility for lobbyists to influence their decisions. Questions of large public attention and import are chiefly determined by considerations of political success and winning the next election. The chief executive, through his political leadership, his ability to mold public opinion, and his command of the resources and imagination of the executive bureaucracy, has the greatest single impact on the shape of public policy. Questions of small technical nature, which attract little public attention, are more subject to lobbying influence. The growth of one lobby group or coalition generally stimulates the development of an opposing group. Most careful observers of governmental decision-making have concluded that the over-all impact of lobbying is relatively minor. This point was made by both lobbyist and congressional respondents and agrees with the observation of other writers on the subject.[18]

If the conclusion that lobbying has a relatively weak impact on policy is added to the conclusions that system controls and legal controls are adequate, that public decisions cannot be bought or stolen, and that the lobbying process is relatively clean, the result is clear: lobbying as we see it today in Washington presents little or no danger to the system. This does not mean that a dangerous situation could not arise or that lobbyists would not engage in unethical or unfair tactics if they believed these would be to their special advantage. The best insurance against danger and corruption in the process is an alert citizenry which elects responsible officials to public office. A wide-open communications system and viable and responsible public media are important preconditions to maintaining public alertness.

THE CONTRIBUTIONS OF LOBBYING

Eckstein raises the most fundamental question about lobbying and pressure groups: "What contributions do pressure groups make to the political system as a whole, and do these contributions tend to make the system more or less viable (stable and effective)? Are their consequences 'dysfunctional' or 'eufunctional' for the larger systems in which they operate?"[19] Though this study focuses on lobbying rather than pressure groups, the question is essentially the same; however, the contribution of these data to an answer is relatively limited.

In this context it is relevant to point out again that lobbying is inevitable and is likely to grow in scope. One lobbyist says it is analogous to automobile drivers: there are a few bad drivers, but people continue to drive, and more cars are added to the road each year. Lobbying is protected by the First Amendment to the Constitution, and government officials are not disposed to hamper its growth or activities.

Granted the inevitability of lobbying, what are its positive contributions to the political process? Lobbyists provide information and other services which are welcomed by governmental decision-makers. These services are costly and somewhat wasteful; the public or the consumer pays for them ultimately; congressional officials even claim they could function quite adequately without them. In another sense, however, they are indispensable. If information from lobbyists and lobby groups was, for some reason, unavailable to government officials, they would be largely dependent on their own staff for information and ideas. Since the Congress is reluctant to staff itself adequately, it would have to turn primarily to the Executive for information. This would create an even further imbalance between Congress and the Executive in policy-making.[20] More important, cutting off lobbying communications would eliminate a valuable, even indispensable, source of creativity. There is no assurance that government institutions can turn up all the possible alternative solutions to policy problems. A decision-maker who has his mind made up may well have to have new points of view forcefully thrust upon him before he can perceive and accept them. The clash of viewpoints between contesting groups is not only informative; it also is creative. Formerly unperceived alternatives may arise from the challenge to previously accepted possibilities.

Eckstein[21] suggests that lobby groups perform two other indispensable functions in the political system: integration and disjunction. Officials must know very specifically what the effects of a given policy will be and how citizens will react to that policy. Lobby groups and lobbyists define opinion for government with a sense of reality and specificity which political parties, the mass media, opinion polls, and staff assistants seldom, if ever, can achieve. Aggregating and defining specialized opinions have both integrative and disjunctive aspects. The function is integrative in that persons with special interests or problems need group action to aggregate their views and communicate the positions to officials. The aggregation process requires some compromise on the part of group members and therefore is integrative. Group opinion is a more manageable consideration for officials than scattered individual opinions.

Specialized opinion is disjunctive as well, in that it encourages multiple group demands. Political parties (especially in a two-party system) strive for a very broad integration in order to win elections. That kind of integration can be achieved only by reaching a very low and vague denominator which may not be very functional for making policy. If special interests were confined to vague representation through political parties, they might begin to feel alienated from a political system which persistently distorts their goals.[22] Affording disparate interests special representation through their own lobby group probably contributes to the stability of the system. There is reason to suppose, then, that the policy-making system produces wiser or more intelligent decisions and functions with more stability than might be the case if lobby groups and lobbyists were not present. If we had no lobby groups and lobbyists we would probably have to invent them to improve the functioning of the system.

NOTES

[1] Edward C. Banfield, *Political Influences* (New York: Free Press of Glencoe, 1961).

[2] James G. March, "Introduction to the Theory and Measurement of Influence," *American Political Science Review,* XLIX (June, 1955), 431–51.

[3] Donald R. Matthews, *U.S. Senators and Their World* (Chapel Hill: University of North Carolina Press, 1960).

[4] Matthews, *op. cit.*, pp. 95–97.

[5] Eckstein, speaking of his own study of pressure groups, said, "In a nutshell, the study suggests (to me, at any rate) that the influence of private groups is greatest when, from the standpoint of democratic values, it matters least whether it is great or small." Harry Eckstein, *Pressure Group Politics: The Case of the British Medical Association* (London: Allen and Unwin, 1960), p. 167.

[6] In each of the six case studies of decisions in Chicago described by Banfield, one group or coalition was opposed by another (Banfield, *op. cit.*, Chapters II–VII). Subsequently, he searched for an "underlying logic" for the decisions and felt that there must have been some "invisible hand" at work (Banfield, *op. cit.*, pp. 327–28). These notions are not far from the concept of a natural self-balancing factor.

[7] Truman also questions the assumption in the argument and calls for further research. David B. Truman, *The Governmental Process* (New York: Knopf, 1951), p. 519.

[8] Even disfranchised, unorganized groups may find some representation because they are potential groups. (Truman, *ibid.*, p. 511). This point is also made in V. O. Key, Jr., *Southern Politics in State and Nation* (New York: Knopf, 1949) and in Arthur F. Bentley, *The Process of Government* (2nd. ed.; Bloomington, Ind.: The Principia Press, 1949).

[9] This argument is made in the General Interim Report of the Buchanan Committee, U.S. Congress. House, Select Committee on Lobbying Activities, *General Interim Report:* 81:2, H. Rep. no. 3138 (Washington, D.C.: Government Printing Office, October 20, 1950).

[10] Wahlke categorizes legislators as facilitators, neutrals, and resistors with respect to their role toward pressure groups. Wahlke *et al.*, "American State Legislator's Role Orientations Toward Pressure Groups," *Journal of Politics*, XXII (May, 1960), 203–27.

[11] Most members of the group of business representatives in Washington who participated in the round-table conference at The Brookings Institution perceived labor unions as their main opponents; they also considered them to be very strong. Paul W. Cherington and Ralph L. Gillen, *The Business Representative in Washington* (Washington: The Brookings Institution, 1962), Chapter V.

[12] The business representatives mentioned in Note 11 apparently felt weak and unsuccessful compared to labor; they reasoned thus partly because they did not mobilize votes the way labor did and partly because they had difficulty agreeing among themselves on policy and tactics. (Cherington and Gillen, *op. cit.*, p. 46). *Redbook* sent a six-page questionaire to 537 members of Congress in the fall of 1961; 174 replied. Members were asked to rate the influence of twenty-eight lobby groups as low, moderate, or high. To only one group was high influence attributed by a majority of those responding; the AFL–CIO was rated high by 58.6 percent, moderate by 36 percent, and low by 5.4 percent. Al Toffluer, "How Congressmen Make Up Their Minds," *Redbook* (February, 1962), pp. 56–57, 126–31.

[13] White picked the farm lobby and the AMA as the strongest in Washington. William S. White, *Citadel: The Story of the U.S. Senate* (New York: Harper, 1956).

[14] DeVries makes such a claim for lobbying in Michigan. Walter DeVries, *The Michigan Lobbyist: A Study in the Bases and Perceptions of Effectiveness*, Unpublished Ph.D. dissertation, Department of Political Science (Michigan State University, 1960).

[15] This is not a liberal-conservative, welfare state vs. free enterprise distinction; nor is it related to defense and offense on specific bills. It is whether the organization in its broad policy is trying to change or to preserve the status quo in society.

[16] Four of the six respondents who report poor success for their organizations represent groups attempting to defend technologically obsolete industries. The decline of such industries probably cannot be stopped by even the most energetic lobbying activity.

[17] The business representatives at the Brookings round table did not think they were very successful; yet it was clear from their remarks that they were primarily defending the status quo. Cherington and Gillen, *op. cit.,* Chapter V.

[18] White, *op. cit.,* pp. 145, 149. Matthews, *op. cit.,* pp. 195–96. Key, Jr., *op. cit.,* Chapter XX.

[19] Eckstein, *op. cit.,* p. 152.

[20] The author is indebted to James A. Robinson for suggesting this point.

[21] Eckstein, *op. cit.,* p. 162.

[22] The Washington representatives at the Brookings round table all represented corporations. They expressed dissatisfaction with general business organizations such as the National Association of Manufacturers and the National Chamber of Commerce and even with their own trade associations for compromising too much on policy, being too vague, and being too slow to take action. Cherington and Gillen, *op. cit.*

PART SIX

Evaluation of Public Policy

CHAPTER 19

Program Budgeting—Applying Economic Analysis to Government Expenditure Decisions

Murray L. Weidenbaum

A fundamental shift is occurring in the focus of *public finance*. As recently as the early 1950's, the textbooks in the field primarily dealt with taxation; a few chapters were devoted to debt and fiscal policy and perhaps a section described the mechanics of governmental budgeting.

The pendulum now appears to be swinging sharply. Recently the emphasis in public finance has been on the expenditure side in attempting to apply economic analysis to governmental expenditure decisions. Benefit/cost comparisons, cost/effectiveness analysis, and *program budgeting* all have become important manifestations of this shift. The most recent and ambitious operational effort along these lines is the Planning-Programming-Budgeting System of the federal government which may, in retrospect, represent a major advance in the application of economic analysis to public sector decision-making.

This article deals mainly with this new development, but in doing so the antecedent efforts will be related to the current budget reform movement. And possible future changes will also be indicated.

On August 25, 1965, President Johnson announced

. . . a very new and very revolutionary system of planning and programming and budgeting throughout the vast federal government—so that through the tools of modern management the full promise of a finer life can be brought to every American at the lowest possible cost.[1]

Before evaluating this governmental innovation, it may be useful to see how earlier developments in the economic analysis of governmental expenditure decisions relate to it. We may then be in a better position to evaluate the "new" and "revolutionary" aspects of the Planning-Programming-Budget System, or PPBS, as it is commonly called.

Reprinted from the *Business and Government Review* (July-August, 1966), pp. 22–31, by permission of the publisher and the author.

ANTECEDENTS OF PPBS

Economists have long been interested in identifying policies that would promote economic welfare, specifically by improving the efficiency with which a society uses its resources. Governmental budgeting provides one important example of this concern.

For a good many years benefit/cost analysis has been applied by a few federal agencies, particularly the Corps of Engineers and the Bureau of Reclamation, to the evaluation of prospective projects. Despite important operational difficulties, such as choosing an appropriate discount rate which would correspond to a realistic estimate of the social cost of capital, the use of benefit/cost analysis has improved the allocation of government resources.

Table 1
Typical B/C Analysis
Water Resource Development Project

	Amortization Period	
	50 yrs.	100 yrs.
	(Thous.)	
Investments		
Total	$3,100	$3,100
Annual Costs		
Interest & amortization	$123.4	$101.6
Operation, maintenance, etc.	25.4	25.9
Total	$148.8	$127.5
Annual Benefits		
Flood damage reduction	$168.0	$206.0
Fish, wildlife, & recreation	32.8	35.5
Total	$200.8	$241.5
Benefit-Cost Ratio		
Ratio	1.4	1.9

It has served as a partial screening device to eliminate obviously uneconomical projects—those whose prospective gains are less than estimated costs. It also has provided some basis for ranking and comparing projects and choosing among alternatives.[2] Perhaps the overriding value of benefit/cost analysis has been in demonstrating the importance of making fairly objective economic analyses of proposed essentially political actions and perhaps narrowing the area in which political forces may operate.

New Pentagon Program

A related development has been the application of cost/effectiveness or cost/utility analysis to military budget decision-making. Much of the development effort was performed at the Rand Corporation under Air Force auspices.[3] For military programs, ordinarily the benefits or results cannot be expressed in dollar terms. However, the end objective, such as the capability to destroy X number of enemy targets under stipulated conditions, can be expressed in quantitative terms. And, more important, the alternative methods of achieving the objective—Y bombers versus Z missiles or some combination—can be priced out and a *least cost* solution arrived at.

This approach has been at the heart of the Planning-Programming-Budgeting System introduced in the Pentagon so successfully by Secretary McNamara and economists Hitch, Enthoven and their associates. It clearly has been the success of the McNamara approach which has led to adoption of a government-wide PPBS effort.

Table 2 illustrates the fundamental shift that has occurred in military

Table 2
Shift in Military Resource Allocation

Old Budget System	New Planning-Budgeting System
Navy:	*Strategic forces:*
Polaris	Polaris
Marine Corps	ICBM's
Carrier task forces	Long range bombers
Air Force:	*General purpose forces:*
ICBM's	Marine Corps
Tactical aircraft	Armored divisions
Air defense aircraft	Tactical aircraft
Long range bombers	Carrier task forces
Army:	*Continental defense forces:*
Air defense missiles	Air defense aircraft
Armored divisions	Air defense missiles

resource allocation. Under the old or pre-McNamara system, each service competed for a larger share of the defense budget and, within the service totals, strategic weapons such as ICBM's competed for funds with tactical programs. Under the new system, close substitutes for performing the same or similar mission are compared with each other, such as ICBM's and submarine launched strategic missiles, although different services are involved.

Performance Budgeting

One other development needs to be acknowledged, in sketching out the origin of the current program budgeting effort, and that is the work on performance budgeting encouraged by the two Hoover Commissions and implemented in part by the United States Bureau of the Budget. By a performance budget the Hoover Commission meant ". . . a budget based upon functions, activities, and projects. . . ." Such an approach, it was contended, would focus attention on the general character and relative importance of the work to be done, rather than upon the things to be acquired.[4] Although it may not appear so, this was a fundamental shift in budgetary thinking at the federal level. Less of the budgetary detail was to be devoted to changes in numbers and types of clerical personnel and office supply usage and more attention given to the activities to be performed. However, implementation was slow and only partial.

The current emphasis on program budgeting may represent the delayed fulfillment of the Hoover Commission recommendation. As we will see, cost/benefit and cost/effectiveness analysis also play important parts in this new budgetary approach.

MECHANICS OF PPBS

The Planning-Programming-Budgeting System which each major federal department and agency is now setting up, in response to the directive from President Johnson, is patterned on the Pentagon approach. It is being developed by the Bureau of the Budget working with the various federal departments and agencies charged with implementation. The entire system is new and its structure has barely been developed or put into operation. Hence, it should be recognized that it is somewhat hazardous to attempt a description, much less an evaluation now.

PPBS is based, according to the Bureau of the Budget, on the introduction of three major concepts into federal government operations:[5]

1. *The development in each government agency of an analytical capability to examine in depth both agency objectives and the various programs to meet these objectives.*

   This is hardly the traditional "green-eye-shade" type of approach to financial management and may be far more difficult to accomplish. However, this does widen the frame of reference of governmental management officials and sets the stage for the next steps.

2. *The formation of a five-year planning and programming process coupled with a sophisticated management information system.*

This should yield an improved basis for decision-making by department heads and the President in that it is designed to provide a comprehensive framework for acting on the myriad of questions that face the management of an organization, public or private.

3. *The last and perhaps fundamental concept to be introduced is the creation of an improved budgeting mechanism which can take broad program decisions, translate them into more refined decisions in a budgetary context, and present the results for Presidential and congressional action.*

This may be more of a statement of ultimate desire and long-term objective to be achieved.

Through the combined planning and budgeting process, it is hoped that broad national goals will be reduced to specific program operations and the most economical method of carrying them out identified. Four major steps have been identified which will need to be taken to accomplish this rather tall order.

Figure 1
The Federal Budget Annual Cycle

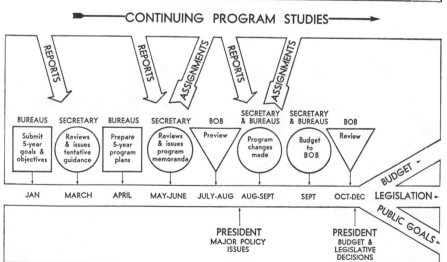

1. Identifying National Goals

The specific goals which are deemed proper and appropriate for the federal government to be seeking will somehow have to be selected in the light of a comprehensive evaluation of national needs and objectives. This is now beginning to get underway in each major department and agency; and there is little indication of the formal methodology, if any, which is employed or available at this step of the process.

2. Relating Broad Goals to Specific Programs

Specific alternative programs which may help to achieve the broad national goals and objectives will then be examined. The ones that appear to be most promising, given the various constraints under which the government operates, will have to be selected. The subject of constraints is not one to be passed over too quickly.

    The typical government agency may find itself with little discretion in selecting the optimum combination of programs which can assist in achieving broad national goals in its area of operations. They may well find that there is little, vague, or conflicting congressional guidance as to the goals to be attained. However, there may be clear and precise congressional directive as to which specific programs—and in what amounts and particulars—are to be conducted. The task here may well be both to infer the goals from the specific programs Congress authorized and then to conjure up new or improved means (other programs) to achieve these goals or objectives.

3. Relating Programs to Resource Requirements

Specific costs of alternative programs will then need to be estimated (in terms of total resources they would require) in order to compare their efficiency in achieving the goals. To those acquainted with benefit/cost or cost/utility analysis, this will be no mean achievement in many illusive program areas. All sorts of specific techniques come to mind here, as well as more informal examinations with less quantification.

    In view of the many theoretical and operational shortcomings of these tools, the user will need to keep in mind that the basic purpose of any of these techniques is the carrying out of broad systems analyses in which alternative programs are compared, with respect to both the costs to be incurred and the gains to be achieved. Recent attempts to apply benefit/cost analysis to fields other than water resources (such as health, education, transportation, and research) reveal the host of pitfalls and short-comings of available techniques and methodology.

4. Relating the Resource Inputs to Budget Dollars

Finally, the manpower, facilities, and other source requirements will need to be translated into budget dollars—all projected several years ahead—so that the costs of the programs can be analyzed over a meaningful period and decisions made to implement the PPBS results. This sounds much easier than it is likely to be in practice. To cite one among numerous possibilities, one may wonder as to how the externalities involved—especially non-federal costs—will be handled. Nevertheless, this four-step procedure sounds both necessary and desirable.

Perhaps the most essential ingredient—and one not prominently mentioned in the available materials on PPBS—is the acceptance, at each line and staff level, of the value of, and need for, the tremendous amount of detail and effort being imposed.[6] To some degree this is inherently both subjective and circular. The better the quality of input into the system, the greater the likelihood of good results. But it will be the value of the results that justify the substantial expenditure (perhaps investment is a more appropriate term) in time and effort involved.

The parallel here, to the introduction of PPBS at the Pentagon, may not be complete. The persons involved in that operation had spent many years at such organizations as Rand where they became intimately knowledgeable of military concepts, organization, requirements, and constraints. They had:

Developed specific methodology for making military systems analysis.
Identified the key points of budgetary decision-making (the selection of weapon systems).
Developed specific formats and concepts for making comparisons among alternative systems, including a sophisticated methodology for costing out alternatives.

One may wonder where the civilian government counterparts of these defense PPBS personnel will come from. The answer is neither obvious nor clear.

FRAMEWORK OF THE SYSTEM

The main product of PPBS is designed to be a comprehensive multi-year program and financial plan for each government agency, which will be updated periodically and systematically. An early and essential step is determining for each the output-oriented categories which cover its total work and area of responsibility.[7] Such a mission-oriented or objectives-oriented program format would be in sharp contrast with present practice—which focuses on the increase in funds over the previous year's budget required to meet rises in the annual expenses of the agency. Thus the present budget review is oriented to organizational units and to inputs such as wages, travel costs, and office equipment.

The *first* level of detail or breakdown in preparing the program and financial plan is termed Program Categories, which are groupings of a department's activities serving the same broad objective or mission. For example, one such broad program objective may be considered to be improvement of higher education. This program category might contain such federal programs as aid to undergraduate, graduate, and vocational education, as well as such auxiliary activities as library support and research assistance.

The *second* level of information is the program sub-categories. These combine activities on the basis of somewhat narrower objectives contributing directly to the broad purposes of the program category as a whole. Thus, expansion of engineering and science training could be a program sub-category within the program category, "improvement of higher education."

The *third* level of detail is the program element, which is the basic building block of the PPBS structure. An element may be a specific product that contributes to the program's objectives. An element could include personnel as well as equipment and facilities. An example of a program element expressed in terms of the objectives served would be the number of teachers to be trained in using the new mathematics as a part of "improvement of elementary education."

Output Measurement Problems

Many difficulties are involved in selecting the measurement of output or performance of a program. Conceptually, only the end-product should be measured rather than intermediate outputs. For example, in the Post Office Department, the end product might reflect the number of letters delivered, and not the number of times these letters were handled at the various stages of their journey.

Similarly, in the case of hospital programs, it may be possible to look at output in terms of patient-days. However, the mission of a hospital might be described better as proper treatment of patients rather than the generation of a number of patient-days. Within a broader framework, the mission of a health program might be viewed as promotion and maintenance of good health and the output measure might reflect prevention of diseases as well as treatment.[8] Legend has it that in better days Chinese patients paid their doctors in times of health and not of illness—a high mark of *output* rather than *input* orientation.

The Bureau of the Budget (the official custodian of PPBS) itself on occasion may mistake the nature of governmental output. In the February 21, 1966 supplement to the PPBS directive, it lists "training *costs* per worker" (italics supplied) as a possible means of measuring output!

The agencies are encouraged to consider comparisons and possible trade-offs among program elements which are close substitutes, even though the activities may be conducted in different bureaus. This attempt to introduce some element of competition is designed to achieve greater effectiveness from the limited budgetary resources utilized for a given program category or sub-category.

Extending the Time Horizon

In sharp contrast to historical budgeting for the next twelve-month fiscal period, PPBS is intended to extend usually five years into the future. In some cases, such as timber production and multiple-purpose water resource projects, longer time-spans may be more appropriate.

Table 3 is a hypothetical sketch of this new approach. Transportation is a good example of a major program category which consists of a variety of activities in different departments, with little attention to gaps or overlapping functions or conflicting objectives.

Major agencies involved are the Bureau of Public Roads and the Maritime Administration in the Department of Commerce, the Federal Aviation Agency, the Corps of Engineers in the Department of the Army, the Forest Service in the Department of Agriculture, the National Park Service in the Department of the Interior, the mass transit assistance program in the Department of Housing and Urban Development, plus a number of regulatory operations, such as the ICC, CAB, Federal Maritime Board, and the Coast Guard among others. Significantly, only a few of these agencies are scheduled to be absorbed by the proposed Federal Department of Transportation.

Table 4 illustrates the possible specific elements which might comprise one of the transportation sub-categories—urban commuter transportation. These elements may vary from the number of miles of way placed under construction (a measure of capital investment) to the number of ton-miles of freight carried (a measure of utilization).

I would doubt whether, in its initial stages, the Planning-Programming-Budgeting System is able to do much toward rationalizing the whole gamut

Table 3

Illustrative Outline*
of a National Transportation Program

Elements

General Inter-City Transport

Interstate Highways
  Interstate Highway Program
  Primary System Highways

Domestic Water Transport
  Inland Waterways Facilities
  Maritime Programs

Aviation
  CAB Subsidies to Airlines
  FAA and NASA Aircraft Technology

Urban Commuter
Transportation

Urban Highway Systems
Urban Transit Systems

Rural Access

Secondary System—Roads
Forest, Public Lands, National Parks Roads
Aid to Local Service Aviation

Military Standby
Transportation

* Columns are provided on the right of the form for fiscal years 1967, 68, 69, 70, 71, 72.

Table 4

Commuter Transportation
Illustrated Elements of a Transportation
Program Category

Urban Highways	Data
Passenger-miles carried	*
Ton-miles of freight carried	*
Miles of way completed	*
Miles of way placed under construction	*
Urban transit system	
Passenger-miles carried	*
Ton-miles of freight carried	*
Miles of way completed	*
Miles of way placed under construction	*

From the above information, comparisons could be made between urban highways and urban transit systems in terms of:
  1. Capital cost per mile of way.
  2. Operating cost per mile of way.
  3. Average commuter travel time per mile of way.

of federal transportation programs. Presumably the current emphasis is on improving the "building blocks," the difficult task of evaluating the individual components. Nevertheless, Tables 3 and 4 are indicative of the broader horizons of the new breed of budgeteers and represents an initial small step along a relatively new path in governmental resource allocation.

LONG-TERM IMPACTS

Assuming that some aspects of PPBS do increasingly become operational —at the departmental, then bureau, and then program level—the decision-making process in the government ultimately may undergo substantial change. With the introduction of sophisticated managerial tools such as benefit/cost, cost/utility, and systems analysis generally, there will be a reduced tendency for decisions on authorizing and financing individual government programs to be made in isolation and solely on the basis of subjective, intuitive judgments. Of course, the computers will not replace managers in making decisions, nor will staff analysts replace line management.

Changes may well occur both in the types of government officials hired and promoted and in the kinds of considerations and information they need to deal with. Nevertheless, even after the implementation of PPBS at the congressional level—which is proceeding at a much slower pace than in the Executive Branch—political consideration will continue to play key roles.

Greater Economic Return

It is possible that the composition of the federal budget will shift substantially as a result. On the basis of preliminary work, it appears that benefit/cost and similar analyses increasingly will show that certain government programs yield a greater economic return (dollar benefit to the nation) than do others.

Federal expenditures for education, training and retraining, and health —so-called investments in "human" resources—are likely to yield estimated benefits substantially in excess of total costs. In contrast, some more traditional construction-oriented activities, notably irrigation, power and other multipurpose water resource projects, are likely to show up far less favorably in this regard. Hence, some shifts from "physical" to "human" capital investment are likely to take place in the federal budget, as PPBS enfolds its long-term influence on the government and the economy.[9]

Also, a *demonstration effect* on state and local governments, and on private companies, will occur as expertise is demonstrated by federal civilian agencies in putting into successful practice these planning concepts and techniques. The initial impact may be transmitted via grant-in-aid programs to states and localities and traditional procurement contracts with business firms.

PROSPECTS FOR PPBS

In testimony before a congressional committee shortly after the presidential announcement of PPBS, Budget Director Schultze stated that he did

. . . not want to leave anybody with the idea that what we are doing is some revolutionary change. It really is an improvement in what we are doing now, a systemization and routinization, if you will . . .[10]

Perhaps the revolutionary has become routine in the Great Society.

As almost every knowledgeable person who has examined the usual budgetary process has concluded, major shortcomings are apparent and fundamental improvements needed.[11] For example, there has been little interest in focusing on the goals and objectives of government spending programs or, as a result, on alternative and more effective ways of achieving them. The future costs of present decisions are often ignored. Hence, it is not surprising that formal planning and systems analysis has had limited effect on budget decisions.

PPBS approach obviously is designed to help remedy these shortcomings. If it succeeds in only a limited way, it will represent a major advance in application of economic analysis to the allocation of public resources. Some initial shortcomings—such as the lack of public availability of the results of the analyses—may be overcome in time.

Possible Difficulties

It obviously is premature to judge the likelihood of PPBS succeeding in what it is attempting to do. Will the vast system of reports generate into a wheel-spinning operation, or will the results become a significant factor in public policy formulation? From one viewpoint, it is too ambitious, in that it is attempting to apply economic and systems analysis to all of the vast gamut of civilian government operations simultaneously. Perhaps some pilot studies, or a few test cases in civilian agency work, would have provided a sounder basis on which to proceed.

From another viewpoint, however, the PPBS approach may be failing to come to grips with the larger choices in allocating federal funds among different agencies and programs. "Would a dollar be more wisely spent for education or for public works?" This fundamental question is not raised anywhere in the budgetary process at the present time—nor is it likely to be answered or even raised under the sub-optimizing approach of PPBS.

This apparent satisfaction with sub-optimization is also evident in the historical experience in the two areas where program budgeting and benefit/cost analysis have been most widely used—national defense and water resource development. For example, much effort has gone into comparing proposed ICBM systems with long range bombers as alternative means of fulfilling a strategic (or general war) requirement. Little, if any, attention has been devoted to determining the optimum allocation of the defense budget between strategic forces and limited war (or general purpose) forces. Yet the latter kind of choice may be the critical or fundamental decision in preparing the defense budget.

Fundamental Questions Raised

Nevertheless, such questions dealing with fundamentals are being raised, in a general way and at the highest levels during the present period of attempting to reduce some expenditures, in order to offset the inflationary impacts of the Viet Nam military buildup. In a recent statement to the National League of Cities, President Johnson urged the mayors to defer or stretch out construction outlays—"I am simply asking you to put first things first." One newspaper commented on this as follows:

What then should be put first? More NASA blast-offs at Cape Kennedy or more youngsters in Head Start and The Job Corps? Better food and better housing or questionable research and development projects?[12]

Perhaps it is inevitable that the formal budget process will continue to fail to come to grips with these basic, but perhaps too elusive, questions. The rule of thumb of budget preparation which I reported to a congressional committee a few years ago still appears to be holding—the smaller and smaller the item the more and more attention is lavished upon it.

In any event, the application of a formalized planning and programming and budgeting mechanism augurs well for extending the use of economic analysis in making governmental expenditure decisions. From one sub-optimization viewpoint, it already has worked wondrously well. The institution of PPBS has resulted in a very brisk labor market in Washington for economists, systems analysts, and possessors of related skills.

NOTES

¹ President Lyndon B. Johnson, announced at a news conference of August 25, 1965 (as reproduced in "Transcript of the President's News Conference on Foreign and Domestic Matters," *New York Times,* Thursday, August 26, 1965).

² Otto Eckstein, *Water Resource Development: The Economics of Project Evaluation* (Cambridge: Harvard University Press, 1958); John D. Krutilla and Otto Eckstein, *Multiple Purpose River Development* (Baltimore: Johns Hopkins Press, 1958); Roland N. McKean, *Efficiency in Government Through Systems Analysis* (New York: John Wiley & Sons, 1958).

³ Charles J. Hitch and Roland N. McKean, *The Economics of Defense in the Nuclear Age* (Cambridge: Harvard University Press, 1960); E. E. Quade (ed.), *Analysis for Military Decisions* (New York: Rand McNally, 1964).

⁴ U.S. Commission on the Organization of the Executive Branch of the Government, *Budgeting and Accounting* (Washington, D.C.: U.S. Government Printing Office, February, 1949), pp. 7–12.

⁵ This section is drawn from statements by Budget Director Charles J. Schultze in Joint Economic Committee, *Fiscal Policy Issues of the Coming Decade,* Hearings before the Subcommittee on Fiscal Policy, July, 1965, pp. 59–96; and Joint Committee on the Organization of the Congress, *Organization of Congress,* Part 12, August-September, 1965, pp. 1775–1835.

⁶ Cf. David Novick (ed.), *Program Budgeting* (Cambridge: Harvard University Press, 1965), especially Part III: Implementation and Operation; George A. Steiner, "Program Budgeting, Business Contribution to Government Management," *California Management Review,* Spring, 1965, pp. 43–51.

⁷ U.S. Bureau of the Budget, *Planning-Programming-Budgeting* (Bulletin No. 66–3, October 12, 1965 and Supplement to Bulletin No. 66–3, February 21, 1966).

⁸ Nestor Terleckyj, "Measurement of Output of Federal Government Programs" (lecture at the U.S. Naval Post-Graduate School, Monterey, California, October 29, 1965), p. 7.

⁹ Some indications may be obtained from comparing results of benefit/cost and return on investment studies in these respective areas. Cf. Robert H. Haveman, *Water Resource Investment and the Public Interest* (Nashville: Vanderbilt University Press, 1965); Eckstein, *op. cit.;* Krutilla and Eckstein, *op. cit.;* Robert Dorfman (ed.), *Measuring Benefits of Government Investments* (Washington, D.C.: Brookings Institution, 1965); Howard G. Schaller (ed.), *Public Expenditure Decisions in the Urban Community* (Baltimore: Johns Hopkins Press, 1962); Theodore W. Schultz, "Reflections on Investment in Man," *Journal of Political Economy,* Part 2 (October, 1962), 1–8; Selma J. Mushkin (ed.), *Economics of Higher Education* (Washington, D.C.: U.S. Department of Health, Education, and Welfare, 1962); Gary Becker, "Underinvestment in College Education?" *American Economic Review* (May, 1960).

¹⁰ Statement of Charles J. Schultze, "U.S. Congress, Joint Committee on the Organization of Congress," *Organization of Congress,* Part 12, p. 1799.

¹¹ Arthur Smithies, *The Budgetary Process in the United States* (New York: McGraw-Hill, 1955); Jesse Burkhead, *Government Budgeting* (New York: John Wiley, 1956); Aaron Wildavsky, *The Politics of the Budgetary Process* (New York: Little, Brown, 1964); Murray L. Weidenbaum and John Saloma, *Congress and the Federal Budget* (Washington, D.C.: American Enterprise Institute, 1965).

¹² Deflating the Great Society," *St. Louis Post Dispatch,* April 6, 1966, p. 2B.

CHAPTER 20

Political Feasibility

Ralph Huitt

If politics is the "art of the possible," as it is often said to be, and the study of it is concerned with "who gets what, when, and how," the question of what is politically feasible would seem to come close to the heart of the matter. But perhaps the empiricism and practicality implicit in these and like definitions suggest why there is little systematic work to suggest what "political feasibility" *is;* it remains the province of the operator, not the theoretician. Pragmatic judgments in politics, as in other human endeavors, nevertheless are based on calculations about how people will behave in certain stable institutional situations, what problems they face, and what resources they can bring to bear on them. If these are largely unconscious and institutional on the part of the operator, they need not be for the student.

It may be that there are certain elements common to "political feasibility" in all political situations, but searching for them would hardly seem to be the way to begin. At first glance it would appear that what is feasible would vary with the enterprise at hand, with the arena in which action must be mounted, in the goals one has in mind, and with the political actor who is deciding what is feasible. The relatively single-minded business of getting elected President of the United States furnishes an example. It clearly is one thing to win primaries, another to capture a national convention—unless, of course, the first is done so successfully that the second is converted into a ratifying device. Mr. Kefauver was eminently proficient at the first but not at the second; Mr. Kennedy and Mr. Goldwater were nominees virtually before their conventions met. Mr. Dewey and his cohorts demonstrated that it is possible to be masters of convention strategy and tactics and still lose two national elections—one when the prospects were poor, it is true, but the other apparently unlosable. This is to say that each stage of the process presents a different "arena," or institutional setting, with its own peculiar requirements of resources, skills, and

Reprinted from Austin Ranney, ed., *Political Science and Public Policy* (Chicago: Markham, 1968), pp. 263–75, with permission of the author.

sense of timing. These differences may make it fairly easy for a candidate and his coterie to succeed at one and impossible to win at another. But even when the auguries are good at each level, it is still possible—to cite the unfortunate Mr. Dewey once more—to bungle the job somewhere.

The two houses of Congress obviously present similar arenas that differ markedly from Presidential electoral arenas. (Perhaps it is not so obvious; more than one gifted senator has failed to recognize it.) The legislative leader learns the mood and rhythm of his house, the kinds of combinations that can be put together on various categories of issues, and the timing necessary to the success of good strategies. It is well established that men who move from state to national legislature, or from House to Senate in Congress, usually are well prepared and content in their new assignments, while former governors often are not.[1] The move from legislator to chief executive surely must entail similar readjustment and socialization, though it probably helps that the incumbent wanted to make the change and probably considers it an advancement.

The question of feasibility in politics also turns upon the goals under consideration. The election of a man to an office is one thing; a change in the drift of national policy clearly is quite another. One is relatively simple, the other enormously complex, requiring skills and good judgment in many arenas. Again, there is the question whether what is wanted is an immediate victory—say, the passage of a bill—or a major change over time. Political education is part of the legislative process, and a succession of defeats may be necessary to prepare the way for an ultimate victory that in retrospect seems inevitable. President Johnson's choice of Independence, Missouri, as the place to sign the Medicare Act, in the presence of Mr. Truman, was acknowledgment that his predecessor had taken the first step toward Medicare when he fought a losing battle for a more sweeping measure almost twenty years earlier. Again, a plan of action which no practical politician would touch might change the climate in which an issue is joined, making feasible what hitherto would have been deemed impossible. The sit-downs in segregated places staged by well-mannered young Negro students a few years ago are a case in point. Much that came later flowed from these simple expressions of courage and dignity, the political feasibility of which at the time could not have been calculated because they were without precedent and because so much depended on the way they were carried out.

A decentralized political system like our own multiplies the actors whose judgments of feasibility significantly affect a policy decision. It would be too much to expect the President and a member of Congress of his party to strike the same balance on an issue affecting their political futures quite differently. A requisite of responsible party government, after all, is to put leaders and rank-and-file as nearly as possible in the same boat. The calculations of the political price to be paid for a course of action, a basic element in a judgment of political feasibility, likewise would vary widely. Two senators otherwise similarly situated, for example, might compute cost quite differently if one aspired to the White House and the other did not.

The purpose of this study is to state some of the conditions of political feasibility which seem to be operative in the making of national policy through the executive and legislative branches and the groups associated with them. The courts, active partners though they are, will not be included because they are somewhat isolated, their reaction is delayed, and the behavior appropriate to them is quite different, and because we shall have trouble enough without them. Moreover, it is policy-making in the here and now that we shall be talking about, not the slow evolution of major change.

I. THE PROBLEM

There are Americans who believe that almost any social problem that can be solved with money is within the competence of the U.S. government if only the attack on the problem is sufficiently massive. Indeed, there are many who seem to believe that *all* social problems could be tackled at once with adequate scope, if only the country would withdraw from Vietnam. Even a casual attention to what went on in congressional committees early in 1966 will bear this out. Again and again members decried attempts to hold down expenditures on this or that problem with the simple contention: But more is needed! And so it was. But the first point to be made is this: that for all its affluence, the American system cannot deal adequately with its acknowledged needs; that this is a system in which an allocation of scarce resources must indeed be made, with all the pain that inevitably entails.

No attempt will be made to catalogue the needs. Anyone can make a list in a few minutes which would overtax resources for years to come. Some samples will suffice. Water-pollution control, which has barely begun, could use $100 billion without wasting a cent. Hospital modernization, to replace 260,000 obsolete beds (and the 13,000 annual increment) would take at least $8 billion. Building 375,000 classrooms in the next five years would cost $15 billion. Building really modern urban transportation, re-creating core cities, breaking the poverty cycle of families by using all the health, education, and welfare resources in a coordinated way—each of these would cost immense sums. Put more accurately, each would call for trained manpower and other resources, which already are in short supply, far beyond any present capacity to meet the demand.

This catalogue of needs, some of them almost catastrophic in proportion, is all the more remarkable in the light of the efforts that have been made. The budget of the Public Health Service, for example, increased in twelve years from $250 million to $2.4 billion in fiscal 1967. The Office of Education spent only $539 million in 1961; in fiscal 1967 its budget was about $3.5 billion. Three sessions of Congress (1963–65) enacted twenty pieces of landmark legislation in health, nineteen in welfare.

The requirement that resources be allocated among needs that cannot be met poses the problem of priorities. Which is more important to society, intensive care for high-risk infants (40 percent of children who die in their first year die in their first day) or artificial kidneys to keep productive adults alive (there are facilities now for continuous treatment of 200 to 300 patients of a possible 10,000 who might be saved)? Head-start programs for disadvantaged preschoolers or basic education for disadvantaged adults? The problem is even harder when the claims of cancer research, say, are compared with the desirability of getting to the moon.

This is an academic discussion of little interest until one is forced by experience to realize that decisions on questions like these actually *do* have to be made and actually *are* being made. What happens to various segments of the population next year depends on these decisions. But what really is appalling is to know upon what flimsy data and partial information these choices often are made. It is perfectly possible, for instance, that it may be decided to increase the funds for adult basic education by a certain amount without the slightest notion of how many people have been taught to read, say, under the existing program. This is not said in criticism of anybody; the men who set the priorities feel their burdens heavily and they get the best help they can. The policy system simply is not geared to let them do better.

What considerations enter into the selection of priorities and the specific program designed to meet them? One, inevitably, is "political feasibility." Will it "go" on the Hill? Will the public buy it? Does it have political "sex appeal"? What "can't be done" is likely to get low priority. An administration bill must be passed if possible, and the men who bear the responsibility for that shrink from taking on one that may discredit them. Political columns like to run a Presidential "box score," and there is no place on it for the bill no one expected to pass, the bill that was introduced as part of the educational process necessary to enact the legislation later on. The "box score" mentality is likely to permeate the discussions of men charged with preparing the President's program. What determines political feasibility therefore is a matter of urgent concern.

Political feasibility as a consideration in national policy-making is, so far as I know, a term of art. It is a seat-of-the-pants judgment, based on the experience of the person making it. It may be shrewd indeed, or appear so, if the men pooling their experience are shrewd and artful men. It may be simply a repetition of some long-accepted and untested cliché about what public or politicians will do. For nearly two decades, for instance, many members of Congress have said in private conversations, "I favor recognizing Red China (or admitting her to the UN), but I wouldn't dare say it. It would be political suicide." How did they know? Again, it may be based on what representatives of interest groups have said, probably in all honesty, but from a remoteness from the currents that run in the country which only a man who spends twenty years in Washington can have. Political feasibility as a target will not track. Any consideration of it that gets anywhere must start from some assumptions and limit the task that is undertaken.

Let us begin therefore by assuming that it is possible to confront the policy system with a set of proposals that actually do maximize the benefits the American people can get from the expenditure of a given amount of appropriations that is, an ideal allocation of scarce resources. As a matter of fact, a process designed to do just that already has been set in motion, a major innovation in the executive branch called Planning-Programming-Budgeting System (PPBS).[2] This system sets out to bring to the conference table where decisions are made an analysis based on the program goals of the government, and the relative success of various programs in achieving them, which will give the decision-makers the materials they need.

PPBS in the federal government originated in the Pentagon, where Secretary McNamara abandoned the old practice of considering a budget for each military service, with the traditional outlays for personnel, operations, equipment, and the like, in favor of a budget based on nine major defense missions. The weapons that could be assigned to each mission were listed without regard to the service that nominally claimed them. All costs of developing, procuring, and operating a weapon were assigned to it and the measure of defense provided by each system was determined. With this kind of information, choices among weapons and systems in terms of their costs and relative effectiveness could be made.

Because the goals of the Defense Department are relatively simple and consistent—deterrence of war, defense of the country, victory in war—PPBS encounters fewer problems there than in departments with many, perhaps conflicting, goals. Nevertheless, in the summer of 1965 President Johnson ordered more than eighty agencies comprising the executive branch to set up staffs capable of establishing the new system. Each agency is to set up broad program goals, with more specific subcategories. All operating programs with similar goals are to be placed in the appropriate category, regardless of the organizational units to which they are attached. If a program goal is stated as "Breaking the Poverty Cycle," for instance, it might require a grouping of programs in education, health, welfare, vocational rehabilitation, poverty, and perhaps others.

The costs of various programs could be established then and measured against specific benefits. The budget would be stated, not in terms of "inputs"—items for personnel, research, planning, etc.—but in the amount of reduction in delinquency, improvement in health or education, and so forth. Thus it would be possible to estimate which programs did more to achieve the goal per dollar expended.

PPBS aims ultimately to do more than help determine which programs contribute most to the same goal. The system would aim in time at measuring one goal against another, so that priorities could be set on the basis of knowledge of comparative benefits.

I have not attempted to explain PPBS in any detail, but rather to set forth its basic assumptions and suggest how it will work. I wish to accept the most extreme claims that could be made for it—to assume that it could produce clear proof that one goal is socially preferable to another, and one way to reach it better than another; that a budget can be drawn which demonstrably gets the most benefits for the resources expended—as a basis for examining some of the structural arrangements in the political system which would have to be taken into account in putting its findings into effect. Of course, it is not necessary for PPBS to achieve anything like these extreme claims to be a highly useful tool of analysis, capable of introducing more rationality in decision-making. Neither is it necessary to postulate a successful PPBS to pose the problem: if pure social intelligence confronted the system with a program, could the system accept it and put it into effect? In a word, would the program be politically feasible?

II. THE EXECUTIVE BRANCH

The classic solution to decentralized national power is more power concentrated in the President. He is the one official elected by the people. He is the one person charged with, and capable of, thinking about the national interest. It would seem therefore that the social intelligence made available by a perfected PPBS would inevitably strengthen his hand. Perhaps it would. Nevertheless, a few more studies that concentrated on the President himself as a political man, trying to survive and have his way (like Neustadt's *Presidential Power*),[3] studies whose authors are not hypnotized by the many hats he wears, might suggest some difficulties the President will have if and when he is confronted by the national program he (or his predecessor) has caused to be made. I have not made such a study and probably never will, but perhaps I can suggest a couple of places a student might look for the answers such a study would provide.

One is the peculiarly vulnerable political position of the President. He is the one American politician who cannot hide. He must be prepared at all times for whatever ill wind may blow. Moreover, his power depends to some extent at least on never surrendering the initiative for very long—or so it must seem to him. When a competitor threatens to propose something good, the temptation is strong for the President to occupy the field first, or to deluge it with something Presidential in scope if he cannot.[4] If there is a carefully constructed legislative proposal at hand, so much the better. If there is not, something may very well be proposed anyway. If he finds himself in congenial company, he, like other men, may suggest what the country needs. Once it has been said, however casually, the machinery works inexorably. Furthermore, the bill that goes up must be passed if possible. Failure catches on much more quickly than success. (Exceptions might occur in election years, when a proposal that cannot pass might make a good campaign issue.) Finally, it is reasonable to doubt whether a President can be the good shepherd of a program someone else has made, even though it be made by his own people and the very best computers. The drama of leadership, of his awful isolation, of his lonely decisions, is the great weapon in his armory.

The second area worth the student's investigation would be the network of executive staff which can truly be called Presidential. This might be stretched to include the Presidential appointees in the agencies, whose loyalty to him usually is dependable, though their lack of intimate knowledge of much of his business reduces their direct usefulness to him almost to the vanishing point. It certainly would not include the bureaucracy, the source of information both branches perforce rely upon, but which in its multitudinous bureaus, divisions, and offices is no more certainly allied to him than to congressional committees or interest groups—or to nobody. Those that remain—the tiny White House staff and the Bureau of the Budget (an effective staff arm whose political judgment often is affected, alas, by its preoccupation with the budget)—are not really a match for the bureaucracy. They are in the sense that they speak for the President and so may have the last word. They are not in the sense of information and expertise. In having the last word, which they must if the President is to have his way, they often overrule the work of months with judgments made in haste and under pressure. Like Congress, they can deal really effectively with the bureaucracy's expertise only by constructing a bureaucracy of their own. If to the weight of experience and expertise which they now bring to the table the bureaucracy could add the authority of PPBS, what then would the President's people do? It must be remembered, after all, that each agency has its own PPBS. Obviously, it is crucial that the ultimate formulations of PPBS would have to be brought under the President's control, with all the very human intrusions on computerized rationality that implies.

The heart of the matter probably is that no intellectual system—and certainly not PPBS—is designed to produce a single right policy, but rather to present policy alternatives, with analyses of the costs and benefits of each. The President would have the advice of his agency heads based on their choices. In all likelihood he would also have his own staff of professional program specialists who would work with agency counterparts and assist him with his own decisions, as members of the Bureau of the Budget staff do now in their own fields. If their advice sometimes reflected their own policy biases, they would be no more guilty of human frailty than are the agency planners. In a word, there are no insurmountable difficulties in the way of getting to the President the kind of advice PPBS can give; the problem would be to get for PPBS the kind of political respectability and acceptance that would cause the President to heed it against the other influences that bear upon him.

The character of the bureaucracy presents problems for unified policy, some of which appear, at least, to be insoluble. First there is the inescapable question of the basis upon which an agency should be organized. By function—health, education, welfare—which augments professionalization and promises a high quality of service? By clientele—labor, farmers, commerce—which has a kind of built-in coherence? By ecological unit—the core city, the river basin for water-pollution control—which encompasses a broad array of related problems? By problem—poverty, crime—which calls for the application and coordination of many services? Each has its justification and all are actually used, of course. No single organizational structure will do for all, nor is it judicious to try to apply logical consistency to their division of labor. If all education were to be placed in the Office of Education, for instance, more than fifty agencies would have to surrender programs to it. The Office of Education would have to administer the three military service academies, the Department of State's foreign service school, Agriculture's graduate school, and the in-service training programs of all the agencies of the federal government—to name only a few. It is safe to say that if any large department tried to claim all the programs that might logically be assigned to it, the federal executive branch would grind to a stop.

Needless to say, overlapping and duplication of effort are inevitable, inspiring the continuous demand for "coordination." But coordination is more easily subscribed to than accomplished. Agencies perforce are parochial; they think in terms of their own statutory authority, operating structure, and clientele. Even plans they make for coordination tend to have agency perimeters. One proposal that has won a high degree of acceptance from all the relevant agencies, to give an example, is the so-called "multi-purpose" (or "one-stop") neighborhood center, containing under one roof all the services that a family is likely to need. But when agencies submit concrete plans, they usually are *single-agency* "multipurpose" centers.

The problem of parochialism is exaggerated by the occupational immobility of the civil service. It is not uncommon for careers to be spent wholly in one department, perhaps in a single bureau. Transfers within the bureaucracy threaten status and a way of life; when they take employees outside the civil service, even to Capitol Hill, they disturb and may temporarily destroy retirement rights, to mention only one of a host of disabilities. But clearly, if the flexibility and innovation implicit in PPBS are to be exploited, it must be possible to reduce, perhaps eliminate, some organizational entities. This is incredibly difficult where employees have a justifiable vested interest in their jobs, which they are quick to protect. When a thirty-year man in the bureauracy takes his grievance to Congress (where occupational immobility is perhaps the supreme value), he is sure of a sympathetic hearing from members he has worked with for years. There is much talk about occupational mobility among officials in the bureaucracy, but little more than talk. What is needed, if PPBS or something like it is to succeed, is a genuine career line in the civil service (not in a particular agency) with easy transferability from one agency to another. More than that, genuine mobility requires an easy flow into and out of private employment, with vested rights in retirement and all the other elements of job security. This would seem to be relatively simple with professionals, whose central loyalty tends to be to their own disciplines, but probably very difficult to achieve with nonprofessionals, whose loyalties and habits are agency-oriented.

To the political people who man the President's program, the relationship of civil servants to Congress is perennially troubling. At one extreme, bureaucrats may resist *all* political considerations, rejecting job applications tainted with congressional recommendations, ignoring legislative intent in administering the laws, and refusing to consider the effect of political reactions on the success of their own legislative and appropriation bills. On the other hand, bureaucrats who know full well the transience of their political superiors may build up mutually advantageous relationships with relevant committees which defy the wishes and will of the President himself. In between are the political "volunteers" who gratuitously help with the legislative process, threatening delicate relationships with sadly misplaced self-confidence. Needless to say, each in his way will obstruct or dilute any coherent Presidential program.

III. THE LEGISLATIVE BRANCH

When a programmatic approach to national policy is mentioned, any student of American government with adequate reflexes is bound to say "Congress." The inability of Congress to consider, at any stage of the legislative process, the whole sweep of a program sponsored by the President is notorious, and a fair number of political scientists have made a respectable living emphasizing it.[5] The outlines hardly need repeating. The party leadership is weak. The committee chairmen, selected by seniority, are strong. The result is a kind of confederation of little legislatures, some of them fragmented even further into subcommittees with specialized jurisdictions which have managed to become small feudalities in their own right. This is the system that baffles the champions of responsible party government, and it is this system that has kept Congress strong. One by one, other national legislatures subservient to party leadership (for which read "executive") have been turned into passive partisans whose hope of sharing power depends upon their climbing into the executive themselves. Not so Congress. Committee chairmen often care about the President's wishes, even when he belongs to the other party. They usually take an administration bill seriously—even if only as a point of departure, which it often is when the President's party is in a minority on the committee. But they cannot be forced by party leadership in either branch. Indeed, when administration spokesmen go as a matter of courtesy to discuss their programs with congressional party leaders, the latter are polite but not much interested. They know that their work begins after the committee has reported a bill.

The organization of Congress around specialized concerns shapes the entire system that makes legislation. It is fashionable to speak of a "legislative system," which includes Congress, the interest groups that serve and influence it, the executive agencies that must deal with it, the press that writes about it, and the constituencies that reward and punish and occasionally know what is going on. It is more accurate, I think, to begin with the committees and speak of the *policy system,* which is focused about each pair of committees that shares similar, if not identical, jurisdiction. There are interest groups that have commitments ranging across a broad sweep of the legislative spectrum, and there are executive departments with similarly large responsibilities. Just the same, none is likely to deal regularly with more than four or five committees in either house, and then there probably is specialization on their legislative staffs. Large newspapers are likely also to develop subject-matter experts on their staffs. More common than the giants by far are the groups with a single interest (albeit a broad one, like higher education), and the executive agency with one or a handful of bills, all of whose business is done with a single committee in each house. The term "constituency" likewise begins to make sense when it signifies numerous specialized interests that are likely to get involved only when those interests are touched. The concept of the mass constituency is hardly more useful analytically than the notion of a mass public.

Two points perhaps should be stressed. The first is the relative isolation that develops around each of these policy systems. They are like planes that cut each other only at points of decision-making, such as the roll-call vote on the floor. One reason for the unresponsiveness of Congress to Presidential pleas for economy in 1966 (in the early days of the session, at least) undoubtedly was the submersion of each committee and its associates in their own work, which they knew to be vitally important. The President was right, of course, but he certainly must have been talking about somebody else. Only after heroic efforts on the President's part did the message begin to sink in that he was talking about, and to, everybody. The sense of isolation is less stark in the Senate, where each member belongs to more than one committee and several subcommittees. But the result ultimately is the same, or worse. The burden of many assignments requires the members to rely heavily on committee staff. Needless to say, these persons are experts if they can be, their fierce specialization unrelieved by the varied life of chamber and constituency which tends to liberate the minds of their principals.

The second point to be emphasized is the very large measure of control over the business in their charge by each of these policy systems. This too may be demonstrated many times over in the second session of the 89th Congress. After unprecedented success with a huge legislative program the year before, President Johnson decided, because of the Vietnam war and threats of inflation, to make only modest increases in most programs and actual cuts in some. One of the latter was aid to school districts that bore the impact of federal installations, in which he proposed a sharp reduction on the ground that the large sums available under new federal education programs justified it. Roughly 315 congressional districts were affected. The two education committees agreed with the powerful impacted-area lobby that it was not worth discussing—and they did not discuss it. The Secretary of Health, Education, and Welfare was not asked a single question about it in either house. In their own good time the committees increased the authorization.

An incident equally revealing concerned the President's proposal to convert the direct loans to students under the National Defense Education Act to private loans guaranteed by the government. The education subcommittee in the House believed the colleges needed to know what they could count on for the next year, whereupon by a simple unanimous vote in executive session they eliminated that title from the bill. It is significant that the colleges could not know what they could count on then unless they had complete confidence the subcommittee action would stand. The subcommittee never doubted they would have that confidence, and they did.

IV. COMMENTS ON POLITICAL FEASIBILITY

If the foregoing sketch of the policy systems that pool their respective programs to make the national policy is reasonably correct, it should be possible now to make some suggestions about political feasibility at the national level.

What is least feasible is what requires serious, responsible consideration of some unitary conception of national need. Congress does not manage it, does not try to do so, and with its present power structure is virtually incapable of trying. With the President the case is not so clear. He does indeed present his "program" in the early months of the year, in successive unveilings marked by messages to Congress. Viewed uncharitably, they represent an agglomeration of most of the programs the policy systems would have insisted on anyway. Nevertheless, they bear his imprint. The President—in the institutional sense at lease and, in what matters most, personally—has considered them all and supplied emphasis. Moreover, his notions of relative weights are expressed in his budget, the only genuinely unitary policy instrument in national life. Congress, it may be said in passing, cannot even pretend to look at national policy whole until it develops an institutional capacity to cope with the concept of a budget. Needless to say, once the budget is delivered to Congress and dismembered among its subcommittees, the President too virtually abandons the unitary view and plays the congressional game; he fights for his bills.

Low feasibility also must be attached to whatever is genuinely new or innovative, especially if it can be successfully labeled as such, and more especially if it rubs an ideological nerve. What is most feasible is what is purely incremental, or can be made to appear so. Paradoxically, it is politically attractive to tout a proposal as "new" so long as it is generally recognized that it is not new at all, but a variation on a familiar theme. But the political art can make feasible what is not feasible by finding halfway houses (what the lawyers might call "quasis") which supply at least part of what is needed under the guise of doing something else. Halfway houses may become so numerous and large they occupy the field; nevertheless, a simple declaration that this is so may cause bitter controversy.

Examples are legion. President Hoover's misfortunes demonstrated for those who could learn that the President must accept, or have thrust upon him, responsibility for the health of the economy. President Roosevelt demonstrated that he had learned the lesson well; his twelve years in the White House were studded with attempts to mend the health and even the structure of the economy. Just the same, a watered-down policy statement of national responsibility for employment had real trouble in Congress as late as 1946. Again, the federal government had been the most important influence in the housing market long before a bill plainly marked "housing" could pass finally in 1949. In education, the three furies— federal interference, racial strife, church and state—never sleep, but they doze; they can be stepped around. Veterans can be helped, federally impacted areas aided, education for national defense fostered, disadvantaged children succored. All this so long as the dread concepts are not invoked by name.

The halfway-house approach comes at a high price, it must be admitted. It cannot face a whole problem frankly and try to do what needs to be done, and usually it cannot deal equitably among respective claimants for federal benefits. Moreover, what is accomplished this way becomes imbedded in law. Beneficiaries may support broader, better laws when the climate is propitious, but they will not let go what they have. The legislative halfway house tends to be as permanent as a temporary government building.

It follows that what is most feasible is what is incremental, what can be made to seem a comfortable next step under a program that has already received the good-conduct medal. Nothing is better than an amendment. A once hated housing law becomes an annual invitation to try to get something else under a respected umbrella, where it may take shelter forevermore. A higher education bill that was killed in conference in 1962 by a telegram and passed with great exertion in 1963 was renewed and extended by the House of Representatives in 1966 under suspension of the rules, without a recorded vote. No one fears the familiar; nothing succeeds like success: in politics the bromides are the best guides.

All of this is not meant to say that the approach to policy represented by PPBS is doomed to futility. Far from it. Even if it is only modestly successful in the kind of analysis it will attempt, its weight in the policy process should not be discounted. Who would deny that the unitary approach represented by the budget has had a real, if incalculable, influence on the conduct of the national government? It is without doubt the most formidable policy tool the President has. So could it be with systematic program planning: a President who can support his values with the authority of science will be a formidable competitor indeed. Rationality is respected, sometimes irrationally, in a democratic society.

The history of the national budget may provide an answer to our original question: if social intelligence could confront the policy system with a program that would maximize the benefits to be received from the exertions of the federal government, could that program ever be made politically feasible? The budget experience suggests it could. The budget was adopted because it had to be; the fiscal system could no longer afford the luxury of irresponsibility. The decentralized policy structure with its many policy systems which has evolved here under our constitutional separation of institutions has many virtues: diversity of skills, creativeness within appointed bounds, easy public access to a multiplicity of decision points, openness in the conduct of public business, hospitality to ideas, continuous political education for those who pay attention, and the enormous stimulation that comes with the opportunity to fashion great careers. Nevertheless, the sheer weight of items on the national agenda will require that choices be made, which in turn could force changes in process and structure to make possible a more coherent approach to the needs of the system.

NOTES

[1] See Donald R. Matthews, *U.S. Senators and Their World* (Chapel Hill: University of North Carolina Press, 1960), pp. 103–9.

[2] See David Novick (ed.), *Program Budgeting . . . Program Analysis and the Federal Budget* (Washington: U.S. Government Printing Office, 1964); *Budgeting for National Objectives* (New York: Committee for Economic Development, 1966); "Planning-Programming-Budgeting System: A Symposium," *Public Administration Review,* 26 (December, 1966), 243–310.

[3] Richard E. Neustadt, *Presidential Power* (New York: John Wiley & Sons, 1960).

[4] An example of the President's need to maintain (or regain) the initiative, especially in an election year, was Mr. Johnson's widely previewed speech in Baltimore on October 10, 1966, asking for changes in the social security system which included a 10 percent benefit increase *in the next session of Congress.* The regular procedures of legislative program-building were bypassed. The Republicans promptly responded by demanding that the changes be made in the 89th Congress, which had less than two weeks of life left to it.

[5] Twenty years after the enactment of the Legislative Reorganization Act of 1946, a joint Committee on the Organization of Congress (one of whose cochairmen was Senator Mike Monroney, who as a member of the House of Representatives had co-authored the 1946 act) tackled anew the problem of congressional reform. Eleven monographs written by political scientists were published by the American Enterprise Institute for Public Policy Research to assist the joint committee. They were later published by American Enterprise under the editorship of Alfred de Grazia as *Congress: The First Branch of Government* (Washington, 1966). Another political science treatise, titled much the same as other books appearing over the two decades, was Roger H. Davidson, David M. Kovenock, and Michael K. O'Leary, *Congress in Crisis: Politics and Congressional Reform* (Belmont, Calif.: Wadsworth, 1966).

CHAPTER 21

Reapportionment and Urban Representation In Legislative Influence Positions: The Case of Georgia

Brett Hawkins
Cheryl Whelchel

Because of its county unit, "rule of the rustics," past,[1] Georgia is one state in which reapportionment might be expected to have a real impact. Georgia's court ordered reapportionment was hailed by its supporters as the beginning of the end of rural domination of the General Assembly. They argued that rapid urbanization and reapportionment would combine to produce an urban-run Legislature and, eventually, more urban-directed policies. Others suggested, however, that reapportionment would not change the operation and decisions of the Georgia Legislature because (1) urban legislators are too diverse a group to act as a bloc, (2) no distinct urban-rural split ever existed in the Legislature, and (3) more experienced rural legislators, representing less socially diverse and politically competitive districts would continue to dominate in positions of influence. Thus one rural Senator told a University of Georgia interviewer, in substance if not in words, that it takes ten years just to find out where to go to the toilet around the General Assembly.

This paper focuses on post-reapportionment changes in influence positions in the General Assembly of Georgia. It also examines the effect on urban position holding of the passage of time after reapportionment. While political scientists and others have made many assumptions about these changes, there are few if any systematic, empirical studies that attempt to specify their nature and direction. This study attempts to do so. It is designed to help answer these and other questions about the effect of reapportionment—questions that seem newly troublesome in the light of recent research.[2]

"Reapportionment and Urban Representation in Legislative Influence Positions: The Case of Georgia" by Brett W. Hawkins and Cheryl Whelchel is reprinted from *Urban Affairs Quarterly*, Volume III, No. 3 (March, 1968), pp. 69–80, by permission of the Publisher, Sage Publications, Inc. and the authors.

METHODS

The statistics analyzed here are indices of proportionate urban and metro-politan representation in each chamber of the Georgia Legislature, and especially in the following influence positions:

1. key committee[3] memberships;
2. key committee chairmanships and vice-chairmanships;
3. major legislative leaders (Speaker of the House, Speaker Pro Tempore of the House, Administration Floor Leader of the House, President Pro Tempore of the Senate, and Administration Floor Leader of the Senate).[4]

Indices are compared on a before-after reapportionment basis.

The above positions are considered to have potential for the exercise of disproportionate influence. The present analysis therefore focuses on the potential for influence inherent in key committee and leadership positions, and not on the direct exercise of influence. Such a positional study, however, provides a basis for inferences about the exercise of influence.

Category three is especially important in a positional study of the Georgia Legislature because in Georgia committee members and officers are picked by the presiding officers of each house.[5] Nevertheless, key committee chairmen are powers in their own right; and some committees remain more influential on the legislative end-product than others.

The indices used here are similar to those used by Matthews in his study of the United States Senate.[6] They are measures of proportionate position-holding, or the degree to which urban representation is higher or lower than one would expect from the operation of chance. For instance, if all Georgia legislators were selected by chance, and without regard to their residence, urban representation could be expected to be the same as the urban composition of the universe from which they were selected; that is, the population of the state. And if influence positions within the legislature were selected by chance, urban representation in such positions could be expected to be the same as the urban composition of the universe from which they were chosen; here the total membership in each house.

Population indices, as used in this study, are based on the percent of Georgia's population that is urban, according to the 1960 census:

membership population index

$$\frac{\text{percent of house membership that is urban}}{\text{percent urban population of the state}}$$

position population index

percent influence positions held by urban legislators

percent urban population of the state

The *legislative index,* in contrast, refers to index numbers based on the percent of each house's membership that is urban:

percent influence positions held by urban legislators

percent urban members in house

The authors began with the expectation that urban position holding after reapportionment would lag behind somewhat because of the lack of seniority of the new urban members. A disproportionate number of the veterans could be expected to be rural in the immediate post-reapportionment sessions. Such a lag would be reflected in the legislative index. However, our investigations showed that this is less a problem than expected. In fact it is no problem at all in the Senate because (1) before reapportionment a rotational system (by county) operated within the 52 three county districts, causing virtually 100 percent turnover after each session and (2) in the first session after reapportionment only four veterans returned, two urban and two rural. Since the first session Senate turnover has declined; but it has been greater for rural legislators than urban.

In the House one is justified in expecting some lag because after reapportionment almost 2/3 of the members were veterans, and 2/3 of those were rural. In the second post-reapportionment House session, however, about 3/4 were veterans and exactly 1/2 of those were urban. Thus House legislative index numbers made up of averages of the two post-reapportionment sessions reflect a declining problem of lag. In addition, legislative indices that drop from *above* 1.0 (more than proportionate representation) to below it are important in their own right. An index number of 1.0 indicates perfectly proportionate representation.

The adjective "urban" as used here refers to those legislators representing districts in which more than 50 percent of the people live in urban places. "Metropolitan" is treated as a subcategory of "urban" and describes legislators from districts in which 75 percent of the people live in urban places.[7]

House of Representatives

The Georgia House was reapportioned in 1965. Indices describing urban and metropolitan representation before reapportionment are averages from the 1961–62, 1963–64, and 1965 sessions. Indices describing representa-

Table 1
Legislative Indices, Population Indices, and Seats: Georgia House of Representatives Before and After Reapportionment

	RURAL			URBAN			METROPOLITAN		
State's Population in % (1960)	44.71			55.29			39.49		
1A	Leg. Index	Pop. Index	Seats %	Leg. Index	Pop. Index	Seats %	Leg. Index	Pop. Index	Seats %
ALL HOUSE MEMBERS									
Before reapportionment	—	1.68	154 (75.12%)	—	.45	51 (24.88%)	—	.28	23 (11.22%)
After reapportionment	—	1.16	106 (51.71%)	—	.87	99 (48.29%)	—	.87	70 (34.15%)
1B	Leg. Index	Pop. Index		Leg. Index	Pop. Index		Leg. Index	Pop. Index	
ALL INFLUENCE POSITION INDICES COMBINED									
Before reapportionment	.86	1.44		1.44	.64		1.17	.33	
After reapportionment	1.21	1.07		.78	.68		.72	.76	
Net Change	+.35	−.37		−.66	+.4		−.45	.62	

Table 1 (continued)

	RURAL			URBAN			METROPOLITAN		
1C	Leg. Index	Pop. Index	Seats %	Leg. Index	Pop. Index	Seats %	Leg. Index	Pop. Index	Seats %
			KEY COMMITTEE MEMBERS						
Before reapportionment	.97	1.63	566 (72.75%)	1.10	.49	212 (27.25%)	1.03	.29	90 (11.57%)
After reapportionment	1.06	1.22	311 (54.56%)	.94	.82	259 (45.44%)	.85	.74	166 (29.12%)
1D	Leg. Index	Pop. Index	Seats %	Leg. Index	Pop. Index	Seats %	Leg. Index	Pop. Index	Seats %
			KEY COMMITTEE CHAIRMEN AND VICE-CHAIRMEN						
Before reapportionment	.86	1.44	31 (64.58%)	1.42	.64	17 (35.42%)	1.49	.42	8 (16.67%)
After reapportionment	.97	1.12	16 (50.00%)	1.04	.90	16 (50.00%)	.82	.71	9 (28.13%)
1E	Leg. Index	Pop. Index	Seats %	Leg. Index	Pop. Index	Seats %	Leg. Index	Pop. Index	Seats %
			HOUSE LEADERS						
Before reapportionment	.74	1.24	5 (55.56%)	1.79	.80	4 (44.44%)	.99	.28	1 (11.11%)
After reapportionment	1.61	1.86	5 (83.33%)	.35	.31	1 (16.67%)	.49	.42	1 (16.67%)

tion after reapportionment are averages from the 1966 and 1967–68 sessions.

The most obvious effect of reapportionment was to boost total urban membership from 24.88 percent of the seats to 48.29 percent. The urban membership population index almost doubled and the same index for metropolitan legislators more than tripled. Interestingly, however, urban membership gains along an absolute scale, and in terms of the state's population, were accompanied by drops in proportionate position-holding. In relation to their numbers in the House, urban legislators before reapportionment enjoyed disproportionate representation in influence positions, with a legislative index of 1.44 for all positions taken together. Metropolitan representatives were similarly overrepresented, with a legislative index of 1.17. With reapportionment, however, both urban and metropolitan legislative indices dropped from well above 1.0 to well below 1.0. See Table 1B. On the other hand rural legislative indices (Tables 1B, C, D, and E) all rose after reapportionment. In proportion to their numbers in the Legislature, therefore, there were fewer urban-metropolitan held positions after than before reapportionment. And almost all legislative indices dropped from above to below the 1.0 mark.

Positional gains were evident in terms of the composition of the state's population, however, but all position population indices remain well below the 1.0 level.

Turning to specific House positions, urban representatives have managed to acquire 50 percent of the key committee chairmanships and vice-chairmanships—as compared with 35.42 percent before. Accompanying this absolute gain, however, was a large drop in the legislative index. See Table 1D. For metropolitan representatives the 67 point drop represents a fall to an index of .82.[8]

In House leadership positions (category 3), substantial changes have accompanied reapportionment, although the numbers involved are necessarily small. The urban legislative and position population indices both dropped after reapportionment—the former by 144 points. At the same time the rural legislative index increased by 87 points. (The Speaker of the House was drawn from rural districts in all sessions studied here: there was no change.)

Senate

Urban Senators, when compared with urban Representatives, are in no better circumstances despite an additional post-reapportionment session. (See Table 2 on pp. 420–21.) The Senate was reapportioned in 1962. Indices representing the situation before reapportionment are averages from the 1959–60 and 1961–62 sessions. Indices representing the situation after reapportionment are averages from the 1963–64, 1965–66, and 1967–68 sessions. Urban Senators held 25.93 percent of all Senate seats before reapportionment and 40.74 percent after. Metropolitan membership jumped even more—from 7.41 percent to 37.04 percent. The latter figure represents a membership population index close to equality (.94).

In all Senate influence positions taken together (Table 2B), however, urban representation as measured by the legislative index fell off 45 points. More surprising, in view of the general pattern, is the fact that the urban population index for all influence positions also fell off, by 9 points. Metropolitan Senators enjoyed a 57 point gain in the position population index, but both groups remain greatly underrepresented in relation to the state's population. All rural legislative indices (Tables 2B, C, D, and E) increased after reapportionment.

As for committee chairmen and vice-chairmen, urban-metropolitan Senators have not fared as well as their House counterparts. See Tables 2D and 1D. Every Senate legislative and population index, for both urban and metropolitan Senators, started at a lower point than in the House and was still at a much lower point after reapportionment. All are now around the .50 mark.[9]

Before reapportionment urban Senators were highly successful in obtaining leadership positions (category 3), although small numbers were involved. See Table 2E. The legislative index here was 2.12 and the position population index was 1.36. After reapportionment both indices dropped, the former by 89 points and the latter by 46 points.

SUMMARY AND DISCUSSION

The overall picture of reapportionment and urban position-holding is as follows. Positional gains in absolute terms, and in relation to the state's urban population, are accompanied by losses in relation to urban members in the Legislature. In addition, most of these losses go from above to below the proportionate mark (1.0) on the legislative index. On the same index, however, rural position-holding has increased after reapportionment in both houses.

Also, urban positional gains in relation to the state's population still fall short of equality. And half of the urban legislative indices in the Senate are lower after reapportionment than in the House, despite an additional post-reapportionment session in the former. This shows more tenacious rural position-holding in the Senate.

In short, gains in total urban membership in Georgia's General

Table 2
Legislative Indices, Population Indices, and Seats:
Georgia Senate Before and
After Reapportionment

	RURAL			URBAN			METROPOLITAN		
State's Population in % (1960)	44.71			55.29			39.49		
2A	Leg. Index	Pop. Index	Seats %	Leg. Index	Pop. Index	Seats %	Leg. Index	Pop. Index	Seats %
			ALL SENATE MEMBERS						
Before reapportionment	—	1.66	40 (74.07%)	—	.47	14 (25.93%)	—	.19	4 (7.41%)
After reapportionment	—	1.10	32 (59.26%)	—	.74	22 (40.74%)	—	.94	20 (37.04%)
2B	Leg. Index	Pop. Index		Leg. Index	Pop. Index		Leg. Index	Pop. Index	
			ALL INFLUENCE POSITION INDICES COMBINED						
Before reapportionment	.78	1.30		1.36	.76		.72	.13	
After reapportionment	1.06	1.41		.91	.67		.75	.70	
Net Change	+.28	+.11		−.45	−.09		+.03	+.57	

Table 2 (continued)

	RURAL			URBAN			METROPOLITAN		
2C	Leg. Index	Pop. Index	Seats %	Leg. Index	Pop. Index	Seats %	Leg. Index	Pop. Index	Seats %
			KEY COMMITTEE MEMBERS						
Before reapportionment	.97	1.61	140 (72.16%)	1.07	.50	54 (27.84%)	1.11	.21	16 (8.25%)
After reapportionment	1.05	1.39	230 (62.33%)	.92	.68	139 (37.67%)	.86	.81	118 (31.98%)
2D	Leg. Index	Pop. Index	Seats %	Leg. Index	Pop. Index	Seats %	Leg. Index	Pop. Index	Seats %
			KEY COMMITTEE CHAIRMEN AND VICE-CHAIRMEN						
Before reapportionment	1.04	1.72	20 (76.92%)	.89	.42	6 (23.08%)	1.04	.19	2 (7.69%)
After reapportionment	1.30	1.72	30 (76.92%)	.57	.42	9 (23.08%)	.48	.45	7 (17.95%)
2E	Leg. Index	Pop. Index	Seats %	Leg. Index	Pop. Index	Seats %	Leg. Index	Pop. Index	Seats %
			SENATE LEADERS						
Before reapportionment	.34	.56	1 (25.00%)	2.12	1.36	3 (75.00%)	0	0	0 (0%)
After reapportionment	.84	1.112	3 (50.00%)	1.23	.90	3 (50.00%)	.90	.84	2 (33.33%)

Assembly have not been matched by proportionate gains in influence positions. Quite the contrary, before reapportionment urban legislators had more than proportionate representation in relation to their numbers in the Legislature; after, they had much less than proportionate representation. Such a "before" situation, of course, qualifies a common criticism of legislatures not apportioned on a population basis. Before reapportionment Georgia's urban legislators enjoyed more than proportionate representation (in relation to their numbers) in influence positions.

Reapportionment in Georgia has not yet produced the positional results expected by its champions. On the contrary, influence positions are now more in rural hands in proportion to their numbers, especially in the Senate. This appears to be due in part to the seniority and greater experience of rural legislators compared with urban and metropolitan, at least in the House, and to a rural-oriented presiding officer in the Senate. The Lieutenant Governor in all post-reapportionment sessions but the last (1967) was the same rural, county-unit bred politician. His appointments, plus the alliances and friendships built up over the years, probably continue to have an effect in the Senate.[10] Still another factor is that with reapportionment urban and metropolitan delegations have become larger and more internally diverse in terms of social status, race, and urban-suburban residence. Diversity is especially great where subdistricting has occurred, as in Fulton County (Atlanta). Large, diverse urban delegations are less unified in pressing for key influence positions than small, homogeneous delegations.[11]

Our findings are not due, however, to partisan discrimination against the small number of Republicans, most of whom represent metropolitan districts. Republicans have enjoyed generous key committee assignments after reapportionment.

Of course, Georgia's reapportionment is a recent phenomenon: the situation with respect to influence positions may change with the passage of time. The present analysis, however, offers only conflicting evidence on that score.

On the one hand, a separate analysis of the first two post-reapportionment Senate sessions shows almost uniformly lower legislative indices than when the third session is included. This suggests a progression with the passage of time toward urban position-holding more proportionate to urban membership. On the other hand, after three sessions urban Senators remain no better represented, proportionately, in influence positions than their House counterparts—and they are much worse off in committee offices—despite one more session and the passage of more time. Thus the important question of the impact of time on the proportionate holding of influence positions is not answerable with these data. Our data do suggest, however, that reapportionment's champions may have to wait longer than expected for urban-metropolitan districts to be proportionately represented in key legislative positions.

NOTES

[1] See William G. Cornelius, "The County Unit System of Georgia: Facts and Prospects," *Western Political Quarterly,* XIV (December, 1961), 942–60; Albert B. Saye, "Georgia's County Unit System of Election," *Journal of Politics,* XII (February, 1950), 93–106; and V. O. Key, *Southern Politics in State and Nation* (New York: Knopf, 1951), Chapter 6.

[2] See Thomas R. Dye, *Politics, Economics, and the Public* (Chicago: Rand McNally, 1966).

[3] Agriculture, Appropriations, Banks and Banking, Education, Highways Judiciary, Rules, and Ways and Means. The latter has no equivalent in the Senate and is excluded from the analysis of the upper chamber.

[4] Until the 1967–68 session, the administration floor leader was also the majority leader—making that position even more influential. Majority leaders of the 1967 session are not included in this analysis because no "before" basis for comparison exists.

[5] The Lieutenant Governor, who usually presides over the Senate, is elected by state-wide vote at the same time as the Governor. He further serves as chairman of the Senate Rules Committee but on the basis of his state-wide election is excluded from committee analyses.

[6] Donald R. Matthews, *U.S. Senators and Their World* (New York: Vintage Books, 1960).

[7] The classifications are based on the urban composition of the entire legislative district—not the county of residence of the legislative position-holder. "Urban places" are those which the Bureau of the Census defines as urban—essentially communities with 2,500 inhabitants or more. The districts here designated "metropolitan" are also classified by the U.S. Census as metropolitan. They include the cities of Albany, Atlanta, Augusta, Columbus, Macon, and Savannah. Baldwin County, with an urban population 82.3 per cent, is classified as metropolitan under our criterion but excluded from the Census listing. The district demographic data were collected under the National Municipal League grant mentioned above.

[8] After reapportionment the important Appropriations and Highways committees had urban officers, whereas before they had none. Metropolitan Representatives also gained key positions on the same two committees after reapportionment, and on Rules also, whereas before they served as officers only of Banking and Judiciary. Even so, the Chairman of the Appropriations Committee has been from a rural district in all sessions examined here.

[9] It may also be of interest that in the two sessions before reapportionment, urban Senators held six of 26 possible positions, but on only four committees. Metropolitan Senators held a chairmanship or vice-chairmanship on each of two committees. After reapportionment, urban Senators held nine positions in the three sessions with but one additional committee involved. After reapportionment, metropolitan Senators have held seven positions involving four committees.

[10] This is indicated by a fight in early 1967 between some of his supporters and those of the new Lieutenant Governor (a man with a more urban-oriented reputation), over the power to name committee officers. The former wanted to eliminate that power, but the latter won. The new man's appointments, however, still do not reflect proportionately the Senate's urban-metropolitan composition.

[11] The authors are indebted to Malcolm E. Jewell for suggesting this point.

CHAPTER 22

Selective Service and Military Manpower: Induction and Deferment Policies in the 1960's*

James Davis, Jr.
Kenneth M. Dolbeare

More than twelve million Americans have enlisted or been inducted into the armed forces in the two decades since the end of World War II. The broad outlines of military manpower procurement policy have remained stable throughout this period: articulating with continuing direct recruiting efforts, conducted by the armed forces, is the selective conscription of men not qualifying for one of several deferred classifications, accomplished by a decentralized civilian agency. Within this basic framework, adjustments in policy applications (in response to changing circumstances) have resulted in a wide range of new accessions to the armed forces from year to year. Force levels have ranged from 1,460,000 in early 1950 to nearly 3,700,-000 at the height of the Korean buildup, down to the post-Korean low of 2,476,000 in 1960, and back up to the mid-1967 level of 3,450,000. The rate of accessions has varied similarly, from 200,000 per year in fiscal 1950 to 1,270,000 in fiscal 1951, and from about 500,000 in 1965 to 1,200,000 in 1966. The proportions of new recruits obtained through enlistment and through induction have also varied sharply during this period, with inductions ranging from 15 percent of new accessions in 1961 to over 30 percent in 1966. The effects of conscription are felt not only by those inducted, of course: 340,000 men were inducted in 1966, for example, but of the 800,000 who enlisted, nearly half did so only after passing their preinduction physical examination.[1]

This military manpower procurement policy, including both conscription and varyingly induced enlistment, has clearly met the critical test of delivering substantial but fluctuating numbers of men to the armed forces. But this is only one effect of these policies, and many other dimensions of their impact remain to be explored. We seek to define the consequences of present conscription policies in more comprehensive fashion by asking such

Reprinted from Austin Ranney, ed., *Political Science and Public Policy* (Chicago: Markham, 1968), pp. 83–121, with permission of the authors.

questions as: What happens to whom by virtue of these policies? What social and economic implications do their effects carry? To what extent are the stated goals of these policies actually realized? What would be the consequences of instituting alternative policies?

Our analysis of conscription policies will employ policy[2] as an independent variable, empirically assessing the impact of deferment and induction policies upon various types of registrants. We shall identify the effects of various components of present policy in such a manner as to permit description of the probable consequences of alternative policies for the society, economy, and polity. By taking policy as the focus of our inquiry, rather than as the dependent product of decision-making activity, we hope to indicate some possibilities of a policy-oriented approach to the study of politics. Two broad categories of potential utility seem to inhere in such an approach. First, analysis of the impact and effects of particular public policies may underscore the consequences of determinative features of the policy-forming process; it may shed new light on the reasons for the political behavior of those affected (directly and indirectly) by the policies; and it may suggest some characteristics of the processes of feedback and support. Second, analysis of present policies which identifies those aspects of policy which produce particular effects may permit empirically defensible predictions concerning alternative policies. Under some conditions, such projections may greatly narrow the range of policy-makers' choices and permit professionally responsible recommendations by political scientists. In both cases, some incremental advances in theoretical development are also possible; in the first, because the output of the system has structuring consequences for popular support and for the nature of future inputs; in the second, because hypotheses may be tested and interpretations refined through experimentation under varying conditions. But these are long-range goals, and our present purposes extend only to the analysis of policy impact and the assessing of alternative policies.[3] We begin by examining the substance of present policies and the conditions under which they are applied.

I. PRESENT POLICY: GOALS, SUBSTANCE, IMPLEMENTATION, CONDITIONS

Conscription has been a part of all major American wars. The more recent peacetime draft laws (the Selective Service Act of 1948 and its direct descendants, the Universal Military Service and Training Act of 1951 and the Military Selective Service Act of 1967) follow the precedent of the act of 1940, itself based on the experience of 1917.[4] The intent of all these statutes has been to induct selectively those men who can best be spared from the civilian and defense economies, with the goal of achieving that equity in liability for military service which is consistent with the national health, safety, and interest.[5] To accomplish this end, deferments have existed under the 1948 act, as extended, for fathers, students, hardship cases, reservists, certain occupations, and physically and mentally unacceptable men.[6] The availability of these deferments has led the Selective Service System to see "channeling" as an important secondary goal. Through the use of deferments, as General Hershey has indicated, men are "channeled" into jobs where they are needed:

A complementary function [to inductions] is to insure, by deferment, that vital activities and scarce skills are protected, and that the patterns of civilian life generally are disrupted no more than necessary by exercise of the duty and privilege of military service. . . . I do not believe that we are so rich in human resources that we can afford deliberately to ignore opportunities we have to channel people into training and the application of training. . . . There are enough factors over which we have no control which interfere with the development of the potential of our citizens, and with the best utilization of that potential when it is developed. By deferment we can influence people to train themselves and to use the skills they acquire in work critical to the nation in civilian or military life.[7]

Implementation of the law is in the hands of the almost 4,100 local boards, which operate under the general supervision of 56 state (or comparable) Selective Service headquarters within the United States and its territories.[8] National headquarters issues policy guidelines for application by the local boards, with the reminder that they are "advisory only." More detailed interpretations of these general guidelines are provided (when deemed necessary) by the various state headquarters to the local boards under their respective jurisdictions. The state headquarters are manned by full-time personnel, chiefly National Guard or reserve officers, but the local boards are made up of civilian volunteers drawn from the local communities in which they sit. This unique design, first tried in World War I, is intended to mitigate local resistance such as was encountered in the Civil War. Local advisers and appeal agents and an internal appeals system consisting of ninety-five appeal boards provide the registrant, at least in form, opportunities for review of his local board's actions and compensate to some extent for the statutory insulation of the system from legal challenge in court.

The individual registrant first encounters conscription within five days of his eighteenth birthday, when he is required to register with his local board. From that day forward, for a possible term of seventeen years (if he ever accepts a deferred classification), and regardless of where his school-ing or occupation may take him, he shares control of his life and career with the members of that local board. He will probably be classified and reclassified several times, as his situation changes and as the needs of the nation and the size of the available manpower pools shift over time. Deferment criteria are modified, and applied with varying rigor even if unmodified in formal fashion, as the level of induction needs rises and falls;[9] for any given individual, therefore, military liability rests on a com-plex of relevant factors including personal, societal, and international conditions.

The goal of conscription policy—provision of rapidly fluctuating numbers of men to the armed forces—is to be accomplished in a context of the twin values of efficiency and equity. By "efficiency" we mean defer-ment, if and when necessary, in order to utilize a man's services in a manner that maximizes his potential contribution to the nation's "defense effort." This is the system's rationale for the existence of all but hardship, dependency, and unfitness deferments. The *Annual Report of the Director* (1966) declares, for example, "It must be continually emphasized that the Selective Service System is no longer just a draft. . . . Its reason for being is to see that men are assigned to the military or retained in the civilian area so that the right man may be in the right place at the right time."[10] By "equity" we understand equalization of burdens. Obviously there may be tension between the two values, for burdens cannot be equalized if some men are deferred to employ their civilian skills while others are inducted. When mobilization is nearly complete, however, as it was in World War II, tensions are low. Full equity was not achieved, because service was not universal; men were deferred in the name of efficiency to work in ship-yards, munition factories, mines, farms, and other places thought essential to the war effort and the civilian economy. But the conflict between efficiency and equity then was tolerable because most eligible men *did* go into the army, and those who did not were in apparently necessary jobs. In the Korean period, the armed forces required a high proportion of the relatively small available manpower pool, and military liability extended to nearly all strata of the society, once again reducing the inevitable tensions.

But conditions of manpower availability in the 1960's have radically altered the situation and given rise to sharp conflict between the two values. Only a fraction of the available manpower is currently needed by the armed forces—even with the Vietnam buildup of 1965–67—and only one out of every seven physically acceptable men will have to be drafted in the 1970's.[11]

Table 1 shows the proportions of twenty-six-year-old men who have had service experience in the last ten years and shows also the proportions

Table 1
Military Service Experience of 26-Year-Old Men,
Selected Years

Year	Total 26-Year-Old Men	Ever Entered Military Service	
		Number	Percent
Actual:			
1958 (Korean-period men)	1,100,000	770,000	70%
1962	1,110,000	640,000	58
1964	1,190,000	610,000	52
1966	1,250,000	580,000	46
Projected:			
1974			
3,000,000 strength	1,870,000	790,000	42
2,700,000 strength	1,870,000	640,000	34

Source: Department of Defense estimates, contained in *Hearings*, p. 10005.

Note: Age 26 is used as the critical age for comparison because it is the practical upper age limit by which time service will have been experienced by all those who are likely to undergo military service at all (except doctors and dentists). The median age of induction dropped to below 20 years in 1966, so that there is considerable time lag before such experience will be reflected in such totals as are here employed; the current expansion in numbers of men in service, however, will probably hold the proportion for 1970–72 at around 44 or 45 percent, and only very large increases could arrest the decisive downward trend in service proportions.

that will see service in the future. Reduced force levels in the late 1950's and early 1960's are responsible for the early sharpness of the drop in service experience, but it is clear that the steeply rising manpower pool of the mid– and late 1960's would by itself cause the proportions shown from about 1968 on. At noncrisis levels, the proportion of men with service experience could drop even lower than the projected 34 percent. This surplus of available manpower over military needs creates conditions quite different from those existing when men were deferred during World War II and the Korean conflict.

Throughout the late 1950's and 1960's, the Selective Service System sought to cope with the relatively low military manpower needs and rising manpower resources by relaxing the stringency of deferment criteria. The tight student deferment standards of the Korean War gave way to the assignment of a student deferment classification without regard to class standing or Selective Service Qualification Test scores,[12] and finally the test itself was abandoned in 1963. In 1956, fathers were placed in the last category in the order of call, with the result in most instances of revoking their Korean-necessitated eligibility. In 1963 they were transferred to a deferred category (III-A), and married men without children were granted the last place in the order of call, again for practical purposes removing them from availability. The purpose of these generous allocations of deferments was to maintain some sense of certainty for those men who remained liable for service (thereby preserving some impetus for enlistments) and to reduce the age at which men were actually called, partly to reduce the disruptive impact of conscription on the economy and society, and partly because the armed forces prefer younger men.

Deferments thus have clearly been shaped by military needs and manpower resources: strict criteria were applied during the years 1951–53, and then these gave way to liberal granting of deferments in the late 1950's and 1960's, with tightening beginning again in 1965. These effects can be clearly seen in Table 2, which compares the proportions of twenty-six-year-old men with service experience and deferred status in 1958 (a year that reflects Korean service levels) with those of 1962 and 1966. (Lest it be assumed that the American male has declined in physical and/or mental capacity since the Korean War, we should note that the Defense Department has modified its standards in the face of manpower surpluses, accepting only those men who meet the higher standards; a separate classification (I-Y) was established for men whose qualifications were such that they would be acceptable only in time of national emergency.) The table shows that the proportion of men who have entered service has steadily decreased, while the proportions in two important deferment categories have increased.

It is not too much to say that those who actually see military service are those who are left over after all possible deferments have been extended. Deferments, originally intended to maximize the efficient use of manpower resources, have been used in effect to reduce the pool of available men to manageable proportions. The obvious question is whether they can be so used without undermining their original justification, and/or creating unanticipated consequences with significant social implications. The critical question becomes: Who gets drafted when many are deferred?

Table 2
Military Service Status of 26-Year-Old Men, Selected Years

Status	1958	1962	1966
Entered service	70%	58%	46%
Not qualified	22	27	30
Dependency (including married nonfathers)	5	12	20
Other deferred and exempt groups	4	4	4

Source: Department of Defense Estimates, 1966. See *Hearings,* p. 10006.

II. POLICY IMPACT: WHO IS DRAFTED?

There are substantial difficulties in the way of discovering the consequences of deferment practices. Neither Selective Service nor the armed forces maintain comprehensive records of the socioeconomic characteristics of registrants, draftees, or enlistees. Selective Service record-keeping is limited to those few items of information that concern a registrant's availability for service, and, in any event, files are confidential by law. There exists, therefore, no ready way to compare those who serve with those who do not, or to ascribe reasons for such patterns. Problems are also introduced by some of the special features of Selective Service operation: because men may still enlist after passing their preinduction physicals or even after being ordered to report for induction, analysis of those *actually* inducted would reach only one-half to one-third of the men *ordered* for induction, probably producing a skewed picture of Selective Service actions. In addition, analyses of mental and physical rejections must provide for the Defense Department's changes of standards in response to manpower needs. But in spite of these difficulties it is possible to make an assessment, however rough, of the impact of deferment policies.

The Defense Department Draft Study of 1964 commissioned a national survey through the Census Bureau and the National Opinion Research Center as part of its effort to ascertain whether adequate force levels could be maintained without the aid of conscription.[13] One by-product of this inquiry was an analysis by educational level of the military service experience of men aged twenty-seven through thirty-four, and these data are presented in Table 3. The lowest and highest educational levels (before

Table 3

**Military Service of Men Age
27–34 in 1964, by Educational
Level**

Educational Level before Service	Percent Who Served
Eighth grade or less	41%
High school dropout	70
High school graduate	74
College dropout	68
College degree	70
Graduate school	27

Source: Albert D. Klassen, *Military Service in the United States: An Overview* (Chicago: National Opinion Research Center, 1966), p. 15.

entering service) experienced the least military service, with high school graduates, college dropouts, and college graduates sharing liability in roughly equal proportions. The same pattern was repeated when father's education or father's occupation was used as the independent variable, and while no income measures were available, it may well be surmised that income would also correlate with service experience in this way. These data appear to suggest that liability for service is lower only for graduate students or for men with an eighth-grade education or less, and that college graduates serve at roughly the same rate as college dropouts, high school dropouts, and high school graduates. The National Advisory Commission on Selective Service presented a chart showing these proportions in its report, with no further interpretation, and the *New York Times* used it as one of two illustrations of the findings of the Commission in its *précis* of that report.

Many of the arguments for the elimination of graduate-student deferment and the retention of undergraduate deferment appear to rely on the data in Table 3. Men aged twenty-seven through thirty-four in 1964 were at prime military liability ages in the Korean War, however, and the comparatively small size of the manpower pool in relation to manpower requirements resulted in a high proportion of service for all strata. College students served at almost the average rates for the entire male population during that period; only graduate students were able to avoid military service. More recent data, applicable to the growing manpower pool and decreasing manpower requirements of the late 1950's and early 1960's, are available from Selective Service itself, and are presented in Table 4. These data show that by 1964 men aged twenty-six who had been to college were much less likely to have served in the armed forces.[14] The difference in the two bodies of data with respect to service experience of college students is not due to the failure of the latter data to segregate graduate students. Only 6 percent of college graduates had student deferments, and even if all of these escaped service, the proportions of service experience on the part of college graduates as a group would still be distinctly lower than at all other educational levels. It is clear that under the manpower surplus conditions of the 1950's and early 1960's, college students as well as graduate students experienced military service at distinctly lower proportions than any other group (except for the lowest levels of education) in the population.[15]

The national data just reviewed say nothing about the impact of the draft at different economic levels. But data from the 1960 census show clearly that college attendance is related to income. According to the census data, only 19 percent of persons from sixteen through twenty-four from families with incomes under $5,000 per year reported some college

Table 4
Military Service of 26-Year-Old Men in 1964, by
Educational Level

	Less than High School	High School	Some College	College Degree	Total
Entered military service	50%	57%	60%	40%	52%
No military service (total)	50	43	40	60	48
	100%	100%	100%	100%	100%
The "no military service" group can be broken down as follows:					
Available for service (I-A)	1%	1%	1%	3%	1%
Married (service unlikely)	. . .	. . .	. . .	2	. . .
Unmarried (service probable)	1	1	1	1	1
Not available for service	50	42	40	56	47
Unacceptable (I-Y, IV-F)	25	12	14	12	18
Student deferments	. . .	. . .	2	6	1
Occupational deferments (II-A, II-C)	. . .	. . .	1	11	2
Dependency deferments	23	29	23	25	25
Other deferred and exempt groups	1	1	1	3	2

Source: Selective Service sample inventory of registrants, reported in *Hearings*, p. 10011. Figures may not add to 100 percent in all instances due to rounding.

attendance, while 33 percent of persons in the $5,000–$7,500-per-year range and 49 percent of those in the $7,500–$10,000 bracket reported college attendance. The implication of these figures is that men from higher income families are less likely to see service than men from lower income families.

This conclusion is supported by data quite different from those so far examined. To examine the impact of the draft further, we analyzed Selective Service classification data on a month-by-month, board-by-board basis for the eighty local boards of Wisconsin.[16] These records included no educational data, nor did they reveal any other socioeconomic characteristics of individual registrants. Therefore, we were able to relate Census Bureau data describing the socioeconomic characteristics of local board jurisdictions only to the classification performances of those boards; however approximate the use of such aggregate data may be, the absence of any other data has led us to make some cautious appraisals on this basis. We should add that our analysis relies on 1965 and 1966 data. The 1967 renewal of Selective Service legislation altered the terms of deferment somewhat (details are discussed in a later section), but in our opinion the status quo was altered so slightly that the analysis that follows is still relevant.

Table 5 shows the state medians in proportions of eligible-age registrants (total registrants less classification V-A, overage) in each of the major classifications during 1965 and 1966, as well as the range between the highest and lowest local boards in 1966. The deferment categories with the most men are dependency/hardship (III-A), unfit for service (IV-F), and student deferment (II-S); the latter increased substantially (by 39 percent) between 1965 and 1966. The table shows that the highest board has ten times as many registrants in II-S and five times as many I-D (reserves) as the lowest board, and there are sharp differences also in occupational-deferment and unfit-for-service classifications. Clearly, the impact of the draft is not the same in every draft-board jurisdiction. Extensive analysis convinces us that this variation is rooted in the socioeconomic differences between these jurisdictions rather than in any systematic pattern of local-board behavior; within this single state we found almost no evidence of systematic variation which could be attributed to local-board idiosyncrasies or localized norms.[17]

Table 5
Percentage of Eligible-Age Registrants in Major
Selective Service Classifications, Wisconsin, 1966

Classification	Description of Classification	Percentage of Eligible-Age Group in Each Classification: State Medians of 80 Boards		Range of Variation between Highest and Lowest Boards, 1966 (in Percent)	
		Fiscal 1965	Fiscal 1966	Lowest	Highest
I-A	Available for service	9.2%	5.8%	4.4%	8.3%
I-C	Now in service	10.8	11.8	8.6	18.1
I-Y	Available in emergency	4.4	6.7	2.4	11.5
I-D	In reserves	3.8	4.8	1.7	8.8
II-A	Occupationally deferred	1.3	1.5	0.3	3.9
II-C	Agriculturally deferred	0.9	1.0	—	5.7
II-S	Student deferments	6.6	9.2	1.9	19.7
III-A	Hardship and dependency deferments	17.4	18.8	12.5	25.2
IV-A	Completed service	18.5	17.1	12.3	23.7
IV-F	Unfit for service	14.4	13.1	9.3	30.7
	Enlistments	2.1	3.3	—	—
	Inductions	0.7	2.0	—	—

Table 5 indicates that nearly 20 percent of the eligible-age group in some boards had student deferments. Table 6 compares proportions of student deferments by income of board jurisdictions. Because many boards in this state cluster about the state median, we have segregated them by the relatively narrow margin of 1 percent of the eligible-age group above and below the median; the sharply contrasting distribution of boards in these two directions correlates closely with income differentials and leads us to conclude, not surprisingly, that educational deferments are more likely to go to men from higher income families.

We can come closer to a specification of this relationship, and of possible exceptions to it, by means of the scatter diagram in Figure 1. In this case, we used proportions of families with incomes under $3,000 per year in the jurisdictions of the boards as the correlate of student deferment for purposes of greater precision, and the general distribution again shows deferment by income level. Some special features make for individualized variability, of course, such as the proximity of colleges and universities or the varying proportions of relatively wealthy persons in each board jurisdiction. We may note also that the greatest range in student-deferment proportions, with relatively little range in income, is found in urban areas, suggesting the relevance of special factors in those areas, such as a proportion of nonwhites within the population.

So far, our data have indicated that many registrants in this state, probably the sons of upper income families, hold educational deferments. The more interesting question is whether those men who obtain student deferments serve in the armed forces after their graduation. Certainly some will, but several pieces of evidence suggest that they will see service at distinctly lower rates than any other group. Our detailed analysis of Wis-

Table 6
Student Deferments by Median Income
of Board Jurisdictions, Wisconsin, 1966

	Median Income of Families	
Fiscal 1966 II-S Levels	Boards in Low-Income Areas (below $5,000) (N = 46)	Boards in High-Income Areas (above $5,000) (N = 34)
More than 1% above state median	11%	56%
Within 1% of state median	44	35
More than 1% below state median	45	9
	100%	100%

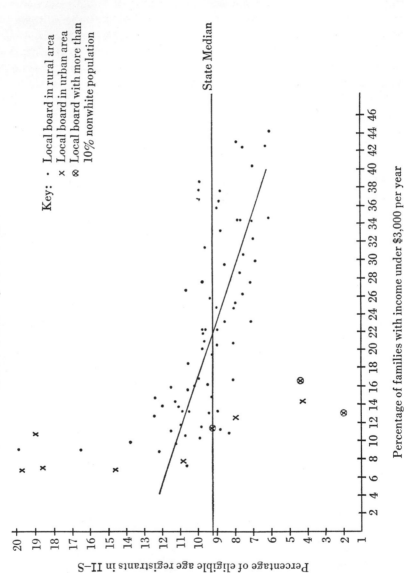

Figure 1
II-S Deferments by Income Levels

Key: · Local board in rural area
x Local board in urban area
⊗ Local board with more than
10% nonwhite population

State Median

Percentage of families with income under $3,000 per year

Percentage of eligible age registrants in II-S

consin experience suggests strongly that registrants from higher income areas undergo military service at lower rates than registrants from lower income areas. Table 7 relates total proportions of military-service experience (current service *and* completed service) to the income levels of the board jurisdictions. The overall incidence of military service is lowest in the higher income area and highest in the lower income areas; the proportion of boards that are above the median decreases sharply as one moves from the lowest to the highest income areas, with only 11 percent of the boards with over-$6,000-income jurisdictions being more than 1 percent above the median.

The close correlation between student deferment and income levels previously noted appears to have carried over to the point of establishing an income-related overall pattern of service experience. But if student deferment has the closest correlations with income, it is not the only factor involved in this relationship. Occupational deferment combines with student deferment to give higher income men a better chance of avoiding military service. Table 4 showed that 11 percent of twenty-six-year-old college graduates held an occupational deferment in July 1964, as compared with 1 percent of all other twenty-six-year-old men. (Military service after age twenty-six was rare then, and is unlikely now; for all practical purposes, such men will never see service.) And among Wisconsin local boards occupational deferments were most numerous in higher income areas.

We have not included men in classification I-D (reserves) in our

Table 7
Service in Armed Forces* by Income of Board
Jurisdictions, Wisconsin, 1966

	Median Family Income of Board Jurisdictions†		
	$3,000-$4,000 (N = 19)	$4,000-$6,000 (N = 42)	Over $6,000 (N = 19)
More than 1% above state median	53%	36%	11%
Within 1% of state median	11	33	37
More than 1% below state median	37	31	53
	101%‡	100%	101%‡

* Includes classifications I-C (in service) and IV-A (completed service).

† Median family income data based on U.S. Census, 1960. In the case of boards comprising less than an entire county (eleven boards), census tracts were allocated geographically to construct socioeconomic profiles of each board jurisdiction.

‡ Figures add to more than 100 percent because of rounding.

computations of men who have seen military service, because we have defined military service as active duty. While some I-D men are former service personnel, most are six-months or no-prior-service men. As of May 1968, few organized reserve units had been called up, and only a small proportion of those men who have had no training at all have been activated during the Vietnam period. Under these conditions, and despite the extended liability of reservists, it appears to be an advantageous classification—and it is available primarily to the higher income, better educated registrants. Among Wisconsin local boards, only the lowest income boards had less than 4 percent of their eligible-age group in class I-D; the higher income boards were all above this figure.

Defense Department comparisons of the educational attainment of men entering the reserves with men entering the services via induction reveal sharp disparities[18] consistent with our contention that service in the reserves is another income-related advantage. The rise in Wisconsin reserves proportions between 1965 and 1966 shown in Table 5 occurred chiefly in the higher income areas. Local-board members concur in the view that deferment policy provides a means for the more fortunate registrant to avoid active service in a time of maximum danger.[19]

The advantage of higher income registrants can be illustrated in another way. To test our hypothesis that the risk of military service for qualified men in low-income areas was higher than the risk for qualified men in higher income areas, we subtracted the "fit only in emergency" (I-Y) and "unfit" (IV-F) classifications from the totals of eligible-age registrants in each board, and then computed the registrants' actual service liability by finding the ratio of the two service categories (I-C and IV-A) to the total. The resulting service liability ratios ranged from 1 to 3.2 in the wealthier urban boards to 1 to 2.5 in the relatively low-income, most heavily Negro board, and 1 to 2.3 in a very low-income rural board. This means that actual military service was experienced by 1 in every 2.3 physically and mentally qualified men in the low-income rural board, but by almost 50 percent less, or 1 in every 3.2 men, in the wealthier urban boards. Here, as elsewhere, we have clear evidence that the income-related advantages in present deferment policies (chiefly the student deferment) are sufficiently great to overcome the counterveiling effects of higher proportions of unfitness in the lower income areas and establish the income-based pattern of military service.

So far, we have been working with data that include all men currently or previously in service, without regard to their avenue of entry. This leaves open the possibility that the lower income registrants may have enlisted in disproportionate numbers, thus in effect voluntarily creating the pattern we have discerned. In order to test this possibility, we have to distinguish enlistments from inductions and compare both with the income levels of board jurisdictions. The results of such an analysis are presented in Table 8.

These proportions are not drastically different, and a shift in a small number of boards would restructure them; but the table is most instructive for its negation of the assumption that the poor enlist. The enlistment rate tends to be *lower* in the lower income jurisdictions and relatively *higher* in the high-income jurisdictions. Conversely, the induction rate is higher in the low-income areas and lower in the high-income areas. This suggests, in response to our original inquiry, that the higher service experience of the low-income boards is *not* due to enlistments, but, quite the opposite, is due to the heavy weight of inductions there. The high-income areas, with their apparently higher enlistment rates, would, in accordance with the formulas for allocating induction calls, receive lower calls for induction from the state headquarters; induction calls would be proportionately higher in those areas that did not provide men through enlistment. This seems to be the case here, with perhaps some additional impact on the lower income areas deriving from the availability of men there.

National data permit a somewhat broader perspective on patterns of enlistment. The question of who enlists is related to the level of induction calls: men with higher levels of educational attainment and higher scores

Table 8
Enlistments and Inductions, by Income Level
of Board Jurisdictions, Wisconsin, 1966

	Boards in Low-Income Areas* (N = 39)	Boards in High-Income Areas† (N = 41)
Enlistment rate‡		
Low	36%	22%
Medium	51	49
High	13	29
	100%	100%
Induction rate§		
Low	33%	49%
Medium	28	36
High	39	15
	100%	100%

* More than 20 percent of families earning less than $3,000 per year.
† Less than 20 percent of families earning less than $3,000 per year.
‡ Based on percentage of eligible-age group enlisting during fiscal 1966. (Low, less than 3 percent; medium, 3–3.99 percent; high, over 4 percent.)
§ Based on percentage of eligible-age group inducted during fiscal 1966. (Low, less than 2 percent; medium, 2–2.49 percent; high, over 2.5 percent.)

on service aptitude tests tend to enlist because of draft pressure, while under conditions of low induction calls, enlistments come proportionately more from lower socioeconomic and aptitude levels.[20] The net results create the patterns shown in Table 9. While the data in the first part of the table reflect the experience of the Korean War and the immediate postwar years, current (though less complete) data regarding enlistments in the last two years are entirely consistent; together they reinforce our point that high-income, high-status men are more likely to enlist and less likely to be drafted than low-income, low-status men. The proportionately higher rates of service which we have found in lower income areas, in short, are not the

Table 9

(A) Enlistment and Induction, by Socioeconomic Status and Race

	Age in 1964			
	27–30		31–34	
Race and SES*	Inducted	Enlisted	Inducted	Enlisted
White	16%	84%	34%	66%
Negro	25	75	51	49
White high SES	11	89	27	73
White low SES	20	80	40	60

* Based on father's occupation and education. See Albert D. Klassen, *Military Service in American Life since World War II: An Overview* (Chicago: National Opinion Research Center, 1966), pp. 37–45, for the bases of the index.

Source: Klassen, *Military Service,* Table A–VI.5d, p. 253 (part of the Defense Department draft study).

(B) Form of Military Service, by Race, October 1964

	White		Nonwhite	
Entered military service	66%		49%	
Inducted		22%		25.0%
Enlisted		30		22.0
Officer programs		4		0.4
Reserve programs		10		1.7
Never entered service	34		51	
Unfit for service		21		42.0
Other deferred and exempt groups		13		8.0
	100%		100%	

Source: National Advisory Commission on Selective Service, *In Pursuit of Equity: Who Serves When Not All Serve?* (Washington: U.S. Government Printing Office, 1967), Table 5.8, p. 158 (based on Census Bureau survey of civilian men aged 16–34 years and Defense Department surveys of active-duty personnel, October 1964).

product of enlistments; they are caused by inductions from those areas. The data in the second part of the table confirm our point that income-related opportunities shape the pattern of service experience. Of those Negroes who see military service, more than half do so via induction; exactly one-third of whites have been inducted while the rest have served via officer programs, reserves, or enlistment. Lower proportions of Negroes experience military service, of course, but the reason lies entirely with the difference in the "unfit for service" category.[21] Indeed, for the physically and mentally acceptable Negro, service prospects are higher than for whites. The National Advisory Commission reported that "proportionately more (30 percent) Negroes of the group qualified for service are drafted than whites (18 percent)—primarily because fewer Negroes are admitted into Reserve or officer training programs."[22]

We may assess the differences in the draft's impact on the two racial groupings in greater detail through comparison of the classification proportions of two adjoining local boards in Milwaukee, one with high-income white residents and the other with a relatively low-income population, almost 50 percent Negro, which is presented as Figure 2. Conspicuous differences between the two boards appear in the student-deferment, occupational-deferment, reserves, and "unfit for service" classifications, all of which conform to our interpretations. It is clear that residents of the two areas have radically different opportunities to claim such deferments; under the circumstances, it is remarkable that service experience is so similar. With a much smaller pool of acceptable men, the Negro board provides nearly the same percentage of men to the armed forces, again indicating that, for those registrants in the Negro board who *are* physically qualified, liability for military service is high indeed.

To conclude the study of the income-related impact of national deferment policies, we examined the record of thirty-seven boards, all in rural areas, where more than 20 percent of families had incomes under $3,000 per year and less than 10 percent of families had incomes over $10,000 per year. Their classification patterns are the same as those previously described, but now in exaggerated form (Table 10). These lowest income areas are dramatically low in II-S deferments, distinctly high in mental and physical unfitness, and high in hardship and dependency deferments. The combined effect of the presence of all these factors is a rate of service experience above the state median, which is not due to high enlistments. We conclude that the absence of the student deferment has overcome the countervailing factors and has exposed these registrants to greater liability. National deferment policies as applied through the mid-1960's (and, so far as we can tell, continuing into the present) have the effect of making the incidence of military service closely related to income levels: men with the

Figure 2
Comparison of Proportions of Registrants in
Selected Classifications, Two Boards

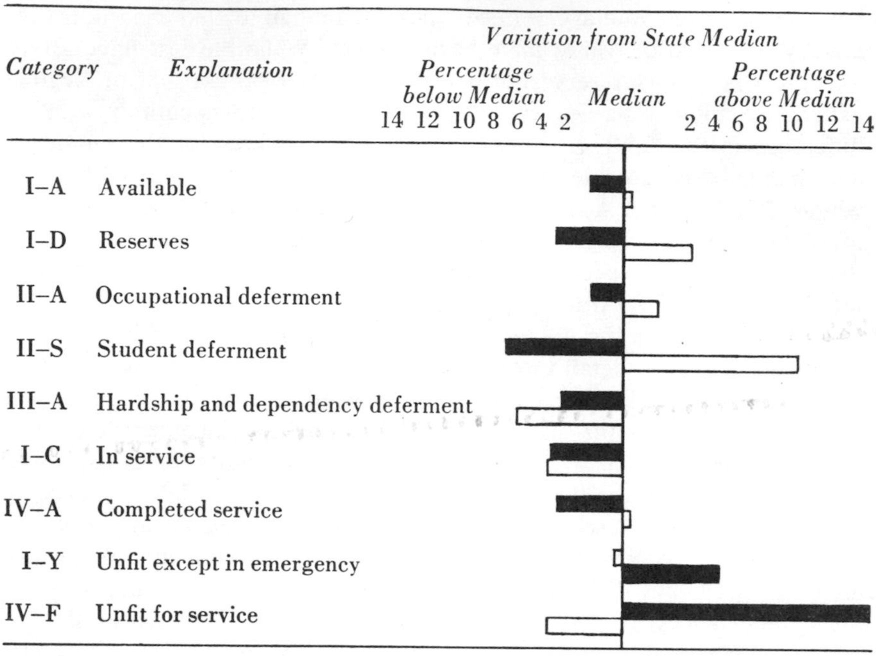

		Variation from State Median		
Category	*Explanation*	*Percentage below Median* 14 12 10 8 6 4 2	*Median*	*Percentage above Median* 2 4 6 8 10 12 14

I–A   Available

I–D   Reserves

II–A   Occupational deferment

II–S   Student deferment

III–A   Hardship and dependency deferment

I–C   In service

IV–A   Completed service

I–Y   Unfit except in emergency

IV–F   Unfit for service

Key: ▆▆▆ Median family income $4,900, approximately 50 percent Negro.

☐ Median family income $8,500, approximately 1 percent Negro.

Table 10
Classification and Enlistment Characteristics of
Low-Income Boards, Wisconsin, 1966*

	Completed Service and In Service (I-C, IV-A)	Student Defer- ments (II-S)	Hardship and De- pendency Deferments (III-A)	Mental and Physical Unfitness I-Y, IV-F)	Enlist- ments
More than 1% above state median	43%	0%	51%	38%	5%
Within 1% of state median	27	49	38	46	92
More than 1% below state median	30	51	11	16	3
	100%	100%	100%	100%	100%

*The 37 boards with jurisdictions in which more than 20 percent of families had incomes under $3,000 *and* less than 10 percent had incomes over $10,000.

advantages of income and education do not experience service at the same rates as their less advantaged contemporaries.

III. SOME FURTHER CONSEQUENCES
OF PRESENT POLICIES

We think the data in the preceding section show that increasing manpower surplus, accompanied by extensive granting of deferments, has precluded realization of the value of equity under present policies. Instead, substantial inequities—discrimination along income-based lines, or by residence or race—have developed. What has happened to the value of efficiency under these conditions? To answer this question, we must examine the means employed to implement conscription as well as the findings already reviewed.

For efficiency to be achieved, four criteria would have to be met. Our evidence suggests that, in the 1960's, none of them has been. First, there would have to be a carefully considered and reasonably appropriate definition of what the national interest requires in the way of manpower. We would argue that such a definition should rest in part on projections of available manpower on a long-term basis, together with projections of both foreign and domestic social and other policy problems on an equally long-term basis, in order that relative priorities could be established. Not only defense-related needs, but also pressing domestic social, educational, and technical requirements should be considered. Priorities defined in Selective Service materials, however, are generalized, short-term, and chiefly scientific and military in character.

Second, the definition of the national interest in manpower usage would have to be communicated to local boards with enough specificity to make possible reasonably close adherence by local boards across the country. National headquarters so far has done no such thing; it has instead stated deferment policies in the broadest terms, and has reminded local boards that such guidelines are "advisory only." No effort has been made to encourage conformity with national policies, and variations that have resulted have been defined as desirable. Some state headquarters have added supplementary interpretations for the benefit of their local boards, and the result is a wide number of conflicting instructions for the nation's local boards. The President's Commission reports one classic example in which the states divided sharply over instructions to local boards regarding what course load would qualify a registrant as a "full-time student." Some said twelve credit hours, some fifteen; some told their boards to adhere to whatever the college considered a full-time student; and some said nothing and permitted their boards to make their own definitions.[23] Illustrations could be multiplied, but the point is made: no clear or consistent view of the nation's interests is communicated to local boards. Indeed, it is possible to identify instances where national or state interpretations reflect the requests of trade associations, particular corporations, or unions for quite specific deferment practices. In dairying Wisconsin, for example, cheese-makers or drivers of milk tank trucks are granted occupational deferment by some boards, but not by others.

Third, the performance of local boards would have to be consistent with the transmitted definition of the national interest, *or* the accumulated body of decisions by the 4,087 local boards of the country would have to be taken as representing the national interest even in the absence of guidance based on broad national consideration of what that interest was. The former seems impossible in the light of the absence of a definition and of any single clear specification of standards; the latter seems impossible unless we are to convert the body of local-board decisions into a version of the national interest by definition or as an act of faith.

The inconsistent performances of different elements of the Selective Service System demonstrate that no single definition of national interest has been trasmitted; rather each local board, appeal board, and state system is left to do its own defining. Although our analysis in Wisconsin indicated, and the research of the President's Commission confirmed, that Wisconsin is a state with low variability between boards in jurisdictions with similar socioeconomic characteristics, this is not the case in all states. The research conducted by the President's Commission revealed substantial variation between boards in similar areas in many states,[24] and this is compounded by the varying instructions issued to local boards by the fifty-six state headquarters of the system. It is compounded further by varying performances by appeal boards in different states, whose decisions normally reflect the interpretations neither of the national nor of the state headquarters, but of the five members of the ninety-five appeal boards. Participant observation in nine urban local boards over a six-month period of 1966 showed that little or no attention was paid to the guidelines from national headquarters, particularly the critical-skills list,[25] and that board members reached their decisions on a wide variety of personalized value premises, experiences, and prejudices. Very little decision-making, interestingly, was based on knowledge of either registrant or the needs of the community, because board members almost never knew registrants and frequently lived outside the particular jurisdiction, and, we may add, their jurisdictions probably had little socioeconomic integrity in any event. The President's Commission evaluated (among other things) occupational deferment classification performance on the part of a sample of 199 local boards, and found that "about half [of the registrants] reclassified into II-A were in neither a critical occupation nor an essential industry as defined by the Department of Labor."[26]

By any measures adopted, we have convincing evidence of dissimilarities in the treatment of similarly situated men. Nonuniformity in classification is a hallmark of the system. The only way in which this performance record can be interpreted as serving the national interest through efficient utilization of manpower resources is by defining the national interest as the sum of the shifting views of 4,087 local boards.

We would have asked as our fourth point that there be some evidence of the effects of the "channeling" accomplished by the system through these deferment policies. We know of no evidence on this, however, except for some scattered indications that some registrants, probably the better educated men, take alternative courses of action in contemplation of the draft. Our sample surveys of the general public and of registrants in Wisconsin indicate that a relatively small number of men have changed their courses of study or their vocational plans principally because of the draft. Some of our respondents were convinced that *others* had acted so as to qualify for deferment, such as by having children or going to school. We do know also that the marriage rate among the immediately affected age groups, and those age groups only, rose by 10 percent during the nine months immediately after President Kennedy declared such men last in the order of call in 1963.[27] But the Selective Service System has never sought to support its argument that men have been channeled into socially productive occupations because of national deferment policies, and, given the premises on which such channeling would have to be based, it is perhaps just as well.

We do not believe that this situation can be characterized as efficient use of manpower resources in the national interest. Recalling the manipulation of deferment criteria for the principal purpose of controlling the size of the manpower pool, and noting that the President's Commission found the performance of some appeal boards to amount to economic protectionism (some boards never reversed an appeal from an out-of-state local board, while others did so as much as 88 percent of the time),[28] we are confident that we have only begun to detail the factors that prevent such an interpretation.

It might be argued that efficiency is served under the present system in the very gross sense that the lower income, less skilled (and most unemployed) segments of the population are drawn into military service while those with other capabilities are deferred. But the lack of any kind of "fit" between unemployability and lack of skills on the one hand and induction on the other—brought about chiefly but not exclusively by high physical and educational standards of acceptability for service—militates against this possibility. So do the arbitrary and idiosyncratic performance of local boards and the demonstrated variability among state boards and appeal boards. If such an argument were not foreclosed by these factors, it would probably raise serious additional value questions and equity-efficiency conflict under our present manpower-surplus conditions.

In any summary evaluation of present policies, we must not lose sight of the fact that the Selective Service System has for more than two decades filled all calls for induction, as well as motivated countless other enlistments, without provoking significant resistance from the society. This is an important benefit, the more important because it appears to be the only benefit. Ranged against it on the cost side are the several dimensions of inequity already fully described; the social dislocations that are the product of the kind of "channeling" which passes for efficient use of manpower in the national interest; and the uncertainties related to induction at a relatively advanced age.

It has been argued that these are by-products of a decentralization that is fundamental to popular acquiescence in conscription, but our sample surveys suggest that the reverse is the case: decentralization and conscription by local men is perceived as one of the *bad* things about the system. Let us digress for a moment to establish this point. Table 11 shows

Table 11
Approval of Local Board Concept by Attitude
toward Fairness of the Draft

	Attitude toward Draft*				
Attitude toward Local Boards†	Fair (41%) (N = 248)	Depends (7%) (N = 40)	Not Fair (35%) (N = 212)	Don't Know, No Answer (17%) (N = 107)	Total (100%) (N = 607)
Good idea	44%	40%	28%	33%	36%
Depends	5	10	10	4	7
Not good idea	44	45	58	31	47
Don't know	7	5	4	32	10
	100%	100%	100%	100%	100%

* Q.1: With regard to your knowledge of the draft here in Wisconsin, would you say it is working in a manner that is fair to all, or not?
† Q.2: What do you think about having local people involved in drafting men? Is this a good idea or not?
Source: Wisconsin Survey Research Laboratory, clustered area probability sample, September 1966.

the responses of the adult population of Wisconsin to our inquiries concerning knowledge about and attitudes toward the conduct of the draft by local draft boards in the state. (A total of 52 percent of respondents knew that the draft was conducted by local boards. All respondents were advised of this fact before being asked the preference question reflected in the table; those who knew of the existence of local boards were more favorable to the idea than those who had not previously been aware that local boards did the drafting, but still split 45 percent to 43 percent against the idea.) The most significant finding from this inquiry is the fact that the local-board concept is not nearly so popular as the Selective Service System and its supporters argue. Not even those who think the draft itself is fair support the local-board concept more than they oppose it; in the state as a whole, 47 percent say local boards are *not* a good idea, while only 36 percent say that they are, and at a time when the draft itself is evaluated as not unfair. We asked those who said that local boards were not a good idea why they felt that way, and almost every respondent answered with some form of allegation of bias or prejudice on the part of boards. The only strata within the state which contained more respondents who favored local boards than opposed them were the higher levels of education and occupation, a finding that is part of a body of evidence, reported elsewhere, which leads us to the conclusion that the draft gains support from the more advantaged and more politically influential elements of the population partially because of their reduced liability combined with their local management of the system. National data indicate that these findings are not unique to the state of Wisconsin; perceptions of the draft as fair correlate with the capacity to qualify for alternatives to military service in the NORC report of their work for the Defense Department Draft Study of 1964.[29]

The evidence reviewed in the course of this brief digression leads us to the conclusion that the consequences we have identified cannot be justified as necessary though perhaps undesirable by-products of an absolutely essential form of organization. Decentralization and local participation are *not* essential to popular acquiescence in conscription; they may be functional in one sense as a means of drawing off resentment and focusing it on the local board rather than on the principle of conscription itself, but in other respects they seem to be dispensable.

Our analysis thus leads us to the conclusion that the present system is producing unnecessarily high costs in exchange for the single essential benefit it returns. Attempts to serve both equity and efficiency in the employment of manpower resources in this way lead to the attainment of neither, and the prospect for the future, with its increasing manpower surplus, is for greater and greater inequities—higher and higher costs—if the present practices are continued. What are the alternatives? We shall consider several briefly, before taking up our own proposals.

IV. ALTERNATIVES TO PRESENT POLICIES

Several alternatives to the present form of conscription have been suggested in recent years, though none has as yet been adopted. In the paragraphs below we comment on several of the proposals that have received the most attention, and offer speculations where applicable upon their consequences.

National Service

Several plans for national service have been put forward, the gist of the major ones being to provide opportunities for service, either military or social, to all the nation's youth, male and female.[30] Some advocates of national service would have it compulsory and others not, but all include as a goal the rehabilitation of disadvantaged youth. Because about eight million persons might be participating at any one time, there are staggering problems of effective employment of such people: what sorts of jobs, where, with what impact on the labor market, at how much cost? There are constitutional issues of the power of the Congress to compel nonmilitary service, practical questions about who would end up in the military, value questions concerning the intrusion on people's lives, and so many other issues that national service seems to us to be beyond the realm of probability if not possibility.

Universal Military Service or Universal Military Training

Another solution to the problem of inequities in military liability is to take every able-bodied male into the service, and some see advantages as well from administering military training to the entire male population, either for personal improvement or for the nation's benefit. The chief objections here are practical, although there are some who reject the idea of universality in military service as inconsistent with democratic values. The practical problems arise from the size of the manpower pool, the costs of absorbing such huge numbers of men in the services, and the incapacity of training facilities to cope with such an influx unless they were radically expanded. The estimates of the future manpower pool are as follows:

Year	Men Reaching 18th Birthday
1966	1,920,000
1968	1,860,000
1970	1,930,000
1972	2,050,000
1974	2,120,000

Source: Defense Department estimates, reported in *Hearings,* p. 10003.

These estimates compare with a total of 1,170,000 in 1950, and their growing numbers will create a total available pool (ages nineteen through twenty-five) nearly 60 percent larger than in 1950. It will be recalled that universal training and service were rejected in 1951, partly for cost reasons and partly for value reasons; it seems even less likely that these approaches will be acceptable as solutions in the future.

A Voluntary Army

The abolition of conscription carries an attraction that unites left and right, but it also encounters both philosophical and practical opposition.[31] Some of the former is based on the belief that in a democracy military service should be widely shared by the citizens. Yet it seems clear that the men most likely to enlist and re-enlist in a voluntary army would be from the less advantaged (though not poverty-level) sectors of the population. Some opponents of a voluntary army argue also that a mercenary army would pose a threat to the society. In addition to these value-based arguments, there are several practical problems presented by a voluntary army.

1. How high would military salaries have to be raised to make service competitive in the labor market, and what total costs would be involved? The Defense Department study of 1964 sought to ascertain whether men would enlist if there were no draft, and to estimate the size of the armed forces that could be sustained solely from volunteers at various pay and unemployment levels. There are so many factors in this equation (including the occurrence of shooting wars) that there is room for wide disagreement over feasibility, but we may cite some basic statistics. Table 12 shows the responses of various groups of men who had enlisted in service to nearly identical variants of the question "Would you have enlisted if there had been no draft?" Asked by the Defense Department in October and

450

Table 12
Proportions of Men Who Had Enlisted in Military Service Whose Service Was Draft-Motivated,* 1964

Officers	% Draft-Motivated	Enlisted Men	% Draft-Motivated	Reserves	% Draft-Motivated
	41%		38%		71%
Breakdown by source:		Breakdown by age:		Breakdown by age:	
ROTC	45	17–19	31	17–19	40
OCS	51	20–25	58	20–21	77
Direct appointment	58			22 and over	89
		Breakdown by education:		Breakdown by education:	
		Non-high school graduate	23	Non-high school graduate	31
		High school graduate	40	High school graduate	59
		Some college or college graduate	58	Some college	71
				College graduate	90

* Based on the responses "No, definitely" or "No, probably" to the question "Would you have enlisted if there had been no draft?"

Source: Defense Department surveys of men in the armed forces, October and November 1964, reported in *Hearings*, pp. 10038, 10039.

November of 1964. In all probability, the proportions would be much higher now, but these are sufficient to show the scope of the problem: not only does the draft provide substantial proportions of new accessions by induction, but a good share of the enlistments are draft-motivated as well.

Proponents of the voluntary army argue that this situation would be drastically changed by paying members of the armed forces the wages their services would be worth in the open market, or by raising wages to the point necessary to fill the armed forces to the levels required. The proponents have a sound point when they argue that current military-service wage rates in effect impose a tax on those who serve,[32] and that both justice and the national economy would be served by paying military personnel wages equivalent to the value of their services in the open labor market. If this were the basis from which increases in wages needed to constitute and maintain a voluntary army were computed, the costs involved would not appear so high. These estimates range all the way from $4 billion to $17 billion to maintain a 2.7-million force level under various possible conditions, with the Defense Department's best estimate of net costs with a 4 percent unemployment rate being $8 billion.[33]

We should emphasize that the feasibility of a voluntary army depends heavily on the force level that is to be maintained. The cost estimates reviewed above are based on a force level of 2.7 million, but in mid-1967 there were 3.45 million men under arms. Not even the strongest advocate of a voluntary army considers it feasible until it is possible to reduce force levels.

The Defense Department's research sought to ascertain the effects of higher pay on enlistments if there were no draft, with some disquieting results for the cause of a voluntary army. Men aged sixteen to twenty-five years were asked, "If there were no draft now, and you had no military obligation at all, which condition would be most likely to get you to volunteer?" Table 13 presents responses by age and educational status. It seems apparent that pay scales comparable to those of the open labor market would not be sufficient, and that substantially greater salaries or other inducements would be necessary. Faced with the characteristics of motivations and potential costs which are intimated in the research reports from the Draft Study of 1964, the Defense Department has understandably been less optimistic about the feasibility of a voluntary army than have the proponents of the cause.

2. A second and to us even more serious problem in the voluntary-army proposals is the problem of flexibility. The present combined compulsory and "voluntary" procurement system has succeeded in meeting rapidly fluctuating demands for manpower, and it does not seem likely that mere manipulation of wage rates could achieve the same results. Experi-

Table 13
Most Important Inducement to Volunteer, by Age
and Educational Status

	Not in School		In School	
Conditions	16–19 Years	20–25 Years	16–19 Years	20–25 Years
Military pay the same as civilian life	4%	5%	2%	3%
Military pay considerably higher than in civilian life	21	25	16	23
If given a $1,000 enlistment bonus	6	3	3	0
If guaranteed training in job or skill useful in civilian life	29	23	20	9
If sent to civilian school at government expense before or during service	18	19	31	30
If given opportunity for civilian school or college after service	8	8	12	12
Other miscellaneous conditions	7	10	6	9
If officer training available	7	7	11	14
	100%	100%	100%*	100%*

* Figures do not add to 100 because of rounding.
Source: U.S. Census Bureau Survey of civilian men, October 1964, reported in *Hearings,* p. 10051.

ence has shown that it is sometimes necessary to draw in a million men the year after taking in less than half that number; would it be possible to raise wages sufficiently (and publicize the fact sufficiently) to induce such numbers to enlist within the time period in which their services were required? Presumably such wage increases would have to be extended to all those already in service, with potentially ballooned costs across the board. Could such wages, if raised in the manner described, be reduced again when the need slackened? The cost issues are secondary to the problem of adding sufficient strength to the military in time of national need, and the voluntary-army advocates have not (perhaps cannot) lay to rest doubts on this score. One route taken is to suggest that some form of the draft be retained as support for the program in the event of such an emergency, but this seems to us to carry with it other problems, such as maintaining an organization without a regular function to perform.

In addition to lacking numbers flexibility, a voluntary army might also lack skills flexibility. At present the enlistment of men from higher educational levels is frequently draft-motivated, and of course some men from the higher educational levels are drafted. It is these men who can be readily trained in languages, intelligence analysis, electronic repair, and other skills necessary for the modern army. Even if the voluntary army could attract the required numbers, it is by no means clear that it could attract men with the necessary attitudes and skills.

The alternatives presented above were rejected, largely because of the problems we have outlined, by the official participants in the 1966–67 draft debate. But the National Advisory Commission on Selective Service, the Civilian Advisory Panel on Military Manpower Procurement, and President Johnson all suggested changes in the system in existence until June 30, 1967. We summarize below their recommendations, together with the major provisions of the Military Selective Service Act of 1967.

National Advisory Commission Proposals

The Commission considered and rejected the alternatives already mentioned and concentrated on altering the existing system more or less incrementally. The Commission's report, *In Pursuit of Equity: Who Should Serve When Not All Serve?* presented data similar to those we have presented and emphasized the inequity of the present system due to economic discrimination and variability among local boards, appeal boards, and the states. The chief recommendations made by the Commission to the President were as follows:

(*a*) Selective Service should be continued.

(*b*) The System should be reorganized to reduce the number of local boards to 300–500, with professional classifiers acting in accordance with nationally uniform classification standards and under a centralized arrangement with eight to ten regional offices. There would be local boards that would hear appeals from the actions of the initial classifier. Data processing equipment and methods should be used to maintain current and uniform handling of all registrants.

(*c*) Student deferments should be eliminated except for officer training programs.

(*d*) With the exception of hardship deferments, all deferments should be eliminated.

(*e*) Men should be inducted on a youngest-first basis at age nineteen.

(*f*) Men should be inducted by a random selection system in which their vulnerability would be limited to the year in which they were age nineteen.

(*g*) Non-prior-service men should not be allowed to enlist in the reserves or National Guard after being classified I-A. If reserve units cannot otherwise maintain their strength, they should be staffed by induction under the random selection system.

The President's Reaction. The President's message to Congress dealing with the draft asked for only two of the Commission recommendations; many of the recommendations were already within his existing authority under the Universal Military Training and Service Act of 1951. Primarily he asked Congress to extend the Selective Service System's authority to induct men who had not previously been deferred, and in addition he asked for standby authority to induct men into the reserves. He announced that he was referring the matter of Selective Service System reorganization to an interagency task force for study and review. He declared his intention of instituting a youngest-first call and said that he was instructing the Director of Selective Service to develop a random selection system in conjunction with the Secretary of Defense. He proposed to defer action on ending undergraduate student deferments for one year pending discussion in the Congress and by the public, but declared his intention to end graduate-student deferments.

The Civilian Advisory Panel Recommendations

This panel, appointed by the chairman of the House Armed Services Committee to aid the Committee in its deliberations and also (apparently) to counterbalance the National (President's) Commission, made recommendations (not, however, based on research) which differed substantially from those of the National Commission. Among their many recommendations were the following:

(*a*) Induction authority should be extended.

(*b*) Care should be taken to ensure that any effort to establish greater uniformity in local board actions avoids diminishing the discretionary authority of local draft boards.

(*c*) Deferment should be granted for bona fide students of institutions of higher education who request and qualify for such deferment, and this deferment should remain in effect until the student terminates his student status, receives his undergraduate degree, or reaches the age of twenty-four.

(*d*) Occupational deferments should be continued.

(*e*) The "Modified Young Age Class System" should be adopted.

(*f*) A lottery should not be adopted to perform any of the functions of the Selective Service System and a data processing system centralized in Washington should not be adopted at this time.

Congressional Action and the Military Selective Service Act of 1967. Congress virtually ignored the recommendations of the National Advisory Commission and enacted changes that followed closely the recom-

mendations of the Civilian Advisory Panel. Undergraduate student deferment was made a matter of right and occupational deferments were
continued. Random selection was prohibited without further legislation by
the Congress, but a youngest-first order of call was left within Presidential
discretion. And men were given the right to enlist in the reserves of National Guard up until the date scheduled for their actual induction. Thus,
every problem that is documented in our analysis, and particularly inequity
in induction patterns and variability among local boards, seems likely to
become more pronounced in the next four years under the act as extended.

V. POLICY ANALYSIS AND POLICY RECOMMENDATION: THE PROBLEM OF SELECTING AMONG ALTERNATIVES

Our analysis of the probable consequences of alternative military manpower procurement policies has clarified the implications of each, and
perhaps it has (at least for practical purposes) simplified the problem of
choice. But it does not, and probably cannot under most circumstances,
fully solve the problem of choice. The critical question therefore is: Can
we, acting as professional political scientists, recommend one alternative
over others? There is no doubt that we could do so in our capacity as
citizens, of course, but do the training expertise, and other professional
skills that we or others may possess *as political scientists* enable us to make
recommendations? We believe that the answer depends upon the state of
knowledge in the particular policy area, the character of the analysis conducted, and the objectivity with which data and interpretations are presented. Not all subject areas will admit of professionally responsible
recommendation, but some aspects of some areas will; in other words, the
issue of professionalism hinges not upon the *fact* of recommendation, but
upon the manner and circumstances in which the recommendations are
made. Let us examine the process of choosing among alternatives in the
military manpower procurement field.

  In one sense, the content of public policy reflects the distribution of
power resources and relative skills in wielding such resources among actors
in the political process. But it also reflects a balance struck among *assumptions* accepted, *conditions* perceived, *goals* established, *value priorities*
asserted, *means* available, and *effects and by-products* considered tolerable. Policies undeniably have, as one of several elements, a value component. But this need not in and of itself prevent the political scientist from
making recommendations. The pressing character of public problems and
the exigencies of governmental needs mandate employment of the social
scientist's research skills and concepts, and those who develop superior
knowledge will be asked to recommend solutions. In any given case, and

whether or not the data and circumstances are sufficient to enable the researcher to act within the bounds of his professional expertise, it may be necessary for him to recommend measures to cope with public problems. In such cases, the social scientist will—and should—do the best he can with the data at his disposal. But some problem contexts may permit more. In three of the six elements just defined as making up the ingredients of the substance of policy, research may produce knowledge that will support recommendation as a professional act. These are the areas of relevant conditions, means available, and effects and by-products produced. Herein lies the strength of the social scientist: through sophisticated use of the current techniques of empirical research, he may be able to identify causes and effects with sufficient precision to be able to advise and recommend. The less we know, the more that remains for mere speculation, and the more we fall back on value preferences; conversely, the more we know, the more it is at least theoretically possible to reduce speculation and both reduce the number of and focus the issues for value choices.

For the social scientist faced with a request to employ his knowledge and respond to the existence of pressing public problems with recommendations for their solution, there are at least three general ways to choose among alternatives. First, he might frankly declare what values he considers appropriate, and seek to defend their propriety in some way. This might be through evidence of their widespread acceptance within the polity, or through evidence of their relevance in the past or under similar circumstances elsewhere, or through justification that sought to demonstrate their propriety by other criteria, such as their harmony with ideals of justice or democracy. Second, he might assume various possible values alternatively, in effect leaving the final choice to others. Among the alternative values considered, the stated goals of the present policy structure could be posited and means prescribed for their fuller attainment. Third, he might so assiduously develop data and refine interpretations of causes and effects in the areas of his peculiar strength (conditions, means, by-products) that the range of value choices would be drastically narrowed and so sharply focused that recommendation would involve a minimum of value preference. These broad categories of alternative-selecting approaches are arbitrary constructs, of course; rather than being really separable or mutually exclusive, they overlap, and any real situation will involve aspects of each. But situations will vary in the proportions in which each is applicable, with some problems of alternative selection favoring one approach more than others. The element of value choice is inescapable. We cannot avoid it, and it is better that we recognize it and confront it fully than consciously or unconsciously to conceal value preferences in the design or presentation of our research. There are, however, varying proportions of value choices involved in different acts of recommendation, and those in which there is a narrow area for value assertion (because of a well-developed set of data and interpretations) are professionally distinguishable.

Recommendation in the area of military manpower procurement, we believe, partakes sufficiently of the third category above that we can choose an alternative as political scientists. Very briefly, let us summarize the extent to which our data fill the requisites about conditions, means, and by-products, and structure the choice to be made. Before doing so, it is imperative that we make clear the parameters within which we operate. This may be done through the vehicle of the other three elements in the policy balance—assumptions, goals, and value priorities. Our assumptions, partly dictated by space exigencies of this paper, are that the United States will continue to have at least the present level of international commitments for the next five to ten years, that the maintenance of an armed force will be necessary, and that this force will at least for the next five years be composed of more than 2.7 million men. These assumptions in company with the data developed eliminate the alternatives of token armed forces and a voluntary army. The shift to a noncoercive procurement policy is an attractive proposal meriting full inquiry, but not even its strongest advocates believe it possible at force levels of nearly 3 million men. We assume also that the demonstrable financial and other costs of national service and universal military training will continue to foreclose their serious consideration. This brings our question down to one of the form of conscription policy. (We do not mean to define away all hard value choices in the course of this illustration; a glance at the range and intensity of the polemics in the draft-law debate of 1966–67 confirms that there is adequate value conflict remaining over the question of what form conscription policy should take to sustain its use for our purposes.)

We understand the goals of present policy to be the staffing of the armed forces on a flexible basis with minimum dislocation to the society and economy, and with maintenance of a level of public support and acquiescence sufficient to permit the accomplishment of the primary task. The major values with which the present policies have been designed are those of efficiency in use of manpower resources, and then equity in liability for military service. For the moment, we take these two as givens, and return to our data and interpretations.

We have seen that the *conditions* that are most significant for military manpower procurement purposes are those of steadily increasing manpower surplus over the armed forces' needs. Sharp increases in the incidence of college attendance have also occurred in the last two decades. The means now employed—decentralized local boards with decision-making power held by civilian volunteers—give rise to variability both within and between states. In part, this variability is based on differential impact of deferment policies on areas of different socioeconomic character, exacerbated by the allocation of quotas and calls to small jurisdictions, but an important share of it is traceable to the discretionary actions of boards themselves. The principal *by-products* identified were inefficiency in utilization of manpower resources, inequities in service liability following income and college-attendance lines, and widespread antipathy to the local-board concept. Close interrelationships exist among these factors: rising manpower surpluses give rise to the need to grant deferments freely, which precludes equity and inhibits efficiency; the use of local boards precludes efficiency and promotes antipathies among many members of the general public.

We think the following conclusions have been established: Present conscription policies have delivered the necessary numbers of men to the armed forces in a flexible manner, no small attainment. But the goals of minimum dislocation have not been met as well as the evidence suggests that they could be, and there is even the indication that public acquiescence in one aspect of conscription is weak. The values of efficiency and equity have not been served, except in symbolic or rhetorical terms; indeed, the inequities revealed by the evidence are a major indictment of present policies, if the stated values of the policies are taken at face value. We think that the evidence suggests that improvements can be made which will enable conscription policy to continue to provide men flexibly, but with fuller realization of some of its other stated goals and reduced dislocations and antipathies.

The conditions of manpower surplus are fixed, short of total mobilization, and college-attendance proportions are probably only slightly less so. Efficiency in the use of manpower resources under such conditions seems so unlikely as to be almost impossible. The local-board system could be eliminated, of course, and replaced by a nationally uniform system of classification based on carefully established criteria of national needs, but this would not assure efficiency; there would also have to be means of checking the continuity of men's employment in jobs that were known to meet the criteria of serving the national interest, perhaps for a period of up to fifteen years per man. The extent of surveillance and controls over the careers of young men requisite to attaining efficiency seems inconsistent with the usually accepted values of this society. We may be in error, of course, but we think this is a predictable and unprovocative value choice which we reasonably can expect to be shared broadly.

If efficiency is unattainable except under circumstances of radically altered means and atypical value choices of controls over personal lives, what are the prospects for achieving greater equity? Here we think the evidence leads in another direction. With a manpower surplus and mass college attendance, it is still possible to achieve equity without undermining flexibility of delivery of men or such efficiency as can be expected under any system. Not surprisingly, our recommendations resemble those of the National Advisory Commission on Selective Service, which we served as consultants. Essentially, we suggest elimination of all but the most essential deferments, induction at an early age (between eighteen and nineteen), and selection in sequence from a randomized order of call established nationally by mechanized randomising processes.

Those deferments that are equally available to all, and which are necessary to the maintenance of an armed force, can remain unchanged. We have no quarrel with the setting of physical or mental requirements, though we are not confident that the present ones reflect minimum standards for all military tasks, and we suspect that standards are in part a reflection of the Army's need for men. We do challenge almost every other deferment as it is presently applied.

The student deferment is in our eyes the most discriminatory and the most vulnerable. We would eliminate it entirely, rather than attempt to limit its duration or prohibit its eventuation into other forms of deferment; under either of these alternatives, the deferment is still available to the higher income registrant, permitting him alone to choose his time of service and avoid the years of maximum danger. Because the services obtain many of their officers from ROTC programs,[34] we would defer ROTC students, as well as medical and dental students, who would be subject to a post-degree draft, just as they are now.

The elimination of fatherhood, occupational, and reserve deferments is not as drastic as may at first appear, when it is realized that we advocate earlier service. Not many men will have claims for such deferment between ages eighteen and nineteen, but we oppose them for those who might. The act of becoming a father should not bring deferment from service, and no injustice would result if the rule is clear in advance and not retroactively applied. The increased cost to the government in the form of dependency allowances seems a small price to pay to close this path of escape from military service. Some hardship cases would probably still have to be granted deferment, although we would want them scrutinized objectively and without regard to the relative costs to the government. Occupational deferments should not be numerous, for few men can be truly irreplaceable in a critical occupation at age eighteen. We propose to use Selective Service to provide men for the reserves on a free and open basis. We will be charged with jeopardizing the integrity of the reserves, but this course will eliminate the economic biases, as well as potential favoritism and, in some states, racial discrimination, which exist in the present reserve selection procedures. The reserves and the National Guard should be freed of their attributes of a private association, and we see no way to accomplish this other than by requiring them to obtain their no-prior-service personnel through conscription processes.

The second part of our three-step proposal is induction between ages eighteen and nineteen. We think this desirable because it involves the least interference with careers and education, and provides the greatest certainty for individuals, educational institutions, and employers. Once a registrant has passed his year of liability, he would no longer be subject to service except in time of great national emergency. With reduced numbers of deferments, the manpower pool of eighteen-year-olds should be large enough to meet service requirements each year. When men emerge from service they could receive some form of government educational assistance if they wanted it. After the first two years of transition to such a system, therefore, the colleges should be able to count on a steady flow of probably greater numbers of students than under the present system. During the transition period, the colleges will suffer the absence of about one in every six male students who would otherwise have been in attendance.

The larger pool of men and the earlier age of service enhance the general desirability of instituting equitable selection procedures. Our third step, therefore, calls for a random selection to be made at age eighteen. This would involve randomized, possibly computerized, ordering of all eligible men to establish an order of call for the year. Registrants would know in advance whether they were likely to be inducted or not, a probability dependent chiefly on world conditions. If their situations changed during the year in such a way as to raise a claim for one of the few possible deferments, they would have recourse to appeals. Students deferred from one round of randomized selection because of their ROTC status could, in the event of failure to maintain good standing, or at their own option, enter the next subsequent selection group for a year of liability.

These three proposals, as a package, would go a long way toward eliminating present faults in the system, yet the advantages of the present system would be retained. Though each man's burden would not be the same (some would have to serve and some would not), at least the risk (or opportunity) of service would be the same for all registrants. Until his year of eligibility was over, no man could be sure he would not have to serve, but at least the period of uncertainty would be shortened. This system would interfere with the lives of individuals no more than the present system, and substantially less than any of the universal proposals. Clearly it has an element of compulsion not in the voluntary system, but it is also more flexible and more surely capable of producing the required numbers of men.

Such a system might be implemented by an organization quite different from the one now in existence. With few deferments and random selection there would be no need for local boards to classify and select men for induction. A much more centralized and professionalized organization could be used to administer the provisions we propose, but we have dealt elsewhere with the matter of organization change.[35] It is sufficient to point out that the kinds of changes we suggest in deferment and selection practices may (and probably would) have implications for the design of the implementing organization.

The foregoing recommendations are somewhat stark, principally because of space limitations. We have not, for example, given any consideration to such factors as the political costs of change in policies. Our focus in this section has been exclusively on the problem of political scientists' capacity to provide various forms of guidance for policy-makers as to the substance of policy and the merits of various possible problem-solving programs. We are aware that the substantively "best" policy may not be practical under given circumstances, and that there are many entirely defensible reasons why policies should not be changed even when "better" ways are acknowledged to be available. Nor have we considered many issues in the detail that their importance and complexity warrant. These too have been sacrificed for the purpose of presenting an illustration of one version of a policy-oriented approach to the study of politics.

Among the several potential payoffs that we think inhere in such an approach, recommendation is only one. And we are more than perfunctorily tentative in our argument that some forms of recommendation are under some circumstances within the range of the professional responsibilities of the political scientist who is inclined to make them. Recommendation was possible here because the areas for speculation were greatly reduced, and the evidence sharply narrowed the range of values that were attainable. This felicitous set of circumstances might not obtain in other subject areas, and perhaps some will feel that they did not exist even here.[36] In either case, the discipline should develop standards that will facilitate the identification of those recommendations that can carry the imprimatur of professional respectability. But even if we should arrive at the point where we sanitize political science entirely against the making of all recommendations except in the capacity of citizens, two vital implications will survive: empirical techniques will increasingly be employed by increasingly sophisticated social scientists to enable governments to respond more adequately to the multitude of pressing public problems in their environments, and we can add much to our understanding of the nature of political life by the study of public policy as an independent variable, its impact and effects, feedback and support processes, and so on, without ever reaching the boundaries of recommendation or immediate relevance to government action.

NOTES

* This paper is in every sense our joint product. The data are drawn in part from our study *Little Groups of Neighbors: The Selective Service System* (Chicago: Markham, 1968), and some of the tables have appeared in the *Wisconsin Law Review* (Fall, 1967), to which we are indebted for permission to reprint them. The research was supported in part by the Institute for Research on Poverty pursuant to the provisions of the Economic Opportunity Act of 1964. We acknowledge our indebtedness to the Institute for its many forms of assistance, and to Barry Gaberman, James Thomas, and Marilyn Wenell for exceptional research assistance. We are also grateful for the opportunity to participate as consultants in the work of the National Advisory Commission on Selective Service, and for the very useful criticism of an earlier draft of this paper by the participants at the SSRC Committee on Governmental and Legal Processes Newagen Conference in August, 1967.

1 Lieutenant General Lewis B. Hershey, director of Selective Service, in testimony before the House Armed Services Committee, June 22, 1966, reported in *Review of the Administration and Operation of the Selective Service System, Hearings before the Armed Services Committee of the House of Representatives,* 89th Cong., 2nd Sess., June 24–26, 28–30, 1966 (hereinafter cited as *Hearings*), p. 9626. Military force level and annual accessions data from Department of Defense totals (*Hearings,* p. 10001).

2 The concept of policy is varyingly employed (as it already has been here) to cover anything from the grand outline of goals and directions of societal movement to specific day-to-day details of bureaucratic decision-making. Henceforth we use the term to signify the substance of the adjustment or accommodation by participants to a problem or goal in their political context, expressed by the actions (or conscious inaction) of governmental bodies. This still leaves a possibility of ambiguity as to scale (i.e., congressional decisions to draft the youngest men first versus a particular local board's decision to draft a specific registrant) and as to the distinction between tangible impact and secondary or symbolic effects. We trust that the context in which we use the term will provide clarity as to the particular referent intended.

3 The approach taken follows in general the statement of the concerns of the Committee on Governmental and Legal Processes, which were as follows: What principal problems are the policies intended to deal with? What principal policy alternatives have been seriously considered? Which ones have been chosen? How effectively have they dealt with the problems? What have been their economic, social, and political costs? How has their choice affected the range of policy alternatives presently available in this field? Where are we likely to go from here? Where *should* we go from here? Implicit throughout the paper is a further question: To what extent can the research skills and professional judgments of political scientists contribute to the resolution of these questions?

4 For histories of Selective Service and comparisons of the various statutes, see Jack Franklin Leach, *Conscription in the United States: Historical Background* (Rutland, Vt.: Charles E. Tuttle, 1952); the Special Monograph Series of the Selective Service System (Washington: U.S. Government Printing Office, 1947–55), containing

volumes on the background, organization, and administration of the system in the Second World War; *Selective Service under the 1948 Act Extended* (Washington: U.S. Government Printing Office, 1953); Clyde E. Jacobs and John F. Gallagher, *The Selective Service Act: A Case Study of the Governmental Process* (New York: Dodd, Mead, 1967), particularly for the congressional debates; and *Hearings*, Appendix II, for the current statute with analysis and a brief description of the Selective Service System.

[5] The congressional statement of "Policy and Intent" at the outset of the Universal Military Training and Service Act (now called the Military Selective Service Act) declares (Sec. 1c), ". . . the obligations and privileges of serving in the armed forces and the reserve components thereof should be shared generally, in accordance with a system of selection which is fair and just, and which is consistent with the maintenance of an effective national economy." The President is authorized to provide for the deferment (Sec. 6h) of those whose employment or whose activity in study, research, or medical, scientific, or other endeavors "is found to be necessary to the maintenance of the national health, safety, or interest."

[6] Classifications established pursuant to the authority just cited fall into the following general groupings, with the proportions of the approximately 33 million living registrants indicated as of the close of fiscal 1966.

Available for service (I–A, I–A–O, I–O)	3.1%
Disqualified (I–Y, fit only in emergency; IV–F, unfit for service)	14.8
Students (I–S, II–S)	7.7
Occupational deferment (II–A, nonfarm; II–C, farm)	.8
Dependency and hardship (III–A)	10.9
All other deferred and exempt categories	.3
In service or completed service (I–C, I–D, IV–A)	18.1
Over age of liability (V–A)	44.3
	100.0%

Note that these proportions are based on the total number of registrants; because the overage group is nearly half the total, the proportions of the effectively available manpower pool represented by each deferment category is almost double the percentage shown. In subsequent analyses of classification performance in Wisconsin, we have used proportions of the eligible age group only.

[7] *Hearings*, pp. 9620, 9623. Other statements of the System have also emphasized the importance of channeling. For example, a press information bulletin says: "One of the major products of the Selective Service classification process is the channeling of manpower into many endeavors, occupations, and activities that are in the national interest. This function is a counterpart and amplification of the System's responsibility to deliver manpower to the armed forces in such a manner as to reduce to a minimum any adverse effect upon the national health, safety, interest, and progress. By identifying and applying this process intelligently, the System is able not only to minimize any adverse effect but to exert an effect beneficial to the national health, safety, and interest."

[8] For descriptions of the organization, see especially *Hearings*, Appendix II; National Advisory Commission on Selective Service, *In Pursuit of Equity: Who Serves When Not All Serve?* (Washington: U.S. Government Printing Office, 1967) (hereinafter cited as *President's Commission Report*), Chapter 3; the operations of the system, together with their legal bases and the registrant's rights, are well summarized on a step-by-step basis by Charles H. Wilson, "The Selective Service System: An Administrative Obstacle Course," *California Law Review*, 1967.

[9] The Selective Service System has made clear that at different times deferments may be granted conservatively or liberally. "The opportunity to enhance the national well being by inducing more registrants to participate in fields which relate directly to the national interest came about as a consequence, soon after the close of the Korean

episode, of the knowledge within the System that there was enough registrant personnel to allow stringent deferment practices employed during wartime to be relaxed or tightened as the situation might require" (from a press information bulletin entitled "Channeling," p. 2).

10 National Headquarters of the Selective Service System, *Annual Report of the Director* (1966) (Washington: U.S. Government Printing Office, 1967), p. 31.

11 Testimony of Assistant Secretary of Defense (Manpower) Thomas D. Morris, April 12, 1967. See *Hearings before the Committee on Armed Services, U.S. Senate, 90th Cong., 1st Sess.*, p. 64.

12 For chronological summaries of changes in deferment practices and other relevant policies and events, see the chronology sections of *Annual Report of the Director of Selective Service* (Washington: U.S. Government Printing Office, 1951–67).

13 The report of the Defense Department Draft Study of 1964, according to Thomas D. Morris, Assistant Secretary of Defense, consists entirely of his prepared statement to the House Armed Services Committee on June 30, 1966 (*Hearings*, p. 9923 ff.), and supplementary data presented as Appendix I to *Hearings*. But others insist that they have examined other unreleased and revised portions of it; see Jean Carper, *Bitter Greetings* (New York: Grossman, 1967), Chapter 11. The study was undertaken in April, 1964 "to assess the possibility of meeting our military manpower requirements on an entirely voluntary basis in the coming decade" (Morris, *Hearings*, p. 9923). As part of the study, opinion sampling was undertaken by the Census Bureau in conjunction with the National Opinion Research Center of the University of Chicago. Self-administered questionnaire data were received from a total of 9,593 civilian male respondents (60 percent nonveterans, 31 percent veterans in the final weighting) between the ages of sixteen and thirty-four, and combined with the responses to a similar questionnaire from 102,000 men on active military service (9 percent in final weighting). The basic source in which these results are reported is Albert D. Klassen, *Military Service in American Life since World War II: An Overview* (Chicago: National Opinion Research Center, 1966), many aspects of which are included among the materials presented by the Defense Department in Appendix I, *Hearings*. Several other publications from the National Opinion Research Center draw on these data; see, for example, Karen Oppenheim, *Attitudes of Younger American Men toward Selective Service* (Chicago: National Opinion Research Center, 1966).

14 The data in Table 4 are probably conservative, since the military service category includes both active service and reserve service. Professor Walter Oi has separated active-duty veterans from the reservists and in an analysis reported in his paper "The Costs and Implications of an All Volunteer Force" shows that in the cohort of men born in 1938, "Over three fourths of qualified high school graduates served in the active duty forces, while less than one-third of college graduates discharged their draft liabilities in this way." See *Hearings before the Committee on Armed Services, U.S. Senate, 90th Cong., 1st Sess., on S. 1432*, "Amending and Extending the Draft Law and Related Authorities," p. 455.

15 It should be noted that the advantages conferred by the student deferment are not limited to increased chances of complete avoidance of military service. The availability of this deferment also permits those financially and otherwise able to go to college in effect to choose their time of service, possibly avoiding those years when military service would involve maximum danger. The increase in the II-S classification (Table 5) demonstrates that this may have occurred between 1965 and 1966.

16 The inquiry was begun in December 1965 and has continuously enjoyed the full cooperation of the Wisconsin State Selective Service System. State Director Bentley Courtenay, with the permission of General Hershey, made the nonconfidential records of his state headquarters available and aided in securing questionnaire responses from 81 percent of all local board members in the state, plus interviews with

forty local board members and thirty members of the state selective service personnel at various levels. We wish to express our appreciation for his assistance and that of his officers. Without their rigorous and detailed review and criticism of our work we might have made factual errors; our judgments are our own, of course, and needless to say, members of the Wisconsin State Selective Service System neither share them nor bear any responsibility for them.

[17] This analysis appears in James W. Davis and Kenneth M. Dolbeare, *Little Groups of Neighbors: The Selective Service System* (Chicago: Markham, 1968), Chapter 6.

[18] *Hearings,* p. 10012, and unpublished Defense Department statistics that show that, in 1964, 15.7 percent of the men joining the reserves had college degrees while only 5.7 percent of the men inducted into active service had degrees.

[19] In a mail questionnaire sent to Wisconsin local board members in September 1966, we asked respondents (among other questions) to indicate their agreement or disagreement with the statement "The reserves and the National Guard are frequently a means whereby registrants successfully avoid the draft," with the following results (from 314 respondents):

Agree strongly	31%
Agree	43
Don't know, depends	11
Disagree	10
Disagree strongly	3
No response	2
	100%

[20] Morris, *Hearings,* p. 9938.

[21] Slight changes in Defense Department minimum standards, such as that made in 1966 for the purpose of bringing in 100,000 men otherwise classifiable as I-Y, can have substantial impact on Negro service proportions. For example, 43 percent of Negroes given preinduction examinations in fiscal 1966 were accepted in contrast to 29 percent in 1965; the effect of the change on whites was less than half as great, from 60 percent to 65 percent (UPI wire story from Army report, May 25, 1967).

[22] *President's Commission Report,* p. 9.

[23] *President's Commission Report,* p. 27.

[24] *President's Commission Report,* Appendix, Sec. 2, p. 83.

[25] See Gary L. Wamsley, "Local Board Behavior," in the forthcoming volume on Selective Service edited by Roger D. Little (New York: Russell Sage Foundation, 1968).

[26] *President's Commission Report,* p. 27.

[27] *Hearings,* p. 10015.

[28] *President's Commission Report,* p. 108.

[29] Oppenheim, *Attitudes,* p. 20. Those men who had heavy investments in education or other civilian-related skills were more likely to think the draft unfair than "light investors"; but in every investment level, those men who would not enter military service, either because they qualified for deferment or because of physical disqualification, were most likely to consider the draft fair, and those who remained draft-eligible tended to think it unfair.

[30] The goal of national service is advocated in publications emanating from the National Service Secretariat, Donald Eberly, Executive Director, 522 Fifth Avenue, New York, N.Y. For a representative statement, see *A Plan for National Service* (November, 1966).

[31] The strongest argument is contained in Bruce Chapman, *Wrong Man in Uniform* (New York: Trident Press, 1967). Examples of scholarly analysis may be found in Stuart Altman and Alan E. Fechter, "The Supply of Military Personnel" (paper presented at the meetings of the American Economic Association, December,

1966) (con, and Walter Y. Oi (unpublished paper read at the Chicago Conference on the Draft, December, 1966) (pro). Milton Friedman, another advocate of a voluntary army, has defended his position in the *New York Times Magazine,* May 14, 1967, p. 23. His case was rebutted in a letter from Stuart Altman which was printed in the June 4 issue, p. 12.

[32] W. Lee Hansen and Burton A. Weisbrod, "Economics of the Military Draft" (unpublished paper, University of Wisconsin, 1966).

[33] *Hearings,* p. 10043.

[34] According to the *Report of the National Advisory Commission,* p. 43: "The military services get almost 80 percent of their new officers from college sources. The most substantial component of these are university ROTC students (about 40 percent of the new officer population) who receive special (class I-D) deferments. The other 40 percent of new officers are college and professional school graduates who receive general II-S student deferments while in college. This includes doctors and dentists, who make up about 17 percent of the new officer group each year."

[35] Davis and Dolbeare, *op. cit.*

[36] Since efficiency is unattainable without an organization and policies that would in all probability be anathema to Americans, and equity seems to be within the reach of possible policy adjustments, manpower procurement policy may seem to be uniquely subject to recommendation. But other areas may be, upon examination, equally susceptible to professional recommendation by political scientists.

If this much be granted, the question may arise as to whether those political scientists who are so inclined have any special discliphine-based expertise to bring to the general area of policy recommendation, or whether they would be interchangeable with, say, competent economists or sociologists. We think that the training and scholarly interest of political science as a discipline create a strong though not exclusive entitlement and responsibility in this area. While the interests and methods of social science disciplines overlap substantially, each discipline also has its own distinctive questions, problems, and areas of expertise. If the policies may be undertaken in part or entirely by governmental institutions; if the impact of these policies must be assessed in comprehensive terms, including the political consequences; if alternative administrative feasibility is relevant; if the alternative values to be maximized must be justified in terms of their demonstrable and probable consequences (past, present, and future); and if an understanding of the contemporary political process and its strengths, weaknesses, and supports is requisite, then political scientists should be included in such endeavors. In short, we see competent political scientists as synthesizing the research products of many disciplines in professional and objective ways, interpreting these findings in terms of target goals and probable consequences within the policy, and formulating recommendations that will serve the nation's needs effectively. Continuously guided by the developing research techniques and findings of the pure empiricist and employing open and assessable evaluative standards in a professionally competent manner, the interested political scientist can add important dimensions to policy recommendation. Not only is he able to make such contributions, but he brings an additional and desirable increment of professional expertise to the task.

Suggestions for Additional Reading

BASIC CONCEPTIONS IN POLICY ANALYSIS

Bauer, Raymond. *Social Indicators* (Cambridge, Mass.: M.I.T. Press, 1967).

Bauer, Raymond; Pool, Ithiel de Sola; and Dexter, Lewis. *American Business and Public Policy: The Politics of Foreign Trade* (New York: Atherton, 1963).

Deutsch, Karl. *The Nerves of Government* (New York: Free Press, 1963).

Easton, David. *A Systems Analysis of Political Life* (New York: Wiley, 1965).

Edelman, Murray. *The Symbolic Uses of Politics* (Urbana: University of Illinois Press, 1967).

Eulau, Heinz, and Eyestone, Robert. "Policy Maps of City Councils and Policy Outcomes: A Developmental Analysis," *American Political Science Review*, 62 (March, 1968), 124–43.

Froman, Lewis A. "An Analysis of Public Policies in Cities," *Journal of Politics*, 29 (February, 1967), 94–108.

Lasswell, Harold. *Who Gets What, When, How?* (New York: McGraw-Hill, 1936).

Lowi, Theodore. "American Business, Public Policy, Case Studies and Political Theory," *World Politics*, 16 (July, 1964), 677–715.

Wiseman, M. Victor. *Political Systems: Some Sociological Approaches* (New York: Praeger).

THE MEASUREMENT OF POLICY

Advisory Commission on Intergovernmental Relations. *Measures of State and Local Fiscal Capacity and Tax Effort* (Washington, D.C.: Government Printing Office, 1962).

Advisory Commission on Intergovernmental Relations. *The Role of Equalization in Federal Grants* (Washington, D.C.: Government Printing Office, 1964).

Burch, Philip. *Highway Revenue and Expenditure Policy in the United States* (New Brunswick, N.J.: Rutgers University Press, 1962).

Cnudde, Charles, and McCrone, Donald. "The Linkage Between Constituency Attitudes and Congressional Voting Behavior," *American Political Science Review,* 60 (March, 1966), 66–72.

Cnudde, Charles, and McCrone, Donald. "Party Competition and Welfare Policies in the United States," *American Political Science Review,* 63 (September, 1969), 858–66.

Davis, Otto; Dempster, M. A.; and Wildavsky, Aaron. "A Theory of the Budgetary Process," *American Political Science Review,* 60 (September, 1966), 529–47.

Dorfman, Robert (ed.). *Measuring Benefits of Government Investment* (Washington, D.C.: Brookings Institution, 1965).

Forbes, Hugh Donald, and Tufte, Edward R. "A Note of Caution in Causal Modelling," *American Political Science Review,* 62 (December, 1968), 1258–64.

Friedman, Robert. "State Politics and Highways," *Politics in the American States,* eds. Herbert Jacob and Kenneth N. Vines (New York: Little, Brown, 1965).

Gardiner, John. "Police Enforcement of Traffic Laws: A Comparative Analysis," *City Politics and Public Policy,* ed. James Q. Wilson (New York: Wiley, 1968).

Gurr, Ted. "A Causal Model of Civil Strife: A Comparative Analysis Using New Indices," *American Political Science Review,* 62 (December, 1968), 1104–24.

Hawkins, Brett W. "Reapportionment Aids Georgia's Urban Bills," *National Civic Review* (March, 1968), 153–56.

Hofferbert, Richard I. "Socio-Economic Dimensions of the American States: 1890–1960," *Midwest Journal of Politics,* 12 (August, 1968), 401–18.

Kaiser, Henry F. "A Measure of the Population Quality of Legislative Apportionment," *American Political Science Review,* 62 (March, 1968), 208–15.

North, Robert. *Content Analysis* (Evanston, Ill.: Northwestern University Press, 1963).

Novick, David (ed.). *Program Budgeting: Program Analysis and the Federal Budget* (Cambridge, Mass.: Harvard University Press, 1967).

Penniman, Clara. "The Politics of Taxation," *Politics in the American States,* eds. Jacob and Vines (New York: Little, Brown, 1965).

Price, H. Douglas. "Are Southern Democrats Different: An Application of Scale Analysis to Senate Voting Patterns," *Politics and Social Life,* eds. Nelson Polsby, *et al.* (New York: Houghton Mifflin, 1964).

Salisbury, Robert. "State Politics and Education," *Politics in the American States,* eds. Jacob and Vines (New York: Little, Brown, 1965).

Schubert, Glendon, and Press, Charles. "Measuring Malapportionment," *American Political Science Review*, 58 (June and December, 1964), 302–27, 966.

Sharkansky, Ira. "Four Agencies and an Apportions Committee: A Comparative Study of Budget Strategies," *Midwest Journal of Political Science*, 9 (August, 1965), 254–81.

Sharkansky, Ira. "Agency Requests, Gubernatorial Support and Budget Success in State Legislatures," *American Political Science Review*, 62 (December, 1968), 1220–31.

Sharkansky, Ira, and Hofferbert, Richard I. "Dimensions of State Politics, Economics and Public Policy," *American Political Science Review*, 63 (September, 1969), 867–79.

Walker, Jack L. "The Diffusion of Innovations Among the American States," *American Political Science Review*, 63 (September, 1969), 880–99.

Webb, Eugene, *et al. Unobtrusive Measures: Nonreactive Research in the Social Sciences* (Chicago: Rand McNally, 1966).

Wood, Robert C. *1400 Governments: The Political Economy of the New York Metropolitan Region* (Cambridge, Mass.: Harvard University Press, 1961).

DETERMINANTS OF PUBLIC POLICY: THE ECONOMY

Bator, Francis. *The Question of Government Spending* (New York: Harper & Row, 1960).

Burkhead, Jesse. *Public School Finance* (Syracuse, N.Y.: Syracuse University Press, 1964).

Campbell, Alan, and Sachs, Seymour. *Metropolitan America* (New York: Free Press of Glencoe, 1967).

Dye, Thomas R. *Politics, Economics and the Public: Policy Outcomes in the American States* (Chicago: Rand McNally, 1966).

Fabricant, Soloman. *The Trend of Government Activity in the United States Since 1900* (New York: National Bureau of Economic Research, 1952).

Fischer, Glenn. "Interstate Variation in State and Local Government Expenditures," *National Tax Journal*, 17 (March, 1964), 57–64.

Lineberry, Robert, and Fowler, Edmund. "Reformism and Public Policies in American Cities," *American Political Science Review*, 61 (September, 1967), 701–16.

Perloff, Harvey, *et al. Regions, Resources and Economic Growth* (Lincoln: University of Nebraska Press, 1965).

Sachs, Seymour, and Harris, Robert. "The Determinants of State and Local Expenditures and Intergovernment Flow of Funds," *National Tax Journal,* 17 (March, 1964), 75–85.

DETERMINANTS OF PUBLIC POLICY: POPULAR DEMANDS AND POLITICAL CULTURE

Agger, Robert, *et al. Rulers and the Ruled: Political Power and Impotence in American Communities* (New York: Wiley, 1964).

Alford, Robert, and Lee, Eugene C. "Voting Turnout in American Cities," *American Political Science Review,* 62 (September, 1968), 796–813.

Alford, Robert, and Scoble, Harry M. "Sources of Local Political Involvement," *American Political Science Review,* 62 (December, 1968), 1192–1206.

Almond, Gabriel, and Verba, Sidney. *The Civic Culture* (Princeton, N.J.: Princeton University Press, 1963).

Berelson, Bernard, *et al. Voting: A Study of Opinion Formation in a Presidential Campaign* (Chicago: University of Chicago Press, 1954).

Campbell, Angus, *et al. The American Voter* (New York: Wiley, 1964).

Campbell, Angus, *et al. Elections and the Political Order* (New York: Wiley, 1966).

Dahl, Robert. *Who Governs?* (New Haven, Conn.: Yale University Press, 1961).

Dennis, Jack. "Major Problems of Political Socialization Research," *Midwest Journal of Political Science,* 12 (February, 1968), 85–114.

Donnelly, Thomas (ed.). *Rocky Mountain Politics* (Albuquerque: University of New Mexico Press, 1940).

Downs, Anthony. *An Economic Theory of Democracy* (New York: Harper & Row, 1957).

Easton, David, and Dennis, Jack. "The Child's Acquisition of Regime Norms: Political Efficacy," *American Political Science Review,* 61 (March, 1967), 25–38.

Elazar, Daniel. *American Federalism: A View from the States* (New York: Thomas Crowell, 1966).

Fenton, John. *Politics in the Border States* (New Orleans: Hauser, 1957).

Fenton, John. *Midwest Politics* (New York: Holt, Rinehart & Winston, 1966).

Froman, Lewis A. *Congressmen and Their Constituencies* (Chicago: Rand McNally, 1963).

Golembiewski, Robert. *Men, Management and Morality* (New York: McGraw-Hill, 1965).

Greenstein, Fred. *Children and Politics* (New Haven, Conn.: Yale University Press, 1965).

Harlow, Robert, and Sharkansky, Ira. "Criticism and Comment," *National Tax Journal,* 21 (June, 1968), 215–19.

Jaros, Dean. "Children's Attitudes Toward the President," *Journal of Politics,* 29 (May, 1967), 368–87.

Jennings, M. Kent, and Niemi, Richard G. "The Transmission of Political Values from Parent to Child," *American Political Science Review,* 62 (March, 1968), 169–84.

Keech, William. *The Impact of Negro Voting* (Chicago: Rand McNally, 1968).

Key, V. O., Jr. *Southern Politics in State and Nation* (New York: Knopf, 1949).

Key, V. O., Jr. *Public Opinion and American Democracy* (New York: Knopf, 1961).

Lane, Robert. *Political Ideology* (New York: Free Press, 1962).

Langton, Kenneth P., and Jennings, M. Kent. "Political Socialization and the High School Civics Curriculum in the United States," *American Political Science Review,* 62 (September, 1968), 852–67.

Lipset, Seymour. *Political Man* (New York: Doubleday, 1959).

Lockard, Duane. *New England State Politics* (Princeton, N.J.: Princeton University Press, 1959).

Matthews, Donald, and Prothro, James. *Negroes and the New Southern Politics* (New York: Harcourt, Brace & World, 1966).

Milbrath, Lester. *Political Participation* (Chicago: Rand McNally, 1965).

Miller, Warren, and Stokes, Donald. "Constituency Influence in Congress," *American Political Science Review,* 57 (March, 1963), 45–56.

Munger, Frank. *American State Politics* (New York: Crowell, 1966).

Owen, Karen, and Peterson, Paul. "Presidential Assassination: A Case Study," *Journal of Politics,* 29 (May, 1967), 388–404.

Parenti, Michael. "Ethnic Politics and the Persistence of Ethnic Indentification," *American Political Science Review,* 61 (September, 1967), 717–26.

Patterson, Samuel. "The Political Cultures of the American States," *Journal of Politics,* 30 (February, 1968), 187–209.

Polsby, Nelson. *Community Power and Political Theory* (New Haven, Conn.: Yale University Press, 1963).

Schattschneider, E. E. *Semi-Sovereign People* (New York: Holt, Rinehart & Winston, 1960).

Sharkansky, Ira. "Economic and Political Correlates of State Government Expenditures: General Tendencies and Deviant Cases," *Midwest Journal of Political Science,* 11 (May, 1967), 173–92.

Sharkansky, Ira. "Some More Thoughts on the Determinants of Government Expenditures," *National Tax Journal,* 20 (June, 1967), 171–79.

Sharkansky, Ira. *Regionalism in American Politics* (Indianapolis: Bobbs-Merrill, 1969).

Sigel, Robert S. "Image of a President: Some Insights into the Political Views of Schoolchildren," *American Political Science Review,* 62 (March, 1968), 216–26.

Wolfinger, Raymond E. and Fred I. Greenstein. "The Repeal of Fair Housing in California: An Analysis of Referendum Voting," *American Political Science Review,* 62 (September, 1968), 753–69.

DETERMINANTS OF PUBLIC POLICY: INDIVIDUAL ACTORS AND INSTITUTIONS IN THE POLICY PROCESS

Altshuler, Alan. *The Politics of the Federal Bureaucracy* (New York: Dodd, 1968).

Anton, Thomas. *The Politics of State Expenditure in Illinois* (Urbana: University of Illinois Press, 1966).

Bailey, Stephen. *Congress Makes a Law* (New York: Columbia University Press, 1950).

Barber, James. *Power in Committees* (Chicago: Rand McNally, 1966).

Bernstein, Marver. *The Job of the Federal Executive* (Washington, D.C.: Brookings Institution, 1958).

Boyer, William. *Bureaucracy on Trial* (Indianapolis: Bobbs-Merrill, 1964).

Crecine, John P. *Government Problem-Solving* (Chicago: Rand McNally, 1968).

David, Paul, and Eisenberg, Ralph. *Devaluation of the Urban and Suburban Vote* (Charlottesville: University of Virginia Bureau of Public Administration, 1961).

Dawson, Richard, and Robinson, James. "Interparty Competition, Economic Variables, and Welfare Policies in the American States," *Journal of Politics,* 25 (May, 1963), 265–89.

Downs, Anthony. *Inside Bureaucracy* (New York: Little, Brown, 1967).

Epstein, Leon. *Political Parties in Western Democracies* (New York: Praeger, 1967).

Fenno, Richard. *The President's Cabinet* (Cambridge, Mass.: Harvard University Press, 1959).

Fenno, Richard. *The Power of the Purse* (New York: Little, Brown, 1966).

Francis, Wayne. *Legislative Issues in the Fifty States* (Chicago: Rand McNally, 1968).

Froman, Lewis A. *The Congressional Process: Strategies, Rules and Procedures* (New York: Little, Brown).

Gore, William. *Administrative Decision-Making* (New York: Wiley, 1964).

Gore, William, and Dyson, James. *The Making of Decisions* (New York: Free Press, 1964).

Greenstone, J. David, and Peterson, Paul E. "Reformers, Machines, and the War on Poverty," *City Politics and Public Policy,* ed. James Q. Wilson (New York: Wiley, 1968).

Grumm, John. "Structural Determinants of Legislative Output," (paper given at Conference on the Measurement of Public Policies in the States, Inter-University Consortium for Political Research, Ann Arbor, Michigan, 1968).

Hagan, Charles B. "The Group in Political Science," *Approaches to the Study of Politics,* ed. Roland Young (Evanston, Ill.: Northwestern University Press, 1958).

Heller, Walter. *New Dimensions of Political Economy* (New York: Norton, 1967).

Hofferbert, Richard I. "The Relation Between Public Policy and Some Structural and Environmental Variables in the American States," *American Political Science Review,* 60 (March, 1966), 73–82.

Jacob, Herbert. "The Consequences of Malapportionment: A Note of Caution," *Social Forces,* 43 (1964), 256–61.

Jewell, Malcolm, and Samuel Patterson, *The Legislative Process in the United States* (New York: Random House, 1966).

Kilpatrick, Franklin, *et al. The Image of the Federal Service* (Washington, D.C.: Brookings Institution, 1964).

Koenig, Louis. *The Chief Executive* (New York: Harcourt, Brace & World, 1964).

Lasswell, Harold. *Psychopathology and Politics* (New York: Viking Press, 1960).

Lindblom, Charles. "Decision-Making in Taxation and Expenditure," *Public Finances: Needs, Sources, and Utilization* (Princeton, N.J.: National Bureau of Economic Research, 1961).

Lindblom, Charles. *Intelligence of Democracy* (New York: Macmillan, 1965).

Lindblom, Charles. *The Policy-Making Process* (Englewood Cliffs, N.J.: Prentice-Hall, 1968).

Lipset, Seymour, *et al. Union Democracy* (New York: Doubleday, 1960).

Manley, John. "The House Committee on Ways and Means," *American Political Science Review,* 59 (December, 1965), 927–39.

Mann, Dean. *The Assistant Secretaries* (Washington, D.C.: Brookings Institution, 1965).

March, James and Simon, Herbert. *Organizations* (New York: Wiley, 1958).

Matthews, Donald. *The Social Background of Political Decision-Makers* (New York: Random House, 1954).

Matthews, Donald. *U.S. Senators and Their World* (Chapel Hill: University of North Carolina Press, 1960).

Milbrath, Lester. *Washington Lobbyists* (Chicago: Rand McNally, 1963).

Morse, Elliot R., *et al.* "Fluctuations in State Expenditures," *Southern Economic Journal,* 33 (April, 1967), 496–516.

Neustadt, Richard. *Presidential Power* (New York: Wiley, 1960).

Peabody, Robert, and Polsby, Nelson. *New Perspectives on the House of Representatives* (Chicago: Rand McNally, 1963).

Polsby, Nelson. "The Institutionalization of the U.S. House of Representatives," *American Political Science Review,* 62 (March, 1968), 144–68.

Pulsipher, Allan G., and Weatherby, James L. Jr. "Malapportionment, Party Competition, and the Functional Distribution of Government Expenditures," *American Political Science Review,* 62 (December, 1968), 1207–19.

Ranney, Austin. *The Doctrine of Responsible Party Government* (Urbana: University of Illinois Press, 1962).

Robinson, James. *The House Rules Committee* (Indianapolis: Bobbs-Merrill, 1964).

Rose, Richard. *Influencing Voters: A Study of Campaign Rationality* (New York: St. Martin's Press, 1967).

Rossiter, Clinton. *The American Presidency* (New York: Harcourt, Brace & World, 1966).

Rothman, Stanley. "Systematic Political Theory: Observations on the Group Approach," *American Political Science Review,* 54 (March, 1960), 15–33.

Schlesinger, Joseph. *Ambition and Politics* (Chicago: Rand McNally, 1966).

Scott, Andrew, and Hunt, Margaret. *Congress and Lobbies: Image and Reality* (Chapel Hill: University of North Carolina Press, 1966).

Sharkansky, Ira. "Agency Requests, Gubernatorial Support, and Budget Success in State Legislatures," *American Political Science Review,* 62 (December, 1968), 1220–31.

Sharkansky, Ira. *The Routines of Politics* (New York: Van Nostrand-Reinhold, 1970).

Sorauf, Frank. *Party Politics in America* (New York: Little, Brown, 1968).

Sorensen, Theodore. *Decision-Making in the White House* (New York: Columbia University Press, 1963).

Steiner, Gilbert. *Social Insecurity* (Chicago: Rand McNally, 1960).

Truman, David. *The Governmental Process: Political Interests and Public Opinion* (New York: Knopf, 1951).

Truman, David. *Congressional Party* (New York: Wiley, 1959).

Wahlke, John, *et al. The Legislative System* (New York: Wiley, 1962).

Warner, Lloyd, *et al. The American Federal Executive* (New Haven, Conn.: Yale University Press, 1963).

White, Theodore. *The Making of the President,* 1960, 1964, 1968 . . . (New York: Atheneum).

Wildavsky, Aaron. *The Politics of the Budgetary Process* (New York: Little, Brown, 1964).

Wildavsky, Aaron. *American Federalism in Perspective* (New York: Little, Brown, 1967).

EVALUATION OF PUBLIC POLICY

Davis, James, Jr., and Dolbeare, Kenneth. *Little Groups of Neighbors: The Selective Service System* (Chicago: Markham, 1968).

Dror, Yehezkel. *Public Policymaking Reexamined* (San Francisco: Chandler, 1968).

Kaufman, Herbert. *Forest Ranger: A Study in Administrative Behavior* (Baltimore: Johns Hopkins Press, 1967).

Lipsky, Michael. *Protest in City Politics: Rent Strikes, Housing and the Power of the Poor* (Chicago: Rand McNally, 1969).

Lyden, Fremont, and Miller, Ernest. *Planning-Programming-Budgeting* (Chicago: Markham, 1968).

Peacock, Alan, and Wiseman, Jack. *The Growth of Public Expenditure in the United Kingdom* (New York: National Bureau of Economic Research, 1961).

"Planning-Programming-Budgeting," Hearings before the Subcommittee on National Security and International Operations of the Senate Committee on Government Operations, 90th Congress.

Sayre, Wallace, and Kaufman, Herbert. *Governing New York City* (New York: Russell Sage, 1960).

Sharkansky, Ira. *Spending in the American States* (Chicago: Rand McNally, 1968).

Vernon, Raymond. *Metropolis 1985* (Cambridge, Mass.: Harvard University Press, 1960).

Wildavsky, Aaron. "Political Implications of Budgetary Reform," *Public Administration Review,* 21 (Autumn, 1961), 183–90.

Wilson, James Q. *City Politics and Public Policy* (New York: Wiley, 1968).